FOUNDATIONS *of* **Health Psychology**

FOUNDATIONS

of

Health Psychology

EDITED BY

Howard S. Friedman and Roxane Cohen Silver

OXFORD
UNIVERSITY PRESS

2007

OXFORD
UNIVERSITY PRESS

Oxford University Press, Inc., publishes works that further
Oxford University's objective of excellence
in research, scholarship, and education.

Oxford   New York
Auckland   Cape Town   Dar es Salaam   Hong Kong   Karachi
Kuala Lumpur   Madrid   Melbourne   Mexico City   Nairobi
New Delhi   Shanghai   Taipei   Toronto

With offices in
Argentina   Austria   Brazil   Chile   Czech Republic   France   Greece
Guatemala   Hungary   Italy   Japan   Poland   Portugal   Singapore
South Korea   Switzerland   Thailand   Turkey   Ukraine   Vietnam

Published by Oxford University Press, Inc.
198 Madison Avenue, New York, New York 10016

www.oup.com

Oxford is a registered trademark of Oxford University Press

Library of Congress Cataloging-in-Publication Data
Foundations of health psychology / edited by Howard S. Friedman and Roxane C. Silver.
    p. cm.
Includes bibliographical references and index.
ISBN-13 978-0-19-513959-4
ISBN 0-19-513959-3
1. Clinical health psychology.   I. Friedman, Howard S.   II. Silver, Roxane Cohen.
R726.7.F68 2007
610.1'9—dc22   2005035996

9 8 7 6 5 4 3 2 1

Printed in the United States of America
on acid-free paper

Preface

Although the formal field of health psychology is only 25 years old, it has burgeoned into a major scientific and clinical discipline. Health psychology has excellent scientific journals, thousands of scientists and practitioners, and many students. Yet there has not been sufficient statement and explication of the underpinning concepts on which this flourishing field is built. The present foundational volume provides this conceptual base.

In 1954, the psychologist Gardner Lindzey edited the first edition of the *Handbook of Social Psychology*. Lindzey noted that it was important to present his rapidly expanding new discipline at a level of difficulty appropriate for graduate students and other scholars new to the field. In a like vein, the current volume is aimed at graduate students, postdoctoral scholars, new researchers, and other investigators seeking the firmest possible basis for successful research and practice—this time in the young field of health psychology. A reader who grasps and internalizes the core concepts in the well-developed, well-integrated, and well-written chapters herein will be soundly prepared for years of work in health psychology.

The chapters are authored by some of the very best health psychology scholars in the world. The contributors were instructed to focus on the background and the *fundamentals* of a particular core area of health psychology—things that will stick with the reader for many years. This volume does not attempt to be exhaustive; indeed, there are many detailed review articles about current research available in health psychology each year. Further, this book does not take a medical model approach. Rather, it is aimed more *theoretically, conceptually,* and *methodologically,* around *psychological levels of analysis.* These are the core unique strengths of health psychology.

The social psychologist Kurt Lewin said that there is nothing so practical as a good theory. We share this view and believe that once one has achieved a deep understanding about how to think about, measure, and study biopsychosocial processes, one can delve into a variety of specific problems, interventions, and conditions. The sophisticated concepts and methods of psychology can inform and help address many problems of the human condition, including matters of health. There are thus here no groupings by disease ("cancer, heart disease," etc.), no surveys of the full applied health psychology landscape, and no fine-grained instructions of technique. Rather, we believe that the most intelligent work in health psychology will develop if it is built on a wise and deep understanding of the intellectual bases of the discipline.

Contents

Contributors

Nancy E. Adler, University of California, San Francisco

Gary G. Berntson, Ohio State University

Kathrin Boerner, Lighthouse International

John T. Cacioppo, University of Chicago

Charles S. Carver, University of Miami

Susan T. Charles, University of California, Irvine

Cindy K. Chung, University of Texas at Austin

Howard S. Friedman (Editor), University of California, Riverside

Virginia Gil-Rivas, University of North Carolina, Charlotte

Judith A. Hall, Northeastern University

Jutta Heckhausen, University of California, Irvine

Robert M. Kaplan, University of California, Los Angeles

Margaret E. Kemeny, University of California, San Francisco

James W. Pennebaker, University of Texas at Austin

Tracey A. Revenson, City University of New York

Karen S. Rook, University of California, Irvine

Debra L. Roter, The Johns Hopkins University

Roxane Cohen Silver (Co-editor), University of California, Irvine

Timothy W. Smith, University of Utah

Annette L. Stanton, University of California, Los Angeles

Shelley E. Taylor, University of California, Los Angeles

J. Lee Westmaas, Stony Brook University

Camille B. Wortman, Stony Brook University

History and Methods

Howard S. Friedman and Nancy E. Adler

The History and Background of Health Psychology

Health psychology, the most modern major domain of psychology, flows from ancient intellectual well-springs. From the biblical proverb which taught that "A merry heart does good like a medicine" (Proverbs 17:22) to the definitional "heart-ache" of Shakespeare's *Hamlet* (act 3, scene 1), the psyche and the soma have long been sensed to be linked. Benjamin Franklin, who uncovered many secrets to a long, successful life, warned against associating with hostile, choleric people; he then developed a self-reinforcing habit chart to discourage himself from drunkenness and gluttony (Franklin, 1794/1906). Yet although such notions of close ties between health and thoughts, feelings, and behaviors date back thousands of years, the scientific discipline of health psychology did not take shape until the 1970s. This emergence was a full century after the beginnings of psychology in the 1870s, and well after the establishment of experimental psychology, social psychology, developmental psychology, physiological psychology, personality psychology, and clinical psychology.

Why is health psychology such a latecomer to the scene, especially given its ancient provenance and the obvious general importance of health and longevity? The answer is a complex one, rooted in long-standing conceptions of disease, illness, and

health and compounded by structural divisions in societal approaches to health and well-being. Health psychology builds on many disciplines, applying their theories and methods to matters of health.

Origins in Ancient Philosophy and Medicine

Early understandings of physical ailments were closely tied to age-old notions of the body's spiritual nature. In early philosophies, the body's health and its spirit are inextricably bound.

In ancient Greece, patients visited temples to be cured by Asclepius, the god of healing. These retreats, probably the first hospitals, often contained gardens and fountains, and included bathing, nutrition, and sometimes exercise in their healing rituals (Longrigg, 1998). In ancient Rome, holistic health promotion became quite sophisticated in the integration of individual well-being and public health, as evidenced in such measures as the building of accessible baths, removing sewage, and constructing aqueducts for clean water, while nourishing the spirit. After the fall of the western Roman Empire and the ensuing decline in science and hygiene, some of the spiritual aspects of these ancient practices were adopted and maintained by early Christians in the Dark Ages (Guthrie, 1945), as healing shrines were set up throughout Europe.

By the fourth century BCE, the Greeks had conceived that the world was composed of air, water, fire, and earth, which in turn had led to the notion of the four bodily humors: blood, phlegm, choler (yellow bile), and melancholy (black bile). This was the age of Hippocrates, who came to be known as the Father of Medicine. Hippocrates and other Greeks of his time had striking skills of observation and laid the basis for much of modern science. In health and medicine, their primary accomplishment was to move conceptions away from supernatural causes and cures. For example, Hippocrates decided that epilepsy was a disease (caused by surplus phlegm in the brain), not a sacred spell or divine affliction. Importantly, their observations demonstrated that the likelihood of certain diseases could be affected by one's food, one's work, one's location, and one's endowment.

It was in the Roman era, several hundred years later, that Greek ideas of health and medicine led to the foundation of what would become modern approaches. Galen, a Greek doctor in second-century Rome, both philosopher and anatomist (who dissected animals), revealed the body to be a beautifully balanced creation, in constant interaction with its environment. Galen used the balance of humors to refer not only to temperament but also to the causes of disease. The predominant humor in a person was thought to produce the dominant temperament, and an excess of a humor led to disease. For example, an excess of black bile was thought to produce a melancholic personality, gluttony, eventual depression, and associated physical illness. Psychology and health, and mental and physical health, were seen as closely related.

Ancient notions of bodily humors have been discarded. Yet the idea that the health-relevant emotional states of individuals can be categorized as sanguine, repressed, hostile, or depressed, as well as balanced or imbalanced, remains with us. This scheme of emotional aspects of personality and health was sufficiently perceptive (or ambiguous) to influence the practice of medicine for 2,000 years. Now, however, we speak of hormones (not humors) associated with optimism, anxiety, anger, and depression.

Analogous concern with balance and harmony emerged in Eastern medicine. Ayurvedic medicine, originating in India more than 2,000 years ago, paralleled Western medicine in the use of herbs, foods, emetics, and bleedings to restore harmony. Like early Western medicine, it had its share of demons, magic spells, and potions, but it also emphasized spiritual balance and personal hygiene. Traditional Chinese medicine was based on balance between the yin and the yang—the active male force and the passive female force (Venzmer, 1972). Acupuncture, the insertion of needles into the skin at strategic points in order to restore the proper "flow" of energy, is an example of ancient Chinese practice that continues to this day, although modern scientific attention in this area has expanded from bodily "forces" to the roles of neurotransmitters.

Religion and Spiritual Healing

The philosophy of the Middle Ages was heavily concerned with religious and spiritual matters, and this speculation about the human soul and its ties to God directed attention away from biology. The pilgrims depicted in Chaucer's fourteenth-century work *The Canterbury Tales,* are on a pilgrimage to the shrine of St. Thomas à Becket, at Canterbury. For more than a thousand years, pilgrims sought such shrines and saints, to heal their illnesses through divine intervention.

On their journeys, European pilgrims often stopped at hospices, a place of rest for travelers, the elderly, and the sick. Hospices were one of the origins of the modern hospital. As modern medicine developed in the twentieth century and hospitals became centers of aggressive medical intervention, the elderly and the dying were often moved out; the emotional and spiritual aspects departed as well. Hospices were eventually reconstituted as programs to care for the terminally ill, a development that dates from St. Christopher's, a London hospice founded by Cicely Saunders in the 1960s (Stoddard, 1978). These programs focus on the psychological and the spiritual needs of the dying, along with traditional medical care. Many modern hospitals have much they could learn from hospices, both ancient and modern (Greer & Mor, 1986).

Cartesian Dualism

With the coming of the Renaissance, the philosopher and mathematician René Descartes (1596–1650) struggled with the relations between the mind or soul and the physical body. By freeing the "body" from its religious, spiritual aspects, Descartes helped establish the science of medical biology, less encumbered by religious orthodoxy. But by separating the mind from the body (including separating the mind from the brain), Descartes created a major philosophical conundrum. Although what we think affects what we do, and what we experience affects what we think and feel, how can an intangible spirit interact with a material physicality?

Struggling with the dichotomy, some subsequent philosophers, such as Spinoza (1632–1677), argued that the mental and the physical are different aspects of the same substance. For Spinoza, the superordinate aspect is God. Others argued that the physical world exists only to the extent that it is perceived by a mind. Still others claimed that the psyche does not exist but is simply an epiphenomenon of the physical workings of the body. This history of dichotomy is important to modern health psychology because seventeenth- and eighteenth-century philosophy had a crucial impact on modern notions of human nature and the proper structure of society.

These issues came to a head in the latter part of the nineteenth century, as new developments in biology (evolution), medicine/physiology (neurology), and psychology (sensation) opened wide new fields of inquiry. Most psychologists thereafter followed the lead of William James (1890/1910) and pushed aside the philosophical mysteries to instead focus directly on thinking, feeling, and learning, and on the brain, the nerves, and the hormonal system (Benjamin, 1988; Boring, 1950). Yet incomplete understanding of mind-body matters continues to challenge modern health psychology.

The Interdisciplinary Scientific Origins

The modern discipline of health psychology is, at its best, an interdisciplinary one, emerging from a confluence of important twentieth-century intellectual trends in the understanding of health.

One key thread in the scientific origins of health psychology traces back to the work of Charles Darwin. In his seminal work, Darwin (1859) not only proposed his theory of evolution but also expended considerable effort describing the biological and anatomical similarities between humans and other species. The revelation that human attributes had many common elements with those of animals reinforced the Cartesian split between those focused on the life of the mind and those concerned with the physical functioning of the body. At the same time, Darwin's observations inspired research, even up to this day, on evolutionary processes affecting human emotion and its relation to well-being (see, e.g., Ekman & Davidson, 1994).

Darwin's work also inspired the Russian physiologist Ivan Pavlov to begin examining the relations among environmental stimulation, learning, and physiological responses, a second important thread of modern health psychology. It contributed directly as well to Sigmund Freud's search for ways in which the hidden workings of the brain might influence health, as he examined the evolutionary significance of mental functioning.

Medical Psychology and Clinical Psychology

In the latter half of the nineteenth century, the American Medical Association (AMA, founded 1847) began to establish minimal standards for medical education and medical practice. This was a time when practices such as bleedings and quack nostrums were widespread, and patients who sought treatment had a greater chance of being harmed than being helped. By the early part of the twentieth century, physicians had organized into guilds and obtained legal status to regulate medical practice. The placing of strict control over the practice of medicine into the hands of physicians had two main results. First, it assured a certain level of quality and standardization in medical care. Second, it concentrated authority into the hands of one group of professionals—physicians—who controlled the definition of health and deemed other (nonmedical) aspects of health care to be ancillary or peripheral.

This professionalization of medicine extended to medical education. The AMA established the Council on Medical Education, with Abraham Flexner charged with surveying the existing medical schools and evaluating their training. The 1910 Flexner report, *Medical Education in the United States and Canada*, became the basis of the reform of medical education, which included standardization of entry requirements and development of a scientifically based curriculum (in which an initial 2 years of laboratory-based science training preceded 2 years of clinical training; Vevier, 1987).

At about the same time, efforts were made to integrate psychology into medical training. In 1911, Shepherd Ivory Franz, a psychologist and director of the Government Hospital for the Insane in Washington, D.C., attended a conference on the integration of psychology and medicine, hosted by the American Psychological Association (APA; Franz, 1912, 1913). Franz discussed such issues as "the success of placebos," in which "the mental effect of knowledge appears to be much greater than the chemical action of the drug" (1912, p. 910). Today, the power of placebos is implicitly recognized in the design of clinical trials of new drugs and procedures, where the "double-blind" randomized trial is the gold standard of evidence. Yet almost a century after Franz's highlighting of placebo responses, the mechanisms accounting for such responses are poorly understood, and discussions of placebo effects remain on the periphery of health care.

Franz chaired an APA committee that surveyed U.S. medical schools and recommended increased cooperation between psychology and medicine, inclusion of psychology in the medical curriculum, and an undergraduate course in psychology as a prerequisite for medical school. By 1928, a psychology professor, E. A. Bott, produced an essay entitled "Teaching of Psychology in the Medical Course." Noting that two decades of debate about the role of psychology in medical education had already occurred, Bott concluded: "There seems to be a wide and growing acceptance of the view that psychological factors have an important place in the life adjustments of persons (and patients) in general, and that our conception of health must be broadened to take these mental factors fully into account. Some orientation of students towards an understanding and appreciation of these factors should therefore be attempted through formal instruction" (p. 291).

Although a limited number of psychologists have served on the faculties of medical schools over the past century and introduced medical students to a psychological perspective, rarely has psychology been viewed by physicians as a basic science for the practice of medicine. Suggestions for requiring preparation in psychology as a prerequisite for medical school admission were also not acted upon. Rather, psychologists in medical schools for the most part have been called upon to address the so-called art of medicine, involving communication skills, the relationship between the physician and patient, and the motivation of patients to follow treatment prescriptions. Because this "art of medicine" clearly involved psychology, psychologists were expected to help in the "humanizing" of doctor-patient relations.

Prior to the establishment of the field of health psychology, matters of the psychological aspects of medical care were often termed *medical psychology*. For the most part, clinical psychologists with appointments in departments of psychiatry focused on mental illness and its treatment, as well as doing liaison psychology consultations for distressed patients with serious chronic disease. In some places and some countries (especially Great Britain), medical psychology was closely tied to psychiatry and the treatment of mental illnesses, but in the United States, medical psychologists also worked in medical schools alongside pediatricians, gerontologists, and even internists.

The presence of a cadre of psychologists in medical settings provided an important contribution to the emergence of health psychology. As other scientific and social forces pushed toward the need for a discipline of health psychology, the medical psychologists were already in place, with tremendous depth of relevant knowledge about medical care. For example, in 1969, clinical psychologist William Schofield analyzed psychological research in health domains and projected evolving demand for psychological service in both prevention and treatment (Schofield, 1969).

Although calls for the integration of psychology "back" into the medical curriculum and medical practice continue (Novack, 2003), psychology was never a core piece of modern medicine and health care. Psychologists were primarily employed to deal with deviant behavior, family crises, and stressful situations (such as cancer, burns, assaults, and other forms of trauma); and of course psychology was often a key part of the practice of psychiatry. Psychology was not, however, seen as central to health, by most physicians or even by most psychologists. A significant part of the problem is that the psychological aspects of health were and are often viewed (incorrectly) as an "art," whereas in reality research and practice in health psychology involve a difficult and complicated science.

Substantial integration of psychological theory and findings into medical school curricula continues to be challenging. Psychological material is often viewed by physicians as marginal because it lies outside the traditional biomedical focus on disease. Nonetheless, some progress has been made, with national boards for medical students now assessing behavioral science knowledge. Moreover, a report from the Institute of Medicine (Cuff & Vanselow, 2004) explicitly addresses the need for such a curriculum, as well as the obstacles to integrating it. The report identified 20 topics that should be included in a medical school curriculum. Many of these topics are within the purview of health psychology, including psychosocial contributions to chronic disease; developmental influences on disease; psychosocial factors in pain; determinants and modification of health-relevant behaviors; patient and physician beliefs, attitudes and values; communication skills; and social disparities in health. It will be important for those responding to such opportunities at integration to be cognizant of the century of repeated calls and failed efforts, so that they appreciate and anticipate the intellectual, conceptual, and structural barriers to such integration.

Psychosomatic Medicine

In the 1930s, the field of psychiatry began to emerge as an important area of medical specialization. The development and use of sulfa drugs in the 1930s and penicillin in the 1940s had given physicians, for the first time, dramatically effective treatments for many acute problems, and "internal medicine" began its rise to prominence. Medical students began receiving extensive training in biochemistry and microbiology. Matters of the "mind" were increasingly left to psychiatry.

Sigmund Freud, influenced by Darwin, began conducting evolutionary research early in his training, but he endeavored to explain rather than discard or diminish complex human attributes and motivations like love and jealousy. Unwilling to reduce psychology to biology, Freud (in the late nineteenth and early twentieth centuries) was fascinated with biopsychological problems such as hysterical paralysis. Physicians interested in mind-body relations thus gravitated to the Freudian and related psychoanalytic concepts. The psychoanalyst Franz Alexander (1950) argued that various diseases are caused by specific unconscious emotional conflicts. For example, he posited that ulcers were linked to oral conflicts (an unconscious desire to

have basic infantile needs satisfied) and asthma to separation anxiety (i.e., an unconscious desire to be protected by one's mother). The Menningers (1936), pioneering and influential psychiatrists, noted that very aggressive and ambitious men seemed prone to heart disease.

Flanders Dunbar at Columbia University postulated that mental disturbance often contributed to organic disease (Dunbar, 1943). In 1938–1939, Dunbar started the journal *Psychosomatic Medicine,* which subsequently became the official journal of the American Psychosomatic Society (founded in 1942) (www.psychosomatic.org). It was believed that inner psychic conflict disrupted normal bodily functioning and that the resolution of these psychological conflicts would contribute to a cure. Interestingly, given current knowledge of disease processes, other conditions of primary interest to the early psychosomatic physicians were colitis, hypertension, diabetes, arthritis, and dermatitis.

Little was known about immunology, psychobiology, and metabolism, especially in relation to psychological processes. Psychosomatic practitioners and researchers of the mid–twentieth century thus amassed clinical observations and proposed links between external stress, internal psychological conflict, and organic disease but developed few validated scientific principles or specific efficacious treatments.

By the 1970s, the growth of biological knowledge (neurobiology, neurochemistry, genetics, neurophysiology) overwhelmed traditional psychosomatic psychiatry, and biological psychiatry rose to prominence. For example, the discovery (in 1982) that the bacterium *Helicobacter pylori* was a contributing factor to the development of ulcers called the psychosomatic basis of ulcers into question. But the two explanations are not mutually exclusive; even in the presence of the bacteria, there is individual variation in the experience of symptoms and in the effects of stress on the stomach environment, which are linked to psychosocial experience. However, a pure "psychosomatic" explanation is inadequate, and certainly obsessive mothers are not the root cause. Analogously, although it is today not uncommon for psychiatrists to treat depression and attention deficit disorder primarily through medication, such biological approaches are often viewed as incomplete (by both psychosomatic practitioners and the general public), with demands for more attention to be directed toward psychological, social, and environmental factors that affect and interact with the biological.

Psychosomatic medicine eventually began using more rigorous research methods and incorporating sociobehavioral science as well as biological science. There was increasing concern with the cumbersome psychoanalytic jargon and the basic premises that did not easily lend themselves to empirical validation. There was also better appreciation of the scientific possibilities of sociobehavioral and epidemiological research. For example, the cardiologists Rosenman and Friedman (Rosenman et al., 1964), noticing a psychological predisposition to heart disease, turned to both psychophysiological studies of stress and longitudinal studies of type A behavior and coronary heart disease. They called for reliable assessment of coronary-proneness and a fully empirical scientific approach. Cardiologists, meanwhile, searched for medical "syndromes" (or complexes of symptoms), and it remained for psychologists to apply multitrait, multimethod assessments and construct validation to this inquiry (Houston & Snyder, 1988).

Social Science: Medical Sociology and Anthropology

Throughout the twentieth century, medical sociology and medical anthropology made important contributions to understanding the social nature of illness and the social roles of patients and healers. Studies across cultures, across ethnicities, and across social classes and social roles made it clear that illness is not simply a biological condition but is inherently social and cultural as well.

In the period following World War II, a period of rapid societal change and medical progress, the influential medical sociologist Talcott Parsons (1902–1979) and his colleagues began documenting the social nature of illness. Parsons began his career as a biologist but moved into social science and primarily worked toward combining structural and functional approaches to understanding basic phenomena of society, including sickness and health. Parsons and the other pioneering medical sociologists described how people in any given society share certain expectations (norms) about the rights and responsibilities of a person who is ill. These roles (such as "sick roles"—norms applied to a category of people, namely, patients) guide and facilitate the functioning of both the individual and

the society. For example, to become a "patient," one must enter the sick role and be treated by a "healer" (usually a physician in American society; Parsons, 1951, 1958). A sick person is relieved from certain responsibilities (such as going to work) but must seek medical help and profess a desire to get well. The doctor can validate this new status (i.e., confirm that the person is ill and can be a patient). A sick person who does not try to get well, does not seem uncomfortable in the role of patient, and simply shirks all usual responsibilities may be removed from the role of patient, that is, called a fake or a malingerer. Such sociological analyses delineated how illness is a social phenomenon (Hollingshead, 1973). Illness must be agreed to or validated by the opinions of others in the society; it is not just a function of some internal organic state.

Such ideas complemented and illuminated the many conundrums of psychosomatic medicine, such as the surprisingly low correlation often found between documentable tissue (organic) damage and patient reports of illness. These perspectives and analyses provided an intellectual opening to such puzzling issues as individual differences in reactions to pain, and individual differences in seeking medical care. Pain is not isomorphic with organic disintegration and indeed is often more heavily determined by upbringing, personality, mood, social roles, and current social circumstances (Pennebaker, 1982).

With regard to help seeking, social influences lead to problems of both too little and too much. On the one hand, many people delay seeking treatment, both for life-threatening emergencies like heart attacks and strokes and for dangerous progressive conditions such as precancerous lesions, infections, and small tumors. On the other hand, many other people are quick to demand medical attention for every minor ache. The shared social definitions of health and illness have serious consequences for both the individual and the society.

Medical anthropologists further illuminated the ways in which symptoms are noticed, interpreted, and reported across cultures and subcultures (Adler & Stone, 1979). For example, Mark Zborowski (1952) and Irving Zola (1966) documented ethnic differences in the experience of pain and responses to it. Further, many conditions that are considered diseases in the United States—ranging from depression to neurasthenia to hearing voices—are ignored, or seen as normal, or conceived with different meanings in other countries and cultures (Foster

& Anderson, 1978; Kleinman, 1986; Scheff, 1967). This work presaged current debates about what conditions represent "illness" and deserve coverage by medical plans or health insurance. It is also relevant to the struggles of clinical health psychologists to receive reimbursements as health practitioners.

The importance of medical sociology and medical anthropology has grown with the increasing cultural diversity of many Western populations, as well as with issues emerging from a global health perspective. Health care workers increasingly are being evaluated in terms of their "cultural competence" and ability to relate to patients from very different backgrounds, taking into account their belief systems as these affect disease prevention, diagnoses, and treatment.

It is now clear that sociocultural, developmental, and sociodemographic forces, including age, gender, class, wealth, ethnicity, family, work, and nationality, are integral parts of a comprehensive understanding of health and illness. Modern health psychology, as a discipline partly rooted in social science, includes such concepts in its theories and its research, and addresses ethnic disparities in health, special issues in women's health, and sociodemographic considerations in health promotion.

Epidemiology and Public Health

The late nineteenth century and the first half of the twentieth century saw great changes in the public health. First, the Industrial Revolution vastly increased the wealth of working people in Western societies and created a substantial middle class. Second, the discovery and increasing recognition of the role of infectious microbes in human disease led to enormous improvements in sanitation and hygiene. (In Greek mythology, Hygieia, the goddess of health and cleanliness, was the daughter of Asclepius.) The work of French chemist Louis Pasteur and his colleagues on microorganisms, and the demonstrations of prevention of infection by English surgeon Joseph Lister (in the 1860s; see Metchnikoff, 1939) and others, led to the construction of germ theory—the idea that many diseases are caused by microorganisms. Together, these developments led to enormous changes in the quality of drinking water, the treatment of sewage, and the handling and storage of food (e.g., refrigeration).

As modern cities and suburbs developed, people gained access to safe drinking water, adequate shelter, flush toilets, trash removal, and inspected, monitored, and nutritious food. On the individual level, hand washing and other sanitary practices also increased, as people came to understand the transmission of infectious disease. Together, all these factors produced a dramatic decrease in the death rate from infectious disease (McKeown, 1976, 1979; Grob, 1983). Life expectancy in North America and Western Europe rose dramatically.

The vivid decline in deaths from many infectious diseases occurred in advance of the availability of antibiotics, and even for diseases for which no vaccinations were available. For example, death rates from measles for children in England fell more than 99% from 1850 to 1950 (McKeown, 1976), even though the measles vaccine was not introduced until the 1960s. Nevertheless, the introduction of vaccinations, beginning with a smallpox vaccine in the 1880s, paralleled the time frame of the introduction of improved sanitation, nutrition, and living conditions and further lowered the death rate and decreased morbidity from infectious agents. Together, these sanitation- and vaccination-related public health measures produced a remarkable improvement in health in the 100 years preceding the 1950s.

Interestingly, life expectancy in developed countries began to level off just as antibiotics entered the scene. As advances in biochemistry research created more and more antimicrobial drugs, the field of internal medicine came into its own, but an unintended side effect was to obscure the broader trends in public health. In other words, the dramatic increase in longevity was overattributed to "miracle drugs" (biomedical cures), rather than properly credited to plunging childhood mortality rates and new control of epidemics. Psychologically speaking, people could better understand cures as a result of miracle drugs than they could make the connections between increased life expectancy and a largely invisible set of public health measures; this phenomenon still hinders public health efforts today.

As mortality from infectious diseases declined, death rates from cardiovascular disease skyrocketed, and it became the leading cause of death. Very slowly, the idea began to emerge (or, more accurately, *reemerge*) that lifestyle—including behaviors such as diet, cigarette smoking, and physical activity—might have significant effects on serious diseases like heart disease. Starting in 1948, about 5,000 residents of Framingham, Massachusetts, began being followed to see what behaviors and other risk factors might affect (predict) heart disease and stroke. Findings from that study indicated that lifestyle-related conditions such as hypertension (high blood pressure) were significant risk factors. By the 1970s, it began to seem both sensible and feasible to try to *prevent* (rather than merely *treat*) the development of cardiovascular disease and other slow-developing conditions as well. The stage was thus set for the new field of health psychology to incorporate a public health perspective as a significant core concept; it would address psychological factors in the prevention of disease, as well as in treatment and recovery. Yet it was not until 1990 that the U.S. government emphatically urged adoption of lifestyles maximally conducive to good health (Healthy People 2000).

The focus on prevention has remained a core concept in public health, as well as in health psychology. The World Health Organization (WHO), an agency of the United Nations, was established in 1948 with a focus on complete physical, mental, and social well-being. It followed a predecessor organization in the League of Nations, set up to help control worldwide epidemics such as typhus and cholera. WHO, along with other organizations addressing global health, has documented that chronic diseases tied to behavioral factors are increasing in the developing world (Yach, Hawkes, Gould, & Hofman, 2004). It is not simply that as infectious diseases are being reduced, there is more opportunity for chronic diseases to account for mortality. Rather, it appears that health-damaging behaviors such as tobacco use and ingestion of excessive amounts of high-calorie foods increase as nations experience economic development. Health promotion is thus a critical component of global health, which has become a domain that requires the expertise of health psychologists.

Although medicine has traditionally paid less attention to prevention than to treatment, some changes in health care organization and delivery have encouraged greater concern. Under fee-for-service arrangements, physicians have little financial incentive to spend time and resources on prevention, since such activity is rarely compensated. In contrast, health maintenance organizations (HMOs) that receive capitated payments (i.e., re-

ceive a lump sum per person per year) have greater motivation to help their patients avoid the need for medical care. HMOs such as Kaiser Permanente (begun in the 1930s in California) and Health Insurance Plan (HIP, begun in 1947 in New York), which care for patients over the long term, tend to invest more in prevention and have often integrated psychologists into their practices. This shift to managing health for populations opens opportunities for health psychologists in concepts, research, and practice.

Biopsychosocial Model

In the 1930s, researcher-physician Adolf Meyer proposed that stressful life events may be important in the etiology of illness (Meyer, 1948). He suggested that these events need not be negative or catastrophic to be pathogenic; they must simply be interpreted by the individual as an important life change.

This work placed a social psychological context around the pioneering efforts of the experimental physiologist and physician Walter Cannon. Cannon, following up on the investigations of the nineteenth-century French physiologist Claude Bernard, focused attention on the stress on the body from emotional activation. Bernard had emphasized the *milieu interne*—the internal environment—the idea that all living things must maintain a constant or balanced internal environment. Bernard (1880) made scientific the study of physiology and homeostasis. Cannon followed up on these ideas, discovering and explaining the relations among stress, the nervous system, and the endocrine system. He proposed one of the most important concepts in health psychology, the so-called *wisdom of the body* (Cannon, 1932).

In 1896, while still a medical student, Cannon began using the newly discovered X-rays to study digestion. He noticed that stomach movements seemed to be affected by emotional state (Benison, Barger, & Wolfe, 1987). Rather than viewing this finding as noisy data interfering with his study of the biology of digestion, Cannon went on to explore what causes our subjective feelings of a "knot in the stomach" when facing a stressful or fear-arousing situation. By 1932, Cannon was able to write a detailed analysis of how bodily alterations occur in conjunction with emotional strife and the experiencing of emotions such as anger or fear (Cannon

1932, 1942). He documented that stress causes an increase in the blood sugar level; a large output of adrenaline (epinephrine); an increase in pulse rate, blood pressure, and respiration rate; and an increase in the amount of blood pumped to the skeletal muscles. Cannon called this the *fight-or-flight response*.

Importantly, according to Cannon and his homeostasis approach, the body has developed a margin of safety, with allowance for contingencies that we count on in times of stress. In other words, the body naturally prepares itself for challenge, including the rare "extra" challenge. This robust internal regulation—this wisdom of the body to self-correct—is built around the hypothalamic-pituitary-adrenal system but extends to systems throughout the body. Cannon also foresaw that the body exists in a social and environmental context, and presciently argued that the study of psychophysiology should not ignore the larger issues of coping with environmental stress.

The idea that sundry noxious stimuli, be they emotional or physical, result in a biological, neuroendocrine response was championed in the 1930s by Hans Selye. Selye (1956) studied the physiological consequences of an ongoing response to threat. In his view, just about any type of threat would produce an arousal in the body's system of defenses against noxious stimuli. But in Selye's model, stress would not necessarily lead to disease unless the adaptive responses are required for a prolonged period, an idea consistent with modern views on stress and disruption of metabolic and immune systems (Cacioppo & Berntson, this volume; Kemeny, this volume).

Harold Wolff (1953), a physician with great influence in psychiatric circles, continued this evolutionary view, with a focus on seeing stress as a response to *perceived* challenge or danger, rather than to a necessarily threatening or noxious stimulus. For Wolff, as for Selye, it was continuing but futile efforts to achieve homeostasis through maladaptive coping (such as constant worrying and arousal) that would lead to illness. Note that these models are more general and nonspecific than the "specific conflict to disease" models typically proposed by Dunbar and other founders of psychosomatic medicine. Even today, within modern neurobiology and psychoneuroimmunology, the debate continues about whether stress phenomena mostly begin with a general weakening and vulnerability, or instead involve mostly disease-specific disruptions of a particular biological mechanism.

More recently, recognizing that stress can either help or hurt the body, McEwen (1998) analyzed how the body adapts to stress by what can be termed *allostasis*—the ability to achieve stability through change. The processes of allostasis use the autonomic nervous system, the hypothalamic-pituitary-adrenal axis, and the cardiovascular, metabolic, and immune systems to respond to challenges. In the short term, this can enhance functioning. However, when these systems are used frequently to help respond to much stress, allostatic load occurs, and the body is damaged. That is, if there is repeated stress over time (many challenges, lack of adaptation, or lingering stress), the ongoing and increased exposure to stress hormones harms many physiological functions. The idea of allostasis, though not radically different from previous notions of stress and homeostasis, emphasizes the processes involved in the constant reestablishment of homeostasis and explains how even small degrees of dysregulation, when cumulated across systems, can contribute to disease susceptibility. It is striking how the most modern notions involve many of the same basic adaptation systems uncovered by Cannon and Selye.

The physiological work on stress response was paralleled by psychological research on the nature of stress and how individuals respond to (i.e., cope with) such stressors. In social psychology, Irving Janis (1958), turning attention toward managing the challenges, examined psychological coping mechanisms in facing the stress of surgery. His research showed that before surgery, some patients were worried about their operation and felt very vulnerable; other patients were somewhat concerned and asked for information about their surgery; still other patients were extremely cheerful and relaxed before their operation and did not want to know anything about it. Reactions differed after surgery, and these differences were related in systematic ways to the presurgery behaviors. The highly fearful and the totally fearless patients experienced poorer postoperative reactions than did patients with a moderate amount of anticipatory fear. These successful patients rehearsed ways of dealing with the stresses they faced, a phenomenon referred to by Janis as "the work of worrying."

Around the same time, Richard Lazarus (1966) began research that showed that an individual's appraisal of the meaning of an event was critical for determining if the event was experienced as stressful. Individuals experience stress when they perceive that they do not have the resources needed to address a given threat. An environmental event is not stressful if the individual appraises (interprets) it as manageable. Along with his collaborator, Susan Folkman, Lazarus elaborated the ways of coping with these threats and the implications of these efforts for health (Lazarus & Folkman, 1984). Such research helped launch the modern era of work on stress and coping (Carver, this volume).

Studying both the new developments in psychosomatic psychiatry and the emerging ideas of coping with stress, the physician George Engel (1968, 1977) helped bring together the various threads of mind-body approaches to health. Engel and his colleagues argued that a "giving up" response in the face of situations of loss may precede the development of various illnesses in individuals who have *predispositions* to the particular illnesses. Engel combined the environment (e.g., loss), the ability or inability to cope, and a set of common biological pathways to various health problems.

On the psychobiological side, health psychology was given a big push forward by Neal Miller (1976) and his colleagues. Miller was an eminent psychological researcher of learning and motivation during several decades at Yale University. In the 1960s, he moved to Rockefeller University (a center of brain research) and focused on integrating learning principles with the new discipline of behavioral neuroscience. As research techniques improved, Miller looked further into how the brain affected motivation and learning, and vice versa. By showing that organisms could sometimes learn to control bodily functions like heartbeat, blood pressure, and intestinal contractions (that are regulated by the autonomic nervous system), Miller helped open the door to rigorous research on such topics as biofeedback, placebo effects, and relaxation training.

Also in the 1960s and 1970s, researchers overturned the assumption that the body's immune system acted autonomously, without input from the nervous system. For example, psychologist Robert Ader, who was studying the classical conditioning of learned taste aversion in rats, was puzzled when the rats that had been injected with an immune-suppressing drug became ill during subsequent experiments, long after the drug was gone from their systems. Ader teamed with immunologist Nicholas Cohen and (using principles of condi-

tioning) found that when the immune-suppressing drug (unconditioned stimulus) was paired with sweetened water (conditioned stimulus), the rats subsequently became ill when they received only the sweetened water (Ader & Cohen 1975, 1985; Kemeny, this volume). This work provided a clear demonstration that the immune system could be classically conditioned. The immune system had learned to respond to the environment and was communicating with the nervous system. Such research helped launch the modern field of psychoneuroimmunology, which postulates that environmental psychosocial challenges may cause or encourage disease through stress effects on suppressing or disrupting the immune system.

Together, these researchers (and others) thus demonstrated the importance of integrating the biological, the psychological, and the social, both conceptually and empirically. The general approach that emerged from the theorizing of Cannon, Selye, Engel, and others has come to be called the *biopsychosocial approach to health*. Still, in the 1950s and 1960s only several hundred articles per year were published in areas now considered within the purview of health psychology, compared with many thousands in medicine and the rest of psychology (Rodin & Stone, 1987). See Figure 1.1 for an overview of the roots of health psychology.

The Establishment of the Field of Health Psychology

By the 1970s, all the major ideas were in place, but the catalyzing structures were needed to launch the field of health psychology.

In 1973, the American Psychological Association appointed the Task Force on Health Research (APA Task Force, 1976). Counseling psychologists, clinical psychologists, and rehabilitation psychologists were increasingly employing a biopsychosocial approach to patient care but were finding that this did not fit well with the traditional medical model being used by their physician colleagues (Wallston, 1997). Simultaneously, social psychologists, developmental psychologists, and community/environmental psychologists were distilling and integrating new concepts of and approaches to health and well-being from the broader social sciences. Topics and issues that were seen as peripheral or puzzling by those in the field of medicine were interesting and

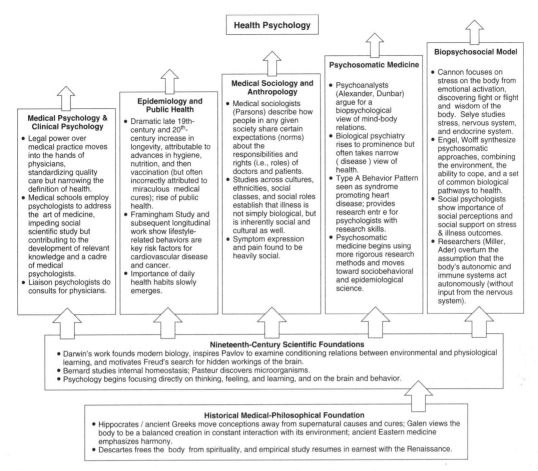

Figure 1.1. Key historical developments in scientific progress of health psychology.

researchable to psychologists—coping with stress, cooperation with treatment, adapting to chronic illness, hospitals as institutions, psychophysiology, environmental challenge, risky behaviors (like smoking), socioeconomic factors and health, gender and health, quality of life, dying with dignity, and more (Friedman & DiMatteo, 1982; Matarazzo, Weiss, Herd, Miller, & Weiss, 1984).

A major organizational step was taken in 1978 when the Division of Health Psychology became the 38th division of the APA, with Joseph Matarazzo as its first president. Matarazzo, who had spent much of his career as a medical psychologist (both clinician and researcher) in a medical school, was well positioned to understand and bring together critical elements from research psychology, clinical psychology, and health care. In a series of papers, he eloquently called for specialty training and research in this new field (Matarazzo, 1980, 1983, 1994).

In 1979, an edited handbook—*Health Psychology*, the first book so titled—was published by George C. Stone, Frances Cohen, and Nancy E. Adler (1979). It defined health psychology as the application of the theory and methods of all branches of psychology to the understanding of physical health and illness. The handbook demonstrated the contributions to this understanding from developmental, social, personality, experimental, physiological, organizational, and clinical psychology. The editors were launching a new doctoral program in health psychology at the University of California, San Francisco, and the handbook was developed to help define the intellectual scope of the new field. The doctoral program was based in a medical school but was run by research psychologists and focused on psychological factors in the etiology, course, and treatment of disease, and in the maintenance of health. This program helped serve as a rallying point for many psychologists in California and then throughout the nation. A number of programs were established soon after, and a wide range of programs are now in place across the country.

The term *behavioral medicine* also began to be used in the 1970s (e.g., Birk, 1973), and an organizational conference on behavioral medicine was held at Yale University in 1977 (Schwartz & Weiss, 1978). This emerging interdisciplinary field was focused on integrating the mind and the body in treatment of disorders and included a large number of psychologists, as well as physicians and other health professionals. There is considerable overlap between health psychology and behavioral medicine, with the latter including a broader set of disciplines and perhaps a somewhat greater relative focus on clinical application.

The field of health psychology gained greater visibility and legitimacy in 1982, as the first issue of the journal *Health Psychology* was published under the editorship of George Stone. The first article, by Stone himself, was entitled "Health Psychology: A New Journal for a New Field" and outlined Stone's wide-ranging model of the "health system." Stone then raised a core issue, asking rhetorically, "With such an enormous range of approaches and topics, it is certainly appropriate to ask whether health psychology can exist as a cohesive and integrated field of specialization" (1982, p. 3). The field of health psychology is still grappling with this matter. Sociobehavioral science research using health as an outcome appears in a wide range of journals, not only those dedicated to health psychology.

The first issue of *Health Psychology* also contained an address from the health psychology division's second president, Stephen M. Weiss, who was head of the recently formed behavioral medicine branch at the National Heart, Lung, and Blood Institute (Weiss, 1982 [speech delivered in 1980]). Weiss, hopeful but somewhat nervous about the future of the small field of health psychology, proclaimed, "If there ever was a time of opportunity for Health Psychology, that time is *now*" (p. 81). These words were a hope and a plea as much as a prediction, but they were indeed prophetic, and the field of health psychology exploded during the next two decades—in research, teaching, and structure.

The founding psychologists recognized that they themselves had not received training in the broad new field of health psychology. Rather, each brought to the field his or her own disciplinary background but with an appreciation that this pro-

vided only part of the picture. They believed that psychologists would be better equipped if they were trained not only in their psychological disciplines but also in the issues in health and health care. It was not obvious, however, what the core training should be for this field. In May 1983, a foundational conference was held at the Arden House, an old mansion on the Hudson River. We attended that gathering—the National Working Conference on Education and Training in Health Psychology (see Stone et al., 1987)—and remember it as an exhilarating blend of differing approaches to the same fundamental questions of psychology and health, with a fitting mountaintop location allowing a glimpse of the promised land.

This conference emphasized the coming rapprochement between psychology and health care. It recommended a focus on quality, a broad, interdisciplinary orientation, and significant attention to ethical, legal, and cultural issues. Anticipating the strain between science and practice, the recommendations also had a strong professional (clinical and public health) component embedded in science, emphasizing an integrated mix of theory and practice, training experience in health care settings, and the licensure of health psychologists (Stone, 1983b). This tension between scientists and practitioners continues to be problematic, as health psychologists immersed in patient care seek specific advice and techniques for interventions while health psychologists focused on the scientific underpinnings of health and health policy tend toward more complex and nuanced concepts and models. Nevertheless, the field of health psychology remains an excellent example of the mutual benefits of reciprocal progress between theory and practice, research and application, and policy and implementation.

In addition to several edited books, authored textbooks began to appear in the 1980s. In 1982, M. Robin DiMatteo and Howard S. Friedman published *Social Psychology and Medicine;* in 1983, *An Introduction to Health Psychology* by Robert J. Gatchel and Andrew Baum appeared; and by 1986, textbooks by Shelley E. Taylor and by Michael Feuerstein, Elise E. Labbé, and Andrzej Kuczmierczyk were on the market. Undergraduate courses in health psychology slowly began to appear. A handbook on psychology and health was launched by Robert Gatchel, Andrew Baum, and Jerome Singer (1982).

Thus, by the end of the 1980s, health psychology was firmly established. The structural foundation was laid and remarkable progress made in a little more than a decade. Division 38 became a fast-growing part of the APA. Today, various pre- and postdoctoral programs have been established, and many undergraduate curricula include a course in health psychology. There are multiple journals, and traditional psychology journals now include a substantial number of articles that deal with matters of health.

Defining Health Psychology

As an academic discipline, health psychology might best be defined as "the scientific study of psychological processes related to health and health care." As a professional and policy field, health psychology might best be defined as "the use of findings from basic psychological theory and peer-reviewed research to understand and encourage thoughts, feelings, and behaviors that promote health."

These definitions are narrower than the foundational definitions from the 1980s, which emphasize the educational, scientific, and professional contributions of psychology to the promotion of health, the maintenance of health, the prevention of illness, the treatment of illness, and the analysis and improvement of the health care system and health policy (Matarazzo, 1980, 1983; Stone, 1983a). Such broad definitions include almost everything having to do with psychology and health. Because almost every aspect of psychology has some implications for well-being, and because almost every aspect of health and health care involves some aspect of psychology (such as decision making, communication, psychophysiology, or behavior), a broad definition of health psychology means that almost everything in psychology and almost everything in health care involves health psychology. Although it is useful to acknowledge the pervasive interrelationship of psychology and health, such breadth also engenders ambiguity. In fact, health psychologists largely focus on a limited number of core psychological processes related to health. These include social support; coping with stress; communication and patient adherence; adaptation to chronic illness; health developmental issues in childhood, adolescence, and aging; health risk behavior; resource allocation and decision making in health care; psychopharmacology; personality and disease; social context and other social influences on health; and the central nervous system, hormones, and immunity.

The Modern Field of Health Psychology

Still growing and evolving, health psychology has not yet established core research paradigms, core bodies of knowledge, or established boundaries. It remains both enhanced and hindered by its diverse intellectual heritage. It has contributed significantly to other areas of psychology and has been enriched from them.

In 2001, the APA added "promoting health" as a key element of its mission statement. This change marked a formal shift in organized psychology from a traditional focus on behavior and mental health to a more direct and broader emphasis on health. It also raised a challenge to health psychology: If a fundamental focus of psychology is promoting health, then why do we need a subfield called "health psychology"?

This fundamental alteration of the APA's mission statement is remarkable. As noted, 25 years earlier, there was not even any formal *subfield* called "health psychology." Even as late as the 1970s and 1980s, few people would have viewed health promotion as an essential ingredient of psychology as a whole. Although a latecomer to the scene, health psychology has rapidly moved to center stage. Yet the field of health psychology has its own views of significant problems to be addressed, its own organizational cultures, its own interfaces with related professions and disciplines, and its own preferred concepts and methods.

Urged on by developments in health psychology and public health, as well as encouragement from the U.S. Congress, the U.S. National Institutes of Health (NIH) opened the Office of Behavioral and Social Sciences Research (OBSSR) in 1995. The OBSSR aims to integrate a biobehavioral perspective across the research areas of the NIH, with an important goal being the initiation and promotion of studies to evaluate the contributions of behavioral, social, and lifestyle determinants in the development, course, treatment, and prevention of illness and related public health problems. The U.S. Centers for Disease Control and Prevention (CDC) likewise have increasingly turned attention toward matters at the core of health psychology, including the promotion of healthy behaviors and the fostering of healthful environments. Funding for health psychology research comes from almost all of the NIH institutes, with major funding provided by

NIMH (mental health), NIDA (drug abuse), NHLBI (heart, lung, blood), NCI (cancer), NICHD (development), and NIA (aging).

In Europe, the establishment of health psychology has accelerated in recent years, often tied to the provision of health care (i.e., medical psychology) and to the establishment of public health principles in national health services. The European Health Psychology Society (EHPS) was formed subsequent to a first meeting at Tilburg (Netherlands) in 1986 and holds annual conferences.

Health Psychology and Health

Perhaps most important, the field of health psychology is bringing together diverse insights into the nature of health itself. By providing a dynamic and multilayered view of what it means to be human, research in health psychology has helped reveal important limits of a traditional medical model that attempts to cure disease. From the perspective of health psychology, it is not the case that we are healthy until we become "sick." Further, it is not the case that mental problems or mental stresses are clearly distinguishable from physical problems or physical stresses. The human organism is launched with a particular genetic endowment into a specific yet complex and ever-changing environment, in which it reacts, copes, learns, strives, and ages.

Startling new insights emerge from this perspective. There may never be a simple "cure" for heart disease, obesity, stress, pain, or aging. It is not necessarily the case that providing more doctors (whether physician or psychologist) is the best way to improve the health and well-being of the population (Kaplan, this volume). Doctors and other health care providers function best when they communicate effectively with their patients, based on a scientific understanding of practitioner-patient relations (Hall & Roter, this volume). How people think about, verbalize, and cope with challenges can have important direct and indirect effects on whether they become ill or enter the medical care system (Carver, this volume; Pennebaker, & Chung, this volume). Studying personality as a predictor of health forces attention beyond a more narrow focus on psychoimmunology or stress or unhealthy habits; it brings the view of how the pieces fit together in the whole person (Friedman, this volume). Social contact with others, a sense of belonging, and participation in social groups have been docu-

mented to be significantly tied to many key aspects of health, and not always in a simple manner (Taylor, this volume). Life-span and life-course perspectives on health emphasize the processes by which well-being is maintained in the face of age-related changes in functioning (Rook, Charles, & Heckhausen, this volume). Research on adaptation to stress and to chronic diseases has led to multifaceted conceptualizations of adjustment, as well as to attention to the reciprocal influences and intersections of emotions, cognition, behaviors, life roles, and culture (Kemeny, this volume; Stanton & Revenson, this volume); sound measurement and research design are key challenges of the complex biopsychosocial model (Smith, this volume; Westmaas, Gil-Rivas & Silver, this volume). Homeostasis models have been confirmed as fruitful, extended to multiple levels, and considered in an evolutionary context (Cacioppo & Berntson, this volume). There are vast clinical implications, as many common assumptions of treatment do not stand up to scientific review (Wortman & Boerner, this volume). The Cartesian dualism is dissolving, the structural impediments to an encompassing view of well-being are slowly dissipating, and a new view of health is emerging.

Acknowledgments.   We thank George Stone for comments on this chapter.

References

Ader, R., & Cohen, N. (1975). Behaviorally conditioned immunosuppression. *Psychosomatic Medicine, 37,* 333–40.

Ader, R., & Cohen, N. (1985). CNS–immune system interaction: Conditioning phenomena. *Behavioral and Brain Sciences, 8,* 379–394.

Adler, N. E., & Stone, G. C. (1979). Social science perspectives on the health system. In G. C. Stone, F. Cohen, & N. E. Adler (Eds.), *Health psychology: A handbook* (pp. 19–46). San Francisco: Jossey-Bass.

Alexander, F. (1950). *Psychosomatic medicine: Its principles and applications.* New York: Norton.

APA Task Force on Health Research. (1976). Contributions of psychology to health research: Patterns, problems, and potentials. *American Psychologist, 31,* 263–274.

Benison, S., Barger, A. C., & Wolfe, E. (1987). *Walter B. Cannon: The life and times of a young scientist.* Cambridge, MA: Harvard University Press.

Benjamin, L.T., Jr. (Ed.). (1988). *A history of psychology: Original sources and contemporary research*. New York: McGraw-Hill.

Bernard, C. (1880). *Leçons de pathologie expérimentale: Et leçons sur les propriétés de la moelle épinière*. Paris: Librarie J.-B. Baillière et fils.

Birk, L. (Ed.). (1973). *Biofeedback: Behavioral medicine*. New York: Grune and Stratton.

Boring, E. (1950). *A history of experimental psychology*. New York: Appleton-Century-Crofts.

Bott, E. A. (1928). Teaching of psychology in the medical course. *Bulletin of the Association of American Medical Colleges, 3*, 289–304.

Cannon, W. B. (1932). *Wisdom of the body*. New York: Norton.

Cannon, W. B. (1942). Voodoo death. *American Anthropologist, 44*, 169–181.

Cuff, P. A., & Vanselow, N. (2004). *Improving medical education: Enhancing the behavioral and social science content of medical school education*. Washington, DC: National Academies Press.

Darwin, C. (1859). *On the origin of species by means of natural selection*. London: J. Murray.

DiMatteo, M. R., & Friedman, H. S. *Social psychology and medicine*. Cambridge, MA: Oelgeschlager, Gunn and Hain, 1982.

Dunbar, F. H. (1943). *Psychosomatic diagnosis*. New York: Hoeber.

Ekman, P., & Davidson, R. J. (Eds.). (1994). *The nature of emotion: Fundamental questions*. New York: Oxford University Press.

Engel, G. L. (1968). A life setting conducive to illness: The giving up–given up complex. *Bulletin of the Menninger Clinic, 32*, 355–365.

Engel, G. L. (1977). The need for a new medical model: A challenge for biomedicine. *Science, 196*, 129–136.

Feuerstein, M., Labbé, E. E. & Kuczmierczyk, A. R. (1986). *Health psychology: A psychobiological perspective*. New York: Plenum Press.

Foster, G. M., & Anderson, B. G. (1978). *Medical anthropology*. New York: Wiley.

Franklin, B. (1794/1906). *The autobiography of Benjamin Franklin*. Boston: Houghton Mifflin.

Franz, S. I. (1912). The present status of psychology in medical education and practice. *Journal of the American Medical Association, 58*, 909–911.

Franz, S. I. (1913). On psychology and medical education. *Science, 38*, 555–566.

Friedman, H. S., & DiMatteo, M. R. (Eds.). (1982). *Interpersonal issues in health care*. New York: Academic Press.

Gatchel, R. J., & Baum, A. (1983). *An introduction to health psychology*. Reading, MA: Addison-Wesley.

Gatchel, R. J., Baum, A., & Singer, J. E. (1982). *Handbook of psychology and health* (Vol. 1). Hillsdale, NJ: Erlbaum.

Greer, D. S., & Mor, V. (1986). An overview of national hospice study findings. *Journal of Chronic Diseases, 39*, 5–7.

Grob, G. N. (1983). *Mental illness and American society, 1875–1940*. Princeton, NJ: Princeton University Press.

Guthrie, D. (1945). *A history of medicine*. London, T. Nelson and Sons.

Healthy People 2000: National health promotion and disease prevention. (1990). Washington, D.C.: U.S. Department of Health and Human Services.

Hollingshead, A. (1973). Medical sociology: A brief review. *Milbank Memorial Fund Quarterly, 51*, 531–542.

Houston, B. K., & Snyder, C. R. (Eds.). (1988). *Type A behavior pattern: Research, theory, and intervention*. New York: Wiley.

James, W. (1890/1910). *The principles of psychology*. New York: Holt.

Janis, I. L. (1958). *Psychological stress: Psychoanalytic and behavioral studies of surgical patients*. New York: Wiley.

Kleinman, A. (1986). *Social origins of distress and disease: Depression, neurasthenia, and pain in modern China*. New Haven, CT: Yale University Press.

Lazarus, R. S. (1966). *Psychological stress and the coping process*. New York: McGraw-Hill.

Lazarus, R. S., & Folkman, S. (1984). *Stress, appraisal, and coping*. New York: Springer.

Longrigg, J. (1998). *Greek medicine: From the heroic to the Hellenistic age: A source book*. New York: Routledge.

Matarazzo, J. D. (1980). Behavioral health and behavioral medicine: Frontiers for a new health psychology. *American Psychologist, 35*, 807–817.

Matarazzo, J. D. (1983). Education and training in health psychology: Boulder or bolder. *Health Psychology, 2*, 73–113.

Matarazzo, J. D. (1994). Health and behavior: The coming together of science and practice in psychology and medicine after a century of benign neglect. *Journal of Clinical Psychology in Medical Settings, 1*(1), 7–39.

Matarazzo, J. D., Weiss, S. M., Herd, J. A., Miller, N. E., & Weiss, S. M. (1984). *Behavioral health: A handbook of health enhancement and disease*. New York: Wiley.

McEwen, B. S. (1998). Stress, adaptation and disease: Allostasis and allostatic load. *Annals of the New York Academy of Sciences, 840*, 33–44.

McKeown, T. (1976). *The modern rise of population*. London: Edward Arnold.

McKeown, T. (1979). *The role of medicine*. Princeton, NJ: Princeton University Press.

Menninger, K. A., & Menninger, W. C. (1936). Psychoanalytic observations in cardiac disorders. *American Heart Journal, 11,* 1–21.

Metchnikoff, E. (1939). *The founders of modern medicine: Pasteur, Koch, Lister; Including Etiology of wound infections, by Robert Koch, The antiseptic system, by Sir Joseph Lister, and Prevention of rabies, by Louis Pasteur* (D. Berger, Trans.). New York: Walden.

Meyer, A. (1948). Selected papers. In A. Lief (Ed.), *The commonsense psychiatry of Dr. Adolf Meyer.* New York: McGraw-Hill.

Miller, N. E. (1976). *Fact and fancy about biofeedback and its clinical implications.* Washington, DC: American Psychological Association.

Novack, D. H. (2003). Realizing Engel's vision: Psychosomatic medicine and the education of physician-healers. *Psychosomatic Medicine, 65,* 925–930.

Parsons, T. (1951). *The social system.* New York: Free Press.

Parsons, T. (1958). Definitions of health and illness in the light of American values and social structure. In E. G. Jaco (Ed.), *Physicians, patients, and illness: Sourcebook in behavioral science and medicine* (pp. 165–187). Glencoe, IL: Free Press.

Pennebaker, J. W. (1982). *The psychology of physical symptoms.* New York: Springer-Verlag.

Rodin, J., & Stone, G. (1987). Historical highlights in the emergence of the field. In G. C. Stone, S. M. Weiss, J. D. Matarazzo, N. E. Miller, J. Rodin, C. D. Belar, et al. (Eds.), *Health psychology: A discipline and a profession* (pp. 15–26). Chicago: University of Chicago Press.

Rosenman, R. H., Friedman, M., Straus, R., Wurm, M., Kositcheck, R., Hahn, W., et al. (1964). A predictive study of coronary disease. The Western Collaborative Group Study. *Journal of the American Medical Association, 189,* 103–110.

Scheff, T. J. (Ed.). (1967). *Mental illness and social processes.* New York: Harper and Row.

Schofield, W. (1969). The role of psychology in the delivery of health services. *American Psychologist, 24,* 565–584.

Schwartz, G. E., & Weiss, S. M. (1978) Yale Conference on Behavioral Medicine. *Journal of Behavioral Medicine, 1,* 3–12.

Selye, H. (1956). *The stress of life.* New York: McGraw-Hill.

Stoddard, S. (1978). *The hospice movement: A better way of caring for the dying.* New York: Vintage.

Stone, G. C. (1982). *Health Psychology,* a new journal for a new field. *Health Psychology, 1,* 1–6.

Stone, G. C. (1983a). The scope of health psychology. In G. C. Stone, S. M. Weiss, J. D. Matarazzo, N. E. Miller, J. Rodin, C. D. Belar, M. J. Follick, & J. E. Singer (Eds.). (1987). *Health psychology: A discipline and a profession* (pp. 27–40). Chicago: University of Chicago Press.

Stone, G. C. (1983b). Summary of recommendations. *Health Psychology, 2*(5), 15–18.

Stone, G. C., Cohen, F., & Adler, N. A. (Eds.). (1979). *Health psychology: A handbook.* San Francisco: Jossey-Bass.

Stone, G. C., Weiss, S. M., Matarazzo, J. D., Miller, N. E., Rodin, J., Belar, C. D., et al. (Eds.). (1987). *Health psychology: A discipline and a profession.* Chicago: University of Chicago Press.

Taylor, S. E. (1986). *Health psychology.* New York: Random House.

Venzmer, G. (1972). *Five thousand years of medicine* (Marion Koenig, Trans.). London: Macdonald.

Vevier, C. (Ed.). (1987). *Flexner 75 years later: A current commentary on medical education.* Lanham, MD: University Press of America.

Wallston, K. A. (1997). A history of Division 38 (Health Psychology). In Donald A. Dewsbury (Ed.), *Unification through division: Histories of the divisions of the American Psychological Association* (Vol. 2, pp. 239–267). Washington, DC: American Psychological Association.

Weiss, S. M. (1982). Health psychology: The time is now. *Health Psychology, 1,* 81–91.

Wolff, H. G. (1953). *Stress and disease.* Springfield, IL: Thomas.

Yach, D., Hawkes, C., Gould, C. L., & Hofman, K. (2004). The global burden of chronic diseases. *Journal of the American Medical Association, 291,* 2616–2622.

Zborowski, M. (1952). Cultural components in responses to pain. *Journal of Social Issues, 8,* 16–30.

Zola, I. K. (1966). Culture and symptoms: An analysis of patients presenting complaints. *American Sociological Review, 31,* 615–630.

2

Timothy W. Smith

Measurement in Health Psychology Research

Health psychology has always held the promise of both a methodologically rigorous basic science and applications for the improvement of health and well-being. Early in the development of the field, book-length discussions illustrated convincingly that scientifically sound approaches to measurement were essential in health psychology's basic and applied agendas (Karoly, 1985; Keefe & Blumenthal, 1982). With increasing methodological sophistication, there has been remarkable progress in fulfilling this dual promise of health psychology (Smith, Kendall, & Keefe, 2002; Smith & Suls, 2004).

From the outset, measurement has posed major challenges in health psychology, in part because the field is based on the biopsychosocial model (Engel, 1977). In contrast to the biomedical model, in which disease is seen as reflecting alterations in biochemistry and the function of cells, organs, and physiological systems, the biopsychosocial view describes health and disease in terms of the interplay of biological, psychological, and social/cultural processes. This framework involves reciprocally interacting and hierarchically arranged levels of analysis (von Bertalanffy, 1968) that shape research questions within and across levels of analysis. Each level of analysis has its own conceptual models, research methods, and related measurement pro-

cedures. The biopsychosocial model requires that these levels be integrated in the process of research. For investigators, this imposes a requirement not only for increased breadth in familiarity of measurement concepts and methods, but also for consideration of processes involved in bringing them together in meaningful ways.

Measurement remains a complex and central concern for the field's progress, yet it rarely garners the attention that advances in basic research and application do. Reports of associations between psychosocial variables and disease or the usefulness of psychosocial interventions in the management of disease often receive considerable notice in the scientific literature, as well as the science media. Even though such developments would not be possible without sound measurement procedures, this essential component of the research infrastructure generates little of the excitement associated with many instances of its use. Grand theories of behavior and health or mind and body, as well as related investigations, are nearly always more noteworthy than the smaller theories and seemingly lesser investigations regarding the associations between measures and the constructs they are intended to assess.

The gap between the centrality of measurement and the attention it receives is not unique to health psychology. Over the much longer history of psychological research, this same situation has been observed many times in many fields. Consider, for example, Judd and McClelland's (1998) observation of the state of measurement research and the usual level of attention to measurement concerns in social psychology, as it could have just as appropriately been written about health psychology:

> So why, one might ask, do we need a *Handbook* chapter on measurement, and why should one read it? The answer, we suggest, is that our discipline's lack of attention to measurement is a common dilemma. While the individual researcher can ignore measurement issues for the most part without consequence, the discipline as a whole suffers when the theories and methods of measurement are undeveloped and unscrutinized. Conceptual advances in science frequently follow measurement advances. The everyday practice of normal science can successfully operate without much attention to measurement issues. But for the discipline as a whole to advance and develop, measurement must be a focus of collective attention. (p. 180)

Definitions of measurement are plentiful and varied, but many share elements of Stevens's (1951, 1959, 1968) articulation of measurement as "the assignment of numbers to aspects of objects or events according to one or another rule or convention" (Stevens, 1968, p. 850). Judd and McClelland (1998) suggested that this view is not sufficient, because the assignment of numbers identified by Stevens as the core of this process actually constitutes measurement "only if the subsequent numbers ultimately represent something of meaning, some regularity of attributes or behaviors that permits prediction" (p. 181). Measuring a person's level of social support by counting the number of pieces of mail he or she receives in a week certainly involves an easily described rule, but at best it is indirectly related to social support as defined in most conceptual approaches and might actually be unrelated to the construct of interest.

Judd and McClelland endorse the refinement of Stevens's definition provided by Dawes and Smith (1985), who maintained that "the assignment of numbers not only must be orderly if it is to yield measurement but must also represent meaningful attributes and yield meaningful predictions" (p. 511).

This emphasis on a systematic relationship between the numbers assigned in the process of observation and meaningful but indirectly observed attributes is a core assumption in most modern approaches to measurement. Judd and McClelland (1998) describe this correspondence as follows:

> The compact model or description that we construct of observations through measurement we will call a scale or a variable. The meaningful attribute or regularity that it is presumed to represent we will call a construct. Accordingly, measurement consists of rules that assign scale or variable values to entities to represent the constructs that are thought to be theoretically meaningful. (p. 181)

Following this definition, the construct of pain could be (and often is) measured with a 100-millimeter visual analogue scale anchored by the descriptors "no pain at all" and "worst pain imaginable." In the rule for assigning numbers to observations, pain is quantified as the distance in millimeters from the "no pain" end to the point respondents mark as corresponding to their level of pain. As discussed at length later, such definitions underscore the fact that measurement is a complex process in which theory and conceptual models play an important role. The selection of constructs as meaningful—and the nonselection of others—is clearly a matter of theoretical models and related assumptions. Similarly, the selection of a method of observation and the rules involved in assigning numbers to observations are also theory-laden decisions. For example, in the visual analogue pain scale, it is assumed that individuals are able and willing to accurately describe their subjective experience. Hence, the process of measurement is itself a theory-driven process (McFall, 2005).

In order for research on the grander theories and questions in health psychology to be maximally useful in the field's basic and applied agendas, these "smaller" embedded theories and questions regarding measurement must also be articulated and tested. Returning to the previous example, one could ask a variety of questions. What is the evidence that this visual analogue scale captures what the researcher intends when he or she sets out to measure "pain"? What constructs instead of or in addition to pain might be captured unintentionally using this method? For the visual analogue scale to be useful in understanding influences on the development of pain or in evaluating the benefits of a new treatment for pain, such questions must be addressed.

In behavioral science generally—and any field within psychology in particular—measurement is an ongoing and complex process. It involves theorizing, measurement development, evaluation, and refinement of both specific measurement techniques and the conceptual models underpinning those techniques. Measurement in health psychology is often particularly complex. A daunting variety of topics, methods, and levels of analysis seemingly requires encyclopedic knowledge within and beyond psychology, and researchers must be flexible and often creative in applying basic principles of measurement to novel questions and domains.

This chapter provides an overview of basic principles and methods of measurement, emphasizing critical issues and illustrating their application in health psychology. This overview cannot replace more thorough reviews of basic measurement principles, but rather will serve to introduce these concepts. Several excellent basic sources are cited in the present chapter, and readers are encouraged to consult them. Similarly, this chapter cannot provide a review of measurement in all areas of health psychology, but it can illustrate application of principles of measurement to the design and critical evaluation of measurement procedures in the main topics in the field.

Before turning to principles of measurement design and evaluation, it is important to discuss several sources of complexity for measurement in health psychology. As discussed in virtually every section of this chapter, clearly articulated conceptual models and theoretical assumptions greatly facilitate sound measurement. In health psychology, several important considerations or contexts influence these conceptual models and several other facets of the design, development, evaluation, and refinement of measurement procedures and techniques (Smith, 2003; Smith & Ruiz, 1999). Measures are useful to the extent that they permit valid inferences in the service of given research goals, and health psychology research encompasses a variety of goals and audiences.

Sources of Complexity for Measurement in Health Psychology

In its emergence and subsequent development, health psychology has drawn heavily from concepts and methods in older fields in psychology, especially social, clinical, personality, experimental, and physiological psychology. Like the related fields of behavioral medicine and psychosomatic medicine, health psychology also draws on several other behavioral and biomedical sciences, particularly medicine, epidemiology, public health, sociology, genetics, and nursing. Research and application in health psychology often—if not usually—involve collaborative efforts with investigators from these other sciences, and the resulting research methods, including measurement, are therefore both shaped by and intended to speak to multiple perspectives.

Three Domains of Health Psychology

One source of complexity for measurement in health psychology is the wide variety of research topics in the field. These can be loosely organized into three overlapping domains (Smith, 2003). The first—*health behavior and prevention*—includes the association between daily habits and other behaviors (e.g., diet, physical activity level, smoking, alcohol use) and subsequent health outcomes. The initial goal of this research area is the identification of robust associations between potentially modifiable behaviors and subsequent health outcomes, as well as moderators of these associations (e.g., age, gender, ethnicity, family history of disease) that might indicate subgroups in which these behavioral risk factors are more or less important. Subsequent research examines determinants of these behavioral risk factors, in order to construct models that will facilitate the design of risk-reducing interventions. The array of influences on health behaviors that can inform intervention efforts is quite broad, including rapidly changing psychological variables (e.g., urges and other motivational variables, affect, appraisals), more stable psychological characteristics (e.g., beliefs, expectancies, attitudes), biological variables (e.g., homeostatic processes, chemical dependencies), and broader social and even cultural factors (e.g., socioeconomic status [SES], education).

Ideally, intervention research follows from the findings of studies of the nature, moderators, and determinants of behavioral risk factors. Intervention studies are intended to ask one or both of two questions. First, does the intervention produce meaningful changes in behavioral risk? In this context, meaningful refers not only to the magnitude of change but also to its duration, as many improvements in health behavior (e.g., smoking cessation, weight loss, increased physical activity) are short-lived. Second, do behavioral changes produced by these interventions reduce the incidence of disease or improve other health outcomes? In prevention research, a very wide variety of intervention approaches can be used, ranging from individual or small-group-based approaches (e.g., behavior therapy, motivational interviewing, family or couple counseling), to larger group approaches (e.g., school, work site, or neighborhood programs), to population-based interventions (e.g., public policy, advertising, and public education).

This first health psychology domain illustrates one of the most important sources of complexity in health psychology measurement—the heterogeneity of constructs to be addressed. The health behaviors to be assessed range from seat belt, sunscreen, and health screening use to smoking, drinking, eating, and physical activity. The health outcomes these behavioral risks influence include longevity, morbidity or mortality from specific causes, and levels of functional activity (i.e., the inverse of disability). The determinants of these behaviors involve biological, psychological, social, cultural, and economic factors, and the types of interventions used to address them are similarly varied. Hence, in this one domain, the conceptual models of the relevant behaviors, moderators of their effects, their determinants, and intervention approaches can be highly varied and often complex. The methods of observation through which these constructs can be assessed and the rules for translating the related observations into numbers are similarly diverse.

The second domain—*stress and health,* or *psychosomatics*—poses similar challenges. Here, the focus is on more direct psychobiological influences on the development and course of disease. Psychological stress, negative emotions, and related personality traits and characteristics of the social environment are hypothesized to influence the onset and course of disease—not through the behavioral mechanisms that are the primary concern in the first topic described earlier but through more direct physiological processes. Psychosocial epidemiology examines the statistical associations of these risk factors with the incidence of disease among initially healthy persons, and with the course of existing disease. These risk factors include characteristics or experiences of persons (e.g., personality traits, stressful life circum-

stances, emotional disorders), their social relationships (e.g., isolation, conflict), and their surroundings (e.g., neighborhood SES). The outcomes of interest include longevity and a variety of indications of the presence, severity, and course of disease that can be either general (e.g., hospitalization) or specific to a given condition (e.g., presence and severity of atherosclerosis, level of inflammation in arthritic joints).

Research in this second domain also tests models of the mechanisms linking these risk factors with disease, including cardiovascular, neuroendocrine, immunologic, and other physiological processes that are plausibly influenced by the psychosocial constructs and also plausibly linked to pathophysiology of disease. Beyond testing long-standing hypotheses about the influence of psychological experiences on health and disease, this research also informs the design of interventions intended to modify these risk factors or interrupt their psychobiological influences on pathophysiology. The outcomes targeted in such interventions (e.g., stress management, cognitive behavioral therapy) include change in the risk factor, alteration of the mediating mechanism, or in some instances health outcomes such as morbidity or even mortality risk. Here again, the wide variety of constructs to be assessed and the complexity of the conceptual models in which they are embedded—often in a single study—pose major challenges in the design, evaluation, refinement, and use of measurement procedures.

The third major domain in health psychology involves *psychosocial aspects of medical illness and care.* Studies in this domain focus on the psychosocial impact of physical illness on patients and their families. The outcomes of interest include emotional, social, and physical functioning (i.e., activity vs. disability), the subjective impact of the condition or side effects of its usual medical/surgical care (e.g., pain, symptom severity), and sometimes the level and cost of health care utilization. The determinants of variations in these effects of illness are a major focus of such research, given that patients differ greatly in these outcomes. Potential influences on these impacts include aspects of the disease (e.g., severity, exacerbations) and its treatment (e.g., medication regimens, surgical procedures), characteristics of the person (e.g., personality, coping responses), and features of his or her social, cultural, and socioeconomic context (e.g., social support, SES, ethnicity). Once determinants of important outcomes have been identified, they can be useful in the design and implementation of adjunctive psychosocial interventions intended to improve well-being and even medical outcomes. Constructs to be measured in intervention research of this type include not only the wide array of psychosocial, biomedical, and even utilization outcomes described previously but also components of the delivery of these interventions (e.g., adherence to treatment protocols) and potential mediators and moderators of the intervention effects.

Levels of Analysis in the Biopsychosocial Model

This brief description of the domains of health psychology indicates the remarkable breadth of research questions and settings where basic principles of measurement must be applied. Much of this breadth stems from the fact noted previously that the biopsychosocial model (Engel, 1977) serves as the fundamental conceptualization in the field (Suls & Rothman, 2004). Typically, research questions in health psychology relate—at least in some manner—to the individual level of analysis, in that the behavior and/or health of individuals is assessed. However, these constructs at the individual level of analysis are often studied in relation to constructs within "higher" levels (e.g., social relations, socioeconomic factors), "lower" levels (e.g., physiological processes, biomedical outcomes), and on occasion both higher and lower levels within a single study. For example, a study might examine the extent to which neighborhood SES as measured by median household income is related to the residents' ambulatory blood pressure levels, and whether that association is mediated by the individual residents' level of self-reported daily stress. Given that specific measures within these levels of analysis are often the purview of different disciplines, they are likely to reflect differing conceptual approaches, methods, and research traditions. As a result, the basic act of measurement in health psychology typically requires integration of a more diverse set of approaches than is typical within other areas of psychology.

Over the last 30 years, this aspect of health psychology has become the norm, rather than an unusual challenge. In fact, it is often seen as one of the novel and exciting characteristics of health psychology research, by both its producers and consumers. The increased demands on expertise can be managed, in part, through interdisciplinary collaboration, but for such efforts to be maximally effective, investigators must often have at least some familiarity with methods outside of their basic discipline.

Age, Sex, Ethnicity, and Culture

The nature of health problems varies as a function of demographic factors. Further, the importance of these factors in health psychology research is increasing, with changes in the age and ethnic composition of the population of the United States and other industrialized nations (Yali & Revenson, 2004). For example, the major sources of morbidity and mortality, psychosocial influences on these health outcomes, and the nature of related interventions change with age. The most prevalent threats to the health of children and adolescents are quite different from those that affect middle-aged adults, who in turn face different health threats than do the elderly. Psychosocial influences on these health outcomes also vary with age, as do health-promoting interventions (Siegler, Bastain, Steffens, Bosworth, & Costa, 2002; Smith, Orleans, & Jenkins, 2004; Williams, Holmbeck, & Greeley, 2002). From the perspective of measurement, this poses challenges not only through the diversity of constructs to be assessed and the variety of conceptual models in which they are embedded. The appropriateness of methods of observation varies with age, as well. For example, pain, emotional distress, and functional activity (i.e., the inverse of disability) are often studied as consequences of chronic physical illness. Self-reports of these impacts of chronic disease are likely to be suspect in very young children, but this method can yield highly useful measures of the same constructs in adults.

This example of age as influencing the strengths and weaknesses of a given measurement procedure illustrates a broader issue. The properties of a measurement procedure are context specific. That is, investigators and consumers of research cannot assume that evidence regarding strengths and limitations of a measure generalizes to populations or settings beyond those where the initial evidence was obtained. Such generalizations constitute hypotheses to be tested in measurement research.

Such generalizations are potentially problematic in health psychology research because the field has often disproportionately included middle- and upper-income white men in research samples (Park, Adams, & Lynch, 1998). Although women's health has received growing attention in recent years, these efforts have not yet eliminated the gender gap in understanding health and disease. Further, SES, ethnicity, and culture are increasingly but still insufficiently studied influences on the nature of health problems, their determinants, and effects of related interventions (Whitfield, Weidner, Clark, & Anderson, 2002; Yali & Revenson, 2004). From the perspective of measurement, these demographic dimensions and categories are themselves important topics for study in health psychology research. Also, the (non)equivalence of properties of any given measurement technique across these dimensions must be evaluated rather than assumed. For example, if a social support scale has been demonstrated to capture the intended construct through measurement research on predominantly Caucasian samples, it must be demonstrated rather than assumed that the scale does so in Latino or other ethnic minority populations.

Multiple Contexts and Audiences in Health Psychology Measurement

Its location at the intersection of several fields has implications for the design and evaluation of measurement procedures in health psychology, as does the fact that health psychology research has audiences beyond psychology. Perhaps the most obvious of these contexts and audiences is *medical science and care*. In the early years of health psychology research, tests of the association between psychosocial variables and subsequent health often used convenient, broad, and nonspecific measures of health outcomes. For example, the effect of stressful life changes on subsequent health was often studied using self-report symptom checklists as measures of health outcomes. Further, nonspecific "black box" models of the mechanisms linking psychosocial inputs and health outcomes were common. That is, it was presumed that effects of stressful life events on subsequent health were mediated by physiological effects of stress and emotion, but these pathophysiological mechanisms were typically not specified, let alone measured. Such work played an important role in the emergence of the field, but it had limited impact beyond psychology, perhaps because research traditions in medicine involve

greater specificity in terms of health outcomes and underlying mechanisms.

One reflection of the maturing scientific status of health psychology research is that it is increasingly informed by current medical standards for assessing specific diseases, as well as an understanding of their pathophysiology. In this newer approach, health psychology research often addresses outcomes and criteria with established significance. Tests of hypotheses regarding psychosocial influences on disease are at least based on explicit and plausible mechanisms. These considerations obviously influence the selection of measures in research on stress and health or psychosomatics. Measures of health outcomes that are established in the context of a specific disease are important, as are established measures of mechanisms through which psychosocial factors might influence outcomes. For example, current research on the effects of depression on the development and course of cardiovascular disease uses widely accepted criteria of establishing the occurrence of disease (e.g., criteria for disease-specific morbidity and mortality) and describes—if not actually tests—autonomic or other physiological mechanisms linking such emotional stress to specific disease processes (Lett et al., 2004).

Similarly, studies of psychosocial adaptation to a given disease should include standard measures of the nature and severity of the condition used in the medical literature (e.g., specific cancer diagnoses, disease stages, related medical treatments). In this way, empirical ties to the medical literature on a given condition will be enhanced, making it more likely that over time health psychology research will have a growing impact on the broader field of health sciences. Similar considerations are important when selecting measures of outcomes for research on the effects of adjunctive psychosocial interventions. If psychosocial interventions have impacts on outcome measures typically used in traditional medical research on a given disease, then this health psychology research is more likely to capture the attention of a broader range of researchers and health care providers outside of psychology.

These suggestions should not be interpreted as an endorsement of uncritical acceptance and incorporation of measurements from medical research. In fact, one of the useful roles health psychologists can play in interdisciplinary research is the application of principles of measurement design and evaluation to traditional medical assessments. Evaluations of reliability, validity, and predictive utility are often relevant to medical assessments, and often the available research on a given medical assessment suggests that such evaluations are not extensive. This process can identify strengths and weaknesses of widely used measures and diagnostic procedures, and the resulting refinements can enhance research in health psychology and the related medical field (Kaplan & Frosch, 2005).

Health care economics and health care financing form an important context for health research. Increasingly, measurement of health outcomes in ways that lend themselves to meaningful estimates of the clinical or practical significance of effects is useful. Ideally, such measurement procedures would lend themselves to comparisons across a wide range of conditions and interventions, in order to facilitate evaluations of the relative importance of observed effects. As discussed in more detail later, Kaplan (1994) has recommended the comprehensive and integrated measurement of several aspects of health status (e.g., symptoms, functional activity level) in standardized units called Quality–Adjusted Life Years. If these general health outcome assessments are used to express health benefits of interventions in standard units, then health psychology interventions can be compared with traditional medical or surgical interventions using the same outcome assessment. If the costs of such interventions are also quantified, then a wide variety of psychosocial and traditional medical interventions can be evaluated in terms of their cost-effectiveness or cost utility (Kaplan & Groessel, 2002). This approach creates a "level playing field" in which the effects of traditional medical approaches are compared using a common and comprehensive metric with those obtained with psychosocial interventions. This important opportunity (Smith & Suls, 2004) is made more likely through developments in measurement (Kaplan, 1994).

Principles of Measurement Design and Evaluation

These sources of complexity in health psychology measurement make this fundamental aspect of the research endeavor challenging. Fortunately, basic principles developed over decades and more recently emerging quantitative methods combine to provide a trustworthy guide to measurement in these complex circumstances.

The Central Role of Theory

In considering the role of theory and conceptual models in health psychology, one might understandably think first about fundamental questions about connections between psychosocial factors and health. Theory guides the basic and applied research in health behavior and prevention, the psychobiology of stress and disease, and the study of psychosocial aspects of medical illness and care. In contrast to such important questions, questions about the nature of the relationship of measures to the constructs they are intended to reflect do not seem to involve "theories" or even conceptual models at all. Yet they involve assumptions and hypotheses, and the field is better served when these are clearly articulated and tested (McFall, 2005).

Not all health psychology researchers would endorse the proposition that theory plays a central role in the development and evaluation of measures. The tradition of *operationism* or *operationalism* equates the concept to be measured with the specific research procedures used to accomplish the task. For example, in a study evaluating the effects of an intervention to reduce chronic pain, pain might be defined (and measured) as the number of specific behaviors (e.g., grimacing, guarded movement) displayed during a structured set of movements. From this conceptual perspective on measurement, if the treatment reduces the frequency of these overt behaviors, it has *by definition* reduced pain. This philosophical view is quite consistent with the behavioral tradition in psychology that was prominent during much of the last century and continues to be influential. Behavioral researchers of this orientation were highly involved in the emergence of health psychology and the overlapping field of behavioral medicine (Gentry, 1984). From this conceptual perspective, any inference or generalization from specific research procedures to unobserved hypothetical constructs is fraught with peril, and "hard-line" versions of this perspective see such inferences as frankly unscientific.

As with the waning prominence of behavioral analysis and other "operational" perspectives in psychology, behavioral medicine and health psychology have implicitly endorsed a broader philosophy of science and as a result a more theory-driven view of measurement. Although the behavioral perspective remains influential, recognition that "operational" procedures of measurement have a complex rather than definitional relationship to the concepts of interest is widespread. As a result, the need for careful delineation of the conceptual context of any measurement instrument or procedure as a critical aspect of the measurement process is more readily acknowledged. Further, although the strong version of operationalism has limited usefulness in current research, the skepticism associated with that tradition regarding inferences and generalizations about unobservable concepts on the basis of research procedures is useful if it is used constructively. That is, inferences about the meaning of measures are hypotheses. As in any research area, measurement research ideally involves the articulation of alternative hypotheses and the design of empirical tests pitting the rivals against each other.

The role of theory in measurement begins with clear and specific definitions of the construct to be assessed. Such definitions include a clear description of the domain or content of the construct, as well as specification of the boundaries or limits of that content. Beyond a sound definition, other characteristics of the conceptual model or theory of a construct must be articulated to guide the development and evaluation of a measure. In a broadly useful discussion of this essential component of the measurement process in personality research, West and Finch (1997, pp. 144–145) outline several questions to be answered in clarifying the nature of the construct.

The first question asks, "What is the expected degree of relationship among items that constitute the measure of the construct?" Although the wording of this question makes clear that it is most relevant to the case of multi-item scales, it is relevant to all cases in which multiple indicators are used in a scale or other summary variable. It is also a more complex question than it first appears.

In perhaps most instances in health psychology research, the association among items within a scale would be expected to be large, given that they are intended to reflect a single construct. Responses to the individual items are in essence *caused* by a latent trait or hypothetical construct (Bollen & Lennox, 1991). Hence, scale items intended to assess the personality trait of conscientiousness would be expected to correlate closely, as responses to scale items would be hypothesized to be caused by a single trait. However, not all sets of items making up scales would be expected to correlate in this way. For example, in measures of overall severity of re-

cent physical symptoms, a variety of symptoms across multiple systems are assessed, and there may be little reason to expect that symptoms of upper respiratory infection (i.e., congestion, sneezing) would correlate highly with symptoms of intestinal or neurological conditions. Indeed, a high level of intercorrelation among such items could indicate that the scale assesses something (e.g., a general tendency for excessive somatic complaints) other than the construct of interest (i.e., a summary of generally unrelated aspects of recent health versus actual illness).

In the case of the conscientiousness scale, responses to individual items are seen as effects of the person's standing on the hypothetical construct, and therefore the items should be highly correlated. In the case of the recent physical symptoms measure, severity of recent physical symptoms is not a general casual construct but instead is a higher-order emergent characteristic or construct that serves as a summary of the specific symptoms captured in individual items. Rather than the respondent's standing on a latent trait of overall sickness "causing" responses to the individual items, the individual items may be more accurately seen as "causes" of the higher-order variable reflected in the summary score for this emergent construct. Thus, a basic distinction among conceptual measurement models that influences the expected associations among indicators has to do with the nature of the causal direction between those indicators and the construct they assess. In "effect indicator" models, variations in item responses or other measured indicators are effects of unmeasured higher-order or latent casual variables or constructs. In "causal indicator" models, the opposite direction of causality is present; variation in the lower-order measured indicators or item responses cause variation in the unmeasured higher-order, emergent constructs (Bollen & Lennox, 1991).

Another example of this sort of emergent latent variable commonly used in health psychology research is SES. As described by Bollen and Lennox (1991; see also Ozer, 1999), many different indicators of SES are available, such as years of education, grade of employment, and income. Yet variation in these indicators is not caused by variations in SES. Rather, education, grade of employment, and income can readily be seen as causes of SES. West and Finch (1997) describe how items within stressful life events scales (e.g., Holmes &

Rahe, 1967) would also not be expected to be highly correlated because these are assumed to be generally unrelated occurrences. Hence, responses to individual items or indicators reflecting specific life events are not *effects* of the individual's standing on the latent variable or construct of major life events. Rather, responses to these items or indicators (or, more accurately, the events such responses are assumed to reflect) can be seen as causes of the person's standing on the construct of interest. As a result, one would not expect high levels of association among items; if low levels of intercorrelation are observed in the process of measurement evaluation, this would not challenge the measurement model. Interestingly, high levels of inter-item correlation in a case such as a stressful life event checklist might raise questions regarding whether or not scale responses are influenced by different constructs or processes, such as general response styles (e.g., social desirability) or the effect of personality on the tendency to experience high versus low levels of stressful life change.

Thus, to answer to the first question posed by West and Finch (1997), one must determine if the measured items or indicators are effects or causes of the constructs they are intended to reflect. Effect indicator measurement models assume at least some intercorrelation among items or indicators, and the latent trait or construct explains these associations (i.e., they reflect a common cause). In causal indicator models, intercorrelations among indicators are not required. Health psychology contains many instances of both types of measurement models. Although inter-item correlations (i.e., internal consistency) would be expected in effect indicator models, high levels of internal consistency could still reflect a measurement problem. If the conceptual domain to be assessed is broad, a high degree of internal consistency might indicate that too narrow a portion of the domain is sampled through the items within the measure. There are no firm guidelines for appropriate levels of inter-indicator correlation, but the observed level should be considered relative to the upper and lower limits implied by the conceptual definition of the construct to be measured.

The second question West and Finch (1997) pose is, "What is the structure of the construct?" Often the assumption is that indicators or items reflect one unidimensional construct. In many instances, however, a construct may consist of multiple, lower-order intercorrelated components, each

of which is assessed through several items or indicators. In the earlier example of the personality trait of conscientiousness, current versions of the five-factor model of personality maintain that this global trait contains distinct facets or components, such as achievement-striving, self-discipline, and deliberation (Costa & McCrae, 1992). As a result, all conscientiousness items or indicators should be correlated, but correlations among items within a subset reflecting the same facet should be larger than correlations among items tapping different facets.

Overall scale scores best represent unidimensional structures. When such structures are assumed rather than established, overall scores may inadvertently combine several specific, though perhaps intercorrelated components. Whether or not the use of overall summary scores for multidimensional measures is informed and intentional or inadvertent, a variety of interpretive and analytic challenges emerge (Carver, 1989; Hull, Lehn, & Tedlie, 1991). Associations of such complex scores with measures of other constructs may mask more specific associations involving components of the overall score. A lack of association between the overall score and other variables (i.e., null results) can similarly mask more specific associations. An early example of this issue was the personality trait of hardiness (Kobasa, 1979), a multifaceted trait that was hypothesized to confer emotional and physical resilience in the face of stressful life circumstances. Hardiness consisted of three specific components—belief in control over the events of one's life, commitment to a meaning or purpose, and viewing change as a challenge rather than threat. Hardiness scales contained subscales measuring these individual components. Therefore, analyses of total hardiness scale scores could mask the effects of the more specific dimensions (Carver, 1989; Hull et al., 1991). Regardless of how such multicomponent measures are managed in subsequent research, the design and evaluation of any measure must be informed by a clear answer to the question about the intended structure. This answer should then become a hypothesis to be tested against other possible structures or measurement models.

The third question is, "What is the stability of the construct?" In health psychology research, some constructs are expected to be quite stable (e.g., personality traits), whereas others should be quite variable (e.g., acute pain, state affect). Still others would be expected to show intermediate levels of stability over time (e.g., health beliefs, disability). Despite the simplicity of this question, it is often overlooked in the selection of specific quantitative evaluations of measurements.

In the final question posed by West and Finch (1997) is a complex issue. "What is the pattern of relationships of measures of the construct of interest with other measures of the same construct and with measures of other constructs?" As these authors note, this refers to what Cronbach and Meehl (1955) called a *nomological net*. A nomological net consists of rules or hypotheses that specify the relationship of observable properties of hypothetical constructs to each other (e.g., associations among measures or other research operations), constructs to observables (i.e., latent variables to indicators or operations), or constructs to each other. Together, these interlocking specifications provide a set of hypotheses that can guide the development and evaluation of measurements. For example, a simple nomological net for the construct of hardiness described earlier might indicate that the three components would be expected to be associated more closely with each other than with conceptually distinct personality characteristics, such as trait anxiety or neuroticism. Hence, the three related component scales should be more closely correlated with each other than with scales assessing the conceptually distinct traits. Interestingly, poor support for this aspect of the nomological net for hardiness has been one of the most troubling challenges for the theory (Funk, 1992).

Nomological nets also contain assumptions about appropriate methods of observation (e.g., self-report, behavioral ratings, psychophysiological assessments) for a given construct, as well as likely levels of intercorrelations or convergence among such multiple indicators. For example, a nomological net for the construct acute lower back pain might specify that self-reports, facial expressions involving grimacing, and psychophysiological measures of increased muscle tension in the lower back would all correlate, and these associations would be larger than correlations of the pain measures with self-reports, facial expressions, and psychophysiological measures (e.g., electrodermal activity) of state anxiety.

In the process of measurement development and evaluation, the elements of nomological nets often emerge and change over time. This is because initial descriptions of the related conceptual models are often limited, and are elaborated and refined as research on the theory and related measurement models accumulates. In many instances, substantive research on a topic can provide relevant evidence regarding the related measurement models, as it typically involves elements of the surrounding nomological net. For example, evidence that scales assessing individual differences in trait anger or hostility are associated with increases in self-reported state anger, physiological arousal, and behavioral displays of aggressive or unfriendly behavior during potentially conflictual social interactions might indicate how these personality traits could influence physical health. Such evidence also supports the nomological net describing these traits and their measured manifestations (Smith, 1992).

Clear and precise conceptual definitions and answers to the questions outlined by West and Finch (1997) are an essential starting point in the design and evaluation of measurements in health psychology. In some instances, measures will have been developed and perhaps even widely adopted without sufficient thought and comment on these issues. In those cases, researchers can do a useful service by "doubling back" and "filling in" this missing work and evaluating the measurement procedure or technique in the new light of a more well-developed conceptual context.

Key Concepts in Measurement

Levels of Measurement

Given the variety of topics, levels of analysis, and disciplines in health psychology research, measurement procedures often involve different levels of measurement. Importantly, levels of measurement are related to the usefulness of the measure in specific applications, as well as to the underlying quantitative models both for evaluating measurement procedures themselves and for testing the substantive questions using these procedures in health psychology research.

Measurements are typically classified in terms of *levels* or *scales*. In the most basic—*nominal* scales —numbers are assigned as labels to classes of objects. That is, numbers simply serve the function of names in identifying and distinguishing in a classification scheme. In *ordinal* scales, numbers are assigned in such a way as to reflect rank ordering on the characteristic of interest. For *interval* scales, numbers are assigned to attributes not only to reflect rank ordering but also so that differences between numbers correspond to meaningful differences on the measured construct. In ordinal scales the difference between numbers refers only to rank order and implies nothing about the size of the difference on the measured characteristic. In contrast, interval scales consist of constant units of measurement, and therefore a given difference between scale values has a constant meaning relative to the measured construct. This consequence of constant units of measurement (i.e., constant meaning of differences between scale values) is true at all points along interval scales. For *ratio* scales, in addition to constant units of measurement, a true zero point can be designated.

In the behavioral sciences the first three levels of measurement are commonly used, and some debate has occurred about whether or not many continuous scale scores (e.g., scores on personality or attitude measures) represent ordinal or interval scales. For example, if it is an interval scale, then the difference between scores of 5 and 10 on the Beck Depression Inventory (BDI) should reflect the same magnitude of difference in the construct of severity of depressive symptoms as does the difference between scores of 25 and 30. Clearly scores on the BDI convey much more information than an ordinal scale, but the difficulty in determining precisely the constancy of units makes it unclear if it is a true interval scale.

Given that scores of zero are possible on the BDI, one might wonder why it is not considered a ratio scale. For measures like the BDI and most measures in behavioral science research, this does not represent a "true zero" because it does not imply the same sort of certainty about the total absence of depressive symptoms as does "zero pounds" in assessing weight or "zero beats per minute" in measuring heart rate. Hence, the BDI cannot be considered a ratio scale.

The distinctions among levels of measurement are important in selecting appropriate statistical analyses and ensuring the accuracy of statistical conclusions. Although not without controversy, it is generally considered appropriate to treat scales or variables that clearly contain more information than ordinal scales but might not meet the precise requirements of constant units of measurement (e.g., state affect questionnaires; pain scales) as interval-level data for the purposes of statistical analy-

sis. In health psychology research, measurement often involves "true" interval and even ratio scales, and it is important to consider the level of measurement prior to selecting approaches to statistical analysis.

Schroeder, Carey, and Vanable (2003a) provide a valuable illustration of the issue of scales of measurement in the case of assessing sexual risk behavior. Most commonly, constructs such as the frequency of unprotected sexual intercourse are assessed through either count measures or relative frequency measures. Count measures ask respondents to indicate the exact number of times (during a specified interval) they engaged in a behavior (e.g., intercourse without a condom). Given the presence of a "true zero" and constant meaning of intervals, these measures in theory constitute true ratio scales. Relative frequency measures, in contrast, ask respondents about the occurrence of the target behavior (e.g., unprotected sexual activity) relative to a broader class of behavior (e.g., all occasions of sexual activity). These approaches to quantifying sexual risk behavior can take the form of several types of scales or levels of measurement, though perhaps most commonly ordinal- or interval-level measurements. These different levels of measurement typically result in different distributions, making different types of statistical analysis appropriate (e.g., parametric vs. nonparametric techniques). Further, count measures may provide a more direct indicator of true risk exposure and therefore may be more useful in some contexts, such as the evaluation of sexual risk reduction interventions.

Except in the case of ratio scales used in health psychology (e.g., blood pressure, weight, plasma lipid levels, etc), most measurements in the field involve metrics that are arbitrary in two respects (Blanchard & Jaccard, 2006); the individual's "true" standing on the construct of interest is unknown, as is the meaning of scale units. Only relative positions on the construct can be inferred. In these common circumstances, care must be taken in interpreting scores as reflecting "low," "medium" or "high" standing on the construct of interest, or differences between individuals or groups as "small," "medium," or "large." Such inferences from arbitrary metrics require additional research relating observed scores to external criteria (Blanton & Jaccard, 2006). This is particularly important in efforts to describe the magnitude and clinical significance of effects in intervention research (Kazdin, 2006).

True Scores, Error, and Reliability

The ability to test any hypothesis in health psychology research depends on the extent to which scores on the measures used reflect the constructs of interest. The extent to which scores reflect the intended construct, in turn, depends on reliability and validity. In classical test theory, any given measurement or observed score (X) contains two components: "true score" (T) and measurement error (E). Hence, $X = T + E$. In this view, T theoretically represents the mean of a large number of measurements of a specific characteristic taken on one individual. E combines a wide variety of random and changing factors that have influenced an observed score. In this model, the reliability of a measure is the ratio of true-score variance to observed-score variance, or the proportion of true-score variance in observed scores. Hence, a reliability coefficient of $r_{xt} = .9$ means that 90% of the variance in observed scores reflects true-score variance; $1 - .9 = .1$ is the proportion of observed score variance that is due to random errors. If true scores reflect the construct of interest (see the following discussion of validity), then increasing levels of reliability in observed scores would translate into more accurate indicators of that construct.

In this view, there are many potential sources of unreliability (i.e., error), and as a result there are several types of reliability coefficients. Coefficients reflecting internal consistency quantify the degree of association or relationship among individual items within a given measure. The most common of these, Cronbach's (1951) coefficient alpha, is the equivalent of the mean of the correlations between all possible split halves of a set of items. This is an important indication or estimate of the reliability of a measure consisting of multiple items intended to sample the same conceptual domain.

It is important to note that a high level of internal consistency does not necessarily indicate that a scale is unidimensional. Cronbach's alpha, for example, is influenced positively by both the interrelatedness of the items and the number of items. Hence, especially in the case of longer scales, high levels of internal consistency can mask a multidimensional structure. Evidence of high levels of internal consistency is typically necessary but never sufficient as an indication of unidimensional structure. Other quantitative methods discussed later are required to evaluate structure. As noted previously,

it is also possible that a high level of internal consistency could indicate that too narrow a range of indicators has been included in a measure of a construct that is conceptually defined as having greater breadth. This potential concern is related to the issue of content validity, discussed in a later section. Short scales often suffer from low internal consistency simply because of their length, and this can be problematic in health psychology research. For example, sometimes in the large surveys used in psychosocial epidemiology, space is at a premium, and researchers are forced to utilize shortened versions of scales intended to assess important risk factors (e.g., personality traits or life experiences). The resulting low reliability can lead to an underestimate of the magnitude of associations between the risk factor and subsequent health outcomes.

Test-retest reliability refers to the stability of scores over time, or the correlation between scores on the same measure administered on two occasions. The level of agreement between independent judges or raters (i.e., interrater reliability) for categorical classification systems (e.g., psychiatric diagnoses) or rating scales (e.g., presence, type, and/or amount of pain behavior) is another common type of reliability assessed in health psychology research. As discussed previously, the relevance of any one type of reliability in the evaluation of a measure depends on the conceptual description of the construct it is intended to assess. Internal consistency of multiple items intended to reflect a single construct is commonly relevant, as is interrater agreement when behavioral observations or diagnostic classifications are used. Temporal stability is often highly relevant, especially if short intervals between testing occasions are employed. However, some constructs are described conceptually as changing rapidly enough (e.g., emotional states, acute pain) that test-retest reliabilities over longer periods are much less relevant. In such cases, high levels of temporal stability might actually raise concerns about the measure, as they suggest that it is not sufficiently sensitive to the expected change in the construct and instead reflects something more stable than implied by the conceptual definition of that construct. These and other potential sources of error can be combined in *generalizability theory*. Rather than treating all sources of error as equivalent, as is the case in the $X = T + E$ model of classical test theory, generalizability theory attempts to partition these sources of error into specific sources.

Reliability is a critical consideration in health psychology research for several reasons. The reliability of a measure sets an upper limit on the magnitude of observed associations that can be obtained with that measure. For example, if depressed mood and self-reported pain have a true correlation of $r = .50$ (i.e., depressed mood accounts for 25% of the variance in pain reports), the size of the observed association will depend on the reliabilities of the measures of depressed mood and pain. If the two measures both have reliability coefficients of .8, then the observed association will average $r = .4$ over multiple occasions of testing this effect. If the measures both have reliabilities of .6, the observed association will be $r = .3$. With perfectly reliable measures, of course, the observed association would be $r = .5$. Hence, low reliability of measures can produce underestimates of substantive associations.

This relationship between reliability of measurement and observed effect sizes has important implications for statistical hypothesis testing. For example, the reduction in observed effect size resulting from low reliability of measurement has a negative effect on statistical power (Cohen, 1992). In some health psychology research, the effects of psychosocial factors on health outcomes are small, given the complex, multifactorial etiology of many diseases. Therefore, reductions in observed effects sizes due to low reliability can produce artifactual null results, unless sample sizes are quite large. Further, these often small effects of psychosocial variables (e.g., social support, depression) on health outcomes often compete in multivariate analyses (e.g., multiple linear or logistic regression) with characteristics that can be measured more reliably (e.g., body mass, cholesterol levels). It is possible that these psychosocial risk factors could appear less important in the prediction of health outcomes in part because of their relatively lower measurement reliability. In a similar vein, low reliability of measures of potential confounding or mediating variables results in the undercorrection of competing or confounding factors when the measured variable is controlled statistically. Because scores on the variable to be controlled contain relatively low levels of "true score," the statistical control procedure fails to adequately capture variance in this construct. Consider, for example, a mediational model in which chronic negative affect mediates the association between low SES and risk of disease (Gallo & Matthews, 2003). If the measure of chronic nega-

tive affect suffers from low reliability, then statistical analyses in which the effect of SES on health is tested with and without controlling the effects of negative affect might falsely contradict the mediational hypothesis.

Defining and Testing Validity

It should be noted that in the preceding discussion of reliability, classical test theory treats all of the measurement variance that is not due to error as "true-score" variance. In fact, true-score variance and error variance in the $X = T + E$ model are more accurately labeled "systematic" and "unsystematic" variance, respectively. Importantly, the systematic component of variance can reflect (a) a single intended construct, (b) a multidimensional construct, (c) a construct other than the intended one, or (d) a combination of these situations. That is, systematic variance is not necessarily a "true score" reflecting only the intended construct; it is not even necessarily a "true score" on only *one* construct. In behavioral science, measures rarely have the precision that the term "true score" seems to imply.

The issue of what the systematic variance captured by a more or less reliable measure actually reflects is called *validity*. Reliability is a necessary precondition for validity, because with increasing levels of error in measurement (i.e., increasing levels of unsystematic variance), there is by definition a decreasing amount of information about the construct of interest contained in any observed score. Hence, just as the (un)reliability of a measure limits the magnitude of its observed statistical association with other measures, (un)reliability limits the magnitude of its association with the intended construct. The task of evaluating the validity of a measure goes beyond consideration of the relative amounts of systematic and unsystematic variance in scores to also involve partitioning the systematic measurement variance. Validity involves the question, "To what extent do observed scores reflect the intended construct as opposed to something else?" Unreliability (i.e., error) of observed scores will limit this correspondence between measure and construct, but so will sources of systematic variance beyond the intended construct. It is essential to note that validity is not a property of measures. Rather, validity is a property of inferences or interpretations that are based on measures (Messick, 1995). That is, researchers do not validate tests or other measurement procedures per se. They validate interpretations, inferences, decisions, or judgments made on the basis of scores obtained with the measure.

Evidence of validity is easier to acquire and evaluate to the extent that the theory of the construct is well developed, including a description of its association with other constructs that could be sources of systematic variance in the observed scores (West & Finch, 1997). For example, a variety of conceptual models hypothesize an association of negative emotional conditions such as depression or anger with chronic pain, such that chronic pain often functions as a cause and/or consequence of negative affect. A statistical association between a measure of pain and a measure of negative affect could be seen as support for these models. However, an alternative interpretation of such an association could be that it reflects a correlation between two measures of a single construct (e.g., general distress). Hence, it would be important to determine the extent to which the measure of chronic pain can be distinguished from the measures of negative affect. That is, it would be useful to evaluate the extent to which the systematic variance in the measure of pain reflected that construct instead of a related but distinct construct such as general distress. Because research evaluating validity for a given measure is never exhaustive and instead is typically ongoing, the validity of interpretations or inferences based on a measure is always at least somewhat tentative and subject to change with new evidence (G.T. Smith, 2005; West & Finch, 1997).

Because validity concerns hypotheses about what test scores mean, the degree of evidence in support of validity is a function of the amount of evidence consistent with the underlying measurement model and the nomological net in which it is embedded. Contradictory or disconfirming evidence, of course, challenges validity of a given interpretation of the measure. Further, the extent of the supportive evidence is in proportion to the cumulative severity of the tests of those hypotheses (Meehl, 1978), where the severity of a test of any given hypothesis refers to the likeliness of obtaining disconfirming results. For example, a simple t-test of the difference between two groups in their mean scores on a given measure evaluates the hypothesis that the groups do not have precisely the same mean level of this characteristic (i.e., $A >$ or $< B$). It is not terribly likely that any two groups would have exactly the same value, and therefore

with a large enough sample size it is not particularly likely that the implicit prediction of "some difference, any difference" would be disconfirmed. Hence, findings of this sort provide weak—if any—evidence of validity. Specifying the direction of the difference between the two groups (i.e., $A > B$) increases the likelihood that the prediction could be disconfirmed, as would adding a third group and generating a more complex pattern prediction (i.e., $A > B > C$). More complex predictions entail a greater likelihood of disconfirmation, and as a result provide stronger evidence in support of the hypothesis.

Consistent with the principle of the importance of falsification in theory testing (Popper, 1959), the degree of support for a given hypothesis or theory is a function of the degree of risk of disconfirmation to which it has been subjected and survived (Meehl, 1978). In measurement research, predictions of patterns of associations involving simultaneous tests of multiple "strands" in the nomological net surrounding the construct and a specific measure provide greater risk of disconfirmation and as a result stronger evidence of validity than does a simple prediction involving a single association. For example, in contrast to a single predicted association (e.g., "Measure A will correlate positively with measure B"), a prediction comprising a pattern of the relative magnitude of two, three, or more associations (e.g., "Measure A will correlate more closely with measure B than it will with measure C") is easier to disconfirm. This is because there are more associations predicted, as well as specific predictions about their relative magnitude. Hence, failure to disconfirm the more complex prediction constitutes stronger evidence of validity than does failure to disconfirm the simpler prediction, providing both patterns are logically consistent with the conceptual description of the construct in the surrounding nomological net.

As described later, simultaneous evidence of larger associations between multiple measures of a single construct *and* smaller associations with measures of different constructs (i.e., convergent *and* divergent or discriminant validity) confers stronger evidence of validity than does the association between the measures of the same construct considered alone (i.e., only convergence). For example, evidence that two measures of social support correlate more closely with each other (association 1) than either of them do with a measure of the personality trait of extroversion (associations 2 and 3) confers stronger evidence of construct validity than does the significant correlation between the two measures of social support (association 1) alone. The former case represents a more complex pattern prediction (association 1 > than 2 and 3) and therefore would have been easier to disconfirm. Hence, support for the measurement model from the more complex and therefore "riskier" test provides stronger evidence of validity.

These "riskier" pattern predictions are particularly informative when they articulate and test plausible alternative interpretations of the simpler patterns. In the preceding example, the large and significant association between the two social support scales might reflect that both are valid measures of the intended construct. Alternatively, they could both be measuring an unintended third variable, such as individual differences in the personality trait extroversion. The more complex pattern prediction essentially articulates this alternative interpretation and pits it against the original interpretation in a context in which both patterns cannot occur; one interpretation must be discarded as unsupported. If the original rather than alternative interpretation is supported, the cumulative evidence of validity is increased.

Taxonomies of types of validity have changed over many years of measurement theory and research. The classic description by Cronbach and Meehl (1955) has been an important foundation for subsequent taxonomies. In their description, *content validity* referred to the extent to which items or other measured indicators of a construct are a representative sample of its conceptual domain. Specifically, a measure possesses content validity to the extent that all indicators fall within the conceptual definition of the construct and the entire domain of the construct is adequately represented in the set of indicators. For example, as in the preceding description of the concept of hardiness, a measure should include items that pertain to the challenge, commitment, and change facets of the construct but not items that pertain to emotional distress. The closely related concept of *face validity* refers to the extent to which indicators or items appear to measure the intended construct. *Criterion validity* refers to the extent to which present (concurrent criterion validity) or future (predictive criterion validity) scores on a relevant criterion or outcome are related to scores on the measure. Finally, *construct*

validity refers to the extent to which variance in scores on the measure reflect variation in the construct of interest as opposed to other constructs.

Subsequent descriptions of types of validity have tended to view construct validity as the overarching concern, with the other types of validity simply aspects of this broader and more important consideration (Loevinger, 1957; Messick, 1989, 1995; G. T. Smith, 2005). Obviously, this more modern view contrasts with the view that observed scores reflect a combination of "true score" and "error" that forms the core of classical test theory (John & Benet-Martinez, 2000). The construct approach holds that observed scores are more accurately seen as consisting of systematic variability (rather than "true-score" variability) and unsystematic variability, rather than "error." More important, however, the current view maintains that systematic variance is further partitioned into variance attributable to the construct of interest and variance attributable to other constructs. Hence, the validity of a measure (or, more accurately, interpretations based on a given measure) increases as the proportion of systematic, construct-relevant variance in scores increases relative to both of these other components—unsystematic or "error" variance and construct-irrelevant systematic variance.

An example of this view is presented in Figure 2.1. Self-reports of illness or physical symptoms have been used to measure the presence and severity of disease. Scores on such measures could reflect three sources, two of which are systematic. The unsystematic component could reflect careless responses to the scale items or other types of "error" (i.e., unreliability). The systematic component could reflect (a) the presence and severity of actual illness (i.e., the intended construct), or (b) individual differences in the tendency to stoically minimize or deny physical illness versus excessive somatic complaints (i.e., an unintended construct). Three scenarios are presented in the figure. The first depicts a desirable level of validity; the construct-relevant component is large relative to the other two. In the second, the measure is invalid primarily because scores contain too much unsystematic variance—that is, the scale is unreliable. In this scenario, use of the scale is likely to produce misleading null results because little systematic variance is available to be involved in statistical covariation with measures of other constructs (e.g., social support). The third scenario indicates that the measure is reliable but invalid because it contains a large proportion of construct-irrelevant but systematic variance. Importantly, in this third scenario, results can produce misleading positive results, in that adequate systematic variance is available for covariation with other measures, but it does not reflect the intended construct.

There are several common sources of systematic construct-irrelevant variance. As a general class of such variance, method variance refers to variance that reflects the method or procedure used to measure the construct, rather than the construct itself. A widely discussed example of method variance involves response biases within self-report measures. Rather than simply reflecting the construct

of interest, responses to self-report measures could reflect the tendency toward socially desirable responding. Situations vary in how strongly they encourage socially desirable responses (e.g., identifiable vs. anonymous responding). In addition, individuals may vary in the tendency to give socially desirable responses. Further, this tendency could reflect a motivation to avoid admitting socially undesirable characteristics to others or to oneself (Paulus, 1991).

In a seminal contribution to the literature on construct validity, Campbell and Fiske (1959) proposed the multitrait, multimethod matrix (MTMM) as a technique for evaluating the extent to which scores on a given measure reflect the construct of interest, a different construct, and/or the method

Figure 2.1. Portions of measurement variance in self-reported health.

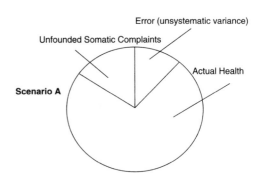

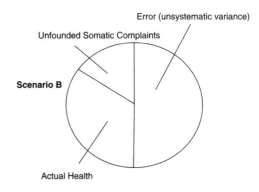

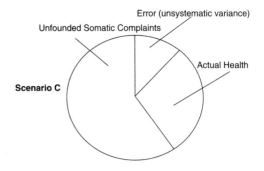

of measurement. The comparison construct(s) in MTMM studies can be either nuisance variables, such as socially desirable response styles, or substantive constructs that are potentially correlated with but distinct from the construct of interest. In this approach two or more methods are used to measure two or more constructs, and the pattern of correlations among the measures is used to evaluate convergent and discriminant (i.e., divergent) validity.

In addition to reliability coefficients (usually presented in the diagonal of MTMM tables), three types of correlations are included. Mono-trait, hetero-method correlations reflect the associations between different methods of assessing the same trait. These pairs of measures share variance due to the fact that they are intended to assess the same construct, but do not share common method variance. As discussed previously, convergent validity refers to the extent to which different measures of a single construct correlate or converge. Discriminant validity refers to the extent to which a measure of a given construct does *not correlate* with (i.e., diverges from) a measure of a conceptually distinct construct. In the MTMM, the two other sets of associations are important in this regard. Hetero-trait, mono-method correlations represent the association between measures of separate constructs that share a common method. Hetero-trait, hetero-method correlations share neither a common construct nor method. As noted previously, these evaluations of convergent and discriminant validity take the form of predictions of patterns of associations. Specifically, in the MTMM design, this pattern prediction is that convergent associations are larger than divergent or discriminant associations.

A recent topic in the study of psychosocial risk factors for cardiovascular disease provides a relevant example of the MTMM approach to construct validity. Suls and Bunde (2005) note that individual differences in anxiety, anger, and depressive symptoms have all been studied as risk factors for coronary heart disease (CHD). Usually, such studies implicitly conceptualize these emotional traits as distinct and typically measure only one of these three characteristics. However, anxiety, anger, and depressive symptoms are correlated components of the broader trait of neuroticism (Costa & McCrae, 1992). Studies of the health consequences of anxiety, depression, and anger rarely establish that measures of these three traits are in fact tapping distinct characteristics. To do so, a researcher could measure each of these three traits with two methods —self-reports and ratings by significant others. The NEO-PI-R (Costa & McCrae, 1992) is available in these two versions and includes scales to assess these dimensions. Given that prior theory and research suggest that anxiety, anger, and depression are components of a common underlying dimension (Costa & McCrae, 1992; Suls & Bunde, 2005), one would expect measures of these subtraits or facets to be correlated rather than truly independent. However, they should not be as closely correlated as two measures of the same subtrait.

Tables 2.1 and 2.2 present hypothetical results for two possible outcomes of an MTMM analysis of this issue. For both sets of hypothetical results, two methods (i.e., self-reports and spouse reports) were used to assess the three traits of interest. In the first scenario, the convergent (i.e., mono-trait, hetero-method) correlations are generally larger than both

Table 2.1. Hypothetical Correlations in Multitrait, Multimethod Analysis of Self and Spouse Reports of Anxiety, Anger, and Depression: Example of Good Convergent and Discriminant Validity

	Self-Reports			Spouse Reports		
	Anxiety	*Anger*	*Depression*	*Anxiety*	*Anger*	*Depression*
Self-Reports						
Anxiety	(.86)*					
Anger	.48	(.90)				
Depression	.55	.44	(.87)			
Spouse Reports						
Anxiety	.60	.32	.36	(.88)		
Anger	.31	.63	.33	.46	(.85)	
Depression	.37	.31	.61	.49	.41	(.89)

*Reliabilities in parentheses.

Table 2.2. Hypothetical Correlations in Multitrait, Multimethod Analysis of Self and Spouse Reports of Anxiety, Anger, and Depression: Example of Poor Convergent and Discriminant Validity

	Self-Reports			Spouse Reports		
	Anxiety	*Anger*	*Depression*	*Anxiety*	*Anger*	*Depression*
Self-Reports						
Anxiety	(.86)*					
Anger	.68	(.90)				
Depression	.71	.67	(.87)			
Spouse Reports						
Anxiety	.51	.52	.55	(.88)		
Anger	.49	.48	.47	.66	(.85)	
Depression	.53	.50	.50	.70	.68	(.89)

*Reliabilities in parentheses.

of the sets of discriminant or divergent correlations (i.e., hetero-trait, mono-method; and hetero-trait, hetero-method). The three dimensions are clearly associated, as reflected in the nonzero, hetero-trait, mono-method and hetero-trait, hetero-method correlations. However, the convergent (i.e., mono-trait, hetero-method) associations are consistently larger. This pattern provides evidence of construct validity of the scales. In addition, the hetero-trait, mono-method correlations tend to be somewhat larger than the hetero-trait, hetero-method correlations, suggesting that some of the systematic variance in scale scores reflects method variance rather than the targeted construct.

In contrast, Table 2.2 depicts a pattern in which there is little evidence that the scales assess distinct dimensions. For example, the mono-trait, hetero-method correlations are generally smaller than the hetero-trait, mono-method associations. There is also clear evidence of method variance, in that the hetero-trait, mono-method associations are consistently larger than the hetero-trait, hetero-method associations. In this latter example, it would be concluded that the scales assess a single global dimension rather than the more specific (albeit, expected to be somewhat correlated) dimensions of anxiety, anger, and depression. Further, scale scores would include both variance reflecting this broad construct and a substantial degree of method variance.

These outcomes serve to illustrate the logic of the MTMM approach in depicting convergent and discriminant validity as essential aspects of construct validity. The actual quantitative evaluation of such studies has advanced in recent years with applications of structural equation modeling, but has remained a challenging undertaking (G. T. Smith, 2005). Full MTMM evaluations of construct validity are not common in most research areas in behavioral science, and certainly they are not common in health psychology. However, the basic logic of construct validation through the simultaneous consideration of convergent and divergent associations (i.e., a pattern prediction) applies in far simpler measurement evaluation designs. The minimal requirement for testing a pattern of convergent and discriminant associations involves two measures of one construct (to examine convergence) and one measure of a different construct (to examine divergence). Given the general lack of measurement research in health psychology, even such minimal approaches can often provide useful information.

Methods in Measurement Evaluation

It is worthwhile to tie some of these basic issues in measurement to quantitative methods used to evaluate them. Many measurement evaluation issues are addressed with basic quantitative procedures that are well known to anyone with basic training in methodology. However, some techniques increasingly used in this context may be at least somewhat unfamiliar to health psychology researchers. This section describes three such techniques. It is well beyond the present scope to review these quantitative methods in detail, but it is useful to consider how these techniques are generally used.

Exploratory and Confirmatory Factor Analysis

Factor analysis is the most commonly used appropriate method to evaluating the structure of a measure. Exploratory factor analysis asks the question, "*What* is the structure of this set of indicators?" As the name implies, this family of analytic techniques holds few advance assumptions about what the structure of a measure might be. In contrast, confirmatory factor analysis asks the question, "*Is this* the structure of this set of indicators?" In this manner, a specific, theory-driven prediction about the structure of a set of items or other indicators of a construct can be compared with the obtained pattern of covariation among indicators in a research sample. Therefore, confirmatory methods can provide "stronger" tests of structural hypotheses because the specific prediction can be disconfirmed by a poor fit with the obtained data. In an even stronger use of confirmatory factor analysis to test structural questions about measures, two or more competing structural hypotheses can be articulated a priori and pitted against each other in model comparison techniques.

For example, in the earlier situation in which anxiety, anger, and depressive symptoms are assessed, one might contrast two models of an 18-item measure containing three 6-item subscales corresponding to each of the affective traits. A model in which these scales are hypothesized to reflect distinct but correlated dimensions (because they are three facets of a broader construct) would predict high levels of correlation among the three sets of 6 items and smaller but still significant correlations across sets. In a model in which these items were hypothesized to reflect indistinguishable aspects of a single broad dimension, correlations among the 18 items would be predicted to be high and generally uniform. These two a priori structural hypotheses can be compared directly in confirmatory factor analysis, with resulting high levels of support emerging from the process given the high risk of disconfirmation. As with most measurement research, the yield from this sort of model testing is greater if the competing models are derived from related theory about the structure of the domain. It is important to note that if exploratory or confirmatory factor analyses indicate that a scale is actually multidimensional, a traditional index of internal consistency for the total scale score (e.g., Cronbach's alpha) is potentially quite misleading. A large value would imply that the total scale is internally consistent (i.e., high reliability across items), when the more appropriate factor analytic methods for evaluating the scale structure suggest something quite different.

A special application of confirmatory factor analysis involves the evaluation of MTMM designs (Marsh & Grayson, 1995). In this case, the hypotheses to be articulated in advance and pitted against one another involve the degree of convergent and discriminant validity reflected in the obtained pattern of intercorrelations, as well as the presence and extent of method variance. Predictions, such as "The multiple measures of a single construct will correlate more closely with each other than with measures of a second construct" and "All measures in the matrix reflect a single construct," can be directly compared. Further, these predictions can be compared with the alternative hypothesis, "Scores of these measures reflect the method used to obtain them, rather than the intended construct." These various hypotheses can be translated into specific expected patterns involving the relative magnitude of the mono-method/hetero-method, hetero-trait/mono-method, and hetero-trait/hetero-method correlations. This application of confirmatory factor analysis has been refined in recent years (Eid, Lischetzke, Nussbeck, & Trierweiler, 2003; G. T. Smith, 2005).

Item Response Theory

Item response theory (IRT) is another relatively recent, complex quantitative method in measurement research (Schmidt & Embretson, 2003). Applied to multi-item or multi-indicator measurements, IRT examines responses to items as a function of the individual's standing on the construct of interest. Specifically, items within a multi-item scale or measure may provide more or less useful information depending on whether the individual displays a low, intermediate, or high level of the construct of interest. For example, in a true-false, self-report scale measuring functional activity versus disability, the item "I have difficulty walking very long distances" might be useful in distinguishing mildly disabled persons from those with moderate levels of disability. This is because the former group is unlikely to endorse the item, whereas the latter is likely to endorse it. However, the item is less useful in distinguishing the moderately disabled from the severely disabled because both groups are likely to endorse it. In contrast, the item "I often have difficulty walking even very short distances" might not be useful in distinguishing the mildly and moderately disabled groups, since neither is likely to endorse the item. However, it could be quite useful in distinguishing the moderately and severely disabled groups.

IRT methods can be used to determine the extent to which a multi-item scale, for example, contains informative items across the full range of the construct as it is conceptually defined. In this way, it is a useful technique for addressing complex aspects of content validity. IRT can also be used in computerized interactive testing contexts to reduce the number of items used in an assessment, by decreasing the sampling of items well above and well below the emerging estimate of the individual's standing on the construct of interest and increasing the sampling with items that are maximally informative around the individual's estimated level. This latter use of IRT is clearly relevant in health psychology measurement, but it is not yet common.

Signal Detection Theory

Another advanced technique in measurement evaluation uses concepts and quantitative methods from signal detection theory (SDT) in evaluations of criterion validity (McFall & Treat, 1999). In many measurement instances, a scale or similar procedure is used to predict an outcome criterion. For example, depressive disorders (i.e., major depression, minor depression, or dysthymia) are potentially serious conditions in need of treatment. They are more common among persons with chronic medical illness than in the general public. Further, in some medical populations such as individuals with coronary heart disease, depression confers increased risk of recurrent coronary events and cardiac mortality (Lett et al., 2004). Definitive clinical diagnoses of depressive disorders are usually made following diagnostic interviewing, a procedure that is typically considered too time-consuming and expensive to be feasible for all coronary patients. Therefore, various self-report or observer rating scales have been used as screening tools to identify patients who are sufficiently likely to be depressed to warrant referral for a more definitive diagnostic evaluation. The basic measurement question in this context involves the relationship of scores on the screening measure to the clinical criterion of diagnosed depressive disorder. This is clearly a question of the validity of such measures.

A variety of factors are considered in such evaluations. *Sensitivity,* or "hit rate," of tests in such applications refers to the proportion of true cases (i.e., actually depressed, according to diagnostic clinical interview) identified as cases on the basis of their score on the screening measure (e.g., scores on the Beck Depression Inventory). *Specificity* refers to the proportion of true noncases identified as such on the basis of scores on the screening measure. Low specificity results in a high number of "false alarms." A critical influence on sensitivity and specificity is the cut point on the screening measure. For example, if a BDI score of equal to or greater than 2 is used to classify a coronary patient as depressed, virtually all truly depressed cases (as determined by subsequent diagnostic interviewing) would be identified. In this case, the screening measure would have high *sensitivity.* However, many truly nondepressed cases would be erroneously labeled as depressed, resulting in a high "false alarm rate" or low *specificity.* In contrast, if a BDI score of 25 was used as the cut point, very few truly nondepressed patients would be identified as depressed on the basis of their screening score, producing few "false alarms" and high specificity. However, many truly depressed patients would be erroneously identified as nondepressed on the basis of having BDI scores below 25, indicating a low "hit rate" or low sensitivity.

In SDT, the function or curve depicting all possible combinations of values for hit rates and false alarm rates at all possible cut points is called a receiver operating curve (ROC). The area under this curve (AUC) can be calculated to quantify the information value for a given measure. Since this value reflects the relative degree of association between the measure and a criterion, it is clearly informative regarding criterion validity. AUC values of 0.50 reflect chance, in that the screening measure with this ROC (along or near the diagonal in a plot of false alarm rates vs. hit rates) does not improve criterion prediction at all. An AUC value of 1.0 is the upper limit, indicating that increasing hit rates does not increase false alarms and decreasing false alarms does not decrease hits. Performance at this level is highly unlikely, of course, and the relative "information value" of measures is reflected in their AUC values.

In an application of this sort, Strik, Honig, Lousberg, and Denollet (2001) compared the criterion validity of several brief self-report scales and ratings in identifying depressed and nondepressed cardiac patients; it is likely that this approach will be increasingly common as health psychology researchers and practitioners alike have become more concerned with quantifying and comparing the utility of measurement and clinical assessment procedures. It is important to note that SDT analyses do not result in specification of optimal cutoffs for scale scores. That process involves judgments about the relative value or importance of specific outcomes. For example, in some applications, false positives are more worrisome than are false negatives (e.g., identifying candidates for an expensive and invasive medical procedure), whereas in other contexts false negatives may be more worrisome (e.g., identifying suicidal risk). These considerations, along with the base rates of the outcome criterion in a given setting and other factors, are important in specifying cut points for decision making (McFall & Treat, 1999), but the SDT approach provides a broadly applicable approach for evaluating and comparing measures.

Examples of Measurement Issues in the Three Domains of Health Psychology

To illustrate further the application of the basic principles and issues discussed previously to research in health psychology, the following section includes topics within each of the field's three major content domains. Across this wide range of specific topics, the importance of theory-driven decisions about the nature of constructs, the optimal methods of measuring them, and alternative interpretations of existing measures is clear.

Health Behavior and Prevention

As in most behavioral and social science research, self-reports play a prominent role in research on health behavior and prevention. Self-reports of health behavior and its determinants are often used when other approaches are available, in large part because of their apparent simplicity and low cost. In other instances, such as survey studies with very large samples, self-reports are used because alternate measurement methods are simply not feasible. Most health behaviors are relatively specific and seemingly easily amenable to self-report (e.g., smoking, physical activity level, dietary intake, seat belt use). However, a large and growing body of research indicates that this measurement method is complex and often limited to the point of producing potentially misleading findings (Stone, Trukkan, et al., 2000).

All the previously described issues having to do with the reliability, structure, and validity of measures are relevant to self-reports of health behavior and self-reports of potential influences on health behavior. Importantly, the use of self-reports assumes that respondents are able and willing to provide accurate—that is, reliable and valid—information about their standing on the construct of interest. This is an implicit component of the nomological net surrounding any use of this method. As discussed previously, the tendency to give socially desirable responses is a pervasive threat to the validity of self-reports and can reflect the individual's interest in withholding information about socially undesirable characteristics from others or from him- or herself (Paulhus, 1991). Any time a self-report measure is used, this sort of method variance must be carefully considered as a potential source of systematic variance. Approaches to minimizing these threats to validity (e.g., anonymous responding) must be considered when designing and using such measures (Schaeffer, 2000).

In the case of health behavior, many if not most specific behaviors have obvious social desirability connotations. Smoking, physical inactivity, excessive calorie intake, alcohol or other substance abuse, unsafe sexual activity, and other unhealthy behaviors are generally seen as undesirable (e.g., Schroeder, Carey, & Vanable, 2003b; Patrick et al., 1994). If a measure of a predictor of health behavior (e.g., personality traits such as anger or hostility, social support or loneliness, participation in religious activity, self-efficacy) also contains systematic variance reflecting social desirability, the association between predictor and health behavior outcome may at least in part reflect this third variable (i.e., shared method variance) rather the presumed association between the intended constructs.

Often, interventions intended to reduce unhealthy behavior and increase better habits communicate clear expectations for positive change. If self-reports of health behavior used as outcome measures in such intervention studies contain systematic variance reflecting the tendency to give socially desirable responses, then treatment effects can reflect—at least in part—an association between the social communication of expectancies for change (i.e., demand characteristics) and the tendency to provide socially desirable responses rather than the substantive effect of the intervention on actual behavior change. In this instance, sources of invalidity in measurement can contribute to an over-estimate of treatment effects. Non-self-report measures can be used as alternative or supplemental outcome measures, such as exhaled carbon monoxide or plasma cotinine as measures of smoking status (Glasgow et al., 1993) or mechanical monitors (e.g., actigraphs) to assess physical activity levels. However, such measures are often not feasible in large-scale interventions or survey studies.

Even if individuals are willing to provide accurate self-reports, they may be unable to do so. A wide variety of cognitive and emotional processes can reduce the accuracy of self-reports (Kihlstrom, Eich, Sandbrand, & Tobias, 2000; Menon & Yorkston, 2000; Tourangeau, 2000). One consequence of these cognitive and affective threats to the accuracy of self-reports is reduced reliability. That is, they are sources of error in the form of unsystematic variance, and therefore would reduce observed effect sizes below "true" levels of association. However, when the accuracy of respondents' self-reports is low, they may rely on other processes in forming responses that are sources of construct-irrelevant systematic variance, thereby reducing the validity of the measure without necessarily reducing its reliability. For example, respondents' mood could influence their estimate of the frequency of health behavior, such that they recall more positive behavior when in a positive mood and less when in a negative mood. Similar to the effects of socially desirable responding, if the predictor variables in related studies share this susceptibility to the influence of mood (or are themselves measures of current or characteristic mood), these influences on self-report measures of health behavior would lead to overestimates of the effects of interest. That is, the observed associations would reflect a combination of shared method variance and the substantive effect under examination.

In some measurement contexts, unreliable and invalid self-reports are more likely when individuals make global reports over long periods of time, as when they describe how much exercise they engage in during the usual week or how many hours of sleep they typically get. For this reason, "real-time" self-reports of daily or momentary experiences and activities obtained in the natural environment have become an important approach in health psychology and related fields (Affleck, Zautra, Tennen, & Armeli, 1999; Bolger, Davis, & Rafaeli, 2003; Kahneman, Krueger, Schkade, Schwartz, & Stone, 2005; Shiffman, 2000; Stone & Shiffman, 2002).

One interesting type of measurement research involves testing the convergence of traditional global self-reports of a construct with measures of the same construct obtained through daily diary or experience sampling approaches. Results of such studies often indicate poor correspondence between global reports of behaviors such as smoking and reports obtained through the much more frequent experience sampling method (Shiffman, 2000). Such findings clearly suggest caution in interpreting traditional self-report measures but also suggest novel approaches to self-report assessment and a valuable paradigm for evaluating construct validity.

A final concern in studies of health behavior involves the measurement of influences on these actions. The potential influences on health behavior include a wide variety of characteristics, ranging from biochemical processes in addiction and appetite to sociocultural factors such as SES and acculturation. Basic issues of reliability and validity of measures of these constructs are obviously essential in the critical evaluation of related studies. Of particular importance is whether or not measures of factors influencing health behavior have sufficient evidence of convergent and discriminant validity to support the inference that it is the specific construct of interest and not another construct that is related to health behavior. As described previously, social desirability is one such alternative construct that has to do with measurement variance. Holding aside method artifacts and considering only substantive alternative constructs, these aspects of construct validity are often a source of concern.

A brief consideration of individual-level influences on health behavior will illustrate this concern. Conceptual descriptions of this domain of influences on health behavior include many individual difference characteristics. For example, simply within the cognitive-social perspective on the determinants of health behavior (S. M. Miller, Shoda, & Hurley, 1996), the list of important constructs includes the categories of health-relevant encodings (e.g., internal representations of health risks, attention to health information), health beliefs and expectations (e.g., outcome expectancies for health behavior, self-efficacy), health goals and values, and several others. Measures of these constructs are often developed for single studies, and even if used more frequently are often not subjected to extensive evaluations of their convergent and discriminant validity. As a result, evidence is often lacking as to the extent to which these scales actually measure the distinct and specific construct of interest *and* do not measure related constructs. Scale names often imply a great deal of specificity. For example, a measure of health-relevant goals implies it assesses goals but not outcome expectancies. However, this implied level of specificity is rarely evaluated through confirmatory structural analyses of the items of a specific scale and those of a scale intended to measure a related but conceptually distinct construct. The implicitly hypothesized structural model would predict the best fit from a two-factor model. However, if the item content is at all similar across the two item sets (and it often is), then a single-factor model is a viable alternative unless tested and discarded as fitting less well.

Further, evaluations of convergent and discriminant validity in the form of even partial MTMM studies are rare. The result is that this literature often seems to support conclusions about specific influences on health behavior that are much more definitive than is warranted given the limited support for the implicit hypothesis that these influences are measured with the level of specificity implied by scale labels. That is, it is possible that distinctly labeled but psychometrically overlapping scales are misinterpreted as supporting unique influences on health behavior. Greater attention to construct validity in this literature might identify broad or overlapping determinants of health behavior.

Stress and Disease

As described previously, in the history of the field, the effects of stress, personality traits, and other psychosocial risk factors on physical health sometimes have been studied using self-report measures of health as the outcome variable. Self-rated health is reliably related to subsequent mortality (Idler & Benyamini, 1997; McGee, Liao, Cao, & Cooper, 1999), persuasively indicating that self-reports of health contain systematic variance related to the construct of interest. However, self-report measures of health also clearly contain systematic variance that is independent of actual health (Barsky, 2000; Pennebaker, 2000). Some individuals tend to report physical symptoms in excess of actual disease, whereas others tend to minimize symptoms. As a result, when a psychosocial predictor is found to

be related to self-reported health, it is not clear if the association involves variance in the outcome measure that reflects actual health, the component that is unrelated to actual health, or a combination of these components.

This situation is further complicated by the fact that a broad individual difference variable—negative affectivity or neuroticism—is related to both actual health outcomes and complaints of health problems that are independent of actual illness (Suls & Bunde, 2005). This broad trait is also associated with measures of many other psychosocial risk factors (Smith & Gallo, 2001). Hence, whenever self-reported health is used as an outcome measure, it is possible that observed effects involve individual differences in the tendency to experience negative affect and report excessive physical health problems. Self-rated health is an important construct in and of itself, but these ambiguities undermine its usefulness when the research question involves the effects of psychosocial factors on actual disease. A similar issue arises when health outcome measures are heavily related to symptom reports rather than objective measures (e.g., reports of angina pectoris as an indicator of coronary disease, as opposed to medically verified myocardial infarction, ischemia, or coronary death). Finally, the tendency to make excessive somatic complaints can alter the process of selection into a medical study sample, potentially producing biases and misleading results. For example, a large literature indicates that the trait of negative affectivity or neuroticism is associated with actual coronary heart disease (Suls & Brunde, 2005). However, in studies of patients undergoing coronary angiography to assess the presence and severity of the underlying coronary artery disease, neuroticism is often found to be unrelated or even inversely related to the presence and severity of coronary disease. This finding could reflect the fact that individuals high in negative affectivity but otherwise healthy complain convincingly enough of possible cardiac symptoms that they are referred for this invasive diagnostic procedure. The resulting overinclusion of disease-free persons with high levels of neuroticism could produce the misleading results.

Similar to the issue of individual difference predictors of health behaviors described previously, studies of psychosocial predictors of subsequent health often use individual difference measures that are insufficiently evaluated. On some occasions the scales used in large epidemiological studies are by necessity quite brief, raising the concern that low reliability could attenuate the magnitude of associations with health outcomes. In other instances, the measures of psychosocial risk factors have not been subjected to even minimal construct validation, such as correlations with other measures of the same construct. It is common for measures to be used that have not been subjected to compelling tests of their convergent and discriminant validity. As a result, it is often possible that the measures used assess constructs that are different than the scale label implies. Further, the proliferation of insufficiently validated scales used in such studies creates the possibility that previously identified risk factors are being "rediscovered" when unvalidated scales with novel labels unintentionally tap established risk constructs.

Several authors have argued that this psychometric cacophony could impede systematic progress in the field, and that the use of established construct validation methods and comparisons with well-validated individual differences in personality and social behavior could help to identify robust, broad risk factors studied under a variety of potentially misleading labels (Costa & McCrae, 1987; Friedman, Tucker, & Reise, 1995; Marshall, Wortman, Vickers, Kusulas, & Hervig, 1994; Smith & Gallo, 2001; Smith & Williams, 1992). Suls and Bunde (2005) provide a recent example of this issue in their review of the literature linking anxiety, depressive symptoms, and anger with the development and course of coronary disease. Without comprehensive measurement of these traits and thoughtful analysis of their overlapping and unique effects, it is difficult to discern if they represent distinct influences on cardiovascular health or aspects of a single broad risk factor involving the tendency to experience negative affect (cf. Friedman & Booth-Kewley, 1987).

The problems associated with the measurement of personality traits and similar psychosocial risk factors arise not only from the failure to employ thorough approaches to construct validation. They also often arise from an initial failure to thoroughly consider conceptual issues such as the relationship of a proposed risk factor to previously established risk factors and well-validated taxonomies of related individual differences. In the latter regard, the five-factor model of personality and the interpersonal circumplex are useful nomological nets. Complete

with clear conceptual definitions and many well-validated assessment procedures using multiple measurement methods, these models can facilitate comparing, contrasting, and integrating psychosocial risk factors (Gallo & Smith, 1998; Marshall et al., 1994; Smith & Williams, 1992).

As in the study of determinants of health behavior, self-reports of psychosocial risk factors for disease such as personality traits, social support, and stressful life experiences are commonly used given their ease of administration and low cost. Given that some of these characteristics involve attitudes and subjective emotional experiences, this is not an unreasonable choice. The measurement model underlying such use implies that individuals can and will provide reliable and valid reports. However, there is some evidence to suggest that this assumption must be made with caution. For example, behavioral ratings of hostility from structured interviewers are more closely related to subsequent health outcomes than are self-reports of similar characteristics (Miller et al., 1996). Similarly, in samples of heart patients, spouse reports of anger and other negative emotional characteristics are more closely related to disease severity and prognosis than are the patients' self-reports of the same characteristics (Ketterer et al., 2004). Low self-awareness of negative characteristics, social desirability artifacts, and patients' denial of emotional distress as they cope with serious illness are all possible sources of invalidity in self-reports of these risk factors. The net effect for research studies would be the tendency to find smaller—and potentially nonsignificant—effect sizes when self-report measures are employed. Hence, the optimal method of measurement is an important aspect of the conceptual model surrounding these risk factors.

The importance of conceptual models guiding measurement can also be seen in the study of mechanisms linking psychosocial risk factors and disease. The construct of cardiovascular reactivity (CVR) provides an important example in this regard. In its general meaning, CVR refers to increases in heart rate and blood pressure in response to stressful stimuli. Such responses are hypothesized to initiate and hasten the development of high blood pressure, atherosclerosis, and other manifestations of cardiovascular disease (Manuck, 1994). However, on careful reading this term is actually used to refer to two conceptually distinct characteristics. In the first, it is considered to be a stable individual difference variable that is consistent across time and situations. That is, some individuals display consistently large cardiovascular responses to potential stressors, whereas others display consistently smaller responses. The former group is hypothesized to be more prone to the development of cardiovascular disease. In an innovative and important application of the principles of measurement, Kamarck, Jennings, Pogue-Geile, and Manuck (1994) have demonstrated that the multiple measurements using multiple stressors increase the reliability of estimates of this trait, much like adding items to a self-report scale can increase estimates of internal consistency. Further, this more reliable estimate of CVR, not surprisingly, is more closely related to health outcomes (e.g., ambulatory blood pressure) than are single measurements of CVR, most likely due to the enhanced reliability of measurement. With this underlying conceptualization of CVR and the related measurement model, increasing the number of measurements and doing so across a wider range of stressors logically improves the measure—up to a point of diminishing returns.

However, CVR also refers to a mechanism hypothesized to link psychosocial risk factors to disease, as in the case of the personality trait of hostility (Williams, Barefoot, & Shekelle, 1985). In this specific model and many others like it, CVR is not necessarily a stable characteristic of the individual that is consistent across time and settings. Rather, it is a situation-specific response that is more pronounced among hostile persons than among their more agreeable counterparts. The personality trait is believed to be stable, as is the tendency for hostile persons to respond to some classes of stimuli (e.g., provocation, conflict, harassment) but not others (e.g., achievement challenge) with heightened CVR. Increasing the frequency of measurements of heart rate and blood pressure in relevant situations might improve the likelihood of detecting the hypothesized association between the personality trait and the unhealthy physiological response, through increased reliability of measurement of situation- specific CVR. However, simply increasing the number of measurements of CVR—if it includes nonrelevant situations—would not be expected to improve the reliability of measurement in this case.

The underlying conceptual model that should guide the measurement of this second conceptual view of CVR is quite different than that guiding assessments of broad cross-situational individual differences in CVR. Different views of the nature and location of the stability of the response, as well as different expectations regarding the stimuli used to evoke it, are implied in the nomological nets surrounding these two constructs, despite the use of the identical label. In the situation-specific view, more recent conceptual models from cognitive-social perspectives in personality (Mischel & Shoda, 1995) would provide a better guide for designing the assessment scheme for CVR than do the traditional views of the assessment of traits that underpin the model of measuring CVR proposed by Kamarck et al. (1994). In this newer perspective, individual differences are reflected in profiles or patterns of responses across specific situations, rather than levels of response across all situations. Measurement should be guided by theory, and care should be taken to make certain that the measurement model appropriately reflects other aspects of the nomological net surrounding the construct to be assessed.

In studies evaluating physiological mechanisms potentially linking psychosocial risk factors and health, care must also be taken in the measurement of the physiological response. For example, the sensitivity of assays to detect neuroendocrine or immune system responses and temporal aspects of these responses must guide the measurement protocol. Otherwise, insensitive or mistimed measures can contribute to erroneous results. Similarly, the measurement of health outcomes must be guided by appropriate consideration of the likely occurrence and level of variability of medical end points during the study period. In studies of psychosocial determinants of the recurrence of myocardial infarction, for example, the likely frequency of recurrent events over follow-up periods of varying lengths must be considered before the protocol for measuring the health outcome of interest is finalized. Such decisions are often best informed through collaborations with other biomedical researchers.

Psychosocial Aspects of Medical Illness and Care

Given the nature of many constructs in this third broad topic area (e.g., pain, emotion), self-reports are an essential approach to measurement. The nomological net surrounding most uses of global self-reports would predict convergence with measures of the same constructs obtained through daily diary or experience sampling methods. However, results often suggest little or no correspondence between these two methods of measuring constructs such as type of coping with stress or change in chronic pain (Porter, Stone, & Schwartz, 1999; Schwartz, Neale, Marco, Shiffman, & Stone, 1999; Stone, Broderick, Shiffman, & Schwartz, 2004; Stone et al., 1998). Hence, interpretations of findings obtained with global self-reports should be made cautiously. Further, the daily experience paradigm and recent variations (Kahneman et al, 2005) once again provide an important alternative for testing theories of adaptation in chronic disease, as well as a valuable context for evaluating other measures. Of course, self-report outcome measures of all types could contain systematic variance reflecting social desirability, again raising the previously described concerns about interpretations of their association with measures of predictor variables that also contain this component and their susceptibility to the inflation of estimates of intervention effects when those treatments contain demand characteristics.

In the measurement of predictors of adaptation in acute or chronic medical illness, the issues about construct validity described in the previous two content areas are again highly relevant. All too often the labels applied to scales measuring predictor variables imply much more specificity than is supported by the available evidence of convergent and discriminant validity. Further, the outcomes these measures are used to predict typically involve emotional and physical distress. As a result, a measurement concern raised in the study of models of emotional adaptation in general is quite relevant here. Specifically, in their classic critique of research on cognitive models of depression, Coyne and Gotlib (1983) noted that some of the self-report measures of key cognitive constructs (e.g., dysfunctional attitudes, cognitive errors) often contain item wording that includes reference to emotional distress. This could result in what the authors described as "thinly veiled tautologies" in which associations between two measures with overlapping content are misinterpreted as evidence of the predicted substantive association between constructs. That is, common method variance in the form of similar item content contributes to—if not fully accounts for—the observed effect. In the literature on psychosocial predictors of adaptation to medical illness and care, few studies have demonstrated

that the predictor measures have sufficient discriminant validity relative to the outcome measures to rule out this artifact as an alternative explanation for observed effects.

The study of adaptation to chronic disease also provides important examples of difficulties arising when measurement models previously studied in one context are applied in a novel context. As noted previously, depression is more common among persons with chronic medical illness than among medically healthy persons, presumably reflecting—at least in part—the stress of living with a serious health problem. Hence, assessment of depression is an important component in studying adaptation to chronic disease. However, most of the measures of depression used in this body of research were initially developed and used to study depression in physically healthy populations. In the physically healthy population, physical symptoms included in depression inventories (e.g., sleep disturbance, fatigue, concerns about appearance) can be highly diagnostic. However, for persons with a serious physical (rather than mental) illness, these symptoms can reflect the medical condition rather than its emotional consequences (Blalock, DeVellis, Brown, & Wallston, 1989; Clark, Cook, & Snow, 1998; Mohr et al., 1997; O'Donnell & Chung, 1997; Peck, Smith, Ward, & Milano, 1989). This could lead to the overestimation of levels of depression in the medically ill. Further, correlates of these depression measures in such populations could in part reflect correlates of the severity of medical illness rather than only the construct of interest. Hence, use of a measure outside of the context where it was initially developed and validated could result in a circumstance in which it captures systematic variability beyond the construct of interest. Further, it is important to note that although scores on self-report depression scales certainly are related to diagnosable clinical depressive disorders, such scales are best seen as measuring a broader dimension of negative affectivity that overlaps—but is not isomorphic with—depressive disorders (Coyne, 1994; Fechner-Bates, Coyne, & Schwenk, 1994). As a result, the scale names can be misleading.

The use of depression measures to assess the emotional impact of medical illness also raises a question about the appropriateness of the underlying conceptual model. Depression is certainly an important concern in this context. However, by conceptualizing emotional adaptation as the presence and severity of symptoms of depression, researchers are implicitly suggesting that varying degrees of emotional maladjustment is a more appropriate approach than is variation in normal affective experience. Models of normal emotional experience (e.g., Watson & Tellegen, 1983) identify two dimensions—positive and negative affect. Chronic disease could have undesirable emotional consequences not only by increasing negative affect (NA) but also by reducing positive affect (PA). Importantly, measures of depression are associated with both higher NA and lower PA, and therefore depression measures combine NA and PA in a nonspecific affective index. Further, in chronic medical illness, NA and PA are influenced by different factors (Smith & Christensen, 1996; Zautra et al., 1995). As a result, use of depression measures to capture the emotional consequences of chronic illness can produce a loss of specificity in identifying influences on multifaceted aspects of adaptation. In this manner, the selection of a conceptual model and corresponding approach to measurement can result in an imprecise view of the phenomenon of interest.

Although increased specificity in measurement of outcomes is often highly desirable, valid global measures are also valuable. Kaplan (1994) has argued convincingly that a common metric for measuring health status would permit the comparative evaluation of the impact of various diseases and a wide range of health interventions. When combined with assessment of costs, such a broadly applicable, common metric also permits cost utility analyses in which health benefits of virtually any intervention for the prevention or management of virtually any condition can be compared relative to their related costs (Kaplan & Groessel, 2002). The Quality-Adjusted Life Year (QUALY; Kaplan, 1994) is one such index in which mortality and quality of life are combined. In this measurement model, quality of life is quantified as a combination of various aspects of morbidity and functional activity. The metric ranges from 0.0 (i.e., death or "zero quality of life") to 1.0 (i.e., asymptomatic, optimal functioning). By multiplying years alive by their quality, a common metric for health outcomes is derived. This is an example of a "cause indicator" measurement model rather than an "effect indicator" model, in that a given QUALY value is a result of the measured variables rather than a hypothetical construct that "causes" variability on the measured variables. It also

is a clear example of how the health economic context of health psychology research and related issues of public policy are an increasingly important influence on the development of new measurement procedures.

Conclusions

As described in the preceding section, important issues involving the application of basic principles of measurement can be found in each of the major content domains of health psychology. This brief presentation merely provided illustrations rather than anything approaching an exhaustive review. There are many additional instances in which widely used measures are in need of further evaluation and refinement. Certainly, there are many research questions in the immediate future of the field where these basic measurement issues should be thoughtfully applied in the development of new measures and the use of existing measures in new contexts.

The interdisciplinary nature of the field creates the need for application of principles of measurement development and evaluation to a wide-ranging set of biomedical, psychological, and social processes. Thorough attention to these issues is an essential aspect of the basic and applied research missions in health psychology. It is best seen as an ongoing process within an active and evolving field that is constantly addressing new research questions and extending the study of established topics to new contexts. As a result, the design, evaluation, and refinement of measurement procedures do not represent a research challenge to be addressed once and dispatched; instead, they must be continually considered when designing new research or evaluating prior work.

Fortunately, long-standing basic principles and a growing array of quantitative methods are available to address these complex challenges. It is essential to note that the application of these principles and techniques must be guided by theory. In this case, it is not the grand theories of health and behavior or mind and body central in the field's history that require consideration. Rather, it is the smaller—but no less important—theories of the construct to be assessed and methods of measurement that guide this work. These nomological nets have rarely been exhaustively studied in health psychology research. Hence, health psychology researchers and consumers of their efforts are well advised to exercise caution in making inferences about what measures actually reflect.

Perhaps more important, these unexplored measurement research questions present opportunities for useful contributions to the field. The evaluation of existing measures and development of new measures can be the primary focus of a research project, but useful contributions can also be made when measurement research is added as a secondary focus to research studies where the primary focus is on some other substantive question. Whether or not measurement is a primary or secondary focus and regardless of the quantitative complexity of the work, careful and clear thinking is the essential element of measurement research in health psychology (McFall, 2005). This includes consideration of the nature and structure of the construct of interest, delineation of the surrounding nomological net, critical evaluation of what can and cannot be concluded on the basis of available evidence, the articulation of alternative or competing interpretations of measures, and the design of "risky" tests of rival explanations. This type of sustained attention to measurement issues will strengthen the empirical foundations of the field and help to make its future as remarkable as its past.

References

Affleck, G., Zautra, A., Tennen, H., Armeli, S. (1999). Multilevel daily process designs for consulting and clinical psychology: A primer for the perplexed. *Journal of Consulting and Clinical Psychology, 67,* 746–754.

Baron, R. M., & Kenney, D. A. (1986). The moderator-mediator variable distinction in social psychological research: Conceptual, strategic, and statistical consideration. *Journal of Personality and Social Psychology, 51,* 1173–1182.

Barsky, A. J. (2000). The validity of bodily symptoms in medical outpatients. In A. A. Stone, J. S. Turkkan, C. A. Bachrach, J. B. Jobe, H. S. Kurtzman, & V. S. Cain (Eds.), *The science of self-report: Implications for research and practice* (pp.339–361). Mahwah, NJ: Erlbaum.

Blalock, S. J., DeVellis, R. F., Brown, G. K., & Wallston, K. A. (1989). Validity of the Center for Epidemiological Studies Depression scale in arthritic populations. *Arthritis and Rheumatism, 32,* 991–997.

Blanton, H., & Jaccard, J. (2006). Arbitrary metrics in psychology. *American Psychologist, 61,* 27–41.

Bolger, N, Davis, A., & Rafaeli, E. (2003). Diary methods: Capturing life as it is lived. *Annual Review of Psychology, 54,* 579–612.

Bollen, K. A., & Lennox, R. (1991). Conventional wisdom on measurement: A structural equation perspective. *Psychological Bulletin, 110,* 305–314.

Campbell, D. T., & Fiske, D. W. (1959). Covergent and discriminant validation by the multitrait-multimethod matrix. *Psychological Bulletin, 56,* 81–105.

Carver, C. S. (1989). How should multifaceted personality constructs be tested? Issues illustrated by self-monitoring, attributional style, and hardiness. *Journal of Personality and Social Psychology, 56,* 577–585.

Clark, D. A., Cook, A., & Snow, D. (1998). Depressive symptom differences in hospitalized medically ill, depressed psychiatric inpatients, and nonmedical controls. *Journal of Abnormal Psychology, 107,* 38–48.

Cohen, J. (1992). A power primer. *Psychological Bulletin, 112,* 155–159.

Costa, P. T., Jr., & McCrae, R. R. (1987). Neuroticism, somatic complaints, and disease: Is the bark worse than the bite? *Journal of Personality, 55,* 299–316.

Costa, P. T., Jr., & McCrae, R. R. (1992). Professional manual: Revised NEO Personality Inventory (NEO-PI-R) and the NEO Five-Factor Inventory (NEO-FFI). Odessa, FL: Psychological Assessment Resources.

Coyne, J. C. (1994). Self-reported distress: Analog or ersatz depression? *Psychological Bulletin, 116,* 29–45.

Coyne, J. C., Gallo, S. M., Klinkman, M. S., & Calarco, M. N. (1998). Effects of recent and past major depression and distress on self-concept and coping. *Journal of Abnormal Psychology, 107,* 86–96.

Coyne, J. C., & Gotlib, J. (1983). The role of cognition in depression: A critical review. *Psychological Bulletin, 94,* 472–505.

Coyne, J. C., & Gottlieb, B. H. (1996). The mismeasure of coping by checklist. *Journal of Personality, 64,* 959–991.

Coyne, J. C., Kruus, L, Racioppo, M., Calzone, K. A., & Armstrong, K. (2003). What do ratings of cancer-specific distress mean among women at high risk of breast and ovarian cancer? *American Journal of Medical Genetics, 116A,* 222–228.

Coyne, J. C., Thompson, R, & Racioppo, M.W. (2001). Validity and efficiency of screening for history of depression by self-report. *Psychological Assessment, 13,* 163–170.

Cronbach, L. J. (1951). Coefficient alpha and the internal structure of tests. *Psychometrika, 16,* 297–334.

Cronbach, L. J., & Meehl, P. E. (1955). Construct validity in psychological tests. *Psychological Bulletin, 52,* 281–302.

Dawes, R. M. (1994). Psychological measurement. *Psychological Review, 101,* 278–281.

Dawes, R. M., & Smith, T. L. (1985). Attitude and opinion measurement. In G. Lindzey & E. Aronson (Eds.), *The handbook of social psychology* (3rd ed., Vol. 1, pp. 509–566). New York: Random House.

Eid, M., Lischetzke, T., Nussbeck, F.W., & Trier-weiler, L.I. (2003). Separating trait effects from trait-specific method effects in multitrait-multimethod models: A multiple-indicator CT-C(M-1) model. *Psychological Methods, 8,* 38–60.

Embretson, S. E. (1996). The new rules of measurement. *Psychological Assessment, 8,* 341–349.

Engel, G. L. (1977). The need for a new medical model: A challenge for biomedicine. *Science, 196,* 129–136.

Fechner-Bates, S., Coyne, J. C., & Schwenk, T. L. (1994). The relationship of self-reported distress to depressive disorders and other psychopathology. *Journal of Consulting and Clinical Psychology, 62,* 550–559.

Friedman, H. S., & Booth-Kewley, S. (1987). The "disease-prone personality": A meta-analytic view of the construct. *American Psychologist, 42,* 539–555.

Freidman, H. S., Tucker, J. S., & Reise, S. P. (1995). Personality dimensions and measures potentially related to health: A focus on hostility. *Annals of Behavioral Medicine, 17,* 245–251.

Funk, S. (1992). Hardiness: A review of theory and research. *Health Psychology, 11,* 333–345.

Gallo, L. C., & Matthews, K. A. (2003). Understanding the association between socio-economic status and physical health: Do negative emotions play a role? *Psychological Bulletin, 129,* 10–51.

Gallo, L. C., & Smith, T. W. (1998). Construct validation of health-relevant personality units: Interpersonal circumplex and five-factor model analyses of the aggression questionnaire. *International Journal of Behavioral Medicine, 5,* 129–147.

Gentry, W. D. (Ed). (1984). *Handbook of behavioral medicine.* New York: Guilford.

Glasgow, R. E., Mullooly, J. P., Vogt, T. M., Stevens, V. J., Lichetenstein, E., Hollis, J. F., et al. (1993). Biochemical validation of smoking status in public health setting: Pros, cons and data from four low-intensity intervention trials. *Addictive Behaviors, 18,* 511–527.

Holmbeck, G. N. (1997). Toward terminological, conceptual, and statistical clarity in the study of mediators and moderators: Examples from the child-clinical and pediatric psychology literatures. *Journal of Consulting and Clinical Psychology, 65,* 599–610.

Holmes, T. H., & Rahe, R. H. (1967). The social readjustment rating scale. *Journal of Psychosomatic Research, 14,* 213–218.

Hull, J. G., Lehn, D. A., & Tedlie, J. C, (1991). A general approach to testing multifaceted personality constructs. *Journal of Personality and Social Psychology, 61,* 932–945.

Idler, E. L., & Benyamini, Y. (1997). Self-rated health and mortality: A review of twenty-seven community studies. *Journal of Health and Social Behavior, 38,* 21–37.

John, O. P., & Benet-Martinez, V. (2000). Measurement: Reliability, construct validation, and scale construction. In H. T. Reis & C. M. Judd (Eds.), *Handbook of research methods in social and personality psychology* (pp. 339–369). Cambridge, England: Cambridge University Press.

Judd, C. M., & McClelland, G. H. (1995). Data analysis: Continuing issues in the everyday analysis of psychological data. *Annual Review of Psychology, 46,* 433–465.

Judd, C. M., & McClelland, G. H. (1998). Measurement. In D. T. Gilbert, S. T. Fiske, & G. Lindzey (Eds.), *Handbook of social psychology* (Vol. 2, pp. 180–232). Boston: McGraw-Hill.

Kahneman, D., Krueger, A. B., Schkade, D. A., Schwartz, N., & Stone, A. A. (2005). A survey method for characterizing daily life experiences: The day reconstruction method. *Science,* 306:1776–1780.

Kamarck, T. W., Jennings, J. J., Pogue-Geile, M., & Manuck, S. B. (1994). A multidimensional measurement model for cardiovascular reactivity: Stability and cross-validation in two adult samples. *Health Psychology, 13,* 471–478.

Kaplan, R. M. (1994). The Ziggy theorem: Toward an outcomes-focused health psychology. *Health Psychology, 13,* 451–460.

Kaplan, R. M., & Frosch, D. L. (2005). Decision making in medicine and health care. *Annual Review of Clinical Psychology, 1,* 525–556.

Kaplan, R. M., & Groessel, E. J. (2002). Applications of cost-effectiveness methodologies in behavioral medicine. *Journal of Consulting and Clinical Psychology, 70,* 482–493.

Karoly, P. (Ed.). (1985) Measurement strategies in health psychology. New York: Wiley.

Kazdin, A.E. (2006). Arbitrary metrics: Implications for identifying evidence-based treatments. *American Psychologist, 61,* 42–49.

Keefe, F. J. (2000). Self-report of pain: Issues and opportunities. In A. A. Stone, J. S. Turkkan, C. A. Bachrach, J. B. Jobe, H. S. Kurtzman, & V. S. Cain (Eds.), *The science of self-report: Implications for research and practice* (pp. 317–337). Mahwah, NJ: Erlbaum.

Keefe, F. J., & Blumenthal, J. A. (Eds.). (1982). *Assessment strategies in behavioral medicine.* New York: Grune and Stratton.

Kenny, D. A., & Kashy, D .A. (1992). Analysis of the multitrait-multimethod matrix by confirmatory factor analysis. *Psychological Bulletin, 112,* 165–172.

Ketterer, M. W., Denollet, J., Chapp, J., Thayer, B., Keteyian, S., Clark, V., et al. (2004). Men deny and women cry, but who dies? Do the wages of "denial" include early ischemic coronary disease? *Journal of Psychosomatic Research, 56,* 119–123.

Ketterer, M. W., Denollet, J., Goldberg, A. D., McCullough, P. A., John, S, Farba, A .J., et al. (2002). The big mush: Psychometric measures are confounded and non-independent in their association with age at initial diagnosis of ischaemic coronary heart disease. *Journal of Cardiovascular Risk, 9,* 41–48.

Kihlstrom, J. F., Eich, E., Sandbrand, D., & Tobias, B. A. (2000). Emotion and memory: Implications for self-report. In A. A. Stone, J. S. Turkkan, C. A. Bachrach, J. B. Jobe, H. S. Kurtzman, & V. S. Cain (Eds.), *The science of self-report: Implications for research and practice* (pp. 81–99). Mahwah, NJ: Erlbaum.

Kobasa, S. C. (1979). Stressful life events, personality and health: An inquiry into hardiness. *Journal of Personality and Social Psychology, 37,* 1–11.

Lett, H. S., Blumenthal, J. A., Babyak, M. A., Sherwood, A., Strauman, T., Robins, C., et al. (2004). Depression as a risk factor for coronary artery disease: Evidence, mechanisms, and treatment. *Psychosomatic Medicine, 66,* 305–315.

Loevinger, J. (1947). A systematic approach to the construction and evaluation of tests of ability. *Psychological Monograph, 61* (No. 4, Whole No. 285).

Loevinger, J. (1954). The attenuation paradox in test theory. *Psychological Bulletin, 51,* 493–504.

Loevinger, J. (1957). Objective tests as instruments of psychological theory. *Psychological Reports, 3,* 635–694.

Manuck, S. B. (1994). Cardiovascular reactivity in cardiovascular disease: "Once more unto the breach." *International Journal of Behavioral Medicine, 1,* 4–31.

Marsh, H. W. (1989). Confirmatory factor analyses of multitrait-multimethod data: Many problems and few solutions. *Applied Psychological Measurement, 13,* 335–361.

Marsh, H. W., & Grayson, D. (1995). Latent variable models of multitrait-multimethod data. In R. H. Hoyle (Ed.), *Structural equation modeling: Concepts, issues, and applications* (pp. 177–198). Thousand Oaks, CA: Sage.

Marshall, G. N., Wortman, C. B., Vickers, R. R., Kusulas, J. W., & Hervig, L. K. (1994). The five-factor model as a framework for personality-health research. *Journal of Personality and Social Psychology, 67,* 278–286.

Martin, R., Watson, D., & Wan, C. K. (2000). A three-factor model of trait anger: Dimensions of affect, behavior and cognition. *Journal of Personality, 68,* 869–897.

McArdle, J. J. (1996). Current directions in structural factor analysis. *Current Directions in Psychological Science, 5,* 11–18.

McCallum, J., Shadbolt, B., & Wong, D. (1992). Self-rated health and survival: A 7-year follow-up study of Australian elderly. *American Journal of Public Health, 84,* 1100–1105.

McFall, R.M. (2005). Theory and utility—key themes in evidence-based assessment: Comment on the special section. *Psychological Assessment, 17,* 312–323.

McFall, R. M., & Treat, T. A. (1999). Quantifying the information value of clinical assessments with signal detection theory. *Annual Review of Psychology, 50,* 215–241.

McGee, D. L., Liao, Y. L. Cao, G. C., & Cooper, R. S. (1999). Self-reported health status and mortality in a multi-ethnic U.S. cohort. *American Journal of Epidemiology, 149,* 41–46.

Meehl, P. E. (1970). Nuisance variables and the ex post facto design. In M. Radner & S. Winokur (Eds.), *Minnesota studies in the philosophy of science: Vol. 4. Analyses of theories and methods of physics and psychology* (pp. 373–402). Minneapolis: University of Minnesota Press.

Meehl, P. E. (1978). Theoretical risks and tabular asterisks: Sir Karl, Sir Ronald, and the slow progress of soft psychology. *Journal of Consulting and Clinical Psychology, 46,* 806–834.

Menon, G., & Yorkston, E. A. (2000). The use of memory and contextual cues in the formation of behavioral frequency judgments. In A. A. Stone, J. S. Turkkan, C. A. Bachrach, J. B. Jobe, H. S. Kurtzman, & V. S. Cain (Eds.), *The science of self-report: Implications for research and practice* (pp. 63–79). Mahwah, NJ: Erlbaum.

Messick, S. (1989). Validity. In R. L. Linn (Ed.), *Educational measurement* (3rd ed., pp. 13–104). New York: Macmillan.

Messick, S. (1995). Validity of psychological assessment: Validation of inferences from persons' responses and performances as scientific inquiry into score meaning. *American Psychologist, 50,* 741–749.

Miller, S. M., Shoda, Y., & Hurley, K. (1996). Applying social-cognitive theory to health protective behavior: Breast self-examination in cancer screening. *Psychological Bulletin, 119,* 70–94.

Miller, T. Q., Turner, C. W., Tindale, R. S., Posavac, E. J., & Dugoni, B. L. (1991). Reasons for the trend toward null findings in research on Type A behavior. *Psychological Bulletin, 110,* 469–485.

Mischel, W., & Shoda, Y. (1995). A cognitive-affective system theory of personality: Reconceptualizing situations, dispositions, dynamics, and invariance in personality structure. *Psychological Review, 102,* 246–268.

Mohr, D. C., Goodkin, D. E., Likosky, W., Beutler, L., Gatto, N., & Langan, M. K. (1997). Identification of Beck Depression Inventory items related to multiple sclerosis. *Journal of Behavioral Medicine, 20,* 407–414.

Morey, L. C. (2003). Measuring personality and psychopathology. In J. A. Schinka & W. F. Velicer (Eds.), *Handbook of psychology: Vol. 2. Research methods in psychology* (pp. 377–405). Hoboken, NJ: Wiley.

O'Donnell, K., & Chung, J. Y. (1997). The diagnosis of major depression in end-stage renal disease. *Psychotherapy and Psychosomatics, 66,* 38–43.

Ozer, D. J. (1999). Four principles for personality assessment. In L. A. Pervin & O. P. John (Eds.), *Handbook of personality: Theory and research* (pp. 671–686). New York: Guilford.

Park, T. L., Adams, S. G., & Lynch, J. (1998). Sociodemographic factors in health psychology research: 12 years in review. *Health Psychology, 17,* 381–383.

Patrick, D. L., Cheadle, A., Thompson, D. C., Diebr, P., Koepsell, T., & Kinne, S. (1994). The validity of self-reported smoking: A review and meta-analysis. *American Journal of Public Health, 84,* 1086–1093.

Paulhus, D. L. (1991). Measurement and control of response bias. In J. P. Robinson, P. R. Shaver, & L. S. Wrightsman (Eds.), *Measures of personality and social psychological attitudes* (pp. 17–59). San Diego, CA: Academic Press.

Peck, J. R., Smith, T. W., Ward, J. R., & Milano, R. (1989). Disability and depression in rheumatoid arthritis: A multi-trait, multi-method investigation. *Arthritis and Rheumatism 32,* 1100–1106.

Pennebaker, J. W. (2000). Psychological factors influencing the reporting of physical symptoms. In A. A. Stone, J. S. Turkkan, C. A. Bachrach, J. B. Jobe, H. S. Kurtzman, & V. S. Cain (Eds.), *The science of self-report: Implications for research and practice* (pp. 299–315). Mahwah, NJ: Erlbaum.

Popper, K. (1959). *The logic of scientific discovery.* New York: Basic Books.

Porter, L. S., Stone, A. A., & Schwartz, J. E. (1999). Anger expression and ambulatory blood pressure: A comparison of state and trait measures. *Psychosomatic Medicine, 61,* 454–463.

Rand, C. S. (2000). I took the medicine like you told me, doctor: Self-report of adherence with medical regimens. In A. A. Stone, J. S. Turkkan, C. A. Bachrach, J. B. Jobe, H. S. Kurtzman, & V. S. Cain (Eds.), *The science of self-report: Implications for research and practice* (pp. 257–276). Mahwah, NJ: Erlbaum.

Reise, F. P., Widaman, K. F., & Pugh, R. H. (1993). Confirmatory factor analysis and item response theory: Two approaches for exploring measurement invariance. *Psychological Bulletin, 114,* 552–556.

Rohrbaugh, M. J., Shoham, V., Coyne, J. C., Cranford, J. A., Sonnega, J. S., & Nicklas, J. M. (2004). Beyond the "self" in self-efficacy: Spouse confidence predicts patient survival following heart failure. *Journal of Family Psychology, 18,* 184–193.

Ryff, C. D., & Singer, B. (1998). The contours of positive human health *Psychological Inquiry, 9,* 1–28.

Schaeffer, N. C. (2000). Asking questions about threatening topics: A selective overview. In A. A. Stone, J. S. Turkkan, C. A. Bachrach, J. B. Jobe, H. S. Kurtzman, & V. S. Cain (Eds.), *The science of self-report: Implications for research and practice* (pp.105–121). Mahwah, NJ: Erlbaum.

Schmidt, K. M., & Embretson, S. E. (2003). Item response theory and measuring abilities. In I. B. Weiner (Series Ed.), J. A. Schinka & W. Velicer (Vol. Ed.), *Comprehensive handbook of psychology. Vol. 2: Research methods* (pp. 429–446). Hoboken, NJ: Wiley.

Schroeder, K. E., Carey, M. P., & Vanable, P. A. (2003a). Methodological challenges in research on sexual risk behavior: I. Item content, scaling, and data analytic options. *Annals of Behavioral Medicine, 26,* 76–103.

Schroeder, K. E., Carey, M. P., & Vanable, P. A. (2003b). Methodological challenges in research on sexual risk behavior: II. Accuracy of self-reports. *Annals of Behavioral Medicine, 26,* 104–123.

Schwartz, J. E., Neale, J., Marco, C., Shiffman, S. S., & Stone, A. A. (1999). Does trait coping exist? A momentary assessment approach to the evaluation of traits. *Journal of Personality and Social Psychology, 77,* 360–369.

Shiffman, S. (2000). Real-time self-report of momentary states in the natural environment: Computerized ecological momentary assessment. In A. A. Stone, J. S. Turkkan, C. A. Bachrach, J. B. Jobe, H. S. Kurtzman, & V. S. Cain (Eds.), *The science of self-report: Implications for research and practice* (pp. 277–298). Mahwah, NJ: Erlbaum.

Siegler, I. C., Bastain, L. A., Steffens, D. C., Bosworth, H. B., & Costa, P. T. (2002). Behavioral medicine and aging. *Journal of Consulting and Clinical Psychology, 70,* 843–851.

Smith, G. T. (2005). On construct validity: Issues of method and measurement. *Psychological Assessment, 17,* 396–408.

Smith, T. W. (1992). Hostility and health: Current status of a psychosomatic hypothesis. *Health Psychology, 11,* 139–150.

Smith, T. W. (2003). Health psychology. In I. B. Weiner (Series Ed.), J. A. Schinka & W. Velicer (Vol. Ed.), *Comprehensive handbook of psychology, Vol. 2: Research methods* (pp. 241–270). Hoboken, NJ: Wiley.

Smith, T. W., & Christensen, A. J. (1996). Positive and negative affect in rheumatoid arthritis: Increased specificity in the assessment of emotional adjustment. *Annals of Behavioral Medicine, 18,* 75–78.

Smith, T. W., & Gallo, L. C. (2001). Personality traits as risk factors for physical illness. In A. Baum, T. Revenson, & J. Singer (Eds.), *Handbook of health psychology.* Hillside, NJ: Erlbaum.

Smith, T.W., Kendall, P.C., & Keefe, F.J. (2002). Behavioral medicine and clinical health psychology: Introduction to the special issue, a view from the decade of behavior. *Journal of Consulting and Clinical Psychology, 70,* 459–462.

Smith, T. W., Orleans, T., & Jenkins, D. (2004). Prevention and health promotion: Decades of progress, new challenges, and an emerging agenda. *Health Psychology, 23,* 126–131.

Smith, T. W., Pope, M. K., Rhodewalt, F., & Poulton, J. L. (1989). Optimism, neuroticism, coping, and symptom reports: An alternative interpretation of the Life Orientation Test. *Journal of Personality and Social Psychology, 56,* 640–648.

Smith, T. W., & Ruiz, J. M. (1999). Methodological issues in adult health psychology. In P. C. Kendall, J. N. Butcher, & G. N. Holmbeck (Eds.), *Handbook of research methods in clinical psychology* (2nd ed., pp. 499–536). New York: Wiley.

Smith, T. W., & Suls, J. (2004). On the future of health psychology: Introduction to the special section. *Health Psychology, 23,* 115–118.

Smith, T. W., & Williams, P. G. (1992). Personality and health: Advantages and limitations of the five-factor model. *Journal of Personality, 60,* 395–423.

Stevens, S. S. (1951). Mathematics, measurement, and psychophysics. In S. S. Stevens (Ed.), *Handbook of experimental psychology* (pp. 1–49). New York: Wiley.

Stevens, S. S. (1959). Measurement, psychophysics, and utility. In C. W. Christensen & P. Ratoosh (Eds.), *Measurement: Definitions and theories* (pp. 18–63). New York: Wiley.

Stevens, S. S. (1968). Measurement, statistics, and the schemapiric view. *Science, 161,* 849–856.

Stone, A. A., Broderick, J. E., Shiffman, S. S., & Schwartz, J. E. (2004). Understanding recall of weekly pain from a momentary assessment perspective: Absolute agreement, between- and within-person consistency, and judged change in weekly pain. *Pain, 107,* 61–69.

Stone A. A., Schwartz, J. E., Neale, J. M., Shiffman, S. Marco, C. Hickox, M., et. al., (1998). A comparison of coping assessed by ecological momentary assessment and retrospective recall. *Journal of Personality and Social Psychology, 74,* 1670–1680.

Stone, A. A., & Shiffman, S. (2002). Capturing momentary, self-report data: A proposal for reporting guidelines. *Annals of Behavioral Medicine, 24,* 236–243.

Stone, A. A., Turkkan, J. S., Bachrach, C. A., Jobe, J. B., Kurtzman, H. S., & Cain, V. S. (Eds.). (2000). *The science of self-report: Implications for research and practice.* Mahwah, NJ: Erlbaum.

Strik, J., Honig, A., Lousberg, R., & Denollet, J. (2001). Sensitivity and specificity of observer and self-report questionnaires in major and minor depression following myocardial infarction. *Psychosomatics, 42,* 423–428.

Suls, J., & Bunde, J. (2005). Anger, anxiety, and depression as risk factors for cardiovascular disease: The problems and implications of overlapping affective disposition. *Psychological Bulletin, 131,* 260–300.

Suls, J., & Rothman, A. (2004). Evolution of the biopsychosocial model: Prospects and challenges for health psychology. *Health Psychology, 23,* 119–125.

Tourangeau, R. (2000). Remembering what happened: Memory errors and survey reports. In A. A. Stone, J. S. Turkkan, C. A. Bachrach, J. B. Jobe, H. S. Kurtzman, & V. S. Cain (Eds.), *The science of self-report: Implications for research and practice* (pp. 29–47). Mahwah, NJ: Erlbaum.

Von Bertalanffy, L. (1968). *General systems theory.* New York: Braziller.

Watson, D., & Pennebaker, J. W. (1989). Health complaints, stress, and distress: Exploring the central role of negative affectivity. *Psychological Review, 96,* 234–254.

Watson, D., & Tellegen, A. (1983). Toward a consensual structure of mood. *Psychological Bulletin, 98,* 219–225.

West, S. G., & Finch, J. F. (1997). Personality measurement: Reliability and validity issues. In R. Hogan, J. Johnson, & S. Briggs (Eds.), *Handbook of personality psychology* (pp. 143–164). Dallas, TX: Academic Press.

Whitfield, K. E., Weidner, G., Clark, R., & Anderson, N. B. (2002). Sociodemographic diversity and behavioral medicine. *Journal of Consulting and Clinical Psychology, 70,* 463–481.

Williams, P. G., Holmbeck, G. N., & Greenley, R. N. (2002). Adolescent health psychology. *Journal of Consulting and Clinical Psychology, 70,* 828–842.

Williams, R. B., Jr., Barefoot, J. C., & Shekelle, R. B. (1985). The health consequences of hostility. In M. A. Chesney & R. H. Rosenman (Eds.), *Anger and hostility in cardiovascular and behavioral disorders* (pp. 173–185). New York: Hemisphere.

Yali, A. M., & Revenson, T. A. (2004). How changes in population demographics will impact health psychology: Incorporating a broader notion of cultural competence into the field. *Health Psychology, 23,* 147–155.

Zautra, A., Burleson, M., Smith, C., Blalock, S., Wallston, K., BeVellis, R, et al. (1995). Arthritis and perceptions of quality of life: An examination of positive and negative affect in rheumatoid arthritis patients. *Health Psychology, 14,* 399–408.

J. Lee Westmaas, Virginia Gil-Rivas,
and Roxane Cohen Silver

Designing and Implementing Interventions to Promote Health and Prevent Illness

3

Warnings in the media are plentiful about the dangers of potential threats to our health such as flu pandemics, mad cow disease, and excessive use of pesticides and antibiotics. Although efforts to prevent such scenarios from becoming reality are well placed, many other health conditions in which individuals can play a role in their prevention are already taking the lives of millions of people. For example, the Centers for Disease Control and Prevention (CDC) estimate that more than 440,000 smokers in the United States die prematurely every year from smoking-related diseases (CDC, 2002). In addition, although HIV infection has been known for more than a decade to be mostly preventable by behaviors such as using a condom, approximately 40,000 persons become infected with HIV each year (Glynn & Rhodes, 2005), and 4.3 million adults worldwide were newly infected with HIV in 2004 (UNAIDS, 2004). These sobering statistics point out the need to develop, and the challenge of developing, effective interventions to promote health and prevent illness.

Although the task of persuading thousands or millions of people to change their behaviors may seem daunting, this is not an unrealistic goal. When the surgeon general announced that cigarette smoking was a leading cause of cancer in 1964, approxi-

mately 42% of the U.S. population smoked (CDC, 2004). Through a combination of laws restricting smoking in public places, bans on various forms of advertisement, tobacco taxes, the availability of cognitive-behavioral programs for smoking cessation, and advances in pharmacotherapies, the rate of smoking in the United States in 2004 was approximately 21% (CDC, 2005), a 50% reduction in prevalence. In the early years of the AIDS epidemic, the increase in safer-sex activities among gay men that accompanied messages about the dangers of unprotected sex was also a remarkable example of the effectiveness of behavior change interventions (Revenson & Schiaffino, 2000; Shilts, 1987). However, the recent increases in HIV infection rate among men who have sex with men (Elford & Hart, 2003) and the increases in smoking rates observed among high school students in the 1990s (CDC, 1999), and among college students in the 2000s (Rigotti, Lee, & Wechsler, 2000; Wechsler, Kelley, Seibring, Juo, & Rigotti, 2001), demonstrate that effective prevention interventions need to be attuned to the dynamic, ongoing, and complex nature of human behavior. This chapter presents important conceptual and practical issues in designing and implementing behavioral and psychological interventions whose goal is to promote health and prevent illness. Our aim is not to present a comprehensive review of each of these issues (readers will be provided with references to articles that provide more in-depth discussions) but to direct attention to their importance and their implications for conducting effective or informative prevention interventions. Examples that illustrate topics under discussion will be taken from the smoking cessation and HIV-prevention literatures, not only because of the substantial morbidity and mortality associated with smoking and HIV infection, but also because these topics have generated a substantial amount of research illustrating the challenges of conducting effective prevention interventions.

Primary, Secondary, and Tertiary Interventions

Interventions can be identified by the point along the health-illness continuum at which they occur. *Primary* prevention focuses on changing behaviors to prevent illness from occurring. For example, a primary prevention program for HIV-negative individuals would aim to prevent infection by promoting the use of condoms and other safe-sex strategies. *Secondary* prevention interventions are those that occur after the individual has been diagnosed with a condition, disease, or illness and seek to stop or reverse its progression. In the case of HIV, a secondary prevention intervention would focus on behavior change to prevent other strains of the virus from infecting those already infected. Current health policy emphasizes secondary prevention, although it has been argued that devoting more resources to primary intervention might benefit population health more substantially (Kaplan, 2000). *Tertiary* prevention interventions seek to control the devastating complications of an illness or negative health condition. An intervention to get hospitalized cancer patients to give up smoking to promote recovery from their surgery is an example of a tertiary prevention intervention.

Levels of Intervention

Interventions to promote health and prevent illness can also attempt to influence behavior at the individual, organizational, community, or societal level. Action at the societal (population) level represents the broadest level of influence; interventions focused on this level of influence seek to motivate

entire communities that differ on sociodemographic and other dimensions. These interventions may use the media and social organizations to educate and encourage people to adopt healthy behaviors and discourage unhealthy ones. For example, advertisements by the government of Canada encouraging physical activity in its populace, the ParticipAction campaign in the 1970s, 1980s, and 1990s emphasized the positive health benefits of exercise and were expected to be viewed and acted upon regardless of age, gender, or socioeconomic status (Canadian Public Health Association, 2004). Population-based efforts usually involve simple messages that can be understood by a majority of a society's members. On their own, however, they can be less effective than other approaches in changing individual behavior. Population approaches can sometimes be cost-effective, however. If only a tiny fraction of the population is motivated to change their behavior as a result of the message, the cost savings resulting from the prevention of illness among these individuals can be significantly greater than the cost of the intervention (Thompson, Cornonado, Snipes, & Puschel, 2003).

Population-wide interventions also include laws that mandate health-promoting behaviors, for example, seat belt use, the wearing of protective headgear for motorcyclists in some jurisdictions, or laws restricting smoking in the workplace. These interventions can lead to behavior change not only by increasing levels of perceived threat but also by influencing individuals' attitudes, beliefs, and appraisals. At the interpersonal level, these campaigns may result in changes in social attitudes and norms that may further contribute to behavioral change. Action at the policy or population level can also provide additional motivation for behavior change among individuals contemplating action as a result of other prevention efforts. For example, county- or statewide restrictions on smoking in workplaces and eating establishments, which have already encouraged thousands of smokers to attempt to quit smoking (Chapman et al., 1999), might need to be combined with steep tobacco taxes to encourage some smokers to quit.

Less broad in their reach are community and organizational activities that seek to promote healthy behavior in their members. Many community interventions have adopted a social ecological perspective, recognizing that behavior change is a result of social and environmental influences. The program components of community-level interventions are often supported by the results of individual-level or clinic-based research. Indeed, it has been argued that the costs of community-wide programs to promote healthy behaviors are justifiable only if prior research supports program components (Sorensen, Emmons, Hunt, & Johnston, 1998). An example of a community intervention to prevent the uptake of smoking in youth was the Healthy for Life Project conducted in the United States. Recognizing the various social influences on smoking, the intervention targeted peers, schools, and parents, as well as community agencies (Piper, 2000). A justification for the use of community prevention approaches is based on the concept of *population-attributable risk*, which refers to how much risk produces a given amount of disease in a population (Rose, 1985). According to the epidemiologist Geoffrey Rose (1992), changing the risk levels of a population to a small degree can impact public health more strongly than substantially changing the risk of a smaller number of people.

Some interventions are limited to specific institutions such as work sites or schools. Considering that many individuals spend a substantial amount of time at places of employment or education, the proliferation of work site and school programs addressing a wide range of health issues such as smoking, weight loss, and physical activity is not surprising.

Individual-level interventions are characterized by higher levels of personal interaction between the targets of the interventions and their providers and are more likely to be based on psychosocial or biomedical explanations for behavior. An example is a program to reduce smoking prevalence by having physicians provide advice and support for smoking cessation (Goldstein et al., 1997). Evaluations of such interventions led to the recommendation in 1996 by the United States Agency for Health Care Policy and Research (AHCPR) that physicians practice the "Four Rs" during their patients' checkups: emphasize the risks of smoking, the rewards of quitting, the relevance of the risks of smoking to the smoker (and the rewards of quitting), and repetition of these messages (Fiore, Jorenby, & Baker, 1997). These recommendations for physician interventions were found to be cost-effective compared with other prevention interventions (Cromwell, Bartosch, Fiore, Hasselblad, & Baker, 1997). Family members or friends can also become involved in

individual-level approaches. For example, social pressure by a spouse or family members to change an individual's behavior (i.e., social control) has been associated with the degree to which spouses reduce their levels of smoking (Westmaas, Wild, & Ferrence, 2002).

Advocates of ecological models of health promotion interventions recommend an integration of these various levels of influence in any effort to change health behaviors (Stokols, Pelletier, & Fielding, 1995). Nonetheless, the decision as to whether an intervention should be at the individual, community, or population level, and whether it should be primary, secondary, or tertiary, will be influenced by a number of factors. These include the amount of financial resources available, political considerations, findings from prior prevention/intervention research, the likelihood of community cooperation, and the believed causes of the behavior or illness in question. Of these, an important first step is to understand the various influences on the illness- or health-promoting behavior and to use a theoretical model to guide the design of the intervention.

Psychosocial and Other Pathways to Disease

Research in the last three decades has provided convincing evidence of the contribution of psychosocial, biological, and behavioral factors in illness and health, and several theories to explain these associations have been elaborated (Schneiderman, 2004). Understanding how psychosocial, behavioral, and biological factors independently and/or interactively contribute to health is an important step in deciding when and how to intervene. Having a theoretical model as a template from which to understand the influence of these variables on health and behavior change is important in designing a successful and cost-effective intervention.

Models of Health Behavior Change

To date, prevention intervention efforts have been largely guided by individual-level theories in which social and cognitive variables play a central role (Kohler, Grimley, & Reynolds, 1999; Rutter & Quine, 2002). Chief among these are the health belief model (HBM; Rosenstock, Strecher, & Becker,

1994); the theories of reasoned action (Ajzen & Fishbein, 1977, 1980) and planned behavior (Ajzen, 1991, 1998); social cognitive (learning) theory (Bandura, 1986, 1997); and the transtheoretical model of change (Prochaska & DiClemente, 1983). These models and theories overlap to a considerable extent, but each emphasizes key concepts that significantly influence health behavior change (Elder, Ayala, & Harris, 1999).

The HBM proposes that behavior change will occur if individuals perceive a threat to their well-being and believe that the benefits of engaging in behavior change outweigh the barriers or costs associated with that behavior. Cues to action (e.g., education, symptoms) are viewed as prompting behavior change, particularly when levels of perceived threat are high (Rosentock, Strecher, & Becker, 1994). The HBM has been used to predict a variety of health behaviors such as breast self-examination (Champion, 1994), safe-sex practices (Zimmerman & Olson, 1994), and exercise (Corwyn & Benda, 1999), among others. Although the HBM has been widely used, the relationship between key elements of the model and behavior change are rather small (Sheeran & Abraham, 1996), suggesting the need to consider the influence of factors in addition to those central to the model. More recently, principles of social-cognitive theory have been incorporated in interventions guided by the HBM in an effort to increase the likelihood of health behavior change.

Social-cognitive (learning) theory (Bandura, 1997, 1998) posits that self-efficacy beliefs, goals, outcome expectations, and perceived barriers or aids involved in enacting a behavior jointly influence human motivation, action, and health (Bandura, 1998). Self-efficacy refers to one's perceived ability to take the action necessary to achieve the desired effects or outcomes. Self-efficacy beliefs are the result of direct and vicarious experience and verbal persuasion. Bandura (1998) suggests that personal self-efficacy beliefs play an influential role in health in two ways: (a) by influencing biological pathways (i.e., sympathetic nervous system activation, immune functioning) involved in the relationship between stress and illness, and (b) by its impact on individuals' decisions to make behavioral changes, their motivation to maintain these changes and their ability to resume those efforts when they face a setback. Outcome expectations regarding the physical effects of a health behavior (e.g., discomfort), the social reactions it evokes, and self-evaluative

reactions to one's behavior are also important influences on health behavior. Barriers to the initiation and maintenance of behavioral change may exist within the individual (such as whether he or she has the resources and skills needed), may be situational, or may be the result of larger social and structural factors. An extensive body of research has documented the influence of self-efficacy beliefs on individuals' efforts to implement and maintain dietary changes (McCann et al., 1995); physical activity and exercise adherence (McAuley, Jerome, Marquez, Elavsky, & Blissmer, 2003); smoking cessation (Shiffman et al., 2000); condom use (Baele, Dusseldorp, & Maes, 2001); alcohol use (Maisto, Connors, & Zywiak, 2000); and drug use (Reilly et al., 1995). Prevention intervention programs based on social-cognitive theory include several components, including an informational component to increase perceptions of the risks and benefits associated with a particular behavior, teaching social and cognitive skills that can be used to initiate behavior change, building self-efficacy to promote behavior maintenance, and building social support to sustain change (Kohler, Grimley, & Reynolds, 1999).

The theories of reasoned action (Ajzen & Fishbein, 1977, 1980) and planned behavior (Ajzen, 1988, 1991) propose that for behavior change to occur, individuals must experience a strong *intention* to change. Behavioral intentions, in turn, are predicted by (a) expectancies that a behavior will produce a particular outcome, (b) attitudes toward the behavior, (c) beliefs about what others think is appropriate behavior (subjective norms) and motivation to comply with others' opinions, (d) perceptions of control over one's behavior, and (e) other behavioral, normative, and control beliefs (Albarracin, Johnson, Fishbein, & Muellerleile, 2001). The application of these theories to prevention intervention efforts and prediction of behavior requires defining the targeted individuals' key beliefs, values, and attitudes and their levels of perceived control (Ajzen & Fishbein, 1980). These theories have been widely used to predict health behaviors and to develop prevention interventions. The empirical evidence, however, suggests a weak to moderate association between key elements of the theory and condom use (Albarracin et al., 2001), contraceptive use (Adler, Kegeles, Irwin, & Wibbelsman, 1990), physical activity (Blue, 1995), alcohol use (Johnston & White,

2003), and smoking (Higgins & Conner, 2003), among others.

The transtheoretical model of change (TMC; Prochaska & DiClemente, 1983) proposes that behavior change is a process. Key elements include stages of change, the process of change, decisional balance (pros and cons of change), and situational self-efficacy. The stages of change are precontemplation (not ready to change within the next 6 months), contemplation (thinking about change within the next 6 months), preparation (ready to change in the next 30 days), action, and maintenance (more than 6 months of sustained action). The TMC posits that tailoring interventions to individuals' readiness to change based on their current stage will be more likely to produce behavioral changes. This theory has been used to predict a wide range of health behaviors, including alcohol and drug use (Prochaska, DiClemente, & Norcross, 1992), physical activity (Marshall & Biddle, 2001), and sexual risk behaviors (Grimley, Prochaska, & Prochaska, 1993), but there have been null effects reported by some interventions using this approach (Adams & White, 2005). Other theoretical models guiding health promotion research include cognitive/information processing (Joos & Hickam, 1990) and social support theories (Gonzalez, Goeppinger, & Lorig, 1990).

Key Elements of Successful Interventions

Based on research demonstrating the value of key concepts from the preceding models in predicting behavior change, Elder et al. (1999) summarized the important ingredients for successful health promotion and prevention programs. Specifically, for a person to change, she or he must

> (1) have a strong positive intention or predisposition to perform a behavior; (2) face a minimum of information processing and physical, logistical, and social environmental barriers to performing the behavior; (3) perceive her/himself as having the requisite skills for the behavior; (4) believe that material, social, or other reinforcement will follow the behavior; (5) believe that there is normative pressure to perform and none sanctioning the behavior; (6) believe that the behavior is consistent with the person's self-image; (7) have a positive affect regarding the behavior; and (8) encounter cues or enablers

to engage in the behavior at the appropriate time and place. (p. 276)

Some interventions have targeted one or more of these requirements for behavior change (e.g., self-efficacy in performing the behavior, outcome expectancies) and have also examined how they influence physical health or physiological outcomes. Sobel (1995) argues that psychosocial variables such as sense of control and optimism, in addition to self-efficacy, not only directly impact health behaviors but also have direct effects on physiological processes that in turn influence health. Interventions that attempt to increase levels of these "shared determinants of health," he believes, are important in changing any health-relevant behavior but have not been given the attention they deserve. For example, although feelings of self-efficacy have been found to be an important predictor of behavior change, few interventions have been developed in which creating feelings of self-efficacy regarding the targeted behaviors is an important goal. The studies of Lorig and colleagues at the Stanford Arthritis Center were offered by Sobel as an example in which the finding that improvement in symptoms (reduced pain) was predicted most strongly by an enhanced sense of control over symptoms led to a change in intervention focus (Lorig & Fries, 1990; Lorig et al., 1989). The result was a restructuring of the intervention to focus on enhancing feelings of self-efficacy based on achievable goals (e.g., walking up two steps rather than a whole flight of stairs), and which produced significant reductions in pain and subsequent physician visits.

The research and interventions of Kemeny with HIV-positive patients have also targeted health behavior change variables such as outcome expectancies (see Kemeny, 2003). Their research program found that in men diagnosed with AIDS, negative expectancies about their future health were the strongest predictor of accelerated time to death, controlling for a variety of confounding factors such as baseline health status or immune functioning. Other important psychosocial predictors were negative appraisals of characteristics of the self and rejection sensitivity. Rejection sensitivity about one's homosexuality was significantly related to the rate of CD4 decline and to faster progression to AIDS and mortality (Cole, Kemeny, & Taylor, 1997). Interventions to alter cognitive appraisals of the disease process among these men, in addition to cognitive-behavioral stress management, have been found to produce significant changes in physiological parameters relevant to HIV, such as CD4 T cells and viral load (Schneiderman, Antoni, & Ironson, 2003).

Social Influences and Health Behavior Change

One psychosocial variable that may be a valuable component of interventions to change health behaviors is providing support for achieving the desired goal. Many interventions have included social support in an effort to delay illness or prolong life (e.g., Zabalegui, Sanchez, Sanchez, & Juando, 2005). For example, interventions to help smokers quit have included strategies to elicit social support from others or have assigned smokers to buddies who provide support during situations with a high risk for relapse (May & West, 2000; Park, Schultz, Tudiver, Campbell, & Becker, 2004).

In many cases, however, the promise of social support has not lived up to expectations. For example, some studies have found null or adverse effects of critical incident stress debriefing (CISD), a form of immediate social support provided to survivors of acute trauma, on the incidence of posttraumatic stress disorder (McNally, Bryant, & Ehlers, 2003). In addition, a recent Cochrane meta-analysis of psychosocial interventions for women with metastatic breast cancer found no evidence of long-term effects, although methodological features of the trials reviewed, as well as insufficient power to detect effects, may have precluded finding effects. Personality factors may also moderate the extent to which social support is beneficial, but few studies have examined how personality factors or other individual differences interact with support provision. Possible candidates are hostility (Lepore, 1995) and defensiveness (Strickland & Crowne, 1963; Westmaas & Jamner, 2006); experimental studies have found these dispositional qualities to moderate the extent to which social support is beneficial in reducing subjective and physiological reactions to stressors.

In the smoking cessation literature, some intervention studies that have sought to increase the amount of social support for smokers likewise have proved to be ineffective (May & West, 2000). However, data suggest that attention to potential moderators such as gender and the use of theoretical models to guide research may be valuable in understanding how social support can be used effectively in interventions. For example, Westmaas and Billings (2005) hypothesized that social support might facilitate smoking cessation by reducing subjective responses to stressors such as negative affect and cravings, responses that in prior research predict the likelihood of lapsing (Kassel, Stroud, & Paronis, 2003). However, they hypothesized that the gender of the support provider and recipient would moderate the effects of support in reducing negative affect and cravings. Prior research on gender and social support suggested to them that among men, emotional support during quitting should originate from a romantic partner, whereas among women, effective sources of support could include same-sex friends or strangers. They found that, indeed, women smokers' negative affect and withdrawal symptoms were minimized during a stress task if a female stranger provided support. However, men smokers' negative affect and withdrawal symptoms increased if the support provider was a female confederate. These results indicated that smoking cessation interventions may need to take into account theory and findings on gender in constructing interventions that include supportive components.

In other areas of health psychology research, gender, age, and sociocultural factors may be important factors in whether the provision of social support is an effective component of interventions. Attention to how social support is defined (structural, emotional, social pressure, etc.) and other methodological factors such as the use of standardized measures and process evaluation, are also important in evaluating the effects of social support components. These methodological factors are discussed in subsequent sections in more detail.

A Social Ecological Approach to Health Behavior Change

Social ecological models of behavior change address multiple sources of influence on health-relevant behaviors. In a model described by Sorensen and colleagues (1998), these sources of influence are explained in terms of lenses through which various disciplines view the behavior or illness:

> At the micro level, the biomedical lens focuses on biophysiological theories of disease causation. . . . The psychosocial lens maintains a primary focus on the individual, investigating questions about individual and social

behaviors such as personality structures, a sense of control, and self-efficacy. . . . The epidemiological lens examines disease patterns within populations and aims to understand differential risk factors, including biological predispositions as well as behavioral and environmental exposures. By contrast, the society-and-health lens brings to the foreground cultural, social, economic, and political processes and aims to understand the ways in which these social structures influence differential risks. The social ecological model cuts across these disciplinary lenses and offers a theoretical framework that integrates multiple perspectives and theories. This framework recognizes that behavior is affected by multiple levels of influence, including intrapersonal factors, interpersonal processes, institutional factors, community factors, and public policy. (p. 390)

Social ecological models to promote healthful behaviors can also address the influence of physical environments. According to Stokols (1992), in a social ecological approach "the healthfulness of a situation and the well-being of its participants are assumed to be influenced by multiple facets of both the physical environment (e.g., geography, architecture, and technology) and the social environment (e.g., culture, economics, and politics)" (p. 7). Of five health-related functions of the sociophysical environment noted by Stokols, one is environment as "an enabler of health behavior exemplified by the installation of safety devices in buildings and vehicles, geographic proximity to health care facilities, and exposure to interpersonal modeling or cultural practices that foster health-promotive behavior" (pp. 13–14).

Multiple Influences on Health Behavior Change: The Case of Smoking

A good example of the multiple levels of influence that comprise a social ecological approach to behavior change is the case of smoking. Smoking is implicated in many illnesses, and the ability to quit appears to be a function of societal, psychosocial, and biological variables. Cigarette smoking is believed to account for approximately 90% of all lung cancer cases (Siemiatycki, Krewski, Franco, & Kaiserman, 1995), but most smokers will not develop lung cancer. Genetic polymorphisms in glu-

tathione s-transferase enzyme activity may influence the degree to which carcinogens in cigarette smoke are metabolized, and by implication the likelihood of developing lung cancer (Harrison, Cantlay, Rae, Lamb, & Smith, 1997; Nyberg, Hou, Hemminki, Lambert, & Pershagen, 1998; Jourenkova-Mironova et al., 1998). These and other advancements, such as the development of a vaccine to prevent nicotine from reaching the brain (Shine, 2000), offer the possibility of future biologically based interventions to prevent the development of lung cancer among smokers (secondary prevention).

Psychosocial factors are also associated with smoking initiation, such as parental or sibling smoking, and perceived norms about the acceptability of smoking. School-based primary interventions have addressed these psychosocial factors. Recent meta-analyses of school-based interventions found that the most effective approaches were those that included a focus on social reinforcement for not smoking, whereas the least effective were those that sought only to increase awareness of the dangers of starting to smoke (Levinthal, 2005).

In addition to psychosocial factors as contributors to smoking behavior, societal-level factors are implicated, such as the price of cigarettes and the portrayal of smoking among actors in movies (Anderson & Hughes, 2000). Community approaches to the prevention of smoking have recognized that in addition to psychosocial factors, these societal-level factors are also important.

Sociodemographic and cultural variables, such as age, gender, ethnicity, and/or socioeconomic status, may moderate the impact of biological, psychosocial, and societal influences on smoking. These variables have taken on increased importance in the design of interventions to reduce or prevent smoking because of recent evidence that smoking initiation is also now occurring at a later age through cigarette promotion activities in bars that cater to college students (Rigotti, Moran, & Wechsler, 2005). This has occurred as laws curbing advertising directed at youth have been enacted (e.g., the Joe Camel campaign). Such recent developments suggest that to appropriately evaluate population-level interventions such as those limiting the advertising or price and availability of cigarettes, age, or educational level will need to be considered as possible moderators of the effectiveness of these activities. Gender or ethnic differences in smoking initiation, in reasons for smoking, and in smoking prevalence or ability to quit have also been demonstrated (Mermelstein, 1999; Perkins, 2001; Perkins, Donny, & Caggiula, 1999), suggesting their potential role as moderators of intervention effectiveness.

Although a social-ecological perspective in designing health promotion interventions has been promulgated and extensively implemented (see reviews by Merzel & D'Afflitti, 2003; Sorensen et al., 1998), a single unifying framework that integrates multiple levels of influence on a particular behavior, and that acknowledges possible interactions among them, has been absent (Merzel, & D'Afflitti, 2003). Goodman and colleagues have also argued that without the specificity of an integrative social-ecological model with which to test hypotheses, it is difficult to properly evaluate the effects of community-level prevention interventions (Goodman, Liburd, & Green-Phillips, 2001).

Designing Interventions

An initial step in designing prevention interventions is deciding who should be the target of the intervention. This decision should be partly related to whether the focus of the intervention is primary, secondary, or tertiary prevention. Many illness-promoting behaviors begin during youth or adolescence, and so primary interventions will often need to target individuals in these age groups. Good examples are school-based interventions to prevent initiation of smoking, to prevent obesity, or to prevent pregnancies and sexually transmitted diseases. However, primary interventions can also target older individuals, such as older HIV-negative men who have sex with men, or college students who are in danger of starting to smoke or binge drink. Age and gender differences are important considerations because they are related to maturational or sociocultural factors that are likely to play a role in the factors influencing health behaviors and whether the behavior is adopted. The use of explicit sexual language in print messages urging gay men to use condoms to prevent HIV infection, for example, while believed to have been effective for this population, could be offensive if applied to young women who are also in danger of becoming infected.

If the target population for an intervention consists of specialized groups such as ethnic and racial minorities, immigrant populations, children, the elderly, or the physically ill, other challenges exist. For example, cultural beliefs may play a significant role in the adoption of the behavior, and culture-appropriate materials may be needed to deliver the intervention. In an intervention to reduce the likelihood of HIV infection among migrant farmworkers in California who have sex with other men, but who would not self-identify as gay, Conner and colleagues distributed a novella (ongoing sagas presented in comic book format) to promote condom use (Mishra, Sanudo, & Conner, 2004). In this particular socioethnic group, such an approach was seen as a legitimate source of information compared with other possible options.

In addition to cultural factors, specialized groups may also differ on other sociodemographic characteristics, such as literacy or socioeconomic status, which will dictate the methods used to deliver the intervention. If English is not the native language of the intended recipients, the intervention will of course need to be presented in their language. If reading ability is limited, print media are not appropriate.

The sociodemographic and cultural characteristics of a targeted population can also influence whether an intervention should be undertaken at the individual, community, or societal level. If the targeted population is difficult to recruit for face-to-face interactions, then community- or society-level interventions, rather than individual-level prevention approaches, may be more appropriate. If individuals from some communities have to endure a long commute to attend a cognitive-behavioral smoking cessation clinic provided by a hospital, or do not have the financial resources to make the trip, public service messages on radio stations or campaigns delivered through church groups may have a better chance at reaching them. For example, Brandon and colleagues recruited recently quit smokers for a relapse-prevention intervention through newspaper, radio, and media advertisements that provided them with a toll-free number to call to register for the program (Brandon et al., 2004). The intervention consisted of brochures that were mailed directly to participants. This technique was effective in decreasing relapse rates.

Sometimes an intervention seeks to target those who are most at risk. If reducing risk in the most at-risk individuals is the overarching goal, it might be assumed that increasing the intensity of the intervention will be needed to change behavior. However, even moderately intense prevention efforts could increase the attrition rate in such a population. Equally important, the intervention will be less likely to show positive effects among those most at risk. For example, the aim of the Community Intervention Trial for Smoking Cessation (COMMIT) was to increase cessation rates among heavy smokers (i.e., those smoking more than 25 cigarettes a day). However, postintervention analyses indicated that COMMIT succeeded in increasing quit rates among light and moderate smokers (i.e., those smoking less than 25 cigarettes a day) but not among heavy smokers (Fisher, 1995).

Another important consideration in selecting participants is how generalizable the results of the intervention are intended to be, which in turn will influence whether the intervention is likely to be adopted by others. The RE-AIM framework, developed by Glasgow and colleagues, is a system of evaluating health promotion interventions that includes an assessment of the representativeness of participants, and the settings in which the intervention was conducted (Glasgow, Bull, Gillette, Klesges, & Dzewaltowski, 2002). Among the components of RE-AIM (Reach, Effectiveness, Adoption, Implementation, Maintenance), Reach refers to "the percentage of potential participants who will take part in an intervention, and to how representative they are of the population from which they are drawn" (p. 63). Glasgow and colleagues evaluated health promotion interventions conducted between 1996 and 2000 that attempted to change dietary, smoking, and physical activity behaviors, and that included a comparison or control group. They found that among 36 studies, although a majority reported on the percentage of eligible patients who participated, few studies reported whether participants, compared with those who declined, differed on sociodemographic or medical variables. Knowing who declined, why they did so, and whether they differed from participants on sociodemographic variables such as sex, age, and socioeconomic status can help in the design and revision of recruitment strategies so that generalizability of an intervention is enhanced.

Selecting the Appropriate Design

To be able to conclude that an intervention is effective, plausible alternative explanations must be ruled out. Randomization of individuals, schools, work sites, or communities to intervention and control groups represents the best strategy for ruling out alternative explanations, but participant responses to and reactions against the randomization process must be attended to and minimized, if possible (Wortman, Hendricks, & Hillis, 1976). In addition, other designs, including longitudinal research, can be used to support causal inferences. However, longitudinal designs are based on the assumption that certain parameters do not change over time, and there is still the possibility of spuriousness that needs to be accounted for in order to make causal inferences (Kenny, 1979).

One threat to the ability to make causal inferences is the problem of selection bias. Selection bias occurs if the units making up the intervention and control groups differ before the intervention is even implemented (Larzelere, Kuhn, & Johnson, 2004). These biases can lead to both overestimating and underestimating the effects of interventions. In some interventions, selection biases operate so that the sickest or riskiest groups are targeted for behavior change. Regression to the mean by these individuals, defined as the tendency over time to approach mean levels of a behavior (Cook & Campbell, 1979), can give the appearance that the intervention produced positive effects. Without randomization to intervention and control groups of the most at-risk individuals, regression to the mean as a plausible alternative interpretation of results cannot be eliminated.

Well-designed randomized clinical trials represent one of the most powerful means of assessing health behavior theories and the effectiveness of interventions. However, as Helgeson and Lepore (1997) note, designing a randomized clinical intervention will often require balancing "the needs of the individual patient with the requirements of the research protocol" and "the practical or logistical issues in conducting an intervention with the theoretical and experimental issues." Helgeson and Lepore further note that this balancing act will sometimes require unforeseen modifications to the research protocol in order to ensure patient recruitment and retention and/or the cooperation of clinic staff. As an example they mention the occasional cancer patient who is dismayed by his or her assignment to the control group and asks to be put in the intervention group. The authors resolved this issue in their own research by favoring patients' well-being (e.g., providing them with referrals to other support groups in the community; see Hohmann

& Shear, 2002, for another discussion of these problems).

When there is nonrandomization of units to intervention and control groups, assessing possible preexisting differences between intervention and control groups on variables that may influence the targeted behavior becomes paramount. These principles have not always been followed in community interventions to prevent the uptake of smoking in young people, however. According to a recent Cochrane database review, among the 17 community intervention studies designed to prevent youth smoking that included control groups and assessed baseline characteristics (their criteria for inclusion in the review), in 8 studies the allocation of communities or schools to the intervention or control groups was nonrandom, and some studies did not account for baseline differences in smoking in their follow-up analyses (Sowden, Arblaster, & Stead, 2005).

In the absence of randomization to intervention and control groups, matching individuals or communities from intervention and comparison groups on variables associated with the targeted behavior is appropriate. In a review of 32 community interventions to reduce smoking in adults that included a control group, however, only 5 studies demonstrated that the intervention and control communities were comparable on demographic variables at baseline (Secker-Walker, Gnich, Platt, & Lancaster, 2005).

In randomized controlled interventions conducted at the community level, the need to maintain scientific rigor through standardization and control can sometimes conflict with community goals and priorities. A certain amount of flexibility in accommodating the needs of participating community organizations is important for ensuring intervention integrity and can ultimately influence the effectiveness of the intervention. Involving communities in the design and implementation process will help both researchers and communities understand each other's perspectives and can ensure that the goals and priorities of both parties are met.

The expense of randomized controlled trials at the community level, in which the unit of allocation to experimental and comparison groups is the community or organization, can be a motivating factor in considering alternative designs, especially if required levels of statistical power are to be achieved. Sorensen and colleagues (1998) have stated that in designing interventions at the community level, "an expanded range of research methodologies is required to address the diverse needs for scientific rigor, appropriateness to research questions, and feasibility in terms of cost and setting" (p. 401). They describe other designs that could supplement the randomized control trial in answering questions about the effectiveness of community interventions, including observational studies, qualitative research methods, and action research methods. For example, qualitative research methods would be appropriate for understanding community needs, priorities, and resources before an intervention is designed.

With the increased popularity of the Internet, a number of Web-based interventions have also been developed. Web-based interventions offer the advantages of accessibility, low cost, data completeness, standardization, personalization or tailoring of information, and potentially greater accuracy of reporting symptoms or illegal or stigmatizing behaviors. Subjects can also participate in program elements in the privacy of their own homes and at their own convenience, and the degree of program participation can be easily assessed. Currently, there is a paucity of well-controlled research on the efficacy of Web-based interventions to promote health behaviors, but there are promising signs. For example, current Web-based interventions addressing smoking cessation, substance use, depression, and post-traumatic stress disorders have demonstrated positive treatment effects compared with control groups (Barr, Taylor, & Luce, 2003; Bock et al., 2004; Copeland & Martin, 2004).

Power Analyses

For any research endeavor, conducting power analyses is an important means of determining the number of units to be assigned to experimental and control groups in order to answer questions about the intervention's effectiveness. If a proposed study is not adequately powered, the absence of reliable (significant) differences between groups could be attributed to lack of power. Power analyses can also determine whether there are sufficient data points to adequately evaluate if intervention effects on outcome variables are moderated by other variables (e.g., motivation to quit smoking or gender). Such analyses represent the testing of "group by moderating variable" interactions and provide valuable information, especially if no main effects are obtained.

In individual-level interventions, the unit of allocation is the participant, with power analyses indicating the number of participants that should be recruited in each group in order to detect significant main or interaction effects at predetermined levels of power (usually 80%). In community interventions, the unit of allocation is the work site, school, hospital, city, or town. Power analysis to determine adequate sample sizes in community interventions need to account for statistical dependencies of responses within each unit or cluster (Donner & Klar, 1996; Koepsell et al., 1992). When only one community receives the intervention, with another community serving as the control group, conducting power analysis is difficult if results are to be analyzed at the cluster level. Indeed, it has been argued that the modest or nonsignificant effects of several community interventions to promote health and prevent illness may have been due to insufficient power to detect positive effects, even small ones (Secker-Walker et al., 2005).

Enlisting Cooperation for Interventions

In clinic-based interventions, the goal is often to evaluate the efficacy of a specific treatment on a specific outcome. An example is determining whether a cognitive-behavioral intervention for smoking cessation is effective in getting hospitalized patients to quit. Clinic-based interventions usually involve nurses, doctors, or other health care professionals (e.g., therapists, psychologists, and psychiatrists). Helgeson and Lepore (1997) provide several guidelines and comments that are useful in enlisting the cooperation of medical personnel. For example, they note that to gain access to a medical population, the first step is to identify a physician who values research and can be convinced that the results of the intervention will translate to benefits for the patient and the medical community. Including physicians in designing the intervention itself may be challenging, given the time constraints that many have, but nurses, whose training emphasizes the psychosocial needs of the patient, can often provide valuable information about patients and the operation of the institution (Holman, 1997). This information can be especially valuable in the design phase of the intervention. Because of the multitude of demands faced by clinic staff, minimizing the amount of work required of them (e.g., in developing a list of eligible patients for the study) will

be important in maintaining their interest and cooperation. Maintaining contact with staff, particularly nurses, who are often vital to the successful implementation of the project, rewarding them for their cooperation, and providing updates and evidence of the intervention's value will also help to achieve this goal (Helgeson & Lepore, 1997; Grady & Wallston, 1988).

For interventions at the community level, the skills and priorities of the individuals, agencies, and institutions participating in the intervention are more varied. Altman (1995a) summarized four recommendations for improving community-level interventions, at least two of which refer to the importance of community cooperation. The four recommendations include "(i) integrate interventions into the community infrastructure, (ii) use comprehensive, multi-level intervention approaches, (iii) facilitate community participation and promote community capacity-building, and (iv) conduct thorough needs assessment/social reconnaissance in order to tailor interventions to the community context." Spending the time to understand the priorities of community organizations, whose assistance is required for the intervention to be implemented, and incorporating their needs into the intervention goals will help to sustain their cooperation during the research phase. At the same time, demonstrating how the intervention goals can benefit the community, and obtaining consensus for their importance, will help ensure that the needs of all parties are adequately met. However, some flexibility is still required on the part of the academically oriented research team so that the intervention is tailored to the community context.

Process Evaluation

Designing, planning, and executing an intervention, especially one that requires the cooperation of researchers, community agencies, workplaces, and media, involves a tremendous amount of effort. To be able to determine whether these considerable efforts are effective in producing the intended changes and are cost-effective, a rigorous evaluation of intervention delivery is required. Without extensive process evaluation, interpreting a lack of differences between intervention and control groups is particularly problematic. For example, if teachers implementing a smoking resistance program among middle schoolers deviate significantly from activities geared to changing norms about smoking and resisting offers to smoke, then nonsignificant effects of the intervention could be attributed to the intervention group having received a weaker dose of the treatment. Ongoing evaluation of program activities and delivery can also be used to appropriately modify program components once the intervention is under way.

A model example of rigorous process evaluation occurred in the COMMIT trial, a five-year community intervention trial to decrease smoking prevalence among heavy smokers (Fisher, 1995). Monitoring of program delivery was extensive, with logs completed by staff and volunteers and computerized record keeping of intervention activities. Process evaluation in other community interventions has included surveys completed by the targeted population and deliverers of the intervention, either by phone or through the mail, focus groups and semistructured interviews, and tracking and documenting program activities. In some trials, these functions were performed by computerized systems (Secker-Walker et al., 2005).

Process evaluation in community interventions can also include a determination of its *reach* and *penetration*. Reach refers to how aware members of the target population are of program activities such as radio or television advertisements, newspaper articles, health fairs, workplace programs, treatment clinics, self-help kits, and so on. Penetration refers to the extent to which the targeted population participated in these activities. Polling of representative samples of individuals from the targeted population can determine reach and penetration, which can be presented as the number or proportion of individuals who partook of intervention activities. This information should be an important part of the dissemination of trial results because low rates of awareness and/or penetration could account for nonsignificant differences between intervention and comparison groups on key outcomes. Penetration (intervention dose) can also be used to determine dose-response relationships, a measure of the effect of the intervention.

A case can be made that assessing the reach and penetration in comparison groups or communities for activities that are similar to intervention components should also be performed. There may be diffusion or "spillover" of the treatment from the experimental group or community into the comparison group or community. At the community level, this is likely to occur if the media extensively cover intervention activities. Comparison communities may also independently conduct their own health fairs, enact legislation, or provide media messages that produce effects similar to those of the intervention. For example, in the Alliance of Black Churches Project to reduce smoking through counseling by church members, the difference between the intervention group and the comparison group in whether they received information about smoking from a church member was 29% versus 20%, respectively (Schorling et al., 1997). In the COMMIT trial, differences in indices of penetration for the intervention and control communities were relatively small.

Secular trends in awareness of and engagement in behaviors that promote health and prevent illness may lead to behavioral changes in the control group that are comparable to those in the intervention group. For example, the decreased social acceptability of smoking, facilitated first by the surgeon general's report and subsequently by tobacco taxes, public health campaigns, and the Master Tobacco Settlement Agreement, may be contributing to a decline in smoking rates in many geographic areas. The secular trend of reducing smoking levels has been cited for the observation of a greater decrease in smoking prevalence in the control compared with the intervention community in the Pawtucket Heart Health program (Carleton, Lasater, Assaf, Feldman, & McKinlay, 1995). Secular trends in smoking reduction may have also precluded finding stronger effects in the COMMIT trial (Bauman, Suchindran, & Murray, 1999). A greater intensity of intervention dosage may be needed to overcome secular trends observed in comparison communities. In addition, to better assess intervention effectiveness, investigators should determine the extent to which secular trends in behavior change are occurring prior to the implementation of the intervention (Secker-Walker et al., 2005).

Outcome Evaluation

For any health promotion or disease prevention intervention, what the outcome variables should be, by what means they should be assessed (questionnaires, interviews, etc.), and how often and when they should be measured, need to be determined. In community-level interventions, outcome variables should be relevant or salient to the individuals from the communities or populations being studied (Hohmann & Shear, 2002). Hohmann and Shear (2002) suggest that while symptoms and diagnostic categories may be important for comparative purposes, for participants the important or expected outcomes may be different (e.g., an increase in level of daily functioning). The use of standardized measures with demonstrated reliability and validity, or measures that have been used in prior research, should be encouraged because they allow for easier comparison with results of prior research.

Who the intervention is targeting, as discussed previously, may play a role in determining which methods should be used to assess outcome variables. Self-report measures are often the most convenient and may be the best option if highly personal information, such as sexual practices or illegal activity, is sought. Structured interviews conducted over the telephone or computer-assisted interviews also provide some degree of anonymity and are probably less subject to the problem of missing data than are questionnaires. Both questionnaire and interview formats allow some degree of control of the testing context and data quality by researchers, but the degree of control needed will depend on the question being asked. For example, in a study investigating why women stay in abusive relationships, Herbert and colleagues used a strategy that ensured that women who completed the sensitive questionnaires could do so without the knowledge of their abusive spouses (Herbert, Silver, & Ellard, 1991).

For interventions conducted at the individual level, demand characteristics are more likely to be a problem. For example, smokers who undergo a cognitive-behavioral intervention to quit smoking may be motivated to misrepresent their actual levels of smoking at the end of the intervention because of the expectation by clinic staff that they should have quit or reduced their smoking. This consideration has led many smoking cessation programs to include biochemical validation of smoking status. In general, however, the more limited the contact between participants and clinic staff, the less likely smokers are to misrepresent their actual levels of smoking (Velicer, Prochaska, Rossi, & Snow, 1992). In addition, findings from randomized experiments document that when research participants respond to questions without interacting directly with an interviewer, they are more likely to reveal sensitive and/or personal information (Lau, Thomas, & Liu, 2000; Turner et al., 1998).

The reliability of participants' responses can also be assessed through the use of collateral reports from subjects' romantic partners, family, and/or friends. Convergence of evidence from these sources provides a greater degree of confidence about the reliability of responses. In addition to self-report or interview format, observational or archival measures can be useful indicators of intervention effectiveness. An example would be documentation of the number of teenage pregnancies before, during, and after an intervention promoting condom use in adolescents.

These methods of assessment differ in convenience and amount of resources required. As noted earlier, Web-based questionnaire assessments have been used with increasing success in health psychology research because of their convenience and low cost, and it is likely that they will be seriously considered for use in future health-promoting interventions. (See also Schlenger & Silver, 2006, for additional information on the pros and cons of the use of the Web for data collection.)

The assessment of outcomes, and of potential mediating or moderating variables, should be conducted before, during, and after the intervention. Assessing outcomes sometime after the intervention has ended can answer important questions about its long-term efficacy. For example, follow-up of cognitive-behavioral smoking cessation programs has found impressive quit rates soon after the intervention ended, but a substantial number of smokers relapse within the subsequent year (USDHHS, 2000). This has led to a focus on devising relapse prevention programs for smokers, some of which have been successful (e.g., Brandon et al., 2004). Many community-level prevention efforts have also led to short-lived behavioral changes. However, some of the health effects of interventions may take years to be realized. This has stimulated efforts to encourage the sustainability or maintenance of interventions after researchers have collected and published their data.

Sustaining Interventions at the Community Level

If intervention activities are to be transferred to community organizations, their leaders should be involved in the planning and implementation of the intervention, which will need to be sensitive to the priorities and limitations of community resources (Altman, 1995b). According to Altman, questions of ownership and control of community programs should be addressed prior to implementation, and any conflicts resolved, so that there is "broad-based support from a cross-section of community constituencies" (p. 529) both during the intervention and after the research phase has ended. An exchange of skills, through education and training, between researchers and community staff, and fostering a sense of empowerment in communities to obtain resources for programs also contribute to sustainability. For example, educating community leaders on effective performance evaluation should foster a sense of empowerment and produce skills that leaders can use to design and implement unique interventions that address the same health behaviors.

Disseminating Research Findings

Although expenditures on health promotive research have been substantial, knowledge of how to disseminate findings from research to primary-care clinics and community agencies that deliver health services is only now emerging as a research endeavor in its own right (Kerner, Rimer, & Emmons, 2005). Much work remains, however, for dissemination research to advance as a science. As Kerner et al. note, the best research methods for evaluating dissemination strategies have not yet been established, which limits the amount of guidance available for researchers who want to conduct dissemination research. These authors also recommend more infrastructure support from private and public sectors, along with greater consensus among journal reviewers and editors on how to evaluate dissemination research projects. Nonetheless, translating the empirical results of scientific investigations into practical recommendations for health care professionals, schools, work sites, and community organizations is critical. Working effectively with the media and others to take research findings to the public—to ensure that they are effectively applied to both policy and practice—should be an important goal of health psychology researchers. With increasing attention to these issues, the efforts devoted to designing effective health-promoting interventions will hopefully translate to evidence-based practices that improve the public health.

Ethical Issues

Any research whose goal is to change behaviors, even health-promoting ones, must attend to ethical issues involving the use of human subjects. Because of concerns regarding the use of community samples in intervention research, nonprofit agencies, health care settings, schools, and work sites may serve as gatekeepers to block access to potential research subjects. Convincing these gatekeepers of the value of one's research often requires demonstrating sensitivity to the ethics of human subject experimentation (Sieber, 1998). Moreover, conducting interventions at any level of analysis must also involve the review of research plans by institutional review boards housed in academic institutions, as well as in individual research settings (e.g., individual hospitals). The provision of an inherently more appealing treatment may require eventually offering it as an option to the control group at a later date (e.g., designing a "waiting list" control group). Designing research on specialized populations, such as geriatric, pediatric, or medically ill samples, requires special attention to issues of informed consent, avoiding coercive procedures, and providing ample opportunity for refusal and termination of participation in the research effort over time. It is important that the individual researcher conduct a careful cost-benefit analysis, weighing the personal rights of individual participants against the potential benefits for society of the research. While ethical issues surrounding the design and implementation of community-based intervention research may be challenging and will undoubtedly require creativity and persistence, conducting methodologically rigorous research on human participants is required for the science of health promotion and illness prevention to advance.

Conclusion

The value of health promotion and intervention programs to improve health and reduce illness has been amply demonstrated in several domains of behavior. Indeed, it can be argued that intervention programs are victims of their own success when individuals in control groups show the same improvements in health behaviors as those in intervention groups. However, for progress to continue in our dynamic environment, where new threats to mental and physical health emerge (e.g., bioter-rorism) and old ones adopt new faces (e.g., water pipes for smoking), lessons learned from prior intervention research must be considered as well as new approaches. Attention to such principles as the use of theoretical models to guide research, consideration of individual, cultural, and socio-demographic differences and their moderating effects on treatment outcomes, the equivalence of intervention and control groups, and the appropriate use of statistical analyses and methods should provide the foundation for health promotion and intervention research. However, to improve the health of the greatest number of individuals, the expertise of others who are invested in advancing our ability to promote health and prevent illness is needed. Their involvement, as well as that of the targets of our research, will necessarily contribute to our understanding the most effective ways to initiate and sustain health behavior change.

References

Adams, J., & White, M. (2005). Why don't stage-based activity promotion interventions work? *Health Education Research, 20,* 237–243.

Adler, N. E., Kegeles, S. M., Irwin, C. E., & Wibbels-man, C. (1990). Adolescent contraceptive behavior: An assessment of decision processes. *Journal of Pediatrics, 116,* 463–471.

Ajzen, I. (1988). *Attitudes, personality and behavior.* Milton Keynes, UK: Open University.

Ajzen, I. (1991). The theory of planned behavior. *Organizational Behavior and Human Decision Processes, 50,* 179–211.

Ajzen, I., & Fishbein, M. (1977). Attitude-behavior relations: A theoretical analysis and review of empirical research. *Psychological Bulletin, 84,* 888–918.

Ajzen, I., & Fishbein, M. (1980). *Understanding attitudes and predicting social behavior.* Englewood Cliffs, NJ: Prentice Hall.

Albarracin, D., Johnson, B. T., Fishbein, M., & Muellerleile, P. A. (2001). Theories of reasoned action and planned behavior as models of condom use: A meta-analysis. *Psychological Bulletin, 127,* 142–161.

Altman, D. (1995a). Strategies for community health intervention: Promises, paradoxes, pitfalls. *Psychosomatic Medicine, 57,* 226–233.

Altman, D. G. (1995b). Sustaining interventions in community systems: On the relationship between

researchers and communities. *Health Psychology, 14,* 526–536.

Anderson, P., & Hughes, J. R. (2000). Policy interventions to reduce the harm from smoking. *Addiction, 95*(Suppl), S9–S11.

Baele, J., Dusseldorp, E., & Maes, S. (2001). Condom use self-efficacy: Effect on intended and actual condom use in adolescents. *Journal of Adolescent Health, 28,* 421–431.

Bandura, A. (1986). *Social foundations of thought and action.* Englewood Cliffs, NJ: Prentice-Hall.

Bandura, A. (1997). *Self-efficacy: The exercise of control.* New York: Freeman.

Bandura, A. (1998). Health promotion from the perspective of social cognitive theory. *Psychology and Health, 13,* 623–649.

Barr Taylor, C., & Luce, K. H. (2003). Computer- and Internet-based psychotherapy interventions. *Current Directions in Psychological Science, 12,* 18–22.

Bauman, K. E., Suchindran, C. M., & Murray, D. M. (1999). The paucity of effects in community trials: Is secular trend the culprit? *Preventive Medicine, 28,* 426–429.

Blue, C. L. (1995). The predictive capacity of the theory of reasoned action and the theory of planned behavior in exercise research: An integrated literature review. *Research in Nursing & Health, 18,* 105–121.

Bock, B. D., Graham, A. L., Sciamanna, C. N., Krishnamoorthy, J., Whiteley, J., Carmona-Barros, R. N. et al. (2004). Smoking cessation treatment on the Internet: Content, quality, and usability. *Nicotine and Tobacco Research, 6,* 207–219.

Brandon, T. H., Meade, C. D., Herzog, T. A., Chirikos, T. N., Webb, M. S., & Cantor, A. B. (2004). Efficacy and cost-effectiveness of a minimal intervention to prevent smoking relapse: Dismantling the effects of amount of content versus contact. *Journal of Consulting and Clinical Psychology, 72,* 797–808.

Canadian Public Health Association. (2004). ParticipAction—The Mouse That Roared: A Marketing and Health Communications Success Story. *Canadian Journal of Public Health, 95*(Suppl), 1–46.

Carleton, R. A., Lasater, T. M., Assaf, A. R., Feldman, H. A., & McKinlay, S.(1995). The Pawtucket Heart Health Program: Community changes in cardiovascular risk factors and projected disease risk. *American Journal of Public Health, 85,* 777–785.

Centers for Disease Control and Prevention. (1999). Cigarette smoking among high school students:

11 States, 1991–1997. *Morbidity and Mortality Weekly Report, 48,* 686–692.

Centers for Disease Control and Prevention. (2002). Cigarette smoking—attributable mortality and years of potential life lost—United States. *Morbidity and Mortality Weekly Report, 42,* 645–649.

Centers for Disease Control and Prevention. (2004). *The health consequences of smoking: A report of the Surgeon General.* Rockville, MD: U.S. Department of Health and Human Services, Public Health Service.

Centers for Disease Control and Prevention. (2005). Cigarette smoking among adults—United States, 2004. *MMWR Highlights, 54*(44), 1121–1124.

Champion V. L. (1994). Strategies to increase mammography utilization. *Medical Care, 32,* 118–129.

Chapman, S., Borland, R., Scollo, M., Brownson, R. C., Dominello, A., & Woodward, S. (1999). The impact of smoke-free workplaces on declining cigarette consumption in Australia and the United States. *American Journal of Public Health, 89,* 1018–1023.

Cole, S. W., Kemeny, M. E., & Taylor, S. E. (1997). Social identity and physical health: Accelerated HIV progression in rejection-sensitive gay men. *Journal of Personality and Social Psychology, 72,* 320–335.

Cook, T., & Campbell, D. (1979). *Quasi-experimental design.* Chicago: Rand McNally.

Copeland, J., & Martin, G. (2004). Web-based interventions for substance use disorders: A qualitative review. *Journal of Substance Abuse Treatment, 26,* 109–116.

Corwyn, R. F., & Benda, B. B. (1999). Examination of an integrated theoretical model of exercise behavior. *American Journal of Health Behavior, 23,* 381–392.

Cromwell, J., Bartosch, W. J., Fiore, M. C., Hasselblad, V., & Baker, T. (1997). Cost-effectiveness of the clinical practice recommendations in the AHCPR guideline for smoking cessation. Agency for Health Care Policy and Research. *Journal of the American Medical Association, 278,* 1759–1766.

Donner, A., & Klar, N. (1996). Statistical considerations in the design and analysis of community intervention trials. *Journal of Clinical Epidemiology, 49,* 435–439.

Elder, J. P., Ayala, G. X., & Harris, S. (1999). Theories and intervention approaches to health-behavior change in primary care. *American Journal of Preventive Medicine, 17,* 275–284.

Elford, J., & Hart, G. J. (2003). If HIV prevention works, why are rates of high risk sexual behaviour increasing among men who have sex with men? *AIDS Education Prevention, 15,* 294–308.

Fiore, M. C., Bailey, W. C., Cohen, S. J., Dorfman, S. F., Goldstein, M. G., Gritz, E. R. et al. (2000). *Treating tobacco use and dependence. Clinical practice guideline.* Rockville, MD: U.S. Department of Health and Human Services, Public Health Service.

Fiore, M. C., Jorenby, D. E., & Baker, T. B. (1997). Smoking cessation: Principles and practice based upon the AHCPR Guideline, 1996. Agency for Health Care Policy and Research. *Annals of Behavioral Medicine, 19,* 213–219.

Fisher, E. B. (1995). The results of the COMMIT trial. *American Journal of Public Health, 85,* 159–160.

Glasgow, R. E., Bull, S. S., Gillette, C., Klesges, L. M., & Dzewaltowski, D. A. (2002). Behavior change intervention research in health care settings: A review of recent reports with emphases on external validity. *American Journal of Preventive Medicine, 23,* 62–69.

Glynn, M., & Rhodes, P. (2005, June). *Estimated HIV prevalence in the United States at the end of 2003.* Poster presented at the National HIV Prevention Conference, Atlanta, GA. Abstract 595.

Goldstein, M. G., Niaura, R., Willey-Lessne, C., DePue, J., Eaton, C., Rakowski, W., et al. (1997). Physicians counseling smokers: A population-based survey of patients' perceptions of health care provider–delivered smoking cessation interventions. *Archives of Internal Medicine, 157,* 1313–1317.

Gonzalez, V., Goeppinger, J., & Lorig, K. (1990). Four psychosocial theories and their application to patient education and clinical practice. *Arthritis, Care, and Research, 3,* 132–143.

Goodman, R. M., Liburd, L. C., & Green-Phillips A. (2001). The formation of a complex community program for diabetes control: Lessons learned from a case study of Project DIRECT. *Journal of Public Health Management and Practice, 7,* 19–29.

Grady, K. E., & Wallston, B. S. (1988). *Research in health care settings.* Newbury Park, CA: Sage.

Grimley, D. M., Prochaska, G. E., & Prochaska, J. O. (1993). Condom use assertiveness and the stages of change with main and other partners. *Journal of Applied Biobehavioral Research, 12,* 152–173.

Harrison, D. J., Cantlay, A. M., Rae, F., Lamb, D., & Smith, C. A. (1997). Frequency of glutathione S-transferase M1 deletion in smokers with emphysema and lung cancer. *Human Experimental Toxicology, 16,* 356–360.

Helgeson, V. S., & Lepore, S. J. (1997). The hurdles involved in conducting a randomized clinical intervention. *Health Psychologist, 18*(4), 4–5, 14–16.

Herbert, T. B., Silver, R. C., & Ellard, J. H. (1991). Coping with an abusive relationship: 1. How and why do women stay? *Journal of Marriage and the Family, 53,* 311–325.

Higgins, A., & Conner, M. (2003). Understanding adolescent smoking: The role of the Theory of Planned Behavior and implementation intentions. *Psychology, Health, and Medicine, 8*(2), 173–186.

Hohmann, A. A., & Shear, M. K. (2002). Community-based intervention research: Coping with the "noise" of real life in study design. *American Journal of Psychiatry, 159,* 201–207.

Holman, E. A. (1997). The nursing profession's role in health psychology research: A reply to Helgeson and Lepore. *Health Psychologist, 19*(2), 8.

Johnston, K. L., & White, K. M. (2003). Binge-drinking: A test of the role of group norms in the Theory of Planned Behavior. *Psychology and Health, 18,* 63–77.

Joos, S., & Hickam, D. (1990). How health professionals influence health behavior: Patient provider interaction and health care outcomes. In K. Glanz, F. Lewis, & B. Rimer (Eds.), *Health behavior and health education: Theory, research and practice* (pp. 216–241). San Francisco: Jossey Bass.

Jourenkova-Mironova, N., Wikman, H., Bouchardy, C., Voho, A., Dayer, P., Benhamou, S., et al. (1998). Role of glutathione S-transferase GSTM1, GSTM3, GSTP1 and GSTT1 genotypes in modulating susceptibility to smoking-related lung cancer. *Pharmacogenetics, 8,* 495–502.

Kaplan, R. M. (2000). Two pathways to prevention. *American Psychologist, 55,* 382–396.

Kassel, J. D., Stroud, L. R., & Paronis, C. A. (2003). Smoking, stress, and negative affect: Correlation, causation, and context across stages of smoking. *Psychological Bulletin, 129,* 270–304.

Kemeny, M. E. (2003). An interdisciplinary research model to investigate psychosocial cofactors in disease: Application to HIV-1 pathogenesis. *Brain, Behavior, and Immunity, 17*(Supplement), S62–S72.

Kenny, D. A. (1979). *Correlation and causality.* New York: Wiley.

Kerner, J., Rimer, B., & Emmons, K. (2005). Introduction to the Special Section on Dissemination. Dissemination research and research dissemination: How can we close the gap? *Health Psychology, 24,* 443–446.

Koepsell, T. D., Wagner, E. H., Cheadle, A. C., Patrick, D. L., Martin, D. C., Diehr, P. H., et al. (1992). Selected methodological issues in evaluating community-based health promotion and disease prevention programs. *Annual Review of Public Health, 13,* 31–57.

Kohler, C. L., Grimley, D., & Reynolds, K. (1999). Theoretical approaches guiding the development and implementation of health promotion programs. In J. M. Raczynski & R. J. DiClemente (Eds.), *Handbook of health promotion and disease prevention* (pp. 23–46). New York: Kluwer/Plenum.

Larzelere, R. E., Kuhn, B. R., & Johnson, B. (2004). The intervention selection bias: An under-recognized confound in intervention research. *Psychological Bulletin, 130,* 289–303.

Lau, J. T. F., Thomas, J., & Liu, J. L. Y. (2000). Mobile phone and interactive computer interviewing to measure HIV-related risk behaviours: The impacts of data collection methods on research results. *AIDS, 14,* 1277–1278.

Lepore, S. J. (1995). Cynicism, social support, and cardiovascular reactivity. *Health Psychology, 14,* 210–216.

Levinthal, C. F. (2005). *Drugs, behavior, and modern society.* Boston: Allyn and Bacon.

Lorig, K., & Fries, J. F. (1990). *The arthritis helpbook: A tested self-management program for coping with your arthritis.* Reading, MA: Addison-Wesley.

Lorig, K., Seleznick, M., Lubeck, D., Ung, E., Chastain, R. L., & Holman, H. R. (1989). The beneficial outcomes of the arthritis self-management course are not adequately explained by behavior change. *Arthritis and Rheumatism, 31,* 91–95.

Maisto, S. A., Connors, G. J., & Zywiak, W. H. (2000). Alcohol treatment, changes in coping skills, self-efficacy, and levels of alcohol use and related problems 1 year following treatment initiation. *Psychology of Addictive Behaviors, 14,* 257–266.

Marshall, S. J., & Biddle, S. J. H. (2001). The Transtheoretical Model of Behavior Change: A meta-analysis of applications to physical activity and exercise. *Annals of Behavioral Medicine, 23,* 229–246.

May, S., & West, R. (2000). Do social support interventions ("buddy systems") aid smoking cessation? A review. *Tobacco Control, 9,* 415–422.

McAuley, E., Jerome, G. J., Marquez, D. X., Elavsky, S., & Blissmer, B. (2003). Exercise self-efficacy in older adults: Social, affective, and behavioral influences. *Annals of Behavioral Medicine, 25,* 1–7.

McCann, J. M., Bovbjerg, V. E., Brief, D. J., Turner, C., Follette, W. C., Fitzpatrick, V., et al. (1995). Relationship of self-efficacy to cholesterol lowering and dietary change in hyperlipidemia. *Annals of Behavioral Medicine, 17,* 221–226.

McNally, R. J., Bryant, R. A., & Ehlers, A. (2003).

Does early psychological intervention promote recovery from post-traumatic stress? *Psychological Science in the Public Interest, 4,* 45–79.

Mermelstein, R. (1999). Ethnicity, gender and risk factors for smoking initiation: An overview. *Nicotine and Tobacco Research, 1*(Suppl 2), S69–S70.

Merzel, C., & D'Afflitti, J. (2003). Reconsidering community-based health promotion: Promise, performance, and potential. *American Journal of Public Health, 93,* 557–574.

Mishra, S. I., Sanudo, F., & Conner, R. F. (2004). Collaborative research toward HIV prevention among migrant farmworkers. In B. P. Bowser & S. I. Mishra et al. (Eds.), *Preventing AIDS: Community-science collaborations* (pp. 69–95). New York: Haworth.

Nyberg, F., Hou, S. M., Hemminki, K., Lambert, B., & Pershagen, G. (1998). Glutathione S-transferase mu1 and N-acetyltransferase 2 genetic polymorphisms and exposure to tobacco smoke in nonsmoking and smoking lung cancer patients and population controls. *Cancer Epidemiology Biomarkers and Prevention, 7,* 875–883.

Park, E., Schultz, J. K., Tudiver, F., Campbell, T., & Becker, L. (2004). Enhancing partner support to improve smoking cessation. *Cochrane Database of Systematic Review, 1,* CD002928.

Perkins, K. A. (2001). Smoking cessation in women: Special considerations. *CNS Drugs, 15,* 391–411.

Perkins, K. A., Donny, E., & Caggiula, A. R. (1999). Sex differences in nicotine effects and self-administration: Review of human and animal evidence. *Nicotine and Tobacco Research, 1,* 301–315.

Piper, D. L. (2000). The Health for Life Project: Behavioral outcomes. *Journal of Primary Prevention, 21,* 47–73.

Prochaska, J. O., & DiClemente, C. C. (1983). Stages and processes of self-change of smoking: Toward an integrative model of change. *Journal of Consulting and Clinical Psychology, 51,* 390–395.

Prochaska, J. O., DiClemente, C. C., & Norcross, J. C. (1992). In search of how people change: Applications to addictive behaviors. *American Psychologist, 47,* 1102–1114.

Reilly, P. M., Sees, K. L., Shopshire, M. S., Hall, S. M., Delucchi, K. L., Tusel, D. J., et al. (1995). Self-efficacy and illicit opioid use in a 180-day detoxification treatment. *Journal of Consulting and Clinical Psychology, 63,* 158–162.

Revenson, T. A., & Schiaffino, K. M. (2000). Community-based health interventions. In J. Rappaport & E. Seidman (Eds.), *Handbook of community psychology* (pp. 471–493). New York: Kluwer Academic/Plenum.

Rigotti, N. A., Lee, J. E., & Wechsler, H. (2000). US college students' use of tobacco products: Results of a national survey. *Journal of the American Medical Association, 9,* 699–705.

Rigotti, N. A., Moran, S. E., & Wechsler, H. (2005). US college students' exposure to tobacco promotions: Prevalence and association with tobacco use. *American Journal of Public Health, 95,* 138–144.

Rose, G. (1985). Sick individuals and sick populations. *International Journal of Epidemiology, 14,* 32–38.

Rose, G. (1992). *The strategy of preventive medicine.* New York: Oxford University Press.

Rosenstock, I. M., Strecher, V. J., & Becker, M. H. (1994). The health belief model and HIV risk behavior change. In R. J. DiClemente & J. L. Peterson (Eds.), *Preventing AIDS: Theories and methods of behavioral interventions* (pp. 5–24). New York: Plenum.

Rutter, D., & Quine, L. (2002). *Changing health behavior: Intervention and research with social cognition models.* Buckingham, PA: Open University Press.

Schlenger, W. E., & Silver, R. C. (2006). Web-based methods in terrorism and disaster research. *Journal of Traumatic Stress, 19,* 185–193.

Schneiderman, N. (2004). Psychosocial, behavioral, and biological aspects of chronic disease. *Current Directions in Psychological Science, 13,* 247–251.

Schneiderman, N., Antoni, M. H., & Ironson, G. (2003). Behavioral medicine in HIV infection. *Psychotherapeutics, 48,* 342–347.

Schorling, J. B., Roach, J., Siegel, M., Baturka, N. Hunt, D. E., Guterbock, T. M., et al. (1997). A trial of church-based smoking cessation interventions for rural African Americans. *Preventive Medicine, 26,* 92–101.

Secker-Walker, R. H., Gnich, W., Platt, S., & Lancaster, T. (2005). Community interventions for reducing smoking among adults. *Cochrane Database of Systematic Review, 1,* CD001745.

Sheeran, P., & Abraham, C. (1996). The Health Belief Model. In M. Conner & P. Norman (Eds.), *Predicting health behaviour: Research and practice with social cognition models* (pp. 23–61). Buckingham, England: Open University Press.

Shiffman, S., Balabanis, M. H., Paty, J. A., Engberg, J., Gwaltney, C. J., Liu, K. S., et al. (2000). Dynamic effects of self-efficacy on smoking lapse and relapse. *Health Psychology, 19,* 315–323.

Shilts, R. (1987). *And the band played on: Politics, people, and the AIDS epidemic.* New York: St. Martin's.

Shine, B. (2000). Nicotine vaccine moves toward clinical trials. *NIDA Notes: Nicotine Research, 15,* 1–2.

Sieber, J. E. (1998). Planning ethically responsible research. In L. Bickman & D. J. Rog (Eds.), *Handbook of applied social research methods* (pp. 127–156). Thousand Oaks, CA: Sage.

Siemiatycki, J., Krewski, D., Franco, E., & Kaiserman, M. (1995). Associations between cigarette smoking and each of 21 types of cancer: A multi-site case-control study. *International Journal of Epidemiology, 24,* 504–514.

Sobel, D. S. (1995). Rethinking medicine: Improving health outcomes with cost-effective psychosocial interventions. *Psychosomatic Medicine, 57,* 234–244.

Sorensen, G., Emmons, K., Hunt, M. K., & Johnston, D. (1998). Implications of the results of community intervention trials. *Annual Review of Public Health, 19,* 379–416.

Sowden, A., Arblaster, L., & Stead, L. (2005). Community interventions for preventing smoking in young people. *Cochrane Database of Systematic Review, 1,* CD001291.

Stokols, D. (1992). Establishing and maintaining healthy environments: Toward a social ecology of health promotion. *American Psychologist, 47,* 6–22.

Stokols, D., Pelletier, K. R., & Fielding, J. E. (1995). Integration of medical care and worksite health promotion. *Journal of the American Medical Association, 273,* 1136–1142.

Strickland, B. R., & Crowne, D. P. (1963). Need for approval and the premature termination of psychotherapy. *Journal of Consulting and Clinical Psychology, 27,* 95–101.

Thompson, B., Coronado, G., Snipes, S. A., & Puschel, K. (2003). Methodological advances and ongoing challenges in designing community-based health promotion programs. *Annual Review of Public Health, 24,* 315–340.

Turner, C. F., Ku, L., Rogers, S. M., Lindberg, L. D.,

Pleck, J. H., & Sonenstein, F. L. (1998). Adolescent sexual behavior, drug use, and violence: Increased reporting with computer survey technology. *Science, 280,* 867–873.

UNAIDS, Joint United Nations Programme on HIV/AIDS (2004). Global summary of the AIDS epidemic. *Aids Epidemic Update—2004.*

Velicer, W. F., Prochaska, J. O., Rossi, J. S., & Snow, M. G. (1992). Assessing outcome in smoking cessation studies. *Psychological Bulletin, 111,* 23–41.

Wechsler, H., Kelley, K., Seibring, M., Juo, M., & Rigotti, N. A. (2001). College smoking policies and smoking cessation programs: Results of a survey of college health center directors. *Journal of American College of Health, 50,* 141–142.

Westmaas, J. L., & Billings, M. (2005). *Gender, social support, and stress reactions in smokers.* Unpublished manuscript.

Westmaas, J. L., & Jamner, L. D. (2006). Paradoxical effects of social support on blood pressure reactivity among defensive individuals. *Annals of Behavioral Medicine, 31,* 238–247.

Westmaas, J. L., Wild, C., & Ferrence, R. (2002). Effects of gender in social control of smoking. *Health Psychology, 21,* 368–376.

Wortman, C. B., Hendricks, M., & Hillis, J. W. (1976). Factors affecting participant reactions to random assignment in ameliorative social programs. *Journal of Personality and Social Psychology, 33,* 256–266.

Zabalegui, A., Sanchez, S., Sanchez, P. D., & Juando, C. (2005). Nursing and cancer support groups. *Journal of Advanced Nursing, 51,* 369–381.

Zimmerman, R. S., & Olson, K. (1994). AIDS-related risk behavior and behavior change in a sexually active, heterosexual sample: A test of three models of prevention. *AIDS Education and Prevention, 6,* 189–205.

Core Concepts

of the Biopsychosocial

Approach to Health

John T. Cacioppo and Gary G. Berntson

The Brain, Homeostasis, and Health

Balancing Demands of the Internal and External Milieu

The biologist Richard Lewontin (2000) characterized living organisms as electromechanical devices made up of articulated physical parts that, for purely thermodynamic reasons, eventually wear out and fail to function. Lithgow and Kirkwood (1996), in their review of research on the biology of aging, observed that it is "disadvantageous to increase maintenance beyond a level sufficient to keep the organism in good shape through its natural life expectancy in the wild, because the extra cost will eat into resources that in terms of natural selection are better used to boost other functions that will enhance fitness" (p. 80). We are only now beginning to understand how the brain integrates the regulatory and restorative forces of the body to foster health and adaptation to environmental challenge. This chapter examines these forces as they relate to psychology and health.

In their normal state, regulatory processes (e.g., homeostasis) buffer organisms from the effects of internal and external changes, and restorative processes (e.g., wound healing, humoral immunity) operate to refresh, buttress, and repair various forms of cellular damage. Regulatory devices work only within certain limits of perturbation in buffering the organism from changes in the internal milieu, however, and the restorative components of

these regulatory devices work only within certain limits to return the organism to an earlier condition. If the disturbance is too great or enduring, the very parameters around which these regulatory devices operate (e.g., basal levels of functioning or set points) can be affected (McEwen, 1998; Cacioppo et al., 2000). Psychological stress has also been shown to influence the operation of these regulatory (Berntson & Cacioppo, 2000) and restorative (Kiecolt-Glaser, Marucha, Malarkey, Mercado, & Glaser, 1995; Kiecolt-Glaser, Page, Marucha, MacCallum, & Glaser, 1998) devices, meaning that anticipated or imagined events as well as specific physical assaults can disrupt mind and biology. For example, the sympathetic activation of the heart and cardiovascular system promotes adaptive responding by adjusting the circulation of blood to sleeping, walking, and running (Sterling & Eyer, 1988). Surges of blood pressure in the face of job stress, however, provide the metabolic support needed for anticipated and actual physical activity; if repeated and persisting, these cardiovascular responses may promote hypertension and atherosclerosis (cf. McEwen, 1998).

Among the peripheral regulatory and restorative devices orchestrated by the brain in mammalian species are the autonomic, endocrine, and immune systems. Not long ago these systems were thought to function largely independently, outside the reach of social and cultural influences. Research on the molecular aspects of neuroimmunomodulation has now shown that the autonomic, endocrine, and immune systems communicate by shared ligands (compounds that bind to receptors and exert functional actions, such as cytokines, hormones, and neurotransmitters) coordinated at multiple levels of the neuraxis (i.e., brain and nervous system; McCann et al., 1998). The nervous system can communicate with the endocrine system through direct innervation, whereas the endocrine system signals the nervous system through hormones and neurotransmitters that cross the blood-brain barrier or act directly on viscera (Brown, 1994; Norman & Litwack, 1987).

The nervous system and endocrine system communicate with the immune system through a variety of means, including autonomic innervation of lymphoid organs and through adrenergic (Madden, Thyagarajan, & Felton, 1998) and glucocorticoid (Bauer, 1983) receptors on immune cells. For example, previous studies have demonstrated the impact of psychological stress on the steady-state expression/reactivation of latent Epstein-Barr virus (EBV). Most adults have been exposed to EBV (mononucleosis), but they do not show symptoms of this virus because the immune system holds it in check. The virus is said to be "latent" in the body. When a person is under stress, cellular immune function can be impaired (through the effects of stress hormones on lymphocytes), resulting in (a) less control over the expression of the latent virus, (b) increases in antibody to the virus, and in some cases (c) the clinical manifestation of the virus. Cacioppo, Kiecolt-Glaser, et al. (2002) investigated whether the steady-state expression of latent EBV in vivo differed between high and low-stress reactors, as defined by sympathetic cardiac reactivity (Cacioppo, Uchino, & Berntson, 1994; Cacioppo, 1994). Results revealed that women who were high-stress reactors were characterized by higher antibody titers to the latent virus than low-stress reactors. Moreover, an in vitro study suggested that the frequency and amplitude of the *release* of pituitary and adrenal hormones such as the powerful stress hormone cortisol likely contributed to this result.

That is, daily stressors can activate the autonomic nervous system and promote the release of pituitary and adrenal hormones, especially in high reactors. The release of these glucocorticoid hormones, in turn, may contribute to the weakened immunologic conditions required for the reactivation of the virus in latently infected cells throughout the body. If these individuals are not able to retreat from the stresses of their environment to recuperate, or, worse yet, if their weakened immunologic state only increases the stressors they are confronting, then a positive feedback system results, which fosters the conditions for the development of frequent and chronic disease. This circumstance is more likely to characterize individuals from low than high socioeconomic status, because they are less likely to be able to afford to miss work due to illness, and individuals who are socially isolated rather than integrated, because they are less likely to have someone help them at least temporarily deal with their daily stresses. One of the implications of this positive feedback system is that it creates physiological conditions that make illness more likely and more ravaging. What physiological forces have evolved to counteract the creation of this positive feedback loop in everyone?

The immune system, long thought to consist of isolated circulating sentinels against disease, is now recognized as communicating with the central nervous system, autonomic nervous system, and endocrine system. Catecholamines and peptides (e.g., neuropeptide Y) modulate lymphocytic actions, and peripheral immune cytokines (lymphocyte secretions) are transduced into a neuronal signal and conveyed to the brain via afferent fibers in the vagus nerve (Maier & Watkins, 1998) and influence behavior (Dantzer, et al., 1998; see Kemeny, this volume). As Maier and Watkins (1998) noted:

> If the immune system is conceived of as a diffuse sense organ that communicates the status of infection- and injury-related events to the brain, it is then sensible to inquire how sense organs generally communicate to the brain. They do not generally do so by accumulating chemical signals in the blood that then cross into the brain. Rather, they do so by activating peripheral nerves that go to the brain. Indeed, there is a nerve that innervates regions of the body in which immune responses occur (the gut, spleen, thymus, lymph nodes, etc.) and provides afferent input to the brain from these regions, which is called the *vagus nerve*. Although the vagus has traditionally been

viewed as an efferent nerve providing parasympathetic input from the brain to visceral organs, modern anatomy has revealed that many of the vagal fibers (roughly 70%) are actually sensory, sending afferent messages from the innervated organs to the brain. (p. 88)

Maier and Watkins (1998) review further evidence that fever, increases in pain responsivity, brain norepinephrine changes, glucocorticoid increases, and conditioned taste aversions produced by cytokines may be attenuated in animals in which the vagus had been lesioned. These results suggest that, in addition to direct actions of immune signals in the brain, the afferent (sensory) aspect of the vagus is an important route through which information from the peripheral immune system (e.g., cytokines) can be conveyed to the brain, where such effects are controlled (Hansen et al., 2000; Hansen, O'Connor, Goehler, Watkins, & Maier, 2001).

In short, communications among the nervous system, neuroendocrine system, and immune system are bidirectional to better balance the demands of the internal and external milieu. By producing feelings of fever and fatigue, not only is the immune system better able to defend against an infection (e.g., invading microbes do not flourish at elevated body temperatures), but the individual who, due to fever and fatigue, withdraws from daily stresses to the comfort of his or her bedroom also diminishes the release of neural and hormonal signals that can compromise immune function.

We organize the present chapter in terms of the historical development of integrative principles regarding the regulatory and restorative forces of the autonomic nervous system, neuroendocrine function, and immune actions and their modulation by the brain in transaction with the environment. Our intention is not to focus in detail on any one regulatory device but to examine from a global perspective how the brain integrates the regulatory and restorative processes of the body to foster health and adaptation to environmental challenges. We begin with an overview of why an integrative analysis may be profitable for understanding health and disease.

The Organism in Transaction with the Environment

The social and behavioral sciences are influenced by societal problems just as the medical sciences are driven by health problems. Changes in society and health over the past century have drawn the social, behavioral, and biological sciences together to address how the brain integrates the regulatory forces of the body to cultivate health while also promoting adaptation to the physical, psychological, and social challenges posed by extended life in contemporary society (see review by Cacioppo, Berntson, Sheridan, & McClintock, 2000). A century ago, antibiotics were nonexistent, public health was underdeveloped, and germ-based diseases were among the major causes of adult morbidity and mortality. The mortality statistics point to the most important killers as being diphtheria, smallpox, tuberculosis, bronchitis, pneumonia, and measles. Medical scientists at the turn of the twentieth century focused on the major health problems of the day about which they could do something. By the end of the twentieth century, public health improvements, widespread vaccinations, and advances in medical and pharmacological treatments were paralleled by diminished mortality from infectious diseases.

The decreased mortality from infectious diseases during the nineteenth and twentieth centuries may not be primarily attributable to these medical or public health innovations, however. Lewontin (2000) notes, for instance, that the death rates from infectious diseases were decreasing by the 1830s, and that more than 90% of the reduction in these death rates had occurred before antibiotics were introduced after World War II. Even improvements in sanitation may not be an adequate explanation for the decreases in deaths from infectious diseases because the principal killers were airborne, not waterborne. Measles, the principal killer of children in the nineteenth century, was still contracted by most children in the first half of the twentieth century, but the mortality rate from the disease had greatly diminished (Lewontin, 2000). Thus, reductions in mortality from infectious diseases could not be explained adequately in terms of measures designed to prevent the spread of diseases (see also McKeown, 1979).

The reduction may be attributable to a general trend of increases in real wage, an increase in the state of nutrition, and a decrease in the number of hours worked—that is, *a decrease in the wear and tear on the organism* and *improved opportunities for the organism to heal itself.* As Lewontin (2000) notes: "As people were better nourished and better clothed and had more rest time to recover from taxing labor, their bodies, being in a less stressed physiological state, were better able to recover from the further severe stress of infection" (p. 104). If this analysis is correct, the social and behavioral sciences have a great deal to contribute to understanding morbidity and mortality, in particular as they help illuminate the operations and dysfunction of regulatory and restorative processes. It also follows that health psychology should consider not only the effects of stress and catabolic processes but also the effects of restorative and anabolic processes.[1]

Demographic changes during the twentieth century have direct implications for health care, problems, and costs. Only 4% of the U.S. population lived to be more than 65 years of age, compared with more than 17% today. The fastest-growing segment of the population is now older adults, with the number of persons under the age 65 in the United States increasing by a factor of three during the twentieth century, while the number of persons 65 and over is increasing by a factor of 11 (Hobbs & Stoops, 2002). Although threats from infectious diseases demand continued vigilance (Garrett, 2000), and research and advances in molecular biology provide powerful new weapons with which to combat the devastation of diseases (Kandel & Squire, 2000), entry into the twenty-first century has brought into view a new set of health problems. Among the leading causes of death in industrialized nations are now heart disease, cancer, cerebrovascular disease, accidents, chronic lung disease, infectious diseases, diabetes, suicide and homicide, and chronic liver disease/cirrhosis (e.g., Blumenthal, Matthews, & Weiss, 1994). Chronic diseases are now the most frequent sources of complaints and the largest causes of morbidity and mortality in older adults, and the cost of these diseases is stunning. According to estimates by Luskin and Newell (1997), by the early 1990s, individuals 65 and older (who at that time accounted for 11% of the U.S. population) accounted for 36% of all hospital stays and 48% of total days of doctor care. These percentages and the corresponding health costs are increasing dramatically, not only because the costs of health care are rising but also because the number of elderly individuals is increasing rapidly (as is the percentage of the total population that is elderly). To better understand the etiology of these new sources of morbidity and mortality, we need to consider the effects of stress and restoration on the cumulative wear and tear of the organism.

Regulated Variables, Perturbations, and Adaptive Responses

With impressive advances in molecular biology and genetics, it is easy to think about the organism as indifferent to the physical and social environment, and health problems as best addressed exclusively at the level of the gene or cell (cf. Temple, McLeod, Gallinger, & Wright, 2001). Claude Bernard's (1878/1974) seminal observations more than a century ago speak eloquently against such a notion. He observed that the extracellular fluid constitutes the immediate environment—the internalized sea—for plants and animals. He noted the relative constancy of this internal milieu and regarded this constancy, and the physiological mechanisms that served to maintain it, as providing protection against the powerful entropic forces that threaten to disrupt the biological order essential for life. Without mechanisms to stabilize the cellular environment, organisms would be confined to a limited ecological niche. In Bernard's terms, the existence of these mechanisms permitted animals to live a *free and independent* existence.

The notion of an integrative regulatory biology in animals that enables a free and independent existence, and the exquisite role of the brain and behavior in this process, is illustrated in the regulatory mechanisms that maintain body temperature. Metabolic activity is impaired at temperatures discrepant from 98.60° F, so this equilibrium point is usually defended by multiple mechanisms. One of the simplest is a self-produced atmosphere that surrounds the human body and helps insulate it from the outer air (Lewontin, 2000). Specifically, the body is surrounded by a layer of higher-density air that is warmed and moistened by the body's metabolic heat and water. (This phenomenon helps explain the windchill factor, which is the result of wind stripping away this insulating layer.) In Lewontin's (2000) terms, "Organisms not only determine what aspects of the outside world are relevant to them by peculiarities of their shape and metabolism, but they actively construct, in the literal sense of the word, a world around themselves" (p. 54) that helps buffer the internal milieu from environmental variations.

In addition, normal metabolic activity such as the breaking down of food to composite packets and energy creates heat in excess of 98.60° F. Consequently, the body activates the eccrine (sweat) glands (to foster perspiration and a consequent loss of body heat) and peripheral vasodilation (to foster a shunting of blood from the hot viscera and muscles to cutaneous tissue beds near the surface of the skin to allow heat to dissipate). These adaptive responses go unnoticed under normal circumstances, leaving the individual's limited cognitive resources and behavioral options untouched. When body temperature falls below 98.60°, eccrine gland activity decreases to minimize perspiration and the consequent loss of body heat, and peripheral vasoconstriction occurs to retain the heated blood within the deep recesses of the brain and body. These automated and unnoticed peripheral adjustments are often sufficient to maintain body temperature within the narrow range needed for orderly metabolic activity, thereby permitting a "free and independent existence."

If the organism is exposed to a greater drain on its heat output, an involuntary rhythmical tensing of small muscles throughout the body (i.e., shivering) begins to occur. Each time a muscle fiber contracts, millions of adenosine triphosphate molecules are cleaved, liberating energy in the form of heat, and the biomechanics of muscle contraction produces yet additional heat. As the need for heat increases, more and larger muscles are recruited. Heat production can increase for several critical minutes, although some muscle coordination is forfeited in the process. Broader systems can be called into action, including additional autonomic (e.g., Collins & Surwit, 2001) and neuroendocrine (e.g., Arancibia, Rage, Astier, & Tapia-Arancibia, 1996) adjustments. Still higher-order regulatory mechanisms are called into play, including attention, behavioral adjustments, and decision making. Although especially well known in cold-blooded animals that have a body temperature that varies with the temperature of its surroundings, if given the opportunity all vertebrates will contribute to thermal regulation by moving to a region of warmer or cooler temperature. The individual notices (i.e., attends to) being cold, and cognitive resources and behavioral options that were available for other tasks are usurped to reestablish a constancy of the balance within. The individual might do so by donning a sweater, turning on a heater, moving to a warmer location, or huddling with others. In doing so, however, the individual surrenders, at least temporarily, some of the freedom and independence of existence that characterizes the integrative physiology of animals. If even these devices prove insufficient, extravagances

of the organism such as coordinated movement, consciousness, and maintenance of appendages are sacrificed, at least temporarily, while the remaining heated blood is directed to the organs (e.g., heart and brain) that are vital to survival, thereby increasing the chances that the physical or social environment changes to restore the balance within and, consequently, the likelihood of survival.

Anticipatory responses, planning, and decision making are also empowered, as individuals can change their behaviors and environments to minimize perturbations to the balance within. Migration to warmer climates with the changing seasons and construction of dwellings to buffer changes in temperature are illustrative. As Claude Bernard (1878/1974) observed, mammals are far from being indifferent to their surroundings but must be in close and intimate relation to it, continually compensating for and counterbalancing external variations. This interplay between organismic and environmental conditions is orchestrated at multiple levels to maintain a balance within.

The same principle applies to the endocrine and immune systems. The latter must defend the organism against an unknowable variety of infectious agents by surveying, identifying, isolating, and eradicating rapidly reproducing microorganisms. Accordingly, the immune system cannot be too insensitive in initiating, developing, or expanding, else effector functions can be overwhelmed by pathogens (e.g., cancer, viral, and infectious diseases; Cohn & Langman, 1990), and it cannot be too sensitive because the cellular and chemical agents meant to combat pathogens are themselves capable of substantial destruction of host tissues (i.e., autoimmune diseases; Germain, 2000). For a review of the regulatory agents and mechanisms that characterize the immune system, see Kemeny (this volume).

In sum, the autonomic, neuroendocrine, and immune systems are orchestrated in part to preserve conditions compatible with life in what Claude Bernard (1878/1974) called the *milieu interieur*—a state Esther Sternberg (2000) has called "the balance within." Humans do not reside in an unchanging, nurturant ecological niche but rather explore, accommodate, and tame hostile and hospitable environments alike. In the process, disturbing forces (e.g., stressors) operate on the *milieu interieur*. The resulting disequilibrium can trigger counteracting normalizing forces (Chrousos, 2000), followed by repair and maintenance.

Homeostasis

It remained for subsequent investigators to delineate the general nature of these regulatory mechanisms. A dominant perspective for most of the twentieth century was Walter Cannon's (1939) notion of homeostasis, in which adaptive reactions were equated with processes that maintained the constancy of the fluid matrix (see Berntson & Cacioppo, 2000). Cannon argued that the variations from basal physiological levels ("set points") do not reach the dangerous extremes that impair the functions of the cells or threaten the existence of the organism because adaptive reactions are automatically triggered to return the affected physiological system to a basal state.

The sympathetic branch of the autonomic nervous system, in Cannon's (1929) model, as the primary homeostatic regulator and the parasympathetic branch provides a fine-tuning of visceral responses. Homeostasis was thought to be maintained by a self-regulating feedback mechanism (i.e., servo-controlled reflexes; Cannon, 1929, 1939). Slight variations in the magnitude of activation notwithstanding, the sympathetic and parasympathetic branches were thought to be reciprocally activated and synergistic in their actions (Berntson & Cacioppo, 2000). The baroreceptor–heart rate reflex, which serves to maintain blood pressure, illustrates this reciprocal relationship between the activation of the sympathetic and parasympathetic branches (Berntson, Cacioppo, & Quigley, 1991). Elevations in blood pressure activate the baroreceptors (pressure-sensitive receptors) mostly within the carotid sinus, which then increase firing in afferent (sensory) fibers to the nucleus of the tractus solitarius (NTS). The activation of the NTS, in turn, inhibits sympathetic motor neurons in the intermediolateral cell column of the spinal cord and excites the parasympathetic source nuclei in the nucleus ambiguous and dorsal motor nucleus of the vagus. That is, increased blood pressure reflexively leads to a decrease in sympathetic activation of the heart and a reciprocal increase in parasympathetic activation of the heart. This decrease in sympathetic activation slows the heart rate and reduces ventricular contractility, whereas the reciprocal increase in parasympathetic activation slows the beat of the heart and reduces cardiac output. Together with reductions in adrenergic vasoconstrictor tone, the baroreceptor actions compensate for the distur-

bance and restore blood pressure to normal levels. The opposite pattern of autonomic control (i.e. sympathetic activation and reciprocal parasympathetic withdrawal) is triggered by a sudden lowering of blood pressure (e.g., during assumption of an upright posture).

As this example illustrates, the baroreflex displays the essential characteristics of a feedback-regulated, homeostatic mechanism that responds to perturbations of blood pressure and acts to restore basal blood pressure. But blood pressure regulation is not *limited* to servomechanisms like the baroreflex. Indeed, blood pressure changes can be seen in anticipation of a perturbation, before any change in baroreceptor afference. Examples include the increased blood pressure just prior to physical exercise, the assumption of an upright posture, or the anticipated confrontation of a threatening or dangerous stimulus. To some extent, these anticipatory changes likely reflect simple Pavlovian conditioning, in which stimuli (environmental or cognitive) that predict an impending perturbation can serve as conditioned stimuli (CS) for an anticipatory, compensatory adjustment (Dworkin & Dworkin, 1995). In addition to this simple form of heterotopic conditioning (i.e., conditioning in which the CS and the unconditioned stimuli, or UCS, are in different modalities), there is a growing probability of homotopic conditioning of the baroreflex and other autonomic systems (Dworkin, 2000). In homotopic conditioning the CS and UCS are in the same modality (e.g., baroreceptor afference), wherein a modest baroreceptor activation (CS) that evokes a small compensatory response (unconditioned response or UCR) may trigger a larger conditioned response (CR) that acts synergistically with the UCR to actually preclude a subsequent perturbation (Dworkin, 2000). This serves to make adjustments that not only precede physiological perturbation but also dampen or eliminate the perturbation. Thus, when fine-tuned by consistent homotopic conditioning, regulatory systems may act preemptively to prevent, rather than simply react to, perturbations.

These specific examples, although not exclusively servomechanisms, still represent homeostasis because they represent negative feedback systems that operate to maintain physiological functioning around a given set point. Conditioned anticipatory responses, however, are not limited to homeostatic effects, as they can also produce a change in set point or an inhibition of set point regulation (Dworkin, Elbert, & Rau, 2000). The reflex-based homeostatic model also has limitations, as the same excitatory stimulus (e.g., stressor) can have profoundly different effects on physiological activation across individuals or life circumstances, and higher-level behavioral circuits come into play. Accordingly, the reciprocal activation of the sympathetic and parasympathetic branches may be true for brain stem baroreceptor reflexes, but it does not provide a comprehensive account of the autonomic responses supporting more complex behaviors (Berntson et al., 1991; Berntson, Cacioppo, & Quigley, 1993).

In an illustrative study, Berntson et al. (1994) quantified the sympathetic and parasympathetic responses to postural (orthostatic) and active coping (e.g., mental arithmetic) stressors using autonomic blockades. At the nomothetic level, orthostatic and psychological stressors produced what appeared to be reciprocal activation—whether individuals moved from a sitting to a standing posture or whether they moved from a quiescent baseline to an active coping task (i.e., mental arithmetic, competitive reaction time, and public speaking tasks), mean sympathetic activation of the heart increased and vagal (parasympathetic) activation of the heart decreased. Based on the known physiology, the postural effect is largely attributable to reciprocal autonomic control by the baroreflex. Indeed, the correlation between the quantitative estimates of sympathetic and parasympathetic contributions to the cardiac response to orthostatic stressor was large and significant, confirming reciprocal cardiac activation at the idiographic level consistent with Cannon's conception of homeostasis. The autonomic determinants of the cardiac responses to the psychological stressors, in contrast, revealed large and reliable individual differences in sympathetic and parasympathetic activation. Unlike what was found for posture, for instance, the correlation between the quantitative estimates of sympathetic and parasympathetic contributions to the cardiac response to psychological stressors were nonsignificant (Berntson et al., 1994). The autonomic control of the heart in response to each of the psychological stressors is modulated by more rostral (higher-order) brain systems. These higher regions of the brain are rich in input from environmental and associative (including personal historical) events (Berntson, Sarter, & Cacioppo, 1998). Accordingly, they produce cardiac responses to psychological

stressors that exceed metabolic demands (Turner, 1989) and reveal more interindividual variation in the mode of cardiac control (Berntson et al., 1994).

To account for these and related findings, Berntson and colleagues (e.g., Berntson et al. 1991, 1993) proposed a model of autonomic space in which sympathetic and parasympathetic activation not only could be reciprocal but could also be uncoupled, coactivated, or coinhibited. Reciprocal activation fosters a rapid and dramatic change in effector status (e.g., heart rate), uncoupled activation affords more fine-tuning (e.g., vagal withdrawal in response to mild exercise), and coactivation or coinhibition can regulate or mute the functional consequences of underlying neural adjustments. These latter adjustments, which fall outside the rubric of homeostasis (Berntson et al., 1991), nevertheless represent regulatory adjustments to support the demands, perceived or real, of the external world. Of what importance is this to health?

Although high blood pressure is generally asymptomatic, approximately 30% of individuals with high blood pressure will suffer some adverse health outcome such as heart disease, and 5% to 10% will die from a stroke (Temple et al., 2001). High heart rate (HR) reactivity to active coping tasks has received considerable attention because of its association with elevated blood pressure and cardiovascular disease in later life (e.g., Light, Dolan, Davis, & Sherwood, 1992). High HR reactivity has also been associated with poorer recovery following myocardial infarction (e.g., Krantz & Manuck, 1984), heightened sympathetic adrenomedullary activity, and impaired cellular immune function (Manuck, Cohen, Rabin, Muldoon, & Bachen, 1991; Sgoutas-Emch et al., 1994).

Although high HR reactivity has been regarded to be a risk factor for hypertension, an individual's classification as high in HR reactivity could originate from elevated sympathetic reactivity, vagal withdrawal, or reciprocal activation of the sympathetic and vagal outflows to the heart. Research on cardiac reactivity, however, has generally emphasized variations in HR reactivity rather than variations in the autonomic origins of HR reactivity. According to Berntson and colleagues' (1991) theory of autonomic organization and function, the classification of individuals in terms of HR reactivity relegates variations in the autonomic origins of HR reactivity to the error term. In other words, one cannot distinguish between a level of HR reactivity that reflects sympathetic activation or vagal with-drawal—and blurring this distinction can obscure relationships between autonomic responses to stres-sors and behavioral, humoral, or clinical outcomes (Cacioppo, 1994). Indeed, reliable differences exist not only in HR reactivity to psychological stressors but also in sympathetic cardiac activation and in vagal cardiac activation (Berntson et al., 1994; Cacioppo, Berntson, et al., 1994; Cacioppo, Uchino, & Berntson, 1994); it is the sympathetic component that best predicts the activation of the hypothalamic pituitary axis and cellular immunity (Benschop et al., 1998; Cacioppo et al., 1995; Uchino, Cacioppo, Malarkey, Glaser, & Kiecolt-Glaser, 1995). In dif-ferent health domains, such as when predicting the recovery from myocardial infarction, both sympa-thetic and vagal components may be important for understanding separable potentially pathophysi-ological mechanisms of action (Berntson et al., 1997).

Sympathetic activation is not the unidimen-sional construct that was ascribed to Cannon, ei-ther. Contrary to the notion that sympathetic nervous activation is global and diffuse, highly specific regional sympathetic activation has been observed in response to stressors (Johnson & Anderson, 1990) even in extreme conditions such as panic attacks (Wilkinson et al., 1998). Obrist, Light, and colleagues demonstrated that active cop-ing tasks (those with which one copes by doing something; e.g., mental arithmetic) tend to elicit beta-adrenergic (e.g., cardiac) activation and in-creased blood pressure, whereas passive coping tasks (those with which one copes by enduring; e.g., cold pressor) tend to elicit alpha-adrenergic (e.g., vasomotor) activation (Light, Girdler, & Hinder-liter, 2003) and increased blood pressure. Again, individual differences have been found, with some individuals showing greater cardiac reactivity and others greater vasomotor reactivity (Kasprowicz, Manuck, Malkoff, & Krantz, 1990; Light, Turner, Hinderliter, Girdler, & Sherwood, 1994; Llabre, Klein, Saab, McCalla, & Schneiderman, 1998; Sher-wood, Dolan, & Light, 1990). An integration of these apparently disparate effects is suggested by the research showing that individuals who approach active coping tasks with the belief that they can meet task demands ("challenge appraisals") also tend to show primarily cardiac activation to the task, whereas those who approach the tasks with the belief that they cannot meet task demands ("threat appraisals") tend to show primarily vascular acti-

vation (Tomaka, Blascovich, Kibler, & Ernst, 1997). Whether it is threat/challenge appraisals or active/passive coping strategies for dealing with the stres-sors that produce the different patterns of sympa-thetic activation remains to be determined, but it is becoming clear that sympathetic activation does not represent a simple arousal mechanism, and that not all responses to stressors are the same (Berntson, Cacioppo, & Sarter, 2003; Hawkley & Cacioppo, 2003).

Allostasis

The research reviewed in the preceding section sug-gests that not all regulatory mechanisms are homeo-static and that the balance within is not maintained by a system of rigid servocontrollers operating around immutable set points. The regulated re-sponse of the brain and body serves a constancy of the internal milieu, not only in an immediate sense like most homeostatic adjustments but also in the long term under conditions of changing physiologi-cal capacities or resilience. The complexity of the regulatory devices required to achieve this con-stancy led Sterling and Eyer (1988) and McEwen and Stellar (1993) to propose the concept of allo-stasis. Thus, the concept of allostasis is an abstrac-tion to guide our study and understanding of the many autonomic, endocrine, and immune dimen-sions that are regulated by multiple, interacting mechanisms that are subjected to broader modu-latory influences, whether from external challenges or endogenous processes.

Allostatic regulation (in contrast to homeostatic regulation) reflects the operation of higher neural systems that serve to control and integrate a broad range of homeostatic reflexes (Berntson & Cacioppo, 2003). Allostatic regulation, therefore, may achieve greater flexibility in maintaining integrative regu-lation both within and across autonomic, neuroen-docrine, and immune function than is possible through homeostasis alone. An illustration is the alteration in body temperature set point associated with a fever (Berntson & Cacioppo, 2000). The increase in body temperature during illness does not represent a failure of homeostasis. Rather, the increased temperature of a fever is actively regulated and defended, and reductions in body temperature are met with active compensatory thermogenic pro-cesses (e.g. shivering, behavioral thermoregulation). The elevation in temperature associated with a fever may be of benefit in slowing bacterial growth and proliferation (Maier & Watkins, 1998). Despite its potential adaptive significance, fever is not readily subsumed within homeostatic regulation because it reflects the adoption of a new regulatory set point.

In sum, the term *allostasis* was coined by Sterling and Eyer (1988) to refer to active deviations from homeostatic levels that often appear under conditions of adaptive challenge.[2] Interestingly, the seeds of this idea can be found in Selye's (1973) concept of heterostasis, in which altered chemical and hormonal conditions associated with exogenous stimuli were seen as contributing to resistance and adaptation by (a) rendering tissues less sensitive to pathogenic stimuli and/or (b) neutralizing or destroying pathogens. The anti-inflammatory effects of adrenocorticoids such as cortisol are an example of the former mechanism, as corticoids make tissue less sensitive to irritation. An example of the latter mechanism is the centrally regulated increase in body temperature (fever) associated with illness, which may promote an optimal host defense.

Short-Term Gains Versus Long-Term Costs

Both homeostasis and allostasis exist in order to buffer organisms from the effects of internal and external changes—for instance, from the effects of environmental stressors. Stressors and stress responses are neither inherently good nor inherently bad, however. Homeostasis and allostasis evolved because there were reproductive benefits to being able to respond to environmental stressors. The counteracting forces triggered by disturbances of the *internal milieu* can have long-term costs but can also promote growth, adaptation, and resilience—especially if the resources that can be marshaled are sufficient to meet adaptive demands and the associated restorative (e.g., anabolic) processes promote adaptive responding to subsequent exposures to the same kind of demands. Learning, muscular development, and humoral immunity are illustrative of the empowering aspects of the restorative powers of the body. A defensive lineman who makes the transition from college to professional football may initially be in awe of the strength of the offensive linemen he must block and muscularly fatigued after practices. The same events, however, become less and less demanding as the lineman's muscles have time to repair and grow following each prac-

tice.[3] Thus, at least some long-term costs of stress may be minimized, or in some cases reversed, if appropriate repair and maintenance processes also unfold. Indeed, vaccinations work in this way. A weakened antigen is inserted to immunologically challenge the body to produce the antibodies needed to eradicate the pathogen and repair the body. An individual who is vaccinated may suffer a brief, mild bout of the illness but subsequently will have an acquired immunity to future exposures to this antigen.

In the remainder of this section, we focus on the short-term benefits and the long-term *costs* of stress responses. We return in a later section on clinical implications to the importance of dealing with these long-term costs not only by decreasing exposures to stressors but also by increasing the opportunity and salubrity of restorative physiological processes.

Sympathetic Adrenomedullary System

Cannon (1929) studied not only the physiological basis of homeostasis but also the influence of emotional disturbances on various physiological processes. This latter work focused on what he termed the *emergency reaction*. In Cannon's (1929) formulation, autonomic and neuroendocrine activation associated with emotional disturbances serve to mobilize metabolic resources to support the requirements of fight or flight, thereby promoting the protection and survival of the organism. The sympathetic nervous system, via a sympathetic nerve called the *splanchnics,* directly stimulates the medullary cells of the adrenal gland, causing the release of the catecholamine hormones epinephrine and norepinephrine. Cannon (1929) believed that the sympathetic-adrenomedullary (SAM) system was activated primarily during fight-or-flight responses and played a role in maintaining homeostasis within the body and adapting to environmental stressors.

The actions of the SAM system—which include an increase in muscular efficiency, release of energy stores (glycogenolysis), and increased arterial blood pressure and muscle blood flow—are attributable in large part to epinephrine. Because of differences in the receptors of the arterial walls, catecholamines cause vasodilation within the internal organs (e.g., via beta-adrenergic receptors in skeletal muscles) and vasoconstriction in the periphery (e.g., by alpha-adrenergic receptors in cutaneous tissue beds). This pattern of perfusion (blood flow) has adaptive utility. By shifting blood flow to muscles, the organism is better able to mobilize and cope with the situation. The constriction of peripheral areas not only facilitates the rapid redistribution of blood within the body but also minimizes the loss of blood should an injury occur. Additionally, with the presence of pressure-sensitive receptors in the arterial walls, circulatory changes initiated by the release of catecholamines can feed back and alter the activity of the brain. Blood pressure elevations, for instance, have been shown to diminish pain—a useful short-term adjustment in response to attack but a costly long-term adjustment if it occurs in response to chronic psychological stress and results in hypertension (Dworkin et al., 2000).

Hypothalamic Pituitary Adrenocortical System

Although sympathetic activation from the release of norepinephrine from sympathetic terminals produces more specific effects than Cannon had envisioned (1928), the SAM response to stress, with the release of epinephrine and norepinephrine into and transport by the blood to visceral organs throughout the body, is capable of producing generalized effects from which the organism recovers more slowly than sympathetic or parasympathetic (i.e., direct neural) activation. Cannon's historic characterization of the SAM response to stress as adaptive but fixed or rigid (i.e., stereotypic) was elaborated upon in Selye's (1956) general adaptation syndrome (GAS) theory, which emphasized the hypothalamic-pituitary-adrenocortical (HPA) response to stressors. The SAM system is directly innervated by the sympathetic nervous system and therefore can respond more quickly to stressors than the HPA system and more slowly than the autonomic nervous system. The HPA system, on the other hand, has more general and enduring effects than either the SAM or the autonomic nervous system.

Briefly, a release of adrenocorticotropic hormone (ACTH) from the pituitary can be initiated from the hypothalamus and cause the adrenal gland to secrete carbohydrate-active steroids (e.g., glucocorticoids) that have wide-ranging effects on the body's metabolism. These include muscular efficiency, energy resources and cellular metabolism, inflammatory and allergic responses, and brain function, including alertness, learning, and memory processes underlying behavioral adaptation. Selye's work on GAS theory provided early support for the notion that physiological activation in response to stressors is beneficial up to a point but excessive or prolonged activation may indeed have long-term costs. The initial physiological reaction in the general adaptation syndrome is an emergency fight-or-flight response believed to be adaptive, at least in most instances in the short term. If ineffective behavioral coping results, additional compensatory actions occur, such as increased and sustained secretions of steroids and decreased secretions of catecholamines, and a consequent alteration in homeostatic levels for a number of physiological systems (e.g., water retention, circulatory pressure). If the stress continues for a protracted period without relief, the physiological coping mechanisms may not be able to prevent permanent physiological damage to organs or the demise of the organism.

Cortisol levels are generally held in check by a negative feedback mechanism, in which dual glucocorticoid and mineralocorticoid receptors in the hippocampal region of the brain inhibit further HPA activity (De Kloet, Vreugdenhil, Oitzl, & Joels, 1998). Relatedly, psychological stress in animals has been shown to increase the number of hippocampal mineralocorticoid receptors and produce greater inhibition of HPA activity (Geising et al., 2001). However, continued glucocorticoid and mineralocorticoid excess, which can result from sustained psychological stress, may contribute ultimately to the down-regulation of these hippocampal receptors and to hippocampal atrophy (Sapolsky, 1996). Such anatomical changes, in turn, diminish the ability of circulating stress hormones to reduce or terminate HPA activation. In other words, chronically elevated circulating cortisol levels can lead to a down-regulation (decreased sensitivity) of the glucocorticoid receptors in the hippocampal region, which in turn decreases the efficacy of the negative feedback mechanism that, under normal conditions, applies brakes to the activation of the hypothalamic pituitary adrenocortical axis. With weakened brakes on this stress system, the individual will come to be characterized by a higher set point for circulating cortisol (McEwen, 1998; Selye, 1973).[4]

Importantly, Selye studied physical stressors in animals, but subsequent work has shown that the same general mechanisms may operate in response to psychological stressors in humans (Mason, 1975). Thus, idiosyncratic construals (i.e., cognitive appraisals; Lazarus & Folkman, 1984) of an event can produce variations in autonomic, neuroendocrine, and immune adjustments to the event (Cacioppo, 1994), as well as variations in recovery (Davidson, 1998; McEwen & Seeman, 2003).

Immune Modulation

The pituitary and adrenal hormones and other neuropeptides (short-chain proteins in the nervous system that are capable of acting as a neurotransmitters) play an important role in the modulation of the immune system (Munck, Guyre, & Holbrook, 1984), as well. Circulating hormones such as epinephrine, norepinephrine, and cortisol can act on visceral as well as cellular immune receptors; they constitute an important gateway through which psychological stressors affect the cellular immune response (Ader, Felton, & Cohen, 2001). As we discussed earlier, psychological stress is associated with increases in antibody titers to latent EBV (mononucleosis). In an early study, Kasl and colleagues (1979) followed cadets at West Point, over a 4-year period, who were seronegative for EBV at entry into the Academy. Consistent with the notion that stress can down-regulate the cellular immune response and adversely affect the body's ability to respond to infection with EBV, they found that poor academic performance, high levels of motivation for a military career, and an overachieving father were associated with a greater risk for seroconversion to EBV, longer hospitalization in the infirmary following infection (i.e., more severe illness episodes), and higher EBV antibody titers among those who seroconverted but had no clinical symptoms. Similarly, using an academic stress model with medical students, Glaser and colleagues measured EBV antibody titers over time, both at baseline periods in which the students were less stressed and during examination periods, when the medical students reported more stress. Results showed reliable changes in antibody titers to EBV virus capsid antigen (VCA) concomitant with the down-regulation of several components of the cellular immune response (Glaser et al., 1987; Glaser et al., 1991; Glaser et al., 1993).

In sum, autonomic and neuroendocrinological activation in response to stressors serves to mobilize metabolic resources to support the requirements of fight or flight. Stress may be necessary for survival, but it can also alter susceptibility to disease. Stress, particularly if prolonged or repeated, can produce cardiovascular changes that can contribute to a narrowing of blood vessels and to heart attacks or strokes and reduce the strength of immunologic activities in the body (Baum, 1994; Cohen, 1996). Stress may obscure symptoms, increase appraisal and patient delays, and reduce medical compliance (Andersen, Cacioppo, & Roberts, 1995). Stress can activate maladaptive behaviors that reflect attempts to cope with negative emotional responses. Persons experiencing psychological stress, for example, may engage in unhealthy practices such as smoking, not eating or sleeping properly, and not exercising; these behaviors may foster accidents, cardiovascular disease, and suppressed immune function (Baum, 1994; Cohen, 1991).

Many of the powerful elicitors of emotion in contemporary society—personal affronts, traffic congestion, pressing deadlines, public speaking engagements, unreasonable bosses, perceived injustices—do not require or even allow behavioral fight or flight, and the reactions in response to these events can substantially exceed metabolic requirements. Thus, although physiological activation in response to stressors is beneficial up to a point, excessive autonomic and neuroendocrine activation can diminish health across time. That is, a design for the brain and stress physiology that worked well in human evolution may have maladaptive aspects that manifest as life expectancy has increased well beyond the reproductive years. Indeed, according to Lithgow and Kirkwood's (1996) disposable soma theory of aging, it may be disadvantageous to increase maintenance beyond a level sufficient to keep the organism in good shape through its natural life expectancy in the wild. Given that the metabolic requirements posed by the psychological stressors in today's society are often minimal, physiological reactivity to quotidian stressors in the absence of restorative breaks may increase the wear and tear on the organism and contribute to broad-based morbidity and mortality.

Allostatic Load

The concept of allostasis was introduced earlier in this chapter. In this section, we introduce the related concept of allostatic load. The damage to the balance within, although potentially occurring in response to acute environmental events during an especially sensitive period of development (Anisman, Zaharia, Meaney, & Merali, 1998; Meaney et al., 1996), more typically reflects the accrual of wear and tear on the regulatory and restorative systems of the body in response to stressors over an extended period of time—an accrual termed *allostatic load* (McEwen 1998). Among the allostatic responses that have been studied most extensively are the autonomic nervous system and the two neuroendocrine systems covered in the preceding section—the SAM and HPA systems. As outlined earlier, the activation of these systems results in the release of neurotransmitters at the viscera, catecholamines from the adrenal medulla, corticotropin from the pituitary, and cortisol from the adrenal cortex. Although inactivation of these systems normally occurs when the perceived danger is past, inefficient inactivation or delayed recovery may result in an overexposure to stress hormones. Thus, high and prolonged exposure to glucocorticoids may result in degenerative changes in the hippocampus, as discussed earlier, with a consequent loss in ability to diminish or terminate potent aspects of the stress response (Sapolsky, 1996).

The adaptive utility of stress reactions is inherent in the concept of allostasis, as is the notion that they come at a cost over the long term. McEwen and Steller (1993) proposed that specific patterns of stress response vary considerably across individuals and contexts, but that they also show common allostatic features. Specifically, in contrast to simple homeostatic systems that are focused on a single dimension (e.g., blood gases) and regulated around a fixed set point, allostatic systems entail multiple dimensions, integrated and orchestrated by central, autonomic, and endocrine processes. Within allostatic systems, functional set points are subject to change, and disturbances in one dimension may lead to compensatory fluctuations in another. McEwen and Stellar (1993) propose that repeated or prolonged allostatic fluctuations extract a physiological cost, a sort of "wear and tear." This wear and tear is seen to be cumulative, largely irreversible, and disposed toward stress pathology. Prolonged stress-related elevations in cortisol and increases in insulin secretion, for instance, accelerate atherosclerosis and contribute to hypertension (McEwen & Stellar, 1993). These latter changes are largely irreversible by normal restorative devices and increase the risk for disease.

McEwen (1998) discussed four specific situations associated with allostatic load. First and most obvious, frequent exposure to stressors increases allostatic load. The frequency of stressors, for instance, has been shown to accelerate atherosclero-

sis and increase the risk of myocardial infarction (e.g., Kaplan & Manuck, 2003). The stressors need not be physically present either, as, for reasons outlined earlier, repeated feelings of threat or worry can also trigger stress reactions that over time contribute to the deterioration of cellular and organ function and regulatory mechanisms (i.e., allostatic load).

Second, allostatic load can result from a failure to adapt or habituate to repeated stressors of the same type. The metabolic requirements posed by the psychological stressors to which people are typically exposed in contemporary society are minimal (e.g., public speaking, daily commutes), yet these stressors continue to elicit strong autonomic and neuroendocrine activation. Individuals who fail to show adaptation to these stressors may also be at risk for pathophysiological developments (Cacioppo et al., 1998; McEwen, 1998).

Third, allostatic load results when there is an inability or inefficiency in terminating the allostatic response after the stressor is removed. Some individuals, for instance, recover more slowly than others from psychological stressors such as mental arithmetic, and the latter are thought to be at greater risk for hypertension (Gehring & Pickering, 1995). Consistent with this reasoning, McEwen (1998) reviews evidence that the failure to efficiently terminate sympathetic and HPA responses to stressors is a feature of an age-related functional decline in nonhuman animals, a process that likely operates in humans, as well.

Finally, inadequate responses by some allostatic systems trigger compensatory increases in others. If cortisol secretion does not increase in response to stress, secretion of inflammatory cytokines, which is usually down-regulated by cortisol, increases, with potentially pathophysiological effects (Munck et al., 1984).

In sum, we have emphasized that what is adaptive or maladaptive, healthy or unhealthy, depends on context, and what may be good for one tissue may be lifesaving, but may have a negative impact on another tissue, with mortal consequences in the long run. The regional positioning of immunocytes in response to acute stress may provide the host with a selective advantage should aggressive behavioral interactions lead to cutaneous wounding and the possibility of infection (Dhabhar & McEwen, 1997). The selective advantage that may accompany acute stress does not extend to chronic forms of stress, however, as the prolonged activation of the HPA axis and sympathetic nervous system seen in chronic stress tends to suppress cellular immunity (Lupien & McEwen, 1997; Sheridan, 1998), reduce response to vaccination (Kiecolt-Glaser, Glaser, Gravenstein, Malarkey, & Sheridan, 1996), and slow the healing of experimental cutaneous and mucosal wounds (Kiecolt-Glaser et al., 1995; Marucha, Kiecolt-Glaser, & Favagehi, 1998; Padgett, Marucha, & Sheridan, 1998). *These complexities underscore the interdependence between organisms and their physical and social environments.* Restorative mechanisms such as a balanced diet, moderate exercise, sleep, and rich social connections can have salutogenic (e.g., stress-buffering) effects, whereas a diet high in fat, the use of tobacco and alcohol, a sedentary lifestyle, and hostility and isolation exacerbate the deleterious effects of chronic stress. Our understanding of the complex regulative and restorative processes of the organism—and the balance within—is therefore fostered by a multilevel integrative analysis.

Clinical Implications

In his book on genetics, evolution, and biology, Lewontin (2000) argued that we would not fully understand living organisms if we continue to think of genes, organisms, and environments as separate entities. "In a curious sense," he suggested, "the study of the organisms is really a study of the shape of the environmental space, the organisms themselves being nothing but the passive medium through which we see the shape of the external world" (p. 44). We have sounded a resonant theme here, suggesting that a multilevel integrative analysis is needed if we are to develop a comprehensive explanation of morbidity and mortality. Given the complexity of the regulatory mechanisms in the brain and body, clinical interventions that target a single peripheral process (e.g., beta-adrenergic blockades) should not be expected to be broadly protective or to have only protective effects. Pharmacological interventions designed to affect peripheral cellular processes, therefore, might best be conceptualized as a component of a broad, multimodal (e.g., behavioral, psychosocial) therapeutic intervention.

The concept of stress has also received a great deal of attention in health psychology, with numerous studies showing that stress is associated with acute responses that mimic pathophysiological states

(e.g., elevated blood pressure, diminished lymphocyte proliferation) and higher rates of morbidity and mortality. It would be easy to conclude from these studies that stress is bad and to develop clinical interventions based on this premise. Clinical interventions designed to either decrease a person's exposure to stressors (e.g., simplify living) or diminish the person's reactivity to stressors (e.g., cognitive behavior therapy; stress buffering by friends and family) certainly have a place, but not all stressors are or should be avoided, and many may offer opportunities for growth or an explanation of capacities.

In these cases, the value of temporary respites from the stresses of everyday life might be considered. As noted in the introductory section of this chapter, stress hormones can diminish important aspects of cellular immunity. If these individuals are not able to retreat from the stresses of their environment to recuperate or, worse yet, if their weakened immunologic state only increases the stressors they are confronting, then a positive feedback system results that fosters the conditions for the development of frequent and chronic disease. That is, a positive feedback loop may be created that makes illness more likely and more ravaging. Unfortunately, the individuals who are least likely to be able to take these respites are, perhaps not coincidentally, those who are also at risk for broad-based morbidity and mortality.

Relatedly, we have reviewed evidence emphasizing not only the potentially different short- and long-term effects of stress reactions but the additional importance of the repair and maintenance processes of the body. Individuals who feel socially connected, for instance, may live longer and healthier lives in part because they enjoy more efficient sleep (and restorative physiological processes) than people who feel socially isolated (Cacioppo, Hawkley, et al., 2002). More scientific and clinical research is needed on how the toxic effects of stressors may be reduced by the repair and maintenance processes of the brain and body.

Conclusion

The topics we have discussed fall under five general principles: (a) the autonomic, neuroendocrine, and immune systems are orchestrated in part to buffer the organism against the effects of internal and external changes by regulatory and restorative devices; (b) disturbances of the constancy of internal conditions trigger counteracting forces that can have both beneficial, acute effects and detrimental, chronic effects for the organism (i.e., what may be good for one tissue may be lifesaving, but may have negative impact on another tissue, with mortal consequences in the long run); (c) the organization of these regulatory devices is not static across circumstances and the life span; (d) whether these adjustments are adaptive or maladaptive, healthy or unhealthy, depends in part on the physical and social environment (external milieu) and in part on the status of the organism and the nature of the response itself (internal milieu); and (5) a design for the brain and stress physiology that worked well in human evolution is now a contributing factor to broad-based morbidity and mortality. These principles operate at the level of the aggregate, covering a range of specific pathophysiological processes.

We have also emphasized that the etiology and course of chronic disease have biological substrates but that these biological substrates are influenced profoundly by the physical and social world. We have discussed a variety of issues bearing on this assertion, including the mechanisms by which adaptive reactions are achieved (e.g., Berntson et al., 1991), including homeostasis and allostasis (McEwen & Stellar, 1993; Sterling & Eyer, 1988). Evidence has been reviewed that allostatic load—the accrued effects of a lifetime of stress—alters the efficiency of effectors, as well as the regulatory and restorative devices that control them. Accordingly, there is profit from conceptualizing organismic functioning within an environmental (physical, psychological, social) context and from confronting the new questions that such a conceptualization brings into focus.

It remains to be determined, for instance, to what extent individual differences in allostatic load are the consequence of differential exposure to stressors, differential reactivity to stressors, and differential recovery from stressors—and why. A good deal is now known about stress physiology (e.g., Chrousos, 2000), but the rostral neurobehavioral systems that orchestrate organismic-environmental transactions (Berntson et al., 1998; Berntson, Cacioppo, & Sarter, 2003) and the psychological transduction mechanisms (e.g., health behaviors, health utilization, stress buffering) remain only partially mapped. "Stress" has been assigned a special role in the development of allostatic load, but

the concept of stress itself is often vaguely (or circularly) defined. Operationalizations and measures across studies, especially across animal and human studies, were regularly so different (e.g., restraint, hypoglycemic, orthostatic, mathematic stressors) that results are sometimes difficult to compare or reconcile (Lovallo, 1997). Stressors are not always negative, either, as positive as well as negative events are considered stressors in studies focused on predicting health (Holmes & Rahe, 1967). Further complicating matters, the measurements of stress within a given study are often so weakly correlated that they provide poor convergent validity for the construct of stress (e.g., Lacey, 1959; Johnson & Anderson, 1990). In short, neither stress nor health is a simple, unitary concept, and the search for a singular universal mechanism relating stress to health is doomed to failure. The concept of allostatic load, too, while useful at a molar level of analysis, is misleading if applied to specific underlying mechanisms as if there were a single cause of wear and tear. The concept is useful because it represents a broad, multifarious category of specific and largely unrelated transduction mechanisms that contribute to the wear and tear on the organism.

Why not simply ignore the molar constructs of integrative physiology and focus on the details of the cellular machinery? As Claude Bernard (1878/1974) opined more than a century ago, and Lewontin (2000) and we (Cacioppo et al., 2000) have echoed more recently, the organization and function of the elemental parts of an organism can be understood comprehensively only within the context of its transactions with its physical and social environment. Lewontin's (2000) analysis suggesting that the reduction in mortality from infectious diseases during the late 1800s and early 1900s is attributable to a general trend of increases in real wage, an increase in the state of nutrition, and a decrease in the number of hours worked—that is, a decrease in the wear and tear on the organism and improved opportunities for the organism to heal itself—hints at causal factors and targets of interventions to which we would be blind if we focused on cellular mechanisms alone. Although we are beginning to understand how the brain integrates the regulatory and restorative forces of the body to foster health and adaptation to environmental challenges, it is clear that health psychology will have much to contribute to this understanding for a long time to come.

Acknowledgments.   Funding was provided by the National Institute of Aging Grant No. PO1 AG18911 and the John Templeton Foundations.

Notes

1. *Catabolic processes* refers to the phase of metabolism in which complex molecules are broken down into simpler ones, often resulting in a release of energy (e.g., stress reactivity), whereas *anabolic processes* refers to the phase of metabolism in which simple substances are synthesized into the complex materials of living tissue.

2. Allostasis further holds that the modulation of homeostatic or regulatory mechanisms can be achieved through local (peripheral) or central processes (Berntson & Cacioppo, 2000).

3. The current framework also points to a qualification in this statement. If the lineman is overtraining—that is, if he is not getting sufficient nutrition and rest to allow his body to repair and grow as a result of the training, then the training will not provide the same physiological benefits.

4. This example also illustrates how the physiological systems activated by events in daily life not only can protect and restore some aspects or functions of the body but can simultaneously damage others, either through behavioral channels (e.g., a person persisting in the face of stressors and thereby putting themselves in a position to suffer additional damage), alteration of the equilibrium or set point of a homeostatic system, increased reactivity to stressors, or slowed and less potent recovery and restoration following stressors.

References

Ader, R., Felton, D. L., & Cohen, N. (Eds.). (2001). *Psychoneuroimmunology* (3rd ed.). San Diego, CA: Academic Press.

Andersen, B. L., Cacioppo, J. T., & Roberts, D. C. (1995). Delay in seeking a cancer diagnosis: Delay stages and psychophysiological comparison processes. *British Journal of Social Psychology, 34,* 33–52.

Anisman, H., Zaharia, M. D., Meaney, M. J., & Merali, Z. (1998). Do early-life events permanently alter behavioral and hormonal responses to stressors? *International Journal of Developmental Neuroscience, 16,* 149–164.

Arancibia, S., Rage, F., Astier, H., & Tapia-Arancibia, L. (1996). Neuroendocrine and autonomous mechanisms underlying thermoregulation in cold environment. *Neuroendocrinology, 64,* 257–267.

Bauer, G. (1983). Induction of Epstein-Barr virus early antigens by corticosteroids: Inhibition by TPA and retinoic acid. *International Journal of Cancer, 31,* 291–295.

Baum, A. (1994). Behavioral, biological, and environmental interactions in disease processes. In S. Blumenthal, K. Matthews, & S. Weiss (Eds.), *New research frontiers in behavioral medicine: Proceedings of the national conference.* Washington, DC: NIH Publications.

Benschop, R. J., Geenen, R., Mills, P. J., Naliboff, B. D., Kiecolt-Glaser, J. K., Herbert, T. B., et al. (1998). Cardiovascular and immune responses to acute psychological stress in young and old women: A meta-investigation. *Psychosomatic Medicine, 60,* 290–296.

Bernard, C. (1878/1974). *Lecons sur les phenomenes de la vie communes aux animaux et aux vegetaux.* Paris: B. Bailliere et Fils [Lectures on the phenomena of life common to animals and plants] (H. E. Hoff, R. Guillemin, & L. Guillemin, Trans.). Springfield, IL: Thomas.

Berntson, G. G., Bigger, J. T., Jr., Eckberg, D. L., Grossman, P., Kaufmann, P. G., Malik, M., et al. (1997). Heart rate variability: Origins, methods, and interpretive caveats. *Psychophysiology, 34,* 623–648.

Berntson, G. G., & Cacioppo, J. T. (2000). From homeostasis to allodynamic regulation. In J. T. Cacioppo, L. G. Tassinary, & G. G. Berntson (Eds.), *Handbook of psychophysiology* (2nd ed., pp. 459–481). New York: Cambridge University Press.

Berntson, G. G., & Cacioppo, J. T. (2003). A contemporary perspective on multilevel analyses and social neuroscience. In F. Kessel, P. Rosenfeld & N. Anderson, (Eds.), *Expanding the boundaries of health and social science: Case studies in interdisciplinary innovation* (pp. 18–40). New York: Oxford University Press.

Berntson, G. G., Cacioppo, J. T., Binkley, P. F., Uchino, B. N., Quigley, K. S., & Fieldstone, A. (1994). Autonomic cardiac control. III. Psychological stress and cardiac response in autonomic space as revealed by pharmacological blockades. *Psychophysiology, 31,* 599–608.

Berntson, G. G., Cacioppo, J. T., & Quigley, K. S. (1991). Autonomic determinism: The modes of autonomic control, the doctrine of autonomic space, and the laws of autonomic constraint. *Psychological Review, 98,* 459–487.

Berntson, G. G., Cacioppo, J. T., & Quigley, K. S. (1993). Cardiac psychophysiology and autonomic space in humans: Empirical perspectives and conceptual implications. *Psychological Bulletin, 114,* 296–322.

Berntson, G. G., Cacioppo, J. T., & Sarter, M. (2003). Bottom-up: Implications for neurobehavioral models of anxiety and autonomic regulation. In R. J. Davidson, K. R. Sherer, & H. H. Goldsmith (Eds.), *Handbook of affective sciences* (pp. 1105–1116). New York: Oxford University Press.

Berntson, G. G., Sarter, M., & Cacioppo, J. T. (1998). Anxiety and cardiovascular reactivity: The basal forebrain cholinergic link. *Behavioural Brain Research, 94,* 225–248.

Blumenthal, S., Matthews, K. A., & Weiss, S. (1994). *New research frontiers in behavioral medicine: Proceedings of the national conference.* Washington, DC: NIH Publications.

Brown, R. E. (1994). *An introduction to neuroendocrinology.* New York: Cambridge University Press.

Burns, V. E., Ring, C., Drayson, M., & Carroll, D. (2002). Cortisol and cardiovascular reactions to mental stress and antibody status following hepatitis B vaccination: A preliminary study. *Psychophysiology, 39,* 361–368.

Cacioppo, J. T. (1994). Social neuroscience: Autonomic, neuroendocrine, and immune responses to stress. *Psychophysiology, 31,* 113–128.

Cacioppo, J. T., Berntson, G. G., Binkley, P. F., Quigley, K. S., Uchino, B. N., & Fieldstone, A. (1994). Autonomic cardiac control. II. Non-invasive indices and baseline response as revealed by autonomic blockades. *Psychophysiology, 31,* 586–598.

Cacioppo, J. T., Berntson, G. G., Malarkey, W. B., Kiecolt-Glaser, J. K., Sheridan, J. F., Poehlmann, K. M., et al. (1998). Autonomic, neuroendocrine, and immune responses to psychological stress: The reactivity hypothesis. *Annals of the New York Academy of Sciences, 840,* 664–673.

Cacioppo, J. T., Berntson, G. G., Sheridan, J. F., & McClintock, M. K. (2000). Multi-level integrative analyses of human behavior: Social neuroscience and the complementing nature of social and biological approaches. *Psychological Bulletin, 126,* 829–843.

Cacioppo, J. T., Burleson, M. H., Poehlmann, K. M., Malarkey, W. B., Kiecolt-Glaser, J. K., Berntson, et al. (2000). Autonomic and neuroendocrine responses to mild psychological stressors: Effects of chronic stress on older women. *Annals of Behavioral Medicine, 22,* 140–148.

Cacioppo, J. T., Hawkley, L. C., Berntson, G. G., Ernst, J. M., Gibbs, A. C., Stickgold, R., et al. (2002). Lonely days invade the nights: Social modulation of sleep efficiency. *Psychological Science, 13,* 384–387.

Cacioppo, J. T., Kiecolt-Glaser, J. K., Malarkey, W. B., Laskowski, B. F., Rozlog, L. A., Poehlmann, K. M., et al. (2002). Autonomic glucocorticoid associations with the steady state expression of latent Epstein-Barr virus. *Hormones and Behavior, 42,* 32–41.

Cacioppo, J. T., Malarkey, W. B., Kiecolt-Glaser, J. K., Uchino, B. N., Sgoutas-Emch, S. A., Sheridan, J. F., et al. (1995). Heterogeneity in neuroendocrine and immune responses to brief psychological stressors as a function of autonomic cardiac activation. *Psychosomatic Medicine, 57,* 154–164.

Cacioppo, J. T., Uchino, B. N., & Berntson, G. G. (1994). Individual differences in the autonomic origins of heart rate reactivity: The psychometrics of respiratory sinus arrhythmia and preejection period. *Psychophysiology, 31,* 412–419.

Cannon, W. B. (1928). The mechanism of emotional disturbance of bodily functions. *New England Journal of Medicine, 198,* 877–884.

Cannon, W. B. (1929). Organization for physiological homeostasis. *Physiological Reviews, 9,* 399–431.

Cannon, W. B. (1939). *The wisdom of the body* (2nd Ed.) London: Kegan Paul, Trench, Trubner.

Chrousos, G. P. (2000). The stress response and immune function: Clinical implications. The 1999 Novera H. Spector Lecture. *Annals of the New York Academy of Sciences, 917,* 38–67.

Cohen, S. (1991). Social supports and physical health: Symptoms, health behaviors and infectious disease. In A. L. Greene, M. Cummings, & K. H. Karraker (Eds.), *Life-span developmental psychology: Perspectives on stress and coping* (pp. 213–234). Hillsdale, NJ: Erlbaum.

Cohen, S. (1996). Psychological stress, immunity, and upper respiratory infections. *Current Directions in Psychological Science, 5,* 86–90.

Cohen, S., Tyrrell, D. A., & Smith, A. P. (1991). Psychological stress and susceptibility to the common cold. *New England Journal of Medicine. 325,* 606–612.

Cohn, M., & Langman, R. E. (1990). The protection: The unit of humoral immunity selected by evolution. *Immunological Review, 115,* 11–147.

Collins, S., & Surwit, R. S. (2001). The beta-adrenergic receptors and the control of adipose tissue metabolism and thermogenesis. *Recent Progress in Hormone Research, 56,* 309–328.

Dantzer, R., Bluthe, R., Laye, S., Bret-Dibat, J., Parnet, P., & Kelley, K. W. (1998). Cytokines and sickness behavior. *Annals of the New York Academy of Sciences, 840,* 586–590.

Davidson, R. J. (1998). Affective style and affective disorders: Perspectives from affective neuroscience. *Cognition and Emotion, 12,* 307–330.

De Kloet, E. R., Vreugdenhil, E., Oitzl, M. S., & Joels, M. (1998). Brain cortico-steroid receptor balance in health and disease. *Endocrine Review, 19,* 269–301.

Dhabhar, F. S., & McEwen, B. S. (1997). Acute stress enhances while chronic stress suppresses cell-mediated immunity in vivo: A potential role for leukocyte trafficking. *Brain, Behavior, and Immunity, 11,* 286–306.

Dworkin, B. R. (2000). Introception. In J. T. Cacioppo, L. G. Tassinary, & G. G. Berntson (Eds.), *Handbook of psychophysiology* (pp. 459–481). Cambridge, England: Cambridge University Press.

Dworkin, B. R., & Dworkin, S. (1995). Learning of physiological responses: II. Classical conditioning of the baroreflex. *Behavioral Neuroscience, 109,* 1119–1136.

Dworkin, B. R., Elbert, T., & Rau, H. (2000). Blood pressure elevation as a coping response. In P. McCabe, N. Schneiderman, T. M. Field, & A. R. Wellens (Eds.), *Stress, coping and the cardiovascular system* (pp. 51–69). Mahwah, NJ: Erlbaum.

Garrett, L. (2000). *Betrayal of trust: The collapse of global public health.* New York: Hyperion.

Gehring, W., & Pickering, T. G. (1995). Association between delayed recovery of blood pressure after acute mental stress and parental history of hypertension. *Journal of Hypertension, 13,* 603–610.

Geising, A., Bilang-Bleurel, A., Droste, S. K., Linthorst, A. C. E., Holsboer, F., & Reul, J. M. H. M. (2001). Psychological stress increases hippocampal mineralocorticoid receptor levels: Involvement of corticotropin-releasing hormone. *Journal of Neuroscience, 21,* 4822–4829.

Germain, R. N. (2000). The art of the probable: System control in the adaptive immune system. *Science, 293,* 240–245.

Glaser, R., Kutz, L. A., MacCallum, R. C., & Malarkey, W. B. (1995). Hormonal modulation of Epstein-Barr virus replication. *Neuroendocrinology, 62,* 356–361.

Glaser, R., Pearson, G. R., Bonneau, R. H., Esterling, B. A., Atkinson, C., & Kiecolt-Glaser, J. K. (1993). Stress and the memory T-cell response to the Epstein-Barr virus in healthy medical students. *Health Psychology, 12,* 435–442.

Glaser, R., Pearson, G. R., Jones, J. F., Hillhouse, J., Kennedy, S., Mao, H., & Kiecolt-Glaser, J. K. (1991). Stress related activation of Epstein-Barr virus. *Brain Behavior Immunology, 5,* 219–232.

Glaser, R., Rice, J., Sheridan, J., Fertel, R., Stout, J., Speicher, C. E., et al. (1987). Stress-related immune suppression: Health implications. *Brain Behavior Immunology, 1,* 7–20.

Hansen, M. K., Daniels, S., Goehler, L. E., Gaykema, R. P., Maier, S. F., & Watkins, L. R. (2000). Subdiaphragmatic vagotomy does not block intraperitoneal lipopolysaccharide-induced fever. *Autonomic Neuroscience, 85*(1–3), 83–87.

Hansen, M. K., O'Connor, K. A., Goehler, L. E., Watkins, L. R., & Maier, S. F. (2001). The contribution of the vagus nerve in interleukin-1β-induced fever is dependent on dose. *American Journal of Regulatory Integrative Comparative Physiology, 280,* R929–R934.

Hawkley, L. C., & Cacioppo, J. T. (2003). Loneliness and pathways to disease. *Brain, Behavior, and Immunity, 17*(Supplement 1), S98–S105.

Hobbs, F., & Stoops, N. (2002). *Demographic trends in the 20th century.* U.S. Census Bureau, Census 2000 Special Reports, Series CENSR-4. Washington, DC: U.S. Government Printing Office.

Holmes, T. H., & Rahe, R. H. (1967). The social readjustment rating scale. *Journal of Psychosomatic Research, 11,* 213–218.

Johnson, A. K., & Anderson, E. A. (1990). Stress and arousal. In J. T. Cacioppo & L. G. Tassinary (Eds.), *Principles of psychophysiology* (pp. 216–252). New York: Cambridge University Press.

Kandel, E. R., & Squire, L. R. (2000). Breaking down scientific barriers to the study of brain and mind. *Science, 290,* 1113–1120.

Kaplan, J. R., & Manuck, S. B. (2003). Monkeying around with coronary disease: Status, stress, and atherosclerosis. In F. Kessel, Rosenfield & N. Anderson, (Eds.), *Expanding the boundaries of health and social science: Case studies in interdisciplinary innovation* (pp. 68–94). New York: Oxford University Press.

Kaplan, J. R., Pettersson, K., Manuck, S. B., & Olsson, G. (1991). Role of sympathoadrenal medullary activation in the initiation and progression of atherosclerosis. *Circulation, 84* (Suppl VI), VI-23–VI-32.

Kasl, S. V., Evans, A. S., & Niederman, J. C. (1979). Psychosocial risk factors in the development of infectious mononucleosis. *Psychosomatic Medicine, 41,* 445–466.

Kasprowicz, A. L., Manuck, S. B., Malkoff, S. B., & Krantz, D. S. (1990). Individual differences in behaviorally evoked cardiovascular response: Temporal stability and hemodynamic patterning. *Psychophysiology, 27,* 605–619.

Kiecolt-Glaser, J. K., Glaser, R., Gravenstein, S., Malarkey, W. B., & Sheridan, J. (1996). Chronic stress alters the immune response to influenza virus vaccine in older adults. *Proceedings of the National Academy of Sciences: United States of America, 93,* 3043–3047.

Kiecolt-Glaser, J. K., Marucha, P. T., Malarkey, W. B., Mercado, A. M., & Glaser, R. (1995). Slowing of wound healing by psychological stress. *Lancet, 346,* 1194–1196.

Kiecolt-Glaser, J. K., Page, G. G., Marucha, P. T., MacCallum, R. C., & Glaser, R. (1998). Psychological influences on surgical recovery. *American Psychologist, 53,* 1209–1218.

Krantz, D. S., & Manuck, S. B. (1984). Acute psychophysiologic reactivity and risk of cardio-vascular disease: A review and methodologic critique. *Psychological Bulletin, 96,* 435–464.

Lacey, J. I. (1959). Psychophysiological approaches to the evaluation of psychotherapeutic process and outcome. In E. A. Rubinstein & M. B. Parloff (Eds.), *Research in psychotherapy* (pp. 160–208). Washington, DC: American Psychological Association.

Lazarus, R. S., & Folkman, S. (1984). *Stress, appraisal, and coping.* New York: Springer.

Lewontin, R. (2000). *The triple helix.* Cambridge, MA: Harvard University Press.

Light, K. C., Dolan, C. A., Davis, M. R., & Sherwood, A. (1992). Cardiovascular responses to an active coping challenge as predictors of blood pressure patterns 10 to 15 years later. *Psychosomatic Medicine, 54,* 217–230.

Light, K. C., Girdler, S. S., & Hinderliter, A. L. (2003). Genetic and behavioral factors in combination influence risk of hypertensive heart disease. In N. Anderson, F. Kessel, & P. Rosen-field (Eds.), *Expanding the boundaries of health: Bio-behavioral-social perspectives* (pp. 41–67). New York: Oxford University Press.

Light, K. C., Turner, J. R., Hinderliter, A. L., Girdler, S. S., & Sherwood, A. (1994). Comparison of cardiac versus vascular reactors and ethnic groups in plasma epinephrine and norepinephrine responses to stress. *International Journal of Behavioral Medicine, 3,* 229–246.

Lithgow, G. J., & Kirkwood, T. B. L. (1996). Mechanisms and evolution of aging. *Science, 273,* 80–81.

Llabre, M. M., Klein, B. R., Saab, P. G., McCalla, J. B., & Schneiderman, N. (1998). Classification of individual differences in cardiovascular respon-sivity: The contribution of reactor type control-ling for race and gender. *International Journal of Behavioral Medicine, 5,* 213–229.

Lovallo, W. R. (1997). *Stress and health.* Thousand Oaks, CA: Sage.

Lupien, S. J., & McEwen, B. S. (1997). The acute effects of corticosteroids on cognition: Integration of animal and human model studies. *Brain Research. Brain Research Reviews, 24,* 1–27.

Luskin, F., & Newell, K. (1997). Mind-body approaches to successful aging. In A. Watkins (Ed.), *Mind-body medicine: A clinician's guide to psychoneuroimmunology* (pp. 251–268). New York: Churchill Livingstone.

Madden, K. S., Thyagarajan, S., & Felten, D. L. (1998). Alterations in sympathetic noradrenergic innervation in lymphoid organs with age. *Annals of the New York Academy of Sciences, 840,* 262–268.

Maier, S. F., & Watkins, L. R. (1998). Cytokines for psychologists: Implications of bidirectional immune-to-brain communication for understand-ing behavior, mood, and cognition. *Psychological Review, 105,* 83–107.

Manuck, S. B., Cohen, S., Rabin, B. S., Muldoon, M. F., & Bachen, E. A. (1991). Individual differences in cellular immune response to stress. *Psychological Science, 2,* 111–115.

Marucha, P. T., Kiecolt-Glaser, J. K., & Favagehi, M. (1998). Mucosal wound healing is impaired by examination stress. *Psychosomatic Medicine, 60,* 362–365.

Mason, J. W. (1975). An historical view of the stress field: Part II. *Journal of Human Stress, 1,* 22–35.

McCann, S. M., Lipton, J. M., Sternberg, E. M., Chrousos, G. P., Gold, P. W., & Smith, C. C. (Eds.). (1998). Neuroimmunomodulation: Molecular aspects, integrative systems, and clinical advances. *Annals of the New York Academy of Sciences, 840.*

McEwen, B. S. (1998) Protective and damaging effects of stress mediators. *New England Journal of Medicine, 338,* 171–179.

McEwen, B. S., & Seeman T. (2003). Stress and affect: Applicability of the concepts of allostasis and allostatic load. In R. J. Davidson, K. R. Sherer, & H. H. Goldsmith (Eds.), *Handbook of affective sciences* (pp. 1117–1138). New York: Oxford University Press.

McEwen, B. S., & Stellar, E. (1993). Stress and the individual: Mechanisms leading to disease. *Archives of Internal Medicine, 153,* 2093–2101.

McKeown, T. (1979). The direction of medical research. *Lancet, 2,* 1281–1284.

Meaney, M. J., Bhatnagar, S., Larocque, S., McCormick, C. M., Shanks, N., Sharma, S., et al. (1996). Early environment and the development of individual differences in the hypothalamic-pituitary-adrenal stress response. In C. R. Pfeffer (Ed.), *Severe stress and mental disturbance in children* (pp. 85–127). Washington, DC: American Psychiatric Press.

Munck, A., Guyre, P. M., & Holbrook, N. J. (1984). Physiological functions of glucocorticoids in stress and their relation to pharmacological actions. *Endocrine Reviews, 5,* 25–44.

Norman, A. W., & Litwack, G. (1987). *Hormones.* Orlando, FL: Academic Press.

Padgett, D. A., Marucha, P. T., and Sheridan, J. F. (1998). Restraint stress slows cutaneous wound healing in mice. *Brain, Behavior and Immunity, 12,* 64–73.

Sapolsky, R. M. (1996). Why stress is bad for your brain. *Science, 273,* 749–750.

Scherer, K., Schorr, A., & Johnstone, T. (2001). *Appraisal processes in emotion.* New York: Oxford University Press.

Selye, H. (1956). *The stress of life.* New York: McGraw-Hill.

Selye, H. (1973). Homeostasis and heterostasis. *Perspectives in Biology and Medicine, 16,* 441–445.

Sgoutas-Emch, S. A., Cacioppo, J. T., Uchino, B., Malarkey, W., Pearl, D., Kiecolt-Glaser, J. K., et al. (1994). The effects of an acute psychological stressor on cardiovascular, endocrine, and cellular immune response: A prospective study of individuals high and low in heart rate reactivity. *Psychophysiology, 31,* 264–271.

Sheridan, J. F. (1998). Stress-induced modulation of anti-viral immunity. *Brain, Behavior and Immunity, 12,* 1–6.

Sherwood, A., Dolan, C. A., & Light, K. C. (1990). Hemodynamics of blood pressure responses during active and passive coping. *Psychophysiology, 27,* 656–668.

Sterling, P., & Eyer, J. (1988). Allostasis: A new paradigm to explain arousal pathology. In S. Fisher & J. Reason (Eds.), *Handbook of life stress, cognition and health* (pp. 629–649). New York: Wiley.

Sternberg, E. (2000). *The balance within.* New York: Freeman.

Temple, L. K. F., McLeod, R. S., Gallinger, S., & Wright, J. G. (2001). Defining disease in the genomics era. *Science, 293,* 807–808.

Tomaka, J., Blascovich, J., Kibler, J., & Ernst, J. M. (1997). Cognitive and physiological antecedents of threat and challenge appraisal. *Journal of Personality and Social Psychology, 73,* 63–72.

Turner, R. J. (1989). Individual differences in heart rate response during behavioral challenge. *Psychophysiology, 26,* 497–505.

Uchino, B. N., Cacioppo, J. T., Malarkey, W. B., Glaser, R., & Kiecolt-Glaser, J. K. (1995). Appraisal support predicts age-related differences in cardiovascular function in women. *Health Psychology, 14,* 556–562.

Wilkinson, D. J., Thompson, J. M., Lambert, G. W., Jennings, G. L., Schwarz, R. G., Jefferys, D., et al. (1998). Sympathetic activity in patients with panic disorder at rest, under laboratory mental stress, and during panic attacks. *Archives of General Psychiatry, 55,* 211–220.

Margaret E. Kemeny

Psychoneuroimmunology

Psychoneuroimmunology is an interdisciplinary field that involves the investigation of the bidirectional relationships between the mind, brain, and immune system and the implications of these relationships for clinical disease. This field is highly relevant to health psychology for a number of reasons. First, studies in this field examine the physiological linkages that explain relationships between psychological factors and the etiology and progression of disease. The immune system is a major pathophysiological system whose dysfunctions can play a critical role in the etiology and progression of a variety of diseases, including infections, the autoimmune diseases (such as rheumatoid arthritis), some forms of cancer, and even cardiovascular disease. By understanding how psychological factors and their neurophysiological correlates affect the immune system, it is possible to flesh out part of the mechanistic pathway that links psychological factors to disease. Specifying a mechanistic or mediational pathway is central to establishing a causal relationship between a specific psychological factor and a health outcome (see Figure 5.1 for an X-Y-Z schematic representation of central components of this pathway; Kemeny, 2003). Psychoneuroimmunology studies can provide evidence for each of the links in this pathway and can point to critical psychological elicitors and mediating systems.

Second, the immune system can affect the brain and alter learning, memory, mood, cognition, and motivation. Findings related to these effects can foster a greater understanding of the psychological sequelae of immune-related diseases and can contribute to the development of effective interventions for reducing the adverse psychological effects of such conditions. For example, alterations in cognition and mood can occur with inflammatory diseases, such as systemic lupus erythematosus (SLE), and there is evidence suggesting that some of these neurophysiological effects may be a function of inflammatory processes acting on the brain. Finally, on a conceptual level, research in psychoneuroimmunology can shed light on the adaptive bidirectional linkages across the neurophysiological, behavioral, and immune systems. For example, the field is demonstrating that behavior can be shaped by products of the immune system as part of an integrated recuperative response following injury or infection.

Historical Overview

The nervous system is known to regulate most organ systems (e.g., the endocrine system, cardiovascu-

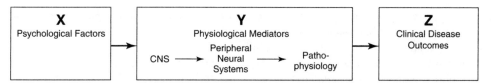

Figure 5.1. The X-Y-Z model for investigating linkages between psychological processes, physiological mediators, and disease progression. Reprinted from M. E. Kemeny, 2003, An interdisciplinary research model to investigate psychosocial cofactors in disease: Application to HIV-1 pathogenesis, *Brain, Behavior, and Immunity, 17,* S67–S72, with permission from Elsevier.

lar system, respiratory system). However, until relatively recently, the immune system was assumed to be autonomous, without major input from the brain. Research in psychoneuroimmunology over the past 20 years has challenged this assumption by documenting bidirectional communication between the central nervous system (CNS; the brain and spinal cord) and the immune system (the cells and organs that play a role in response to pathogens). The earliest findings formed the groundwork for the conceptual leap that was necessary for investigators to begin to consider possible linkages between these two systems. For example, in the early 1960s, Rasmussen and colleagues (Solomon, 1969) demonstrated that stressor exposure in animals could affect the course of viral infections. A critical first chapter in our recognition that the CNS is capable of modulating immune processes began with the work of the psychologist Robert Ader and the immunologist Nicholas Cohen. In 1975, Ader and Cohen reported that the immune system could be classically conditioned. Using a rodent model, an immunosuppressive drug, cyclophosphamide (the unconditioned stimulus), was paired with saccharin (the conditioned stimulus), resulting in immune suppression. Subsequent exposure to saccharin alone was able to induce immune suppression. Clearly, learning occurs in the brain, so these studies were the first to demonstrate communication from the brain to the immune system. At about the same time, Russian investigators made another significant contribution at a neurophysiological level by demonstrating that lesions of the hypothalamus in rodents could alter immune responses in the periphery (Korneva, 1967).

The first "speculative theoretical integration" that laid out a framework for understanding possible linkages between the brain and the immune system was written in 1964 by George Solomon and Rudolph Moos, They suggested that neuroendocrine processes could regulate immunity and introduced the notion that "experience" could impact this system. Solomon and his immunologist colleague Alfred Amkraut went on to show effects of early experience, stressors, and spontaneous behavior on immunity in animals. Another critical milestone was the demonstration by David Felten and Suzanne Felten (1988) that sympathetic nervous system fibers innervate immune organs and alter the activity of resident immune cells, thereby providing a "hardwired" link between the brain and the immune system. The field was catapulted forward in the early 1980s, when the team headed by Janice Kiecolt-Glaser and Ronald Glaser began its program of research documenting the effects of stressful experience on a wide array of immune functions in humans (Kiecolt-Glaser et al., 1984). It was not until the 1990s, however, that researchers began to recognize that not only could behavior and the CNS affect the immune system but immune products could affect the brain and behavior, suggesting a fully bidirectional relationship across these systems.

An Adaptive Integrated System

The changes in immune processes coincident with exposure to stressors and particular psychological responses and behaviors are likely not mere side effects of the neurophysiological impact of such exposures. Activation of stress-responsive systems, such as the hypothalamic-pituitary-adrenal axis (HPA), in response to a threat involves a coordinated and adaptive set of physiological changes, such as the release of bodily fuels to ready the organism for action. Until recently, however, the immunologic changes that often occur following such provocations were believed to be nonfunctional side effects of activation of these stress systems. There is growing evidence that some immune system changes play a critical adaptive role in responding not only to pathogen assault but also to behavioral conditions. These immune changes can be viewed as part of an integrated psychobiological response to specific eliciting conditions (Weiner, 1992).

It is now clear that the brain and the immune system have the "hard-wiring" to allow this kind of ongoing communication to occur. As described in more detail later in the chapter, there are a variety of ways that the brain can "talk" to the immune system. For example, immune cells express receptors not only for proteins produced by other immune cells but also for molecules produced by the brain and neuroendocrine system. Thus, the immune system is equipped to "hear" the messages communicated by these molecules and to be regulated by these systems. In addition, all types of immune organs are innervated by autonomic nervous system fibers, which have functional connections with the immune cells resident in these organs. This neural hard-wiring allows the autonomic nervous system to directly influence the activities of these immune cells, regulating their response to pathogens.

It appears that the immune system can play an adaptive role in three behavioral responses—the fight-or-flight response, recuperation from injury or infection, and a more general disengagement-withdrawal response. The well-articulated *fight-or-flight response* involves higher brain region recognition of a threat that may necessitate physical action and the mobilization of resources to promote bodily systems that can be utilized in such a situation, while down-regulating systems that are not a priority under threatening conditions, such as growth and reproduction (Sapolsky, 1993). This goal shift from resource building in a nonthreat context to resource utilization during a threat activates the sympathetic nervous system, the HPA, and other regulatory systems. Under these circumstances, patterned changes in the immune system are also occurring. Across animal species, white blood cells are shunted from the bloodstream to immune organs such as lymph nodes, bone marrow, the gastrointestinal tract, and the skin (Dhabhar, 2003), and "first line of defense" cells such as natural killer cells are increased in number. Dhabhar and McEwen (2001) argue that this redistribution of immune cells to immune organs may be an integral part of the fight-or-flight response,

which mobilizes physiological systems that can adaptively respond to physical threats, such as predation. One part of this adaptive response may be preparation for the challenge of wounding or infection that may occur during physical stressors that involve fighting or fleeing for example (Dhabhar, 2003; Dhabhar & McEwen, 2001). Higher levels of white blood cells in these "battle station" organs would increase the likelihood of effective response to wounding and infection. A rapid increase in a particular subclass of white blood cells called first line of defense cells would also allow for rapid and nonspecific killing of pathogens that may enter the system through wounds or other injuries (Kemeny & Gruenewald, 2000). Thus, just as activation of stress systems increases respiratory rate and heart rate to prepare the organism for a challenge, these fight-or-flight systems may also ready the organism for wounding and increase chances of survival from resulting infectious agents. Mediation of these acute effects may be via the sympathetic nervous system (SNS), since SNS products increase heart rate and, at the same time, influence the trafficking of white blood cells, as well as the expression of immune molecules that play a central role in trafficking (Ottaway & Husband, 1992).

The immune system also plays a major role in supporting *behavioral recuperation* following infection or injury. As will be described in more detail later, proteins called *pro-inflammatory cytokines* are released during an infection or injury, and these substances orchestrate a number of the immune activities that play a role in killing the pathogen and repairing damaged tissue. At the same time, these molecules act on the brain and cause the animal to withdraw from its normal activities (sexual behavior, exploration, grooming) and engage in recuperative activities, including sleeping. This reorganization of priorities, with resulting changes in behavior, is adaptive because it lowers energy utilization so that available energy can support processes necessary to fight the infection (e.g., fever); it also facilitates the restorative processes required to recuperate from illness and injury (Maier & Watkins, 1998).

In addition to the behavioral disengagement required for efficient recuperation from injury or infection, the immune system can play a role in a more generalized behavioral disengagement in response to specific psychological stressors. A number of studies in humans and animals demonstrate that the pro-inflammatory cytokines that are induced with infection can also be activated with exposure to psychological stressors, outside the context of infection or injury (Maier & Watkins, 1998). The behavioral disengagement that is produced as a result of activation of these cytokines would be a particularly adaptive response to uncontrollable stressors, such as confrontation with a more aggressive or dominant animal (Kemeny, Gruenewald, & Dickerson, 2005). In such contexts, cytokine-induced behaviors such as withdrawal and inhibition of aggression, sexual behavior, and social exploration would be adaptive in that they would reduce the likelihood of attack and injury. The notion of a link between pro-inflammatory cytokine activity and adaptive behavioral disengagement in response to uncontrollable threats is supported by studies of social reorganization using an intruder confrontation model. Pro-inflammatory cytokine responses to confrontation depend on the behavior of the animal. Social reorganization (introducing a dominant rodent into the home cage of other rodents) increases the inflammatory response to an infectious agent and increases systemic levels of corticosterone in home caged animals, suggesting a state of "glucocorticoid resistance" in immune cells. In other words, since corticosteroids are normally immunosuppressive, this pattern of results suggests that the immune cells are *resistant* to the effects of this hormone. Further work confirmed that the subordinate animals in the context of social reorganization show glucocorticoid resistance, resulting in elevated pro-inflammatory cytokine levels, and the level of glucocorticoid resistance was correlated with the frequency of submissive behaviors (Avitsur, Stark, & Sheridan, 2001).

These correlational findings are corroborated in an experimental model in which healthy animals are injected with a pro-inflammatory cytokine. In response to a confrontation with another animal, animals typically display offensive behavior and then switch to defensive behavior if it becomes clear that the contest is uncontrollable and they are likely to lose. However, animals injected with a pro-inflammatory cytokine display no offensive behavior but instead display only defensive elements such as upright defensive posture and submissive posture (Cirulli, De Acetis, & Alleva, 1998). Thus, an uncontrollable social threat may induce the release of these cytokines or resistance to the anti-inflammatory effects of corticosteroids, resulting in increased levels of pro-inflammatory cytokines, which then pro-

motes or maintains the behavioral disengagement that is observed in subordinate animals exhibiting submissive behavior and a defeated posture. Since subordinate animals are more likely to be wounded than dominants, this cytokine activation would also be adaptive in promoting wound healing.

In some human studies of acute laboratory stressors, levels of pro-inflammatory cytokines are increased, but in other cases they are not. A perusal of the elicitors across these studies indicates that those studies that utilized an uncontrollable social threat (performing difficult tasks without the possibility of success in front of an evaluative audience) showed consistent increases in these cytokines, whereas those without this type of uncontrollable social threat did not (Ackerman, Martino, Heyman, Moyna, & Rabin, 1998; Dickerson, Gruenewald, & Kemeny, 2004). Uncontrollable social threats may represent a set of uncontrollable conditions that are capable of activating the production of pro-inflammatory cytokines and eliciting behavioral disengagement in animals and humans.

Although activation of stress systems and resulting alterations in the immune system may be adaptive under certain circumstances in the short run, persistent alteration in these systems could result in vulnerability to disease. Allostatic load, a concept coined by Bruce McEwen (1998), refers to the consequences of prolonged exposure to stress hormones, or a cumulative toll on the body due to chronic overactivation of stress-responsive systems. These response patterns are thought to increase the risk of a number of negative health outcomes, such as diabetes, hypertension, cancer, and cardiovascular disease (McEwen, 1998). In the case of the immune system, long-term down-regulation of certain immune parameters as a result of chronic exposure to stressors could increase vulnerability to infection or, in certain cases, tumors. At the same time, chronic *overactivation* of certain immune processes, as in the systems described earlier that regulate inflammation, could increase vulnerability to autoimmune disorders (which involve overactivity of certain immune processes) or cardiovascular disease (which can be promoted by inflammatory mediators).

The Immune System

The immune system serves a variety of functions, including destruction and clearance of foreign pathogens (viruses, bacteria) and destruction of host cells that have become altered, as in the case of the formation of tumor cells. A number of "key players" form the central cellular components of the immune response. Immune cells are leukocytes or white blood cells that fall into three classes: polymorphonuclear granulocytes (e.g., neutrophils), lymphocytes (e.g., T cells, B cells), and monocytes. These cells can be found in the bloodstream, in the lymphatic vessels and nodes, and in a variety of immune organs such as the bone marrow, thymus, spleen, and gastrointestinal tract. When a pathogen enters the body (e.g., is breathed in) and is not ejected or destroyed by the body's nonimmunological defenses (e.g., coughing), it can come into contact with immune cells in the local tissue or in the lymphatic vessels or nodes. Without adequate defense, the consequence of infection of local tissue can be tissue damage and organ impairment. For example, viruses can infect host cells, replicate within those cells, and destroy them.

A *first line of defense* against invading organisms is the process of inflammation. Inflammation is a complex set of events that bring immune cells into infected areas so that pathogens can be destroyed or inactivated and damage to the infected area can be limited. As a result of the production of mediators of inflammation, blood vessels to the infected area are dilated and become more permeable so immune products can enter the area. Immune cells are chemically attracted to the area (chemotaxis), the tissue swells from increased release of immune fluids, the invader is attacked and often destroyed, and the area is walled off and tissue is repaired. Systemic fever is induced as part of this adaptive response because immune cells can proliferate more efficiently at higher than normal temperatures and many pathogens are less effective at these temperatures.

One cell plays a primary role in the initial first line of defense process—the *macrophage*. Macrophages (also called *monocytes*) can engulf, digest, and process foreign organisms, alert other cells to the infection, and produce specific proteins called *proinflammatory cytokines,* which promote inflammatory reactions. A number of pro-inflammatory cytokines play a key role in this process, including interleukins 1 and 6 (IL-1, IL-6) and tumor necrosis factor α. There are also anti-inflammatory cytokines, such as interleukin-4, 5, and 10, that dampen the inflammatory response and inhibit specific immune cell functions relevant to inflammation.

Another cell that is capable of acting quickly in a nonspecific way at this early stage is the natural killer (NK) cell. NK cells are lymphocytes that can kill virally infected cells and can produce substances (called *interferon*) that inhibit viral replication. These cells can also kill tumor cells in vitro and may play this role in the body as well.

The *second line of defense* involves two other types of cells, the T and B cells, and requires specificity (a match between the immune cell and the specific pathogen or pathogen component, called the *antigen*). The CD8 suppressor/cytotoxic T cell is capable of killing virally infected cells. The CD4 helper T cell releases a variety of types of cytokines that promote the functioning of cytotoxic T cells and B cells, for example (see Table 5.1). B cells produce antibody molecules that can neutralize pathogens, participate in a number of other immune responses (such as the complement cascade), and facilitate cytotoxicity by T cells and NK cells. T and B cells are involved in specific immunity in that they require a match in surface receptors with the pathogen before activation and cell function can occur. A great deal of the orchestration and balance of help and suppression of various immune processes results from the activities of various types of the communication molecules called *cytokines* (Sherwood, 1993).

A number of methods of assessing immune processes are used to determine if psychological factors are capable of altering this system. First, immune cells can be enumerated, or counted. Knowing the impact of a stressor, for example, on the number and proportion of various immune subsets is important, since an immune response requires adequate numbers of the various subclasses of cells. For example, the HIV virus is capable of infecting and killing the CD4 helper T cell, resulting in significant loss of these cells. This loss plays a major role in the immune deficiency that can result from HIV infection, leaving the host vulnerable to a range of diseases. The number of CD4 helper T cells (per cubic millimeter of blood) is a critically important value that predicts AIDS onset and mortality.

Second, immune assays can test the functions of immune cells. For example, assays can determine if immune cells produce antibody in response to stimuli, are capable of killing virally infected cells or tumor cells, produce different classes of cytokines, and so on. There is no one immune assay that can determine the capacity of the immune system to

Table 5.1. Immune Cell Functions
(% of Total Leukocytes)

Macrophage/monocytes (2–8%)
  • Engulf/digest organism
  • Antigen presentation
  • Cytokine production (IL-1, IL-6, TNF-α)
Lymphocytes (20–40%)
  Natural killer cell
    • Kills virally infected cells nonspecifically
    • Produces interferon
    • Kills tumor cells
  T helper (CD4) cell
    • Cytokine production (II-2, γ IFN)
    • Activates T cytotoxic cells
    • Stimulates B cell maturation and antibody
      production
  T cytotoxic/suppressor (CD8) cell
    • kills virally infected cells specifically
  B cell
    • Antibody production
    • Neutralizes viruses
    • Destroys viruses via complement cascade or
      facilitation of T or NK cytotoxicity
Polymorphonuclear granulocytes (50–70%)
  Neutrophils
    • Digest bacteria
  Eosinophils
    • Kill parasites
  Basophils
    • Increase vessel permeability in inflammatory
      response

defend the body from pathogens, but functional testing can determine the capacity of cells to engage in a wide array of essential immune functions. Three immune assays are commonly utilized in psychoneuroimmunology studies. The *natural killer cell activity assay* (NKCA) determines whether natural killer cells are capable of killing tumor cells in a test tube. *Lymphocyte proliferative capacity* captures a central function of lymphocytes, the ability to proliferate in response to a foreign challenge. This proliferation (cell division) provides the "army" of cells required to mount a defense against a particular pathogen. *Cytokine production* can be determined so that the ability of cells to produce these critical communication molecules can be determined. There is a great deal of interest in cytokines, since these proteins coordinate a variety of immune functions.

Although most immune cells utilized in these methods are derived from the bloodstream, it is important to determine the functioning of immune cells in immune organs and tissues that are directly involved in the immune response to pathogens. For example, investigators are now creating injuries or wounding of the skin and looking at tissue repair and *wound healing* mechanisms. Also, substances (e.g., antigens) can be placed under the skin to elicit an immune response, and the tissue can be examined using immunohistochemistry to determine, for example, which cells are present and activated. Cells from the lungs, gastrointestinal tract, and other organs can be obtained for assessments similar to those used to examine the functions of immune cells in the blood.

Physiological Systems That Affect the Immune System

How does the brain come in contact with the immune system and play a role in its regulation? One pathway is via the autonomic nervous system. The second pathway is via factors released in the brain that activate organs to produce hormones that affect immune cells and organs. The HPA axis that releases the glucocorticoids (e.g., cortisol) is a major endocrine relay from the CNS to the immune system.

Hypothalamic-Pituitary-Adrenal Axis

The hypothalamic-pituitary-adrenal (HPA) is a system that can become activated in response to specific stressful stimuli. Neural pathways link perception and appraisal of a stimulus to an integrated response in the hypothalamus, which results in the release of corticotropin releasing hormone (CRH). CRH travels to the anterior pituitary gland and stimulates adrenal cells to release adrenocorticotropic hormone (ACTH) into the bloodstream. ACTH travels to the adrenal glands and causes the adrenal cortex to release cortisol into the bloodstream. These changes occur as a part of normal physiological functioning and can become accentuated during stressful encounters. The glucocorticoids are part of a complicated signaling system that integrates brain and body in response to the environment, regulating behaviors such as wake-sleep cycles with physiological responses such as metabolism (McEwen et al., 1997).

Cortisol can have profound effects on a variety of physiological systems, including the immune system. Cortisol can act on lymphocytes and inhibit a wide variety of lymphocyte functions, including the ability to proliferate. It can also slow integrated immune responses such as wound healing. Cortisol can be considered the body's own anti-inflammatory because it can act on immune cells to inhibit the production of pro-inflammatory cytokines (such as IL-1, IL-6), just as its synthetic form, cortisone, reduces inflammation on the skin or in various organs. At the same time, pro-inflammatory cytokines can activate the HPA, causing the release of cortisol. Over the past 10 years, it has become clear that there is a bidirectional cytokine-HPA network that is responsive to exposure to stressful circumstances.

Autonomic Nervous System

The autonomic nervous system (ANS) is divided into three parts, the sympathetic nervous system, the parasympathetic nervous system, and the enteric nervous system (which regulates the gastrointestinal tract). The sympathetic nervous system controls a variety of involuntary bodily functions that must be up-regulated in response to threats, for example, the cardiovascular system and the respiratory system. It is considered to be a system designed for mobilization. Thus, in response to acute stressors, individuals often experience symptoms that reflect activation of this system (e.g., acceleration of heart rate, breathing rate). The parasympathetic nervous system controls involuntary resting functions (such as digestion, reproduction) and activates organ systems to play a restorative role when the organism is not threatened. In addition, it actively inhibits sympathetic activity, for example, by inhibiting heart rate, resulting in a calming of the individual. The neurotransmitter released by sympathetic fibers is norepinephrine (noradrenalin), and the neurotransmitter released by parasympathetic fibers is acetylcholine. Walter Cannon, in the 1930s, demonstrated that exposure to emergency situations resulted in the release of the hormone epinephrine (adrenalin) from the adrenal medulla. Sympathetic innervation of the adrenal medulla and release of norepinephrine cause the release of epinephrine from the adrenal medulla into the bloodstream.

Autonomic nervous system fibers are directly connected to the immune system. Noradrenergic fibers innervate virtually all immune organs, including primary immune organs (thymus and bone marrow) and secondary organs (lymph nodes, Peyer's patches in the gut). These neural fibers release their neurotransmitters in close proximity to immune cells in these organs. Immune cells express receptors for these neurotransmitters (α and β adr-

energic receptors), allowing them to be affected by the ANS. Studies that involve interfering with ANS connections to immune organs (e.g., by chemically denervating these organs) demonstrate alterations in the functioning of resident immune cells, thus indicating a functional link between the ANS and the activity of cells residing in these organs (Bellinger et al., 2001).

A variety of human studies demonstrate linkages between these two systems. For example, administration of epinephrine can greatly alter the number of circulating CD4 helper T cells within 15 minutes. Evidence also suggest that sympathetic activity mediates effects of acute stressful experience on certain immune functions, since administration of beta blockers, which block the activity of sympathetic hormones, can eliminate effects of acute stressors on certain immune functions (Elenkov, Wilder, Chrousos, & Vizi, 2000).

Other Physiological Systems

Other physiological systems also affect the immune system and may play a role in the relationship between psychological factors and immune processes. For example, other hormones, such as growth hormone and prolactin, can alter immune functions. Other neuropeptides, such as the opioids (including beta-endorphin and the enkaphalins), have been shown to influence immune functions in vitro (Carr & Weber, 2001).

Learning and the Immune System

One of the most definitive sets of studies demonstrating a link between the mind, brain, and immune system involves the ability of the immune system to be classically conditioned. As noted earlier, Ader and Cohen first demonstrated in 1975 that the taste of saccharin initially paired with an immunosuppressive drug acquired the ability to suppress antibody response in a classical conditioning paradigm. These findings have been replicated and extended to studies of different conditioned and unconditioned stimuli and different responses. For example, conditioned immunoenhancement has also been demonstrated (Solvason, Ghanta, & Hiramoto, 1988). The mechanisms that underlie these effects are unclear; however, Ader and colleagues have demonstrated that they are not due to a conditioned stress response, since these effects can be elicited in animals whose adrenal glands have been removed. An interesting question regards the nature of the constraints on these effects. Can any kind of immunologic alteration be "learned" and therefore affected by the CNS, or are there specific limits to the nature of the effects that can be conditioned?

One of the important implications of this area of research is the possibility that such paradigms could be used to alter immune processes in such a way as to benefit health. These conditioned immune changes, although small, have in fact been shown to be clinically significant in animals. Specifically, the conditioning paradigm was applied to mice genetically susceptible to a systemic lupus erythematosus (SLE)-like autoimmune disease. In these mice, the immunosuppressive drug cyclophosphamide prolongs life because it controls the overactive immune response that is central to this autoimmune disease. Mice given a schedule of saccharin-flavored water that had been paired with cyclophosphamide showed prolonged survival (Ader & Cohen, 1982). These studies confirm that the CNS can control immunoregulatory processes and suggests that these relationships have clinical significance (an example of X-Y-Z mechanistic pathways). A few studies suggest that immune responses may be able to be conditioned in humans as well. For example, nausea following chemotherapy can become conditioned to the hospital environment, explaining the frequent observation that cancer patients begin to become nauseous once they enter the hospital for their chemotherapy treatments (Bovjberg et al., 1990).

A number of possible applications of this area of research may follow from this body of work. For example, it may be possible to pair an innocuous substance with an effective drug that has toxic side effects and then, following conditioning, reduce the dosage of the toxic drug, substituting the conditioned substance for some dosages. The innocuous substance could not fully replace the pharmacological agent, however, since the conditioned effects would eventually extinguish. Also, it may be possible to determine whether certain negative physiological or health effects are conditioned to particular environments or other stimuli. If so, detrimental health effects could be reduced via extinction processes. Given the findings mentioned earlier, nausea associated with chemotherapy that has become conditioned to the hospital environment could be reduced with trials of exposure to the hospital environment without subsequent chemotherapy.

Another potentially useful application of our understanding of classical conditioning of the immune system relates to placebo effects in immune-relevant diseases. In the placebo literature, there is evidence of improvement in a variety of diseases with administration of placebo pills or other nonspecific treatments (Guess, Kleinman, Kusek, & Engel, 2002). There is a great deal of controversy in this area regarding the symptoms and conditions amenable to placebo effects; renewed interest in this area should lead to findings that can determine when, under what conditions, and how placebo effects occur. One area of interest and investigation focuses on whether or not some placebo effects are due to prior experience with the pairing of an effective treatment (the unconditioned stimulus) with pill taking (the conditioned stimulus) such that pill taking alone (without the pharmacological stimulus; i.e., the placebo) can elicit similar beneficial physical responses. For example, a placebo pill for the treatment of pain related to joint inflammation may reduce pain because patients have had experience taking effective treatments for reducing these symptoms in the past. In this case, pill taking has been paired with effective pharmacological agents and can therefore alter symptom experience alone. In other words, one possibility is that "harnessing the power of the placebo" might depend on setting up a conditioning trial to maximize the efficacy of the conditioned stimulus (Ader, 2000). An alternative explanation for placebo effects centers on potential mediation by positive treatment-specific expectancies induced by receiving treatment (see the section on expectancy later in the chapter). Research involving a placebo manipulation in the context of pain supports the notion that representations of expectations within certain brain regions may modulate neural activity relevant to placebo outcomes (Wager et al., 2004).

Stress and the Immune System

A large literature indicates that "stress" can impact the immune system. The literature often uses the term *stress* in a vague and inconsistent way, sometimes referring to stress as a stimulus, sometimes as a psychological response, and sometimes as the physiological responses to stressful circumstances. A number of more specific terms can be used instead. *Stressors* or stressful life experiences are circumstances that threaten a major goal. The prototype is a predator attack that threatens the goal of maintaining survival and physical integrity. Other major goals include the maintenance of a positive social self (status), social connectedness, and resources. *Distress* is a negative psychological response to goal threats that can involve a variety of affective and cognitive responses, including fear, hopelessness, sadness, anxiety, frustration, and so on. In the research literature, acute laboratory stressors involve exposure to 20 to 30 minutes of stressful procedures. Acute or short-term naturalistic stressors are time-limited circumstances that last days to weeks, such as taking school exams. Chronic stressors are prolonged, lasting weeks, months, or years, with a waxing and waning of impact (bereavement, job loss, separation).

Exposure to a wide variety of *naturalistic* stressors can impact the immune system. In animals, stressors such as electric shock, restraint, cold water swim, maternal separation, and social defeat have been shown to cause both enumerative and functional alterations in the immune system (Ader, Felten, & Cohen, 2001). In humans, short-term stressors such as medical school examinations, major life change events such as the death of a spouse or divorce, and chronic ongoing difficulties such as caregiving for a loved one with Alzheimer's disease have been found to be associated with changes in the number and proportion of various lymphocyte subsets. Often, following a stressful circumstance, the number of helper T cells, cytotoxic T cells, and natural killers cells is reduced. In addition, these stressors are associated with deficits in the ability of immune cells in vitro to proliferate, kill tumor cells, produce antibody, respond to cytokine signals, and engage in other immune functions (Segerstrom & Miller, 2004). Stressors, such as taking exams, have also been associated with increased levels of antibody to latent viruses such as the Epstein-Barr virus and the herpes simplex virus (HSV), suggesting a decreased capacity of the immune system to control viral latency (Kiecolt-Glaser & Glaser, 2001). Using medical school examinations as a model, Kiecolt-Glaser and Glasser have demonstrated reliable alterations in the immune system with acute naturalistic stressor exposure (Kiecolt-Glaser et al., 1984; Kiecolt-Glaser et al., 1986). More recently, whole integrated local immune responses have been evaluated; for example, naturalistic stressors have been shown to slow wound healing (Kiecolt-Glaser, Marucha, Malarkey, Mercado, & Glaser, 1995). It

does not appear that these stress-related immune alterations are due solely to alterations in health behaviors such as drug or alcohol use, exercise, or altered nutrition.

Stressor exposure can also *enhance* certain immune functions. For example, it appears that certain stressors can increase the inflammatory response by increasing levels of pro-inflammatory cytokines. Although inflammation is an adaptive response to orchestrate the elimination of pathogens and repair damaged tissue, chronic and inappropriate inflammation is believed to play a role in the etiology and progression of inflammatory diseases, such as rheumatoid arthritis, and inflammatory bowel disease, along with other factors. Evidence suggests that the ability of stressor exposure to increase mediators of inflammation may be a result of a stress-related reduction in the sensitivity of immune cells to the inhibitory effects of cortisol, which has been called the *glucocorticoid resistance model* (Miller, Cohen, & Ritchey, 2002). Specifically, immune cells express glucocorticoid receptors that allow them to be affected by cortisol; for example, cortisol inhibits the production of a variety of cytokines. When these receptors are down-regulated, however, the cells do not respond to cortisol signals, so that they do not become inhibited when exposed to increased levels of cortisol. Exposure to chronically stressful experience has been shown to reduce the sensitivity of immune cells to the inhibitory effects of cortisol, thus leading to increases in inflammatory mediators normally constrained by cortisol (Miller, Cohen, et al., 2002).

The size of the effects of stressors on the immune system varies widely, depending on the nature and chronicity of the stressor and the type of immune parameter evaluated. In most cases, it is not known whether the types of immune alterations generated as a result of stressor exposure can in fact increase vulnerability to disease (discussed in more detail later in this chapter).

A large number of studies have demonstrated that acute exposure to *laboratory* stressful experiences can also alter immune processes. Typical laboratory paradigms expose individuals to brief (e.g., 20-min) stressors, such as mental arithmetic, loud noise, difficult puzzles, or giving a speech. Blood is drawn before and immediately after the stressful task. As with naturalistic studies, these brief exposures can impair lymphocyte functions such as the proliferative response and decrease the number of B cells and CD4 helper T cells (Herbert & Cohen, 1993b). However, in contrast to effects of naturalistic studies, natural killer cell activity and the number of natural killer cells (as well as CD8 cells) *increase* after an acute laboratory stressor. These functional changes may be due to increases in the number of natural killer cells in the bloodstream following a stressor, not to changes in the function of cells on a per cell basis. The immune effects observed with acute laboratory stress occur quickly, within 5 minutes, and return to baseline within 30 minutes to 1 hour. The presence of chronic life stressors may accentuate the effects of acute laboratory stressors on certain immune functions (Pike et al., 1997).

Stressor Specificity

Different types of stressors and stressor characteristics can elicit distinctive patterns of immunologic alteration. The duration, intensity, and timing of a stressor can impact the nature of the immune effects. For example, an increasing number of foot shocks per session progressively decreased the proliferative response in rats (Lysle, Lyte, Fowler, & Rabin, 1987). Continuous versus intermittent stress can have different immune consequences in rodents (Shavit et al., 1987). However, little is known about the relationship between stressor characteristics and immune effects in humans. While acute laboratory stressors versus acute naturalistic stressors have different immune effects, as described earlier, it is unclear whether these differences are due to the length of the stressors, the context, or other parameters, for example, timing or the specific nature of the stressors. For example, laboratory stressors (such as giving a speech) are shorter than naturalistic stressors (such as final exams), do not have the lengthy anticipatory period, have different potential consequences and different social contexts, and therefore may induce different cognitive and affective responses. These distinctive psychological responses may then have different neurohormonal correlates and immunologic outcomes.

It is possible that the specific nature of the stressor, apart from timing issues, may elicit a distinctive pattern of neurobiological and peripheral changes to support an adaptive response to the specific nature of the context (Weiner, 1992). Studies in humans that systematically vary these stressor characteristics have not been conducted, so it is unclear which factors explain the different pattern of immune effects. However, evidence that different types of stressors elicit distinct patterns of physiological changes in systems that affect the immune system, such as the HPA and ANS, suggests that the specific nature of the stressor may also be relevant to the pattern of immune effects (Blascovich & Tomaka, 1996; Dickerson & Kemeny, 2004; Pacak & Palkovits, 2001).

Physiological Mediators of Stressor Effects

Sympathetic arousal appears to mediate some of the effects of acute stressors on NKCA and other immune outcomes. For example, in a study of parachute jumping as a stressor, significant elevations in measures of sympathetic arousal occurred during and after the jump, including increases in heart rate, respiratory rate, and release of epinephrine and norepinephrine. In addition, the number of natural killer (NK) cells and NKCA increased during the stressor (the numbers doubled on average). Sympathetic mediation of NK effects was suggested by the fact that the greater the level of norepinephrine produced during the jump, the greater the NKCA increase (Schedlowski et al., 1993). The increases in NK number and activity following acute *laboratory* stressors also appear to be mediated by sympathetic arousal again, because of the correlation between sympathetic activation and NK enhancement (Herbert et al., 1994). Strong support for the mediating role of ANS products comes from studies that show that similar immune effects can be induced with an injection of epinephrine (Van Tits et al., 1990) and that stress effects on this aspect of immunity can be abolished with a β-adrenergic antagonist (Benschop et al., 1994).

Because exposure to some stressors can increase levels of glucocorticoids, and glucocorticoids are potent immunosuppressive substances, it has long been assumed that the HPA axis plays a major mediating role in the effects of stressors on the immune system. Although data are available to support this contention, a number of studies fail to find this relationship. For example, stress-induced immunosuppression can occur in animals whose adrenal glands have been removed (Keller, Weiss, Schleifer, Miller, & Stein, 1983). In some cases, it appears that the glucocorticoids can permit the induction of stress-related immune changes, but they may not be sufficient by themselves (Moynihan & Stevens,

2001). Other systems that have been shown to affect the immune system and mediate stress effects include the opioid peptides. It is likely that the physiological mediation of stress effects will involve multiple, interacting systems and depend on a number of factors, including the nature of the stressor, the condition of the host, the presence of pathogens, and the specific immune parameters under study. Thus, simple pathways from stress to immunity are uncommon.

Individual Difference Factors

Although stressors impact a variety of immune parameters, the effects are not uniform across individuals. Even when the specific nature of the stressor and other contextual factors are held constant as much as is possible, some individuals show immune alterations and some do not. There is a great deal of variability in the magnitude of the changes, their trajectory (speed of onset and recovery), and the aspects of immune function that become altered. There are a variety of potential sources of this variance, including the genetic makeup of the individuals, their health status, the impact of behaviors on their immune status (including recreational drug and alcohol use, exercise, nutrition, smoking), the medication they are taking, and so forth. Despite the relative paucity of research on, for example, the moderating role of genetic factors on the relationship between stressor exposure and immune alteration in humans, it is likely to be a highly fruitful area of research that will produce much more useful findings than studies of environmental or psychological factors alone. For example, studies of strain differences using Lewis versus Fischer rats led to a wealth of information on the linkage between the HPA and inflammatory disease. Specifically, Sternberg and colleagues (Sternberg, 1997) found that Lewis and Fisher rats, which differ in the reactivity of the HPA, also vary in their susceptibility to experimentally induced rheumatoid arthritis and encephalomyelitis. Lewis rats show reduced activity in an open field (a measure of anxiety), have lower HPA activity, and are much more susceptible to these autoimmune diseases.

Individual difference factors related to psychological states and traits are of great interest in the field of psychoneuroimmunology. There can be a great deal of difference in the psychological response to stressors across individuals and within individuals over time. These responses can be tied to individual differences in stable characteristics such as personality and temperament. The specific nature of the psychological response to a stressor may play a critical role in shaping the neurophysiological and consequent immunologic responses observed (Kemeny & Laudenslager, 1999; Segerstrom, Kemeny, & Laudenslager, 1999). Key individual differences in response to circumstances would include the cognitive appraisal and the affective response.

Affect and the Immune System

There is growing evidence that affective response may play an important role in determining the immunologic changes associated with exposure to a stressor. One major support for this premise rests on the emerging evidence that distinctive affective states have different CNS and ANS correlates. For example, neuroimaging studies find that different regions of the brain become activated with different emotional states (Damasio et al., 2000; Lane, Reiman, Ahern, Schwartz, & Davidson, 1997). Studies that induce diverse affective states have shown different patterns of autonomic arousal with certain emotional states (Ekman, Levenson, & Friesen, 1983). For example, skin temperature increases more with anger than with fear. These distinct neural patterns may result in different effects on the immune system, since autonomic fibers innervate immune organs and regulate the activity of the resident immune cells.

Most of the immune studies in this area focus on affective states rather than traits. A few studies suggest a relationship between affective traits and basal immune status or response to stressors, but the results are somewhat limited at this time. One area that appears promising is the utilization of recording of brain electrical activity in the left and right prefrontal cortex as a measure of affectivity. Davidson (1998) has shown that greater relative right prefrontal activation is associated with less positive and more negative trait affect. Individuals with this activation pattern also respond more strongly to negative affective challenges and have higher basal cortisol levels (Kalin, Larson, Shelton, & Davidson, 1998). Davidson and his colleagues have shown lower basal immune function (NKCA) and a greater reduction in function after an examination stressor in individuals with greater right prefrontal activation (Davidson, Coe, Dolski, &

Donzella, 1999; Kang et al., 1991). Thus, this neurophysiological emotion-relevant pattern may predict both basal and stressor-induced immune changes. Other emotion regulation styles, such as trait worry and repressive style, have also been shown to predict immune response to laboratory and naturalistic stressors in some studies (Esterling, Antoni, Kumar, & Schneiderman, 1990; Segerstrom, Glover, Craske, & Fahey, 1999; Segerstrom, Solomon, Kemeny, & Fahey, 1998).

A great deal is known about the relationship between depression and the immune system. Major depression is associated with immune alterations, including functional changes that are similar to those observed with naturalistic stressors (Irwin, Daniels, Bloom, & Weiner, 1986; Schleifer et al., 1984). A meta-analytic review has shown that depression is associated with reliable increases in certain immune subsets (e.g., neutrophils) and decreases in others (B and T cells). Decrements in proliferative capacity, as well as in NKCA, are common (Herbert & Cohen, 1993a). Depressed individuals most vulnerable to immune suppression appear to be those with more severe depression, older age, and melancholia (severe depression with more psychomotor and vitality disturbance), and those who also have a sleep disorder or alcoholism (Irwin, 2001). There is also some evidence that increases in these immune functions can be observed in depressed patients following treatment (Irwin, Lacher, & Caldwell, 1992)

Evidence suggests immune *enhancement* can also occur with depression. In a series of studies by Maes and his colleagues, patients with depressive symptoms or syndromal depression showed evidence of increased levels of pro-inflammatory cytokines, although these findings are not always consistent (Maes et al., 1994). Controlling for a host of potential alternative explanations, such as presence of other medical conditions, medications, and health behaviors such as cigarette smoking, individuals meeting criteria for clinical depression have been shown to have higher levels of IL-6 when compared with demographically matched controls (Miller, Stetler, et al., 2002). In some studies, pharmacological treatment was associated with a reduction in these levels. It has been argued that the relationship between depression and increased levels of pro-inflammatory cytokines may be mediated by glucocorticoid resistance, as described earlier in relation to exposure to chronic stressors.

One of the most provocative aspects of the research on depression and pro-inflammatory cytokines is the hypothesis that these cytokines may play an etiologic role in depression. Four sets of findings support this possibility. First, studies, as described earlier, demonstrate a link between a diagnosis of depression and increased levels of these cytokines. Second, injections of pro-inflammatory cytokines in humans can induce depression-like symptoms, including dysphoria, anhedonia, helplessness, fatigue, and apathy, which regress when treatment has ended (Dunn, Swiergiel, & de Peurepaire, 2005). Third, patients with inflammatory diseases that are often accompanied by elevated levels of pro-inflammatory cytokines have an increased risk for depression. Finally, animals injected with these cytokines either peripherally or centrally show an increase in a number of behaviors that have overlap with depression (Dantzer et al., 2001; Kent, Bluthe, Kelley, & Dantzer, 1992). Specifically, these cytokines can induce what is called "sickness behavior," which includes locomotor retardation, immobility, sleep disorders, anorexia, hyperalgesia, decreased social exploration, inhibition of sexual behavior, and anhedonia. These are symptoms of many illnesses, but most also overlap with the vegetative symptoms of depression. The behavioral changes observed following administration of a pro-inflammatory cytokine are not the result of physical weakness or debilitation but the expression of a shift in motivational state that alters priorities to deal preferentially with combating infection (Dantzer et al., 2001). The changes are adaptive in that they reduce the utilization of unnecessary energy, which can then be redirected to energy-draining aspects of the inflammatory process, such as the development of a fever (Maier & Watkins, 1998). Interestingly, sickness behavior in rats due to injection with pro-inflammatory cytokines can be prevented if the animals are pretreated with certain antidepressant medications (Castanon, Bluthe, & Dantzer, 2001).

Maier and Watkins (1998) have argued that exposure to stressors can increase the production of pro-inflammatory cytokines, which then contributes to the onset of depression via cytokine effects on the CNS. In other words, the known association between exposure to stressful life experience and depression may be mediated, in some cases, by stress-induced increases in the pro-inflammatory cytokines and the sickness behaviors that are engendered. This notion is supported by the research reviewed earlier in the chapter, which indicates that a variety of acute stressors have been associated with elevations in these cytokines, in both animals and humans. However, it appears that *uncontrollable* stressors may preferentially activate this network, leading to depression, since the motivational shifts demonstrated following an injection of IL-1β are consistent with behavioral responses to uncontrollable contexts. As described previously, animals injected with IL-1 exhibit defensive and defeated postures during a confrontation, postures they would assume if the context was uncontrollable and they were destined to lose. Animals that are socially defeated show a greater production of these cytokines than those who are not (Avitsur et al., 2001; Stark et al., 2001). In humans, the results are inconclusive. However, among the small number of laboratory stress studies conducted, those that utilize an uncontrollable social evaluative threat demonstrate a consistent increase in these cytokines, whereas those without this social threat do not (Ackerman et al., 1998). It would be adaptive for uncontrollable stressors to be capable of eliciting cytokine-induced depression-like disengagement from a conservation-withdrawal perspective, for example. However, these behavioral indicators of depression would be maladaptive in response to a controllable circumstance. Other affective states associated with motivational disengagement may also be linked to increases in pro-inflammatory cytokines (see evidence for increases in these cytokines with shame; Dickerson, Kemeny, Azia, Kim, & Fahey, 2004).

A growing but still limited literature suggests that positive affective states may also be associated with immune system changes (Pressman & Cohen, in press). Older literature suggests that positive affect is associated with increases in secretory immunoglobulin A (SIga), an antibody found in the mucosal immune system (e.g., in saliva). Increases have been demonstrated in response to positive mood inductions, such as watching a funny movie, and in tandem with positive mood measured on a day-to-day basis. However, the relevance of this type of change to disease is not clear. Positive affect may also be correlated with increases in the number of certain subsets of white blood cells, although the results are not entirely consistent, and the direction of effects is similar to that found with a stressor exposure. Few studies have examined the relationship between positive affect and functional measures of immune response or whole integrated immune responses (e.g., placing an antigen under the skin and examining the immune response on the skin; Pressman & Cohen, 2005).

Different affective states may have distinctive effects on the immune system. For example, Futterman, Kemeny, Shapiro, and Fahey (1994) conducted an experimental study that manipulated positive and negative mood over a 25-minute period. Results indicated that both positive and negative mood increased NKCA; however, the proliferative response was increased with positive mood and decreased with negative mood. Differential antigen-specific IgA antibody responses have been found to be associated with positive and negative daily mood ratings (Stone, Cox, Valdlmarsdottir, Jandorf, & Neale, 1987). Less work has been conducted differentiating immune correlates of different negative emotions. In a disclosure study, participants wrote about a trivial topic or a situation in which they blamed themselves, in order to elicit the experience of shame (Dickerson, Kemeny, et al., 2004). The self-blame condition induced significantly more shame and guilt than other emotions and also increased the levels of TNF-α receptor, a marker of pro-inflammatory cytokine activity. The greatest increases in TNF were observed in those individuals who reported the greatest increases in shame during the mood induction, while changes in other emotions were not correlated with this immune parameter. These findings suggest that acute affective experience may have immunologic correlates, and that the nature and extent of the immune change may depend on the specific nature of the emotion experienced.

Cognitive Representations and the Immune System

Individuals differ in the way in which they think about themselves, their lives, and others. Representations of the *self* have been investigated in psychology as powerful contributors to mood and motivation. A number of studies suggest that self-representations may also affect neurophysiological systems and the immune system. As described later in the chapter, negative appraisals of self have been shown to predict activation of the HPA in healthy individuals, as well as important immune and health end points in those infected with HIV (Dickerson, Gruenewald, et al., 2004). In addition, following priming of self-representations, greater self discrepancy (or the difference between one's perceived "actual" self and one's "ought" self or "ideal" self) was associated with lower NKCA (Strauman, Lemieux, & Coe, 1993). Along a similar line, a negative attributional style (attributing blame for negative events to internal, stable, and global—rather than specific— causes) has been associated with lower basal phenotypic and functional immune parameters.

Representations of the *future* have also been studied. Whereas dispositional optimism, or the tendency to expect positive outcomes, has been shown to predict a variety of health outcomes, there have been a number of studies that have not found health correlates of this style, reflecting the possibility that this disposition may be adaptive in some contexts and for some individuals but not across the board. However, *state* representations of the future (e.g., expectations about future health) have been shown to predict health outcomes in HIV (see the section on HIV research later in the chapter). Affective states are proposed to mediate the relationships between cognitive representations and physiological parameters; however, it is also possible that cognitive states and their neural substrates can activate physiological changes without the intermediary role of affect (Kemeny & Gruenewald, 2000).

Social Context

There is a long tradition of study of the role that *social support* plays in promoting and maintaining physical health. Across a large number of studies, individuals with confidants (someone they can talk to about problems) and those who have more satisfying social relationships have superior physical health than those with less social support. One possible mechanism of some of these effects is via the immune benefits associated with social support. Individuals who have greater social support may have stronger immune systems (main effect hypothesis), or social support may buffer the effects of stressors on immune processes (buffering hypothesis), or both (Cohen & Wills, 1985).

Increasing evidence indicates that social support is capable of moderating the effects of stressful experience on the immune response. For example, in infant squirrel monkeys, the presence of peers moderated both the hormonal and the immunologic effects of maternal separation (Coe, Rosenberg, & Levine, 1988). In medical students confronting major exam periods, the extent of immune alteration (NKCA, antibody response to EBV) was associated with the degree of loneliness experienced (Kiecolt-

Glaser et al., 1984). In another context, the extent of immune alteration following separation or divorce depended on the level of attachment to the ex-spouse (Kiecolt-Glaser et al., 1984). These conclusions are bolstered by the literature demonstrating protective effects of social support with regard to physiological systems that impact the immune system, such as the autonomic nervous system and the HPA.

Another important social process that appears to play a critical role in regulating social relationships in almost all animal species and humans is *social hierarchy*. Dominant and subordinate animals do not manifest the same neurophysiological and immunologic changes in response to social confrontations. Submissives show more negative physiological alterations (inhibited production of antibody) even three weeks after an encounter with dominant animals (Fleshner, Laudenslager, Simons, & Maier, 1989). The amount of time spent in the defeated posture and antibody levels were highly correlated in this study ($r = -.80$). Immune differences in dominant versus subordinate animals have been demonstrated in a variety of species, including fish, rodents, and primates. For example, in one set of studies by Stefanski and colleagues (Stefanski, 1998), rats were exposed to social confrontation, and the behavioral response of the intruder was characterized as either submissive (defeat posture) or subdominant (without defeat). Basal immune parameters did not differ across the groups; however, after 7 days of confrontation, shifts in lymphocyte subsets were observed, with the largest decreases in the subdominant. Sheridan and colleagues (Avitsur et al., 2001) showed that when rodents were confronted with a very aggressive intruder, they demonstrated nonverbal displays of social defeat and more glucocorticoid resistance than animals that were not exposed to this confrontation. The degree of glucocorticoid resistance correlated with the extent of submissive displays. A larger literature indicates that submissive animals also show increased levels of corticosteroid, with the level correlated positively with the amount of displayed submissive behavior. Thus, altered patterns of HPA activation could mediate immune correlates of low status. Extrapolation of these findings to status differences in humans has been undertaken (Kemeny et al., 2005).

Interventions

If stressors, negative mood, and negative cognitive appraisals can adversely affect the immune system, can psychological interventions that reduce negative states of mind induce immune improvements? At least 100 intervention studies have been conducted with immune end points in healthy individuals, or those with cancer, autoimmune disease, and other conditions. A number of studies have demonstrated short-term immune enhancement following interventions, although the extent of benefit appears to depend on the type of intervention and the aspect of immunity examined (Kemeny & Miller, 1999; Miller & Cohen, 2001).

One of the interesting unexpected findings in this area of research relates to the fact that the interventions that have been found in the past to show the most robust effects on depression, for example, do not appear to show the strongest effects on the immune system. For example, *cognitive behavioral* interventions, which focus on altering maladaptive cognitive responses and have shown psychological benefits for individuals with depression, have shown immunologic effects in some contexts and not in others This may be due to the fact that the majority of participants in these intervention studies do not have elevated levels of depression and are therefore less likely to derive the benefit that a depressed sample would derive (Miller & Cohen, 2001).

Disclosure paradigms involve writing essays about traumatic events. Writing takes place in short sessions (e.g., 20 minutes) over 4 or more days. Engaging in this form of expressive writing has been found to positively impact health care utilization, autonomic nervous system reactivity, and other processes; however, effects on the immune system are mixed. For example, benefits were shown by Petrie, Booth, Pennebaker, Davison, & Thomas (1995), who studied disclosure in 40 medical students who were given a hepatitis B vaccine with boosters at 1 and 4 months after disclosure sessions. Antibody titers to hepatitis B were significantly higher at 1, 4, and 6 months after vaccination in the disclosure group than in the control group. Effects on other immune parameters, including NKCA and lymphocyte subsets, were not observed. Consistent effects of disclosure on specific immune parameters have not yet been demonstrated.

Despite the large literature documenting reductions in distress and physiological arousal with *relaxation,* research does not suggest consistent immune benefits (Miller & Cohen, 2001). In these studies, a wide array of techniques were used to induce a relaxed state, including progressive muscle relaxation, biofeedback, imagery, and meditation or combinations of these techniques. In some cases, significant benefits were obtained. For example, in an early study of older individuals in nursing homes, participants were randomly assigned to receive relaxation exercises once a week for 6 weeks, social contact with a college student over the same time frame, or no intervention (Kiecolt-Glaser et al., 1985). Significant increases in NKCA and decreases in antibody to HSV (suggesting more control over viral latency) were found immediately after the intervention. HSV effects were maintained at the 1-month follow-up. The social support condition showed no benefits. On the other hand, other relaxation intervention studies have shown no immune benefits. It may be that certain relaxation approaches are more beneficial than others. For example, a study demonstrated that an 8-week mediation program (mindfulness-based stress reduction) significantly increased antibody levels to a flu vaccine compared with a control condition (Davidson et al., 2003). Interestingly, significantly greater left prefrontal cortex activation resulted from the intervention, using recordings of brain electrical activity from the scalp. As described earlier, Davidson and colleagues have shown that individuals with greater relative left prefrontal activation report less negative and more positive dispositional mood and respond less negatively to emotional challenges (Davidson, 1998). Meditation can impact a variety of psychological processes, for example, attention and awareness, and it may be these effects, rather than relaxation effects, that explain the benefits observed.

On the other hand, there is more consistent evidence of immune benefit for *hypnosis* and *conditioning*. These interventions are interesting because, rather than focusing on decreasing negative mood and distress, they involve a directed manipulation of "expectation" about the specific immune processes being examined. Thus, these studies are based on the premise that it is possible to manipulate the direction of an immune response via neurophysiological pathways. There are a number of other ways in which these studies differ from the other intervention studies. For example, many studies of the impact of hypnosis and conditioning evaluated hypersensitivity reactions as outcomes. An antigen is placed under the skin, and the wheal that forms is measured as an index of the immune response to the antigen. These studies are unique in that an entire in vivo immune response is measured rather than an in vitro assay that isolates immune cells from their biological context. Also, only highly hypnotizable participants are included in the hypnosis studies. Any of these factors may explain the successes in this area.

Development

Early experience can have a profound effect on the developing immune system, as well as on adult immunity. For example, in very early work in rats, Solomon and colleagues (Solomon, 1968) showed that handling in the first 21 days of life was associated with more vigorous antibody responses in adulthood. Maternal separation has been studied in young nonhuman primates as it relates to immune outcomes. Maternal separation results in elevations in a variety of markers of distress, alterations in sleep patterns, and effects on the CNS, the SNS, the HPA, and other hormone systems. The extent and nature of these changes depend on the species, presence of others, length of the separation, and so forth. Alterations in a wide variety of immune parameters are also observed, including reductions in the proliferative response and the primary antibody response, as well as increases in markers of macrophage activation (Worlein & Laudenslager, 2001). Effects depend on behavioral response, with evidence that more vocalized distress and more behavioral withdrawal may be associated with greater physiological alteration. Even brief separations at an early age can affect adult behavioral patterns and physiological responses, including immune responses.

Do Stress-Related Immune Changes Explain the Relationship Between Stress and Disease?

Although stressor exposure and psychological responses can influence the immune system, and these psychological processes have also been found to be risk factors for certain diseases, it remains unclear whether immune changes mediate the stress-disease relationship. A major thrust of research in health psychology is examining these links, as described in the X-Y-Z model (Kemeny, 1991; see Figure 5.1). In the area of cancer, animal studies have shown that alterations in NK cell activity may mediate the effects of stress on metastases to the lung in rats with a breast tumor (Ben-Eliyahu, Yirmiya, Liebeskind, Taylor, & Gale, 1991). In the

area of infectious disease, HSV pathogenesis following exposure to a stressor may be related to suppression of HSV-specific cytotoxic T cells and NK cell activity in rodents (Bonneau, Sheridan, Feng, & Glaser, 1991a, 1991b).

However, similar mediation has not been affirmed in humans. For example, excellent work has been done to show that chronic exposure to stressful experience is associated with vulnerability to a respiratory infection following inoculation with a rhinovirus (Cohen et al., 1998). However, the immune (or other physiological) mediators of this relationship have yet to be determined.

Predictors of HIV Disease

HIV-1 infection has been used as a model for studying psychoneuroimmunologic relationships and disease end points for a variety of reasons, but particularly because immune and virologic processes that are highly predictive of disease course are known and easily quantifiable. This fact may not seem particularly noteworthy; but it is important to recognize that even for diseases known to be affected by the immune system, such as infectious or autoimmune diseases, immune assays whose values can predict disease course in humans are often not readily available. This problem has limited the ability of researchers to conduct studies of psychological factors, immune mediators, and disease etiology or course. In addition, HIV is a good model because there is a great deal of unexplained variability in disease course even with the advent of powerful antiretrovirals. Also, some of the immunologic processes that can contain the virus have been shown to be modifiable in other populations by stressful life experience and psychological factors. And because HIV infection occurs frequently in younger, otherwise healthy individuals, comorbidities do not complicate models. Finally, many HIV-positive individuals are exposed to the same profoundly stressful circumstances (e.g., death of close others to HIV, stigma), providing an opportunity to compare physiological processes and disease course in samples differing on psychological responses to these stressors.

A number of studies have shown that psychological factors can predict HIV disease course, controlling for demographic, behavioral, and medical factors. For example, HIV-positive individuals with high levels of depression show accelerated rates of clinical disease progression, as well as evidence of more rapid immune decline in some studies, but relationships vary depending on the disease outcome measured (Cole & Kemeny, 2001). A simple count of the number of stressful life events encountered over intervals such as the past year does not consistently predict disease course. However, the presence of significant stressors defined in terms of the nature of the individual's specific context has predicted immune decline in HIV-positive individuals (Leserman et al., 2000). These findings are supported by studies in rhesus macaques inoculated with the simian immunodeficiency virus (SIV), showing that exposure to social stressors, such as housing changes and separation, predicts accelerated disease progression and immune alteration (Capitanio & Lerche, 1998; Capitanio, Mendoza, Lerche, & Mason, 1998).

As described earlier, cognitive appraisal processes can have profound effects on psychological and physiological responses to threats. A number of studies suggest that one set of appraisal processes, expectations of disease course, predicts clinical and immunologic evidence of HIV disease progression. Even at the same stage of disease, individuals with HIV vary widely in their expectations about the future course of their disease. Some expect to remain healthy, whereas others are "preparing" for disease progression and death. Longitudinal studies show that those with more pessimistic expectations develop HIV-related symptoms more quickly and die of AIDS more rapidly (Reed, Kemeny, Taylor, & Visscher, 1999; Reed, Kemeny, Taylor, Wang, & Visscher, 1994). Expectations also predict an array of immune changes that are associated with disease progression, including CD4 T cell decline, deficits in proliferative capacity, and high levels of immune activation (which have been shown to trigger replication of the virus and CD4 T cell death; Kemeny et al., 2005). These associations, across studies, are strongest in HIV-positive individuals who have lost a close friend to AIDS in the past year. Pessimistic expectations in this context may lead to a "giving up" or goal disengagement, which is then associated with immune alteration (Kemeny, Reed, Taylor, Visscher, & Fahey, 2006).

A second consistent cognitive predictor of immune changes relevant to HIV progression is negative appraisals of the self. A growing literature suggests that threats to one's "social self" or threats to social esteem, status, and acceptance are associated with specific negative cognitive and affective responses, including shame and humiliation. More recently, evidence suggests that such threats are also accompanied by specific physiological changes (Dickerson, Gruenewald, et al., 2004). Social self preservation theory argues that these affective and physiological responses are integral components of a coordinated psychobiological response to threats to "social self preservation," in the same way that fear and its physiological correlates are aspects of the response to threats to physical self preservation (Kemeny et al., 2005). Although these affective and physiological changes may be adaptive in an acute threat context, persistence of these psychobiological responses may have negative consequences for health. Persistence could occur under two conditions: chronic exposure to conditions of social self threat (such as evaluative, rejecting conditions as experienced by those with a stigma), or the presence of individual difference factors that increase vulnerability to experience negative self-related emotions and cognitions (e.g., rejection sensitivity). HIV is a good model for investigations in this area because HIV infection often occurs among stigmatized groups (gay and bisexual men; minority individuals; drug abusers) and is a stigmatizing sexually transmitted disease itself.

Consistent with theoretical predictions, HIV-positive gay and bisexual men who are particularly sensitive to rejection around their homosexuality show more rapid progression of HIV disease than those who are less sensitive to these social self threats. Specifically, individuals with more rejection sensitivity around their homosexuality showed faster CD4 T cell decline and faster times to AIDS onset and death over a 9-year follow-up period (Cole, Kemeny, & Taylor, 1997). Rejection-sensitive individuals died, on average, 2 years faster than their less sensitive counterparts. Effects were not explained by health behaviors, medications, demographics, or other possible confounding factors. In addition, rejection sensitivity predicts response to antiviral medication. Among HIV-positive men initiating the highly active antiretroviral therapy (HAART) regimen to control viral replication, those with psychological characteristics that include increased sensitivity to rejection showed a weaker response to the medication over the next year than the less sensitive individuals. Specifically, those who were less rejection sensitive showed greater beneficial changes in HIV viral load (amount of HIV in the blood) and CD4 T cell levels (Cole, Kemeny,

Fahey, Zack, & Naliboff, 2003). This relationship was mediated by increased autonomic nervous system arousal to a variety of stimuli in the more sensitive individuals.

Perceptions of rejection and negative self-related cognitions also predict indicators of HIV progression. In a multiethnic sample of women with HIV and a sample of HIV-positive men, the interpersonal rejection/self-reproach component of depression predicted accelerated CD4 T cell decline over time, when the other depression components did not (Kemeny & Dean, 1995; Lewis et al., 2003). HIV-positive gay men who characteristically blame themselves for negative events showed more rapid CD4 declines than those who did not manifest this attributional style (Segerstrom, Taylor, Kemeny, Reed, & Visscher, 1996). Thus, cognitions associated with self-blame and social rejection are capable of predicting indicators of HIV progression, whether or not they occur in the context of depression.

Social self preservation theory predicts that the experience of shame and related self-conscious emotions is the key affective component of the psychobiological response to social self threats. One study has shown that the persistent experience of shame about HIV infection can predict CD4 T cell decline over a 7-year follow-up period among HIV-positive gay men (Weitzman, Kemeny, & Fahey, 2006). Other HIV-specific emotional responses, as well as more general responses such as depression, did not predict. Overall, these findings may help to reconcile the inconsistent pattern of results regarding the ability of depression to predict various indictors of HIV progression. In a highly stigmatized group, the perceived social rejection or negative self component of depression and the experience of the shame family of emotions may be more salient feelings that have more powerful and persistent physiological correlates.

These findings suggest that for individuals with a stigmatized social identity, sensitivity to rejection, negative self-related cognitions, and the persistent experience of shame may have physiological correlates that can play a role in immunologic control of this latent virus, although confirmation of the causal direction of these relationships awaits studies that can alter these responses and demonstrate health benefits.

Two potential physiological pathways that may explain the relationships between psychological factors and HIV progression have been studied. The first pathway centers on the HPA. Glucocorticoids may play a role in HIV progression, since elevated levels of cortisol predict HIV progression indices in vivo (Capitanio et al., 1998; Leserman, 2000). Also, in vitro studies show that corticosteroids can enhance HIV-1 replication (Markham, Salahuddin, Veren, Orndorff, & Gallo, 1986) and may prolong viral gene expression (Ayyavoo et al., 1997).

Social self threats can activate the HPA axis, resulting in increased levels of cortisol. In a meta-analytic review of 208 laboratory stress studies, those laboratory conditions that involved uncontrollable social self threats (e.g., uncontrollable motivated performance tasks in front of an evaluative audience) showed higher cortisol responses and slower recovery times than those that did not contain this threat (Dickerson & Kemeny, 2004). A subsequent experiment confirmed this synthesis—exposure to a motivated performance task that included an evaluative audience provoked the HPA, resulting in elevations of cortisol, whereas exposure to tasks without this component did not (Gruenewald, Kemeny, Aziz, & Fahey, 2004). In animals, social threats such as social defeat and subordination are associated with activation of the HPA (Shively, Laber-Laird, & Anton, 1997). These data support the notion that social self threats and their affective sequelae in humans and other animals are associated with activation of the HPA. This activation may serve as one mediator of the effects of social self threat on HIV progression.

A second pathway linking psychological factors to HIV progression involves the autonomic nervous system. Cole and colleagues have shown that individuals who demonstrate higher SNS activity to a variety of challenging tasks show poorer benefit following initiation of HAART—they show less suppression of viral replication (Cole et al., 2001). Supporting these findings, the SNS neurotransmitter, norepinephrine (NE), has been shown to enhance HIV replication in vitro, and there is a dose-response relationship between level of NE and replication rate (Cole, Korin, Fahey, & Zack, 1998; Cole et al., 2001). This effect involves the cyclic AMP/protein kinase A signaling pathway (Cole et al., 1998; Cole et al., 2001). As described earlier, SNS fibers innervate immune organs and release NE in close proximity to lymphocytes, which express beta adrenoreceptors capable of responding to this signal. Since stressful experience and psychological factors have been shown to activate the SNS, this system may mediate effects of psychological processes on HIV replication, CD4 T cell decline, and clinical disease progression.

Cardiovascular Disease

Cardiovascular disease is another excellent model for studies in psychoneuroimmunology and disease. In the past, risk factors for cardiovascular disease have centered on hypertension, lipids, diabetes, and so forth. More recently, however, increasing attention has been focused on the role of inflammatory processes in atherosclerotic diseases. Inflammation plays a role in atherogenesis (Fahdi, Gaddam, Garza, Romeo, & Mehta, 2003) and contributes to plaque instability. Increases in markers of inflammation, such as C-reactive protein (CRP), have been shown to predict a higher risk of stroke and myocardial infarction in healthy individuals (Ridker, Cushman, Stampfer, Tracy, & Hennekens, 1997). These inflammatory processes may explain the consistent ability of depression to predict increased risk of first and recurrent cardiac events within relatively short time intervals (Kop, 1999), since depression is associated with elevated levels of a variety of mediators of inflammation, as described previously. It is notable that increased levels of inflammatory cytokines, particularly IL-6, have been shown to shown to predict a variety of diseases. In fact, elevated IL-6 levels in healthy adults have been found to predict all-cause mortality (Ershler & Keller, 2000). Thus, the bidirectional interaction between psychological factors and the inflammatory network is a critically important area of psychoneuroimmunology.

It is important not to presume immune mediation in the relationship between psychological factors and disease progression, even when a particular psychological state can predict both end points. The problem with this assumption can be clearly seen in the results of an intervention study conducted with patients with malignant melanoma. The impact of a psychoeducational group intervention was evaluated in relation to mood, coping, the NK system, melanoma recurrence and mortality over a 6-year period (Fawzy, Cousins, et al., 1990; Fawzy et al., 1993; Fawzy, Kemeny, et al., 1990). The intervention involved health education, training in problem-solving skills, stress management, and social support. Those randomly assigned to the 6-week intervention showed improved mood and active coping relative to the controls, as well as increases in the number of NK cells and in NKCA at 6 months. Most significantly, the intervention group had fewer melanoma recurrences and fewer deaths during the 5- to 6-year follow-up period than did the control group. Despite the fact that NK cells may play a role in tumor surveillance, however, results indicated that the NKCA activity changes induced by the intervention did not mediate the health benefits observed. Thus, health effects may have been due to other unmeasured immune or nonimmune physiological changes produced by the intervention, or to behavioral changes of some kind.

Conclusions and Implications

Stressful life circumstances can suppress aspects of immune functioning. Although true, this oversimplification does not do justice to the complexity of the bidirectional relationships between the mind and the immune system. First, the "mind" is not included in the equation. Whereas the majority of research focuses on stressful life experience, it is becoming increasingly clear that it is one's perception of circumstances, and the neurophysiological activations that accompany those perceptions, that play a central role in shaping the bodily response to context. In other words, a "stress response," involving activation of the HPA and SNS, along with consequent alterations in the immune system, depends more heavily on individuals' patterns of responses to their life contexts than on the specific nature of the circumstance presented to them. Studies demonstrate that when appraisals are manipulated, distinctive physiological effects can result (Gross & John, in press; Tomaka & Blascovich, 1994).

The potential health effects of these psychological response differences are highlighted in a study predicting mortality in HIV-positive individuals. In this study, HIV-positive gay and bisexual men who concealed their homosexuality, that is, were "in the closet," showed accelerated rates of HIV progression, including a more rapid loss of CD4 T cells and a more rapid onset of AIDS and death (Cole, Kemeny, Taylor, & Visscher, 1996), controlling for biobehavioral confounds. However, the relationship between concealment and HIV progression also depended on the extent to which these men were sensitive to rejection around their homosexuality. Concealing one's homosexuality was unrelated to disease progression among men who were highly rejection sensitive, presumably because failing to tell others about one's sexual identify reduced the likelihood of experiencing the outright rejection that these individuals fear (Cole et al., 1998). Overall, then, there may have been a health "price of passing" in individuals due potentially to the inhibition of a core aspect of one's identity or the chronic fear of the consequences of being discovered. However, among rejection-sensitive individuals, concealment appeared to be protective. Thus, the relationship between one's social context—whether or not the social world is aware of one's stigma—and health depended on one's level of sensitivity to rejection from members of that social world. These interactions between context and psychological response provide a much clearer and more sophisticated picture of the relationship between the mind and health. Adding to these models other critical moderators, such as genetic predispositions and behavioral factors that play a critical role in disease etiology and progression, will improve our ability to predict disease outcomes.

It is also important to note that a relationship between a psychological factor and a change in the immune system may be due to the impact of the mind on the immune system, the effects of the immune system on the mind, both, or neither. Simple cross-sectional correlations across these systems can no longer be interpreted in a unidirectional way. It is now becoming clearer that the immune system can impact the way we think and feel, even in individuals without illness or disease. This research area has provided a new and novel way to understand the predictors of disengagement-related affective states, in particular depression. These findings and new conceptualizations of depression may lead to the development of innovative therapeutic strategies to control these difficult states of mind.

At a conceptual level, we can include the immune system in the list of stress-relevant systems that may play a central role in shaping adaptive responses to both pathogen threats and other environmental threats. Many years ago, fever was viewed as a nuisance side effect of exposure to infectious agents, to be eliminated as soon as possible. Now fever is widely recognized to be an important physiological response to pathogens that supports the body's ability to fight infection. Findings in the field of psychoneuroimmunology have demonstrated that the same molecules that control temperature regulation can also regulate our motivation and behavior in the service, again, of supporting immunologic defense mechanisms and recovery from illness. It has also been argued that these immune products play a role in adaptation to stressful circumstances and are a fundamental component of the adaptive physiological response to certain environmental threats. Future research will more carefully spell out the elicitors of this response and the way in which it is integrated with the other important aspects of the body's adaptive reaction to stressful situations.

References

Ackerman, K. D., Martino, M., Heyman, R., Moyna, N. M., & Rabin, B. S. (1998). Stressor-induced alteration of cytokine production in multiple sclerosis patients and controls. *Psychosomatic Medicine, 60*(4), 484–491.

Ader, R. (2000). The placebo effect: If it's all in your head, does that mean you only think you feel better? *Advances in Mind-Body Medicine, 16*(1), 7–11.

Ader, R., & Cohen, N. (1975). Behaviorally conditioned immuno-suppression. *Psychosomatic Medicine, 37,* 333–340.

Ader, R., & Cohen, N. (1982). Behaviorally conditioned immunosuppression and murine systemic lupus erythematosus. *Science, 215,* 1534–1536.

Ader, R., Felten, D. L., & Cohen, N. (Eds.). (2001). *Psychoneuroimmunology* (3rd ed.). New York: Academic Press.

Avitsur, R., Stark, J. L., & Sheridan, J. F. (2001). Social stress induces glucocorticoid resistance in subordinate animals. *Hormones and Behavior, 39*(4), 247–257.

Ayyavoo, V., Rafaeli, Y., Nagashunmugam, T., Mahalingham, S., Phung, M. T., Hamam, A., et al. (1997). HIV-1 viral protein r (VPR) as a regulator of the target cell. *Psychoneuroendocrinology, 22*(Suppl 1), S41–S49.

Bellinger, D. L., Brouxhon, S. M., Lubahn, C., Tran, L., Kang, J. I., Felten, D. L., et al. (2001). Strain differences in the expression of corticotropin-releasing hormone immunoreactivity in nerves that supply the spleen and thymus. *Neuroimmunomodulation, 9*(2), 78–87.

Ben-Eliyahu, S., Yirmiya, R., Liebeskind, J. C., Taylor, A. N., & Gale, R. P. (1991). Stress increases metastatic spread of a mammary tumor in rats: Evidence for mediation by the immune system. *Brain, Behavior, and Immunity, 5,* 193–205.

Benschop, R. I., Nieuwenhuis, E., Tromp, E., Godaert, G., Ballieux, R. E., & van Doomen, L. (1994). Effects of β-adrenergic blockade on immunologic and cardiovascular changes induced by mental stress. *Circulation, 89,* 762–769.

Blascovich, J., & Tomaka, J. (1996). The biopsychosocial model of arousal regulation. *Advances in Experimental Social Psychology, 28,* 1–51.

Bonneau, R. H., Sheridan, J. F., Feng, N., & Glaser, R. (1991a). Stress-induced suppression of herpes simplex virus (HSV)-specific cytotoxic t lymphocyte and natural killer cell activity and enhancement of acute pathogenesis following local HSV infection. *Brain, Behavior, and Immunity, 5,* 170–192.

Bonneau, R. H., Sheridan, J. F., Feng, N., & Glaser, R. (1991b). Stress-induced effects on cell mediated innate and adaptive memory components of the murine immune response to herpes simplex virus infection. *Brain, Behavior, and Immunity, 5,* 274–295.

Bovjberg, D. H., Redd, W. H., Maier, L. A., Holland, J. C., Lesko, L. M., Niedzwiecki, D., et al. (1990). Anticipatory immune suppression in women receiving cyclic chemotherapy for ovarian cancer. *Journal of Consulting and Clinical Psychology, 58,* 153–157.

Capitanio, J. P., & Lerche, N. W. (1998). Social separation, housing relocation, and survival in simian aids: A retrospective analysis. *Psychosomatic Medicine, 60*(3), 235–244.

Capitanio, J. P., Mendoza, S. P., Lerche, N. W., & Mason, W. A. (1998). Social stress results in altered glucocorticoid regulation and shorter survival in simian acquired immune deficiency syndrome. *Proceedings of the National Academy of Sciences of the United States of America, 95*(8), 4714–4719.

Carr, D. J. J., & Weber, R. J. (2001). Opioidergic modulation of the immune system. In R. Ader, D. Felten, & N. Cohen (Eds.), *Psychoneuroimmunology* (3rd ed., pp. 405–414). New York: Elsevier.

Castanon, N., Bluthe, R. M., & Dantzer, R. (2001). Chronic treatment with the atypical antidepressant tianeptine attenuates sickness behavior induced by peripheral but not central lipopolysaccharide and interleukin-β in the rat. *Psychopharmacology, 154*(1), 50–60.

Cirulli, F., De Acetis, L., & Alleva, E. (1998). Behavioral effects of peripheral interleukin-1 administration in adult cd-1 mice: Specific inhibition of the offensive components of intermale agonistic behavior. *Brain Research, 791*(1–2), 308–312.

Coe, C. L., Rosenberg, L. T., & Levine, S. (1988). Effect of maternal separation on the complement system and antibody response in infant primates. *International Journal of Neuroscience, 40,* 289–302.

Cohen, S., Frank, E., Doyle, W. J., Skoner, D. P., Rabin, B. S., & Gwaltney, J. M., Jr. (1998). Types of stressors that increase susceptibility to the common cold in healthy adults. *Health Psychology, 17*(3), 214–223.

Cohen, S., & Wills, T. A. (1985). Stress, social support, and the buffering hypothesis. *Psychological Bulletin, 98,* 310–357.

Cole, S. W., & Kemeny, M. E. (2001). Psychosocial influences on the progression of HIV infection. In R. Ader, D. L. Felten, & N. Cohen (Eds.), *Psychoneuroimmunology* (3rd ed., Vol. 2, pp. 583–612). New York: Academic Press.

Cole, S. W., Kemeny, M. E., Fahey, J. L., Zack, J. A., & Naliboff, B. D. (2003). Psychological risk factors for HIV pathogenesis: Mediation by the autonomic nervous system. *Biological Psychiatry, 54,* 1444–1456.

Cole, S. W., Kemeny, M. E., & Taylor, S. E. (1997). Social identity and physical health: Accelerated HIV progression in rejection-sensitive gay men. *Journal of Personality and Social Psychology, 72*(2), 320–335.

Cole, S. W., Kemeny, M. E., Taylor, S. E., & Visscher, B. R. (1996). Elevated physical health risk among gay men who conceal their homosexual identity. *Health Psychology, 15,* 243–251.

Cole, S. W., Korin, Y. D., Fahey, J. L., & Zack, J. A. (1998). Norepinephrine accelerates HIV replication via protein kinase a–dependent effects on cytokine production. *Journal of Immunology, 161*(2), 610–616.

Cole, S. W., Naliboff, B. D., Kemeny, M. E., Griswold, M. P., Fahey, J. L., & Zack, J. A. (2001). Impaired response to HAART in HIV-infected individuals with high autonomic nervous system activity. *Proceedings of the National Academy of Sciences of the United States of America, 98*(22), 12695–12700.

Damasio, A. R., Grabowski, T. J., Bechara, A., Damasio, H., Ponto, L. L., Parvizi, J., et al. (2000). Subcortical and cortical brain activity during the feeling of self-generated emotions. *Nature Neuroscience, 3*(10), 1049–1056.

Dantzer, R., Bluthe, R., Castanon, N., Cauvet, N., Capuron, L., Goodall, G., et al. (2001). Cytokine effects on behavior. In R. Ader, D. L. Felten, & N. Cohen (Eds.), *Psychoneuroimmunology* (3rd ed., Vol. 1, pp. 703–727). New York: Academic Press.

Davidson, R. I. (1998). Affective style and affective disorders: Perspectives from affective neuroscience. *Cognition and Emotion, 12,* 307–330.

Davidson, R. J., Coe, C. C., Dolski, I., & Donzella, B. (1999). Individual differences in prefrontal activation asymmetry predict natural killer cell activity at rest and in response to challenge. *Brain, Behavior, and Immunity, 13*(2), 93–108.

Davidson, R. J., Kabat-Zinn, J., Schumacher, J., Rosenkranz, M., Muller, D., Santorelli, S. F., et al. (2003). Alterations in brain and immune function produced by mindfulness meditation. *Psychosomatic Medicine, 65*(4), 564–570.

Dhabhar, F. S. (2003). Stress, leukocyte trafficking, and the augmentation of skin immune function. *Annals of the New York Academy of Sciences, 992,* 205–217.

Dhabhar, F. S., & McEwen, B. S. (2001). Bidirectional effects of stress and glucocorticoid hormones on immune function: Possible explanations for paradoxical observations. In R. Ader, D. L. Felten, & N. Cohen (Eds.), *Psychoneuroimmunology* (3rd ed., Vol. 1, pp. 301–338). New York: Academic Press.

Dickerson, S. S., Gruenewald, T. L., & Kemeny, M. E. (2004). When the social self is threatened: Shame, physiology, and health. *Journal of Personality, 72*(6), 1191–1216.

Dickerson, S. S., & Kemeny, M. E. (2004). Acute stressors and cortisol responses: A theoretical integration and synthesis of laboratory research. *Psychological Bulletin, 130*(3), 355–391.

Dickerson, S. S., Kemeny, M. E., Aziz, N., Kim, K. H., & Fahey, J. L. (2004). Immunological effects of induced shame and guilt. *Psychosomatic Medicine, 66*(1), 124–131.

Dunn, A. J., Swiergiel, A. H., & de Peurepaire, R. (2005). Cytokines as mediators of depression: What can we learn from animal studies? *Neuroscience and Biobehavioral Reviews, 29,* 891–909.

Ekman, P., Levenson, R. W., & Friesen, W. V. (1983). Autonomic nervous system activity distinguishes among emotions. *Science, 221*(4616), 1208–1210.

Elenkov, I. J., Wilder, R. L., Chrousos, G. P., & Vizi, E. S. (2000). The sympathetic nerve—an integrative interface between two supersystems: The brain and the immune system. *Pharmacological Reviews, 52*(4), 595–638.

Ershler, W. B., & Keller, E. T. (2000). Age-associated increased interleukin-6 gene expression, late-life diseases, and frailty. *Annual Review of Medicine, 51,* 245–270.

Esterling, B. A., Antoni, M. H., Kumar, M., & Schneiderman, N. (1990). Emotional repression, stress disclosure responses, and Epstein-Barr viral capsid antigen titers. *Psychosomatic Medicine, 52,* 397–410.

Fahdi, I. E., Gaddam, V., Garza, L., Romeo, F., & Mehta, J. L. (2003). Inflammation, infection, and atherosclerosis. *Brain, Behavior, and Immunity, 17*(4), 238–244.

Fawzy, F. I., Cousins, N., Fawzy, N. W., Kemeny, M. E., Elashoff, R., & Morton, D. (1990). A structured psychiatric intervention for cancer patients: I. Changes over time in methods of coping and affective disturbance. *Archives of General Psychiatry, 47*(8), 720–725.

Fawzy, F. I., Fawzy, N. W., Hyun, C. S., Elashoff, R., Guthrie, D., Fahey, J. L., et al. (1993). Malignant melanoma. Effects of an early structured psychiatric intervention, coping, and affective state on recurrence and survival 6 years later. *Archives of General Psychiatry, 50*(9), 681–689.

Fawzy, F. I., Kemeny, M. E., Fawzy, N. W., Elashoff, R., Morton, D., Cousins, N., et al. (1990). A structured psychiatric intervention for cancer patients: II. Changes over time in immunological measures. *Archives of General Psychiatry, 47*(8), 729–735.

Felten, D. L., & Felten, S. Y. (1988). Sympathetic noradrenergic innervation of immune organs. *Brain, Behavior, and Immunity, 2*(4), 293–300.

Fleshner, M., Laudenslager, M. L., Simons, L., & Maier, S. F. (1989). Reduced serum antibodies associated with social defeat in rats. *Physiology and Behavior, 45*(6), 1183–1187.

Futterman, A. D., Kemeny, M. E., Shapiro, D., & Fahey, J. L. (1994). Immunological and physiological changes associated with induced positive and negative mood. *Psychosomatic Medicine, 56*(6), 499–511.

Gross, J. J., & John, O. P. (in press). Wise emotion regulation. In L. F. Barrett & P. Salovey (Eds.), *The wisdom of feelings: Psychological processes in emotional intelligence.* New York: Guilford.

Gruenewald, T. L., Kemeny, M. E., Aziz, N., & Fahey, J. L. (2004). Acute threat to the social self: Shame, social self-esteem and cortisol activity. *Psychosomatic Medicine, 66,* 915–924.

Guess, H. A., Kleinman, A., Kusek, J. W., & Engel, L. W. (2002). *The science of the placebo: Toward an interdisciplinary research agenda.* London: BMJ Books.

Herbert, T. B., & Cohen, S. (1993a). Depression and immunity: A meta-analytic review. *Psychological Bulletin, 113,* 472–486.

Herbert, T. B., & Cohen, S. (1993b). Stress and immunity in humans: A meta-analytic review. *Psychosomatic Medicine, 55,* 364–379.

Herbert, T. B., Cohen, S., Marsland, A. L., Bachen, E. A., Rabin, B. S., Muldoon, M. F., et al. (1994). Cardiovascular reactivity and the course of immune response to an acute psychological stressor. *Psychosomatic Medicine, 56,* 337–344.

Irwin, M. (2001). Depression and immunity. In R. Ader, D. L. Felten, & N. Cohen (Eds.), *Psychoneuroimmunology* (3rd ed., Vol. 2, pp. 383–398). New York: Academic Press.

Irwin, M., Daniels, M., Bloom, E. T., & Weiner, H. (1986). Life events, depression, and natural killer cell activity. *Psychopharmacology Bulletin, 22*(4), 1093–1096.

Irwin, M. R., Lacher, U., & Caldwell, C. (1992). Depression and reduced natural killer cytotoxicity: A longitudinal study of depressed patients and control subjects. *Psychological Medicine, 22,* 1045–1050.

Kalin, N. H., Larson, C., Shelton, S. E., & Davidson, R. I. (1998). Asymmetric frontal brain activity, cortisol, and behavior associated with fearful temperament in rhesus monkeys. *Behavioral Neuroscience, 112,* 286–292.

Kang, D. H., Davidson, R. I., Coe, C. L., Wheeler, R. W., Tomarken, A. J., & Ershler, W. B. (1991). Frontal brain asymmetry and immune function. *Behavioral Neuroscience, 105,* 860–869.

Keller, S. E., Weiss, J. M., Schleifer, S. J., Miller, N. E., & Stein, M. (1983). Stress-induced suppression of immunity in adrenalectomized rats. *Science, 221,* 1301–1304.

Kemeny, M., Reed, G., Taylor, S., Visscher, B., & Fahey, J. L. (2006). Negative HIV-specific expectancies and goal disengagement predict immunologic evidence of HIV progression. Manuscript in preparation.

Kemeny, M. E. (1991). Psychological factors, immune processes and the course of herpes simplex and human immunodeficiency virus infection. In N. Plotnikoff, A. Murgo, R. Faith, & J. Wybran (Eds.), *Stress and immunity* (pp. 199–210). Boca Raton, FL: CRC Press.

Kemeny, M. E. (2003). An interdisciplinary research model to investigate psychosocial cofactors in disease: Application to HIV-1 pathogenesis. *Brain, Behavior, and Immunity, 17,* 62–72.

Kemeny, M. E., & Dean, L. (1995). Effects of AIDS-related bereavement on HIV progression among New York City gay men. *AIDS Education and Prevention, 7*(Suppl), 36–47.

Kemeny, M. E., & Gruenewald, T. L. (2000). Affect, cognition, the immune system and health. In E. A. Mayer & C. B. Saper (Eds.), *The biological basis for mind body interactions* (Vol. 122, pp. 291–308). New York: Elsevier Science.

Kemeny, M. E., Gruenewald, T. L., & Dickerson, S. S. (2005). Social self-preservation theory: Psychobiology of threats to the social self. Manuscript in preparation.

Kemeny, M. E., & Laudenslager, M. (1999). Beyond stress: The role of individual differences factors in psychoneuroimmunologic relationships. *Brain, Behavior, and Immunity, 13,* 73–75.

Kemeny, M. E., & Miller, G. (1999). Effects of psychosocial interventions on the immune system. In M. Schedlowski & U. Tewes (Eds.), *Psychoneuroimmunology: An interdisciplinary introduction* (pp. 373–416). New York: Plenum.

Kent, S., Bluthe, R. M., Kelley, K. W., & Dantzer, R. (1992). Sickness behavior as a new target for drug development. *Trends in Pharmacological Sciences, 13,* 24–28.

Kiecolt-Glaser, J. K., Garner, W., Speicher, C., Penn, G. M., Holliday, J., & Glaser, R. (1984). Psychosocial modifiers of immunocompetence in medical students. *Psychosomatic Medicine, 46,* 7–17.

Kiecolt-Glaser, J. K., Glaser, J., Williger, D., Stout, J., Messick, G., Sheppard, S., et al. (1985). Psychosocial enhancement of immunocompetence in a geriatric population. *Health Psychology, 4,* 25.

Kiecolt-Glaser, J. K., & Glaser, R. (2001). Psychological stress and wound healing: Kiecolt-Glaser et al. (1995). *Advances in Mind-Body Medicine, 17*(1), 15–16.

Kiecolt-Glaser, J. K., Glaser, R., Strain, E. C., Stout, I. C., Tarr, K. L., Holliday, I. E., et al. (1986). Modulation of cellular immunity in medical students. *Journal of Behavioral Medicine, 9,* 5–21.

Kiecolt-Glaser, J. K., Marucha, P. T., Malarkey, W. B., Mercado, A. M., & Glaser, R. (1995). Slowing of wound healing by psychological stress. *Lancet, 346*(8984), 1194–1196.

Kop, W. J. (1999). Chronic and acute psychological risk factors for clinical manifestations of coronary artery disease. *Psychosomatic Medicine, 61*(4), 476–487.

Korneva, E. A. (1967). The effect of stimulating different mesencephalic structures on protective immune response patterns. *Sechenov Physiological Journal of the USSR, 53,* 42–50.

Lane, R. D., Reiman, E. M., Ahern, G. L., Schwartz, G. E., & Davidson, R. J. (1997). Neuroanatomical correlates of happiness, sadness, and disgust. *American Journal of Psychiatry, 154*(7), 926–933.

Leserman, J. (2000). The effects of depression, stressful life events, social support, and coping on the progression of HIV infection. *Current Psychiatry Reports, 2*(6), 495–502.

Leserman, J., Petitto, J. M., Golden, R. N., Gaynes, B. N., Gu, H., Perkins, D. O., et al. (2000). Impact of stressful life events, depression, social support, coping, and cortisol on progression to AIDS. *American Journal of Psychiatry, 157*(8), 1221–1228.

Lewis, T. T., Kemeny, M. E., Myers, H. F., & Wyatt, G. E. (2003). Perceived interpersonal rejection and CDd4 decline in a community sample of women infected with HIV. Manuscript in preparation.

Lysle, D. T., Lyte, M., Fowler, H., & Rabin, B. S. (1987). Shock-induced modulation of lymphocyte reactivity: Suppression, habituation, and recovery. *Life Sciences, 41,* 1805–1814.

Maes, M., Scharpe, S., Meltzer, H. Y., Okayli, G., Bosmans, E., D'Hondt, P., et al. (1994). Increased neopterin and interferon-gamma secretion and lower availability of l-tryptophan in major depression: Further evidence for an immune response. *Psychiatry Research, 54,* 143–160.

Maier, S. F., & Watkins, L. R. (1998). Cytokines for psychologists: Implications of bidirectional immune-to-brain communication for understanding behavior, mood, and cognition. *Psychological Review, 105,* 83–107.

Markham, P. D., Salahuddin, S. Z., Veren, K., Orndorff, S., & Gallo, R. C. (1986). Hydrocortisone and some other hormones enhance the expression of HTLV-III. *International Journal of Cancer, 37*(1), 67–72.

McEwen, B. S. (1998). Protective and damaging effects of stress mediators. *New England Journal of Medicine, 338,* 171–179.

McEwen, B. S., Biron, C. A., Brunson, K. W., Bulloch, K., Chambers, W. H., Dhabhar, F. S., et al. (1997). The role of adrenocorticoids as modulators of immune function in health and disease: Neural, endocrine and immune interactions. *Brain Research, 23*(1–2), 79–133.

Miller, G. E., & Cohen, S. (2001). Psychological interventions and the immune system: A meta-analytic review and critique. *Health Psychology, 20*(1), 47–63.

Miller, G. E., Cohen, S., & Ritchey, A. K. (2002). Chronic psychological stress and the regulation of pro-inflammatory cytokines: A glucocorticoid resistance model. *Health Psychology, 21,* 531–541.

Miller, G. E., Stetler, C. A., Carney, R. M., Freedland, K. E., & Banks, W. A. (2002). Clinical depression and inflammatory risk markers for coronary heart disease. *American Journal of Cardiology, 90*(12), 1279–1283.

Moynihan, J. A., & Stevens, S. Y. (2001). Mechanisms of stress-induced modulation of immunity in animals. In R. Ader, D. Felten, & N. Cohen (Eds.), *Psychoneuroimmunology* (3rd ed.). New York: Elsevier.

Ottaway, C. A., & Husband, A. J. (1992). Central nervous system influences on lymphocyte migration. *Brain, Behavior, and Immunity, 6*(2), 97–116.

Pacak, K., & Palkovits, M. (2001). Stressor specificity of central neuroendocrine responses: Implications for stress-related disorders. *Endocrine Reviews, 22*(4), 502–548.

Petrie, K. L., Booth, R. J., Pennebaker, J. W., Davison, K. P., & Thomas, M. G. (1995). Disclosure of trauma and immune response to a hepatitis B vaccination program. *Journal of Consulting and Clinical Psychology, 63,* 787–792.

Pike, J. L., Smith, T. L., Hauger, R. L., Nicassio, P. M., Patterson, T. L., McClintick, J., et al. (1997). Chronic life stress alters sympathetic, neuroendocrine, and immune responsivity to an acute psychological stressor in humans. *Psychosomatic Medicine, 59*(4), 447–457.

Pressman, S., & Cohen, S. (2005). Does positive affect influence health? *Psychological Bulletin, 131,* 925–971.

Reed, G. M., Kemeny, M. E., Taylor, S. E., & Visscher, B. R. (1999). Negative HIV-specific expectancies and AIDS-related bereavement as predictors of symptom onset in asymptomatic HIV-positive gay men. *Health Psychology, 18*(4), 354–363.

Reed, G. M., Kemeny, M. E., Taylor, S. E., Wang, H. Y., & Visscher, B. R. (1994). Realistic acceptance as a predictor of decreased survival time in gay men with AIDS. *Health Psychology, 13*(4), 299–307.

Ridker, P. M., Cushman, M., Stampfer, M. J., Tracy, R. P., & Hennekens, C. H. (1997). Inflammation, aspirin, and the risk of cardiovascular disease in apparently healthy men. *New England Journal of Medicine, 336*(14), 973–979.

Sapolsky, R. M. (1993). Endocrinology alfresco: Psychoendocrine studies of wild baboons. *Recent Progress in Hormone Research, 48,* 437–468.

Schedlowski, M., Jacobs, R., Alker, J., Prohl, F., Stratmann, G., Richter, S., et al. (1993). Psychophysiological, neuroendocrine and cellular immune reactions under psychological stress. *Neuropsychobiology, 28,* 87–90.

Schleifer, S. J., Keller, S. E., Meyerson, A. T., Raskin, M. J., Davis, K. L., & Stein, M. (1984). Lymphocyte function in major depressive disorder. *Archives of General Psychiatry, 41,* 484.

Segerstrom, S., Kemeny, M. E., & Laudenslager, M. (1999). Individual differences in immunologic reactivity. In R. Ader, D. L. Felten, & N. Cohen (Eds.), *Psychoneuroimmunology* (3rd ed., pp. 87–110)). New York: Academic Press.

Segerstrom, S. C., Glover, D. A., Craske, M. G., & Fahey, J. L. (1999). Worry affects the immune response to phobic fear. *Brain, Behavior, and Immunity, 13*(2), 80–92.

Segerstrom, S. C., & Miller, G. E. (2004). Psychological stress and the human immune system: A meta-analytic study of 30 years of inquiry. *Psychological Bulletin, 130*(4), 601–630.

Segerstrom, S. C., Solomon, G. F., Kemeny, M. E., & Fahey, J. L. (1998). Relationship of worry to immune sequelae of the Northridge earthquake. *Journal of Behavioral Medicine, 21*(5), 433–450.

Segerstrom, S. C., Taylor, S. E., Kemeny, M. E., Reed, G. M., & Visscher, B. R. (1996). Causal attributions predict rate of immune decline in HIV-seropositive gay men. *Health Psychology, 15*(6), 485–493.

Shavit, Y., Martin, F. C., Yirmiya, R., Ben-Eliyahu, S., Terman, G. W., Weiner, H., et al. (1987). Effects of a single administration of morphine or footshock stress on natural killer cell cytotoxicity. *Brain, Behavior, and Immunity, 1*(4), 318–328.

Sherwood, L. (1993). *Human physiology: From cells to systems* (2nd ed.). St. Paul, MN: West.

Shively, C. A., Laber-Laird, K., & Anton, R. F. (1997). Behavior and physiology of social stress and depression in female cynomolgus monkeys. *Biological Psychiatry, 41*(8), 871–882.

Solomon, G. (1969). Stress and antibody response in rats. *Archives of Allergy, 35,* 97–104.

Solomon, G. F. (1968). Early experience and immunity. *Nature, 220*(169), 821–822.

Solomon, G. F., & Moos, R. H. (1964). Emotions, immunity, and disease: A speculative theoretical integration. *Archives of General Psychiatry, 11,* 657–674.

Solvason, H. B., Ghanta, V. K., & Hiramoto, R. N. (1988). Conditioned augmentation of natural killer cell activity: Independence from nociceptive effects and dependence on interferon-beta. *Journal of Immunology, 140,* 661–665.

Stark, J. L., Avitsur, R., Padgett, D. A., Campbell, K. A., Beck, F. M., & Sheridan, J. F. (2001). Social stress induces glucocorticoid resistance in macrophages. *American Journal of Physiology: Regulatory, Integrative, Comparative, Physiology, 280*(6), R1799–R1805.

Stefanski, V. (1998). Social stress in loser rats: Opposite immunological effects in submissive and subdominant males. *Physiology and Behavior, 63,* 605–613.

Sternberg, E. M. (1997). Neural-immune interactions in health and disease. *Journal of Clinical Investigation, 100,* 2641–2647.

Stone, A. A., Cox, D. S., Valdlmarsdottir, H., Jandorf, L., & Neale, J. M. (1987). Evidence that secretory IgA antibody is associated with daily mood. *Journal of Personality and Social Psychology, 52,* 988–993.

Strauman, T. J., Lemieux, A. M., & Coe, C. L. (1993). Self-discrepancy and natural killer cell activity: Immunological consequences of negative self-evaluation. *Journal of Personality and Social Psychology, 64,* 1042–1052.

Tomaka, J., & Blascovich, J. (1994). Effects of justice beliefs on cognitive appraisal of and subjective, physiological, and behavioral responses to potential stress. *Journal of Personality and Social Psychology, 67*(4), 732–740.

Van Tits, L. J. H., Michel, M. C., Grosse-Wilde, H., Rappel, M., Eigler, F. W., Soliman, A., et al. (1990). Catecholamines increase lymphocyte β 2-adrenergic receptors via a β 2-andrenergic, spleen-dependent process. *American Journal of Physiology, 258,* E191–E202.

Wager, T. D., Rilling, J. K., Smith, E. E., Sokolik, A., Casey, K. L., Davidson, R. J., et al. (2004). Placebo-induced changes in FMRI in the anticipation and experience of pain. *Science, 303*(5661), 1162–1167.

Weiner, H. (1992). *Perturbing the organism: The biology of stressful experiences.* Chicago: University of Chicago Press.

Weitzman, O., Kemeny, M. E., & Fahey, J. L. (2006). HIV-related shame and guilt predict CD4 decline. Manuscript submitted for publication.

Worlein, J. M., & Laudenslager, M. L. (2001). Effects of early rearing experiences and social interactions on immune function in non-human primates. In R. Ader, D. L. Felten, & N. Cohen (Eds.), *Psychoneuroimmunology* (3rd ed., Vol. 2, pp. 73–85). New York: Academic Press.

6

Charles S. Carver

Stress, Coping, and Health

This chapter addresses the confluence of two sets of processes as they come to bear on a class of outcomes. The processes are stress and coping. The outcome is health. This topic is enormous in its scope. The literature of stress itself is broad enough to have had a handbook devoted to it (Goldberger & Breznitz, 1993); the same is true of the literature on coping (Zeidner & Endler, 1996). Although those handbooks are by now dated, the years since their publication have brought only further growth in their respective literatures (Folkman & Moskowitz, 2004). It will be obvious, then, that this chapter does not survey the literature of stress and coping in its entirety. Rather, it addresses a set of basic issues, problems, and conceptual themes that have arisen within the literature bearing on stress, coping, and health.

To begin, we must consider some questions. First, exactly what defines the experience of stress? Several models have been proposed over the years, and although they differ in focus, it appears possible to extract from them a common core of shared themes. Next, what defines coping? Further, what sorts of distinctions among coping are useful, or even necessary? Finally, how do the processes of stress and coping interweave to influence health? Addressing this last question entails confronting at

least two further issues: placing boundaries around the construct of "health," and characterizing pathways by which health might be affected by stress and coping. After considering these issues, I describe some selected evidence from several areas of research on how stress and coping influence health.

What Is Stress?

What is the nature of stress? In my view, it is important to place stress within the context of behavior more generally. For that reason, before I try to define stress per se, I briefly sketch a view of some processes I believe are involved in behavior. Although there are many ways to think about how people regulate their activities, the family of viewpoints with which I am most familiar (and which tends to dominate discussions of motivated action today) derives from a long tradition of expectancy-value models of motivation.

Self-Regulation of Action

A common view among contemporary theorists is that human behavior is organized around the pursuit of goals or incentives (Austin & Vancouver,

1996; Bandura, 1986; Carver & Scheier, 1998; Elliott & Dweck, 1988; Higgins, 1987, 1996; Pervin, 1989). Such a view assumes that goals energize and direct activities, that people's goals give meaning to their lives, that understanding a person means understanding that person's goals. Indeed, in this view it is often implicit that the self consists partly of the person's goals (starting with the ideal sense of self and ranging downward or outward to goals of less complexity) and the organization among them.

Some goals have a static end-point quality (to have a task completed), but others are quite dynamic. The goal of taking a vacation is not to be sitting in your driveway at the end of two weeks but to experience the events of the vacation. The goal of developing a relationship is not a static ending (or, at least, it shouldn't be), because relationships continue to grow and evolve over time. Some goals even are moving targets. For example, career development has that character. Just about the time you reach the level of complexity you had in mind for your career, you realize there is something else you want to add in. Goals also vary in their breadth. Some goals concern what kind of person you want to be; some goals concern activities that are more concrete, focused, and circumscribed.

Goals provide the "value" in the expectancy-value model of motivation. When a person has an aspiration, a desired goal, the incentive value is what pulls behavior into motion. In this view, if there were no goals (not even trivial ones), there would be no action. A goal, an incentive, provides something to strive toward. This is true even when the goal is mundane and trivial—for example, reaching to pick up a piece of toast at breakfast.

The process of moving toward a goal can be viewed in many terms, but I have long argued that a useful model of goal pursuit is the discrepancy-reducing feedback loop (Carver & Scheier, 1998; Powers, 1973). This construct is used extensively in areas of psychology that deal with physiological self-regulation. It is an organization of four elements (Miller, Galanter, & Pribram, 1960; MacKay, 1956; Wiener, 1948): an input function, a reference value, a comparator, and an output function. The reference value is a goal; the comparator compares it against an input, a perception of the present situation. If the goal has not already been attained at the moment of the comparison, a discrepancy is noted between the desired and the actual, and an adjust-

ment in output is made, in an effort to reduce the discrepancy. Thus, behavior occurs.

Although it may be less obvious, there are also what might be viewed as "anti-goals": values, end points, or events that people want to avoid and distance themselves from. Easy examples of anti-goals are traffic tickets, public ridicule, and physical pain. Sometimes people's behavior is motivated by the attempt to escape or avoid these sorts of values, rather than by the attempt to approach incentives.

It is now widely believed that avoidance is managed by one set of neural mechanisms and approach by a different set (e.g., Davidson, 1984, 1998; Fowles, 1993; Gray, 1990, 1994). Sometimes both sets of processes are engaged at once, because sometimes the situation is one in which attaining a desired incentive will simultaneously forestall a threat that the person wants to avoid. Sometimes, however, behavior is dominated by either approach or avoidance. This distinction becomes relevant to thinking about stress and coping processes later on.

If goals provide the "values" in expectancy-value models of motivation, the "expectancy" is provided by, well, expectancies. Expectancies are the sense of confidence or doubt that a given outcome can be attained successfully. Sometimes this is expressed as a probability of attaining the outcome; sometimes it is expressed instead as a dichotomy between confidence and doubt. Effects of confidence and doubt can be seen even before a behavior is undertaken. If the person is doubtful enough about a successful outcome, the behavior will not even be attempted. It requires a degree of confidence to try, and it requires a degree of confidence to keep trying when things get difficult. Goal-directed efforts often are bogged down by impediments of various sorts, obstacles both expected and unexpected. A variety of theories propose that even under conditions of extreme impediment, people's efforts will be determined by their expectancies of success (e.g., Bandura, 1986; Brehm & Self, 1989; Wright, 1996; Carver & Scheier, 1981, 1998; Klinger, 1975; Wortman & Brehm, 1975).

No model of action would be complete without emotions. Emotions often arise when people engage in (or even think about) behavior. Emotions are also an important aspect of stress. Carver and Scheier (1990, 1998) have argued that feelings arise from a system that monitors the effectiveness with which people move toward incentives and away from threats. In essence, feelings are an internal signal that progress toward a goal either is too slow (negative affect) or is faster than necessary (positive affect). Although the details of that view become complex (see Carver & Scheier, 1998, chaps. 8 and 9), the point at present is simply that negative feelings arise when there are obstacles to goal attainment (or anti-goal avoidance). These negative feelings are related to the sense of confidence versus doubt, but they are also partly distinct from that sense.

Mentioning obstacles brings us to the realization that not every behavior produces its intended outcome. Sometimes people stop trying, and sometimes they give up the incentive they had been pursuing. There is a basis for arguing that certain kinds of negative feelings are critical to the process by which people turn aside from one incentive and search for another one (Klinger, 1975; Nesse, 2000). As long as the person remains committed to a particular goal, inability to move in the appropriate direction remains distressing. If the person is able to disengage from commitment to that goal, however, there no longer is a basis for the distress. It may be that the level of the distress (along with its longevity) provides the impetus to give up.

There are further issues here, which complicate the picture more. For example, unimportant goals are easy to disengage from; important ones are harder to give up. Even a goal that looks concrete can be important, if its attainment contributes to a particularly important value of the self. That concrete goal can be difficult to abandon.

Once a goal is abandoned, it is important that the person eventually take up another. The absence of a goal can yield a sense of emptiness that itself is quite problematic (Carver & Scheier, 2003). Disengagement seems to be a valuable and adaptive response *when it leads to—or is tied to—the taking up of other goals* (Aspinwall & Richter, 1999; Wrosch, Scheier, Miller, Schulz, & Carver, 2003). By taking up an attainable alternative, the person remains engaged in activities that have meaning for the self, and life continues to have purpose.

An alternative to giving up on an unattainable goal is to scale it back to something in the same general domain but more restricted (Carver & Scheier, 2003). This is a kind of limited disengagement, in the sense that the initial goal no longer remains in place once the scaling back has occurred.

It avoids a complete disengagement from the domain in question, however, by substituting the more restricted goal. This shift thus keeps the person involved in that area of life, at a level that holds the potential for successful outcomes.

The principles described in this section are about behavior in general. I think they also have a good deal of value when thinking more specifically about stress and coping. Let us now turn to models of stress and see how that may be so.

Stress: Lazarus and Folkman

Most contemporary views of stress and coping trace in one way or another to the work of Richard Lazarus and Susan Folkman and their colleagues (e.g., Lazarus, 1966, 1999; Lazarus & Folkman, 1984). The model they developed assumes that stress exists when a person confronts circumstances that tax or exceed his or her ability to manage them. This places the experience of stress squarely in the domain of behavior in which obstacles or difficulties are being confronted. When people find themselves hard-pressed to deal with some impediment or some looming threat, the experience is stressful.

The Lazarus and Folkman model incorporates several themes that have had a large impact on others' thinking. One theme is that stress arises from the person's *appraisal* of circumstances, rather than the objective circumstances. The appraisal depends both on information contained in the situation and on information inside the person. Stress in this model begins with a perception of either threat, harm, or challenge (though challenge has held up less well as a stressor than have the other two perceptions). Threat appraisal is the perception of the impending occurrence of an event that is bad or harmful. Harm appraisal is the perception that something bad has already happened. Challenge appraisal, in contrast, is the perception that one can gain or grow from what nonetheless will be a demanding encounter.

In all these cases, there are impediments to desired conditions either looming or already in place. Work in the Lazarus and Folkman tradition has typically focused on the experience of the stress per se, rather than on the broader matrix of behavior within which the stressor emerges. However, it seems clear that threats often represent imminent interference with pursuit of desired activities, goals, or conditions. For example, a serious illness threatens one's life goals, one's golf game, and one's perception of reality. In the same way, many kinds of harm are actually instances of *loss* (a term that people sometimes use in place of *harm*). Loss is the perception that a desired object or condition is no longer present or available. Loss thus precludes the continued existence of a desired state of affairs. For example, the death of a spouse prevents the continuation of the relationship (cf. Millar, Tesser, & Millar, 1988).

Sometimes threat and harm involve impediments to desired goals. But sometimes threat and harm appraisal involve impending anti-goals. For example, consider the experience of pain (e.g., Affleck, Tennen, Pfeiffer, & Fifield, 1987). It is true that chronic pain disrupts effort to engage in desired activities (i.e., to move toward goals), but that usually is a secondary effect of pain. Pain is, at its core, an aversive state that the person would rather not experience (i.e., an anti-goal). Some harm events represent the occurrence of such anti-goals (pain being only one example). Some threats similarly represent perceptions of the imminent arrival of an anti-goal. Thus, threat and harm can involve the avoidance motivational system as well as the approach system.

Here are some examples. With respect to approach, a person can be threatened by doubt about receiving a sought-after promotion. With respect to avoidance, a person can be threatened by a sudden movement in a dark alley or the sound of a tornado. There apparently are differences in the affects that arise from failing in approach and failing in avoidance (Carver, 2001; Carver & Scheier, 1998; Higgins, 1996; Higgins, Shah, & Friedman, 1997). Thus, threat or loss in an approach context should yield frustration, anger, sadness, and dejection, whereas threat or loss in an avoidance context should yield anxiety and fear (Carver, 2004).

Challenge in the Lazarus and Folkman model is a special case, one that is quite different conceptually from those of threat and harm. A challenge appraisal reveals a situation in which the person's efforts must be fully engaged, but in which the person perceives an opportunity for gain or growth—a chance to move forward. Challenge is a situation in which the person confronts what might be thought of as an "optimal" obstacle—an obstacle that appears surmountable (given appropriate effort) and the removal of which will lead to a better state of affairs than just a return to the status quo (see also Carver, 1998). Challenge is an experience that in many respects resembles "flow" (Csikszentmihalyi, 1990), a state in which both demands and capabilities are said to be perceived as high (with capabilities exceeding demands by just enough to keep behavior moving seamlessly forward).

Challenge seems to involve the engagement of the approach system of motivation, but not the avoidance system. Further, challenge seems to imply confidence about being able to reach the goal (unless the challenge is accompanied by threat). Affects stemming from challenge are such positive feelings as hope, eagerness, and excitement (Lazarus & Folkman, 1984). Although Lazarus and Folkman posited challenge to be a stressful experience, its characteristics (and its consequences) appear to be sufficiently different from those of threat and loss as to cast doubt on that view.

Another theme embedded in the Lazarus–Folkman model is that there is a dynamic, continuous evaluation of both the situation and one's readiness to respond to it. That is, there is a second appraisal process. People don't always respond to stressful encounters in a reflexive, automatic way. Rather, they often appraise their chances of being able to deal with the stressor effectively. They weigh various options and consider the consequences of those options before acting. Decisions about how to cope depend in part on implicit confidence or doubt about the usefulness of a particular strategy of responding. Thus, issues of confidence and doubt, as well as the disruption of intended courses of behavior, are embedded in this theoretical model.

The two appraisal processes are presumed to be interwoven, so that they mutually influence each other. For example, if a threat is appraised as being strong enough, it begins to cast doubt on one's ability to handle it adequately. Similarly, the recognition that one has a perfect response available for use can diminish the experience of threat. Although the Lazarus and Folkman model is usually presented as a sequence of processes, its authors were explicit in indicating that both processes are continuous and interdependent.

Conservation of Resources: Hobfoll

Another view on the experience of stress, developed by Stevan Hobfoll (1989, 1998), begins with the idea that people have an accumulation of resources that they try to protect, defend, and conserve. A person's resources can be physical (e.g., a house, a car, clothing); they can be conditions of one's current life (e.g., having friends and relatives, stable employment, sound marriage); they can be personal qualities (e.g., a positive view of the world, work skills, social prowess); or they can be energy resources (e.g., money, credit, or knowledge). Resources are anything that the person values.

This theory holds that people try to sustain the resources that they have, and they try to acquire further resources. From this viewpoint, stress occurs when resources are threatened or lost, or when people invest resources and fail to receive an adequate return on the investment. Hobfoll (1989) argued that loss of resources is the central experience in stress (see also Hobfoll, Freedy, Green, & Solomon, 1996; Holahan & Moos, 1986). Threat is an impending loss. One might think of the failure to receive an adequate return on investment of resources as being the loss of an anticipated new resource.

Hobfoll (1989) has argued that this theory differs in important ways from other models of stress (and he has in fact generated hypotheses that would not be as readily derived from other models). His stress theory uses an economic metaphor for human experience, which differs from the orientation of other models. In this metaphor, people acquire resources, defend them, and use them to acquire more resources. Stress occurs when the market has a downturn in the value of your resources or when an event of some sort wipes out part of your resource base.

Of particular importance may be social and psychological resources. Holahan, Moos, Holahan, and Cronkite (1999) followed a large sample of adults across a 10-year period, assessing negative and positive life events and changes in personal and social resources. They found that an increase in the balance of negative events to positive events was associated with a decline in social and personal resources, whereas a decrease in negative events was related to increase in resources. These changes in resources, in turn, predicted increases and decreases, respectively, in depression. They concluded that the resources that people use to protect themselves against stresses are themselves vulnerable to being eroded by stress. They subsequently replicated this pattern in a sample of people who were followed after treatment for depression (Holahan, Moos, Holahan, & Cronkite, 2000).

Although the economic metaphor is a useful one, I would argue that it is important to step back from the resources and ask what their usefulness is. In my view (and I do not think anything about this view intrinsically contradicts Hobfoll's theoretical position), these resources matter to people inasmuch as they facilitate people's movement toward desired goals or avoidance of anti-goals. What use is a car? It can take you places you want to go and it can make an impression on other people. What use are friends? They can help you feel better when you are upset, and you can do interesting things of mutual enjoyment with them. What use is a positive life view? It keeps you moving toward a variety of other goals. Work skills permit you to complete projects, achieve things, and hold a job that fosters continued movement toward goals. Money and influence are means to a variety of ends.

In short, I would assert that, for most people, resources are intimately bound up in the continuing pursuit of goals. Thus, the attempt to conserve resources typically occurs in the implicit service of continued goal attainment. A loss of resources represents a threat to that continued goal attainment. Once again, I think there are strong implicit connections to general principles of self-regulation.

Bereavement and Loss: Stroebe and Stroebe

Another view on an aspect of stress that I would like to address briefly is that of Margaret Stroebe, Wolfgang Stroebe, and their colleagues (e.g., Stroebe, Stroebe, & Hansson, 1993). Their work has been conducted within the context of grieving over loss—particularly bereavement (see also Nolen-Hoeksema & Larson, 1999). Their theory is very social in its focus, aimed at understanding how the bereaved person handles both the loss of a relationship and the potential development of new relationships. The perspective they put forward assumes two potential focuses on the part of the bereaved person. The first focus is on the person who has been lost and the relationship of the bereaved with that person. The second focus is on potential relationships with other persons.

Traditionally, many approaches to bereavement have held that the task of the bereaved is to disengage from the lost relationship and move on to new attachments (e.g., Worden, 1991). This sequence is not unlike that described more generally in self-regulatory models as a disengagement of commitment to one incentive to take up another incentive (Klinger, 1975). From this view, the key to successful adaptation for the bereaved person is finalizing the past well enough to make a start toward a future of involvement with others (cf. Tait & Silver, 1989).

There is no question that movement forward is important. Stroebe (1994) reviewed the literature on bereavement and mortality and found that people who die after bereavement, but not those who survive the period of bereavement, tend to lack contact with others during bereavement. Those vulnerable to dying do not remarry, they do not have people to talk to on the phone, they live alone, and they feel isolated. The general picture of those at risk that Stroebe uncovered is one of loneliness and little integration with other people.

The Stroebes and their colleagues have argued, however, that the optimal solution is not always to completely disengage psychologically from the person who has been lost. Rather, it may be better for some people to reconfigure the psychological bond with that person into something different, something that remains positive but is more restricted than it was. Thus the person can continue to draw on that connection psychologically, in ways that provide benefits to him or her (for broader treatment, see Klass, Silverman, & Nickman, 1996), albeit in smaller ways than was once the case. People may differ in whether it is more beneficial to retain a bond with the person who has been lost or loosen the ties and move on (Stroebe, Schut, & Stroebe, 2005).

This reconfiguration of the sense of the lost relationship resembles the scaling-back process of the self-regulation model described earlier. By letting go and disengaging from attempts to reach the unreachable (a continuation of life as it was), the bereaved person becomes free for potential attachments to others. By disengaging only partly, the person retains a sense of connection with the disrupted relationship and draws sustenance from it. To the extent that the positive value of the disrupted relationship can be encapsulated and used by the bereaved as a psychological resource, the residual sense of attachment might help the bereaved person return to activities and connections with other people. If the limited disengagement did *not* return the person to an active life, however, the resolution would not be adaptive.

Section Summary

The preceding sections outlined some of the principles that are widely used to think about stress (for discussions of how to measure stress, see Cohen, Kessler, & Gordon, 1997). These sections also suggested ways in which several models of the experience of stress resemble the general principles of self-regulation that were described initially. Most basically, the experience of stress occurs when a person perceives a threat (either an impending antigoal or the impending inability to attain a goal) or perceives loss or harm (the actual occurrence of an anti-goal or removal of access to a goal). From the self-regulatory view, these experiences constitute the broad and very general realm of behavior under adversity. People respond to their perceptions of threat or loss in a variety of ways. Such responses, described more concretely and in greater detail, are the subject of the next section.

What Is Coping?

The words *stress and coping* are often used together as a phrase, as though the two concepts were intimately joined. After all, there can hardly be coping without the existence of a stressor, and where there is a stressor there usually are coping efforts. Indeed, Lazarus and Folkman's analysis includes the effort to cope as a component of the stress experience. What, then, is coping?

Coping is often defined as efforts to deal in some manner with the threatening or harmful situation, to remove the threat or to diminish the various ways in which it can have an impact on the person. This sort of definition covers a lot of ground. Indeed, it covers so much ground that theorists have had to make several distinctions within the concept (see also Folkman & Moskowitz, 2004).

Problem-Focused and Emotion-Focused Coping

A distinction that was made early on by Lazarus and Folkman (1984) and their colleagues is between problem-focused coping and emotion-focused coping. Problem-focused coping is aimed at the stressor itself. It may involve taking steps to remove the obstacle that the threat represents or to evade the threatening stimulus. For example, if you are driving on a highway and a car jumps the median strip and heads in your general direction, steering out of its path would be problem-focused coping. If you are driving to an important appointment and unexpected work being done on the highway disrupts traffic and threatens to make you late, you can exit the highway and drive around the obstacle via side streets. This would also be problem-focused coping. These two kinds of coping would allow you to evade or escape from the threat.

Other kinds of problem-focused coping do not evade the threat completely but rather diminish its impact. For example, if a hurricane is forecast, people can put up shutters and bring potted plants and patio furniture into the garage. When the storm does hit, the likelihood of damage to the home is thereby reduced. This sort of coping is problem focused because it deals with the physical impact of the stressor. As another example, if a person knows that the company he works for is on a shaky financial footing, he can try to put some savings aside. If the company fails and he loses his job, he will have something to fall back on. This is also problem-focused coping because it deals with the financial impact of the stressor.

Emotion-focused coping stems from the fact that stress experiences typically incorporate distress emotions. Emotion-focused coping is aimed at reducing those emotions. There are many ways to try to reduce feelings of distress. Thus, many coping responses have been characterized as being emotion focused. If the point of a given response is to try to make oneself feel better, that response would thereby seem to be emotion-focused coping. Relaxation exercises would represent emotion-focused coping; going to the movies to take one's mind off the problem might be seen as emotion-focused coping; for some people, shopping is emotion-focused coping.

Another important kind of emotion-focused coping is accommodation to the stressor's existence, or acceptance of its reality, or perhaps a reframing of the situation to emphasize its positive aspects (Carver, Scheier, & Weintraub 1989; Wade et al., 2001). This sort of response seems to permit the person both to feel better about the situation and to remain engaged in other kinds of coping efforts (Carver et al., 1993; Connor-Smith, Compas, Wadsworth, Thomsen, & Saltzman, 2000; Kennedy et al., 2000).

Yet another sort of emotion focused coping is called *emotional approach coping* (Stanton et al.,

2000). This term refers to actively processing and expressing one's emotions, in a fashion that represents an engagement with, rather than a venting of, the feelings. Emotional approach coping entails an effort to be clear about what feelings mean and acceptance that these feelings are important. This approach can result in less distress later on, as long as it does not turn into rumination (Stanton et al., 2000; see also Stanton & Revenson, this volume).

Sometimes coping is individual, focusing on one's own stress experience without regard to anyone else, but sometimes coping is communal, taking significant others into account when engaging in coping (Wells, Hobfoll, & Lavin, 1997). For example, a person might delay taking action on a problem if that action could be anticipated to produce distress for someone who is part of his or her family. There is evidence that women use such communal coping responses more than men (Dunahoo, Hobfoll, Monnier, Hulsizer, & Johnson, 1998).

The distinction made between problem-focused and emotion-focused coping initially led people to classify every coping responses as being either one or the other. This probably was not a wise thing to do. Some reactions that people have when confronting threat or loss appear not to be motivated either by an attempt to remove the stressor or by an attempt to dampen distress emotions. For example, people under stress sometimes engage in self-blame. Although self-blame is often characterized as emotion-focused coping, it is hard to see how it represents an attempt to diminish negative feelings (Kiecolt-Glaser & Williams, 1987).

Making the distinction between problem-focused and emotion-focused coping brings up several other points, as well. For one thing, these classes of response probably differ in their frequency as a function of the nature of the stressor. Problem-focused coping presumably is most likely if the stressor is something that the person views as controllable; emotion-focused coping presumably is more likely if the person sees the stressor as uncontrollable (e.g., Park, Armeli, & Tennen, 2004; Terry & Hynes, 1998; Vitaliano, DeWolfe, Maiuro, Russo, & Katon, 1990). Threats vary in their controllability. However, usually there is nothing that can be done about loss, which makes loss experiences less controllable than threats. In general, the more the situation can be characterized as one that simply has to be endured (as is the case in instances of harm and loss), the less common is the attempt to engage in problem-focused coping.

Another issue this distinction raises is what sorts of responses qualify as problem focused and emotion focused. The answer is that the immediate goal of the response defines which category it belongs to. Indeed, some coping strategies can serve either function, depending on the focus of their use. An example is the use of social support (e.g., Carver et al., 1989). People can turn to others for emotional support and reassurance, which would represent emotion-focused coping. Alternatively, people often can turn to others for physical assistance (e.g., putting up those shutters before the storm hits). This mobilizing of instrumental assistance is problem-focused coping.

Problem-focused and emotion-focused coping are distinguishable from each other on the basis of their immediate, proximal goal. However, it should also be noted that these two kinds of responses can have interrelated effects on one another. If a person engages in effective problem-focused coping, the threat may now seem to be diminished. If so, the distress emotions prompted by the threat should also diminish. Thus, problem-focused coping can result in the reduction or prevention of emotional upheaval. Similarly, if a person engages in effective emotion-focused coping, he or she can now consider the problem more calmly. This may permit the person to undertake problem-focused coping more effectively. It may even permit him or her to think of problem-focused responses that were not previously apparent. Thus, emotion-focused coping can result in better problem-focused coping.

A final point that should be raised is an issue that weaves through the last few paragraphs but was not noted explicitly. That issue is that attempts to cope are not always effective in producing the desired outcome. An attempt to ward off the approaching hurricane by hanging amulets around the house would be problem-focused coping, but it is unlikely to be very effective. Similarly, the attempt to deal with distress from a loss by numbing oneself with alcohol or other drugs would be emotion-focused coping, but it is unlikely to be effective in the long run. In general, when people talk about coping, they usually are referring to coping that is effective and beneficial. However, coping efforts do not always fulfill the functions they are intended to serve (see also Folkman & Moskowitz, 2004). This issue is perhaps most salient with respect to another

distinction that has been made with respect to coping responses.

Avoidance Coping

This distinction makes a contrast between engagement or approach coping, in which the effort is aimed at dealing with the stressor either directly or indirectly (via emotion regulation), and what is often called *avoidance coping* or *disengagement coping* (e.g., Moos & Schaefer, 1993; Roth & Cohen, 1986). Approach coping is essentially everything that was described in the preceding section. Avoidance coping is the effort to escape from having to deal with the stressor, in one fashion or other.

Avoidance coping often is emotion focused, because the effort being made often is an attempt to evade or escape from feelings of distress. Sometimes avoidance coping is almost literally an effort to act as though the stressor does not exist, so that it does not have to be reacted to at all, behaviorally or emotionally. Wishful thinking and fantasy, for example, can remove the person from the stressor, at least temporarily. Denial can also create a boundary between the stressor's reality and the person's experience.

Sometimes the concept of avoidance coping is extended to include giving up on goals the stressor is threatening (Carver et al., 1989). This sort of avoidance coping differs conceptually from the others just described in that it deals with both the stressor's existence and its emotional impact by giving up an investment in something else. By disengaging from the goal that is being threatened, the person avoids the negative feelings associated with the threat.

As just indicated, avoidance coping often is considered to be emotion focused, because it often is an attempt to evade or escape from feelings of distress. Avoidance coping is not always successful in escaping distress, however. In fact, it might be argued that avoidance coping is *generally* ineffective in escaping distress—especially when the stressor is a threat, rather than a loss. The core problem with avoidance coping is that it does nothing about the stressor's existence and its eventual impact. If you are experiencing a real threat in your life and you respond by going to the movies, the threat will remain when the movie is over. Eventually it must be dealt with.

Indeed, many stressful experiences have a time course that is difficult to change. The longer you avoid dealing with a problem of this sort, the less time is available to deal with the problem when you finally turn to it. This can make the situation worse, in any number of ways. Yet another potential problem with avoidance coping is that some kinds of avoidance create additional problems of their own. Excessive use of alcohol or drugs can create social and health problems. Shopping as an escape sometimes leads to unwise spending binges.

There is some evidence that avoidance coping is not as dysfunctional in cases of loss as it is in cases of threat. Bonnano, Keltner, Holen, and Horowitz (1995) studied bereaved persons at 6 months after bereavement and again 8 months later. They separated participants according to the degree to which they were displaying signs of emotional avoidance at the 6-month point. They found that persons who displayed this pattern at 6 months were also more likely to display lower grief symptoms 8 months later. Even in this sort of case, however, evidence is mixed. In another study Folkman and her colleagues found that bereaved men who tried to distance themselves from thoughts about the loss of their partner had more depression over time than those who did not try to distance themselves (Folkman, Chesney, Collette, Boccellari, & Cooke, 1996).

One reason there is controversy over the role of avoidance coping as a way of dealing with loss is that there is a more general controversy about exactly what a recovery from loss entails (Wortman & Silver, 1989). For example, it is commonly held that loss must be mourned, "worked through," examined, questioned, and assimilated. Meaning must be found in the loss, so that the person can come to terms with it. If this were so, avoidance coping would interfere with this process. However, there is evidence that not everyone goes through this process, and that engagement in this process is not good for everyone. For some people, failing to dwell on the loss seems to be the way to get past it (Stroebe, Schut, & Stroebe, 2005; Wortman & Silver, 1989).

Involuntary Versus Intentional Responses

Another issue worth noting is the extent to which coping is an involuntary reaction versus being an intentional response. Certainly some instances of what appears to be coping are relatively reflexive; others appear just as clearly to be planful and intentional. Some people have responded to this issue

by disregarding it. For example, the COPE inventory, a measure of diverse coping responses (Carver et al., 1989), includes some responses that seem relatively reactive (e.g., denial of the reality of the situation) along with others that seem more thoughtful (e.g., planning, use of social support, active coping).

Others working in the field have been more explicit about wishing to restrict the concept of coping to voluntary responses. For example, Compas and his colleagues regard coping as people's conscious, volitional attempts to regulate cognitive, emotional, behavioral, and physical responses to stress (e.g., Compas, Connor, Osowiecki, & Welch, 1997; Compas, Connor-Smith, Saltzman, Thomsen, & Wadsworth, 2001; Connor-Smith et al., 2000). These researchers recognize, however, that stress also evokes involuntary responses, deriving from such sources as temperament and prior conditioning experiences, which are not under the person's control. Examples would be rumination and thought intrusions, and cognitive interference and mental freezing. On the other hand, although Compas and colleagues make this distinction in principle between voluntary and involuntary responses, they do measure both kinds of responses in their research.

Preventive or Proactive Coping

Although most approaches to coping emphasize the role of coping during the experience of threat and loss, not all do so. Aspinwall and Taylor (1997) have argued that a good deal of coping occurs well before the actual occurrence of any stressor. They refer to such actions as *proactive coping*. Proactive coping is not necessarily different in nature from other sorts of coping, but it is intended to prevent threatening or harmful situations from arising. Aspinwall and Taylor distinguished between proactive coping and what they called anticipatory coping, on the ground that the latter involves preparation for an upcoming stressful event that is very likely to occur. As an example, putting up shutters for an approaching hurricane would be anticipatory coping rather than proactive coping. In contrast, proactive coping is aimed at keeping the stressful experience from ever arriving, or at least from arriving in a fully potent form.

Aspinwall and Taylor argued that proactive coping is nearly always active rather than emotion focused. This is consistent with the idea that emotion-focused coping is most common in situations where the stressor involves harm or loss, which by definition has already happened and thus is inaccessible to proactive coping. Proactive coping is largely a matter of accumulating resources that will be useful in the event of a stressor (including resources pertaining to the ability to accurately appraise emerging threats) and scanning the experiential horizon for signs that a threat may be building. Should the beginnings of a threat be perceived, the person can put into motion strategies that will prevent it from appearing or that will remove the person from its path.

Proactive coping has a number of potential payoffs. Most important, if the anticipation of an emerging threat helps the person to avoid the occurrence of the stressful event, the person will experience fewer really stressful experiences and will experience stress of less intensity when the experiences are unavoidable. To the extent that stressful experiences can be averted or minimized, the person will have a lower level of chronic stress. Keeping chronic stress at a low level is likely to have many positive side effects.

There are at least a couple of potential liabilities to this strategy, however. Most obviously, people who are ever-vigilant to the possibility of threat may already be creating stress experiences for themselves by placing themselves in the continuous posture of vigilance.

Positive Emotions and Positive Coping Responses

An issue that has begun to emerge as important in the coping literature concerns the possible role played by positive experiences during the period of the stressful event. People experience distress emotions during a period of stress, but they also experience positive emotions during the same period (e.g., Andrykowski, Brady, & Hunt, 1993). There is some basis for thinking that positive emotions can have positive effects on health (e.g., Folkman & Moskowitz, 2000, 2004; Fredrickson, Mancuso, Branigan, & Tugade, 2000). A review suggests, however, that such effects are fairly mixed (Pressman & Cohen, 2005). The effects of positive emotions may depend in part on their intensity and on the current health of the person who is experiencing them; at low intensities in persons whose health is not severely impaired, they may have benefit.

Another positive experience that is sometimes associated with stress is variously referred to as *stress-related growth* (Park, Cohen, & Murch, 1996), *post-traumatic growth* (Tedeschi & Calhoun, 2004), or *benefit finding* (Tomich & Helgeson, 2004). Many persons who are under great stress report finding meaning in the stressor or experiencing other positive life changes as a consequence of the stressor (Affleck & Tennen, 1996; Bower, Kemeny, Taylor, & Fahey, 1998; Carver & Antoni, 2004; Cordova, Cunningham, Carlson, & Andrykowski, 2001; Park & Folkman, 1997; Taylor, 1983; Tomich & Helgeson, 2004). Such reactions can be induced by a therapeutic intervention as well as occurring spontaneously (Antoni et al., 2001). This topic has generated substantial interest (Park, Lechner, Stanton, & Antoni, in press).

Some Methodological Issues in Coping Research

Before I conclude this discussion of coping, at least brief mention should be made of several methodological issues in the study of coping. These issues are raised here as cautionary points, but unfortunately there is no clear resolution to any of them. The existence of the issues should be kept in mind, however, in considering evidence later on pertaining to the relationships between stress and coping and health.

One very basic issue is that coping can be examined concurrently with the relevant outcome, or coping can instead be examined as a prospective predictor of the outcome. It is clear that any cross-sectional analysis of coping and health (or stress and health, for that matter) is subject to important limitations on inferences. Given only concurrent relations, it is impossible to draw any conclusions about causal influence. After all, ill health can create stress and induce certain kinds of coping responses, just as easily as it can be influenced by stress and coping responses. With concurrent associations, there is no way to untangle the meaning of the association. Measuring coping (or stress) at one point and health outcomes at a subsequent point permits one to establish temporal precedence of the one, compared with the other. Although this still falls short of demonstrating cause and effect, it at least establishes the plausibility of a causal relation.

Another set of issues concerns the attempt to measure coping over an extended period of time rather than at a specific moment. What should be the time frame for assessment? Should participants in the study be asked about their current coping (i.e., at this moment) with a particular stressor, repeatedly over multiple instances? Should participants be asked instead to rate the extent to which they have used each of a set of coping reactions with the accumulated stressors of the day or the week? Attempting to measure coping with specific stressors repeatedly over time is a labor-intensive enterprise. Yet there are important reasons to consider such a strategy. Most important, there is evidence that people do not do a very good job of remembering what they did to cope with even fairly salient stressors, once some time has passed (Ptacek, Smith, Espe, & Raffety, 1994), though they do better when the time frame is more limited (Todd, Tennen, Carney, Armeli, & Affleck, 2004).

Another, related issue is how long a time lag to use in examining prospective effects of coping. Should you measure coping on one day and the outcome variable the next day? A week later? A month later? Three months later? With some outcome variables, it would seem to be necessary to permit a fairly substantial delay before assessment of the outcome. With others it is less clear. How much sense does it make, for example, to measure coping with a stressor at one time point, then measure emotional well-being a year later? Tennen, Affleck, Armeli, and Carney (2000) have argued for the usefulness of a strategy in which coping and outcomes are measured daily, at least for certain kinds of coping effects.

Another set of questions concerns how to deal with people's responses on self-reports of coping. Typically people are asked to indicate the extent to which they used (or involuntarily experienced) each of several responses to the stressor, on a rating scale that ranges from zero to some high value. One question that has been raised occasionally is this: What if a particular coping response is very important, but different people need to do more of it in order to function adaptively? If the study combines these people, some who report moderate use of the strategy will be using it more than enough, and some might be using it less than they need to. Yet they will be treated as using the strategy equivalently in the analyses. This can obscure a potentially important relationship between the coping strategy and the outcome.

Another question concerns how to deal with the fact that some people report many different coping reactions at a given time, whereas others report far fewer. Should the researcher assume that the extent of use of each strategy is the critical issue? Or should the researcher assume that a person who used this strategy and almost nothing else is relying on this one more than a person who used this strategy and six others as well? Tennen et al. (2000) have proposed that people typically use emotion-focused coping largely after they have tried problem-focused coping and found it to be ineffective. This suggests an approach to examining coping in which the question is whether the individual changes from one sort of coping to another across successive days as a function of lack of effectiveness of the first coping response used.

These various ways of viewing the information lead to very different analytic strategies. The first view presented would treat the raw information as predictors of the outcome. The second view might lead the researcher to create an index of the percentage of total coping that was devoted to this particular coping strategy (cf. Vitaliano, Russo, Young, Teri, & Maiuro, 1991). The third view entails use of multilevel analytic strategies (see Tennen et al., 2000). Yet another possibility is to use all available information about coping to create aggregations of people whose profiles of coping responses are similar, through such techniques as cluster analysis. If several common profiles can be identified, perhaps these more accurately reflect coping differences in large samples of people.

As indicated earlier, the various issues raised in this section are unresolved. It is clear that some strategies have built-in problems (e.g., cross-sectional studies cannot be informative about causality). With respect to other issues (such as the use of raw scores or indices), there is no clear indication that one approach is right and the other wrong. Readers should be aware, however, that different positions on these issues were taken in various studies that bear on stress, coping, and health. These are not the only issues we have to worry about, though. Further issues are raised when we add in the concept of health.

Stress Effects on Health: Issues

In considering how stress and coping may influence health, we must decide what we mean by "health." At first glance, health seems a simple concept with an obvious meaning. However, further reflection reveals that it has some fuzzy boundaries.

What Is Health?

A good deal of research has been conducted on the impact of stress and coping on emotional well-being. Emotional well-being is important in its own right, and there are some indications that variations in emotional well-being influence health. However, for the purposes of this chapter, we must consider emotional responses as being at least a step away from health.

A literature is also beginning to develop regarding the impact of stress and coping on physiological parameters of various sorts, such as blood pressure, neurotransmitters, and immune activity. Should these variables be thought of as constituting health? This question is harder to answer (see also Cohen & Rodriguez, 1995).

Shifts in the values of some physiological indices are considered to be disorders in and of themselves. An example is blood pressure. When resting blood pressure is consistently above a certain level, the person is diagnosed as having the illness called *hypertension*. In other cases, it is less clear that shifts in a physiological parameter—even fairly extreme shifts—would be viewed as reflecting illness or disorder. In general, changes in these parameters are viewed as perhaps having direct influences on health, but not as representing health effects per se.

Generally, when we talk about health in this context, we are talking about the presence or absence of a diagnosable, verifiable illness or disorder. Even within that framework, however, there is a great deal of potential diversity (cf. Carver & Scheier, 1998: chap. 18). In some cases research focuses on what is called disease *promotion,* where the issue is who comes down with the disease and who does not. An example is research on women who have the human papiloma virus, which is a predisposing factor for cervical cancer. Some of these women will develop cancer; others will not. In other cases the issue is disease *progression,* how quickly an early form of a disease evolves into a more advanced form. In yet other cases the focus is on *recurrence* of a disease that has been successfully treated. An example is studies of women who have been treated successfully for breast cancer and are continuing their posttreatment lives. Sometimes research even examines illness that is a *side effect* of treatment for a different illness. An example is the rehospitalization for infection that often follows successful heart surgery. Finally, in some cases, the

health outcome is literally life or death. In these studies the focus is on *mortality* rates or *survival times* among people who have a disease that is more severe. For example, do stress and coping processes influence the longevity of AIDS patients?

All the possibilities described in the preceding paragraph are legitimately regarded as studies of "health." The diversity among them, however, raises further issues. For example, it might be the case that stress and coping variables play a role in some kinds of health outcomes but not in others—perhaps stress influences disease promotion but not survival time, or vice versa. The possibility of an influence on specific health outcomes rather than health outcomes more broadly means that nonsupportive findings must be evaluated more tentatively. What becomes important is patterns of effects on particular classes of outcomes.

Behavioral Pathways of Influence

Other issues to be considered are the functional pathways by which stress and coping might influence health. There are, in fact, several possibilities, which have very different implications.

Some potential pathways are quite behavioral. These are pathways in which health consequences arise from the nature of the behaviors themselves. For example, people sometimes engage in risky behaviors such as unprotected sex. If risky behaviors are more likely when people are under stress, the result would be that stress creates greater potential for exposure to sexually transmitted diseases (see Antoni, 2002).

Other behavioral pathways to disease derive from the fact that certain kinds of behavior, such as smoking and drug use, are intrinsically antagonistic to health. If such behaviors are more likely when people are under stress (cf. Cohen, Schwartz, Bromet, & Parkinson, 1991; Holohan, Moos, Holohan, Cronkite, & Randall, 2003; Horwitz & White, 1991), the result would be that stress increases exposure to harmful agents (in these cases, chemical agents) and ultimately causes adverse health effects. Indeed, the use of drugs and alcohol can have further ripple effects, increasing the tendency to engage in other kinds of risk behaviors (e.g., Ostrow et al., 1990).

Yet another area of behavioral influence concerns adherence to medical regimens. Failure to adhere to a prescribed medical regimen can seriously compromise the benefit of the treatment. If nonadherence or erratic adherence is more likely when people are under stress, the result would be a reduced exposure to the curative agent and eventually poorer medical outcomes (Dunbar-Jacob & Schlenk, 1996; Sherbourne, Hays, Ordway, DiMatteo, & Kravitz, 1992). A parallel case can be made for maintaining exercise and a well-balanced diet. Exercise and proper eating are often the first things to be disregarded when stress arises, and doing so keeps the person from benefits he or she would otherwise experience (Smith & Leon, 1992).

A final sort of behavioral effect is the failure to seek either diagnosis or treatment for a condition that turns out to be an illness (Andersen & Cacioppo, 1995). Failure to seek medical consultation can result in the progression of the disease well beyond its initial level. The result sometimes is that a medical condition that would have been fairly easily treated becomes sufficiently advanced as to be more difficult to treat effectively.

Each of these cases represents a purely "behavioral" pathway to illness. That is, each case involves either an increase in potential exposure to a pathogen or a decrease in exposure to a beneficial agent as a result of the person's action. However, none of these cases assumes a direct link between the person's behavior (or psychological state) and changes in aspects of the body's internal functioning.

I will say very little more about these behavioral pathways. They obviously are important. Dysfunctional coping tactics such as smoking, drinking, binge eating, and high-risk sex represent clear ways in which adverse health effects can be created (for review of issues and findings, see Dunbar-Jacob, Schlenk, & Caruthers, 2002). To the extent that failure to seek diagnosis or treatment (or to follow instructions regarding treatment) can be thought of as avoidance coping, such pathways would reflect yet further instances in which avoidance coping produces adverse effects. These effects are quite straightforward. For the remainder of this chapter, however, I focus on other pathways that appear to involve links between psychological responses and physiological responses.

Psychophysiological Pathways of Influence

Many kinds of psychological experiences produce involuntary physiological changes within the body. Some of these changes are disruptive of important

health-protective functions. In these hypothesized pathways, stress and coping processes influence the body's reactions in some way that renders the person more vulnerable to the promotion or progression of disease.

Typically, this sort of pathway is assumed to begin with the experience of emotional distress (although that aspect of the sequence is not always addressed directly in the research). Intense emotional states are associated with a variety of cardiovascular responses and neuroendocrine changes. Given the broad array of responses that are associated with negative emotions, there again are diverse potential pathways of influence on health.

For example, one line of reasoning holds that extensive and repeated cardiovascular stress responses place an abnormally high burden on arteries, resulting (over the long term) in small tears and the depositing of protective plaques. Too much depositing of plaques, however, eventually turns into a case of atherosclerosis (e.g., Krantz & McCeney, 2002; Rozanski, Blumenthal, & Kaplan, 1999; Smith & Ruiz, 2002). Similarly, the processes by which blood pressure is regulated may be responsive over repeated cardiovascular demands, leading to eventual development of hypertension (cf. Fredrikson & Matthews, 1990). Nor are these the only mechanisms by which stress can contribute to cardiovascular disease.

Another focal point in analyses of stress-related physiological responding is the hypothalamic-pituitary-adrenocortical (HPA) axis. This set of structures has proved to have major involvement in the body's stress response (Michelson, Licinio, & Bold, 1995). I will not describe the functioning of the HPA axis in any detail here, except to say that it is involved in sympathetic nervous system activation under stress (for a broader treatment, see the chapter in this volume by Cacioppo and Berntson; see also Chrousos, 1995; Michelson et al., 1995). This pattern of physiological changes represents the body's pattern of preparation for intense physical activity (Maier, Watkins, & Fleshner, 1994), more colloquially known as the *fight-or-flight response*. HPA activation is reflected in increased levels of several hormones, including the catecholamines (ephinephrine and norepinephrine) and cortisol.

Cortisol is believed to be a particularly important stress hormone because of its links to other processes in the overall stress response. Perhaps most important, elevation of cortisol can suppress immune functions (Maier et al., 1994). The effects include decreasing antibody production, decreasing numbers of T cells, decreasing lymphocyte proliferative responses, and inhibition of natural killer cell (NK) activation (Kronfol, Madhavan, Zhang, Hill, & Brown, 1997). Maier et al. (1994) argued that this suppression stems from a very simple principle: The body can devote its energies either to the fight-or-flight response or to elimination of internal pathogens, but it cannot easily do both at the same time. When strong demands are made on one (fight-or-flight), the other (immune surveillance) is suppressed (see also Miller, Cohen, & Ritchey, 2002).

Indeed, another target in analyses of stress-related physiological responding is the immune system itself (Segerstrom & Miller, 2004). The immune system obviously is another aspect of the body that has important implications for health. The immune system is the body's main line of defense against disease agents, ranging from bacteria to cancer cells. If immune functioning is impaired, the person thereby becomes more vulnerable both to opportunistic infectious agents and to agents of disease that had already been at work in the body. The result may be either disease promotion or disease progression (Glaser & Kiecolt-Glaser, 1994). The immune system is far more complicated than was assumed two decades ago, and there are several ways in which stress can influence immune function (Kemeny, this volume; Kiecolt-Glaser, McGuire, Robles, & Glaser, 2002; Robles, Glaser, & Kiecolt-Glaser, 2005).

One last point should perhaps be made here about the nature of psychophysiological response patterns. One of the earliest writers in the literature of stress, Hans Selye (1956), described the course of stress using the phrase *general adaptation syndrome*. It consists of three stages. First there is an alarm reaction, in which an array of physiological changes occur, in an immediate effort to counter the damaging agent. If the stress continues, a stage of resistance develops in which the body develops inflammation and bodily resources are expended to heal any damage that has occurred. If the stress is severe enough or if it continues for long enough, a third stage ensues: exhaustion. The depletion of resources that defines exhaustion produces a cessation of struggling.

Most of the focus on psychophysiological pathways in today's health psychology is on the phases of the stress response that Selye termed *alarm* and *resistance*. Generally we are looking for signs of struggle from the mechanisms of the body. However, sometimes it is the exhaustion part of the response that is critical to the impact of stress on health (Segerstrom & Miller, 2004). Selye's depiction of exhaustion has some commonality with the psychological state of depression. Depression represents a condition in which the person has given up struggling to move forward. Giving up can also have adverse effects, though the experience differs in many ways from that of a repeated or prolonged struggle.

Section Summary

Let me summarize parts of what I have said thus far and preview some things that are yet to be described, by means of a visual illustration. Figure 6.1 depicts a set of hypothetical links among stress, coping, emotional distress, physiological responses, and health. One way to read the links in the figure is as paths of potential influence. Another way to read them is as relationships that might be examined in a given study. (I hasten to note, however, that I know of no study that has examined all the relationships that are shown in Figure 6.1.)

Models of stress and illness that are not primarily behavioral in focus often assume a logic involving the paths that are aligned in a vertical column in the center of Figure 6.1: That is, adverse events (actual or anticipated) induce the stress experience (path 1), which causes negative emotions (path 2). These emotions incorporate a variety of physiological changes. If the emotional reactions are intense, prolonged, or repeated, there is a potential for disruption in one or more physiological system (path 3). In one way or another, this disruption then makes disease more likely (path 4).

Most studies, however, jump past one or more of these steps. Some examine the impact of stress on physiological changes (path 5); some examine the impact of stress on disease outcomes (path 6). Some start with emotional distress rather than stress, and examine its impact on disease outcomes (path 7). The ideal study would incorporate data on all the classes of variables shown in Figure 6.1: stress level, coping responses, emotional distress, physiological parameters, and disease outcomes. However, this ideal is not often encountered in the literature.

Coping is shown in this figure as a moderator, which potentially interacts at three places in the

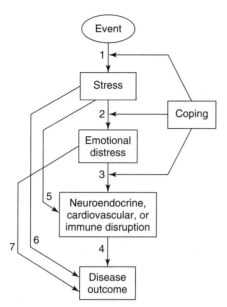

Figure 6.1. Hypothetical pathways by which stress and coping might influence disease outcomes. Each path can also be read as an association that might be examined in a given study. It should be noted that this diagram is an oversimplification, in several respects. For one thing, at least some of the arrows actually go in both directions, rather than just one.

evidence. At present, that hypothesis must be viewed as a line of reasoning that appears worth testing explicitly.

From Stress to Distress and the Role of Coping

With respect to the link between stress and distress, the path is unquestionable. There is no doubt that stressful events produce emotional distress. A variety of studies of chronic stress make this case readily, as do studies of acute stress. As an example, it has been shown that poorer marital quality relates to higher levels of depression (Kiecolt-Glaser, Fisher, et al., 1987), as does being a caregiver for someone with Alzheimer's disease (Kiecolt-Glaser, Glaser, et al., 1987). These findings are straightforward, and there are many more that make conceptually similar points.

There is also not much doubt that coping can have an influence on the link between stress and distress—effects that range from the helpful to the harmful. One example of these effects of coping comes from a study of how women deal with treatment for early-stage breast cancer across the first year after treatment (Carver et al., 1993). In this study, coping with the diagnosis and treatment of the cancer and mood were assessed the day before surgery, 10 days after surgery, and at three follow-ups. Because all the women in this study had just been diagnosed with early-stage breast cancer, the stressor they were exposed to was roughly uniform (differences in stage, surgical treatment, and adjuvant therapy were also examined, however).

Several coping tactics related to distress. Coping that revolved around accepting the reality of the situation (acceptance), placing as good a light on it as possible (positive reframing), and trying to relieve the situation with humor all related to less concurrent distress, both before surgery and afterward. Coping that involved trying to push the reality of the situation away (denial) and giving up the attempt to reach threatened goals (behavioral disengagement) related to greater concurrent distress at all measurement points.

There were also prospective effects, both from coping to distress and from distress to coping. Indeed, these effects seemed to form a spiral of influence. Presurgical acceptance predicted less postsurgical distress (controlling for presurgical distress); postsurgical distress, in turn, predicted greater use

stream of influence. In each case, if the coping is effective, it would dampen the response that is next in line; if the coping is dysfunctional, it might increase the next response. Coping can be proactive, and if engaged sufficiently, it can prevent the stress from arising in the first place (path 1). Coping can influence how intense or prolonged are the distress emotions involved in the event (path 2). And coping can potentially change how emotions are translated into physiological disruptions (path 3). Of course, if a particular study were to disregard emotional distress, or physiological reactions, any interaction that involved coping might instead appear as impinging on paths 5, 6, or 7 (interactions that are omitted from Figure 6.1).

Impact of Stress on Psychological and Physiological Responses

Let us now turn to some of the evidence bearing on some of the pathways shown in Figure 6.1. With respect to the effects of preventive or proactive coping (Aspinwall & Taylor, 1997), there is as yet little of denial and disengagement at the 3-month point. Finally, denial and disengagement at 3 months predicted more distress at 6 months after surgery (controlling for 3-month distress), whereas use of humor at 3 months predicted less distress at 6 months. Additional evidence of such a spiral was reported by Culver, Arena, Antoni, and Carver (2002).

This pattern makes several points. First, it is clear that some coping responses were helpful with regard to future distress (acceptance, use of humor), and others were disruptive (denial and disengagement). Second, the coping responses that were most useful in this situation were emotion focused (acceptance and use of humor). There was little to be done in this situation except to adapt to it and follow the doctors' orders. As a result, the responses that were most useful were those that involved accommodation. Finally, the overall pattern of findings appears to be consistent with elements of the self-regulation model of behavior described earlier.

This study is only a single example of a large number of studies of how differences in coping reactions can result in different levels of emotional distress among persons dealing with stresses. The literature is a very broad one (see also Folkman & Moskowitz, 2004). A couple of caveats about this literature should be kept in mind, however. First, as indicated earlier in the chapter, many studies of stress, coping, and distress are cross-sectional rather than prospective. Although there sometimes are good reasons for using cross-sectional designs, the design also has serious drawbacks.

A second caveat concerns the nature of the effect observed, even when the study is prospective. Specifically, the logic underlying studies of this topic is that coping interacts with stress to determine level of emotional distress. Adequately testing such a moderator, or "stress buffering," hypothesis (Cohen & Wills, 1985) requires that there be varying levels of both stress and coping. In the study just described (Carver et al., 1993), this was not the case. All participants in that study were cancer patients, with roughly equivalent stressors. Thus the study does not deal with the question of whether coping would have had a comparable set of relations to distress level even among women who were not experiencing the stresses associated with breast cancer. Such a finding might be interpretable, but it would not fit the interactive view depicted in Figure 6.1.

Links From Emotional Distress to Physiological Responses

The next step in the logical chain shown in Figure 6.1 is from distress emotions to physiological responses. There are a great many potential physiological responses, and evidence has accumulated pertaining to many of them. Consider first cardiovascular effects. There is no question that many negative emotions such as anxiety and anger produce increases in cardiovascular responses (e.g., Blascovich & Katkin, 1993; Krantz & McCeney, 2002).

An illustration of such effects comes from research on marital interactions. In this research, married couples are asked to discuss a topic on which they have a conflict, and their physiological responses are monitored over time. One early study of this design found that when hostile behavior occurred during these interactions, it produced sizable changes in blood pressure (Ewart, Taylor, Kraemer, & Agras, 1991). In fact, a more recent study found that simply recalling an instance of marital conflict is enough to raise a person's blood pressure (Carels, Sherwood, & Blumenthal, 1998). These findings are particularly compelling because they focus on an experience that is very common in day-to-day life: conflict with significant others.

Emotional distress has also been related to elevations of cortisol and other neuroendocrines (Biondi & Picardi, 1999; Michelson et al., 1995), particularly in the context of social threat (Dickerson & Kemeny, 2004). Research on marital interaction also provides a nice illustration of these effects. Hostile behavior during marital conflict has been found to lead to increases in epinephrine and norepinephrine, both among newlyweds (Malarkey, Kiecolt-Glaser, Pearl, & Glaser, 1994) and among couples in long-term marriages (Kiecolt-Glaser et al., 1997). Among wives, elevations in norepinephrine and cortisol were also found when their own negative behavior was met by withdrawal on the part of their husbands (Kiecolt-Glaser, Newton, et al., 1996), which is a pattern that has also been linked to marital distress (e.g., Heavey, Layne, & Christensen, 1993). Indeed, elevations in neuroendocrine function predict likelihood of divorce 10 years later (Kiecolt-Glaser, Bane, Glaser, & Malarkey, 2003).

These marital interaction effects on neuroendocrines are typically stronger among women than men (Kiecolt-Glaser & Newton, 2001). Interestingly, however, cortisol reactivity to harassment by an experiment accomplice has been found to be twice as great among men as among women (Earle, Linden, & Weinberg, 1999), perhaps because the harassment is experienced by men as a threat to their social dominance (cf. Smith, Allred, Morrison, & Carlson, 1989; Smith, Nealey, Kircher, & Limon, 1997; Smith, Ruiz, & Uchino, 2000).

Thus, distress associated with social challenge often leads to increases in cortisol (Dickerson & Kemeny, 2004). There is also evidence from other sources that elevation of cortisol can suppress immune function (Antoni & Schneiderman, 1998; Kronfol et al., 1997; O'Leary, 1990). Thus, it would seem reasonable to assert that distress can influence immune function. Indeed, that does seem to be true. For example, depression has been related to suppressed immune function in many studies (see Herbert & Cohen, 1993, for a meta-analytic review; see Robles et al., 2005, for a more recent analysis of depression and cytokines). There also seems to be a synergistic effect between depression and other adverse factors. One study found that depression status interacts with smoking, with the lowest NK cell activity appearing in depressed smokers (Jung & Irwin, 1999).

Other research has linked the long-term stress of caring for a demented spouse to adverse immune effects. In one study (Glaser, Sheridan, Malarkey, MacCallum, & Kiecolt-Glaser, 2000), participants received a pneumococcal bacterial vaccination and had immune measures collected at several points afterward. Caregivers showed poorer antibody responses at 3 and 6 months after the vaccination than did controls.

There appear to be two different patterns of cortisol response and related immune response (Segerstrom & Miller, 2004). Loss, epitomized by bereavement, tends to relate to increases in cortisol production and decreased NK cytotoxicity. In contrast, trauma and post-traumatic disorders tend to relate to decreases in cortisol production. That decrease has consequences for immune function, but consequences that are different from those associated with chronic stress.

Recall that Figure 6.1 placed cardiovascular, neuroendocrine, and immune disruptions at the same step of the hypothetical sequence of processes. As is suggested by the preceding paragraph, however, it is not clear whether such an equivalent placement actually is warranted (cf. Maier et al., 1994). Some studies appear to suggest that one set of these physiological parameters influences another set. On the other hand, there is also evidence that several systems are mutually entrained. For example, Cacioppo et al. (1998) found that brief psychological stressors increased cardiac sympathetic activation, elevated catecholamines, and affected cellular immune responses. Persons who showed the greatest stress-related changes in HPA activation also showed the greatest reduction in cellular immune response. Everything seemed tied to everything else in these data, which would be consistent with the portrayal in Figure 6.1.

As if all this were not complicated enough, there is also evidence that influence can be exerted in the opposite direction. Reichenberg and colleagues (2001) injected volunteer research participants with two different substances at two different times. One was a mild dose of a toxin; the other was a placebo. Participants' bodies reacted to the toxin by producing an immune response—reflected, for example, in increasing circulating levels of interleukin-6. An hour after the injection of the toxin (but not the placebo), participants reported an elevation in anxiety. Two hours after that (while the immune response was still elevated), they reported an elevation in depressed feelings. This pattern of findings suggests the possibility that emotional responses can be influenced by the body's immune response.

As indicated by this brief review of a handful of studies, there is a great deal of information linking stress and distress to physiological reactions of diverse types. This sort of research is ongoing, and the picture of how different systems interweave or influence each other should become clearer in the next decades. As noted earlier, however, there is a considerable difference between showing that stress and distress predict changes in physiological responses and showing that stress and distress play a role in actual health outcomes. I now turn to the question of whether stress and coping have implications for physical well-being over the longer term.

Stress and Health

The evidence on the links between stress and physical well-being is scattered across many literatures. There remain many questions about mechanisms of influence. There appears to be no question, however, that such a relationship does exist.

From Stress to Cardiovascular Disruption and Disease

One burgeoning literature bearing on this relationship focuses on cardiovascular diseases (see, e.g., Krantz & McCeney, 2002; Rozanski et al., 1999; Smith & Ruiz, 2002). The studies range from laboratory and field research on humans to studies of infrahuman animals. The stresses range from acute to chronic. The outcome measures range from the very focalized and specific (such as myocardial ischemia, and the occurrence of myocardial infarction), to broader and longer-term (such as development of atherosclerosis).

Part of this literature examines the impact of chronic stress on cardiovascular disease. Chronic work stress seems to exert a variety of pathophysiological effects, including raising blood pressure (Schnall et al., 1990; Schnall, Schwartz, Landsbergis, Warren, & Pickering, 1998). Although people tend to think of chronic stress solely in terms of work, social disruptions can also create chronic stress, which can lead to cardiovascular problems. As an example, many years ago Ratcliffe and Cronin (1958) described the impact of social disruption among animals at a zoo. They argued that crowding and disruption of normal social patterns had led to an increase in atherosclerosis among the animals. More recently, it was found that social isolation, as well as crowding, can create similar problems (Shively, Clarkson, & Kaplan, 1989). In the latter study, monkeys housed alone had four times as much atherosclerosis as those housed in social groups.

Emotional distress has also been studied as a predictor of cardiovascular problems over the long term (Krantz & McCeney, 2002). Among initially healthy persons, symptoms of anxiety and depression have been found to predict incidence of coronary heart disease (CHD) later on (Barefoot & Schroll, 1996; Ford et al., 1998; Kubzansky et al., 1997). Furthermore, among patients who already have clinical evidence of CHD, symptoms of anxiety and depression predict recurrent coronary events and earlier death (Ahern et al., 1990; Barefoot et al., 1996; Barefoot et al., 2000; Frasure-Smith, Lesperance, & Talajic, 1995; Moser & Dracup, 1996; for a review, see Januzzi, Stern, Pasternak, & DeSanctis, 2000). Depression has also proved to be a risk factor for CHD among persons with diabetes (Kinder, Kamarck, Baum, & Orchard, 2002). Other constructs related to depression, such as symptoms of

exhaustion (Appels, Golombeck, Gorgels, de Vreede, & van Breukelen, 2000), pessimism (Scheier et al., 1999), and hopelessness (Everson et al., 1996; Everson, Kaplan, Goldberg, Salonen, & Salonen, 1997), also predict adverse effects and more negative prognoses relating to CHD.

It is not just chronic stress that influences cardiovascular disease. Acute stressors can also have major cardiovascular effects (Krantz & McCeney, 2002). An acute stressor that has long been associated with elevated rates of cardiac events is bereavement (Kaprio, Koskenvuo, & Rita, 1987; Parkes, 1964). In one very large study (95,647 persons followed for 4 to 5 years), the highest relative mortality by heart attack occurred immediately after bereavement (Kaprio et al., 1987). During the first month after bereavement, men's risk of sudden death doubled, and women's risk tripled. After the first month, mortality rates returned to population levels.

Bereavement is probably the best known of acute stressors with cardiovascular implications, but it is not the only one. For instance, during the Los Angeles earthquake of 1994, the number of sudden cardiac deaths rose from a daily average of 4.6 in the preceding week to 24 on the day of the earthquake (Leor, Poole, & Kloner, 1996). Similarly, there was a sharp increase in the number of deaths on the first day of missile strikes on Israeli cities during the Gulf War of 1991 (Meisel et al., 1991). Even an event as simple as a bout of anger can trigger myocardial infarction (MI; Mittleman et al., 1995). In this study, a sample of post-MI patients were asked to reconstruct the events preceding their infarctions. Their reports revealed a relative risk of MI that was more than double after an anger episode.

Research on animals shows that acute stress can have a wide range of very specific adverse effects on the cardiovascular system. Among other things, there is evidence that acute stress can trigger myocardial ischemia, promote arrhythmias, stimulate platelet function, and increase blood viscosity (for more detail concerning mechanisms, see Rozanski et al., 1999). Consistent with this view, there is evidence from a number of studies linking the experience of anxiety to elevated risk of fatal ischemic heart disease (Hemingway & Marmot, 1999). Indeed, one review has concluded that of anger, anxiety, and depression, the evidence was strongest for anxiety as a causal factor in ischemic heart disease (Kubzansky & Kawachi, 2000). On the other hand, a wide variety of research has linked anger proneness to other aspects of coronary heart disease (Krantz & McCeney, 2002; Miller, Smith, Turner, Guijarro, & Hallet, 1996; Williams et al., 2000).

From Stress to Viral Infection

The effects of stress on the cardiovascular system represent one very important aspect of today's research on stress and health, but there are many other focuses as well. Another body of work that is particularly interesting examines vulnerability to infection. Vulnerability or resistance to infection can be shown in a great many ways, and research bearing on the issue has approached it from several directions. One line of research concerns an infection that most people encounter repeatedly over the course of a lifetime: the common cold.

Does stress influence who catches a cold and who does not? The procedure used in research on this question has been to collect a sample of healthy participants, assess them in several ways, expose them to various doses of cold virus in a carefully controlled environment, then see what happens. Cohen, Tyrrell, and Smith (1991) did this, assessing participants' preexisting stress level (using a measure that blended stress and subjective distress). Lower stress levels predicted greater resistance to infection.

Subsequent work has found several other things about this vulnerability (Cohen, 2005). For example, relatively brief stressful events (less than a month in length) did not predict relative infection risk, but chronic stress (events lasting a month or longer) did (Cohen et al., 1998). The long-term stresses in this study were primarily unemployment (or underemployment) and long-lasting interpersonal problems with family or friends. In other research, having chronically high positive emotionality was protective against infection (Cohen, Doyle, Turner, Alper, & Skoner, 2003). Evidence from a study of monkeys indicates that vulnerability to colds is greater among individuals of lower status than among those of higher status (Cohen et al., 1997)

The investigators carrying out this line of research also collected a variety of other measures to determine the pathway by which stress (or emotional distress) exerts its effects. These measures included endocrine and immune measures that were collected before the exposure to the virus.

Interestingly enough, the relation between stressors and susceptibility to colds could not be explained by changes occurring in these other variables. How was the effect mediated?

The answer, which has begun to emerge in subsequent studies (Cohen, 2005), requires going deeper into the immune system, to examine pro-inflammatory cytokines. These are the substances that trigger the symptoms associated with upper respiratory viral infections. The evidence suggests that stress impairs the body's ability to turn off the production of these cytokines when they are no longer needed (e.g., Miller et al., 2002). Cohen (2005) has pointed out that the conclusion was rather different from what had originally been expected: This stress effect occurs not because stress *suppresses* an immune function, but because stress interferes with the ability of the overall immune system to regulate itself properly—to turn the immune function off when it should turn off.

The common cold provides a good example of research on stress, coping, and health partly because it is an experience to which we can all relate. However, it is perhaps important to point out that the viruses responsible for colds stand as representatives of a far broader class of pathogen. Although it is unclear how far the findings described here will generalize, there is reason to think the principles are likely to be applicable to susceptibility to infection from other viral agents, as well (see Cohen & Herbert, 1996).

Stress and Wound Healing

Another focus for research dealing with infectious agents has been on the processes by which wounds, or breaks in the skin, heal over time. Wound healing is a complex process that involves a variety of immune functions. Research on this topic has included both examination of the immune response per se and study of the overall time required for the wound to heal. Some of this research creates wounds in the form of blisters; more recently a common procedure has been to create a punch wound of a controlled diameter and depth.

Glaser et al. (1999) reported data bearing on an immune effect that may represent the first step toward wound healing. This is the inflammatory response that occurs shortly after the event causes the wound. Glaser et al. created blisters on participants' forearms, had participants rate their stress levels, and also measured the presence of two cytokines that are responsible for the inflammation response. The participants who reported higher levels of stress also produced lower levels of these cytokines, which are important for the first stages of wound healing.

And what of wound healing per se? A number of studies have now been reported on this topic. Kiecolt-Glaser and colleagues (Kiecolt-Glaser, Marucha, Malarkey, Mercado, & Glaser, 1995) investigated the effects of the stress resulting from caring for a relative with Alzheimer's disease on wound healing. They compared women caring for demented relatives with control women matched for age and family income. All these women underwent a wound that was carefully controlled in size. Healing was assessed by photography of the wound and by response to hydrogen peroxide (healing defined as no foaming). Wound healing took significantly longer in caregivers than in controls. There was secondary evidence from this study that the caregivers were also experiencing immune suppression.

Another demonstration of this stress effect on wound healing made use of dental students as research participants (Marucha, Kiecolt-Glaser, & Favagehi, 1998). These students underwent punch wounds at two different times: 3 days before the first major exam of the semester (a highly stressful time), and during a vacation period (a low-stress time). On average the students took 40% longer (3 days longer) to heal during the high-stress period than during the control period. This study also found a decline in production of a substance relevant to the immune response during the exam period, again suggesting a possible immune pathway. However, the researchers did not test the path statistically, leaving open the question of whether the difference in immune response was behind the difference in healing time.

Another study examined wound healing as a function of perceived stress at the time of the wound (Ebrecht, Hextall, Kirtley, Taylor, Dyson, & Weinman, 2004). Those reporting lower stress levels experienced faster healing. They also were less likely to display a morning elevation in cortisol. Although the authors suggested that the cortisol elevations played a role in the difference in wound healing, again there was no statistical test for mediation.

The question of how stress influences wound healing is one that has very important practical implications. For instance, it seems likely that the same processes as are involved in healing of these small, controlled wounds are also involved in the process of recovery from major surgery (Broadbent, Petrie, Alley, & Booth, 2003; Kiecolt-Glaser, Page, Marucha, MacCallum, & Glaser, 1998). If so, a better understanding of how to foster healing may have a large payoff in promoting faster recovery from surgery.

Section Summary

The preceding sections have touched on research in several areas in which there is evidence that stress (or distress) plays a role in some aspect of physical health. This description is clearly not anywhere close to exhaustive. Even in the areas I did touch on, a great deal more information exists than was presented here. There are also many other areas in which research is actively examining questions about stress, coping, and physical health—areas that include (but are by no means limited to) such diseases as cancer, HIV and AIDS, and rheumatoid arthritis.

Concluding Comment

This chapter has addressed a set of questions concerning the interrelations among stress, coping, and health. I began by considering some definitions of stress and coping, and trying to link those experiences to a general model of motivation and self-regulated action. In so doing, I tried to make the case that coping is not a special event but is normal behavior that is taking place under circumstances of adversity. Stress is the adversity; coping is the attempt to make it go away or to diminish its impact.

These experiences are important to the behavioral scientist, but they are also important to the health scientist. Dealing with adversity creates emotional responses. It also changes the activities of the systems that handle the flow of blood to various parts of the body, the systems that manage immune responses, and the systems that manage communication among other subsystems. These various consequences of stress and coping change the person's internal environment in ways that ultimately influence health. The attempt to understand how this happens is an important part of health psychology.

The efforts to untangle these links have been ongoing for decades, but in a sense they are only just beginning. The human body is very complex; the reasons for many of its functions are not well understood. The paths of influence shown earlier, in Figure 6.1, represent a simplified view of how experience may create a long-lasting adverse impact on the body. The diagram is far too simple to be complete, and it may even be quite wrong. For example, it is possible that the effects of stress on health depend less on emotional reactions than is now generally believed. Similarly, today's understanding of the neuroendocrine system and the immune system remains limited. Perhaps the keys to disease processes lie in areas that are as yet unexplored.

We know now that stress has several kinds of adverse effects on health. Establishing that fact in effect took health psychologists through the first level of the puzzle. The key questions now are different. They are questions about the mechanisms by which disease is created and worsened. An increasing focus on mechanisms of causality will force health scientists to refine and extend their research strategies. One change that is certain to come in the near future will be an increased emphasis on studies (and on statistical analyses) that test pathways of influence from one variable to another to another, in order to obtain a closer grasp of the mechanisms of action. Only in this way will we really be able to claim that we understand how stress and coping influence health.

References

Affleck, G., & Tennen, H. (1996). Construing benefits from adversity: Adaptational significance and dispositional underpinnings. *Journal of Personality, 64,* 899–922.

Affleck, G., Tennen, H., Pfeiffer, C., & Fifield, J. (1987). Appraisals of control and predictability in adapting to a chronic disease. *Journal of Personality and Social Psychology, 53,* 273–279.

Ahern, D. K., Gorkin, L., Anderson, J. L., Tierney, C., Hallstrom, A., Ewart, C., et al. (1990). Biobehavioral variables and mortality or cardiac arrest in the Cardiac Arrhythmia Pilot Study (CAPS). *American Journal of Cardiology, 66,* 59–62.

Andersen, B. L., & Cacioppo, J. T. (1995). Delay in seeking a cancer diagnosis: Delay stages and psychophysiological comparison processes. *British Journal of Social Psychology, 34,* 33–52.

Andrykowski, M. A., Brady, M. J., & Hunt, J. W. (1993). Positive psychosocial adjustment in potential bone marrow transplant recipients: Cancer as a psychosocial transition. *Psychooncology, 2,* 261–276.

Antoni, M. H. (2002). HIV and AIDS. In A. J. Christensen & M. H. Antoni (Eds.), *Chronic physical disorders: Behavioral medicine's perspective* (pp. 191–219). Oxford, England: Blackwell.

Antoni, M. H., Lehman, J. M., Kilbourn, K. M., Boyers, A. E., Culver, J. L., Alferi, S. M., et al. (2001). Cognitive-behavioral stress management intervention decreases the prevalence of depression and enhances benefit finding among women under treatment for early-stage breast cancer. *Health Psychology, 20,* 20–32.

Antoni, M. H., & Schneiderman, N. (1998). HIV/AIDS. In A. Bellack & M. Hersen (Eds.), *Comprehensive Clinical Psychology* (pp. 237–275). New York: Elsevier Science.

Appels, A., Golombeck, B., Gorgels, A., de Vreede, J., & van Breukelen, G. (2000). Behavioral risk factors of sudden cardiac arrest. *Journal of Psychosomatic Research, 48,* 463–469.

Aspinwall, L. G., & Richter, L. (1999). Optimism and self-mastery predict more rapid disengagement from unsolvable tasks in the presence of alternatives. *Motivation and Emotion, 23,* 221–245.

Aspinwall, L. G., & Taylor, S. E. (1997). A stitch in time: Self-regulation and proactive coping. *Psychological Bulletin, 121,* 417–436.

Austin, J. T., & Vancouver, J. B. (1996). Goal constructs in psychology: Structure, process, and content. *Psychological Bulletin, 120,* 338–375.

Bandura, A. (1986). *Social foundations of thought and action: A social cognitive theory.* Englewood Cliffs, NJ: Prentice-Hall.

Barefoot, J. C., Brummett, B. H., Helms, M. J., Mark, D. B., Siegler, I. C., & Williams, R. B. (2000). Depressive symptoms and survival of patients with coronary artery disease. *Psychosomatic Medicine, 62,* 790–795.

Barefoot, J. C., Helms, M. S., Mark, D. B., Blumenthal, J. A., Califf, R. M., Haney, T. L., et al. (1996). Depression and long-term mortality risk in patients with coronary artery disease. *American Journal of Cardiology, 78,* 613–617.

Barefoot, J. C., & Schroll, M. (1996). Symptoms of depression, acute myocardial infarction, and total mortality in a community sample. *Circulation, 93,* 1976–1980.

Biondi, M., & Picardi, A. (1999). Psychological stress and neuroendocrine function in humans: The last two decades of research. *Psychotherapy and Psychosomatics, 68,* 114–150.

Blascovich, J., & Katkin, E. S. (Eds.). (1993). *Cardiovascular reactivity to psychological stress and disease.* Washington, DC: American Psychological Association.

Bonnano, G. A., Keltner, D., Holen, A., & Horowitz, M. J. (1995). When avoiding unpleasant emotions might not be such a bad thing: Verbal-autonomic response dissociation and midlife conjugal bereavement. *Journal of Personality and Social Psychology, 69,* 975–989.

Bower, J., Kemeny, M., Taylor, S., & Fahey, J. (1998) Cognitive processing, discovery of meaning, CD4 decline, and AIDS-related mortality among bereaved HIV-seropositive men. *Journal of Consulting and Clinical Psychology, 66,* 979–986.

Brehm, J. W., & Self, E. A. (1989). The intensity of motivation. *Annual Review of Psychology, 40,* 109–131.

Broadbent, E., Petrie, K. J., Alley, P. G., & Booth, R. J. (2003). Psychological stress impairs early wound repair following surgery. *Psychosomatic Medicine, 65,* 865–869.

Cacioppo, J. T., Berntson, G. G., Malarkey, W. B., Kiecolt-Glaser, J. K., Sheridan, J. F., Poehlmann, K. M., et al. (1998). Autonomic, neuroendocrine, and immune responses to psychological stress: The reactivity hypothesis. In S. M. McCann, J. M. Lipton, et al. (Eds.), *Annals of the New York Academy of Sciences. Vol. 840: Neuroimmuno-modulation: Molecular aspects, integrative systems, and clinical advances* (pp. 664–673). New York: New York Academy of Sciences.

Carels, R. A., Sherwood, A., & Blumenthal, J. A. (1998). Psychosocial influences on blood pressure during daily life. *International Journal of Psychophysiology, 28,* 117–129.

Carver, C. S. (1998). Resilience and thriving: Issues, models, and linkages. *Journal of Social Issues, 54,* 245–265.

Carver, C. S. (2001). Affect and the functional bases of behavior: On the dimensional structure of affective experience. *Personality and Social Psychology Review, 5,* 345–356.

Carver, C. S. (2004). Negative affects deriving from the behavioral approach system. *Emotion, 4,* 3–22.

Carver, C. S., & Antoni, M. H. (2004). Finding benefit in breast cancer during the year after diagnosis predicts better adjustment 5 to 8 years after diagnosis. *Health Psychology, 26,* 595–598.

Carver, C. S., Pozo, C., Harris, S. D., Noriega, V., Scheier, M. F., Robinson, D. S., et al. (1993). How coping mediates the effect of optimism on distress: A study of women with early stage breast cancer. *Journal of Personality and Social Psychology, 65,* 375–390.

Carver, C. S., & Scheier, M. F. (1981). *Attention and self-regulation: A control-theory approach to human behavior.* New York: Springer Verlag.

Carver, C. S., & Scheier, M. F. (1990). Origins and functions of positive and negative affect: A control-process view. *Psychological Review, 97,* 19–35.

Carver, C. S., & Scheier, M. F. (1998). *On the self-regulation of behavior.* New York: Cambridge University Press.

Carver, C. S., & Scheier, M. F. (2003). Three human strengths. In L. G. Aspinwall & U. M. Staudinger (Eds.), *A psychology of human strengths: Perspectives on an emerging field.* Washington, DC: American Psychological Association.

Carver, C. S., Scheier, M. F., & Weintraub, J. K. (1989). Assessing coping strategies: A theoretically based approach. *Journal of Personality and Social Psychology, 56,* 267–283.

Chrousos, G. (1995). The hypothalamic-pituitary-adrenal axis and immune-mediated inflammation. *New England Journal of Medicine, 332,* 1351–1362.

Cohen, S. (2005). The Pittsburgh common cold studies: Psychosocial predictors of susceptibility to respiratory infectious illness. *International Journal of Behavioral Medicine, 12,* 123–131.

Cohen, S., Doyle, W. J., Turner, R. B., Alper, C. M., & Skoner, D. P. (2003). Emotional style and susceptibility to the common cold. *Psychosomatic Medicine, 65,* 652–657.

Cohen, S., Frank, E., Doyle, W. J., Skoner, D. P., Rabin, B. S., & Gwaltney, J. M., Jr. (1998). Types of stressors that increase susceptibility to the common cold in healthy adults. *Health Psychology, 17,* 214–223.

Cohen, S., & Herbert, T. B. (1996). Health psychology: Psychological factors and physical disease from the perspective of human psychoneuro-immunology. *Annual Review of Psychology, 47,* 113–142.

Cohen, S., Kessler, R. C., & Gordon, L. U. (Eds.). (1997). *Measuring stress: A guide for health and social scientists.* New York: Oxford University Press.

Cohen, S., Line, S., Manuck, S. B., Rabin, B. S., Heise, E. R., & Kaplan, J. R. (1997). Chronic social stress, social status, and susceptibility to upper respiratory infections in nonhuman primates. *Psychosomatic Medicine, 59,* 213–221.

Cohen, S., & Rodriguez, M. S. (1995). Pathways linking affective disturbances and physical disorders. *Health Psychology, 14,* 374–380.

Cohen, S., Schwartz, J. E., Bromet, E. J., & Parkinson, D. K. (1991). Mental health, stress, and poor health behaviors in two community samples. *Preventive Medicine, 20,* 306–315.

Cohen, S., Tyrrell, D. A., & Smith, A. P. (1991). Psychological stress and susceptibility to the common cold. *New England Journal of Medicine, 325,* 606–612.

Cohen, S., & Wills, T. A. (1985). Stress, social

support, and the buffering hypothesis. *Psychological Bulletin, 98,* 310–357.

Compas, B. E., Connor, J. K., Osowiecki, D. N., & Welch, A. (1997). Effortful and involuntary responses to stress: Implications for coping with chronic stress. In B. Gottlieb (Ed.), *Coping with chronic stress* (pp. 105–132). New York: Plenum.

Compas, B. E., Connor-Smith, J. K., Saltzman, H., Thomsen, A. H., & Wadsworth, M. E. (2001). Coping with stress during childhood and adolescence: Problems, progress, and potential in theory and research. *Psychological Bulletin, 127,* 87–127.

Connor-Smith, J. K., Compas, B. E., Wadsworth, M. E., Thomsen, A. H., & Saltzman, H. (2000). Responses to stress in adolescence: Measurement of coping and involuntary stress responses. *Journal of Consulting and Clinical Psychology, 68,* 976–992.

Cordova, M. J., Cunningham, L. L. C., Carlson, C. R., & Andrykowski, M. A. (2001). Posttraumatic growth following breast cancer: A controlled comparison study. *Health Psychology, 20,* 176–185.

Csikszentmihalyi, M. (1990). *Flow: The psychology of optimal experience.* New York: Harper and Row.

Culver, J. L., Arena, P. L., Antoni, M. H., & Carver, C. S. (2002). Coping and distress among women under treatment for early stage breast cancer: Comparing African Americans, Hispanics, and non-Hispanic whites. *Psycho-Oncology, 11,* 495–504.

Davidson, R. J. (1984). Affect, cognition, and hemispheric specialization. In C. E. Izard, J. Kagan, & R. Zajonc (Eds.), *Emotion, cognition, and behavior* (pp. 320–365). New York: Cambridge University Press.

Davidson, R. J. (1998). Affective style and affective disorders: Perspectives from affective neuroscience. *Cognition and Emotion, 12,* 307–330.

Dickerson, S. S., & Kemeny, M. E. (2004). Acute stressors and cortisol responses: A theoretical integration and synthesis of laboratory research. *Psychological Bulletin, 130,* 355–391.

Dunahoo, C. L., Hobfoll, S. E., Monnier, J., Hulsizer, M. R., & Johnson, R. (1998). There's more than rugged individualism in coping. Part 1: Even the Lone Ranger had Tonto. *Anxiety, Stress, and Coping: An International Journal, 11,* 137–665.

Dunbar-Jacob, J., & Schlenk, E. A. (1996). Treatment adherence and clinical outcome: Can we make a difference? In R. J. Resnick, & R. H. Rozensky (Eds.), *Health psychology through the life span: Practice and research opportunities* (pp. 323–343). Washington, DC, American Psychological Association.

Dunbar-Jacob, J., Schlenk, E. A., & Caruthers, D. (2002). Adherence in the management of chronic disorders. In A. J. Christensen & M. H. Antoni (Eds.), *Chronic physical disorders: Behavioral medicine's perspective* (pp. 69–82). Oxford, UK: Blackwell.

Earle, T. L., Linden, W., & Weinberg, J. (1999). Differential effects of harassment on cardiovascular and salivary cortisol stress reactivity and recovery in women and men. *Journal of Psychosomatic Research, 46,* 125–141.

Ebrecht, M., Hextall, J., Kirtley, L.-G., Taylor, A., Dyson, M., & Weinman, J. (2004). Perceived stress and cortisol levels predict speed of wound healing in healthy male adults. *Psychoneuroendocrinology, 29,* 798–809.

Elliott, E. S., & Dweck, C. S. (1988). Goals: An approach to motivation and achievement. *Journal of Personality and Social Psychology, 54,* 5–12.

Everson, S. A., Goldberg, D. E., Kaplan, G. A., Cohen, R. D., Pukkala, E., Tuomilehto, J., et al. (1996). Hopelessness and risk of mortality and incidence of myocardial infarction and cancer. *Psychosomatic Medicine, 58,* 113–121.

Everson, S. A., Kaplan, G. A., Goldberg, D. E., Salonen, R., & Salonen, J. T. (1997). Hopelessness and 4-year progression of carotid atherosclerosis. *Arteriosclerosis, Thrombosis, and Vascular Biology, 17,* 1490–1495.

Ewart, C. K., Taylor, C. B., Kraemer, H. C., & Agras, W. S. (1991). High blood pressure and marital discord: Not being nasty matters more than being nice. *Health Psychology, 10,* 155–163.

Folkman, S., Chesney, M., Collette, L., Boccellari, A., & Cooke, M. (1996). Postbereavement depressive mood and its prebereavement predictors in HIV+ and HIV–gay men. *Journal of Personality and Social Psychology, 70,* 336–348.

Folkman, S., & Moskowitz, J. T. (2000). Positive affect and the other side of coping. *American Psychologist, 55,* 647–654.

Folkman, S., & Moskowitz, J. T. (2004). Coping: Pitfalls and promise. *Annual Review of Psychology, 55,* 745–774.

Ford, D. E., Mead, L. A., Chang, P. P., Cooper-Patrick, L., Wang, N., & Klag, M. J. (1998). Depression is a risk factor for coronary artery disease in men. *Archives of Internal Medicine, 158,* 1422–1426.

Fowles, D. C. (1993). Biological variables in psychopathology: A psychobiological perspective. In P. B. Sutker & H. E. Adams (Eds.), *Comprehensive handbook of psychopathology* (2nd ed., pp. 57–82). New York: Plenum.

Frasure-Smith, N., Lesperance, F., & Talajic, M. (1995). The impact of negative emotions on prognosis following myocardial infarction: Is it more than depression? *Health Psychology, 14,* 388–398.

Fredrickson, B. L., Mancuso, R. A., Branigan, C., & Tugade, M. M. (2000). The undoing effect of positive emotions. *Motivation and Emotion, 24,* 237–258.

Fredrikson, M., & Matthews, K. A. (1990). Cardiovascular responses to behavioral stress and hypertension: A meta-analytic review. *Annals of Behavioral Medicine, 12,* 30–39.

Glaser, R., & Kiecolt-Glaser, J. K. (Eds.). (1994). *Handbook of human stress and immunity.* San Diego, CA: Academic Press.

Glaser, R., Kiecolt-Glaser, J. K., Marucha, P. T., MacCallum, R. C., Laskowski, B. F., & Malarkey, W. B. (1999). Stress-related changes in proinflammatory cytokine production in wounds. *Archives of General Psychiatry, 56,* 450–456.

Glaser, R., Sheridan, J., Malarkey, W. B., MacCallum, R. C., & Kiecolt-Glaser, J. K. (2000). Chronic stress modulates the immune response to a pneumococcal pneumonia vaccine. *Psychosomatic Medicine, 62,* 804–807.

Goldberger, L., & Breznitz, S. (Eds.). (1993). *Handbook of stress: Theoretical and clinical aspects* (2nd ed.). New York: Free Press.

Gray, J. A. (1990). Brain systems that mediate both emotion and cognition. *Cognition and Emotion, 4,* 269–288.

Gray, J. A. (1994). Personality dimensions and emotion systems. In P. Ekman & R. J. Davidson (Eds.), *The nature of emotion: Fundamental questions* (pp. 329–331). New York: Oxford University Press.

Heavey, C. L., Layne, C., & Christensen, A. A. (1993). Gender and conflict structure in marital interaction: A replication and extension. *Journal of Consulting and Clinical Psychology, 61,* 16–27.

Hemingway H., & Marmot, M. (1999). Psychosocial factors in the aetiology and prognosis of coronary heart disease: Systematic review of prospective cohort studies. *British Medical Journal, 318,* 1460–1467.

Herbert, T., & Cohen, S. (1993). Stress and immunity in humans: A meta-analytic review. *Psychosomatic Medicine, 55,* 364–379.

Higgins, E. T. (1987). Self-discrepancy: A theory relating self and affect. *Psychological Review, 94,* 319–340.

Higgins, E. T. (1996). Ideals, oughts, and regulatory focus: Affect and motivation from distinct pains and pleasures. In P. M. Gollwitzer & J. A. Bargh (Eds.), *The psychology of action: Linking cognition and motivation to behavior* (pp. 91–114). New York: Guilford.

Higgins, E. T., Shah, J., & Friedman, R. (1997). Emotional responses to goal attainment: Strength of regulatory focus as moderator. *Journal of Personality and Social Psychology, 72,* 515–525.

Hobfoll, S. E. (1989). Conservation of resources: A new attempt at conceptualizing stress. *American Psychologist, 44,* 513–524.

Hobfoll, S. E. (1998). *Stress, culture, and community.* New York: Plenum.

Hobfoll, S. E., Freedy, J. R., Green, B. L., & Solomon, S. D. (1996). Coping in reaction to extreme stress: The roles of resource loss and resource availability. In M. Zeidner & N. S. Endler (Eds.), *Handbook of coping: Theory, research, applications* (pp. 322–349). New York: Wiley.

Holahan, C. J., & Moos, R. H. (1986). Personality, coping, and family resources in stress resistance: A longitudinal analysis. *Journal of Personality and Social Psychology, 51,* 389–395.

Holahan, C. J., Moos, R. H., Holahan, C. K., & Cronkite, R. C. (1999). Resource loss, resource gain, and depressive symptoms: A 10-year model. *Journal of Personality and Social Psychology, 77,* 620–629.

Holahan, C. J., Moos, R. H., Holahan, C. K., & Cronkite, R. C. (2000). Long-term posttreatment functioning among patients with unipolar depression: An integrative model. *Journal of Consulting and Clinical Psychology, 68,* 226–232.

Holahan, C. J., Moos, R. H., Holahan, C. K., Cronkite, R. C., & Randall, P. K. (2003). Drinking to cope and alcohol use and abuse in unipolar depression: A 10-year model. *Journal of Abnormal Psychology, 112,* 159–165.

Horwitz, A. V., & White, H. R. (1991). Becoming married, depression, and alcohol problems among young adults. *Journal of Health and Social Behavior, 32,* 221–237.

Januzzi, J. L., Stern, T. A., Pasternak, R., & DeSanctis, R. W. (2000). The influence of anxiety and depression on outcomes of patients with coronary artery disease. *Archives of Internal Medicine, 160,* 1913–1921.

Jung, W., & Irwin, M. (1999). Reduction of natural killer cytotoxic activity in major depression: Interaction between depression and cigarette smoking. *Psychosomatic-Medicine, 61,* 263–270.

Kaprio J., Koskenvuo, M., & Rita, H. (1987). Mortality after bereavement: A prospective study of 95,647 persons. *American Journal of Public Health, 77,* 283–287.

Kennedy, P., Marsh, N., Lowe, R., Grey, N., Short, E., & Rogers, B. (2000). A longitudinal analysis of psychological impact and coping strategies following spinal cord injury. *British Journal of Health Psychology, 5,* 157–172.

Kiecolt-Glaser, J. K., Bane, C., Glaser, R., & Malarkey, W. B. (2003). Love, marriage, and divorce: Newlyweds' stress hormones foreshadow relationship changes. *Journal of Consulting and Clinical Psychology, 71,* 176–188.

Kiecolt-Glaser, J. K., Fisher, L. D., Ogrocki, P., Stout, J. C., Speicher, C. E., & Glaser, R. (1987). Marital quality, marital disruption, and immune function. *Psychosomatic Medicine, 49,* 13–34.

Kiecolt-Glaser, J. K., Glaser, R., Cacioppo, J. T., MacCallum, R. C., Snydersmith, M., Kim, C., et al. (1997). Marital conflict in older adults: Endocrinological and immunological correlates. *Psychosomatic Medicine, 59,* 339–349.

Kiecolt-Glaser, J. K., Glaser, R., Shuttleworth, E. C., Dyer, C. S., Ogrocki, P., & Speicher, C. E. (1987). Chronic stress and immunity in family caregivers of Alzheimer's disease victims. *Psychosomatic Medicine, 49,* 523–535.

Kiecolt-Glaser, J. K., Marucha, P. T., Malarkey, W. B., Mercado, A. M., & Glaser, R. (1995). Slowing of wound healing by psychological stress. *Lancet, 346,* 1194–1196.

Kiecolt-Glaser, J. K., McGuire, L., Robles, T. F., & Glaser, R. (2002). Emotions, morbidity, and mortality: New perspectives from psychoneuroimmunology. *Annual Review of Psychology, 53,* 83–107.

Kiecolt-Glaser, J. K., & Newton, T. L. (2001). Marriage and health: His and hers. *Psychological Bulletin, 127,* 451–471.

Kiecolt-Glaser, J. K., Newton, T., Cacioppo, J. T., MacCallum, R. C., Glaser, R., & Malarkey, W. B. (1996). Marital conflict and endocrine function: Are men really more physiologically affected than women? *Journal of Consulting and Clinical Psychology, 64,* 324–332.

Kiecolt-Glaser, J. K., Page, G. G., Marucha, P. T., MacCallum, R. C., & Glaser, R. (1998). Psychological influences on surgical recovery: Perspectives from psychoneuroimmunology. *American Psychologist, 53,* 1209–1218.

Kiecolt-Glaser, J. K., & Williams, D. A. (1987). Self-blame, compliance, and distress among burn patients. *Journal of Personality and Social Psychology, 53,* 187–193.

Kinder, L. S., Kamarck, T. W., Baum, A., & Orchard, T. J. (2002). Depressive symptomatology and coronary heart disease in type I diabetes mellitus: A study of possible mechanisms. *Health Psychology, 21,* 542–552.

Klass, D., Silverman, P. R., & Nickman, S. L. (Eds.). (1996). *Continuing bonds: New understandings of grief.* Washington, DC: Taylor and Francis.

Klinger, E. (1975). Consequences of commitment to and disengagement from incentives. *Psychological Review, 82,* 1–25.

Krantz, D. S., & McCeney, M. K. (2002). Effects of psychological and social factors on organic disease: A critical assessment of research on coronary heart disease. *Annual Review of Psychology, 53,* 341–369.

Kronfol, Z., Madhavan, N., Zhang, Q., Hill, E. E., & Brown, M. B. (1997). Circadian immune measures in healthy volunteers: Relationship to hypothalamic-pituitary-adrenal axis hormones and sympathetic neurotransmitters. *Psychosomatic Medicine, 59,* 42–50.

Kubzansky, L. D., & Kawachi, I. (2000). Going to the heart of the matter: Do negative emotions cause coronary heart disease? *Journal of Psychosomatic Research, 48,* 323–337.

Kubzansky, L. D., Kawachi, I., Spiro, A., III, Weiss, S. T., Vokonas, P. S., & Sparrow, D. (1997). Is worrying bad for your heart? A prospective study of worry and coronary heart disease in the Normative Aging Study. *Circulation, 95,* 818–824.

Lazarus, R. S. (1966). *Psychological stress and the coping process.* New York: McGraw-Hill.

Lazarus, R. S. (1999). *Stress and emotion: A new synthesis.* New York: Springer.

Lazarus, R. S., & Folkman, S. (1984). *Stress, appraisal, and coping.* New York: Springer.

Leor, J., Poole, W. K., & Kloner, R. A. (1996). Sudden cardiac death triggered by an earthquake. *New England Journal of Medicine, 334,* 413–419.

MacKay, D. M. (1956). Toward an information-flow model of human behavior. *British Journal of Psychology, 47,* 30–43.

Maier, S. F., Watkins, L. R., & Fleshner, M. (1994). Psychoneuroimmunology: The interface between behavior, brain, and immunity. *American Psychologist, 49,* 1004–1017.

Malarkey, W., Kiecolt-Glaser, J. K., Pearl, D., & Glaser, R. (1994). Hostile behavior during marital conflict alters pituitary and adrenal hormones. *Psychosomatic Medicine, 56,* 41–51.

Marucha, P. T., Kiecolt-Glaser, J. K., & Favagehi, M. (1998). Mucosal wound healing is impaired by examination stress. *Psychosomatic Medicine, 60,* 362–365.

Meisel, S. R., Kutz, I., Dayan, K. I., Pauzner, H., Chetboun, I., Arbel, Y., et al. (1991). Effects of Iraqi missile war on incidence of acute myocardial infarction and sudden death in Israeli civilians. *Lancet, 338,* 660–661.

Michelson, D., Licinio, J., & Bold, P.W. (1995). Mediation of the stress response by the hypothalamic-pituitary-adrenal axis. In M. J. Friedman, D. S. Charney, & A. Y. Deutch (Eds.), *Neurobiological and clinical consequences of stress* (pp. 225–238). Philadelphia: Lippincott-Raven.

Millar, K. U., Tesser, A., & Millar, M. G. (1988). The

effects of a threatening life event on behavior sequences and intrusive thought: A self-disruption explanation. *Cognitive Therapy and Research, 12,* 441–458.

Miller, G. E., Cohen, S., & Ritchey, A. K. (2002). Chronic psychological stress and the regulation of pro-inflammatory cytokines: A glucocorticoid-resistance model. *Health Psychology, 21,* 531–541.

Miller, G. A., Galanter, E., & Pribram, K. H. (1960). *Plans and the structure of behavior.* New York: Holt, Rinehart, and Winston.

Miller, T. Q., Smith, T. W., Turner, C. W., Guijarro, M. L., & Hallet, A. J. (1996). A meta-analytic review of research on hostility and physical health. *Psychological Bulletin, 119,* 322–348.

Mittleman, M. A., Maclure, M., Sherwood, J. B., Mulry, R. P., Tofler, G. H., Jacobs, S. C., et al., for the Determinants of Myocardial Infarction Onset Study Investigators. (1995). Triggering of acute myocardial infarction onset by episodes of anger. *Circulation, 92,* 1720–1725.

Moos, R. H., & Schaefer, J. A. (1993). Coping resources and processes: Current concepts and measures. In L. Goldberger & S. Breznitz (Eds.), *Handbook of stress: Theoretical and clinical aspects* (2nd ed., pp. 234–257). New York: Free Press.

Moser, D. K., & Dracup, K. (1996). Is anxiety early after myocardial infarction associated with subsequent ischemic and arrhythmic events? *Psychosomatic Medicine, 58,* 395–401.

Nesse, R. M. (2000). Is depression an adaptation? *Archives of General Psychiatry, 57,* 14–20.

Nolen-Hoeksema, S., & Larson, J. (1999). *Coping with loss.* Mahwah, NJ: Erlbaum.

O'Leary, A. (1990). Stress, emotion, and human immune function. *Psychological Bulletin, 108,* 363–382.

Ostrow, D. G., VanRaden, M., Fox, R., Kingsley, L. A., Dudley, J., & Kaslow, R. A. (1990). Recreational drug use and sexual behavior change in a cohort of homosexual men. *AIDS, 4,* 759–765.

Park, C. L., Armeli, S., & Tennen, H. (2004). Appraisal–coping goodness of fit: A daily internet study. *Personality and Social Psychology Bulletin, 30,* 558–569.

Park, C. L., Cohen, L. H., & Murch, R. L. (1996). Assessment and prediction of stress-related growth. *Journal of Personality, 64,* 71–105.

Park, C. L., & Folkman, S. (1997). Meaning in the context of stress and coping. *Review of General Psychology, 1,* 115–144.

Park, C. L., Lechner, S. C., Stanton, A. L., & Antoni, M. H. (Eds.). (in press). *Positive life changes in the context of medical illness.* Washington DC: American Psychological Association.

Parkes, C. M. (1964). Effects of bereavement on physical and mental health: A study of the medical records of widows. *British Medical Journal, 2,* 274–279.

Pervin, L. A. (Ed.). (1989). *Goal concepts in personality and social psychology.* Hillsdale, NJ: Erlbaum.

Powers, W. T. (1973). *Behavior: The control of perception.* Chicago: Aldine.

Pressman, S. D., & Cohen, S. (2005). Does positive affect influence health? *Psychological Bulletin, 131,* 925–971.

Ptacek, J. T., Smith, R. E., Espe, K., & Raffety, B. (1994). Limited correspondence between daily coping reports and retrospective coping recall. *Psychological Assessment, 6,* 41–49.

Ratcliffe, H. L., & Cronin, N. T. (1958). Changing frequency of atherosclerosis in mammals and birds at the Philadelphia Zoological Garden. *Circulation, 18,* 41–52.

Reichenberg, A., Yirmiya, R., Schuld, A., Kraus, T., Haack, M., Morag, A., & Pollmacher, T. (2001). Cytokine-associated emotional and cognitive disturbances in humans. *Archives of General Psychiatry, 58,* 445–452.

Robles, T. F., Glaser, R., & Kiecolt-Glaser, J. K. (2005). Out of balance: A new look at chronic stress, depression, and immunity. *Current Directions in Psychological Science, 14,* 111–115.

Roth, S., & Cohen, L. J. (1986). Approach, avoidance, and coping with stress. *American Psychologist, 41,* 813–819.

Rozanski, A., Blumenthal, J. A., & Kaplan, J. (1999). Impact of psychological factors on the pathogenesis of cardiovascular disease and implications for therapy. *Circulation, 99,* 2192–2217.

Scheier, M. F., Matthews, K. A., Owens, J. F., Schulz, R., Bridges, M. W., Magovern, G. J., Jr., et al. (1999). Optimism and rehospitalization after coronary artery bypass graft surgery. *Archives of Internal Medicine, 159,* 829–833.

Schnall, P. L., Pieper, C., Schwartz, J. E., Karasek, R. A., Schlussel, Y., Devereux, R. B., et al. (1990). The relationship between job strain, workplace diastolic blood pressure, and left ventricular mass index. *Journal of the American Medical Association, 263,* 1929–1935.

Schnall, P. L., Schwartz, J. E., Landsbergis, P. A., Warren, K., & Pickering, T. G. (1998). A longitudinal study of job strain and ambulatory blood pressure: Results from a three-year follow-up. *Psychosomatic Medicine, 60,* 697–706.

Segerstrom, S. C., & Miller, G. E. (2004). Psychological stress and the human immune system: A meta-analytic study of 30 years of inquiry. *Psychological Bulletin, 130,* 601–641.

Selye, H. (1956). *The stress of life.* New York: McGraw-Hill.

Sherbourne, C. D., Hays, R. D., Ordway, L., DiMatteo, M. R., & Kravitz, R. L. (1992). Antecedents of adherence to medical recommendations: Results from the Medical Outcomes Study. *Journal of Behavioral Medicine, 15,* 447–468.

Shively, C. A., Clarkson, T. B., & Kaplan, J. R. (1989). Social deprivation and coronary artery atherosclerosis in female cynomolgus monkeys. *Atherosclerosis, 77,* 69–76.

Smith, T. W., Allred, K. D., Morrison, C. A., & Carlson, S. D. (1989). Cardiovascular reactivity and interpersonal influence: Active coping in a social context. *Journal of Personality and Social Psychology, 56,* 209–218.

Smith, T. W., & Leon, A. S. (1992). *Coronary heart disease: A behavioral perspective.* Champaign-Urbana, IL: Research Press.

Smith, T. W., Nealey, J. B., Kircher, J. C., & Limon, J. P. (1997). Social determinants of cardiovascular reactivity: Effects of incentive to exert influence and evaluative threat. *Psychophysiology, 34,* 65–73.

Smith, T. W., & Ruiz, J. M. (2002). Coronary heart disease. In A. J. Christensen & M. H. Antoni (Eds.), *Chronic physical disorders: Behavioral medicine's perspective* (83–111). Oxford, UK: Blackwell.

Smith, T. W., Ruiz, J. M., & Uchino, B. N. (2000). Vigilance, active coping, and cardiovascular reactivity during social interaction in young men. *Health Psychology, 19,* 382–392.

Stanton, A. L., Danoff-Burg, S., Cameron, C. L., Bishop, M., Collins, C. A., et al. (2000). Emotionally expressive coping predicts psychological and physical adjustment to breast cancer. *Journal of Consulting and Clinical Psychology, 68,* 875–882.

Stroebe, M. S. (1994). The broken heart phenomenon: An examination of the mortality of bereavement. *Journal of Community and Applied Social Psychology, 4,* 47–61.

Stroebe, M. S., Schut, H., & Stroebe, W. (2005). Attachment in coping with bereavement: A theoretical integration. *Review of General Psychology, 9,* 48–66.

Stroebe, M. S., Stroebe, W., & Hansson, R. O. (Eds.). (1993). *Handbook of bereavement: Theory, research, and intervention.* Cambridge, England: Cambridge University Press.

Stroebe, W., Schut, H., & Stroebe, M. S. (2005). Grief work, disclosure, and counseling: Do they help the bereaved? *Clinical Psychology Review, 25,* 395–414.

Tait, R., & Silver, R. C. (1989). Coming to terms with major negative life events. In J. S. Uleman & J. A. Bargh (Eds.), *Unintended thought: The limits of awareness, intention, and control* (pp. 351–381). New York: Guilford.

Taylor, S. E. (1983). Adjustment to threatening events: A theory of cognitive adaptation. *American Psychologist, 38,* 1161–1173.

Tedeschi, R. G., & Calhoun, L. G. (2004). Posttraumatic growth: Conceptual foundations and empirical evidence. *Psychological Inquiry, 15,* 1–18.

Tennen, H., Affleck, G., Armeli, S., & Carney, M. A (2000). A daily process approach to coping: Linking theory, research, and practice. *American Psychologist, 55,* 626–636.

Terry, D. J., & Hynes, G. J. (1998). Adjustment to a low-control situation: Reexamining the role of coping responses. *Journal of Personality and Social Psychology, 74,* 1078–1092.

Todd, M., Tennen, H., Carney, M. A., Armeli, S., & Affleck, G. (2004). Do we know how we cope? Relating daily coping reports to global and time-limited retrospective assessments. *Journal of Personality and Social Psychology, 86,* 310–319.

Tomich, P. L., & Helgeson, V. S. (2004). Is finding something good in the bad always good? Benefit finding among women with breast cancer. *Health Psychology, 23,* 16–23.

Vitaliano, P. P., DeWolfe, D. J., Maiuro, R. D., Russo, J., & Katon, W. (1990). Appraised changeability of a stressor as a modifier of the relationship between coping and depression: A test of the hypothesis of fit. *Journal of Personality and Social Psychology, 59,* 582–592.

Vitaliano, P. P., Russo, J., Young, H., Teri, L., & Maiuro, R. D. (1991). Predictors of burden in spouse caregivers of individuals with Alzheimer's disease. *Psychology and Aging, 6,* 392–402.

Wade, S. L., Borawski, E. A., Taylor, H. G., Drotar, D., Yeates, L. O., & Stancin, T. (2001). The relationship of caregiver coping to family outcomes during the initial year following pediatric traumatic injury. *Journal of Consulting and Clinical Psychology, 69,* 406–415.

Wells, J. D., Hobfoll, S. E., & Lavin, J. (1997). Resource loss, resource gain, and communal coping during pregnancy among women with multiple roles. *Psychology of Women Quarterly, 21,* 645–662.

Wiener, N. (1948). *Cybernetics: Control and communication in the animal and the machine.* Cambridge, MA: MIT Press.

Williams, J. E., Paton, C. C., Siegler, I. C., Eigenbrodt, M. L., Nieto, F. J., & Tyroler, H. A. (2000). Anger proneness predicts coronary heart disease risk:

Prospective analysis from the Atherosclerosis Risk in Communities (ARIC) study. *Circulation, 101,* 2034–2039.

Worden, W. J. (1991). *Grief counseling and grief therapy: A handbook for the mental health practitioner* (2nd ed.). New York: Springer-Verlag.

Wortman, C. B., & Brehm, J. W. (1975). Responses to uncontrollable outcomes: An integration of reactance theory and the learned helplessness model. In L. Berkowitz (Ed.), *Advances in experimental social psychology* (Vol. 8, pp. 277–336). New York: Academic Press.

Wortman, C., & Silver, R. (1989). The myths of coping with loss. *Journal of Consulting and Clinical Psychology, 57,* 349–357.

Wright, R. A. (1996). Brehm's theory of motivation as a model of effort and cardiovascular response. In P. M. Gollwitzer & J. A. Bargh (Eds.), *The psychology of action: Linking cognition and motivation to behavior* (pp. 424–453). New York: Guilford.

Wrosch, C., Scheier, M. F., Miller, G. E., Schulz, R., & Carver, C. S. (2003). Adaptive self-regulation of unattainable goals: Goal disengagement, goal re-engagement, and subjective well-being. *Personality and Social Psychology Bulletin, 29,* 1494–1508.

Zeidner, M., & Endler, N. S. (Eds.). (1996). *Handbook of coping: Theory, research, applications.* New York: Wiley.

Shelley E. Taylor

Social Support

Group living is perhaps the most significant adaptation of primate species, including human beings. Whereas other animals are armed with weapons, such as sharp teeth or claws, and defensive resources, such as thick skin and speed, primate species depend critically on group living for survival (Caporeal, 1997; Dunbar, 1996). This tendency to come together is especially great under threat. Even chimpanzees, known for their solitary behavior, may abandon this style in favor of group activity when there is an enhanced risk of predation (Boesch, 1991). In times of intense stress, humans are much the same. Following the September 11 terrorist attacks, some of the most common methods people reported using to cope with this threatening event involved turning to others, including family, friends, and even strangers (Galea et al., 2002). There are, of course, tangible benefits to social affiliation under threat. For example, following a disaster, such as a fire, a flood, or a bombing, the presence of many hands can locate survivors and get them to safety. But the presence of others has long been known to foster adjustment to threatening events in other ways, specifically by protecting against adverse changes in mental and physical health that may otherwise occur in response to stress. Social support is now so widely acknowl-

edged as a critical resource for managing stressful occurrences that more than 1,100 articles on the topic appear in the research and clinical literatures each year.

What Is Social Support?

Social support is defined as the perception or experience that one is loved and cared for by others, esteemed and valued, and part of a social network of mutual assistance and obligations (Wills, 1991). Social support may come from a partner, relatives, friends, coworkers, social and community ties, and even a devoted pet (Siegel, 1993). Taxonomies of social support have usually classified support into several specific forms. *Informational support* occurs when one individual helps another to understand a stressful event better and to ascertain what resources and coping strategies may be needed to deal with it. Through such information or advice, a person under stress may determine exactly what potential costs or strains the stressful event may impose and decide how best to manage it. *Instrumental support* involves the provision of tangible assistance such as services, financial assistance, and other specific aid or goods. Examples include driving an injured friend to the emergency room or providing food to a bereaved family. *Emotional support* involves providing warmth and nurturance to another individual and reassuring a person that he or she is a valuable person for whom others care. But as the definition makes clear, social support can also involve simply the *perception* that such resources are available, should they be needed. For example, knowing that one is cared for and/or that one could request support from others and receive it may be comforting in its own right. Thus, social support may involve specific transactions whereby one person explicitly receives benefits from another, or it may be experienced through the perception that such help and support are potentially available.

Social support is typically measured in terms of either the structure of socially supportive networks or the functions that network members may provide (e.g., Wills, 1998). Structural social support, often referred to as *social integration,* involves the number of social relationships in which an individual is involved and the structure of interconnections among those relationships. Social integration measures assess the number of relationships or social roles a person has, the frequency of contact with various network members, and the density and interconnectedness of relationships among the network members. Functional support is typically assessed in terms of the specific functions (informational, instrumental, and emotional) that a specific member may serve for a target individual and is often assessed in the context of coping with a particular stressor. Thus, an individual might be asked how much of different kinds of support each member of a supportive network provided during a stressful event.

An early debate in the social support literature centered on the circumstances under which social support may be beneficial. One hypothesis, known as the *direct effects hypothesis,* maintains that social support is generally beneficial to mental and physical health during nonstressful times as well as during highly stressful times. The other hypothesis, known as the *buffering hypothesis,* maintains that the health and mental health benefits of social support are chiefly evident during periods of high stress; when there is little stress, social support may have few physical or mental health benefits. According to this hypothesis, social support acts as a reserve and resource that blunts the effects of stress or enables an individual to deal with stress more effectively, but otherwise is less consequential for mental

and physical health (Cohen & Wills, 1985). After decades of research, evidence for both types of effects has emerged. Measures of social integration typically show direct associations with mental and physical health, but not buffering effects (Thoits, 1995). In contrast, the perception that emotional support is available is associated both with direct benefits to physical and mental health and also with buffering effects (e.g., Wethington & Kessler, 1986).

Benefits of Social Support and Reasons for the Benefits

Mental and Physical Health Benefits

Research consistently demonstrates that social support reduces psychological distress such as depression or anxiety during times of stress (e.g., Sarason, Sarason, & Gurung, 1997; Fleming, Baum, Gisriel, & Gatchel, 1982; Lin, Ye, & Ensel, 1999). It has been found to promote psychological adjustment to chronically stressful conditions, such as coronary artery disease (Holahan, Moos, Holahan, & Brennan, 1997), diabetes, HIV (Turner-Cobb et al., 2002), cancer (Penninx et al., 1998; Stone, Mezzacappa, Donatone, & Gonder, 1999), rheumatoid arthritis (Goodenow, Reisine, & Grady, 1990), kidney disease (Dimond, 1979), childhood leukemia (Magni, Silvestro, Tamiello, Zanesco, & Carl, 1988), and stroke (Robertson & Suinn, 1968), among other disorders. Social support also protects against cognitive decline in older adults (Seeman, Lusignolo, Albert, & Berkman, 2001).

Social support also contributes to physical health and survival. In a classic study that documented this point, epidemiologists Lisa Berkman and Leonard Syme (1979) followed nearly 7,000 California residents over a 9-year period to identify factors that contributed to their longevity or early death. They found that people who lacked social and community ties were more likely to die of all causes during the follow-up period than those who cultivated or maintained their social relationships. Having social contacts predicted an average 2.8 years increased longevity among women and 2.3 years among men; these differences persisted after controlling for socioeconomic status, health status at the beginning of the study, and health habits (Berkman & Syme, 1979). Of particular significance was the fact that the positive impact of social ties on health was as powerful, and in some cases more powerful, a predictor of health and longevity than well-established risk factors for chronic disease and mortality. For example, their absence or loss is a major risk for morbidity and mortality, with effect sizes on a par with smoking, blood pressure, lipids, obesity, and physical activity (House, Landis, & Umberson, 1988).

These benefits are realized in part by the fact that social support appears to help people to stave off illness altogether. For example, Cohen, Doyle, Skoner, Rabin, and Gwaltney (1997) intentionally infected healthy community volunteers with a cold or flu virus by swabbing the inside of their nasal passages with virus-soaked cotton swabs. They found that people experiencing a high level of stress were more likely to develop infections than people under less stress, and the colds and flus they developed were more serious as well. However, those with more social ties were less likely to become ill following exposure to the virus, and if they did, they were able to recover more quickly than those with fewer social ties (Cohen, Doyle, Skoner, Rabin, & Gwaltney, 1997). On the whole, however, evidence for the impact of social support on the likelihood of becoming ill is not as consistently positive as its impact on course of illness or recovery (Seeman, 1996; Taylor & Seeman, 2000). It may be that social contacts contribute to illness likelihood, as through contagion or the creation of stress (e.g., Hamrick, Cohen, & Rodriguez, 2002), but also promote health via social support, leading, on balance, to the only moderately positive net effect on illness likelihood.

Social support has been tied to a variety of specific health benefits among individuals sustaining health risks. These include fewer complications during pregnancy and childbirth (Collins, Dunkel-Schetter, Lobel, & Scrimshaw, 1993); less susceptibility to herpes attacks among infected individuals (VanderPlate, Aral, & Magder, 1988); lower rates of myocardial infarction among individuals with diagnosed disease; a reduced likelihood of mortality from myocardial infarction (Bruhn, 1965; Wallston, Alagna, DeVellis, & DeVellis, 1983; Kulik & Mahler, 1993; Wiklund et al., 1988); faster recovery from coronary artery disease surgery (King, Reis, Porter, & Norsen, 1993; Kulik & Mahler, 1993); better diabetes control (Marteau, Bloch, & Baum, 1987); and less pain among arthritis patients (DeVellis, DeVellis, Sauter, & Cohen, 1986).

The impact of social support on mortality is also clearly established, as the seminal study by Berkman and Syme (1979) suggests. In prospective studies controlling for baseline health status, people with a higher quantity and quality of social relationships have consistently been shown to be at lower risk of death (Seeman, 1996), and in studies of both humans and animals, social isolation has been found to be a major risk factor for mortality (House et al., 1988).

Pathways Linking Social Support to Health

Considerable effort has gone into understanding the pathways whereby social support is beneficial to health. Early research explored the possibility that social support may be associated with good health habits that, in turn, beneficially affect health. For example, family living has been tied to a broad array of good health habits, including a lower likelihood of drug or alcohol abuse and smoking, and an enhanced likelihood of a balanced diet and good sleep habits (e.g., Umberson, 1987). Social isolation has been tied to unhealthy responses to stress, such as smoking and alcohol abuse, which can adversely affect health (Broman, 1993). However, although social support initially may be helpful to people in developing or changing health habits, such as stopping smoking, it may have less consistent effects on maintenance (Carlson, Goodey, Bennett, Taenzer, & Koopmans, 2002). If the social support network itself is engaged in a behavior change program, social support may affect ongoing maintenance. In one study (Fraser & Spink, 2002), for example, women for whom exercise had been prescribed for medical problems were less likely to drop out if they experienced social support in the group. Similarly, when families are engaged in behavior change programs (such as dietary change following diagnosis of cardiovascular disease), such involvement may promote better adherence to an otherwise taxing set of changes (Wilson & Ampey-Thornhill, 2001). Social support may also increase commitment to medical regimens because it enhances feelings of self-efficacy (Resnick, Orwig, Magaziner, & Wynne, 2002). But some social networks may actually promote unhealthy behaviors, such as smoking, drug abuse, and drinking (Wills & Vaughan, 1989). On the whole, the impact of social support on health appears to exist over and above any influence it exerts on health habits.

Accordingly, researchers have focused heavily on potential physiological, neuroendocrine, and immunologic pathways by which social support may achieve its health benefits. What are these pathways? During times of stress, the body releases the catecholamines epinephrine and norepinephrine with concomitant sympathetic nervous system (SNS) arousal and may also engage the hypothalamic-pituitary-adrenocortical (HPA) axis, involving the release of corticosteriods, including cortisol. These responses have short-term protective effects under stressful circumstances because they mobilize the body to meet the demands of pressing situations. However, with chronic or recurrent activation, they can be associated with deleterious long-term effects with implications for health (e.g., Seeman & McEwen, 1996; Uchino, Cacioppo, & Kiecolt-Glaser, 1996). For example, excessive or repeated discharge of epinephrine or norepinephrine can lead to the suppression of cellular immune function, produce hemodynamic changes such as increases in blood pressure and heart rate, provoke abnormal heart rhythms such as ventricular arrhythmias, and produce neurochemical imbalances that may relate to psychiatric disorders (McEwen & Stellar, 1993). Intense, rapid, and/or long-lasting sympathetic responses to repeated stress or challenge have been implicated in the development of hypertension and coronary artery disease.

Stress may increase the risk for adverse health outcomes by suppressing the immune system in ways that leave a person vulnerable to opportunistic diseases and infections. Corticosteroids have immunosuppressive effects, and stress-related increases in cortisol have been tied to decreased lymphocyte responsivity to mitogenic stimulation and to decreased lymphocyte cytotoxicity. Such immunosuppressive changes may be associated with increased susceptibility to infectious disorders and to destruction of neurons in the hippocampus as well (McEwen & Sapolsky, 1995).

An immunosuppression model does not explain how stress might influence diseases whose central feature is excessive inflammation (Miller, Cohen, & Ritchey, 2002); such diseases include allergic, autoimmune, rheumatologic, and cardiovascular disorders, among other disorders that are known to be exacerbated by stress. Miller and colleagues (2002) hypothesized that chronic stress may diminish the immune system's sensitivity to glucocorticoid hormones that normally terminate the inflammatory cascade that occurs during stress. In

support of their hypothesis, they found a clear buffering effect of social support on this process, such that among healthy individuals, glucocorticoid sensitivity bore no relation to social support; however, among parents of children with cancer (a population under extreme stress), those who reported receiving a high level of tangible support from others had higher glucocorticoid sensitivity. This is the first known study to document that social support can buffer inflammatory processes in response to stress.

Extensive evidence suggests that all these systems—the HPA axis, the immune system, and the SNS—influence each other and thereby affect each other's functioning. For example, links between HPA axis activity and SNS activity suggest that chronic activation of the HPA axis could potentiate overactivation of sympathetic functioning (Chrousos & Gold, 1992). Pro-inflammatory cytokines, which are involved in the inflammatory processes just noted, can activate the HPA axis and may contribute not only to the deleterious effects that chronic activation of this system may cause but also, potentially, to depressive symptoms, which have previously been tied to HPA axis activation (Maier & Watkins, 1998; Capuron, Ravaud, & Dantzer, 2000). To the extent, then, that social support can help keep SNS or HPA axis responses to stress low, it may have a beneficial impact on other systems as well (Seeman & McEwen, 1996; Uchino et al., 1996). In turn, these benefits may affect health in a positive direction.

A variety of empirical studies have yielded evidence consistent with these hypotheses. For example, a considerable experimental literature demonstrates that the presence of a supportive person when one is completing a stressful task can reduce cardiovascular and HPA axis responses to stress; these benefits can be experienced whether the supportive person is a partner, a friend, or a stranger (e.g., Christenfeld et el., 1997; Gerin, Pieper, Levy, & Pickering, 1992; Gerin, Milner, Chawla, & Pickering, 1995; Kamarck, Manuck, & Jennings, 1990; Kors, Linden, & Gerin, 1997; Lepore, Allen, & Evans, 1993; Sheffield & Carroll, 1994; see Lepore, 1998, for a review).

Not all research shows beneficial effects of social support in challenging circumstances, however. Sometimes the presence of a friend or stranger actually increases sympathetic reactivity among those undergoing stress (e.g., Allen, Blascovich, Tomaka,

& Kelsey, 1991; Mullen, Bryant, & Driskell, 1997). For example, Allen et al. (1991) found that relative to a control condition in which they remained alone, women who completed a stressful task in the presence of a female friend had higher physiological reactivity and poorer performance (see also Kirschbaum, Klauer, Filipp, & Hellhammer, 1995; Smith, Gallo, Goble, Ngu, & Stark, 1998). Whereas the presence of a partner seems to reduce stress-related physiological and neuroendocrine reactivity among men, the presence of a male partner more reliably enhances reactivity among women (Kiecolt-Glaser & Newton, 2001). The presence of a friend or partner may increase evaluation apprehension over whether important others' perceptions of the self may decline, and so this apprehension may eliminate any effect of support (Lepore, 1998). In addition, the variable findings may reflect different pathways by which social support affects health, increasing efforts to cope in some situations and decreasing harmful physiological responses in others (Hilmert, Kulik, & Christenfeld, 2002).

There may be other biological processes that underlie benefits of social support as well. A growing literature suggests a potential role for oxytocin (OT) in the neuroendocrine and physiological benefits of social support. In response to stress, animals and humans experience a cascade of hormonal responses that begins, at least in some stressors, with the rapid release of oxytocin. Consistent evidence suggests that (1) oxytocin signals gaps in significant social relationships (Taylor, Gonzaga, Klein, Greendale, Hu, & Seeman, 2006); (2) oxytocin is released in response to stress; (3) oxytocin is associated with affiliative activities in response to stress; and (4) oxytocin is associated with reduced SNS and HPA axis responses to stress (see Taylor, Dickerson, & Klein, 2002).

For example, social contact is enhanced and aggression is diminished following central administration of oxytocin in estrogen-treated prairie voles (Witt, Carter, & Walton, 1990), and experimental studies with female rats have found that the administration of oxytocin causes an increase in social contact and in grooming (Argiolas & Gessa, 1991; Carter, De Vries, & Getz, 1995; Witt, Winslow, & Insel, 1992). Animal studies suggest that oxytocin may also be implicated in the modulation of sympathetic and HPA axis responses to stress. For example, oxytocin is associated with parasympathetic (vagal) functioning that plays a counterregulatory

role in fear responses to stress (e.g., McCarthy, 1995; Dreifuss, Dubois-Dauphin, Widmer, & Raggenbass, 1992; Sawchenko & Swanson, 1982; Swanson & Sawchenko, 1980). In experimental studies, oxytocin enhances sedation and relaxation, reduces anxiety, and decreases sympathetic activity (Altemus, Deuster, Galliven, Carter, & Gold, 1995; Uvnäs-Moberg, 1997). Exogenous administration of oxytocin in rats results in decreases in blood pressure, pain sensitivity, and corticosteroid levels, among other findings indicative of a reduced stress response (Uvnäs-Moberg, 1997).

Oxytocin also appears to inhibit the secretion of adrenocorticotropin (ACTH) hormone and cortisol in humans (Chiodera & Legros, 1981; Legros, Chiodera, & Demy-Ponsart, 1982). Uvnäs-Moberg (1996) found that women who were breastfeeding (and therefore very high in plasma oxytocin [OT] concentration), perceived themselves to be calmer and rated themselves as more sociable than age-matched women not breastfeeding or pregnant; the level of plasma oxytocin correlated strongly with the level of calm reported.

The role of oxytocin in the down-regulation of SNS and HPA axis responses to stress is supported by a great deal of animal evidence and some human evidence. Thus, the evidence suggests that OT may be implicated in a pathway by which social support may exert protective effects on health. A compelling investigation demonstrating the potential role of oxytocin in the health-related aspects of social contact was conducted by Detillion, Craft, Glasper, Prendergast, and DeVries (2004). Female Siberian hamsters received a cutaneous wound and then were exposed to immobilization stress. Stress increased cortisol concentrations and impaired wound healing in the isolated, but not the socially housed, hamsters. Adrenalectomy eliminated the effects of stress on wound healing in isolated hamsters, suggesting that the effects of isolation and stress on the healing process was mediated via the HPA axis. Treatment of the isolated hamsters with oxytocin blocked the stress-induced increases in cortisol concentrations and facilitated wound healing. In contrast, treating socially-housed hamsters with an OT antagonist delayed wound healing. Taken together, these data suggest that social interactions buffer against stress and promote wound healing through a mechanism that involves OT-induced suppression of the HPA axis. This study then provides evidence consistent with a potential mechanism implicating OT in the beneficial effects of social support on an important aspect of health.

There may be roles for other hormones both in promoting social support initially and in regulating its biological effects, which include vasopressin, norepinephrine, serotonin, prolactin, and endogenous opioid peptides (Nelson & Panksepp, 1998; Taylor, Dickerson, & Klein, 2002).

Why Is Social Support Beneficial?

Much early research on social support took for granted that its impact on mental and physical health came largely from the specific benefits furnished by social support transactions. That is, when one person helps another, that other is benefited tangibly or emotionally in ways that can contribute to the well-documented beneficial outcomes described. A variety of observations, however, have led researchers to rethink whether all the benefits, or indeed, the primary benefits, of social support come from its actual utilization.

The fact that structural measures of social support are associated with mental and physical health benefits is implicit support for questioning this account. If merely knowing the number of social ties an individual has leads to insights about that individual's health, then it would appear that the activation of those ties may not be essential for benefits to be experienced. Research suggests that the mere perception of social support, whether or not it is actually utilized, can be stress reducing, with concomitant benefits for well-being. For example, Broadwell and Light (1999) brought married men and women into the laboratory and had them fill out a questionnaire about how much support they felt they had at home (or a questionnaire assessing matters unrelated to support). Each person was then put through several stressful tasks such as computing difficult arithmetic problems in his or her head. The men who reported much support from their families had lower blood pressure responses to the stressful tasks than those who had less social support, suggesting that their families were providing support to them, even though they were not physically present; the effect was not significant for women. In fact, beliefs about the availability of emotional support appear to exert stronger effects on mental health than the actual receipt of social support does (e.g., Wethington & Kessler,

1986; Dunkel-Schetter & Bennet, 1990; see Thoits, 1995, for discussion).

This point suggests that actual receipt of social support may have costs. In an important study, Bolger, Zuckerman, and Kessler (2000) documented that actually making use of one's social support network can be associated with enhanced rather than reduced stress. In their studies, couples completed daily diaries regarding the stressors they experienced, how distressed they were in response to them, and whether they had provided or received support from their partner. Supportive acts that were reported by the support recipient did not promote adjustment to stress but, rather, were associated with poorer adjustment, suggesting that when explicit support is provided, there can be emotional costs to the recipient. However, when supportive acts were reported by the support provider but were unrecognized by the recipient, stress-protective effects were found. The results suggest that the most effective support is "invisible" to the recipient, that is, it occurs without his or her awareness. Thus, it may be that one set of benefits that social support confers is the availability of a supportive network that may act in a supportive manner without one's realization, thereby reducing distress in response to threatening events.

An important implication of results like these is that, at least under some circumstances, people can carry their social support networks around in their heads to buffer them against stress without ever having to recruit their networks in active ways that may produce the costs just noted. Findings like these suggest that it is important to distinguish exactly when supportive efforts from others may be beneficial for mental and physical health and when people may not experience these benefits.

When Is Social Support Beneficial?

Whether social contacts are experienced as supportive may depend on several factors. These include how large or dense one's social support networks are; whether the support provided is appropriate for meeting the stressor; and whether the right kind of support comes from the right person.

Considerable research has explored the characteristics of socially supportive networks. As noted, people who belong to both formal and informal organizations in their communities, such as church groups, the PTA, clubs, and the like, enjoy the health and mental health benefits of social support. This may be because such people are more socially skilled to begin with and thus seek out contacts from others, or it may be a direct consequence of participation in supportive networks. Social networks may also be important for accessing specific types of assistance during times of stress (such as social services; Lin & Westcott, 1991). However, the beneficial effects of social support are not cumulative in linear fashion. It is clear that having a confidant (such as a spouse or a partner) may be the most effective social support (Collins & Feeney, 2000; Cohen & Wills, 1985), especially for men (e.g., Broadwell & Light, 1999; Wickrama, Conger, & Lorenz, 1995). Accordingly, married people report higher perceived support than do unmarried people (Thoits, 1995). With respect to friends, research documents the benefits of having at least one close friend, but having a dozen or more close friends may be little more beneficial for health and mental health than having a few (Langner & Michael, 1960). Indeed, one of the risks of social support networks is that overly intrusive social support may actually exacerbate stress (Shumaker & Hill, 1991). People who belong to dense social networks of friends or family who are highly interactive may find themselves overwhelmed by the advice they receive and interference that occurs in times of stress. As comedian George Burns noted, "Happiness is having a large, loving, caring, close-knit family in another city."

Sometimes support providers give poor advice, fail at providing tangible assistance, or provide inappropriate or too little emotional support, thereby reducing or eliminating the effectiveness of the effort (Bolger, Foster, Vinokur, & Ng, 1996; Burg & Seeman, 1994). Social support efforts, too, may be well intentioned but perceived as controlling or directive by the recipient. For example, when a spouse is pulled into the management of a chronic disease, such as coronary artery disease, the "support" of encouraging exercise and changing a partner's diet may be perceived as interference by the patient. Although such well-intentioned support may achieve some benefits in modifying behaviors in a healthy direction, the potential to produce interpersonal conflict and psychological distress is clearly present as well (e.g., Fisher, La Greca, Greco, Arfken, & Schneiderman, 1997; Lewis & Rook,

1999; Wortman & Lehman, 1985). Socially supportive efforts may misfire for other reasons. When a significant other's response to a person's expression of symptoms or distress is contingent on that expression, such "support" may unwittingly reinforce symptom experiences and actually enhance emotional distress (Itkowitz, Kerns, & Otis, 2003).

Effective social support may depend on an appropriate balance between the needs of the recipient and what that recipient gets from those in the social network (Cohen & McKay, 1984; Cohen & Wills, 1985). This "matching hypothesis" suggests that, to be supportive, the actions of the provider must meet the specific needs of the recipient (Thoits, 1995). Thus, for example, if a person needs emotional support but receives advice instead, the misfired effort at support may actually increase psychological distress (Horowitz et al., 2001; Thoits, 1986). Research generally supports this hypothesis. Different kinds of support, for example, may be valued from different members of a social support network. Emotional support may be most helpful from intimate others and actually resented when casual friends attempt to provide it, whereas information and advice may be especially valuable from experts but regarded as inappropriate from well-intentioned friends or family with questionable expertise (e.g., Benson, Gross, Messer, Kellum, & Passmore, 1991; Dakof & Taylor, 1990). Consistent with this perspective, Helgeson and Cohen (1996) reviewed research on the impact of social support on adjustment to cancer. They found that emotional support was most desired by patients and appeared to have the greatest beneficial influence on adjustment. However, peer support group interventions whose goal was providing emotional support did not, for the most part, have benefits; rather, educational groups that provided information were perceived more positively. Although there are several possible interpretations of these findings, it may be that emotional needs were best met by those close to cancer patients, rather than by the relative strangers in the peer group, and that educational interventions in peer groups better met the cancer patients' specific informational needs.

Other threats to obtaining social support may come from the support recipient. People who are under extreme stress often express their distress to others and, over time, can drive their social support networks away (Matt & Dean, 1993; McLeod,

Kessler, & Landis, 1992). For example, depressed, disabled, or ill people can inadvertently repel their families and friends by persistently expressing their negative emotions (Alferi, Carver, Antoni, Weiss, & Duran, 2001; Coyne et al., 1987; Fyrand, Moum, Finset, & Glennas, 2002). In a longitudinal investigation of 405 elderly individuals, Gurung, Taylor, and Seeman (2003) found that men and women who were more depressed or who had greater cognitive dysfunction reported more problems with social relationships at follow-up several years later (see also Honn & Bornstein, 2002; Alferi et al., 2001). They concluded that those most in need of social support were potentially less likely to receive it and to instead experience gaps in their social support.

The positive impact of social support on adjustment to stressful events may be attenuated in especially high-stress environments. For example, Ceballo and McLoyd (2002) found that the usually positive impact of social support on parenting behavior was attenuated in high-stress neighborhoods. Gurung, Taylor, Kemeny, and Myers (2004) found that, although high levels of social support were associated with lower levels of depression in a sample of low-income HIV-seropositive women, social support resources were not sufficient to moderate the relation between chronic burden and high levels of depression. Thus, like most resources, the effectiveness of social support in reducing distress due to stressful circumstances may have its limits at especially high levels of stress. Related to these observations is the fact that the perception of social support as available is positively correlated with socioeconomic status (SES; Thoits, 1984; Taylor & Seeman, 2000).

A recent *New Yorker* cartoon shows one woman enthusiastically telling another woman that what she likes best about their friendship is that they never have to see each other or talk. Indeed, many relationships may be better for the having of them than for the using of them. Social relationships are fraught with the potential for discord as well as support, and so relationships are a potential double-edged sword. In a study of 120 widowed women, Rook (1984) found that negative social interactions were consistently and more strongly related (negatively) to well-being than were positive social interactions. Having one's privacy invaded by family and friends, having promises of help not come through, and being involved with people who provoked con-

flict or anger were among the events that worsened adjustment in this vulnerable sample. Similarly, Schuster, Kessler, and Aseltine (1990) found that negative interactions with a spouse or close friends augmented depression more than positive, supportive interactions reduced it. These findings not only underscore the double-edged nature of social relationships but also imply that avoiding social relationships or situations that actually tax well-being may be helpful for managing stress.

Origins of Social Support

Who Gets Social Support?

The fact that social relationships can be either supportive or unhelpful and the fact that support recipients substantially affect which outcome occurs raise an intriguing issue. Is social support largely "outside" in the social environment or "inside" the person, in the form of abilities to extract support from the environment or construe support as available? Although social support no doubt involves aspects of both, attention to the qualities of the support recipient has yielded some important findings.

Research has suggested that there may be heritable aspects of social support. Specifically, research using twin study methodology has uncovered a moderately high degree of heritability, either in the ability to construe social support as available or in the ability to experience one's network of friends and relatives as supportive (Kessler, Kendler, Heath, Neale, & Eaves, 1992). Although there are a number of potential interpretations of these findings, at the very least, they suggest that heritable factors may play a role in some of the benefits of social support.

Some of these heritable factors may involve social competence. Some people are more effective than others in extracting the social support they need, suggesting that social support involves a considerable degree of skill. For example, Cohen, Sherrod, and Clark (1986) assessed incoming college freshman as to their social competence, social anxiety, and self-disclosure skills to see if these skills influenced whether the students were able to develop and use social support effectively and whether these same skills could account for the positive effects of social support in combating stress. Those students who began college with greater social competence, lower social anxiety, and better self-disclosure skills developed more effective social support and were more likely to form friendships, lending credibility to the idea that the use of social support reflects, in part, a set of competencies rather than an external resource that is available or not in a specific environment. Being a socially competent individual appears to be especially important for getting emotional support, but it may not predict as strongly the ability to get tangible assistance or information (Dunkel-Schetter, Folkman, & Lazarus, 1987).

A Developmental Approach to Social Support

The fact that social support may have heritable aspects and that it may depend, in part, on social skills suggests that focusing on its early familial antecedents may help explain why this vital resource seems to come so easily to some people and more rarely to others. The thesis to be offered here is that (a) the beneficial effects of social support on physical and mental health begin with supportive familial contact; (b) these contacts, in turn, lay the groundwork for the development of social competencies and corresponding abilities to enlist and provide social support and/or construe social support as available; (c) these skills are transferred intergenerationally, through both genomic and nongenomic pathways.

Evidence that socially supportive contacts in early life have beneficial effects on responses to stress, mental health, and health is manifold and may be readily seen in both human and animal studies. In some of the earliest work on this topic, Harlow and Harlow (1962) found that monkeys that were raised with an artificial terrycloth mother and were isolated from other monkeys during the first 6 months of life showed disruptions in their adult social contacts. They were less likely to engage in normal social behavior, such as grooming, their sexual responses were inappropriate, mothering among the females was deficient, and they often showed either highly fearful or abnormally aggressive behavior toward their peers. Not surprisingly, these social behaviors led to peer rejection. In sum, a broad array of social skills were compromised by the absence of early nurturant contact with the mother.

Building on work like this, Meaney and colleagues (Francis, Diorio, Liu, & Meaney, 1999; Liu et al., 1997) explicitly linked early nurturant maternal contact to the development of stress responses in offspring and showed that these contacts affect emotional and neuroendocrine responses to stress across the life span. In their paradigm, infant rats are removed from the nest, handled by a human experimenter, and then returned to the nest. The response of the mother to this separation and reunification is intense licking and grooming and arched-back nursing, which provides the pup with nurturant and soothing immediate stimulation. On the short term, this contact reduces SNS and HPA axis responses to stress in the pups (and in the mother as well). Over the long term, this maternal behavior results in a better-regulated HPA axis response to stress and novelty, and better regulation of somatic growth and neural development, especially hippocampal synaptic development in the pup. These rat pups also showed more open field exploration, which suggests lower levels of fear. This compelling animal model suggests that nurturant stimulation by the mother early in life modulates the responses of offspring to stress in ways that have permanent effects on the offspring's HPA axis responses to stress, on behavior suggestive of anxiety/fearfulness, and on cognitive function (see also Suomi, 1999).

Warm, nurturant, and supportive contact with a caregiver affects physiological and neuroendocrine stress responses in human infants and children just as in these animal studies. Early research on orphans reported high levels of emotional disturbance, especially depression, in infants who failed to receive nurturant stimulating contact from a caregiver (Spitz & Wolff, 1946). More recent findings from Eastern European abandoned infants confirm that, without the affectionate attention of caregivers, infants may fail to thrive, and many die (Carlson & Earls, 1997).

Not surprisingly, attachment processes are implicated in these relations. Gunnar and her associates, studying 15-month-old children receiving well-baby examinations, found that securely attached infants were less likely to show elevated cortisol responses to normal stressors such as inoculations than were less securely attached infants (Gunnar, Brodersen, Krueger, & Rigatuso, 1996; see also Nachmias, Gunnar, Mangelsdorf, Parritz, & Buss, 1996). The protective effects of secure attachment were especially evident for socially fearful or inhibited children (see also Levine & Wiener, 1988; Hart, Gunnar, & Cicchetti, 1996; see Collins & Feeney, 2000, for a discussion of attachment in adult supportive relationships).

Research also consistently suggests that families characterized by unsupportive relationships have damaging outcomes for the mental, physical, and social health of their offspring, not only on the short term but across the life span. Overt family conflict, manifested in recurrent episodes of anger and aggression, deficient nurturing, and family relationships that are cold, unsupportive, and/or neglectful, have been associated with a broad array of adverse mental and physical health outcomes long into adulthood (Repetti, Taylor, & Seeman, 2002; Taylor, Lerner, Sage, Lehman, & Seeman, 2004). The chronic stress of unsupportive families produces repeated or chronic SNS activation in children, which, in turn, may lead to wear and tear on the cardiovascular system. Over time, such alterations may lead to pathogenic changes in sympathetic or parasympathetic functioning or both. Such changes may contribute to disorders such as essential hypertension (e.g., Ewart, 1991) and coronary heart disease (e.g., Woodall & Matthews, 1989).

As appears to be true in the animal studies previously described, early nurturant and supportive contacts appear to be important for human offspring's emotional responses to stress as well, especially those involving anxiety or fear. Infants begin life with emergent abilities to monitor the environment, especially for potential threats. The amygdala is activated any time there is something new or unexpected in the environment, especially if it involves suggestions of danger. Early in life, the amygdala sends off many messages of alarm. Any loud noise, for example, will alarm an infant, and a few months later strangers typically provoke distress. Through the comforting attentions of parents, infants begin to learn about and adjust to the social world. Over time they learn that strangers are not necessarily threatening and that loud noises are not inevitably associated with danger, among other moderations of automatic responses to threat. As the prefrontal cortex develops, children learn additional ways to moderate the signals that they get from the amygdala, storing information about both the threatening and the comforting aspects of the social world.

The development of this system is critically affected by early nurturant contact. Infants form bonds with others that are comforting and, in turn, give rise to the emotion regulation skills and social skills that ultimately enable children to manage potentially threatening events autonomously, skills that

become vital to managing stress across the life span (Taylor, 2002). That is, a broad array of evidence demonstrates that children from supportive families are more likely than those from unsupportive families to develop effective emotion regulation skills and social competencies (Repetti et al., 2002); such children are perceived by their teachers as having better emotion regulation skills and social competencies, and their peers rate them as more popular (e.g., Demaray & Malecki, 2002; see Repetti et al., 2002 for a review). Similarly, adults whose interpersonal styles are marked by hostility and cynicism, a style that has been tied to an unsupportive or conflict-ridden early family environment, are less likely to report having social support (e.g., Smith, 1992), and/or support may be a less effective buffer against stress (e.g., Lepore, 1995).

In essence, then, the early family environment may provide the groundwork for social competence and the abilities to enlist social support across the life span. In families that are warm and nurturant, children learn to manage threat effectively with a lesser physiological/neuroendocrine toll, and through exposure to good models they may develop social skills of their own. If they are raised in cold, non-nurturant, or conflict-ridden families, children instead experience threatening events more commonly and learn fewer social competencies, with the result that social support networks may be difficult to develop or use effectively. As such, early nurturance of offspring in response to stress might be thought of as a prototype for social support, which is mirrored throughout life in the many more modest supportive contacts a person encounters across the life span.

Are the benefits of being raised in a socially supportive environment conferred genetically or through the environment? In other words, do particularly nurturant parents have particularly socially skilled offspring by virtue of their shared genetic heritage, or does nurturance itself play a role in the acquisition of social skills? Both mechanisms appear to be involved. On the one hand, certain species show genetically based high levels of "licking and grooming" in response to stress (Liu et al., 1997), which are transmitted to offspring as styles that appear in the offspring's nurturant behavior. On the other hand, by cross-fostering offspring to high or low nurturant caretakers, the impact of the behavior itself on physiological and social functioning becomes clear. For example, Suomi (1987) assigned rhesus monkeys selectively bred for differences in temperamental reactivity to foster mothers that were either unusually nurturant or within the normal range of mothering behavior. Highly reactive infants cross-fostered to normal mothers exhibited deficits in social behavior, and in adulthood they tended to drop and remain low in the dominance hierarchy (Suomi, 1991). Highly reactive infants cross-fostered to exceptionally nurturant females, in contrast, showed higher levels of social skills and in adulthood were more likely to rise to the top of the dominance hierarchy. When highly reactive females became mothers, they adopted the maternal style of their foster mothers, independent of their own reactivity profile (Suomi, 1987). That is, highly reactive females raised by especially nurturant foster mothers not only showed lower reactivity themselves but also learned effective parenting, which they then passed on to their own offspring. Studies like these provide evidence of the behavioral intergenerational transfer of nurturance over and above genetic predispositions (see also Francis et al., 1999).

These studies are significant for several reasons. First, they suggest clear developmental origins for social competencies that may affect social support availability across the life span. Second, they provide clear evidence that maternal nurturance can moderate genetic risks typically associated with the potential for maladaptive social behavior. Third, they demonstrate the nongenomic intergenerational transfer of social skills via exposure to nurturant supportive behavior. In short, then, whereas genetic factors may contribute to whether or not an individual is able to develop social competence, early nurturant experience can also be a contributing factor that may extend not only across one's own life span but to one's offspring as well. Although the evidence for such a model is primarily from animals, one would expect that genomic and nongenomic factors may be involved in the intergenerational transfer of social skills and deficits in humans as well.

Gender, Culture, and Social Support

Gender and Social Support

The previous discussion places a heavy role on mothering, at least in the animal studies implicating nurturance in offspring's social and physiological behavior. This raises the question of whether there are gender differences in the ability to provide social support to others, in its extraction from others, and in its benefits. The research evidence suggests that women provide more social support to others, draw on socially supportive networks more consistently in times of stress, and may be more benefited by social support.

Although men typically report larger social networks than do women, in part because of men's historically greater involvement in employment and in community organizations, studies find that women are consistently more invested in their relationships and that their relationships with others are more intimate (Belle, 1987). Women are more involved than men in both giving and receiving social support (Thoits, 1995). Across the life cycle, women are more likely to mobilize social support, especially from other women, in times of stress. Adolescent girls report more informal sources of support than do boys, and they are more likely to turn to their same-sex peers than are boys (e.g., Copeland & Hess, 1995; see Belle, 1987, for a review). College student women report more available helpers and report receiving more support than do college men (e.g., Ptacek, Smith, & Zanas, 1992; see Belle, 1987, for a review). Adult women maintain more same-sex close relationships than do men, they mobilize more social support in times of stress than do men, they turn to female friends more often than men turn to male friends, they report more benefits from contacts with their female friends and relatives (although they are also more vulnerable to psychological stress resulting from stressful network events), and they provide more frequent and more effective social support to others than do men (Belle, 1987; McDonald & Korabik, 1991; Ogus, Greenglass, & Burke, 1990).

Women are also more invested in their social networks than are men. They are better at reporting most types of social network events, and they are more likely to report getting involved if there is a crisis in the network (Wethington, McLeod, & Kessler, 1987). In an extensive study of social networks, Veroff, Kulka, and Douvan (1981) reported that women were 30% more likely than men to have provided some type of support in response to network stressors. These findings appear to generalize across a number of cultures as well (Whiting & Whiting, 1975; Edwards, 1993).

Studies of caregiving also bear out these observations. More than 80% of this care is provided by mothers, daughters, and wives. For example, in the United States, the typical caregiver is a 60-year-old, low-income woman with a disabled or ill spouse. However, daughters care for aging parents (sons are only one fourth as likely to give parental care), mothers care for disabled children, and a growing number of caregivers are grandmothers caring for the offspring of their own children who may have drug or alcohol problems or HIV infection (Taylor, 2002). Several studies suggest that men, in contrast, are more likely to institutionalize their wives in response to common causes of the need for caregiving, such as stroke or Alzheimer's disease (Freedman, 1993; Kelly-Hayes et al., 1998).

As the previous analysis suggests, women not only are disproportionately the providers of social support but also are more likely to seek social support in response to stress. Early studies of affiliation in response to stress by Schachter (1959) found that college student women were inclined to wait with another person when they anticipated going through a laboratory stressor, specifically laboratory shock; men did not demonstrate this tendency to affiliate in anticipation of stress. Subsequent research on affiliation under stress tended to use primarily female participants for this reason. Nonetheless, some research has compared male and female responses to stress. Bull and colleagues (1972) found that exposure to noise stress led to decreased liking among male participants but increased liking among female participants toward familiar others. Bell and Barnard (1977) found that males preferred less social interaction in response to stress, whereas females preferred closer interpersonal distance. Two meta-analyses (Luckow, Reifman, & McIntosh, 1998; Tamres, Janicki, & Helgeson, 2002) examined gender differences in coping with stress and found that women were significantly more likely to seek and use social support to deal with a broad array of stressors. For example, in the review by Luckow et al. of the 26 studies that tested for gender differences in coping via social support, 1 showed no differences and 25 showed that women favored social support more. These gender differences are more apparent in the domain of seeking emotional support than for other types of social support.

One might expect that if women seek social support more, are more invested in their social support networks, and report that social support is more important to them than is the case for men, they might benefit more from social support. A meta-analysis conducted by Schwarzer and Leppin (1989) found support for this hypothesis. Across many investigations, the correlation between social support and good health was approximately .20 for women, but for men the correlation was only .08.

Women also may be somewhat more effective providers of social support than are men. For example, Wheeler and colleagues (Wheeler, Reis, & Nezlek, 1983) studied students who remained at college during the December holidays to see who became depressed and lonely in response to this stressful circumstance. The students kept track of how they spent their days, with whom they spent them, and what emotions they experienced during that period. The strongest determinant of how lonely the students were was how much contact they had each day with women. The more time a student, whether man or woman, spent with women, the less lonely he or she was. The amount of time spent with men, for the most part, did not affect mental health.

Research consistent with this point has also come from studies of the differences between men's and women's abilities to provide social support for each other in times of stress and the protective effects of such efforts. An array of evidence suggests that women may be better providers of social support to men than men are to women (Thoits, 1995). For example, when men are asked where their emotional support comes from, most name their wife as their chief source of social support, and many name her as the only person to whom they confide their personal problems or difficulties (see Glaser & Kiecolt-Glaser, 1994; New England Research Institute, 1997; Phillipson, 1997); women report that they are likely to turn to a female friend or relative as well as to their spouse.

These differences appear to translate directly into health benefits. Although marriage benefits both men and women, it benefits men more (Chesney & Darbes, 1998). Thus, for example, the health of married men is better than that of single men, but the health of women is less strongly influenced by marital status. Mortality rates among widowed men are higher than among widowed women, and widowed men who remarry die later in life than those who do not remarry; among widowed women, remarrying has no effect on age of death (Helsing, Szklo, & Comstock, 1981; Stroebe & Stroebe, 1983). As noted earlier, in experimental studies, when women and men are asked to bring their partner with them when they undergo stressful laboratory tasks, men's SNS and HPA axis responses to stress tend to be buffered by the presence of a female partner, but women's responses to stress are often stronger in the presence of a partner than when alone (see Kiecolt-Glaser, & Newton, 2001). Moreover, the downside of social contacts discussed earlier, namely, the potential for conflict and other negative interactions, appears to weigh more heavily on women than on men. Specifically, in a large-scale review, Kiecolt-Glaser and Newton (2001) report that wives show stronger heart rate, blood pressure, and HPA axis changes during marital conflict than do husbands.

In a theoretical model that provides a framework for these observations, Taylor and colleagues (2000) suggested that gender differences in the seeking and giving of social support may reflect, in part, a robust and biologically based difference in how men and women cope with stress. They suggested that, whereas the behaviors of fight-or-flight, namely, aggression or withdrawal in response to stress, may be especially characteristic of men, a pattern termed *tend-and-befriend* may be more characteristic of women in response to stress. Tending involves nurturant activities designed to protect the self and offspring that may promote safety and reduce distress. Befriending is the creation and maintenance of social networks, especially those involving other women, that may aid in this process. Taylor and colleagues' argument is predicated on the evolutionary assumption that, during human prehistory, men and women faced somewhat different adaptive challenges, and as a result may have developed different stress responses to meet those challenges. Specifically, females of most species, including humans, have primary responsibility for the early nurturing of offspring through pregnancy, nursing, and care in early life. Stress responses in females, then, are likely to have evolved in such a way as to simultaneously protect mothers and offspring. Whereas fight and flight constitute responses to stress that can protect an individual well, tending to offspring and befriending others in a social group may facilitate the joint protection of self and offspring.

Taylor and colleagues suggested that these stress responses may be influenced, in part, by neuroendocrine underpinnings such as oxytocin and endogenous opioid peptides. As noted earlier, oxytocin is thought to be an affiliative hormone that may underlie at least some forms of maternal and social contact. Because the impact of oxytocin is enhanced by the effects of estrogen, oxytocin's effects are thought to be stronger in females than in males and may be implicated in the maternal tending of offspring seen in response to stress (Taylor et al., 2000).

In summary, then, although both men and women benefit from social support, women tend to give and receive social support from different sources. Women are disproportionately the support providers to children, to men, and to other women. The support that they provide also appears to translate directly into health benefits. When men seek social support, on the other hand, they are most likely to do so from a partner, and they show clear health benefits from having a marital partner. Overall, women are somewhat more likely to give social support, seek it out in times of stress, and benefit from it, patterns that may have evolutionary significance and biological underpinnings (Taylor et al., 2000; Taylor, 2002).

Culture and Social Support

Culture is another variable that may moderate how social support is perceived or received. On the one hand, there is a large literature to suggest that the benefits of social support for mental and physical health extend across many cultures. On the other hand, the possibility that support is experienced differently in different cultures is an important issue that has not been widely addressed. Is there any reason to believe that particular cultural dimensions might be related to how and whether social support is experienced or used in response to stress?

One such dimension is independence/interdependence. In Western cultures, there is a strong emphasis on individuality and how one can best distinguish oneself from others by discovering and making use of one's unique talents. This sense of self has been referred to as *independence* (Markus & Kitayama, 1991). In contrast, the interdependent view of the self, characteristic of many Asian, southern European, and Latin cultures consists of seeing oneself as part of encompassing social relationships and recognizing that one's behavior is determined and dependent on what one perceives to be the thoughts, feelings, actions, and norms in a given social setting. From this viewpoint, the self becomes meaningful and complete largely within the context of social relationships, rather than through independent, autonomous action.

To the extent that this distinction is related to social support, one might hypothesize that those with an independent self-construal would try to solve their problems individually, without necessarily drawing on social support, whereas those from interdependent cultures would be more likely to call upon their social support networks for aid in times of stress. An alternative viewpoint, however, leads to a different hypothesis. Those with an independent sense of self tend to see resources, including ongoing relationships, in terms of their personal needs (e.g., Kim & Markus, 1999; Fiske, Kitayama, Markus, & Nisbett, 1998). As such, to the extent that social support is perceived to be a resource, those with an independent sense of self may seek the explicit help of family and friends in order to help themselves cope more successfully with stressful events. In contrast, those with an interdependent sense of self, especially in Asian cultural contexts, view the maintenance of harmony within the social group as an overarching goal. Any effort to bring one's personal problems to the attention of others to enlist their help may be seen as undermining that harmony or making inappropriate demands on the social group, and the appreciation of such social norms may lead people to avoid taxing the system by bringing their problems to the attention of others for the purpose of enlisting social support.

Taylor et al. (2004) explored cultural differences in the use of social support. In one study, European American and Korean students were asked about their ways of coping with stress, including both their individual coping methods and social coping methods. Significantly fewer Korean than American students reported explicitly drawing on their social relationships to help them cope. A second study, comparing Asian American and European American students, similarly found that Asian Americans were significantly less likely to draw on social support for coping with stress than were European American students (see also Hsieh, 2000; Shin, 2002; Liang & Bogat, 1994). A third study demonstrated that mediators of the lesser use of social support by Asians/Asian Americans, relative to European Americans, were concern over disrupting the harmony of the group, concern over social criticism or losing face, and the belief that one should be self-reliant in solving one's personal problems.

Results such as these underscore the importance of understanding cultural differences in how support may be experienced or used. They imply, for example, that the construal of social support that has been dominant in the psychological literature—namely, as transactions involving the specific and intentional efforts to extract or provide help or solace from others—may be a particularly Western way of thinking about social support; such a conceptualization may not generalize to cultures that view relationships in terms of interdependent harmony, rather than as resources. Instead, individuals from at least some interdependent cultures, such as East Asian cultures, may draw on implicit social support, which involves the feeling that one is a member of an interdependent, harmonious community to which one has obligations and responsibilities.

Like the research on perceived support noted earlier, social support that is implicit may have many of the same mental health and health benefits as social support that is explicitly drawn on in times of stress. There is a potential broader lesson to be learned from these beginning studies of cultural differences in the experience of social support. As research has clarified the ways in which extracting support from others may be costly, the potential benefits of just knowing that others care for you have come into view.

Providing Social Support

Costs and Benefits of Providing Social Support

Conceptualizations of social support have been guided by the implicit assumption that support is beneficial for the recipient but costly for the provider. On the surface, this is a fairly sensible assumption. The provision of advice, emotional support, or tangible assistance can be costly to a support provider, at least in time, and potentially in resources as well. Virtually all acts of social support, ranging from listening to a friend's woes about her marriage to taking in family members who are out of work, involve an outlay of at least some resources.

This viewpoint may also have been shaped by evolutionary perspectives on altruism, which encompasses some of the actions usually construed as social support. Altruistic behavior has presented something of a problem for traditional evolutionary theory. Put in its most simple form, the paradox is, how do we pass on our altruistic genes to future generations if those very genes can put us at risk, thereby reducing the probability that we will pass on our genes at all? The warning cry of the sentinel, common to some rodent species, is often presented as an example. On the lookout for danger, the sentinel sees a predator such as a hawk and then lets out a loud, distinctive warning cry that not only sends its companions scampering for safety but attracts the attention of the predator, potentially increasing the likelihood that the sentinel itself will be the predator's meal. Although the kinds of social support that we commonly find in contemporary society do not typically put people at potentially fatal risk, in our early prehistory, giving aid to another person facing a severe threat, such as a predator, may well have done so under at least some circumstances, and thus the question is a fair one (Taylor, 2002).

Altruism has largely been rescued by the concept of reciprocal altruism (Hamilton, 1963; Trivers, 1971), which maintains that altruists do not dispense altruism at random but are more likely to aid genetically related others and behave altruistically toward others when there is some expectation of reciprocity. Providing social support is normative, and to the extent that people typically spend their time in the company of familiar social networks of mutual obligation, there is every reason to expect that a favor done by one person may be reciprocated by another at another time.[1]

The idea that support provision is inherently costly is also given credence by research on caregiving. Many people are involved in giving care to elderly parents, spouses, and disabled children. The costs of caregiving can be substantial, as it can be a difficult, grinding, chronic stressor. More than half of contemporary caregivers work outside the home, and many need to modify their job or reduce their hours to accommodate their caregiving. For older people, such caregiving can be a fatal undertaking, with caretakers at high risk for physical and mental health problems. Nearly 60% of elderly caregivers show signs of clinical depression. Evidence of immunocompromise is often present in caregivers, which can leave them vulnerable to flu and respiratory disorders; caretakers also show a poorer response to the influenza vaccine (Kiecolt-Glaser, Glaser, Gravenstein, Malarkey, & Sheridan, 1996; Newsom & Schulz, 1998; see also Esterling, Kiecolt-

Glaser, & Glaser, 1996; Kiecolt-Glaser et al., 1996). Other studies have found that the stress of caregiving can have adverse effects on wound repair (Kiecolt-Glaser, Marucha, Malarkey, Mercado, & Glaser, 1995), on the regulation of SNS responses to stress (Mills et al., 1997), and on natural killer (NK) cell function (Esterling et al., 1996). Moreover, these immune alterations can persist well after caregiving activities have ceased (Esterling, Kiecolt-Glaser, Bodnar, & Glaser, 1994). Caregivers shake off infectious disease very slowly and are at heightened risk for death. Schulz and Beach (2000), for example, found that the chances of dying in a given 4-year period for an elderly person involved in stressful caregiving were 63% higher than for elderly people without these responsibilities (see also Cacioppo et al., 2000; King, Oka, & Young, 1994; Spitze, Logan, Joseph, & Lee, 1994; Wu et al., 1999).

Evidence like this would seem to bear out the viewpoint that giving social support is costly. However, the majority of these studies have focused on populations in which any adverse effects of providing care would be expected to be seen. A number of the situations studied involve particularly burdensome caregiving. A number of the samples involved the elderly, who are at particular risk for health problems. Many others have focused on samples with extreme demands on their time. It is reasonable to think that, although caregiving may provide a glimpse into the extremes of social support provision, it may not characterize support provision generally.

In recent years, the potential benefits of giving social support have become better understood. There are a number of reasons to believe that providing social support to another might be stress reducing for the provider, as well as for the recipient. As the reciprocal altruism perspective just described suggests, providing support to others, as in the form of specific aid, increases the likelihood that there will be people there for you when your needs arise, a perception that can be comforting in its own right, as the perceived social support literature shows. Giving support to others may cement a personal relationship, provide a sense of meaning or purpose, and signify that one matters to others, all of which have been found to promote well-being (e.g., Taylor & Turner, 2001; Batson, 1998). Empirical research suggests that helping others may reduce distress (Cialdini, Darby, & Vincent, 1973; Midlarsky, 1991) and contribute to good health (Luoh & Herzog, 2002; Schwartz & Sendor, 2000). A recent study by Brown, Nesse, Vinokur, and Smith (in press) assessed giving and receiving social support in an older married sample and related it to mortality over a 5-year period. Death was significantly less likely for those people who reported providing instrumental support to friends, relatives, and neighbors and to those who reported providing emotional support to their spouses. Receiving support did not affect mortality, once giving support was statistically controlled. The study also statistically controlled for a wide variety of potential contributors to these effects, and the relationships held. This study, thus, provides important evidence that the giving of support can promote health and/or retard illness progression.

Although the exact mechanisms underlying the benefits of support provision are not yet understood, the animal studies on the impact of nurturant behavior on offspring that were described earlier may be instructive. These studies found not only that offspring were soothed by nurturant contact but also that the animal providing the nurturant contact was benefited as well. Specifically, benefits to offspring were mirrored in the nurturers in the form of reduced sympathetic arousal and higher reported feelings of calm (Wiesenfeld, Malatesta, Whitman, Grannose, & Vile, 1985; Uvnäs-Moberg, 1996; see also Adler, Cook, Davison, West, & Bancroft, 1986; Altemus et al., 1995). Thus, it is possible that the benefits of providing social support operate through some of the same physiological and neuroendocrine pathways whereby the receipt of support from others seems to achieve its benefits. In addition, if oxytocin and other hormones are implicated in the provision of social support, the anxiolytic properties of oxytocin, coupled with its established role in down-regulating SNS and HPA axis responses to stress, may provide a second potential point of departure for understanding the health benefits of providing social support, as well as receiving it.

Social Support Interventions: Clinical Implications

The implications of social support research for clinical practice and interventions are substantial. As one of the best-established resources contributing to

psychological well-being and health, clinical efforts to enhance or improve social support are well placed. Moreover, when people are experiencing intensely stressful events, social support is not inevitably forthcoming. Even when people in a social network make efforts to provide social support, those efforts may not always be effective, as noted earlier. Consequently, a broad array of clinical support interventions have arisen to augment social support, especially for those experiencing gaps in the support they receive from others.

Some of these are family support interventions. For example, when a person has been diagnosed with a chronic condition or illness, the family's participation in an intervention may be enlisted to improve the diagnosed patient's adjustment to the condition. In addition, as noted earlier, involving the family in health behavior change programs may be beneficial for effective management of the disorder (see Taylor, 2006).

Family support interventions may also be emotionally soothing to family members, in part by alleviating anxiety that may be generated by incomplete understanding or misinformation. Explaining exactly what the patient's condition is, what treatments will be needed, and how the family can help can mean that support provided by family members may be more forthcoming and effective. In addition, family members may receive guidance in well-intentioned actions that should nonetheless be avoided because they are experienced as aversive by patients (e.g., Dakof & Taylor, 1990; Martin, Davis, Baron, Suls, & Blanchard, 1994).

For the most part, people who need help managing stressful events turn to their family, to friends, and to experts, such as medical caregivers, for the support they need in times of stress. In some cases, however, that support is not forthcoming. Family and friends may be ill equipped to provide the kind of support that a person needs for any of several reasons. Some conditions for which a person may require social support are stigmatized ones, such as HIV, cancer, or epilepsy, and stigmatized conditions can drive friends and family away (Wortman & Dunkel-Schetter, 1979). In other cases, a person's particular problems, such as the discovery of a chronic disease, can lead to questions and concerns that can be answered only by people with similar problems. Consequently, social support groups have arisen as potentially low-cost and efficient vehicles for meeting unmet social support needs. As of 1979, more than 15 million Americans were using social support groups as a primary vehicle for their mental health services (Evans, 1979), and those numbers have grown over the past 25 years. Recent studies estimate that about 25 million individuals participate in support groups at some point during their life (Kessler, Mickelson, & Zhao, 1997), with whites and women more likely to participate than nonwhites and men (Davison et al., 2000).

Social support groups were originally conceived of as small, face-to-face voluntary groups of individuals who came together to solve a problem or help each other cope with handicaps or illnesses, especially through the provision of emotional support (Katz & Bender, 1976). Some of these groups originally were grassroots organizations formed by patients themselves, but more commonly, these support groups included a professional clinician, either as an initiator and organizer, or as an ongoing counselor who facilitated group interaction. Self-help groups, a particular type of social support group, do not include the participation of a trained professional, once the group is established (Katz & Bender, 1976). Originally, social support groups developed to treat a broad array of problems, disorders, and disabilities, including alcoholism, drug abuse, chronic diseases, loss of a partner through divorce or death, and, most commonly, obesity (see Taylor, Falke, Shoptaw, & Lichtman, 1986, for an early review).

Social support groups continue to be a vital resource for the chronically ill and to people managing problems such as obesity and alcoholism. These groups provide a format for discussions of mutual concern that arise as a result of illness, provide specific information about how others have dealt with similar problems, and provide people with the opportunity to share their emotional responses with others sharing the same problem (Gottlieb, 1988). Such groups can potentially fill gaps in social support not filled by family and friends or may act as an additional source of support provided by those going through the same event.

How effective are these groups? A large number of studies have evaluated the efficacy of social support groups by comparing people who have actually participated in such groups with those who have been waitlisted for participation and/or with nonparticipants, and these studies have generally found beneficial effects (see Hogan & Najarian, 2002, for a review). For example, social support groups have been found to reduce psychological distress for rheumatoid arthritis patients (e.g., Bradley et al., 1987), cancer patients (e.g., Telch & Telch, 1986), and patients who have had a myocardial infarction (e.g., Dracup, 1985), among many others. As noted, self-help groups may especially benefit those with disorders that are stigmatized, such as AIDS, alcoholism, breast and prostate cancer, and epilepsy (Davison, Pennebaker, & Dickerson, 2000; Droge, Arntson, & Norton, 1986).

Other benefits include helping patients to develop the motivation and techniques to adhere to complicated treatment regimens (Storer, Frate, Johnson, & Greenberg, 1987). Support groups may encourage adherence for several reasons. In the course of interacting with others, a participant may learn techniques that others have used successfully to maintain adherence or to cope effectively with a disorder, and may adopt those techniques to combat his or her particular barriers to adherence. Because people may commit themselves to change their behavior in front of others in the support group, they may be especially motivated to maintain adherence (e.g., Cummings, Becker, Kirscht, & Levin, 1981). Emotional support and the encouragement that others with similar problems provide can also encourage adherence to treatment.

Although social support groups have the potential to provide both emotional and informational support to participants, there is some evidence that they may be better at providing educational than emotional support efforts. In a review of cancer support groups described earlier, Helgeson and Cohen (1996) found that educational groups were more effective in meeting patients' needs than were support groups specifically aimed at the provision of emotional support. As noted, because relationships among support group members may seem artificial or not as intimate as "natural" relationships, relations in the support group may be more appropriate for providing information about the target problem or coping with it, whereas family or close friends may be better sources of emotional support.

A controversial issue in the support group literature has been whether participation in support groups among the chronically or terminally ill may promote better health and long-term survival. An early study of advanced breast cancer patients in a weekly cancer support group provided evidence that participants survived longer than nonparticipants (Spiegel, Bloom, Kraemer, & Gottheil, 1989).

However, a follow-up investigation was unable to replicate this finding (Spiegel, 2001), and so whether support group participation has the ability to retard disease progression remains at issue.

Social support groups were widely heralded early in their history because they presaged a low-cost, convenient treatment option for people who might otherwise not have therapeutic vehicles to deal with a wide variety of problems in an efficient, cost-effective manner. Some studies, however, suggested that self-help groups actually reach only a small proportion of potentially eligible members (Taylor et al., 1986), appealing disproportionately to well-educated, middle-class, white women. Not only is this the segment of the population that is already served by traditional treatment services, but at least one study (Taylor et al., 1986) suggested that participants in self-help groups were actually the same individuals who were using support services of all kinds, including therapists, ministers, family, friends, and medical experts.

Other factors can limit the effectiveness of support groups as well. In an evaluation of sources of satisfaction and dissatisfaction among members of cancer support groups, reported difficulties included logistical problems of getting to the face-to-face support group on a regular basis; irritation or annoyance over a particular individual or individuals in the group; concerns that meetings were too large; and concern that topics were too narrow and did not cover the issues in which prospective participants were interested (Taylor, Falke, Mazel, & Hilsberg, 1988).

The limited appeal of face-to-face groups has been somewhat offset by the rise of formal and informal Internet support groups (Davison et al., 2000). Although such groups do not provide the benefit of face-to-face social contact, they are logistically much easier to access, they are inexpensive (once one has a computer and an Internet connection), they provide opportunities to come and go at will and at times of personal need, and they may be a more acceptable mode of help seeking for men than traditional support groups have been. The wealth of information that is now available on the Web also means that many specific questions can be answered without long-term participation in a support group.

Because Internet-based support groups are a rapidly growing means of providing social support, especially for individuals with chronic illnesses or other stressful conditions, efforts have now gone into evaluating their effectiveness. For example, in one study (Barrera, Glasgow, McKay, Boles, & Feil, 2002), 160 patients with type 2 diabetes were randomized into one of four conditions: diabetes information only, a personal self-management coach, a social support intervention, or a personal self-management coach coupled with the social support intervention. All four conditions were implemented via the Internet. After three months, individuals in the two social support conditions (both with and without the personal coach) reported significant increases in perceived support, both with respect to their disease specifically and in general.

Internet social support can be useful with children as well. For example, STARBRIGHT World is a computer network that serves hospitalized children, providing interactive health education and opportunities to meet online with children in other hospitals who have similar disorders (Hazzard, Celano, Collins, & Markov, 2002). In one study evaluating the effectiveness of this program, children who participated reported more support, were found to be more knowledgeable about their illness and were rated as lower in negative coping.

To date, a large-scale evaluation of Internet social support resources has not been undertaken, largely because it is difficult to identify all the sources that are available and all the ways in which people distinctively use them. What research literature there is, however, suggests that these Internet resources are used for many of the same purposes as are face-to-face groups (Davison et al., 2000), and that, as such, they can be a valuable source of both informational and emotional support.

Conclusions

Across the life span, nurturant, supportive contact with others, a sense of belonging or mattering to others, and participation in social groups have been tied to a broad array of mental health and health benefits. Indeed, the social environment appears to be instrumental in helping people develop the abilities to build emotionally supportive ties with others and to construe social support as available.

Socially supportive ties are clearly beneficial in times of stress and may achieve these benefits, in large part, by helping individuals to control their emotional responses to stressful situations, such as anxiety and depression, and by keeping physiological, neuroendocrine, and immunologic responses to stress at low levels or by promoting faster recovery of these systems following stress. As such, social support has translated into health benefits across numerous studies.

Social relationships are inherently double-edged, and so ties with others are not inevitably supportive; gaps in support, misfired efforts at support, and blatantly unsupportive behavior from others in times of stress are well documented. In part because of these observations, researchers and practitioners are increasingly recognizing that the perception of social support, even in the absence of its utilization, may account for much of the benefits of support.

Many important issues remain for investigation. Among the most important conceptual issues is the integration of social support into our understanding of the psychological and biological concomitants of relationships more generally. The growing literature on developmental antecedents of social support may be especially helpful in building such an integrative model. The biological mechanisms underlying the benefits of social support also merit continued investigation. In particular, animal studies have been very useful for identifying underlying mechanisms relating social contacts to health outcomes, and this rich source of insights should continue to be mined. Much emphasis has been placed on SNS and HPA axis responses to stress as primary pathways affected by social support. Continued exploration of the possible roles of oxytocin, endogenous opioid peptides, and other hormones is warranted.

Why the mere perception of support has such strong effects on well-being and health merits continued consideration. Does perceived support operate through similar mechanisms as actual social support, or are other factors, such as genetic predispositions, more meaningful influences? Some issues that will merit additional research are only just being recognized; these include cultural differences in the experience of social support and the psychological/biological benefits of providing support to others. On the clinical side, perhaps the most compelling and provocative issues center on the potential health benefits of social support groups and the enormous role that Internet support increasingly plays in people's lives.

What is, perhaps, most striking about social support research is the astonishing expansion of contexts and vehicles that have arisen to provide support and to address potentially unmet support needs. Once the value of social support for health and mental health was identified, it became understood for the valuable resource it is. As such, social support is a cornerstone of the important insights that health psychology has yielded.

Acknowledgments. Preparation of this chapter was supported in part by grants from the NIMH (MH056880) and NSF (BCS-9905157).

Note

1. Of interest in this context is the observation that in communal relationships, there are norms explicitly *against* reciprocity (Clark & Mills, 1979), favoring instead the notion that a communal relation with another transcends what would otherwise be obligations for reciprocity.

References

Adler, E. M., Cook, A., Davison, D., West, C., & Bancroft, J. (1986). Hormones, mood and sexuality in lactating women. *British Journal of Psychiatry, 148,* 74–79.

Alferi, S. M., Carver, C. S., Antoni, M. H., Weiss, S., & Duran, R. E. (2001). An exploratory study of social support, distress, and life disruption among low-income Hispanic women under treatment for early stage breast cancer. *Health Psychology, 20,* 41–46.

Allen, K. M., Blascovich, J., Tomaka, J., & Kelsey, R. M. (1991). Presence of human friends and pet dogs as moderators of autonomic responses to stress in women. *Journal of Personality and Social Psychology, 61,* 582–589.

Altemus, M. P., Deuster, A., Galliven, E., Carter, C. S., & Gold, P. W. (1995). Suppression of hypothalamic-pituitary-adrenal axis response to stress in lactating women. *Journal of Clinical Endocrinology and Metabolism, 80,* 2954–2959.

Argiolas, A., & Gessa, G. L. (1991). Central functions of oxytocin. *Neuroscience and Biobehavioral Reviews, 15,* 217–231.

Barrera, M., Jr., Glasgow, R. E., McKay, H. G., Boles, S. M., & Feil, E. G. (2002). Do Internet-based support interventions change perceptions of social support? An experimental trial of approaches for supporting diabetes self-management. *American Journal of Community Psychology, 30,* 637–654.

Batson, C. D. (1998). Altruism and prosocial behavior. In D. T. Gilbert & S. T. Fiske (Eds.), *The handbook of social psychology* (Vol. 2, pp. 282–316). New York: McGraw Hill.

Bell, P. A., & Barnard, S. W. (1977, May). *Sex differences in the effects of heat and noise stress on personal space permeability.* Paper presented at the Rocky Mountain Psychological Society annual meetings, Albuquerque, NM.

Belle, D. (1987). Gender differences in the social moderators of stress. In R. C. Barnett, L. Biener, & G. K. Baruch (Eds.), *Gender and stress* (pp. 257–277). New York: Free Press.

Benson, B. A., Gross, A. M., Messer, S. C., Kellum, G., & Passmore, L. A. (1991). Social support networks among families of children with craniofacial anomalies. *Health Psychology, 10,* 252–258.

Berkman, L. F., & Syme, S. L. (1979). Social networks, host resistance, and mortality: A nine-year followup study of Alameda County residents. *American Journal of Epidemiology, 109,* 186–204.

Boesch, C. (1991). The effects of leopard predation on grouping patterns in forest chimpanzees. *Behaviour, 117,* 220–242.

Bolger, N., Foster, M., Vinokur, A. D., & Ng, R. (1996). Close relationships and adjustments to a life crisis: The case of breast cancer. *Journal of Personality and Social Psychology, 70,* 283–294.

Bolger, N., Zuckerman, A., & Kessler, R. C. (2000). Invisible support and adjustment to stress. *Journal of Personality and Social Psychology, 79,* 953–961.

Bradley, L. A., Young, L. D., Anderson, K. O., Turner, R. A., Agudelo, C. A., McDaniel, L. K., et al. (1987). Effects of psychological therapy on pain behavior of rheumatoid arthritis patients: Treatment outcome and six-month followup. *Arthritis and Rheumatism, 30,* 1105–1114.

Broadwell, S. D., & Light, K. C. (1999). Family support and cardiovascular responses in married couples during conflict and other interactions. *International Journal of Behavioral Medicine, 6,* 40–63.

Broman, C. L. (1993). Social relationships and health-related behavior. *Journal of Behavioral Medicine, 16,* 335–350.

Brown, S. L., Nesse, R. M., Vinokur, A. D., & Smith, D. M. (2003). Providing social support may be more beneficial than receiving it: Results from a prospective study of mortality. *Psychological Science, 14,* 320–327.

Bruhn, J. G. (1965). An epidemiological study of myocardial infarction in an Italian-American community. *Journal of Chronic Diseases, 18,* 326–338.

Bull, A. J., Burbage, S. E., Crandall, J. E., Fletcher, C. I., Lloyd, J. T., Ravenberg, R. L., et al. (1972). Effects of noise and intolerance of ambiguity upon attraction for similar and dissimilar others. *Journal of Social Psychology, 88,* 151–152.

Burg, M. M., & Seeman, T. E. (1994). Families and health: The negative side of social ties. *Annals of Behavioral Medicine, 16,* 109–115.

Cacioppo, J., Burleson, M., Poehlmann, K., Malarky, W., Kiecolt-Glaser, J., Bernston, G., et al. (2000). Autonomic and neuroendocrine responses to mild psychological stressors: Effects of chronic stress on older women. *Annals of Behavioral Medicine, 22,* 140–148.

Caporeal, L. R. (1997). The evolution of truly social cognition: The core configuration model. *Personality and Social Psychology Review, 1,* 276–298.

Capuron, L., Ravaud, A., & Dantzer, R. (2000). Early depressive symptoms in cancer patients receiving interleukin-2 and/or interferon alpha-2b therapy. *Journal of Clinical Oncology, 18,* 2143–2151.

Carlson, L. E., Goodey, E., Bennett, M. H., Taenzer, P., & Koopmans, J. (2002). The addition of social support to a community-based large-group behavioral smoking cessation intervention: Improved cessation rates and gender differences. *Addictive Behaviors, 27,* 547–559.

Carlson, M., & Earls, F. (1997). Psychological and neuroendocrinological sequelae of early social deprivation in institutionalized children in Romania. *Annals of the New York Academy of Sciences, 807,* 419–428.

Carter, C. S., DeVries, A. C., & Getz, L. L. (1995). Physiological substrates of mammalian mo-nogamy: The prairie vole model. *Neuroscience and Biobehavioral Reviews, 19,* 303–314.

Ceballo, R., & McLoyd, V. C. (2002). Social support and parenting in poor, dangerous neighborhoods. *Child Development, 73,* 1310–1321.

Champoux, M., Byrne, E., Delizio, R. D., & Suomi, S. J. (1992). Motherless mothers revisited: Rhesus maternal behavior and rearing history. *Primates, 33,* 251–255.

Chesney, M., & Darbes, L. (1998). Social support and heart disease in women: Implications for intervention. In K. Orth-Gomer, M. Chesney, & N. K. Wenger (Eds.), *Women, stress, and heart disease* (pp. 165–182). Mahwah, NJ: Erlbaum.

Chiodera, P., & Legros, J. J. (1981) L'injection intraveineuse d'osytocine entraine unediminution de la concentration plasmatique de cortisol chez l'homme normal. *Comptes Rendus des Seances de la Societe de Biologie et de ses Filiales (Paris), 175,* 546.

Christenfeld, N., Gerin, W., Linden, W., Sanders, M., Mathur, J., Deich, J. D., et al. (1997). Social support effects on cardiovascular reactivity: Is a stranger as effective as a friend? *Psychosomatic Medicine, 59,* 388–398.

Chrousos, G. P., & Gold, P. W. (1992). The concepts of stress and stress system disorders: Overview of physical and behavioral homeostasis. *Journal of the American Medical Association, 267,* 1244–1252.

Cialdini, R. B., Darby, B. L., & Vincent, J. E. (1973). Transgression and altruism: A case for hedonism. *Journal of Experimental Social Psychology, 9,* 502–516.

Clark, M. S., & Mills, J. (1979). Interpersonal attraction in exchange and communal relationships. *Journal of Personality and Social Psychology, 37,* 12–24.

Cohen, S., Doyle, W. J., Skoner, D. P., Rabin, B. S., & Gwaltney, J. M. Jr. (1997). Social ties and susceptibility to the common cold. *Journal of the American Medical Association, 277,* 1940–1944.

Cohen, S., & McKay, G. (1984). Social support, stress, and the buffering hypothesis: A theoretical analysis. In A. Baum, S. E. Taylor, & J. Singer (Eds.), *Handbook of psychology and health* (Vol. 4, pp. 253–268). Hillsdale, NJ: Erlbaum.

Cohen, S., Sherrod, D. R., & Clark, M. S. (1986). Social skills and the stress-protective role of social support. *Journal of Personality and Social Psychology, 50,* 963–973.

Cohen, S., & Wills, T. A. (1985). Stress, social support, and the buffering hypothesis. *Psychological Bulletin, 98,* 310–357.

Collins, N. L., Dunkel-Schetter, C., Lobel, M., & Scrimshaw, S. C. M. (1993). Social support in pregnancy: Psychosocial correlates of birth outcomes and post-partum depression. *Journal of Personality and Social Psychology, 65,* 1243–1258.

Collins, N. L., & Feeney, B. C. (2000). A safe haven: An attachment theory perspective on support seeking and caregiving in intimate relationships. *Journal of Personality and Social Psychology, 78,* 1053–1073.

Copeland, E. P., & Hess, R. S. (1995). Differences in young adolescents' coping strategies based on gender and ethnicity. *Journal of Early Adolescence, 15,* 203–219.

Coyne, J. C., Kessler, R. C., Tal, M., Turnbull, J., Wortman, C. B., & Greden, J. F. (1987). Living with a depressed person. *Journal of Consulting and Clinical Psychology, 55,* 347–352.

Cummings, K. M., Becker, M. H., Kirscht, J. P., & Levin, N. W., (1981). Intervention strategies to improve compliance with medical regimens by ambulatory hemodialysis patients. *Journal of Behavioral Medicine, 4,* 111–128.

Dakof, G. A., & Taylor, S. E. (1990). Victims' perceptions of social support: What is helpful from whom? *Journal of Personality and Social Psychology, 58,* 80–89.

Davison, K. P., Pennebaker, J. W., & Dickerson, S. S. (2000). Who talks? The social psychology of illness support groups. *American Psychologist, 55,* 205–217.

Demaray, M. K., & Malecki, C. K. (2002). Critical levels of social support associated with student adjustment. *School Psychology Quarterly, 17,* 213–241.

Detillion, C. E., Craft, T. K., Glasper, E. R., Prendergast, B. J., & DeVries, C. (2004). Social facilitation of wound healing. *Psychoneuroendocrinology, 29,* 1004–1011.

DeVellis, R. F., DeVellis, B. M., Sauter, S. V. H., & Cohen, J. L. (1986). Predictors of pain and functioning in arthritis. *Health Education Research, 1,* 61–67.

Dimond, M. (1979). Social support and adaptation to chronic illness: The case of maintenance hemodialysis. *Research in Nursing and Health, 2,* 101–108.

Dracup, K. (1985). A controlled trial of couples' group counseling in cardiac rehabilitation. *Journal of Cardiopulmonary Rehabilitation, 5,* 436–442.

Dreifuss, J. J., Dubois-Dauphin, M., Widmer, H., & Raggenbass, M. (1992). Electrophysiology of oxytocin actions on central neurons. *Annals of the New York Academy of Science, 652,* 46–57.

Droge, D., Arntson, P., & Norton, R. (1986). The social support function in epilepsy self-help groups. *Small Group Behavior, 17,* 139–163.

Dunbar, R. (1996). *Grooming, gossip, and the evolution of language.* Cambridge, MA: Harvard University Press.

Dunkel-Schetter, C., & Bennet, T. L. (1990). Differentiating the cognitive and behavioral aspects of social support. In B. R. Sarason, I. G. Sarason, & G. R. Pierce (Eds.), *Social support: An interactional view* (pp. 267–296). Oxford, England: Wiley.

Dunkel-Schetter, C., Folkman, S., & Lazarus, R. S. (1987). Correlates of social support receipt. *Journal of Personality and Social Psychology, 53,* 71–80.

Edwards, C. P. (1993). Behavioral sex differences in children of diverse cultures: The case of nurturance to infants. In M. E. Pereira & L. A. Fairbanks (Eds.), *Juvenile primates: Life history, development, and behavior* (pp. 327–338). New York: Oxford University Press.

Esterling, B. A., Kiecolt-Glaser, J. K., Bodnar, J. C., & Glaser, R. (1994). Chronic stress, social support, and persistent alterations in the natural killer cell response to cytokines in older adults. *Health Psychology, 13,* 291–298.

Esterling, B. A., Kiecolt-Glaser, J. K., & Glaser, R. (1996). Psychosocial modulation of cytokine-induced natural killer cell activity in older adults. *Psychosomatic Medicine, 58,* 264–272.

Evans, G. (1979). *The family-wise guide to self-help.* New York: Ballantine, 1979.

Ewart, C. K. (1991). Familial transmission of essential hypertension: Genes, environments, and chronic anger. *Annals of Behavioral Medicine, 13,* 40–47.

Fisher, E. B., La Greca, A. M., Greco, P., Arfken, C., & Schneiderman, N. (1997). Directive and nondirective social support in diabetes management. *International Journal of Behavioral Medicine, 4,* 131–144.

Fiske, A. P., Kitayama, S., Markus, H. R., & Nisbett, R. E. (1998). The cultural matrix of social psychology. In D. T. Gilbert, S. T. Fiske, & G. Lindzey (Eds.), *Handbook of social psychology* (Vol. 2, pp. 915–981). Boston: McGraw-Hill.

Fleming, R., Baum, A., Gisriel, M. M., & Gatchel, R. J. (1982, September). Mediating influences of social support on stress at Three Mile Island. *Journal of Human Stress,* 14–23.

Francis, D., Diorio, J., Liu, D., & Meaney, M. J. (1999). Nongenomic transmission across generations of maternal behavior and stress responses in the rat. *Science, 286,* 1155–1158.

Fraser, S. N., & Spink, K. S. (2002). Examining the role of social support and group cohesion in exercise compliance. *Journal of Behavioral Medicine, 25,* 233–249.

Freedman, V. A. (1993). Kin and nursing home lengths of stay: A backward recurrence time approach. *Journal of Health and Social Behavior, 34,* 138–152.

Fyrand, L., Moum, T., Finset, A., & Glennas, A. (2002). The impact of disability and disease duration on social support of women with rheumatoid arthritis. *Journal of Behavioral Medicine, 25,* 251–268.

Galea, S., Ahern, J., Resnick, H., Kilpatrick, D., Bucuvalas, M., Gold, J., et al. (2002). Psychological sequelae of the September 11 terrorist attacks in New York City. *New England Journal of Medicine, 346,* 982–987.

Gerin, W., Milner, D., Chawla, S., & Pickering, T. (1995). Social support as a moderator of cardiovascular reactivity: A test of the direct effects and buffering hypothesis. *Psychosomatic Medicine, 57,* 16–22.

Gerin, W., Pieper, C., Levy, R., & Pickering, T. (1992). Social support in social interaction: A moderator of cardiovascular reactivity. *Psychosomatic Medicine, 54,* 324–336.

Glaser, R., & Kiecolt-Glaser, J. K. (Eds.). (1994). *Handbook of human stress and immunity.* San Diego, CA: Academic Press.

Goodenow, C., Reisine, S. T., & Grady, K. E. (1990). Quality of social support and associated social and psychological functioning in women with rheumatoid arthritis. *Health Psychology, 9,* 266–284.

Gottlieb, B. H. (Ed.). (1988). *Marshalling social support: Formats, processes, and effects.* Newbury Park, CA: Sage.

Gunnar, M. R., Brodersen, L., Krueger, K., & Rigatuso, J. (1996). Dampening of adrenocortical responses during infancy: Normative changes and individual differences. *Child Development, 67,* 877–889.

Gurung, R. A. R., Taylor, S. E., Kemeny, M. E., & Myers, H. (2004). "HIV is not my only problem": Predictors of depression in an ethnically diverse sample of women at risk for AIDS. *Journal of Social and Clinical Psychology, 23,* 490–511.

Gurung, R. A. R., Taylor, S. E., & Seeman, T. (2003). Social support in later life: Insights from the MacArthur studies of successful aging. Psychology and Aging, 18, 487–496.

Hamilton, W. D. (1963). The evolution of altruistic behavior. *American Naturalist, 97,* 354–356.

Hamrick, N., Cohen, S., & Rodriguez, M. S. (2002). Being popular can be healthy or unhealthy: Stress, social network diversity, and incidence of upper respiratory infection. *Health Psychology, 21,* 294–298.

Harlow, H. F., & Harlow, M. K. (1962). Social deprivation in monkeys. *Scientific American, 207,* 136–146.

Hart, J., Gunnar, M., & Cicchetti, D. (1996). Altered neuroendocrine activity in maltreated children related to symptoms of depression. *Development and Psychopathology, 8,* 201–214.

Hazzard, A., Celano, M., Collins, M., & Markov, Y. (2002). Effects of STARBRIGHT World on knowledge, social support, and coping in hospitalized children with sickle cell disease and asthma. *Children's Health Care, 31,* 69–86.

Helgeson, V. S., & Cohen, S. (1996). Social support and adjustment to cancer: Reconciling descriptive, correlational, and intervention research. *Health Psychology, 15,* 135–148.

Helsing, K. J., Szklo, M., & Comstock, G. W. (1981). Factors associated with mortality after widowhood. *American Journal of Public Health, 71,* 802–809.

Hilmert, C. J., Kulik, J. A., & Christenfeld, N. (2002). The varied impact of social support on cardiovascular reactivity. *Basic & Applied Social Psychology, 24,* 229–240.

Hogan, B. E., & Najarian, B. (2002). Social support interventions: Do they work? *Clinical Psychology Review, 22,* 381–440.

Holahan, C. J., Moos, R. H., Holahan, C. K., & Brennan, P. L. (1997). Social context, coping strategies, and depressive symptoms: An expanded model with cardiac patients. *Journal of Personality and Social Psychology, 72,* 918–928.

Honn, V. J., & Bornstein, R. A. (2002). Social support, neuropsychological performance and depression in HIV infection. *Journal of the International Neuropsychological Society, 8,* 436–447.

Horowitz, L. M., Krasnoperova, E. N., Tatar, D. G., Hansen, M. B., Person, E. A., Galvin, K. L., et al. (2001). The way to console may depend on the goal: Experimental studies of social support. *Journal of Experimental Social Psychology, 37,* 49–61.

House, J. S., Landis, K. R., & Umberson, D. (1988). Social relationships and health. *Science, 241,* 540–545.

Hsieh, C. (2000). Self-construals, coping, and the culture fit hypothesis: A cross-cultural study. *Dissertation Abstracts International, 61* (1–B), 588. (UMI No. 95014–309)

Itkowitz, N. I., Kerns, R. D., & Otis, J. D. (2003). Support and coronary heart disease: The importance of significant other responses. *Journal of Behavioral Medicine, 26,* 19–30.

Kamarck, T. W., Manuck, S. B., & Jennings, J. R. (1990). Social support reduces cardiovascular reactivity to psychological challenge: A laboratory model. *Psychosomatic Medicine, 52,* 42–58.

Katz, A. H., & Bender, E. I. (1976). Self-help in society: The motif of mutual aid. In A. Katz & E. Bender (Eds.), *The strength in us: Self-help groups in the modern world* (pp. 2–13). New York: New Viewpoints.

Kelly-Hayes, M., Wolf, P. A., Kannel, W. B., Sytkowski, D., D'Agostino, R. B., & Gresham, G. E. (1988). Factors influencing survival and need for institutionalization following stroke: The Framingham Study. *Archives of Physical and Medical Rehabilitation, 69,* 415–418.

Kessler, R. C., Kendler, K. S., Heath, A. C., Neale, M. C., & Eaves, L. J. (1992). Social support, depressed mood, and adjustment to stress: A genetic epidemiological investigation. *Journal of Personality and Social Psychology, 62,* 257–272.

Kessler, R. C., Mickelson, K. D., & Zhao, S. (1997). Patterns and correlates of self-help group membership in the United States. *Social Policy, 27,* 27–46.

Kiecolt-Glaser, J. K., Glaser, R., Gravenstein, S., Malarkey, W. B., & Sheridan, J. (1996). Chronic stress alters the immune response to influenza virus vaccine in older adults. *Proceedings of the National Academy of Science USA, 93,* 3043–3047.

Kiecolt-Glaser, J. K., Marucha, P. T., Malarkey, W. B., Mercado, A. M., & Glaser, R. (1995). Slowing of wound healing by psychological stress. *Lancet, 346,* 1194–1196.

Kiecolt-Glaser, J. K., & Newton, T. L. (2001). Marriage and health: His and hers. *Psychological Bulletin, 127,* 472–503.

Kim, H., & Markus, H. R. (1999). Deviance or uniqueness, harmony or conformity? A cultural analysis. *Journal of Personality and Social Psychology, 77,* 785–800.

King, A., Oka, B., & Young, D. (1994). Ambulatory blood pressure and heart rate responses to stress of work and caregiving in older women. *Journal of Gerontology, 49,* 239–245.

King, K. B., Reis, H. T., Porter, L. A., & Norsen, L. H. (1993). Social support and long-term recovery from coronary artery surgery: Effects on patients and spouses. *Health Psychology, 12,* 56–63.

Kirschbaum, C., Klauer, T., Filipp, S., & Hellhammer, D. H. (1995). Sex-specific effects of social support on cortisol and subjective responses to acute psychological stress. *Psychosomatic Medicine, 57,* 23–31.

Kors, D., Linden, W., & Gerin, W. (1997). Evaluation interferes with social support: Effects on cardiovascular stress reactivity. *Journal of Social and Clinical Psychology, 16,* 1–23.

Kulik, J. A., & Mahler, H. I. M. (1993). Emotional support as a moderator of adjustment and compliance after coronary artery bypass surgery: A longitudinal study. *Journal of Behavioral Medicine, 16,* 45–64.

Langner, T., & Michael, S. (1960). *Life stress and mental health.* New York: Free Press.

Legros, J. J., Chiodera, L., & Demey-Ponsart, D. Inhibitory influence of exogenous oxytocin on adrenocorticotrophin secretion in normal human subjects. *Journal of Clinical Endocrinology and Metabolism, 55,* 1035–1039.

Lepore, S. J. (1995). Cynicism, social support, and cardiovascular reactivity. *Health Psychology, 14,* 210–216.

Lepore, S. J. (1998). Problems and prospects for the social support–reactivity hypothesis. *Annals of Behavioral Medicine, 20,* 257–269.

Lepore, S. J., Allen, K. A. M., & Evans, G. W. (1993). Social support lowers cardiovascular reactivity to an acute stress. *Psychosomatic Medicine, 55,* 518–524.

Leucken, L. J. (1998). Childhood attachment and loss experiences affect adult cardiovascular and cortisol function. *Psychosomatic Medicine, 60,* 765–772.

Levine, S., & Wiener, S. G. (1988). Psychoendocrine aspects of mother-infant relationships in nonhuman primates. *Psychoneuroimmunology, 13,* 143–154.

Lewis, M. A., & Rook, K. S. (1999). Social control in personal relationships: Impact on health behaviors and psychological distress. *Health Psychology, 18,* 63–71.

Liang, B., & Bogat, G. A. (1994). Culture, control, and coping: New perspectives on social support. *American Journal of Community Psychology, 22,* 123–147.

Lin, N., & Westcott, J. (1991). Marital engagement/ disengagement, social networks, and mental health. In J. Eckenrode (Ed.), *The social context of coping* (pp. 213–237). New York: Plenum.

Lin, N., Ye, X., & Ensel, W. (1999). Social support and depressed mood: A structural analysis. *Journal of Health and Social Behavior, 40,* 344–359.

Liu, D., Diorio, J., Tannenbaum, B., Caldji, C., Francis, D., Freedman, A., et al. (1997). Maternal care, hippocampal glucocorticoid receptors, and hypothalamic-pituitary-adrenal responses to stress. *Science, 277,* 1659–1662.

Luckow, A., Reifman, A., & McIntosh, D. N. (1998, August). *Gender differences in coping: A meta-analysis.* Poster session presented at the 106th Annual Convention of the American Psychological Association, San Francisco.

Luoh, M., & Herzog, A. R. (2002). Individual consequences of volunteer and paid work in old age: Health and mortality. *Journal of Health and Social Behavior, 43,* 490–509.

Magni, G., Silvestro, A., Tamiello, M., Zanesco, L., & Carl, M. (1988). An integrated approach to the assessment of family adjustment to acute lymphocytic leukemia in children. *Acta Psychiatrica Scandinavia, 78,* 639–642.

Maier, S. F., & Watkins, L. R. (1998). Cytokines for psychologists: Implications of bidirectional immune-to-brain communication for understanding behavior, mood, and cognition. *Psychological Review, 105,* 83–107.

Markus, H. R., & Kitayama, S. (1991). Culture and the self: Implications for cognition, emotion, and motivation. *Psychological Review, 98,* 224–253.

Marteau, T. M., Bloch, S., & Baum, J. D. (1987). Family life and diabetic control. *Journal of Child Psychology and Psychiatry, 28,* 823–833.

Martin, R., Davis, G. M., Baron, R. S., Suls, J., & Blanchard, E. B. (1994). Specificity in social support: Perceptions of helpful and unhelpful provider behaviors among irritable bowel syndrome, headache, and cancer patients. *Health Psychology, 13,* 432–439.

Matt, G. E., & Dean, A. (1993). Social support from friends and psychological distress among elderly persons: Moderator effects of age. *Journal of Health and Social Behavior, 34,* 187–200.

McCarthy, M. M. (1995). Estrogen modulation of oxytocin and its relation to behavior. In R. Ivell & J. Russell (Eds.), *Oxytocin: Cellular and molecular approaches in medicine and research* (pp. 235– 242). New York: Plenum.

McDonald, L. M., & Korabik, K. (1991). Sources of stress and ways of coping among male and female managers. *Journal of Social Behavior and Personality, 6,* 185–198.

McEwen, B. S., & Sapolsky, R. M. (1995). Stress and cognitive function. *Current Opinion in Neurobiology, 5,* 205–216.

McEwen, B. S., & Stellar, E. (1993). Stress and the individual: Mechanisms leading to disease. *Archives of Internal Medicine, 153,* 2093–2101.

McLeod, J. D., Kessler, R. C., & Landis, K. R. (1992). Speed of recovery from major depressive episodes in a community sample of married men and women. *Journal of Abnormal Psychology, 101,* 277– 286.

Midlarsky, E. (1991). Helping as coping. *Prosocial Behavior.* Thousand Oaks, CA: Sage.

Miller, G. E., Cohen, S., & Ritchey, A. K. (2002). Chronic psychological stress and the regulation of pro-inflammatory cytokines: A glucocorticoid-resistance model. *Health Psychology, 21,* 531–541.

Mills, P. J., Ziegler, M. G., Patterson, T., Dimsdale, J. E., Haugher, R., Irwin, M., et al. (1997). Plasma catecholamine and lymphocyte beta2-adrenergic alterations in elderly Alzheimer caregivers under stress. *Psychosomatic Medicine, 59,* 251–256.

Mullen, B., Bryant, B., & Driskell, J. E. (1997). Presence of others and arousal: An integration. *Group Dynamics: Theory, Research, and Practice, 1,* 52–64.

Nachmias, M., Gunnar, M. R., Mangelsdorf, S., Parritz, R. H., & Buss, K. (1996). Behavioral inhibition and stress reactivity: The moderating role of attachment security. *Child Development, 67,* 508–522.

Nelson, E. E., & Panksepp, J. (1998). Brain substrates of infant-mother attachment: Contributions of opioids, oxytocin, and norepinephrine. *Neuroscience and Biobehavioral Reviews, 22,* 437–452.

New England Research Institutes. (1997, Spring/ Summer). Gender differences in social supports: Data from the Massachusetts Male Aging Study and the Massachusetts Women's Health Study. *Network, 12.*

Newsom, J. T., & Schulz, R. (1998). Caregiving from the recipient's perspective: Negative reactions to being helped. *Health Psychology, 17,* 172–181.

Ogus, E. D., Greenglass, E. R., & Burke, R. J. (1990).

Gender-role differences, work stress and depersonalization. *Journal of Social Behavior and Personality, 5,* 387–398.

Penninx, B. W. J. H., van Tilburg, T., Boeke, A. J. P., Deeg, D. J .H., Kriegsman, D. M. W., & van Eijk, J. Th. M. (1998). Effects of social support and personal coping resources on depressive symptoms: Different for various chronic diseases? *Health Psychology, 17,* 551–558.

Phillipson, C. (1997). Social relationships in later life: A review of the research literature. *International Journal of Geriatric Psychiatry, 12,* 505–512.

Ptacek, J. T., Smith, R. E., & Zanas, J. (1992). Gender, appraisal, and coping: A longitudinal analysis. *Journal of Personality, 60,* 747–770.

Repetti, R. L., Taylor, S. E., & Seeman, T. E. (2002). Risky families: Family social environments and the mental and physical health of offspring. *Psychological Bulletin, 128,* 330–366.

Resnick, B., Orwig, D., Magaziner, J., & Wynne, C. (2002). The effect of social support on exercise behavior in older adults. *Clinical Nursing Research, 11,* 52–70.

Robertson, E. K., & Suinn, R. M. (1968). The determination of rate of progress of stroke patients through empathy measures of patient and family. *Journal of Psychosomatic Research, 12,* 189–191.

Rook, K. S. (1984). The negative side of social interaction: Impact on psychological well-being. *Journal of Personality and Social Psychology, 46,* 1097–1108.

Sarason, B. R., Sarason, I. G., & Gurung, R. A. R. (1997). Close personal relationships and health outcomes: A key to the role of social support. In S. Duck (Ed.), *Handbook of personal relationships* (pp. 547–573). New York: Wiley.

Sawchenko, P. E., & Swanson, L. W. (1982). Immunohistochemical identification of neurons in the paraventricular nucleus of the hypothalamus that project to the medulla or to the spinal cord in the rat. *Journal of Comparative Neurology, 205,* 260–272.

Schachter, S. (1959). *The psychology of affiliation.* Stanford, CA: Stanford University Press.

Schulz, R., & Beach, S. (2000). Caregiving as a risk factor for mortality: The caregiver health effects study. *Journal of the American Medical Association, 282,* 2215–2219.

Schuster, T. L., Kessler, R. C., & Aseltine, R. H., Jr. (1990). Supportive interactions, negative interactions, and depressed mood. *American Journal of Community Psychology, 18,* 423–438.

Schwartz, C., & Sendor, M. (2000). Helping others helps oneself: Response shift effects in peer support. In K. Schmaling (Ed.), *Adaptation to changing health: Response shift in quality-of-life research* (pp. 43–70). Washington, DC: American Psychological Association.

Schwarzer, R., & Leppin, A. (1989). Social support and health: A meta-analysis. *Psychology and Health, 3,* 1–15.

Seeman, T. E. (1996). Social ties and health: The benefits of social integration. *Annals of Epidemiology, 6,* 442–451.

Seeman, T. E., Lusignolo, T. M., Albert, M., & Berkman, L. (2001). Social relationships, social support, and patterns of cognitive aging in healthy, high-functioning older adults: MacArthur Studies of Successful Aging. *Health Psychology, 20,* 243–255.

Seeman, T. E., & McEwen, B. (1996). Impact of social environment characteristics on neuroendocrine regulation. *Psychosomatic Medicine, 58,* 459–471.

Sheffield, D., & Carroll, D. (1994). Social support and cardiovascular reactions to active laboratory stressors. *Psychology and Health, 9,* 305–316.

Shin, J. Y. (2002). Social support for families of children with mental retardation: Comparison between Korea and the United States. *Mental Retardation, 40,* 103–118.

Shumaker, S. A., & Hill, D. R. (1991). Gender differences in social support and physical health. *Health Psychology, 10,* 102–111.

Siegel, J. M. (1993). Companion animals: In sickness and in health. *Journal of Social Issues, 49,* 157–167.

Smith, T. W. (1992). Hostility and health: Current status of a psychosomatic hypothesis. *Health Psychology, 11,* 139–150.

Smith, T. W., Gallo, L. C., Goble, L., Ngu, L. Q., & Stark, K. A. (1998). Agency, communion, and cardiovascular reactivity during marital interaction. *Health Psychology, 17,* 537–545.

Spiegel, D. (2001). Mind matters: Group therapy and survival in breast cancer. *New England Journal of Medicine, 345,* 1767–1768.

Spiegel, D., Bloom, J. R., Kraemer, H. C., & Gottheil, E. (1989). Effect of psychosocial treatment on survival of patients with metastatic breast cancer. *Lancet, 2,* 888–890.

Spitz, R. A., & Wolff, K. M. (1946). Anaclitic depression: An inquiry into the genesis of psychiatric conditions in early childhood, II. In A. Freud et al. (Eds.), *The psychoanalytic study of the child* (Vol. 2., pp. 313–342). New York: International Universities Press.

Spitze, G., Logan, J., Joseph, G., & Lee, E. (1994). Middle generation roles and the well-being of men and women. *Journal of Gerontology, 49,* 107–116.

Stone, A. A., Mezzacappa, E. S., Donatone, B. A., &
Gonder, M. (1999). Psychosocial stress and social
support are associated with prostate-specific antigen
levels in men: Results from a community screening
program. *Health Psychology, 18,* 482–486.

Storer, J. H., Frate, D. M., Johnson, S. A., & Greenberg, A. M. (1987). When the cure seems worse
than the disease: Helping families adapt to
hypertension treatment. *Family Relations, 36,*
311–315.

Stroebe, M. S., & Stroebe, W. (1983). Who suffers
more? Sex differences in health risks of the
widowed. *Psychological Bulletin, 93,* 279–301.

Suomi, S. J. (1987). Genetic and maternal contributions to individual differences in rhesus monkey
biobehavioral development. In N. A. Krasnagor,
E. M. Blass, M. A. Hofer, & W. P. Smotherman
(Eds.), *Perinatal development: A psychobiological
perspective* (pp. 397–420). New York: Academic
Press.

Suomi, S. J. (1991). Up-tight and laid-back monkeys:
Individual differences in the response to social
challenges. In S. Brauth, W. Hall, & R. Dooling
(Eds.), *Plasticity of development* (pp. 27–56).
Cambridge, MA: MIT Press.

Suomi, S. J. (1999). Attachment in rhesus monkeys.
In J. Cassidy & P. Shaver (Eds.), *Handbook of
attachment: Theory, research, and clinical applications* (pp. 181–197). New York: Guilford.

Suomi, S. J., & Levine, S. (1998). Psychobiology of
intergenerational effects of trauma: Evidence from
animal studies. In Y. Danieli (Ed.), *Intergenerational handbook of multigenerational legacies*
(pp. 623–637). New York: Plenum.

Swanson, L. W., & Sawchenko, P. E. (1980).
Paraventricular nucleus: A site for the integration
of neuroendocrine and autonomic mechanisms.
Neuroendocrinology, 31, 410–417.

Tamres, L., Janicki, D., & Helgeson, V. S. (2002). Sex
differences in coping behavior: A meta-analytic
review. *Personality and Social Psychology Review, 6,*
2–30.

Taylor, J. & Turner, R. J. (2001). A longitudinal study
of the role of significance of mattering to others
for depressive symptoms. *Journal of Health and
Social Behavior, 42,* 310–325.

Taylor, S. E. (2002). *The tending instinct: How
nurturing is essential to who we are and how we live.*
New York: Holt.

Taylor, S. E. (2006). *Health psychology* (6th ed.). New
York: McGraw-Hill.

Taylor, S. E., Dickerson, S. S., & Klein, L. C. (2002).
Toward a biology of social support. In C. R.
Snyder & S. J. Lopez (Eds.), *Handbook of positive
psychology* (pp. 556–569). London: Oxford
University Press.

Taylor, S. E., Falke, R. L., Mazel, R. M., & Hilsberg,
B. L. (1988). Sources of satisfaction and
dissatisfaction among members of cancer support
groups. In B. Gottlieb (Ed.), *Marshalling social
support* (pp. 187–208). Beverly Hills, CA: Sage.

Taylor, S. E., Falke, R. L., Shoptaw, S. J., & Lichtman,
R. R. (1986). Social support, support groups, and
the cancer patient. *Journal of Consulting and
Clinical Psychology, 54,* 608–615.

Taylor, S. E., Gonzaga, G., Klein, L. C., Hu, P.,
Greendale, G. A., & Seeman S. E. (2006).
Relation of oxytocin to psychological and
biological stress responses in older women.
Psychosomatic Medicine, 68, 238–245.

Taylor, S. E., Klein, L. C., Lewis, B. P., Gruenewald,
T. L., Gurung, R. A. R., & Updegraff, J. A.
(2000). Biobehavioral responses to stress in
females: Tend-and-befriend, not fight-or-flight.
Psychological Review, 107, 411–429.

Taylor, S. E., Lerner, J. S., Sage, R. M., Lehman, B. J.,
& Seeman, T. E. (2004). Early environment,
emotions, responses to stress, and health. *Journal
of Personality, 72,* 1365–1393.

Taylor, S. E., & Seeman, T. E. (2000). Psychosocial
resources and the SES-health relationship. In
N. Adler, M. Marmot, & B. McEwen (Eds.),
*Socioeconomic status and health in industrial nations:
Social, psychological, and biological pathways*
(pp. 210–225). New York: New York Academy of
Sciences.

Taylor, S. E., Sherman, D. K., Kim, H. S, Jarcho, J.,
Takagi, K., & Dunagan, M. S. (2004). Culture
and social support: Who seeks it and why?
Journal of Personality and Social Psychology, 87,
354–362.

Telch, C. F., & Telch, M. J. (1986). Group coping
skills instruction and supportive group therapy
for cancer patients: A comparison of strategies.
Journal of Consulting and Clinical Psychology, 54,
802–808.

Thoits, P. A. (1984). Explaining distributions of
psychological vulnerability: Lack of social support
in the face of life stress. *Social Forces, 63,* 453–
481.

Thoits, P. A. (1986). Social support as coping
assistance. *Journal of Consulting and Clinical
Psychology, 54,* 416–423.

Thoits, P. A. (1995). Stress, coping and social support
processes: Where are we? What next? *Journal of
Health and Social Behavior, 36*(Extra Issue), 53–
79.

Trivers, R. L. (1971). The evolution of reciprocal
altruism. *Quarterly Review of Biology, 46,* 35–37.

Turner-Cobb, J. M., Gore-Felton, C., Marouf, F.,
Koopman, C, Kim, P., Israelski, D., et al. (2002).
Coping, social support, and attachment style as

psychosocial correlates of adjustment in men and women with HIV/AIDS. *Journal of Behavioral Medicine, 25,* 337–353.

Uchino, B., Cacioppo, J., & Kiecolt-Glaser, J. (1996). The relationship between social support and physiological processes: A review with emphasis on underlying mechanisms and implications for health. *Psychological Bulletin, 119,* 488–531.

Umberson, D. (1987). Family status and health behaviors: Social control as a dimension of social integration. *Journal of Health and Social Behavior, 28,* 306–319.

Uvnäs-Moberg, K. (1996). Neuroendocrinology of the mother-child interaction. *Trends in Endocrinology and Metabolism, 7,* 126–131.

Uvnäs-Moberg, K. (1997). Oxytocin linked antistress effects: The relaxation and growth response. *Acta Psychologica Scandinavica, 640*(Suppl), 38–42.

VanderPlate, C., Aral, S. O., & Magder, L. (1988). The relationship among genital herpes simplex virus, stress, and social support. *Health Psychology, 7,* 159–168.

Veroff, J., Kulka, R., & Douvan, E. (1981). *Mental health in America: Patterns of help-seeking from 1957 to 1976.* New York: Basic Books.

Wallston, B. S., Alagna, S. W., DeVellis, B. M., & DeVellis, R. F. (1983). Social support and physical health. *Health Psychology, 2,* 367–391.

Wethington, E., & Kessler, R. C. (1986). Perceived support, received support, and adjustment to stressful life events. *Journal of Health and Social Behavior, 27,* 78–89.

Wethington, E., McLeod, J. D., & Kessler, R. C. (1987). The importance of life events for explaining sex differences in psychological distress. In R. C. Barnett, L. Biener, & G. K. Baruch (Eds.), *Gender and stress* (pp. 144–156). New York: Free Press.

Wheeler, L., Reis, S., & Nezlek, J. (1983). Loneliness, social interaction, and sex roles. *Journal of Personality and Social Psychology, 45,* 943–953.

Whiting, B., & Whiting, J. (1975). *Children of six cultures.* Cambridge, MA: Harvard University Press.

Wickrama, K., Conger, R. D., & Lorenz, F. O. (1995). Work, marriage, lifestyle, and changes in men's physical health. *Journal of Behavioral Medicine, 18,* 97–111.

Wiesenfeld, A. R., Malatesta, C. Z., Whitman, P. B., Grannose, C., & Vile, R. (1985). Psychophysiological response of breast- and bottle-feeding

mothers to their infants' signals. *Psychophysiology, 22,* 79–86.

Wiklund, I., Oden, A., Sanne, H., Ulvenstam, G., Wilhemsson, C., & Wilhemsen, L. (1988). Prognostic importance of somatic and psychosocial variables after a first myocardial infarction. *American Journal of Epidemiology, 128,* 786–795.

Wills, T. A. (1991). Social support and interpersonal relationships. In M. S. Clark (Ed.), *Prosocial behavior* (pp. 265–289). Newbury Park, CA: Sage.

Wills, T. A. (1998). Social support. In E. A. Blechman, & K. D. Brownell (Eds.), *Behavioral medicine and women: A comprehensive handbook* (pp. 118–128). New York: Guilford.

Wills, T. A., & Vaughan, R. (1989). Social support and substance use in early adolescence. *Journal of Behavioral Medicine, 12,* 321–340.

Wilson, D. K., & Ampey-Thornhill, G. (2001). The role in gender and family support on dietary compliance in an African-American adolescent hypertension prevention study. *Annals of Behavioral Medicine, 23,* 59–67.

Witt, D. M., Carter, C. S., & Walton, D. (1990). Central and peripheral effects of oxytocin administration in prairie voles (*Microtus ochrogaster*). *Pharmacology, Biochemistry, and Behavior, 37,* 63–69.

Witt, D. M., Winslow, J. T., & Insel, T. R. (1992). Enhanced social interactions in rats following chronic, centrally infused oxytocin. *Pharmacology, Biochemistry, and Behavior, 43,* 855–886.

Woodall, K. L., & Matthews, K. A. (1989). Familial environment associated with type A behaviors and psychophysiological responses to stress in children. *Health Psychology, 8,* 403–426.

Wortman, C. B., & Dunkel-Schetter, C. (1979). Interpersonal relationships and cancer: A theoretical analysis. *Journal of Social Issues, 35,* 120–155.

Wortman, C. B., & Lehman, D. R. (1985). Reactions to victims of life crises: Support attempts that fail. In I. G. Sarason & B. R. Sarason (Eds.), *Social support: Theory, research, and applications* (pp. 463–489). Dordrecht, Netherlands: Martinus Nijhoff.

Wu, H., Wang, J., Cacioppo, J. T., Glaser, R., Kiecolt-Glaser, J. K., & Malarkey, W. B. (1999). Chronic stress associated with spousal caregiving of patients with Alzheimer's dementia is associated with downregulation of B-lymphocyte GH mRNA. *Journal of Gerontology. Series A, Biological Sciences and Medical Sciences, 54,* M212–M215.

Howard S. Friedman

Personality, Disease, and Self-Healing

Why do some people become sick, whereas other seemingly similar people remain healthy or quickly recover from disease? Is it true that people with "hurry sickness" suffer heart attacks, and worriers develop ulcers, and shy people face cancer? Is relaxation an elixir, and will having a smile on your face make you live longer?

The relationships among individual differences, disease, and health have been investigated scientifically for more than 100 years, and many thousands of findings have been reported. The general verdict (subject to numerous exceptions and qualifications) is that a person who is chronically irritated, depressed, hostile, impulsive, bored, frustrated, lonely, or powerless is indeed more likely to develop illnesses and to die prematurely than is someone who generally feels emotionally balanced and effective, is in a satisfying job, has stable and supportive social relationships, and is well integrated into the community (Booth-Kewley & Friedman, 1987; Cohen & Williamson, 1991; Friedman & Booth-Kewley, 1987; House, Landis, & Umberson, 1988; Kiecolt-Glaser, Glaser, Cacioppo, & Malarkey, 1998; Miller, Smith, Turner, Guijarro, & Hallett, 1996; Repetti, Taylor, & Seeman, 2002; Smith & Gallo, 2001). Yet the various efforts to measure and

characterize such people have often led to a muddle of weak and hard-to-replicate findings.

To help clarify this muddle with a more structured and scientific framework, I developed the constructs termed *disease-prone personalities* and *self-healing personalities* (Friedman 1991/2000; 1998; Friedman & Booth-Kewley, 1987; Friedman & VandenBos, 1992). These constructs direct theory and research away from associations between single predictors and single outcomes, focusing instead on multiple-predictor, multiple-outcome developments over long periods of time. For example, instead of a medical focus on type A behavior and myocardial infarction, attention moves to biopsychosocial homeostasis and overall well-being and mortality risk, in a sociocultural context. As we shall see, some clarity can emerge from a modern and theoretically sophisticated approach to these matters, but the conceptual and methodological issues are complex.

All too often, when dealing with illness, medical investigators, as well as laypersons, think they are asking the question, "Why do people become sick?" when instead they are really studying "Who becomes sick?" There is astounding variability in susceptibility to various illnesses and in the speed and likelihood of recovery. This variability in vulnerability and recuperation is usually at least as important as the average levels of disease, but yet is underappreciated and understudied.

So-called risk factors mostly do a poor job of predicting who will succumb, and when and why they will do so. Most cookie lovers do not develop breast cancer, most couch potatoes do not suffer strokes, and it is even the case that most smokers do not develop lung cancer. Typically, a solitary risk factor, even if well documented (as many are not), produces only a marginal increase in an individual's risk for a particular disease, again revealing the marked variability. Multiple risk factors, if coupled with detailed knowledge of sociobehavioral environments, can, however, do a fairly good job of predicting subpopulation risk.

Despite the limits on prognostic power, there is a striking motivation to look for simple causal models of health and longevity. When one hears of someone becoming ill or dying at a young age, an immediate thought is, "What can I (as an individual) do to avoid that fate?" (Or, "Why am I different?") Importantly, even when scientists and physicians hear of an association between a stable characteristic or persistent activity and morbidity, there is a strong tendency to think about fairly simple causal links. For example, a well-done study of milk consumption in midlife and the future risk of Parkinson's disease found those in the highest intake group were at a substantially increased risk when compared with those who consumed no milk, even controlling for overall calcium intake and certain other factors (Park et al., 2005). A primary conclusion was: "Whether observed effects are mediated through nutrients other than calcium or through neurotoxic contaminants [in milk] warrants further study" (p. 1047). In other words, the search for explanation quickly turns to a straightforward biomedical model of direct biochemical mediation. Overall, even though scientists well appreciate (in theory) that correlation does not mean causation, the research corpus is full of single-variable models and potentially misleading or erroneous assumptions of causality. Such matters point to the existence of a more fundamental conceptual problem regarding disease-proneness. That is, we need better ways of and new models for thinking about staying healthy.

Many people are exposed to harmful bacteria, viruses, and other microorganisms but do not become ill. This situation was documented a half century ago in a study by two pediatricians who followed a number of families for about a year, doing throat cultures for streptococcal bacteria every few weeks. In a surprising result, they found that most of the time, the strep infections did not produce any symptoms of illness. The strep bacteria by themselves did not cause illness. When the people and families were stressed, however, the strep illness was more likely to develop (Meyer & Haggerty, 1962). On the other hand, no one developed the strep illness without exposure to the bacteria. Today, we have the paradoxical situation that social stress is generally taken for granted as an influence on upper respiratory illness (Cohen, Doyle, & Skoner, 1999), but yet the focus of medical practice remains on the microorganism.

Traditional approaches to health are dominated by the biomedical model of disease, in which health care is seen primarily as a curing or repair system, needed when medical problems strike. It emphasizes physiology, pathology, procedures, and pharmaceuticals. Although it is well known that many biopsychosocial factors influence whether an individual will stay well, the dominant biomedical model of disease exerts constant pressure to focus either on internal genetics or on the external threats of infectious agents and toxins. In contrast, consideration of the individual and his or her personality forces a broader and deeper analysis, which is closer to the true complexity of illness and well-being. This topic is the subject of this chapter.

Historical Context

The idea of links between personality and health dates back thousands of years and clearly appears in the writings of Hippocrates, Galen, and their followers. The ancient Greeks, keen observers of the human condition, saw four essentials—the so-called bodily humors—as key to both individuality and health. People with a healthy, balanced supply of blood would likely turn out to be sanguine—having the healthy temperament and ruddy complexion characteristic of a person dominated by this humor. (*Sanguine* nowadays refers to someone who is cheerful, confident, passionate, and optimistic.) Excessive black bile (or melancholy—sadness, gloom, splenic moroseness) might lead to depression and degenerative diseases or cancer. Yellow bile (or choler—peevish, angry, bilious people) would produce (if present in excess) a bitter, angry personality and associated feverish diseases. Finally, phlegm was said to be characteristic of a phlegmatic (sluggish, unemotional), cold apathy, associated, for example, with rheumatism. Although notions of bodily humors have been discarded, the underlying conception that individuals can be categorized as sanguine, depressed, hostile, and repressed remains with us.

The ancient Greek notion of humoral balance likewise appears in modern ideas of biopsychosocial homeostasis, which developed from the psychophysiological models of the French physiologist Claude Bernard (1880) and the "fight-or-flight" discoverer Walter Cannon (1932). Physicians no longer regularly, intentionally bleed and purge their patients, but they do search for anomalies as signs of illness. In the late 1940s, a number of medical students at Johns Hopkins University were studied in terms of their biological and psychological characteristics, categorized as either slow and solid (wary, self-reliant), rapid and facile (cool, clever), or irregular and uneven (moody, demanding). They were then followed for 30 years, during which time about half of them developed some serious health problem. Most (77%) of the previously labeled "irregular and uneven" types developed a serious disorder during these 30 years, but only about a quarter of the rest suffered a major health setback. In a follow-up, the "irregular and uneven" temperament types were again much more likely to have developed disease or to have died (Betz & Thomas, 1979). A later study found those physicians who seemed to have social and emotional problems (were repressed loners) were more likely to develop cancer (Shaffer, Graves, Swank, & Pearson, 1987). Analogously, a study of lung cancer in 224 men and women followed patients who had been diagnosed within the prior few months and found that those who were more likely to die within the year were patients who had a personality that was either much more sober or much more enthusiastic than average (Stavraky, Donner, Kincade, & Stewart, 1988). Such early work on personality balance helped set the stage for the current-day focus on allostasis—the ability to achieve stability through change (McEwen, 1998). The processes of allostasis use the autonomic nervous system, the hypothalamic-pituitary-adrenal axis, and the cardiovascular, metabolic, and immune systems to respond to challenge.

With the dominance of psychoanalytic and neo-analytic theory in the emergence of the field of psychiatry in the first half of the twentieth century, many interesting ideas in psychosomatic medicine grew out of the psychodynamic framework. (Freud himself used hypnosis and related psychodynamic techniques in the 1890s to cure hysterical paralysis [Freud, 1955].) In classic work beginning in the 1930s, Flanders Dunbar (1955) described conflicted patients such as one named Agnes, an unhappy and unattractive woman of 50 plagued with a serious heart condition that her doctors labeled "cause unknown." Agnes went in and out of hospitals until, finally, she died in the hospital on her birthday because, Dunbar said, Agnes had always wanted to show her resentment at being born. The influential psychoanalyst Alexander (1950) suggested that various diseases are caused by specific unconscious emotional conflicts. For example, ulcers were linked to oral conflicts (an unconscious desire to have basic infantile needs satisfied), and asthma to separation anxiety (i.e., an unconscious desire to be protected by one's mother). Thus, although internal medicine exploded in influence on the medical scene in the 1950s and 1960s with pharmaceuticals based on biochemistry, there was a substantial but underappreciated history in medicine that considered the importance of the psychology of the individual (see Friedman & Adler, this volume). However, like much psychoanalytic work, most of the early psychosomatic work could not be studied directly in a scientific manner. In this context, modern research on personality and health was launched (or at least greatly boosted) in the 1950s, when two cardiologists, Meyer Friedman and Ray Rosenman (1974), proposed the idea of the type A behavior pattern.

The Example of Coronary-Proneness, Type A Behavior, and Heart Disease

Perhaps the most researched topic in personality and disease involves the long-observed association between certain patterns of emotional behavior and the development of heart disease. The topic is of special interest in part because cardiovascular disease (heart disease and stroke) is by far the greatest cause of premature mortality in Western countries. Of course it has been known for thousands of years that excitement increases pulse rate and that emotions like fear and love can cause pain in one's chest. But in the late nineteenth century, the medical educator Sir William

Osler proposed a direct link between high-pressure activity and coronary heart disease (CHD; Leibowitz, 1970). In the 1930s, Karl and William Menninger (1936), well-known American psychiatrists, asserted that CHD is related to repressed aggression.

Despite extensive clinical observations, systematic study of the association between emotional behavior and heart disease did not begin until the 1950s, when type A people were defined as those involved in a constant struggle to do more and more things in less and less time, and who are often quite hostile or aggressive in their efforts to achieve them. Type A people always seem to be under the pressure of time and to live a life characterized by competitiveness. They are hasty, impatient, impulsive, hyperalert, and tense. When under pressure, most people may exhibit some behaviors that are similar to this pattern, but type A individuals exhibit this behavior very often, for example, turning even the most potentially relaxing situation (recreational sports such as tennis) into a high-pressure event (Chesney & Rosenman, 1985).

The initial aim was to simplify and objectify the concept by choosing a neutral term (type A), viewing it as a medical syndrome of coronary-proneness, and avoiding related psychological (especially psychodynamic) concepts and theories. However, it soon became apparent that the disease-relevant characteristics and patterns of individuals cannot be adequately explained in such a sterile manner. That is, researchers soon turned to trying to understand the trait correlates of type A behavior, the components of type A behavior, the developmental bases of type A behavior, the various consequences of type A behavior, and the health aspects of type A behavior beyond coronary disease. Furthermore, in a formulation where type A behavior is defined as synonymous with coronary-proneness, the approach begs the question of whether this type of personality does indeed *predict* coronary disease.

Interestingly, people who do not show type A characteristics are called type B. Consistent with the traditional biomedical approach to disease, type B was considered a default state, with no independent consideration as to what a healthy personality style might be. This approach shunned the usual scientific practice of establishing construct validity by showing that (1) the assessment is related to what it should theoretically be related to (convergent validation) and (2) the assessment is not related to what it should not be related to (discriminant vali-

dation; Campbell & Fiske, 1959). This purposeful disregard of construct validity did not make the phenomenon simpler to study but, on the contrary, led to numerous meandering and unspecified studies. Further, only a theory can tell us what our construct should and should not relate to, and the early type A approach lacked such a theory. It was not proposed to be related or unrelated to any other psychological phenomenon.

A half century and thousands of studies on the possible links between type A and heart disease have produced mixed results (Booth-Kewley & Friedman, 1987; Dembroski, Weiss, Shields, Haynes, & Feinlieb, 1978; Houston & Snyder, 1988; Jenkins, 1979; Matthews, 1982; Miller, Turner, Tindale, Posavac, & Dugoni, 1991). The type A pattern is reliable and can be best assessed through the type A structured interview (rather than through questionnaires). Excessive competitiveness and constant hostility do seem, for some people in some circumstances, to increase the likelihood of CHD (see the section on neuroticism later in the chapter). But being hurried and working hard at one's job are generally not risk factors. Thus the original formulation was only partly confirmed. By inspiring so much empirical research, the flawed type A idea helped the establishment of a broader and deeper approach. For example, the construct of a disease-prone personality (Friedman & Booth-Kewley, 1987) as applied to this issue simultaneously considers multiple aspects of personality (such as chronic anger, chronic anxiety, or chronic depression) and multiple diseases. Conversely, the construct of a self-healing personality (Friedman, 1991/2000) examines a multidimensional healing emotional style involving a match between the individual and the environment, which maintains a physiological and psychosocial homeostasis, and through which good mental health promotes good physical health. Such perspectives encourage and even necessitate a conceptually and methodologically more appropriate concern with rich theoretical traditions, multiple predictive measures, and multiple outcomes across time. For example, rather than an uninformative "Type B" default formulation, self-healing personalities emerge as similar to the mentally healthy orientations that have been extensively described by humanistic and positive psychologists. Such approaches in turn lead to sophisticated concern with mediators, moderators, and constraints on the associations between personality and health.

Extended Typologies

Other researchers subsequently also have pursued the typology approach, looking for a pattern or a collection of psychobiological symptoms associated with a particular disease. For example, some have added the effects of repressed emotions on health, offering the type C personality, which is hypothesized to be cancer-prone (Temoshok et al., 1985). This personality is repressed, apathetic, and hopeless. A type D personality describes distressed people who are supposedly at increased risk of cardiac events (Denollet, 2000). Type D people are high on both negative affectivity (tendency to experience negative emotions) and social inhibition (tendency to inhibit the expression of emotions). As we shall see, such conceptions remain popular because they do capture certain elements of the full relationship between personality and health.

On the other side of the coin, pioneering work by Salvador Maddi and Suzanne C. Ouellette Kobasa (1984) on *hardiness* helped provide a basic framework for thinking about staying healthy in the face of challenge. First, they suggest that a healthy personality maintains a sense of control. This is not necessarily a wild sense of optimism but rather a sense that one can control one's own behaviors. Second, there is a commitment to something that is important and meaningful in one's life, such as important values and goals. Third, hardy people welcome challenge. For example, they may view change as an exciting opportunity for growth and development. Hardiness generally involves a productive orientation, in which one shows a zest for life. Although drawing much-needed attention to the positive side of personality and health (the idea derives from humanistic-existential personality theories), early approaches to hardiness had a number of flaws. Most basically, the problems revolved around unreliable or narrow measurement, and piecemeal research, that could not capture the richness of a healthy personal style (Ouellette & DiPlacido, 2001). Such deficiencies again point to the need for a more comprehensive approach.

What Is Personality and Why Is It Important to Health and Disease?

Despite the interest from the psychoanalytically inspired psychosomatic researchers, the relation of personality and disease has been mostly neglected by modern medicine. Why worry about a difficult-to-define construct like personality when one could concentrate directly on infectious agents, antimicrobial drugs, disease processes, and so on? The answer is that a focus on the individual not only captures the individual's characteristic health-relevant patterns—his or her psychobiological predispositions, usual behaviors, and emotional reactions—but also apprehends the individual's perception of the social milieu and why some people are more likely to be exposed to the infectious agents or stress-inducing situations in the first place.

Personality can be defined as the biopsychosocial forces that make people uniquely themselves; it is a useful "unit of analysis" for studying health because it corresponds to the whole biological organism rather than to components or collectives. In other words, it is a person who is born, a person who behaves, and a person who ultimately dies. There are many reasons to believe that there is some coherence to or something systemic about being an individual; individuals are not merely random collections of cells and organs. Similarly, although persons are born into families and communities, there is some independence of the individual from what happens to the broader social collectives. For example, although people of lower socioeconomic status are at higher risk for morbidity and premature mortality, there is substantial individual variation.

Why is personality especially significant to health promotion and disease prevention? The question is an important one because it leads directly to the issue of causal linkages. In other words, personality is of interest here to the extent that it allows better intervention to improve health or, at the very least, good prediction of future health and disease. By studying personality and health, we are forced to gather research on psychoimmunology, stress, and unhealthy habits and see how the pieces fit together in the whole person. Similarly, after examining social relations or socioeconomic status or social integration, we are forced to return to study how these forces affect the individual. In the applied sphere, the study of personality encourages a focus on individual differences in reactions to interventions, and it cultivates attention to the individual's selection of health-relevant environments (Friedman, 2000).

In short, personality is important because it is the individual person who lives a unique life path, becomes ill or stays well, and lives long or dies prematurely. It matters to some extent whether one's cells or organs are uninfected and functioning well, but only because these affect the whole person. It matters whether a city has polluted air or uncooperative patients, but only because these may affect or characterize the individual. There is no isomorphism between risk factors and an individual's outcomes. Indeed, any health care provider comes to appreciate the complexity and resiliency of the human organism over time.

Models of Linkages Between Personality and Health

At conception, a genetic endowment is inherited from the mother and the father, but the developing organism immediately encounters a unique environment. The in utero environment varies in its supplies of nutrition, toxins, and hormones, thus affecting genetically programmed development, including physiology, the sensory organs, and especially the developing brain. For example, sex hormones affect later sexual behaviors and masculinity-femininity; stress hormones and mother's personality may affect later robustness (Copper et al., 1996; Lobel, DeVincent, Kaminer, & Meyer, 2000; Parsons, 1980). Nine months later, the newborn enters the world with certain predispositions and orientations.

The newborn's body and brain are still rapidly developing and changing, and so early experiences can have long-term significant effects, on both biological and psychological adaptability and resistance to challenge. Importantly, the newborn, who already has an incipient personality of sorts, immediately begins to affect his or her environment. For example, one infant may cry incessantly, thereby affecting the behaviors of the mother and perhaps the whole family (in a manner significantly different from that of quiet baby who soon sleeps through most of the night). However, mothers differ in how they respond to a crying infant, thus further complicating the individual patterns.

By the time the child enters preschool or other significant social interactions with peers at around age 3, certain relatively consistent patterns of response are apparent. Some toddlers are more shy or fearful or irritable or impulsive or distractible or sociable (Thomas, Chess, & Korn, 1982; Kagan, 1994; Plomin, 1986). These consistencies in emotional and motivational responses are often termed

temperament. Temperament captures these biopsychological patterns of responses that have begun to stabilize in the toddler years. But because these patterns will strongly interact with experiences of childhood, especially cognitive and social experiences, it is useful to distinguish them from personality, which begins to stabilize later in childhood.

By age 5 or 6, when formal schooling and more extensive cognitive and social influences begin, the relations among the health-relevant characteristics are already complex. The genetic endowment at conception already has been influenced in myriad ways, and so only the strongest genetic influences (such as trisomy 21/Down syndrome, or ganglioside accumulation in the brain/Tay-Sachs) would be expected to have straightforward, direct effects on personality and health. Most influences of genetics, in utero experiences, and sensory/emotional/cognitive inclinations will be much more subtle and complicated.

Throughout life, aspects of personality may change, though usually gradually (Twenge, 2000, 2001, 2002). Personality captures a combination of genetic, familial, experiential, and sociocultural elements, and so it provides a useful approach to the big picture. But because personality and health are affected by so many internal, external, and interactional variables, the causal links are multidimensional. Nonetheless, there is reason to believe that broad socioeconomic policies that improve children's well-being along many dimensions can be fruitfully considered to be policies of health promotion (Hayward & Gorman, 2004).

A key problem for personality researchers is that we cannot randomly assign a person to personality (at least not until the Human Genome Project develops further, as one wag put it). So because we are stuck with correlational designs, we need rich data collected across many years. The studies with the best research designs are longitudinal and use time-lagged correlational statistics and survival analyses to uncover associations between personality and health. Such longitudinal studies can ascertain whether and when personality is a reliable predictor of health. Unfortunately, most investigations of personality and disease usually focus on adults and are cross-sectional or of limited time frame. Even with longitudinal studies, it is easy to slip into unjustified conclusions about causal relations. For example, if people with repressed emotions are found to be more prone to develop cancer, it is often implicitly or explicitly (and incorrectly) assumed that decreasing one's repression will necessarily decrease one's risk of cancer.

There are a number of key models of causal linkages between personality and health, each of which may have its own subsets and variations. In many instances, more than one linkage is simultaneously causing an observed association. Most study designs, however, are not set up to detect multiple causal linkages.

Personality-Caused Disease: The Behavioral Route

A commonly investigated causal model proposes that personality can lead directly to disease through patterns of unhealthy behaviors such as poor diet and lack of physical activity. A frequent and sensible step in examining links between personality and disease is thus to isolate and control for known behavioral causes of disease, such as cigarette smoking's strong effects on lung disease. Mediational analyses of behavior help point to likely causal pathways. For example, if extroverted or anxious people are more likely to smoke (and to be ill), and controlling for smoking eliminates (statistically explains) a link between personality and a smoking-relevant disease, then these findings are evidence (but not proof) that cigarettes are a smoking gun linking personality and disease. It might also be the case, however, that other factors are correlated with smoking, extroversion, and the disease. Further, note that even if such a link is established, alterations in extroversion or treatments for the anxiety will not necessarily prevent the disease unless the smoking is also affected. Even if the mediator (e.g., smoking) is affected, the disease risk many not diminish if another unhealthy behavior (such as overeating) takes its place.

Sometimes researchers improperly use statistics to control behavioral variables like smoking to eliminate "known risk factors," rather than systematically testing mediator models. For example, if controlling for socioeconomic status eliminates the extroversion to disease association, it would be improper to dismiss extroversion as an irrelevant abstraction. (Socioeconomic status is a very broad variable and with no unitary explanatory power as to mechanism of disease causation.) Simple approaches may overlook a more complex but important web of associations among individual dif-

ferences, environments, behaviors, and disease. The full models need to be developed and tested.

Broadly speaking, evidence supports the idea that health-relevant behavior can be an important mediator of some of the associations between personality and health (Kassel, Stroud, & Paronis, 2003; Smith & Gallo, 2001). Personality does predict a wide variety of health-relevant behaviors. The evidence is much weaker, however, that limiting certain unhealthy behaviors will eliminate disease risk. For example, public health warnings in the 1980s to reduce cholesterol and fat intake did little to improve the dietary and obesity profile of Americans 20 years later. Similarly, it is not known whether directly targeting the relevant unhealthy personality will be generally effective.

Behavioral Mediating Mechanisms

We need to think about how a personality trait will play out in the situations one commonly encounters, *and* the situations to which it will lead us. This is the well-known interaction of personality and situation. Psychologists talk a lot about this, but too often they ignore it in practice.

Special research attention should be directed at smoking because smoking is by far the most powerful common behavioral influence on health. Smoking is often discussed in a broader health behavioral context—of dietary changes such as eating more vegetables, and alcohol use such as eliminating that double martini at lunch, and moderate exercise such as taking the stairs instead of the elevator—but, in fact, such other behavioral interventions usually will have only a relatively minor effect compared with stopping smoking. The importance of smoking has implications for research design and analysis because smoking is likely to emerge as such a potent mediator in many populations where it is present. Note also that although Americans (especially men) smoked a lot in the 1950s through the 1970s, today smoking has dropped by more than half in many states. Thus a certain personality characteristic that might predispose one to smoke in some times or places might be much less relevant in other times and places. Alcohol and drug abuse are other common and potent behavioral mediators, although they also vary by time and place and are of minor import in countries that strictly ban or limit these substances.

Injury—violence and accidents—is a health outcome that is often strongly affected by personality-influenced health behaviors; this is especially true before middle age (Zuckerman & Kuhlman, 2000). Risky sports, unsafe driving, and exposure to violent situations (including those that increase the risk of homicide and suicide) are a major threat to health and longevity, but usually the causes are multifactorial.

Personality-Caused Disease: The Psychophysiological Route

Personality can affect disease directly through physiological mechanisms. That is, individual reaction patterns can trigger unhealthy neurohormonal states. This pathway is the one that laypersons most often assume when they speak about individual differences and disease.

Models of personality causing disease through psychophysiological mediating mechanisms often begin with a focus on poor coping with stress. Depending on the challenge, individuals who are depressed, introverted, repressed, unconscientious, or otherwise unbalanced are often less successful in bringing to bear necessary psychological, social, and behavioral resources to face challenge (Aspinwall & Taylor, 1997).

Psychophysiological Mediating Mechanisms

There is no doubt that the resulting psychosocial stress involves harmful bodily reactions (Cacioppo & Berntson, this volume; Kemeny, this volume). The key questions concern which links are important and common for which kinds of people. Further, there is not yet a body of longitudinal work showing relations among well-measured personality characteristics, subsequent psychophysiological meditating mechanisms, and consequent disease outcomes.

Stress affects the cardiovascular system and metabolism through both the nervous system and the neuroendocrine system (hormones), and so mechanisms have been sought in such matters as changes in heart rate, blood pressure, and plasma lipids, with generally encouraging results. There is also good evidence that chronic psychological states are related to immune functioning, and immune functioning is related to disease susceptibility (Kemeny, this volume). But again here, there is only weak evidence that psychoneuroimmunological effects are a key factor in explaining links between personality and health (Segerstrom, 2000; Segerstrom

& Miller, 2004). It may turn out that psychoneuroimmunological mechanisms will need to be understood in conjunction with stable biological predispositions, health-relevant behaviors, and selection and interpretation of situations for a robust explanatory picture to emerge. Interestingly, cardiovascular and metabolic investigations (usually focused on coronary heart disease) have almost always proceeded independently of psychoneuroimmunological investigations (usually focused on cancer or HIV), thus lessening the chances that common pathways and processes (such as inflammation) will be discovered.

More speculative and rarely investigated are mechanisms involving consciousness and the so-called will to live. Some individuals appear able to employ mental efforts to improve their physiological function, but reports of such successes tend to be isolated and speculative. That is, although there are many well-documented reports of extraordinary individuals and startling recoveries, there is generally not a well-replicated and scientifically sound body of rigorous follow-up research. Advances in brain imaging may lead to better understanding of emotion, motivation, and well-being, as relevant to these phenomena (Rosenkranz et al., 2003; Urry et al., 2004).

Personality-Caused Disease: Selection Into Situations

One of the least understood but most interesting sources of the causal link between personality and disease involves gravitating toward or even choosing unhealthy situations. The usual model of a person randomly encountering various stressful events is untenable; the fact is that the individual helps create and select events (Bolger & Zuckerman, 1995). For example, neuroticism tends to predict negative life events. That is, neurotic people are more likely to experience objectively more stressful events (Magnus, Diener, Fujita, & Payot, 1993; Taylor, Repetti, & Seeman, 1997). Others, who are well socialized, conscientious, and agreeable, are more likely to wind up well educated and surrounded by mature adults.

A hostile, aggressive child may disrupt his family interactions (thereby creating an unsettled home environment) and may then run out to spend the evening with a like-minded gang. Or in terms of a more a clearly biological example, so-called supertasters have more receptors (taste buds) on their tongues and are three times as sensitive to bitterness than people of low taste sensitivity (Bartoshuk et al. 2001); such people might be likely to avoid eating various vegetables, thereby missing the health-protective effects. Many such biologically based individual differences have not yet been discovered or applied to the implications for healthy or unhealthy pathways and choices.

In short, in such examples, it is not that personality leads directly to unhealthy behaviors or unhealthy psychophysiological reactions, but rather that the personality facilitates entering the unhealthy situations.

Biological Underlying (Third) Variables

Genetic endowments and early experiences can affect both later personality and later health. In the simplest or most extreme case, there is a severe genetic defect shaping both personality and disease. For example, people with Down syndrome (trisomy 21) are at high risk for congenital heart disease as well as for premature mortality, usually dying before age 50. Although personality varies, there are clearly differences from people without this condition, such as in average mental acuity. Another chromosomal disorder, Angelman syndrome (deleted area in chromosome 15), leads to children who are unusually happy and laugh excessively. They develop movement disorders, seizure disorders, and mental retardation.

In such cases there is an association between personality and health, but changing the health would not change the personality, and influencing the personality would not change the health. Only an intervention that affected the biological sequelae of the genetic abnormality would have consequences. Yet such examples are a useful entry to thinking about more subtle and complex underlying biological variables. In many people, biological third variables are affecting both personality and health.

When challenged, some people react more than others do, with changes in their blood pressure and heart rate. That is, there are individual differences in psychophysiological reactivity (also called cardiovascular reactivity). Someone who is easily aroused emotionally, who tends to perceive threats to the self in the environment, and whose coping resources are taxed is likely to respond to stressful events with high levels of unhealthy physiological

arousal—symptoms of chronic catecholamine release. However, it is not yet clear the extent to which this variable is a reliable individual difference that is relevant to both personality and overall disease risk (Suls & Rittenhouse, 1990; Swain & Suls, 1996).

Hans Eysenck argued that such temperament-related psychobiological systems produce many associations between personality and disease, but also that some psychobiological characteristics are potentially modifiable, thus producing changes in both personality and disease risk. Eysenck's Big Three construct of psychoticism (Eysenck & Eysenck, 1976; Eysenck, 1991, 1992) describes a predisposition toward sociopathic or psychotic behavior (but high scorers are not necessarily "psychotic" in the clinical sense). Individuals high on this dimension are hostile, solitary, impulsive, novelty-seeking, manipulative, and without fear. This dimension may be linked to health in a number of ways—both behaviorally and psychophysiologically. More recently, researchers have focused on individual differences in neurotransmitters, looking at relations between dopamine and sensation seeking; serotonin and conscientiousness; and norepinephrine and extroversion or reward seeking (Bond, 2001; Cloninger, 1998). Overall, the study of the genetic and early biological influences on personality and associations to disease is still in its infancy.

Finally, it is also the case that people with chronic anxiety are more likely to feel pain and other symptoms. They also may be especially vigilant about bodily sensations (Pennebaker, 1982). This is discussed further in the section on neuroticism later in the chapter. In such relationships (of biological underlying third variables), interventions addressing personality will not necessarily do anything to affect health and/or longevity.

Disease-Caused Personality Changes

Many observed associations between personality and health are the result of patterns that follow from the onset of disease. That is, the disease "causes" (affects) the personality. However, this area is understudied, and the extent of this phenomenon is unknown.

Brain Mediated

Not surprisingly, diseases that affect the brain also have a dramatic impact on personality. Consider

Parkinson's disease and Parkinson-like syndromes, characterized by tremor, muscle rigidity, and movement problems. It has long been noticed that people with Parkinson's disease tend to appear stoic. Because Parkinson's disease involves a deficiency of dopamine (as neurons in the substantia nigra degenerate), it may be that this defect produces this aspect of personality. This process is likely both genetically and environmentally influenced. Even here, there can be multiple causal links, although the cause is usually unknown. For example, Parkinson's may sometimes result from brain infection, which then affects personality; but there also can be an underlying third variable, as when people who mine manganese or live in regions with volcanic soil (high in manganese) sometimes become compulsive fighters and later develop Parkinson's (due to this heavy metal poisoning). Ironically, professional boxers who receive multiple blows to the head can also develop Parkinson's as a result (so-called pugilistic Parkinson's syndrome).

There is well-documented personality change associated with excessive alcohol consumption. Alcoholism can lead to anxiety and depression, although it is sometimes anxiety and depression that contributed to the drinking. At the extreme, in Wernicke-Korsakoff syndrome, there are memory problems, confusion, and delusions, due to brain damage from severe deficiency of thiamine (vitamin B_1) in malnourished chronic alcoholics. Analogously, drugs such as cocaine and LSD can occasionally produce long-lasting, dramatic alterations in personality.

Other diseases that commonly affect personality through effects on the brain include strokes (which affect personality differentially as a function of the location of the stroke), metabolic disorders involving the thyroid, or conditions such as diabetes that involve glycemic control. Sometimes the personality changes result from medical treatment effects, as in long-term mental status changes after coronary bypass surgery (Newman et al., 2001), occasionally nicknamed "pump head." Further, many widely prescribed drugs, especially psychotropic drugs like tranquilizers, sleeping pills, and antidepressants, may have significant effects on personality. The psychological side effects of many prescription drugs are underinvestigated.

With diseases that may develop slowly, such as Alzheimer's, syphilis, and AIDS, the changes in personality may become apparent before the changes in organic brain function are diagnosed. Thus it may appear that the personality is predicting or even causing the disease when the reality is that the disease is changing the personality (Woodward, 1998).

Psychologically Mediated

Encounters with serious illness, such as suffering a myocardial infarction or receiving a diagnosis of cancer, can sometimes precipitate a dramatic change in personality. This is similar in some respects to a religious conversion (and indeed sometimes a religious conversion is the response).

Behaviorally Mediated

Disease may cause changes in motivation (or cravings) and in social status, as occurs if a stroke or cancer victim loses a job, gets divorced, and becomes hostile and depressed. New pressures and social groups may then alter the likelihood of smoking, drinking, risky behavior, and so on, thereby further changing both the individual's personality and health.

Social Psychologically Mediated

Illness often changes the reactions of others to the ill person. For example, the well-documented physical attractiveness stereotype (Dion, 1972) shows positive expectations and subsequent behavioral effects of "beautiful" people; the opposite kinds of effects can sometimes be expected of people stigmatized due to disease (Crocker, Major, & Steele, 1998; Goffman, 1963).

In all these cases, there is a link between personality and disease, but it is caused by the disease or the treatment.

Person-Situation Interactions

Many times it is important to know about both the personality and the situation to understand the links to health.

Widely prescribed legal drugs such as tranquilizers (Valium), sleeping pills (Halcion), and various antidepressants (Prozac), as well as widely available illegal drugs such as cocaine, are known to have short-term and sometimes long-term effects on personality. Importantly, it is not random who takes these drugs; certain personalities are more likely to seek them, or have them prescribed, or become addicted. Furthermore, when encountering a significant life stress, there is more likely to be a significantly negative effect on health if there is a predisposing genetic condition. That is, there can be a gene-by-environment interaction, in which an individual's response to environmental insults is moderated by his or her genetic makeup (Caspi et al., 2003).

Or consider the case in which a person is tending toward unhealthy environments but these environments are inaccessible. For example, if an impulsive, unstable person is raised in a supportive family, with safe schools, in a tight-knit supportive community, with perhaps a supportive religion, then the opportunity for unhealthy behavior greatly diminishes.

The various ways in which personality tends to remain stable even though it is possible to change has been summarized in a model termed *cumulative continuity* (Roberts & Caspi, 2003). By interpreting situations as similar, by eliciting similar reactions from others, and by seeking out certain similar situations, as well as by responding to stable genetic influences and stable environments (social and economic), the average adult maintains a fairly consistent personality. Understanding these individual consistencies, without oversimplifying them, can likely take us a long way toward understanding personality and health. Note, however, that unusual circumstances (such as the major psychosocial disruptions of a war, economic depression, or natural disaster) can produce dramatic personality change and unexpected effects on health.

In sum, when we examine development across long periods of time, we find a complex but understandable interplay between traits and situations. Especially with a focus on processes, the development of healthy or unhealthy states becomes predictable (Friedman, 2000; Roberts & Pomerantz, 2004).

Self-Healing

Although most research focuses on disease, it is equally important to examine those people in whom there is a self-healing personality, which maintains a physiological and psychosocial homeostasis (Friedman, 1991/2000). Such individuals tend to wind up in certain healthy environments, evoke positive reaction from others, and have a healing emotional style that matches the individual with the environment. In these people, good mental health tends to promote good physical health, and good physical health tends to promote good mental health. Various healthy patterns go together, which can be termed *co-salubrious effects*.

As one good pattern or reaction leads to another, positive results cumulate. There is evidence that a process of "broaden-and-build" develops, as coping skills improve, social networks expand, and recuperation processes improve (Fredrickson, 2001). Because medical care is typically focused on pathology, such links have been mostly ignored in health care.

Specific Traits and Health

There is a variety of evidence that good mental health is associated with good physical health. That is, people who are well adjusted are at lower risk for serious conditions like heart disease than those who are seriously or chronically hostile, depressed, anxious, or unstable. Another way of viewing this association is to say that health is health, and that the distinction between mental and physical health is not of greater scientific utility than distinctions among various illnesses. However, one major distinction involves age: chronically hostile and depressed people in their 20s are not likely to die of cancer or heart disease until their 50s or 60s (no matter what the relation between personality and disease). It makes sense to examine specific personality traits and health because certain recognizable patterns of responding, when considered over long periods, put one at higher or lower risk for various chronic diseases and for premature mortality. This is especially true when personality is considered in conjunction with the social, economic, and physical environments. Then, one must consider the various causal models described earlier in this chapter, to see which are applicable in each case.

Personality psychologists use sundry theories, perspectives, methods, and classifications (Friedman & Schustack, 2006). To organize the voluminous literature here, I have employed an expanded version of the five-factor approach to traits. The factors, which often emerge from factor analyses of trait labels, are conscientiousness, agreeableness, neuroticism, extroversion, and openness. I have added and included other characteristics (such as "optimism" to the agreeableness category) to simplify matters, but all the characteristics considered under each of the five trait factors should not be considered to be synonymous. Indeed, there are often important distinctions among related trait constructs.

Conscientiousness

Conscientiousness is a consistent tendency to be prudent, planful, persistent, and dependable. One of the major dimensions of the five-factor approach to personality, conscientiousness is not highly related to personality concepts and measures historically used in health research (Booth-Kewley & Vickers, 1994; Friedman, Tucker, & Reise, 1995; Marshall, Wortman, Vickers, Kusulas, & Hervig, 1994). I will use the example of conscientiousness, which increasing evidence reveals to be highly relevant to pathways to health, as a detailed illustration of fruitful conceptual models and revealing methods of analysis.

For more than 15 years, my colleagues and I have studied personality and longevity in the Terman cohort, derived from the Terman Gifted Children Study that began in 1921. The 1,528 Terman participants were, for the most part, first studied as elementary school children and have been followed ever since. It is the longest study of a single cohort ever conducted so intensively, with rich data collected regularly throughout the life span (from childhood to late adulthood and death). The sample was later characterized as a productive, intelligent segment of twentieth-century middle-class American men and women (mostly White; Sears, 1984; Subotnik, Karp, & Morgan, 1989). Importantly, we have collected death certificates and have professionally coded date and cause of death (Friedman, Tucker, Schwartz, Tomlinson-Keasey et al., 1995).

Starting with the childhood data, our project first tested whether variables representing major dimensions of personality could predict longevity across the life span (Friedman et al., 1993). We examined all items collected by Terman in 1922 that seemed relevant to personality. In 1922, one of each participant's parents (usually the mother, or both parents together) and each participant's teacher were asked to rate the participant on 25 trait dimensions (using a 13-point scale) chosen to measure intellectual, volitional, moral, emotional, aesthetic, physical, and social functioning. The scales used are remarkably modern in their appearance, and we constructed a measure of conscientiousness–social dependability that included the four items of

prudence, conscientiousness, freedom from vanity/egotism, and truthfulness. This corresponds roughly to the five-factor model (McCrae & John, 1992) dimension of conscientiousness, and we have documented the correspondence between conscientiousness measured with this scale and the contemporary NEO PI-R conscientiousness (although the measure is not identical to the NEO-PI measure; Martin & Friedman, 2000). Childhood conscientiousness was clearly related to survival in middle to old age. For example, a person at the 75th percentile on conscientiousness had only 77% of the risk of a person at the 25th percentile of dying in any given year (Friedman et al., 1993).

We then derived (from the archival Terman data) personality measures for adulthood that we likewise validated by showing them to be consistent with the five-factor contemporary conceptions (Martin & Friedman, 2000; Martin & Friedman Schwartz, in press). Adult conscientiousness was "measured" when the participants were in their 30s and 40s. As of the year 2000, 70% of the men and 51% of the women in this sample had verified deaths. We again found conscientiousness (now measured in adulthood) to be significantly related to mortality risk. Those low on adult conscientiousness died sooner.

The Friedman et al. findings on conscientiousness and longevity have been confirmed in follow-up studies by others. One study examined the relation of personality to mortality in 883 older Catholic clergy members, about two thirds of whom were female. The NEO Five Factor Inventory was administered at baseline, and the clergy were followed for a little more than 5 years, during which time 182 died. Those scoring very high on conscientiousness were about half as likely to die as those with a very low score (Wilson, Mendes de Leon, Bienias, Evans, & Bennett, 2004). Another key study examined participants in a Medicare demonstration study with more than 1,000 participants, aged 65–100 (Weiss, Costa, Karuza, Duberstein, & Friedman, 2004). Importantly, the participants in this prospective study were older, sicker, and more representative of the elderly population. Over the 5 years of follow-up, persons high in conscientiousness were significantly less likely to die.

There are now many other solid studies of conscientiousness and health. For example, a study of conscientiousness and renal deterioration in patients with diabetes found that time to renal failure was longer in those with high conscientiousness (Brickman, Yount, Blaney, Rothberg, & De-Nour, 1996). Another prospective study of chronic renal insufficiency found that patients with low conscientiousness had a substantially increased mortality rate over the 4-year term of the study (Christensen et al, 2002). (Both of these studies also found effects of neuroticism.) Evidence of the generality of the importance of conscientiousness comes from a study using the Midlife Development in the United States Survey, a nationally representative sample of 3,032 noninstitutionalized civilian adults (Goodwin & Friedman, in press). This study examined the association between the five-factor traits of personality and common mental and physical disorders. The results showed that conscientiousness (protectively) was reliably associated with reduced risk of illness: those with diabetes, hypertension, sciatica, urinary problems, stroke, hernia, TB, joint problems, and a variety of mental illnesses and substance abuse problems had significantly lower levels of conscientiousness than did those without each disorder. Review work and meta-analyses confirm the relevance of conscientiousness to health (Bogg & Roberts, 2004; Clark & Watson, 1999), with commonly used concepts of past decades including impulse control, self-control, disinhibition, and sense of responsibility.

Such pervasive associations between conscientiousness and health go well beyond adherence effects, as is well illustrated by a randomized study of medication after a myocardial infarction (Horwitz et al., 1990). Patients who did not adhere to their prescribed treatment regimen (i.e., who took less than 75% of the prescribed medication) were 2.6 times more likely than good adherers to die within a year of follow-up. Most interestingly, the unconscientious adherers (poor adherers) had an increased risk of death whether they were on the beta-blocker propranolol (odds ratio = 3.1) or *placebo* (odds ratio = 2.5). This effect was not accounted for by the severity of the myocardial infarction, marital status, education, smoking, or social isolation. In other words, being conscientious enough to fully cooperate with treatment (even if with a placebo) emerged as a more important predictor of mortality risk than the medication.

In short, research following the Friedman et al. (1993) study has shown substantial confirmation of the importance of conscientiousness to health and longevity. Studies include not only self-report

outcomes but also longevity, which is a much more reliable and valid outcome than is self-reported health. Although surprising because of the traditional emphasis on frustration and hostile moods, it turns out that conscientiousness is a key personality predictor of health and longevity.

Models

The question then arises as to *why* conscientiousness is related to health. It turns out that many of the various models of personality and health and longevity described here are plausibly relevant, but the causal pathways are probably not simple ones.

First, as noted, there is reason to suspect that conscientiousness is a good predictor of health because of its many associations with healthy behaviors. A meta-analysis of 194 studies examined conscientiousness-related traits and leading behavioral contributors to mortality—tobacco use, diet and activity patterns, excessive alcohol use, violence, risky sexual behavior, risky driving, suicide, and drug use (Bogg & Roberts, 2004). The researchers conducted database searches for conscientiousness-related terms and relevant health-related behavior terms. They found that conscientiousness-related traits were negatively related to all these risky health-related behaviors and positively related to all these beneficial health-related behaviors.

Among the Terman participants, possible behavioral mechanisms for the robust association between conscientiousness and longevity were examined by gathering cause-of-death information and by considering the possible mediating influences of drinking alcohol, smoking, and overeating (Friedman, Tucker, Schwartz, Martin, et al., 1995). Survival analyses suggested that the protective effect of conscientiousness was somewhat but not primarily due to accident avoidance. Only 9% of the low-conscientious quartile, and only 5% of the high-conscientious quartile, died as a result of injury (accidents and violence); those who died from injury were more likely to be in the low-conscientiousness quartile; but, overall, few people died as the result of injury, and so the overall effect of conscientiousness was not simply explained. Similarly, the protective effect of conscientiousness could not be mostly explained by abstinence from unhealthy substance intake. Conscientious Terman children were less likely to grow up to be heavy drinkers and smokers, but these health behaviors alone did not explain away the effect. Conscientiousness seems to have a more far-reaching and general involvement.

Second, there is emerging evidence for various kinds of psychophysiological mechanisms linking conscientiousness and health. For example, one study examined conscientiousness (NEO-PI) and subclinical cardiovascular disease (atherosclerosis) in a healthy community sample of 353 (51% female). This study used sonography to measure intima-media thickness and collected physiological measures, including 24-hour urinary catecholamines. As expected, conscientiousness was associated with less thickening, with urinary norepinephrine emerging as a partial mediator (Witzig, Kamarck, Muldoon, & Sutton-Tyrrell, 2003).

It is not known the extent to which conscientious people develop more modulated physiological reaction patterns or whether an underlying biopsychological tendency leads to both conscientiousness and salutary reaction patterns. In terms of psychophysiological mechanisms involving underlying third variables, there are some hints that serotonin function may be relevant (Williams et al., 2004). For example, serotonergic functioning influences individual variability on dimensions such as aggression and impulse control, although the degree to which this might be true in the general population or restricted to particular clinical groups is less clear. Manuck and colleagues (1998) demonstrated an inverse relationship between serotonergic functioning and both aggression and impulse control in a nonclinical sample. Johns Hopkins University researchers studying the effects of a mu-opioid receptor mutation found not only that chemical blocking of opioids results in differential cortisol responses and increases in adrenocorticotrophic hormone (ACTH) for those with the variant polymorphism but also that these individuals also scored significantly lower on NEO PI-R conscientiousness than did those without it (Wand et al., 2002). These researchers suggest that those with the variant serotonin transporter might have abnormal HPA axis responses to stress and corresponding personality traits that are regulated by mu-opioid receptor activation.

Third, there is evidence that conscientious individuals seek out or find themselves in healthier environments. Most obviously, in many cultures, imprudent, impulsive people are more likely to find themselves in environments and subcultures that are dangerous, involving, for example, smoking, fast driving, unprotected sexual activity, or gang or military violence. People lacking persistence and dependability are likewise more likely to face and have poor career prospects and lower socioeconomic status, with all the accompanying threats to health (Adler et al., 1994). Those who are more controlled, secure, and hardworking by age 18 are headed to better careers within a decade, which in turn can further enhance their health and their subsequent conscientiousness (Hogan & Ones, 1997; Judge & Ilies, 2002; Roberts, Caspi, & Moffitt, 2003).

Even social support is relevant here because there is self-selection and partner selection into marriage. There is a heritable influence on propensity to marry (Johnson, McGue, Krueger & Bouchard, 2004), with conscientious college women experiencing lower rates of divorce (Roberts & Bogg, 2004). Early individual traits affect later marital stability (Larson & Holman, 1994); divorce is not a random stressor but rather is somewhat predictable. For example, the association between marital history at midlife (in 1950) and mortality (as of 1991) was investigated in the Terman dataset (Tucker, Friedman, Wingard, & Schwartz, 1996). Consistently married individuals lived longer than those who had experienced marital breakup, but this was not due only to the protective effects of marriage itself. Participants who were currently married but had previously experienced a divorce were at significantly higher mortality risk than were consistently married individuals. Consistently married individuals had been more conscientious children than were inconsistently married individuals, and there was evidence for selection into marriage. That is, part of the relationship between marital history and mortality risk was explained by childhood conscientiousness, associated with both future marital history and mortality risk.

In short, the example of conscientiousness reveals the complexity of the relations among personality, physiology, behavior, environments, and health. Multiple pathways likely coexist, and it is unwise to focus on only one path. Further, although conscientiousness is a valuable predictor, interventions to improve health will profitably take advantage of knowledge of this complexity.

Agreeableness, Optimism, and Cheerfulness

Common research findings tend to confirm the popular assumption that people who are happier, optimistic, and better adjusted are also healthier, but such findings are especially susceptible to an uncritical overinterpretation. Because studies almost never manipulate happiness and optimism and then show a direct and lasting effect on physical health, there is scant empirical justification for advising people to "cheer up" as a means of promoting their health. Rather, it appears that almost all the causal pathways described earlier in this chapter play a role in these associations.

There is fairly good evidence that cheerful people, who are generally in good moods, are healthier, at least over the short term (Pressman & Cohen, in press; Salovey, Rothman, Detweiler, & Steward, 2000). But note that this summary statement does not mean that good moods lead to good health. Further, good moods are not a simple and strong correlate of any basic aspect of personality. For example, agreeable people—who are straightforward, altruistic, trusting, and modest—may find themselves in long-term situations in which they are not particularly happy.

Much of the research on this topic focuses on psychophysiological mediation and derives from the idea that challenge is not stressful if it is not interpreted as stressful (Carver, this volume; Segerstrom et al., 1998). That is, construal (cognitive appraisal) is key (F. Cohen & Lazarus, 1983). Various lines of research thus examine the positive cognitions (or rose-colored glasses) through which some individuals cope with life's challenges, thus avoiding stressful physiological arousal. Further, people with good coping skills can be resilient in the face of stress and strain (Garmezy, 1993; Ryff & Singer, 2001).

There is considerable evidence that positive illusions can lead to better health, especially when there is little one can do objectively to reduce the threat or vulnerability (Taylor & Brown, 1988; Taylor et al., 1992). Similarly, individuals with an optimistic explanatory style tend to be healthier, although this may primarily be due to an avoidance of the health threats associated with depression (Peterson et al., 2001; Peterson, Seligman, Yurko, Martin, & Friedman, 1998). On the other hand, the case has often been made that people who think that they or their situation is better than it really is are less in touch with the true demands of reality and with the actions that are needed to deal effectively with challenge, including threats to health (Aldwin, 1994; Colvin & Block, 1994; Colvin, Block, & Funder, 1995; Lazarus & Folkman, 1984).

These contradictory conceptions about positive illusions often cannot be resolved until the particular implications of the cognitive states or illusions are addressed. For example, if adherence to a difficult treatment regimen is health promoting, then those individuals who can use their good coping or good humor to stick with it are likely to be more successful. Similarly, if the situation is relatively uncontrollable, then accepting one's condition with good humor may prove adaptive. However, if one's cheerfulness leads one to ignore the difficult regimen with the idea that "everything will work out anyway," then the positive illusion is maladaptive.

Despite the general association between optimism and health, there has long been an underlying thread of theory and research questioning this generalization. As noted, various ways of coping can be either good or bad, depending on the context. (See also the chapter by Wortman & Boerner in this volume.) Moreover, highly positive moods can be a sign of emotional imbalance. For example, a study of survival in patients with end-state renal disease found those who had "an even mixture of unhappiness and happiness" lived longer than those who were very happy (Devins et al., 1990). Importantly, some people show irrational decision-making processes, such as believing that "I don't smoke too much and don't inhale deeply." Many individuals show a reliable tendency to believe that they are less likely than their peers to suffer harm, and this tendency is difficult to challenge (Weinstein & Klein, 1995).

Sometimes people are happy and optimistic because they have successfully overcome a health challenge; the better health is thus causing their sense of well-being. Such effects may even occur over the long term, such as if one gets in great physical condition during the decade after suffering a mild heart attack. At other times, a cheerful persona may actually be an attempt to cover up some difficult emotional or health challenge. That is, humor can sometimes be an attempt to deal with stress or a difficult childhood (Dixon, 1980). Comics do not live any longer than their peers (Rotton, 1992), and many face addiction or substance abuse. Furthermore, if people are feeling bad about their challenges but cannot get themselves to put on a smile or learn optimism, they might instead spiral downward (Held, 2004).

In the Terman life-span study, children who were rated by their parents and teachers as more cheerful/optimistic and as having a sense of humor died *earlier* in adulthood than those who were less cheerful (Friedman et al, 1993). A follow-up study attempted to see whether cheerful children were less willing to take precautions, took more risks, were less prepared for future stressful challenges, or were covering up some psychological problem (Martin et al., 2002). The cheerful children did grow up to drink more alcohol, smoke more cigarettes, and engage in more risky hobbies and activities, but these had only a minor effect in explaining the relation of cheerfulness and mortality risk. Further, the cheerful children did not grow up to show evidence of poor adjustment. Unrealistic optimism or insufficient caution (Weinstein, 1982) remains a possible explanation, although the findings were weak in this regard.

One circumscribed situation in which optimism and cheerfulness might be expected to have a regular and significant effect on health involves those people facing a difficult and trying medical challenge. For example, an optimistic elderly person facing a painful and difficult medical regimen may be more likely to persevere and thus survive. This conception is consistent with the idea that optimism functions as a self-regulating mechanism, with optimistic people more likely to persevere in goal-directed behavior (Carver & Scheier, 1981). A feeling of self-efficacy often predicts a healthy response to challenge.

The medical sociologist Aaron Antonovsky (1979, 1987) proposed a theory of salutogenesis— a theory of how people stay healthy. Central to successful coping with the challenges of the world is what Antonovsky calls a *sense of coherence*—the person's confidence that the world is understandable, manageable, and meaningful. The world must not necessarily be controllable but controlled—for example, such as occurs in someone with a strong sense of divine order (cf. Wallston et al., 1999). Hopelessness is generally found to be associated with poor health (Everson et al., 1996), but the reasons for this association are probably multifactorial. Antonovsky's approach grew in part from the insightful observation of those in Nazi concentration camps, who noticed that the quickest inmates to die were those who had their sense of identity and purpose taken away from them (Bettelheim, 1960; Frankl, 1962; see also Lutgendorf Vitaliano, Tripp-Reimer, Harvey, & Lubaroff, 1999). One large-scale study that followed more than 20,000

European adults for up to 6 years found that those with a strong sense of coherence were 30% less likely to die, even after adjusting for risk factors such as smoking, blood pressure, cholesterol, social class, hostility, and neuroticism (Surtees, Wainwright, Luben, Khaw, & Day, 2003).

Disagreeableness and pessimism are often associated with hostility and depression. Much of this research as related to health is done under the rubric of neuroticism, which is considered next.

Neuroticism: Worrying, Hostility, and Depression

Perhaps the most complex associations between personality and health involve neuroticism. *Neuroticism,* or *emotional instability,* refers to people who tend to be anxious, high-strung, tense, and worrying; they are also often impulsive, hostile, and prone to depression because they cope poorly with stress. There is long-standing, incontrovertible evidence that many diseases are associated with higher levels of hostility, anxiety, and depression (Barefoot & Schroll, 1996; Friedman & Booth-Kewley, 1987; Goodwin & Friedman, in press; Kubzansky, Kawachi, Weiss, & Sparrow, 1998; Miller et al. 1996; Schulz, Martire, Beach, & Scheier, 2000), but the causal pathways have rarely been elucidated.

Neurotic people are more likely to feel and report symptoms, and disease can cause distress (Costa & McCrae, 1987; Watson & Pennebaker, 1989). Hence, some links of neuroticism to disease are correlational, artifactual, or reverse causal. Even so, such associations do not in any way mean that neuroticism is not also sometimes a causal factor in disease. If neuroticism is correlated with disease because of artifacts associated with the way that disease is assessed, then we should find such associations stronger when medical diagnosis depends on interviews and self-report measures (as does the assessment of personality). Fortunately, this artifact has become less worrisome as studies have focused less on the self-reported, little-varying "health" of college students and more on physician-diagnosed health and longevity.

In 1987, a meta-analysis revealed that not only anxiety and hostility but also depression was reliably associated with cardiovascular disease (Booth-Kewley & Friedman, 1987). This finding ran counter to the prevailing wisdom about the importance of type A behavior and was viewed skeptically at the time (Mathews, 1988). However, the general association between depression and risk of heart disease has since been confirmed in many studies. Depression and related states of chronic anxiety, pessimism, and vital exhaustion predict risk of heart disease in both initially healthy persons and those who already have heart disease (Appels, Golombeck, Gorgels, de Vreede, & van Breukelen, 2000; Barefoot & Schroll, 1996; Barefoot et al., 2000; Ford et al., 1998; Januzzi, Stern, Pasternak, & DeSanctis, 2000; Frasure-Smith, Lesperance, & Talajic, 1995; Rugulies, 2002; Scheier et al., 1999). Further, when the appropriate broader framework is used, depression also predicts other adverse health outcomes.

With a typical approach that views a risk factor as a direct causal agent, many clinicians began treating depression in an effort to prevent the exacerbation of heart disease. Surprising to some researchers, treating depression in recent heart attack patients does not reduce the risk of death or second heart attack (ENRICHD, 2003). Given the societal toll taken by heart disease, such a rush to intervention is understandable, but the confusion that then results from an unexpected research result is reminiscent of the confusion and disappointment that surrounded failed type A intervention studies decades earlier. How and why is depression predicting heart disease, and why only in some people? Viewing depression as a simple "medical risk factor" outside the interconnected web of associations is short-sighted.

Neurotic people, including depressives, are more likely to encounter negative events and to interpret them in a more negative manner (Bolger & Zuckerman, 1995; Magnus et al., 1993; Mroczek & Almeida, , 2004; Taylor et al., 1997). Neuroticism is also associated with a host of psychophysiological states, many of which are generally harmful. Much attention has been paid to the associations between depression and impaired immunity (Herbert, & Cohen, 1993) and between hostility and cardiovascular damage (Schneiderman, Weiss, & Kaufmann, 1989; Williams, 1994). Much more attention, however, needs to be paid to ongoing, long-term pathways. For example, immune alterations tend to be greater in older and sicker samples, suggesting longer-term processes are at work.

The elements of neuroticism—depression, anxiety, and anger-hostility—are predictive of and play some causal role in illness, but their interrelations are not much studied (Friedman & Booth-Kewley, 1987; Suls & Bunde, 2005). We do not really understand whether one of these elements often leads to another (e.g. chronic anger leading to depression), whether these elements have independent or additive effects, and whether they are being optimally conceptualized and assessed (Suls & Bunde, 2005). Also, little is known about how they relate to patterns of healthy social support (Gallo & Smith, 1999), although anger and hostility are clearly implicated in multiple links to disease, including psychosocial pathways (Smith, Glazer, Ruiz, & Gallo, 2004).

What about the other side of the coin? Can neuroticism sometimes be healthy, thus explaining inconsistent findings? Consider now a broader view, which adds the context of worrying about health and of feeling and reporting symptoms. Neurotic people sometimes have the motivation to be very vigilant about avoiding dangerous or polluted environments, noting symptoms needing attention, keeping up with medical developments, and cooperating with treatment. Such a worrying neurotic person (a health nut) might remain very healthy (Friedman, 2000). There is indeed scattered evidence for this view.

In a study of renal deterioration (Brickman et al., 1996), patients moderate in neuroticism did better than patients who were low in neuroticism (and also better than those too high in neuroticism). Aspects of neuroticism, such as self-reports of psychological distress and mental strain, sometimes predict lower mortality risk (Gardner & Oswald, 2004; Korten et al., 1999). Analogously, a paradox was found in the well-known Western Collaborative Group study of type A and heart disease, in which type A clearly predicted heart disease; but *after* a heart attack, type A patients (male) were less likely to die during the subsequent dozen years (Ragland & Brand, 1988). It may be that these type A victims worked especially hard at their treatment regimen for recovery. Further, even before disease develops, some people thrive on challenge and competition, and so there are "healthy type As"; these are people who rush around with heavy workloads but do not want to live any other way (Friedman, Hall, & Harris, 1985). In short, it appears that there are two distinct sorts of health-related outcomes that result from neuroticism, some positive and some negative. The strength of any causal role for neuroticism in disease (out of context) is difficult to ascertain without a broad conceptual and methodological approach.

There are many subject (patient) selection artifacts in personality and health studies, especially relevant to neuroticism. These can arise as a function of the control group used in a study, if certain people are more likely than others to enter the health care system. For example, people who are neurotic and complain about chest pain are much more likely to have angiograms than people who are stoic. This artifact changes the association between depression and observed artery blockage from positive to negative (Friedman, 2000). That is, because random samples of the full population are rarely taken for invasive or risky studies, people who are less neurotic and complaining are unknowingly left out of the study.

By not taking a broader view of overall disease-proneness, studies in this area are also susceptible to faulty inferences that result from restriction of range. The range or variance of the predictor or the outcome (or both) may be unduly restricted. For example, type A behavior is associated with coronary heart disease in initially healthy samples but not in high-risk samples selected from clinical populations (Miller et al., 1991). It appears that restriction of range hides a phenomenon that may truly be there in a more representative (broader) sample. One should be alert for such artifacts whenever the sample is selected on the basis of clinical diagnosis (e.g., angry men) or on the basis of disease (e.g., myocardial infarction, death from heart disease).

To add yet another complication, sometimes the neuroticism is not apparent because it is repressed. A number of studies find poor health associated with repressed anxiety or "repressive coping" (e.g., Jensen, 1987; Matthews, Owens, Kuller, Sutton-Tyrrell, & Jansen-McWilliams, 1998; Pettingale, Morris, Greer, & Haybittle, 1985; see also Pennebaker & Chung, this volume) or suppressed anger (Wilson, Bienias, de Leon, Evans, & Bennett, 2003). A similar pattern in which individuals are unable to express emotion and seem at higher risk for disease progression is sometimes studied under the rubric of "alexithymia" (a condition described by the ancient Greeks as an absence of words for emotions, a condition in which individuals are apathetic, stoic, unemotional, or repressed; Marchesi, Brusamonti, & Maggini, 2000). There is speculation and scattered research that such conditions promote the development or the progression of some cancers (Butow, Hiller, Price, Thackway, Kricker, & Tennant, 2000), but

as usual, the relationship of this constellation of traits to other traits, other behaviors, and other illnesses has not been adequately investigated.

With all these clarifications and caveats surrounding neuroticism and disease, it is not surprising that simple and clear associations have failed to appear. For example, people with migraines and ulcers and related pain are very likely to be high on anxiety, but the relations have been shown to occur through a wide variety of pathways, including recall bias, general distress, a variety of unhealthy behaviors, pituitary-adrenal activation, altered blood flow, and more. These combinations of causal pathways lead to varying results and failures to replicate specific links from study to study.

Extroversion and Sociability

When it comes to matters of health, extroversion is a double-edged sword. Extroverted people are warm, assertive, sociable, active, talkative, and seeking of stimulation and excitement. This tendency has been shown to lead to both health-promoting and health-damaging behavioral patterns.

The seeking of stimulation and excitement can of course be health damaging, especially for young men in today's societies. Even children with accident-related injuries tend to be more extroverted (Vollrath, Landolt, & Ribi, 2003). Extroverts are generally at greater risk for smoking and alcohol abuse, although most of the evidence comes from adolescents or young adults (Grau & Ortet, 1999; Martsh & Miller, 1997; Tucker et al., 1995). Studies confirm that such associations with extroversion are best understood in context (Ham & Hope, 2003; Watson, 2000). Although extroverts may perform risky behaviors, it is generally to increase positive rewards and experiences; in certain circumstances the health effects may be different. For example, to the extent that extroverts sometimes tend to be more physically active, they gain the health benefits of activity (exercise), despite some risk of injury.

If sociability leads to good social relations and social integration, then the sociability aspect of extroversion is likely to be health promoting. However, the most sociable people do not necessarily have the best social relations. An example of the context-dependent effects of sociability comes from the Terman study. Using ratings by parents and teachers in childhood, sociability was defined in terms of fondness for large groups, popularity, leadership, preference for playing with several other people, and preference for social activities such as parties. Sociable individuals did not live longer than their unsociable peers (Friedman et al., 1993). There was simply no evidence that sociable children were healthier or lived longer across many decades. In fact, sociable children were somewhat more likely to grow up to smoke and drink (Tucker et al., 1995). To further analyze this finding, Terman's own grouping of the men in the sample into "scientists and engineers" versus "businessmen and lawyers" was examined. (Terman had found the former group much more unsociable and less interested in social relations at school and in young adulthood.) It turned out that those in the scientist and engineer group were at slightly *less* risk of premature mortality, despite their unsociable nature (Friedman et al., 1994). For example, these studious men often ended up in the well-adjusted, socially stable, and well-integrated life situations well known to be healthy.

Some research suggests that sociability is associated with greater resistance to developing colds when persons were experimentally exposed to a cold virus (thus controlling for differential exposure; Cohen, Doyle, Turner, Alper, & Skoner, 2003). However, extensive efforts failed to uncover any likely mediators for this effect. Here again, it may be that sociability is too broad a construct or too tied to the co-occurring contexts to be simply understood.

Because extroversion seems closely tied to the sensitivity of the nervous system (Eysenck, 1990, 1991), it may also be the case that extroversion has a genetic basis that is linked to physiological processes that directly affect proneness to disease. The relation could be an underlying third variable that produces a spurious association. Or, the physiological processes may produce strong motivations toward certain sociobehavioral patterns. Such causal models of extroversion and health have not been the focus of much research.

A somewhat different approach to understanding the possible deleterious effects of introversion or unsociability is to focus on the psychological construct of loneliness—feelings of social isolation—a path that has been taken by John Cacioppo and others (Cacioppo et al., 2002; Hawkley, Burleson, Berntson, & Cacioppo, 2003; Hawkley & Cacioppo, 2004). Characteristics of lonely people include a poorer quality of sleep and subtle alter-

ations in cardiovascular function (total peripheral resistance) and immune health. But no striking behavioral or psychophysiological (e.g., hormonal) differences have emerged. Such findings are consistent with the idea that a narrow focus on unsociability will be less fruitful than a broader consideration of what it means to be embedded in a social network.

Openness and Intelligence

People high on openness tend to be creative and to value aesthetic and intellectual pursuits, and they tend to seek a wide range of experiences. In some personality schemes, openness is closely tied to intelligence, but in other schemes it is more related to creativity and imagination (McCrae & Costa, 1987; Peabody & Goldberg, 1989).

Popular stereotypes that intelligent people are frail, weak, and "nerdy," as compared with their robust but not-so-clever counterparts, have long been discredited by research; bright people tend to be healthy (Friedman & Markey, 2003; Terman & Oden, 1947). The issue here again, however, is a complex one, because intelligence may serve as a marker for various other health factors and conditions. Further, although intelligence and openness potentially provide a number of health advantages, these advantages are sometimes outweighed by other factors.

Some well-conducted life-span longitudinal research indicates that more intelligent people are at lower risk of disease and premature mortality (Deary & Der, 2005; Deary, Whiteman, Starr, Whalley, & Fox, 2004; Osler et al., 2003). This relation sometimes holds even after correcting for education, occupational social class, and smoking. Similarly, people with lower intellectual abilities among the elderly in the Berlin Aging Study were at higher mortality risk (Maier & Smith, 1999). But many different causal links may be simultaneously operating.

First, it is possible that intelligence and openness are frequently related to health and longevity due to a variety of biological factors. These include genetic, developmental, and behavioral influences. In fact, IQ has been posited as an indirect measure of both bodily insults and system integrity (Whalley & Deary, 2001.) In terms of underlying variables, healthy early developmental experiences combined with robust genes set the stage for both high-functioning brains and long-living bodies. It is also the case that individuals who resist disease suffer fewer brain insults; because the brain is a biological organ that communicates in various ways with the rest of the body, it is not surprising that it is impaired by many diseases. Further, it has been suggested that high levels of cognitive functioning may delay the clinical expression of disease and postpone the physical decline associated with aging (Snowdon, 1997; Snowdon et al., 1996).

Second, socioeconomic status is often correlated with both intelligence and health-related behaviors and activities. It is well established that people of higher income and education are healthier and live longer (the so-called SES-health gradient; Adler et al, 1994), probably for a myriad of reasons. It is generally very difficult to fully disentangle the various interrelated causes, but at the very least, socioeconomic status often both leads to and results from higher cognitive abilities and interests.

Third, bright individuals are certainly better able to receive and understand health information, and so may be able to avoid harmful substances (e.g., tobacco products, pesticides, saturated fats) and better utilize beneficial substances (e.g., medication). Further, high intelligence might lead to better decision making in regard to health and health care utilization. Nonetheless, creative and smart people die at high rates in their 60s and 70s, just as do less intelligent people. Creative, avant-garde individuals might, in some circumstances, also be more likely to use illegal recreational drugs, drink excessively, travel to exotic locations with exotic pathogens, and weaken their community ties. In some highly intellectual, aesthetic subgroups, dangerous sexual activity may be more common.

In the Terman cohort, when the participants' mortality rates are compared with those of the general U.S. population born in 1910, the Terman sample lives longer than their general population peers, even after taking into account the fact (artifact) that these participants, by study design, lived at least until age 10. However, the patterns of mortality risk and overall risk later in life are not strikingly different. That is, the risk pattern is remarkably similar to that of the full 1910 birth cohort of the United States (although somewhat delayed; Friedman & Markey, 2003). The Terman men were more likely to drink significant amounts of alcohol than was the general male population; they also smoked more, in keeping with the fashionable expectations

of the time. Overall, the highly intelligent Terman participants, just like their peers of average intelligence, were highly susceptible to behavioral and psychosocial threats to health and longevity.

Conclusion

There is remarkable variability in susceptibility to illness and in the likelihood of recovery. Traditional biological and behavioral risk factors such as blood pressure and diet do a mediocre job of telling us when or why someone will be well or ill. The search for understanding of individual differences is thus scientifically necessary, but it also leads to a wider and deeper analysis, closer to the true nature of illness and well-being. Employing the methods of the science of personality to study health, we are pressed to see how the various pieces of the bio-psychosocial organism fit together and develop across time.

Studies (and newspaper headlines) continually appear, claiming that personality is (or is not) related to some disease. Such articles are not much more sophisticated than approaches that query, Does the mind really affect the body? It is not helpful to keep asking whether there is a cancer-prone personality, or whether a smiling face makes you live longer. Further, it is practically useless to give general advice to patients to "relax," "cheer up," and "avoid stress." Instead, we need research attention that focuses on the complex links and pathways associated with better or worse health, and interventions that point and move individuals to their own best pathways.

First, we need to understand which causal mechanisms are common in certain subpopulations and which are present in any given instance. If the personality is being influenced by the disease, or if both the personality and the disease are being influenced by underlying genetic or physiological factors, then there is often no value in focusing on changing personality to improve health. Second, we need to understand the relevant context to see what influences (if any) will pull a person toward or away from available healthy environments. Finally, if personality is exerting a causal influence on health, we need to specify the interrelated sets of mediating mechanisms and interrelated outcomes.

There are many individual differences in likelihood of illness and recovery that go well beyond chance expectations. Personality psychology provides a window into these processes and the research tools to investigate them. Risky behavior, harmful psychophysiological patterns, and unsupportive social environments are not independent but generally tend to cluster. Analogously, self-healing patterns are just that—they are patterns rather than litanies of random health components. As the example of conscientiousness well illustrates, there are various links between personality and health and longevity, sometimes operating simultaneously and sometimes more important for different people at different times. For example, conscientiousness is closely tied to many health behaviors; it is linked to impulsive risk taking; it is associated with levels of hormones and neurotransmitters; and it often predicts whether individuals will seek out or find themselves in healthier environments.

Approaching health with the biomedical model of disease leads one to focus on genetics or on infectious agents and toxins. In most cases, such approaches are substantially incomplete; although a large number of diseases can be mostly understood in biomedical terms, they account for a small proportion of morbidity and mortality in developed countries. Rather, most of the major threats to life and the common serious chronic illness conditions—including cardiovascular disease, cancer, diabetes, injury, and addiction—are most often best prevented and addressed by considering long-term biopsychosocial patterns. Consideration of the individual and his or her personality forces a more profound analysis, which is closer to the true complexity of illness and well-being.

Acknowledgments. Preparation of this chapter was supported in part by NIA grant AG08825. The views expressed are those of the author.

References

Adler, N. E., Boyce, T., Chesney, M., Cohen, S., Folkman, S., Kahn, R. L. & Syme, S. L. (1994). Socioeconomic status and health: The challenge of the gradient. *American Psychologist, 49,* 15–24.

Aldwin, C. M. (1994). *Stress, coping, and development: An integrative perspective.* New York: Guilford.

Alexander, F. (1950). *Psychosomatic medicine.* New York: Norton.

Antonovsky, A. (1979). *Health, stress, and coping.* San Francisco: Jossey-Bass.

Antonovsky, A. (1987). *Unraveling the mystery of health: How people manage stress and stay well.* San Francisco: Jossey-Bass.

Appels, A., Golombeck, B., Gorgels, A., de Vreede, J., & van Breukelen, G. (2000). Behavioral risk factors of sudden cardiac arrest. *Journal of Psychosomatic Research, 48,* 463–469.

Aspinwall, L. G., & Taylor, S. E. (1997). A stitch in time: Self-regulation and proactive coping. *Psychological Bulletin, 121,* 417–436.

Barefoot, J. C., Brummett, B. H., Helms, M. J., Mark, D. B., Siegler, I. C., & Williams, R. B. (2000). Depressive symptoms and survival of patients with coronary artery disease. *Psychosomatic Medicine, 62,* 790–795.

Barefoot, J. C., & Schroll, M. (1996). Symptoms of depression, acute myocardial infarction, and total mortality in a community sample. *Circulation, 93,* 1976–1980.

Bartoshuk, L. M., Duffy, V. B., Fast, K., Kveton, J. F., Lucchina, L. A., Phillips, M. N., et al. (2001). What makes a supertaster? *Chemical Senses, 26,* 1074.

Bernard, C. (1880). *Leçons de pathologie expérimentale: Et leçons sur les propriétés de la moelle épinière.* Paris: Librairie J.-B. Baillière et fils.

Bettelheim, B. (1960). *The informed heart: Autonomy in a mass age.* Glencoe, IL: Free Press.

Betz, B., & Thomas, C. (1979). Individual temperament as a predictor of health or premature disease. *Johns Hopkins Medical Journal, 144,* 81–89.

Bogg, T., & Roberts, B. W. (2004). Conscientiousness and health-related behaviors: A meta-analysis of the leading behavioral contributors to mortality. *Psychological Bulletin, 130,* 887–919.

Bolger, N., & Zuckerman, A. (1995). A framework for studying personality in the stress process. *Journal of Personality and Social Psychology, 69,* 890–902.

Bond, A. J. (2001). Neurotransmitters, temperament and social functioning. *European Neuropsychopharmacology, 11,* 261–274.

Booth-Kewley, S., & Friedman, H. S. (1987). Psychological predictors of heart disease: A quantitative review. *Psychological Bulletin, 101,* 343–362.

Booth-Kewley, S., & Vickers, R. R., Jr. (1994). Associations between major domains of personality and health behavior. *Journal of Personality, 62,* 282–298.

Brickman, A. L., Yount, S. E., Blaney, N. T., Rothberg, S. T., & De-Nour, A. K. (1996). Personality traits and long-term health status: The influence of neuroticism and conscientiousness on renal deterioration in Type-1 diabetes. *Psychosomatics: Journal of Consultation Liaison Psychiatry, 37,* 459–468.

Butow, P. N., Hiller, J. E., Price, M. A., Thackway, S. V., Kricker, A., & Tennant, C. C. (2000). Epidemiological evidence for a relationship between life events, coping style, and personality factors in the development of breast cancer. *Journal of Psychosomatic Research, 49,* 169–181.

Cacioppo, J. T., Hawkley, L. C., Crawford, L. E., Ernst, J. M., Burleson, M. H., Kowalewski, R. B., et al. (2002). Loneliness and health: Potential mechanisms. *Psychosomatic Medicine, 64,* 407–417.

Campbell, D. T., & Fiske, D. W. (1959). Convergent and discriminant validation by the multitrait-multimethod matrix. *Psychological Bulletin, 56,* 81–105.

Cannon, W. B. (1932). *Wisdom of the body.* New York: Norton.

Carver, C. S., & Scheier, M. F. (1981). *Attention and self-regulation: A control-theory approach to human behavior.* New York: Springer-Verlag.

Caspi, A., Sugden, K., Moffitt, T. E., Taylor, A., Craig, I. W., Harrington, H., et al. (2003). Influence of life stress on depression: Moderation by a polymorphism in the 5-HTT gene. *Science, 301,* 291–293.

Chesney, M. A., & Rosenman, R. H. (Eds.). (1985). *Anger and hostility in cardiovascular and behavioral disorders.* New York: Hemisphere.

Christensen, A. J., Ehlers, S. L., Wiebe, J. S., Moran, P. J., Raichle, K., Ferneyhough, K., et al. (2002). Patient personality and mortality: A 4-year prospective examination of chronic renal insufficiency. *Health Psychology, 21,* 315–320.

Clark, L. A., & Watson, D. (1999). Temperament: A new paradigm for trait psychology. In L. Pervin & O. John (Eds.), *Handbook of personality: Theory and research* (2nd ed., pp. 399–423). New York: Guilford.

Cloninger, C. R. (1998). The genetics and psychobiology of the seven-factor model of personality. In K. R. Silk (Ed.), *Biology of personality disorders* (pp. 63–92). Washington, DC: American Psychiatric Press.

Cohen, F., & Lazarus, R. S. (1983). Coping and adaptation in health and illness. In D. Mechanic (Ed.), *Handbook of health, health care, and the health professions* (pp. 608–635). New York: Free Press.

Cohen, S., Doyle, W. J., & Skoner, D. P. (1999). Psychological stress, cytokine production, and severity of upper respiratory illness. *Psychosomatic Medicine, 61,* 175–180.

Cohen, S., Doyle, W. J., Turner, R. B., Alper, C. M., & Skoner, D. P. (2003). Sociability and susceptibility to the common cold. *Psychological Science, 14,* 389–395.

Cohen, S., & Williamson, G. M. (1991). Stress and infectious disease in humans. *Psychological Bulletin, 109,* 5–24.

Colvin, C. R., & Block, J. (1994). Do positive illusions foster mental health? An examination of the Taylor and Brown formulation. *Psychological Bulletin, 116,* 3–20.

Colvin C. R., Block, J., & Funder, D. C. (1995). Overly positive self-evaluations and personality: Negative implications for mental health. *Journal of Personality and Social Psychology, 68,* 1152–1162.

Copper, R. L., Goldenberg, R. L., Das, A., Elder, N., Swain, M., Norman, G., et al. (1996). The preterm prediction study: Maternal stress is associated with spontaneous preterm birth at less than thirty-five weeks' gestation. *American Journal of Obstetrics and Gynecology, 175,* 1286–1292.

Costa, P. T., & McCrae, R. R. (1987). Neuroticism, somatic complaints, and disease: Is the bark worse than the bite? *Journal of Personality, 55,* 299–316.

Crocker, J., Major, B., & Steele, C. (1998). Social stigma. In D. T. Gilbert, S. T. Fiske, & G. Lindzey (Eds.), *The handbook of social psychology* (Vol. 2, 4th ed., pp. 504–531). Boston: McGraw-Hill.

Deary, I. J., & Der, G. (2005). Reaction time explains IQ's association with death. *Psychological Science 16*(1), 64–69.

Deary, I. J., Whiteman, M. C., Starr, J. M., Whalley, L. J., & Fox, H. C. (2004). The impact of childhood intelligence on later life: Following up the Scottish Mental Surveys of 1932 and 1947. *Journal of Personality and Social Psychology, 86,* 130–147.

Dembroski, T. M., Weiss, S. M., Shields, J. L., Haynes, S. G., & Feinlieb, M. (Eds.). (1978). *Coronary-prone behavior.* New York: Springer-Verlag.

Denollet, J. (2000). Type D personality: A potential risk factor refined. *Journal of Psychosomatic Research, 49,* 255–266.

Devins, G. M., Mann, J., Mandin, H., Paul, L. C., Hons, R. B., Burgess, E. D., et al. (1990). Psychosocial predictors of survival in end-stage renal disease. *Journal of Nervous and Mental Disease, 178,* 127–133.

Dion, K. (1972). Physical attractiveness and evaluation of children's transgressions. *Journal and Personality and Social Psychology, 24,* 207–213.

Dixon, N. F. (1980). Humor: A cognitive alternative to stress? In I. G. Sarason & C. D. Spielberger (Eds.), *Stress and anxiety* (Vol. 7, pp. 281–289). Washington, DC: Hemisphere.

Dunbar, F. (1955). *Mind and body: Psychosomatic medicine.* New York: Random House.

ENRICHD Investigators. (2003). Effects of treating depression and low perceived social support on clinical events after myocardial infarction: The enhancing recovery in coronary heart disease patients (ENRICHD) randomized trial. *Journal of the American Medical Association, 289,* 3106–3116.

Everson, S. A., Goldberg, D. E., Kaplan, G. A., Cohen, R. D., Pukkala, E., Tuomilehto, J., et al. (1996). Hopelessness and risk of mortality and incidence of myocardial infarction and cancer. *Psychosomatic Medicine, 58,* 113–121.

Eysenck, H. J. (1990). Biological dimensions of personality. In L. A. Pervin (Ed.), *Handbook of personality: Theory and research* (pp. 244–276). New York: Guilford.

Eysenck, H. J. (1991). *Smoking, personality, and stress: Psychosocial factors in the prevention of cancer and coronary heart disease.* New York: Springer-Verlag.

Eysenck, H. J. (1992). Four ways five factors are not basic. *Personality and Individual Differences, 13,* 667–673.

Eysenck, H. J., & Eysenck, S. B. G. (1976). *Psychoticism as a dimension of personality.* London: Hodder and Stoughton.

Ford, D. E., Mead, L. A., Chang, P. P., Cooper-Patrick, L., Wang, N., & Klag, M. J. (1998). Depression is a risk factor for coronary artery disease in men. *Archives of Internal Medicine, 158,* 1422–1426.

Frankl, V. E. (1962). *Man's search for meaning: An introduction to logotherapy* (Rev. ed.; I. Lasch, Trans.). Boston: Beacon.

Frasure-Smith, N., Lesperance, F., & Talajic, M. (1995). Depression and 18–month prognosis after myocardial infarction. *Circulation, 91,* 999–1005.

Fredrickson, B. L. (2001). The role of positive emotions in positive psychology: The broaden-and-build theory of positive emotions. *American Psychologist, 56,* 218–226.

Freud, S. (1955). *Collected works: Vol. 2. Studies of Hysteria.* New York: Hogarth Press.

Friedman, H. S. (1991/2000). *Self-healing personality: Why some people achieve health and others succumb to illness.* New York: Re-published by: http://www.iuniverse.com.

Friedman, H. S. (1998). Self-healing personalities. In H. S. Friedman (Editor-in-chief), *Encyclopedia of mental health* (Vol. 3, pp. 453–459). San Diego, CA: Academic Press.

Friedman, H. S. (2000). Long-term relations of personality and health: Dynamisms, mechanisms, tropisms. *Journal of Personality, 68,* 1089–1108.

Friedman, H. S., & Booth-Kewley, S. (1987). The "disease-prone personality": A meta-analytic view of the construct. *American Psychologist, 42,* 539–555.

Friedman, H. S., Hall, J. A. & Harris, M. J. (1985). Type A behavior, nonverbal expressive style, and health. *Journal of Personality and Social Psychology, 48,* 1299–1315.

Friedman, H. S., & Markey, C. N. (2003). Paths to longevity in the highly intelligent Terman cohort. In C. E. Finch, J-M. Robine, & Y. Christen (Eds.), *Brain and longevity* (pp. 165–175). New York: Springer.

Friedman, H. S., & Schustack, M. W. (2006). *Personality: Classic theories and modern research* (3rd ed.). Boston: Allyn and Bacon.

Friedman, H. S., Tucker, J. S., Martin, L. R., Tomlinson-Keasey, C., Schwartz, J. E., Wingard, D. L., et al. (1994). Do non-scientists really live longer? *Lancet, 343,* 296.

Friedman, H. S., Tucker, J. S., & Reise, S. (1995). Personality dimensions and measures potentially relevant to health: A focus on hostility. *Annals of Behavioral Medicine, 17,* 245–253.

Friedman, H. S., Tucker, J., Schwartz, J. E., Martin, L. R., Tomlinson-Keasey, C., Wingard, D., et al. (1995). Childhood conscientiousness and longevity: Health behaviors and cause of death. *Journal of Personality and Social Psychology, 68,* 696–703.

Friedman, H. S., Tucker, J. S., Schwartz, J. E., Tomlinson-Keasey, C., Martin, L. R., Wingard, D. L., et al. (1995). Psychosocial and behavioral predictors of longevity: The aging and death of the "Termites." *American Psychologist, 50,* 69–78.

Friedman, H. S., Tucker, J., Tomlinson-Keasey, C., Schwartz, J., Wingard, D., & Criqui, M. H. (1993). Does childhood personality predict longevity? *Journal of Personality and Social Psychology, 65,* 176–185.

Friedman, H. S., & VandenBos, G. (1992). Disease-prone and self-healing personalities. *Hospital and Community Psychiatry: A Journal of the American Psychiatric Association, 43,* 1177–1179.

Friedman, M., & Rosenman, R. H. (1974). *Type A behavior and your heart.* New York: Knopf.

Gallo, L. C., & Smith, T. W. (1999). Patterns of hostility and social support: Conceptualizing psychosocial risk factors as characteristics of the person and the environment. *Journal of Research in Personality, 33,* 281–310.

Gardner, J., & Oswald, A. (2004). How is mortality affected by money, marriage and stress? *Journal of Health Economics, 23,* 1181–1207.

Garmezy, N. (1993). Children in poverty: Resilience despite risk. *Psychiatry, 56,* 127–136.

Goffman, E. (1963). *Stigma: Notes on the management of spoiled identity.* Englewood Cliffs, NJ: Prentice-Hall.

Goodwin, R. G., & Friedman, H.S. (in press). Health

status and the Five Factor personality traits in a nationally representative sample. *Journal of Health Psychology.*

Grau, E., & Ortet, G. (1999). Personality traits and alcohol consumption in a sample of non-alcoholic women. *Personality and Individual Differences, 27,* 1057–1066.

Ham, L. S., & Hope, D. A. (2003). College students and problematic drinking: A review of the literature. *Clinical Psychology Review, 23,* 719–759.

Hawkley, L. C., Burleson, M. H., Berntson, G. G., & Cacioppo, J. T. (2003). Loneliness in everyday life: Cardiovascular activity, psychosocial context, and health behaviors. *Journal of Personality and Social Psychology, 85,* 105–120.

Hawkley, L. C., & Cacioppo, J. T. (2004). Stress and the aging immune system. *Brain, Behavior, and Immunity, 18,* 114–119.

Hayward, M. D., & Gorman, B. K. (2004). The long arm of childhood: The influence of early-life social conditions on men's mortality. *Demography, 41,* 87–107.

Held, B. B. (2004). The negative side of positive psychology. *Journal of Humanistic Psychology, 44,* 9–46.

Herbert, T. B., & Cohen, S. (1993). Depression and immunity: A meta-analytic review. *Psychological Bulletin, 113,* 472–486.

Hogan, J., & Ones, D. S. (1997). Conscientiousness and integrity at work. In R. Hogan, J. A. Johnson, & S. R. Briggs (Eds.), *Handbook of personality psychology* (pp. 849–870). San Diego, CA: Academic Press.

Horwitz, R. I., Viscoli, C. M., Berkman, L., Donaldson, R. M., Horwitz, S. M., Murray, C. J., et al. (1990). Treatment adherence and risk of death after a myocardial infarction. *Lancet, 336,* 542–545.

House, J. S., Landis, K. R., & Umberson, D. (1988). Social relationships and health. *Science, 241,* 540–545.

Houston, B. K., & Snyder, C. R. (1988). *Type A behavior pattern: Research, theory and intervention.* New York: Wiley.

Januzzi, J. L., Stern, T. A., Pasternak, R., & DeSanctis, R. W. (2000). The influence of anxiety and depression on outcomes of patients with coronary artery disease. *Archives of Internal Medicine, 160,* 1913–1921.

Jenkins, C. D. (1979). The coronary prone personality. In W. D. Gentry & R. B. Williams (Eds.), *Psychological aspects of myocardial infarction and coronary care* (2nd ed., pp. 5–30). St. Louis, MO: Mosby.

Jensen, M. R. (1987). Psychobiological factors predicting the course of breast cancer. *Journal of Personality, 55,* 317–342.

Johnson, W., McGue, M., Krueger, R. J., & Bouchard, T. J., Jr. (2004). Marriage and personality: A genetic analysis. *Journal of Personality and Social Psychology, 86,* 285–294.

Judge, T. A., & Ilies, R. (2002). Relationship of personality to performance motivation: A meta-analytic review. *Journal of Applied Psychology, 87,* 797–807.

Kagan, J. (1994). *Galen's prophecy: Temperament in human nature.* New York: Basic Books.

Kassel, J. D., Stroud, L. R., & Paronis, C. A. (2003). Smoking, stress, and negative affect: Correlation, causation, and context across stages of smoking. *Psychological Bulletin, 129,* 270–304.

Kiecolt-Glaser, J. K., Glaser, R., Cacioppo, J. T., & Malarkey, W. B. (1998). Marital stress: Immunologic, neuroendocrine, and autonomic correlates. In S. M. McCann, & J. M. Lipton (Eds.), *Annals of the New York Academy of Sciences, Vol. 840: Neuroimmunomodulation: Molecular aspects, integrative systems, and clinical advances* (pp. 656–663). New York: New York Academy of Sciences.

Korten, A. E., Jorm, A. F., Jiao, Z., Letenneur, L., Jacomb, P. A., Henderson, A. S., et al. (1999). Health, cognitive, and psychosocial factors as predictors of mortality in an elderly community sample. *Journal of Epidemiology and Community Health, 53,* 83–88.

Kubzansky, L. D., Kawachi, I., Weiss, S. T., & Sparrow, D. (1998). Anxiety and coronary heart disease: A synthesis of epidemiological, psychological, and experimental evidence. *Annals of Behavioral Medicine, 20,* 47–58.

Larson, J. H., & Holman, T. B. (1994). Premarital predictors of marital quality and stability. *Family Relations: Interdisciplinary Journal of Applied Family Studies, 43,* 228–237.

Lazarus, R. S., & Folkman, S. (1984). *Stress, appraisal, and coping.* New York: Springer.

Leibowitz, J. O. (1970). *The history of coronary heart disease.* Berkeley: University of California Press.

Lobel, M., DeVincent, C. J., Kaminer, A., & Meyer, B. A. (2000). The impact of prenatal maternal stress and optimistic disposition on birth outcomes in medically high-risk women. *Health Psychology, 19,* 544–553.

Lutgendorf, S. K., Vitaliano, P. P., Tripp-Reimer, T., Harvey, J. H., & Lubaroff, D. M. (1999). Sense of coherence moderates the relationship between life stress and natural killer cell activity in healthy older adults. *Psychology and Aging, 14,* 552–563.

Maddi, S. R., & Kobasa, S. C. (1984). *The hardy executive: Health under stress.* Homewood, IL: Dow Jones-Irwin.

Magnus, K., Diener, E., Fujita, F., & Payot, W. (1993). Extraversion and neuroticism as predictors of objective life events: A longitudinal analysis. *Journal of Personality and Social Psychology, 65,* 1046–1053.

Maier, H., & Smith, J. (1999). Psychological predictors of mortality in old age. *Journals of Gerontology: Series B: Psychological Sciences and Social Sciences, 54B,* 44–54.

Manuck, S. B., Flory, J. D., McCaffery, J. M., Matthews, K. A., Mann, J. J., & Muldoon, M. F. (1998). Aggression, impulsivity, and central nervous system serotonergic responsivity in a nonpatient sample. *Neuropsychopharmacology, 19,* 287–299.

Marchesi, C., Brusamonti, E., & Maggini, C. (2000). Are alexithymia, depression, and anxiety distinct constructs in affective disorders? *Journal of Psychosomatic Research, 49,* 43–49.

Marshall, G. N., Wortman, C. B., Vickers, R. R., Jr., Kusulas, J. W., & Hervig, L. K. (1994). The five-factor model of personality as a framework for personality-health research. *Journal of Personality and Social Psychology, 67,* 278–286.

Martin, L. R., & Friedman, H. S. (2000). Comparing personality scales across time: An illustrative study of validity and consistency in life-span archival data. *Journal of Personality, 68,* 85–110.

Martin, L. R., Friedman, H. S., & Schwartz, J. E. (in press). Personality and mortality risk across the lifespan. *Health Psychology.*

Martin, L. R., Friedman, H. S., Tucker, J. S., Tomlinson-Keasey, C., Criqui, M. H., & Schwartz, J. E. (2002). A life course perspective on childhood cheerfulness and its relation to mortality risk. *Personality and Social Psychology Bulletin, 28,* 1155–1165.

Martsh, C. T., & Miller, W. R. (1997). Extraversion predicts heavy drinking in college students. *Personality and Individual Differences, 23,* 153–155.

Matthews, K. A. (1982). Psychological perspectives on the type A behavior pattern. *Psychological Bulletin, 91,* 293–323.

Matthews, K. A. (1988). Coronary heart disease and type A behaviors: Update on and alternative to the Booth-Kewley and Friedman (1987) quantitative review. *Psychological Bulletin, 3,* 373–380.

Matthews, K. A., Owens, J. F., Kuller, L. H., Sutton-Tyrrell, K., & Jansen-McWilliams, L. (1998). Are hostility and anxiety associated with carotid atherosclerosis in healthy postmenopausal women? *Psychosomatic Medicine, 60,* 633–638.

McCrae, R. R., & Costa, P. T., Jr. (1987). Validation of the five-factor model of personality across instruments and observers. *Journal of Personality and Social Psychology, 52,* 81–90.

McCrae, R. R., & John, O. (1992). An introduction to the five-factor model and its applications. *Journal of Personality, 60,* 175–215.

McEwen, B. S. (1998). Stress, adaptation and disease: Allostasis and allostatic load. *Annals of the New York Academy of Sciences, 840,* 33–44.

Menninger, K. A., & Menninger, W. C. (1936). Psychoanalytic observations in cardiac disorders. *American Heart Journal, 11,* 1–12.

Meyer, R., & Haggerty, R. (1962). Streptococcal infections in families. *Pediatrics, 29,* 539–549.

Miller, T. Q., Smith, T. W., Turner, C. W., Guijarro, M. L., & Hallet, A. J. (1996). A meta-analytic review of research on hostility and physical health. *Psychological Bulletin, 119,* 322–348.

Miller, T. Q., Turner, C. W., Tindale, R. S., Posavac, E. J., & Dugoni, B. L. (1991). Reasons for the trend toward null findings in research on type A behavior. *Psychological Bulletin, 110,* 469–485.

Mroczek, D. K., & Almeida, D. M. (2004). The effect of daily stress, personality, and age on daily negative affect. *Journal of Personality, 72,* 355–378.

Newman, M. F., Kirchner, J. L., Phillips-Bute, B., Gaver, V., Grocott, H., Jones, R. H., et al. (2001). Longitudinal assessment of neurocognitive function after coronary-artery bypass surgery. *New England Journal of Medicine, 344,* 395–402.

Osler, M., Andersen, A.-M. N., Due, P., Lund, R., Damsgaard, M. T., & Holstein, B. E. (2003). Socioeconomic position in early life, birth weight, childhood cognitive function, and adult mortality: A longitudinal study of Danish men born in 1953. *Journal of Epidemiology and Community Health, 57,* 681–686.

Ouellette, S. C., & DiPlacido, J. (2001). Personality's role in the protection and enhancement of health: Where the research has been, where it is stuck, how it might move. In A. Baum, T. A. Revenson, & J. Singer (Eds.), *Handbook of health psychology* (pp. 175–194). Mahwah, NJ: Erlbaum.

Park, M., Ross, G. W., Petrovitch, H., White, L. R., Masaki, K. H., Nelson, J. S., et al. (2005). Consumption of milk and calcium in midlife and the future risk of Parkinson disease. *Neurology, 64,* 1047–1051.

Parsons, J. E. (1980). *The psychobiology of sex differences and sex roles.* Cambridge, England: Hemisphere.

Peabody, D., & Goldberg, L. R. (1989). Some determinants of factor structures from personality-trait descriptors. *Journal of Personality and Social Psychology, 57,* 552–567.

Pennebaker, J. W. (1982). *The psychology of physical symptoms.* New York: Springer-Verlag.

Peterson, C., Bishop, M. P., Fletcher, C. W., Kaplan,

M. R., Yesko, E. S. Moon, C. H., et al. (2001). Explanatory style as a risk factor for traumatic mishaps. *Cognitive Therapy and Research, 25,* 633–649.

Peterson, C., Seligman, M. E. P., Yurko, K. H., Martin, L. R., & Friedman, H. S. (1998). Catastrophizing and untimely death. *Psychological Science, 9,* 49–52.

Pettingale, K. W., Morris, T., Greer, S., & Haybittle, J. L. (1985). Mental attitudes to cancer: An additional prognostic factor. *Lancet, 1,* 750.

Plomin, R. (1986). *Development, genetics, and psychology.* Hillsdale, NJ: Erlbaum.

Pressman, S. D., & Cohen, S. (in press). The influence of positive affect on health: A review. *Psychological Bulletin.*

Ragland, D. R., & Brand, R. J. (1988). Type A behavior and mortality from coronary heart disease. *New England Journal of Medicine, 318,* 65–69.

Repetti, R. L., Taylor, S. E., & Seeman, T. E. (2002). Risky families: Family social environments and the mental and physical health of offspring. *Psychological Bulletin, 128,* 330–366.

Roberts, B. W., & Bogg, T. (2004). A longitudinal study of the relationships between conscientiousness and the social environmental factors and substance use behaviors that influence health. *Journal of Personality, 72,* 325–353.

Roberts, B. W., & Caspi, A. (2003). The cumulative continuity model of personality development: Striking a balance between continuity and change in personality traits across the life course. In R. M. Staudinger & U. Lindenberger (Eds.), *Understanding human development: Lifespan psychology in exchange with other disciplines* (pp. 183–214). Dordrecht, Netherlands: Kluwer Academic Publishers.

Roberts, B. W., Caspi, A., & Moffitt, T. (2003). Work experiences and personality development in young adulthood. *Journal of Personality and Social Psychology, 84,* 582–593.

Roberts, B. W., & Pomerantz, E. M. (2004). On traits, situations, and their integration: A developmental perspective. *Personality and Social Psychology Review, 8,* 402–416.

Rosenkranz, M. A., Jackson, D. C., Dalton K. M., Dolski, I., Ryff, C. D., Singer, B. H., et al. (2003). Affective style and *in vivo* immune response: Neurobehavioral mechanisms. *Proceedings of the National Academy of Sciences, 100,* 11148–11152.

Rotton, J. (1992). Trait humor and longevity: Do comics have the last laugh? *Health Psychology, 11,* 262–266.

Rugulies, R. (2002). Depression as a predictor for coronary heart disease: A review and meta-analysis. *American Journal of Preventive Medicine, 23,* 51–61.

Ryff, C. D., & Singer, B. H. (Eds.). (2001). *Emotion, social relationships, and health.* New York: Oxford University Press.

Salovey, P., Rothman, A. J., Detweiler, J. B., & Steward, W. (2000). Emotional states and physical health. *American Psychologist, 55,* 110–121.

Scheier, M. F., Matthews, K. A., Owens, J. F., Schulz, R., Bridges, M. W., Magovern, G. J., Jr., et al. (1999). Optimism and rehospitalization after coronary artery bypass graft surgery. *Archives of Internal Medicine, 159,* 829–833.

Schneiderman, N., Weiss, S. M., & Kaufmann, P. G. (Eds.). (1989). *Handbook of research methods in cardiovascular behavioral medicine.* New York: Plenum.

Schulz, R., Martire, L. M., Beach, S. R., & Scheier, M. F. (2000). Depression and mortality in the elderly. *Current Directions in Psychological Science, 9,* 204–208.

Sears, R. R. (1984). The Terman gifted children study. In S. A. Mednick, M. Harway, & K. M. Finello (Eds.), *Handbook of longitudinal research* (vol. 1, pp. 398–414). New York: Praeger.

Segerstrom, S. C. (2000). Personality and the immune system: Models, methods, and mechanisms. *Annals of Behavioral Medicine, 22,* 180–190.

Segerstrom, S. C., & Miller, G. E. (2004). Psychological stress and the human immune system: A meta-analytic study of 30 years of inquiry. *Psychological Bulletin, 104,* 601–630.

Segerstrom, S. C., Taylor, S. E., Kemeny, M. E., & Fahey, J. L. (1998). Optimism is associated with mood, coping, and immune change in response to stress. *Journal of Personality and Social Psychology, 74,* 1646–1655.

Shaffer, J., Graves, P. L., Swank, R. T., & Pearson, T. A. (1987). Clustering of personality traits in youth and the subsequent development of cancer among physicians. *Journal of Behavioral Medicine, 10,* 441–444.

Smith, T. W., & Gallo, L. C. (2001). Personality traits as risk factors for physical illness. In A. Baum, T. Revenson, & J. Singer (Eds.), *Handbook of health psychology* (pp. 139–172). Hillsdale, NJ: Erlbaum.

Smith, T. W., Glazer, K., Ruiz, J. M., & Gallo, L. C. (2004). Hostility, anger, aggressiveness, and coronary heart disease: An interpersonal perspective on personality, emotion, and health. *Journal of Personality, 72,* 1217–1270.

Snowdon, D. A. (1997). Aging and Alzheimer's disease: Lessons from the Nun Study. *Gerontology, 37,* 150–156.

Snowdon, D. A., Kemper, S. J., Mortimer, J. A., Greiner, L. H., Wekstein, D. R., & Markesbery, W. R. (1996). Linguistic ability early in life and cognitive function and Alzheimer's disease in late life: Findings from the Nun Study. *JAMA, 275,* 528–532.

Stavraky, K. M., Donner, A. P., Kincade, J., & Stewart, M. A. (1988). The effect of psychosocial factors on lung cancer mortality at one year. *Journal of Clinical Epidemiology, 41,* 75–82.

Subotnik, R. F., Karp, D. E., & Morgan, E. R. (1989). High IQ children at midlife: An investigation into the generalizability of Terman's Genetic Studies of Genius. *Roeper Review, 11,* 139–145.

Suls, J., & Bunde, J. (2005). Anger, anxiety, and depression as risk factors for cardiovascular disease: The problems and implications of overlapping affective dispositions. *Psychological Bulletin, 131,* 260–300.

Suls, J., & Rittenhouse, J. D. (1990). Models of linkages between personality and disease. In H. S. Friedman (Ed.), *Personality and disease* (pp. 38–64). New York: Wiley.

Surtees, P., Wainwright, N., Luben, R., Khaw, K. T., & Day, N. (2003). Sense of coherence and mortality in men and women in the EPIC-Norfolk United Kingdom prospective cohort study. *American Journal of Epidemiology, 158,* 1202–1209.

Swain, A., & Suls, J. (1996). Reproducibility of blood pressure and heart rate reactivity: A meta-analysis. *Psychophysiology, 33,* 162–74.

Taylor, S. E., & Brown, J. D. (1988). Illusion and well-being: A social psychological perspective on mental health. *Psychological Bulletin, 103,* 193–210.

Taylor, S. E., Kemeny, M. E., Aspinwall, L. G., Schneider, S. G., Rodriguez, R., & Herbert, M. (1992). Optimism, coping, psychological distress, and high-risk sexual behavior among men at risk for acquired immune deficiency syndrome. *Journal of Personality and Social Psychology, 63,* 460–473.

Taylor, S. E., Repetti, R. L., & Seeman, T. (1997). Health psychology: What is an unhealthy environment and how does it get under the skin? *Annual Review of Psychology, 48,* 411–447.

Temoshok, L., Heller, B. W., Sagebiel, R., Blois, M., Sweet, D. M., DiClemente, R. J., et al. (1985). The relationship of psychosocial factors to prognostic indicators in cutaneous malignant melanoma. *Journal of Psychosomatic Research, 29,* 139–154.

Terman, L. M., & Oden, M. H. (1947). *The gifted child grows up: Twenty-five years' follow-up of a superior group.* Stanford, CA: Stanford University Press.

Thomas, A., Chess, S., & Korn, S. J. (1982). The reality of difficult temperament. *Merrill-Palmer Quarterly, 28,* 1–20.

Tucker, J., Friedman, H. S., Tomlinson-Keasey, C., Schwartz, J. E., Wingard, D. L., & Criqui, M. H. (1995). Childhood psychosocial predictors of adulthood smoking, alcohol consumption, and physical activity. *Journal of Applied Social Psychology, 25,* 1884–1899.

Tucker, J. S., Friedman, H. S., Wingard, D. L., & Schwartz, J. E. (1996). Marital history at mid-life as a predictor of longevity: Alternative explanations to the protective effect of marriage. *Health Psychology, 15,* 94–101.

Twenge, J. M. (2000). The age of anxiety? Birth cohort change in anxiety and neuroticism, 1952–1993. *Journal of Personality and Social Psychology, 79,* 1007–1021.

Twenge, J. M. (2001). Birth cohort changes in extraversion: A cross-temporal meta-analysis, 1966–1993. *Personality and Individual Differences, 30,* 735–748.

Twenge, J. M. (2002). Birth cohort, social change, and personality: The interplay of dysphoria and individualism in the 20th century. In D. Cervone & W. Mischel (Eds.), *Advances in personality science* (pp. 196–218). New York: Guilford.

Urry, H. L., Nitschke, J. B., Dolski, I., Jackson, D. C., Dalton, K. M., Mueller, C. J., et al. (2004). Making a life worth living: Neural correlates of well-being. *Psychological Science, 15,* 367–372.

Vollrath, M., Landolt, M. A., & Ribi, K. (2003). Personality of children with accident-related injuries. *European Journal of Personality, 17,* 299–307.

Wallston, K. A., Malcarne, V. L., Flores, L., Hansdottir, I., Smith, C. A., Stein, M. J., et al. (1999). Does God determine your health? The God Locus of Health Control Scale. *Cognitive Therapy and Research, 23,* 131–142.

Wand, G. S., McCaul, M., Yang, X., Reynolds, J., Gotjen, D., Lee, S., et al. (2002). The mu-opioid receptor gene polymorphism (A188G) alters HPA axis activation induced by opioid receptor blockade. *Neuropsychopharmacology, 26,* 106–114.

Watson, D. (2000). *Mood and temperament.* New York: Guilford.

Watson, D., & Pennebaker, J. W. (1989). Health complaints, stress, and distress: Exploring the central role of negative affectivity. *Psychological Review, 96,* 234–254.

Weinstein, N. D. (1982). Unrealistic optimism about susceptibility to health problems. *Journal of Behavioral Medicine, 5,* 441–460.

Weinstein, N. D., & Klein, W. M. (1995). Resistance of personal risk perceptions to debiasing interventions. *Health Psychology, 14,* 132–140.

Weiss, A., Costa, P. T., Karuza, J., Duberstein, P. R., & Friedman, B. (2004, March). *Personality as predictors of cardiovascular disease and mortality in patients aged 65–100.* Poster presented at the 62nd annual meeting of the American Psychosomatic Society, Orlando, FL.

Whalley, L. J., & Deary, I. J. (2001). Longitudinal cohort study of childhood IQ and survival up to age 76. *British Medical Journal, 322,* 819–829.

Williams, R. (1994). *Anger kills.* New York: HarperCollins.

Williams, R. B., Kuhn, C. M., Helms, M. J., Siegler, I. C., Barefoot, J. C., Ashley-Kocy, A., et al. (2004, March). *Central nervous system (CNS) serotonin function and NEO-PI personality profiles.* Poster presented at the 62nd annual meeting of the American Psychosomatic Society, Orlando, FL.

Wilson, R. S., Bienias, J. L., de Leon, C. F. M., Evans, D. A., & Bennett, D. A. (2003). Negative affect and mortality in older persons. *American Journal of Epidemiology, 158,* 827–835.

Wilson, R. S., Mendes de Leon, C. F., Bienias, J. L., Evans, D. A., & Bennett, D. A. (2004). Personality and mortality in old age. *Journal of Gerontology B: Psychological Sciences and Social Science, 59,* 110–116.

Witzig, M. E., Kamarck, T. W., Muldoon, M. F., & Sutton-Tyrrell, K. (2003, March). *Examining the relationship between conscientiousness and atherosclerosis: The Pittsburgh healthy heart project.* Poster presented at the 61st annual meeting of the American Psychosomatic Society, Phoenix, AZ.

Woodward, J. L. (1998). Dementia. In H. S. Friedman (Editor-in-chief), *Encyclopedia of mental health* (Vol. 1, pp. 693–713). San Diego, CA: Academic Press.

Zuckerman, M., & Kuhlman, D. M. (2000). Personality and risk-taking: Common bisocial factors. *Journal of Personality, 68,* 999–1029.

Applications to Health Promotion and Effective Treatment

Annette L. Stanton

and Tracey A. Revenson

Adjustment to Chronic Disease: Progress and Promise in Research

In 1961, a seminal, observational study of adjustment to chronic disease appeared in the *Archives of General Psychiatry* (Visotsky, Hamburg, Goss, & Lebovits, 1961). Its authors posed questions regarding adjustment to polio that continue to stimulate research on chronic disease today: "How is it possible to deal with such powerful, pervasive, and enduring stresses as are involved in severe polio? What are the types of coping behavior that contribute to favorable outcomes?" (p. 28). Four decades later, theoretical and empirical consideration of these questions has produced multifaceted conceptualizations of adjustment to chronic disease, theoretical frameworks for understanding determinants of adjustment, and empirical evidence regarding factors that contribute to untoward or favorable outcomes. In this chapter, we begin with a brief discussion of the prevalence and impact of chronic disease and then consider what is meant by adjustment to chronic disease. We go on to discuss themes in theories of contributors to adjustment. Finally, we address implications for intervention and future research.

The knowledge base on adjustment to major chronic diseases (e.g., cancer, cardiovascular disease, diabetes, arthritis, AIDS) is large and growing. In this chapter, we attempt to offer cross-cutting observations that have emerged from our analysis of relevant theory and research. Although we attempt to draw broadly from the literature on adjustment to various chronic diseases, the reader will notice an emphasis on those diseases closer to our own areas of expertise (i.e., cancer and rheumatic disease). We focus on psychosocial processes as they influence adjustment to chronic disease rather than as causal factors in chronic disease, although we provide references to this burgeoning literature where relevant. Further, we do not address the important areas of adjustment to chronic disease in childhood (e.g., Roberts, 1995) or caregiver adjustment (Schulz, O'Brien, Bookwala, & Fleissner, 1995; Vitaliano, Zhang, & Scanlan, 2003).

Definitions and Impact of Chronic Disease

The Centers for Disease Control and Prevention (CDC) define *chronic disease* as "illnesses that are prolonged, do not resolve spontaneously, and are rarely cured completely" (CDC, 2003). According to this broad definition, more than 90 million Americans live with chronic diseases, with women and racial minority populations affected disproportionately. A few sobering statistics are all that is needed to make this point: Three chronic diseases—heart disease, cancers, and stroke—account for almost 60% of all deaths in the United States. Women constitute more than half the people who die each year of cardiovascular disease, and African Americans are more likely than Whites are to die from breast, cervical, colon, and prostate cancer. In addition, human immunodeficiency virus (HIV) disease is among the three leading causes of death for non-Hispanic Black women and men aged 25 to 44 years (Anderson & Smith, 2003).

In addition to shortening survival, chronic diseases are the leading cause of disability, which leads to economic, social, and psychological declines. Approximately 13% of adults report some limitation of activity caused by a chronic condition, and this percentage triples to 37% for those aged 65 and older (Eberhardt, Ingram, & Makuc, 2001). Arthritis (of which there are more than 100 forms) is the most common cause of disability in the United States, affecting nearly 25% of the population (CDC, 2004). Chronic diseases account for 75% of medical care costs in the United States (CDC, 2004).

The number of people living with one or more chronic conditions is projected to increase in the next decades (Institute for the Future, 2000). Many infectious diseases have been eradicated. Increases in life expectancy and the proportion of older people are accompanied by an increased prevalence of chronic disease. Thanks to medical advances, many diseases that were formerly considered to be acute and/or rapidly terminal—including HIV disease and some types of cancer—are now being redefined as chronic.

Chronic diseases vary along several dimensions, and even individual chronic diseases reveal a good deal of heterogeneity. No standard exists for defining what is meant by *chronic*. From a psychological perspective, the definition of chronic disease is complex: When does one stop being a cancer patient? Is it when treatment is completed? When one is informed by the medical team that no detectable cancer is present? When disease- and treatment-related symptoms subside? When one celebrates the 5-year anniversary after diagnosis? The meaning of chronicity, as with so many other aspects of disease, lies in the eye of the beholder, although researchers probably would concur that the disease process must persist over at least several months to constitute *chronic* disease.

Rapidity of onset, degree of ambiguity in symptom presentation, level of life threat, prominence

of pain, disease course (e.g., progressive versus relapse-remitting), degree of daily life disruption from symptoms and treatment, and treatment effectiveness represent other dimensions that demonstrate variability across and within chronic diseases. Although some of the consequences of chronic disease are sudden and obvious, such as the surgical excision of a body part, others are gradual and insidious, such as losing muscle strength and flexibility (Thompson & Kyle, 2000). Compromised performance of roles and daily activities, progressive fatigue, and changes in interpersonal relations can proceed subtly and with an uneven course. It is with acknowledgment of this great variation in what constitutes *chronic disease* that we attempt to present some generalizations culled from our analysis of the literature on adjustment to chronic disease. In attempting to address questions regarding what constitutes "optimal" adjustment to chronic disease, however, it is clear to us from the outset that there is no such thing as "one size fits all."

What Does It Mean to Adjust to Chronic Disease?

Prior to considering determinants of adjustment to chronic disease, we must define what it means to adjust. The words *adjustment* and *adaptation* often are used interchangeably in the literature, and will be in this chapter as well. Our analysis of the scientific literature leads us to the conclusions that (1) chronic disease necessitates adjustment in multiple life domains; (2) both positive and negative indicators of adjustment are relevant; (3) adjustment is not static but rather represents a process that unfolds over time; (4) adjustment cannot be described adequately without reference to the individual's context; and (5) heterogeneity in adjustment is the rule rather than the exception.

Adjustment Is Multifaceted

Studies such as that of Visotsky and colleagues (1961) marked an early attempt to broaden conceptualization of adjustment to chronic disease from a sole focus on (the absence of) psychopathology and toward multifaceted conceptualizations. At least five related conceptualizations of adjustment to chronic disease appear consistently in the literature (Stanton, Collins, & Sworowski, 2001): mastery of the adaptive tasks of disease; maintenance of adequate functional status; absence of diagnosable psychological disorder; reports of relatively low negative affect; and perceived quality of life in various domains.

Reviewing observational studies of adjustment to major life transitions, including serious disease, Hamburg and Adams (1967) suggested several central adaptive tasks: keeping distress within manageable limits; maintaining a sense of personal worth; restoring relations with significant other people; enhancing prospects for recovery of bodily functions; and increasing the likelihood of attaining a personally valued and socially acceptable situation once maximum physical recovery has been accomplished. Taylor's (1983) theory of cognitive adaptation to threatening events, which used adjustment to breast cancer as its exemplar, also emphasized self-esteem enhancement and preservation of a sense of mastery over one's life, and added resolution of a search for meaning as a central adaptive task. (The search for meaning will be discussed in more depth later in this chapter.) Others have suggested the importance of more specific, disease-related tasks (e.g., Clark et al., 1991). Moos and Schaefer (1984) added the disease-related tasks of managing pain and symptoms, negotiating the medical treatment environment, and maintaining adequate relationships with health care professionals. A related conceptualization of adjustment focuses on functional status as the central indicator (e.g., Spelten, Sprangers, & Verbeek, 2002). Operationalizations of functional status include resumption of paid employment or routine activities, mobility, and adherence to a prescribed physical rehabilitation protocol or other medical regimen.

The presence or absence of diagnosed psychological disorder often is used as a marker of adjustment to chronic disease (e.g., Cordova et al., 1995; Derogatis et al., 1983). Most often, low or nonclinical levels of anxiety and depression are used to indicate adjustment. (In many cases, the measure is of depressive symptoms and not a diagnosable disorder.) Other researchers examine reports of negative or positive affect rather than evaluating diagnostic categories. In their review of the literature on coping with rheumatoid arthritis (RA), Zautra and Manne (1992) found that the majority of studies relied on the absence of negative affect to indicate adjustment. Reports of life quality in various domains also denote adjustment to chronic disease. In this regard, researchers often examine health-related quality of life in physical, functional, social, sexual, and emotional domains (e.g., Cella, 2001; Eton & Lepore, 2001; Eton, Lepore, & Helgeson, 2001; Fitzpatrick, 2004; Ganz, Rowland, Desmond, Meyerowitz, & Wyatt, 1998; Lutgendorf, Antoni, Schneiderman, Ironson, & Fletcher, 1995; Majerovitz & Revenson, 1994; Nayfield, Ganz, Moinpour, Cella, & Hailey, 1992; Ramsey et al., 2000).

These conceptualizations of adjustment to chronic disease reveal that adjustment is multidimensional, including intrapersonal and interpersonal domains, as well as cognitive, emotional, physical, and behavioral components. Further, domains of adjustment are interrelated. For example, negative emotions (e.g., anxiety, depression) contribute to functional status (e.g., poor glycemic control) in people with diabetes (Lustman, 1988; Lustman et al., 2000), and restriction of daily activities accounts for significant variance in depressive symptoms among samples of breast cancer patients (Williamson, 2000) and arthritis patients (DeVellis, Revenson, & Blalock, 1997). An important review by Kiecolt-Glaser, McGuire, Robles, and Glaser (2002) suggests that negative emotions can intensify a variety of health threats, including chronic conditions such as cardiovascular disease, osteoporosis, and cancer.

Adjustment Involves Both Positive and Negative Outcome Dimensions

It is understandable that researchers primarily have studied psychological disorder and negative affect in individuals who confront chronic disease. The growth of American clinical psychology in the latter half of the twentieth century emphasized pathological processes and an individually based approach (Sarason, 1989). Moreover, identifying the prevalence of and contributors to maladjustment is important for the development of effective interventions aimed at reducing distress and life disruption. A relative lack of attention to more positive psychosocial and behavioral processes has persisted until recent years, despite early observations that "many patients are remarkably resourceful even in the face of a catastrophic situation" (Hamburg & Adams, 1967, p. 278).

There are a number of good reasons for evaluating positive indicators of adjustment. First, positive adjustment may more accurately represent the experience of most individuals with chronic disease than does psychopathology. Studies of long-term cancer survivors suggest the greatest degree of distress and disruption within the first year after diagnosis, which corresponds to the initial treatment phase, with adjustment indicators returning to pre-illness levels after that (Dorval, Maunsell, Deschenes, Brisson, & Masse, 1998; Ganz et al., 1998; Levy et al., 1992; Tomich & Helgeson, 2002).

Second, positive adjustment is not simply the absence of psychopathology—a disease that provokes distress in some realms will not necessarily preclude the experience of life's joys. For example, HIV-positive and HIV-negative caregivers of men with AIDS evidenced the combined presence of high depressive symptoms and positive morale (Folkman, Moskowitz, Ozer, & Park, 1997). Although positive and negative affect may become less differentiated under stressful conditions (e.g., Zautra, Smith, Affleck, & Tennen, 2001), focusing solely on psychopathology will result in a limited understanding of adjustment.

Third, positive and negative indicators of adjustment may have different determinants. Distinct coping strategies are related to positive and negative indicators of adjustment (e.g., Echteld, van Elderen, & van der Kamp, 2003; Felton & Revenson, 1984; Stanton, Tennen, Affleck, & Mendola, 1992). Zautra et al. (2001) found that the presence of positive affect reduced the size of the relationship between pain and negative affect among fibromyalgia and arthritis patients.

Fourth, the social construction of chronic disease as guaranteeing clinical depression or unremitting suffering may carry negative consequences. This negative stereotype may provoke inordinate fear or despair in those who initially face serious disease and may even discourage some individuals from seeking lifesaving medical treatments. It also may result in stigmatization of the chronically ill by the layperson, the withholding of support by friends and family, or the overprescription of psychological intervention or psychoactive medications by health care professionals.

Finally, understanding the environmental, interpersonal, and intrapsychic dynamics of individuals who remain resilient or adjust well to chronic disease may enhance our ability to specify protective factors. A recent development in the literature on adjustment to chronic disease is its increasing consideration of positive aspects of adjustment. Two areas that have received attention are post-

traumatic (or stress-related) growth and resilience. Both approaches challenge the assumption that good adjustment is signaled by a return to baseline or premorbid levels of mental health or physical functioning (O'Leary & Ickovics, 1995). Instead, individuals can experience increases in self-awareness, mastery, and enjoyment of life, or even make quantum changes in their life trajectories (Ickovics & Park, 1998).

A number of studies show that people faced with chronic disease not only have high levels of positive affect but also report personal growth that arose out of the disease experience. Echoing many other personal accounts, three-time Tour de France–winning cyclist Lance Armstrong said that cancer was the best thing that ever happened to him, in part because it made him take his sport more seriously, as if he were given a second chance (Specter, 2002). Research is providing more generalizable evidence for these personal testimonies. For example, women have reported more post-traumatic growth associated with their experience of breast cancer, particularly in life appreciation, relations with others, and spiritual change, than have age- and education-matched healthy comparison women reporting on changes experienced during the same time period (Cordova, Cunningham, Carlson, & Andrykowski, 2001).

This phenomenon cuts across chronic disease groups. In a study of married couples coping with one partner's rheumatic disease (Revenson, 2003), even the most psychologically distressed couples reported high levels of personal growth because of the disease. Similarly, large percentages of people with RA (Danoff-Burg & Revenson, 2005), lupus, (Katz, Flasher, Cacciapaglia, & Nelson, 2001), HIV/AIDS (Siegel & Schrimshaw, 2000), and heart disease (Affleck, Tennen, Croog, & Levine, 1987) have reported experiencing benefits as a result of their illness experience. Although questions remain regarding the conceptualization, operationalization, and correlates of posttraumatic growth (see Tedeschi & Calhoun, 2004 [target article and commentaries]; Tomich & Helgeson, 2004), many people with chronic disease appear able to thrive. In addition, positive affect experienced during chronic illness may influence health outcomes (e.g., Moskowitz, 2003).

Of course, unbalanced attention to positive adjustment has a downside. Social construction of the unfailingly "strong" patient allows the chronically ill little room for having a bad day (or a bad year). Worse is the possibility that presenting a positive face becomes so prescriptive that one falls prey to the notion that any distress or negative thinking contributes to physical disease. Holland and Lewis (2000) referred to the "tyranny of positive thinking" (p. 14) in cautioning against such a prescription.

Adjustment Is a Dynamic Process

Although psychologists tend to use language suggesting that adjustment is a static outcome ("Women who were well-adjusted . . ." or "These factors lead to good/bad adjustment . . ."), we are of the view that adjustment to chronic disease is a dynamic process. As treatment demands, life threat, disability, and prognosis change over time, so do the adaptive tasks of illness. As a result, the process of adaptation to disease is continuous but not constant. Although stage theories of adaptation to disease or traumatic events have been proposed, there is little evidence supporting such stage models (Wortman & Silver, 1989, 2001). Owing to changing contextual factors, adaptation is neither linear nor lockstep. Medical advances such as the development of potent antiretroviral therapies for AIDS (Catz & Kelly, 2001), twists and turns in disease progression such as a cancer recurrence or an arthritis flare, and changes in the individual's life context such as taking on new family or work roles create more circuitous pathways.

A breast cancer diagnosis provides a vivid illustration of how adaptation must be seen as a dynamic process. Upon being informed that a breast lump is malignant, women are faced with making medical decisions, informing family members, setting aside, at least temporarily, other demands in one's life (e.g., work), and acknowledging the threat that the diagnosis places on survival. During the postoperative phase, patients are faced with new treatment decisions and then may undergo noxious physical side effects of treatment. During treatment and in the reentry period following treatment, patients are working to maintain interpersonal relationships, resume or reconfigure work and family roles, and grapple with the long-term meaning of the disease. Women also may be faced with an altered self-concept, late effects of medical treatments, repeated or novel treatments, fears of disease recurrence, and, in some cases, actual disease recurrence.

Disease progression clearly colors the adaptational process. Initial severity and prognosis of the disease, how fast or slow the disease worsens, and whether there are symptomatic and asymptomatic periods (and how long they last) all shape adjustment. For example, a slower disease process may allow a gradual and smoother adaptation, as people cope with their disease in smaller bites and anticipatory coping efforts are made for future problems. A disease course marked with frequent transitions from relative health to illness or ability to disability— sometimes without warning—may prove a harder road to follow. For example, the nature of RA involves a long time horizon with periods of relative severity of joint pain, swelling, and stiffness alternating with periods of relative comfort. Medications may be effective for some time and then stop working, necessitating adjustment to a new medical regimen. Interactions with health care providers also change, as patients move from crisis phases to more stable, long-term phases of medical care (Newman, Fitzpatrick, Revenson, Skevington, & Williams, 1996: chap. 6). Moreover, interactions with intimate others can involve alternating periods of relative independence and dependence in functional and emotional realms.

Adjustment Is Embedded in Context

Adjustment to chronic disease can be understood only in conjunction with the life context in which disease occurs (Revenson, 1990, 2003). Adaptive tasks vary within and across diseases. Sociodemographic characteristics such as gender, age, and social class provide culturally acceptable modes of coping and adjustment and, at the same time, place boundaries around coping resources. For example, in a multiethnic sample of women treated for early-stage breast cancer, women's strongest concerns included cancer recurrence, pain, death, harm from adjuvant treatment, and financial issues (Spencer et al., 1999). However, concerns varied as a function of patient characteristics, such that younger women had more prominent sexual and partner-related concerns than older women, and Hispanic women reported a greater degree of concern in almost all areas than African American or non-Hispanic White women.

Moreover, contextual factors are often interdependent. Chronic disease and functional disability are more prevalent in old age, and women live longer than men; therefore, women are likely to be living with at least one chronic condition for some part of their life (and the statistics bear this out). It also is important to consider whether the disease is occurring "on-time" or "off-time" in the normative life cycle (Neugarten, 1979). The onset of a disease that is "off-time," for example, being diagnosed with Parkinson's disease in one's 30s, is likely to be more stressful than when the disease occurs "on-time." One is not prepared for the life transitions or bodily changes that disease brings—there is no period of anticipatory coping. And, relatively few age peers are simultaneously experiencing the same life situation, so there are fewer individuals with whom to share concerns.

Heterogeneity in Adjustment Is the Rule

Research reveals substantial diversity in individuals' adjustment to chronic disease, with most reporting generally positive adjustment, and the minority evidencing significant distress or life disruption. For example, Stewart and colleagues (1989) assessed 9,385 adults at medical office visits in three U.S. cities. Fifty-four percent had at least one of nine chronic conditions (i.e., hypertension, myocardial infarction, congestive heart failure, arthritis, diabetes, angina, chronic lung problems, back problems, gastrointestinal complaints). Compared with those who had no chronic disease, chronic disease patients (except those with hypertension) reported lower functioning in physical, social, and mental health, health perceptions, pain, and role-related domains. However, mental health was the domain least affected by chronic condition, and chronic condition presence explained only a minority of variance in functioning and well-being. Cassileth and colleagues (1984) studied the status on the Mental Health Index of 758 patients with arthritis, diabetes, cancer, renal disease, dermatologic disorders, or depression versus the general public. Patients with chronic disease had more positive psychological status than did depressed outpatients. Psychological status was comparable across groups with different physical diseases and between those groups and the general public.

Research examining clinical levels of psychological dysfunction in groups with chronic disease suggests that the minority manifests such disorders, although rates vary widely across studies. Reviewing research with validated instruments that as-

sessed psychological sequelae of cancer, van't Spijker, Trijsburg, and Duivenvoorden (1997) reported that 0% to 46% of patients qualified for depressive disorder and 0.9% to 49% for anxiety disorder across studies. In a review of the literature on end-stage renal disease, Christensen and Ehlers (2002) reported that 12% to 40% of patients meet criteria for depressive disorder, rates that varied as a function of assessment methods and diagnostic criteria used. In a meta-analysis of 12 studies comparing individuals with RA and healthy controls on measures of depression, Dickens, McGowan, Clark-Carter, and Creed (2002) reported a greater rate of depressive symptoms in the group with RA, although effect sizes were heterogeneous across studies ($r = .07–.43$). In a meta-analytic review of 42 studies of depression in adults with type 1 or type 2 diabetes (Anderson, Clouse, Freedland, & Lustman, 2001), prevalence estimates ranged from 0% to 60.7%. Rates varied as a function of a number of factors, with depression more prevalent in diabetic women than men, uncontrolled than controlled studies, and clinical than community samples, and when assessed by self-report questionnaires versus standardized diagnostic interviews.

Rather than potentiating global psychological dysfunction, chronic disease is likely to carry more circumscribed impact for most people. Andersen and colleagues (e.g., Andersen, Anderson, & deProsse, 1989a, 1989b; Andersen, Woods, & Copeland, 1997) observed that cancer is more likely to produce "islands" of life disruption in particular life realms and at specific points in the disease trajectory than to confer substantial risk for global maladjustment. For example, the most stressful problems endorsed by a heterogeneous group of cancer patients were fear or uncertainty about the future (41%), limitations in physical ability (24%), and pain (12%; Dunkel-Schetter, Feinstein, Taylor, & Falke, 1992). Common sources of distress for persons with diabetes include worry about long-term complications and anxiety/guilt when problems in self-management occur (Polonsky et al., 1995). Any specific disease represents multiple potential stressors or adaptive tasks, which are differentially relevant to individuals in particular life contexts and at different times in the disease's life cycle. Thus, theoretical frameworks that specify risk and protective factors for (mal)adjustment should acknowledge the marked variability in adjustment to chronic disease across persons, time, and settings and should aid in accounting for this variation. Specification of such contributors will allow targeting for intervention individuals and groups with particular characteristics or experiencing particular contexts.

Determinants of Adjustment to Chronic Disease

Over the past quarter century, general psychological theories of stress and coping, self-regulation, personality, and social processes have formed the foundation for understanding adjustment to chronic disease. Rather than describing discrete theories, we adopt the approach of specifying constructs that emerge *across* theories as important determinants of adjustment. We focus on personality orientations, cognitive appraisals, coping processes, and interpersonal support as more proximal determinants of adjustment and on socioeconomic variables, culture, ethnicity, and gender roles as more macro-level determinants of adjustment.

Dispositional Factors

Dispositional variables are likely to have both a direct influence on adjustment to chronic disease and an indirect effect, mediated through appraisals and coping processes. Optimism (Scheier & Carver, 1985), a generalized expectancy for positive outcomes, serves as an example in this regard. Direct relations with adjustment were demonstrated in a study of ischemic heart disease patients, such that optimism assessed 1 month after hospital discharge predicted lower depressive symptoms 1 year later, controlling for depressive symptoms and other variables at study entry (Shnek, Irvine, Stewart, & Abbey, 2001). Assessed prior to coronary artery bypass graft surgery, optimism was associated with more problem-focused coping and lower denial, and optimism predicted faster in-hospital recovery and return to normal life activities 6 months later (Scheier et al., 1989). Controlling for prior distress, optimism predicted lower distress in women with breast cancer at 3, 6, and 12 months after surgery, relations that were mediated partially through coping strategy use, particularly greater acceptance and lower avoidance (Carver et al., 1993; cf. Stanton & Snider, 1993). Optimism also was related to the use of active coping strategies and with lower distress in a sample of HIV-positive and HIV-negative men

(Lutgendorf et al., 1995). These findings suggest that generalized expectancies for favorable outcomes may constitute a protective factor for individuals adjusting to chronic disease.

Dispositional factors also may interact with other variables to influence adjustment. For example, interpersonal stress predicted increases in negative affect and disease activity among arthritis patients only for individuals who had excessive dispositional sensitivity to others' feelings and behavior (Smith & Zautra, 2002). In a sample of breast cancer patients (Stanton et al., 2000), coping through emotional expression predicted decreased distress and fewer medical appointments for cancer-related morbidities for women high in hope, a cognitive-motivational construct reflecting a sense of goal-directed determination and ability to generate plans to achieve goals (Snyder et al., 1991).

Dispositional factors can be assessed in the earliest phases of diagnosis to identify those who might be most at risk for unfavorable adjustment. Understanding the mechanisms through which dispositional variables contribute to adjustment will enable researchers to target mediating mechanisms for intervention. For example, Antoni and colleagues (2001) demonstrated that a cognitive-behavioral stress management intervention was effective in increasing perceived cancer-related benefits for breast cancer patients who were low in dispositional optimism. Whether such psychosocial interventions will promote changes of sufficient magnitude and endurance to affect health and well-being for individuals with long-standing dispositional risk requires further study.

Cognitive Appraisal Processes

Theories of adjustment to chronic disease converge to suggest that how individuals view their disease is a central determinant of subsequent actions, emotions, and adjustment (although theories differ in the specific cognitive processes that receive emphasis). A man who believes that his diagnosis of prostate cancer is a death sentence is likely to make very different decisions regarding treatment than one who sees his cancer as curable, and the two men are likely to manifest distinct adjustment trajectories. In his stress and coping paradigm that underlies much of the literature on adjustment to disease, Richard Lazarus (Lazarus, 1981; Lazarus &

Folkman, 1984; Lazarus & Launier, 1978) assigned central importance to cognitive appraisals in determining subsequent coping processes and adjustment. Two sets of appraisal processes are crucial: primary appraisal, which involves assessment of the degree and nature of threat (i.e., potential for harm) and challenge (i.e., potential for benefit), and secondary appraisal, which reflects an evaluation of the situation's changeability or controllability and the individual's available coping resources. Cognitive variables that have received considerable theoretical and empirical attention as determinants of disease-related adjustment include perceived threats to health and life goals, disease-related expectancies, and finding meaning in the disease experience. Because these have been the central constructs in the past 20 years of research, each will be reviewed briefly.

Perceived Threats to Life Goals

Many theorists have emphasized cognitive appraisals of disease with regard to consequences for one's life goals. In 1991, Lazarus revised his conceptualization of primary appraisal to include dimensions of goal relevance, goal congruence, and type of ego involvement (e.g., meaning of the disease for specific aspects of the self). The self-regulation theory of Carver and Scheier (e.g., 1998), applied to chronic disease (Scheier & Bridges, 1995, pp. 261–262), posits that "illness represents one general and significant class of events that can interfere with the pursuit of life's activities and goals, both those that are health related and those that are not. . . . [Illness] can interfere, to a greater or lesser extent, with the general set of plans and activities that give a person's life its form and meaning." To the extent that one perceives chronic disease as blocking cherished life goals, psychological distress is likely. For example, primary appraisals of threat and harm/loss were important predictors of subsequent anxiety and depression in a study of 372 male cardiac patients (Waltz, Badura, Pfaff, & Schott, 1988). In a daily process study with fibromyalgia patients, Affleck et al. (2001) found that goal-oriented processes (e.g., perceived goal barriers) were associated with pain and fatigue across time; moreover, dispositional optimism affected the relations among goal processes, fatigue, and pain. In a study of Latina women with arthritis, Abraído-Lanza (1997) found that inability to perform valued roles (including housewife/homemaker) as a result of the disease was associated with worse mental health

outcomes. And Lepore and Eton (2000) found that men with prostate cancer who accommodated to their illness by changing significant life goals were less negatively affected by physical dysfunction than men who did not make such accommodations.

The self-regulation theory of Leventhal and his colleagues (e.g., Nerenz & Leventhal, 1983; Leventhal, Leventhal, & Cameron, 2001) also points to the centrality of individuals' appraisals and emphasizes perceived threats to the self-system. As such, coping and adjustment are determined by the individual's cognitive representation of the disease in relation to the self. These relations can be "total," in which the self and the disease are inseparable; "encapsulated," in which a part of the self is diseased but many components are disease free; and "at-risk," in which the self in total or part faces an enduring threat of disease outbreaks. Influences on the link between the self-system and the disease representation include cultural factors, interpersonal interactions, and subjective experiences (e.g., changes in energy level). Individuals with a well-differentiated self-system are likely to acknowledge that the chronic disease may set limits on activities and longevity, but that much of daily life is unaffected by these limits. Thus, those who encapsulate their disease are postulated to be more likely to adapt successfully.

Disease-Related Expectancies

Expectancies regarding the controllability of chronic disease and its consequences are an important cognitive contributor to adjustment (e.g., Lazarus & Folkman, 1984; Thompson & Kyle, 2000). Chronic disease can undermine perceptions of control in several realms, including control of bodily integrity and functioning, daily schedules, performance in valued roles, and life itself. A hallmark of chronic disease is that individuals' active participation in medical treatments and lifestyle modifications cannot ensure control over its course and outcome. Most individuals are likely to discover controllable aspects of their experience, perceiving greater control over disease consequences (e.g., symptoms, daily management) than over disease outcome (e.g., Affleck, Tennen, Pfeiffer, & Fifield, 1987, on RA; Thompson, Nanni, & Levine, 1994, on AIDS; Thompson, Sobolew-Shubin, Galbraith, Schwankovsky, & Cruzen, 1993, on cancer).

Reviewing research on control perceptions among people with chronic disease, Thompson and

Kyle (2000) reported nearly uniform findings that greater general and disease-specific perceived control is associated with favorable psychosocial outcomes and suggestive evidence that physical parameters also are affected. A sense of control predicted less angina in patients following coronary artery bypass grafts (Fitzgerald, Tennen, Affleck, & Pransky, 1993) and better functional status for osteoarthritis surgery patients (Orbell, Jonston, Rowley, Espley, & Davey, 1998). Control appraisals also influence the choice of coping strategies, in that higher perceived control is associated with the use of more approach-oriented coping strategies (e.g., Felton, Revenson, & Hinrichsen, 1984; Folkman, Chesney, Pollack, & Coates, 1993).

Thompson and Kyle (2000) did note that the relation between perceived control and adjustment outcomes varied according to how control and adjustment were measured. However, they could not discern a ready explanation for the inconsistencies across studies. They suggested that having control over aspects of the disease is useful only to the extent that one desires such control. They also concluded that expectancies for control did not need to match realistic opportunities for control to be useful, although others have suggested that the adaptive potential of control appraisals may depend on whether the threat is responsive to control attempts (Christensen & Ehlers, 2002; Helgeson, 1992; Stanton et al., 2001). For example, Thompson and her colleagues (1993) found that cancer patients' belief that they could control daily emotional and physical symptoms was a stronger predictor of adjustment than was perceived control over long-term disease progression. Affleck and colleagues (1987) found that individuals with severe rheumatic disease who perceived more control over *symptoms* reported less mood disturbance, whereas those who perceived more control over *disease course* had greater mood disturbance. Schiaffino and Revenson (1992) further elaborated on these processes, showing that perceived control over symptoms—an aspect of RA that is controllable—as opposed to perceived control over the course of the disease was instrumental in generating positive affect and better adjustment.

Individuals' expectancies regarding their own disease-related responses, efficacy, and disease outcomes also may contribute to adjustment. For example, self-efficacy expectancies predict symptom management and adjustment in individuals

with arthritis and other chronic conditions (DeVellis & DeVellis, 2001; Keefe, Smith, et al., 2002; Schiaffino, Revenson, & Gibofsky, 1991). In a study of breast cancer patients, Montgomery and Bovbjerg (2001) found that response expectancies regarding nausea predicted anticipatory nausea prior to the third chemotherapy infusion, even after controlling for severity of prior posttreatment nausea and prior anticipatory nausea. Focusing on outcome expectancies, Carver and his colleagues (Carver et al., 2000; Carver & Scheier, 1998) argued that the crucial element in predicting well-being is an expectancy of *whether* a desired outcome is likely to occur rather than *how* it will occur (e.g., through personal control). Thus, perceived control is important to the extent that it contributes to positive outcome expectancies. These researchers reported that the expectancy of remaining cancer free was related to lower distress in two samples of breast cancer patients, but that perceived control over disease outcome was not (Carver et al., 2000). The expectancy that a desired outcome (e.g., cure) will occur may be the final common pathway through which other determinants of adjustment (e.g., perceived control) operate.

Commenting on the Carver et al. findings, Folkman and Moskowitz (2000) noted that the relative importance of outcome versus control expectancies may depend on the person-environment context, including stable preferences for control and consequences of control attempts for other life arenas. In another commentary, Tennen and Affleck (2000) argued that the question of the importance of personal control may need to be supplanted by other, more precise questions that consider the complexities of expectancies, adjustment, and contextual factors: "'When in the course of a medical threat are control perceptions most important?' 'How do the targets of control change over time?' and 'Which aspects of adjustment are most influenced by the perception of personal control?'" (p. 153). Clearly, several types of disease-related expectancies (e.g., response, control, and outcome expectancies) may affect adaptive outcomes, and their relative predictive power in specific contexts requires continued scrutiny.

Finding Meaning

What does it mean to "find meaning" in chronic disease (Park & Folkman, 1997; Tedeschi & Calhoun, 1995; Thompson & Janigian, 1988)? Janoff-Bulman and Frantz (1997) wrote of two different forms of meaning sought by individuals in the aftermath of trauma, which may be applicable in the context of chronic illness. First, meaning as comprehensibility represents an attempt to determine whether and how an event makes sense and often involves causal attribution processes. In her cognitive adaptation theory, Taylor (1983) focused on the search for meaning as an individual's attempts to address the question, "Why me?" Taylor found that more than 90% of a breast cancer sample advanced some causal attribution for the cancer. The specific content of the attribution was not important for psychological adjustment, but simply making some attribution for the cancer was related to adjustment. In a review addressing the experience of threatening events in general, including chronic disease, Tennen and Affleck (1990) reported a consistent relationship between the specific external attribution of blaming others for an event and poorer well-being.

According to Janoff-Bulman and Frantz (1997), a second form of finding meaning involves meaning as significance, which reflects the value of the experience to the individual. The two forms of finding meaning are linked in that the search for comprehensibility often prompts a newfound awareness of personal vulnerability and randomness, which in turn paves the way for an attempt to create meaning in life "by generating significance through appraisals of value and worth" (Janoff-Bulman & Berger, 2000, p. 33). If the diagnosis of chronic disease is sufficiently disruptive to core beliefs (i.e., meaningfulness of the world, benevolence of others, self-worthiness), it should prompt such a search for meaning and concomitant greater awareness of and attention to living. Commenting on this enhanced awareness, a participant in the first author's research lamented that she was beginning to lose "the edge." She went on to explain that, 2 years after her breast cancer diagnosis, she found herself living more on "automatic pilot," losing the sense of immediacy and appreciation for the present moment that her cancer diagnosis had catalyzed.

Janoff-Bulman and Berger (2000) argued that if the reality of death is prompted by the trauma, then a greater appreciation for what it means to be alive can ensue: "That which we may lose suddenly is perceived as valuable" (p. 35). If benevolence and self-worth are questioned, then others' reactions can assume special significance and, depending on their content, can promote greater appreciation for inti-

mate relationships. Self-appreciation also can increase as individuals discover their own competencies in overcoming adversity. Thus, the search for meaning as significance can lead one to find benefits in the chronic disease experience, perhaps particularly to the extent that the disease is perceived as life-threatening.

Although no comprehensive review specific to chronic disease is available, Tennen and Affleck (2002) reviewed the literature on the association between benefit finding and adjustment to adversity, including studies of HIV infection, life-threatening disease, and natural disaster. Fourteen of 20 cross-sectional studies revealed an association of benefit finding and better adjustment. Moreover, 6 longitudinal studies and 2 daily process studies demonstrated that perceiving benefits predicted enhanced psychological adjustment and decreased morbidity, and in one study of bereaved HIV-positive men (Bower, Kemeny, Taylor, & Fahey, 1998), benefit finding also predicted decreased mortality and lowered daily functional impairment. Tennen and Affleck (2002) went on to pose alternative views of the conceptualization of benefit finding (e.g., benefit finding as a personality attribute, a reflection of growth/change, an explanation of temperament, a temporal or other comparison), a construct that deserves increased theoretical and empirical attention.

Coping Processes

It is difficult to imagine that the behaviors the individual initiates in response to the demands of chronic disease would not make a difference in that person's ensuing adjustment. Indeed, although limited by problems in conceptualization, measurement, and methodology (Coyne & Gottlieb, 1996; Coyne & Racioppo, 2000; Danoff-Burg, Ayala, & Revenson, 2000; Somerfield & McCrae, 2000), findings from the large literature on coping processes as contributors to adjustment warrant a conclusion that coping matters.

Broadly, coping efforts may be directed toward relative approach or avoidance of aspects of the experience of chronic disease (Roth & Cohen, 1986; Suls & Fletcher, 1985; Tobin, Holroyd, Reynolds, & Wigal, 1989). This approach-avoidance continuum also reflects a fundamental motivational construct in humans and other animals (Carver & Scheier, 1998; Davidson, Jackson, & Kalin, 2000;

Fox, 1991) and thus maps easily onto broader theories of functioning. Examples of approach-oriented or active coping processes are information seeking, problem solving, seeking social support, actively attempting to identify benefits in one's experience, and creating outlets for emotional expression. Coping oriented toward avoidance involves both cognitive (e.g., denial, distraction, suppression) and behavioral strategies (e.g., behavioral disengagement). Other processes, such as spiritual coping, potentially can serve either approach-oriented or avoidance goals (e.g., Abraído-Lanza, Guier, & Revenson, 1996).

Because chronic disease is by definition a long-term stressor, both the types of coping strategies that are used and their utility are likely to vary over time and across specific disease-related adaptive tasks. Although avoidant coping may be useful at specific, acute points of crisis, reviewers of the literature on chronic disease concur that avoidance typically is associated with maladjustment over time (Maes, Leventhal, & De Ridder, 1996; Stanton et al., 2001; but see Bonanno, 2004, regarding repressive coping). An example is Levine and colleagues' (1987) longitudinal study of male cardiac patients. In this sample, men who denied their disease spent fewer days in the coronary care unit and had fewer indications of cardiac dysfunction during hospitalization than nondeniers. However, deniers were less adherent to exercise training and had more days of rehospitalization in the year after discharge. As another example, breast cancer patients who were high on coping through cognitive avoidance prior to breast biopsy reported more distress at that point, after cancer diagnosis, and after surgery than did less avoidant women (Stanton & Snider, 1993; see also Carver et al., 1993). Coping through avoidance may involve harmful behaviors (e.g., alcohol use), paradoxically prompt intrusion of disease-relevant thoughts and emotions (Wegner & Pennebaker, 1992), or impede other coping attempts.

Are active coping processes oriented toward approaching stressful aspects of chronic disease more useful than avoidant strategies? Although the findings are not as consistent as those for avoidant coping (Maes et al., 1996; Stanton et al., 2001), evidence exists for the utility of approach-oriented strategies. For example, Young (1992) concluded from the literature on RA that "active, problem-focused coping attempts (e.g., information seeking, cognitive restructuring, pain control, and rational

thinking) were consistently associated with positive affect, better psychological adjustment, and decreased depression" (p. 621; see also Keefe, Smith, et al., 2002). The demonstrated efficacy of interventions that encourage the use of approach-oriented strategies such as problem solving and cognitive or emotional processing also suggests the utility of approach-oriented coping (e.g., Antoni et al., 2000; Smyth, Stone, Hurewitz, & Kaell, 1999).

Why is there inconsistent support for the contribution of approach-oriented coping to adjustment in naturalistic studies? Determining the association between approach-oriented coping and adaptive outcomes is complicated by the likelihood that some approach-oriented strategies (e.g., problem solving) may not be particularly effective for immutable aspects of the disease. Further, avoidant coping may be the more powerful predictor of adjustment when both approach and avoidant coping strategies are examined simultaneously. In addition, avoidance- and approach-oriented strategies may be differentially predictive of negative and positive outcomes (e.g., Blalock, DeVellis, & Giorgino, 1995; Echteld et al., 2003). Thus, the exclusion of positive adjustment indicators in many studies may obscure the potentially beneficial effects of approach-oriented coping processes.

Finally, coping is likely to contribute to adjustment in the context of other factors. For example, the combination of high avoidance-oriented coping and low social support was identified as a risk factor for posttransplant psychological disturbance in adults awaiting bone marrow transplant for cancer (Jacobsen et al., 2002), and coping interacted with control perceptions in a study of breast cancer patients (Osowiecki & Compas, 1999), such that women who had high perceived personal control had low distress when they used active, problem-focused coping strategies. It is unreasonable to expect that coping processes alone would determine adjustment to chronic disease. Rather, coping strategies are likely to mediate relations between more enduring personality attributes and adjustment and to interact with other factors in contributing to adjustment. For example, in a longitudinal study of women with RA, avoidance coping both mediated and moderated the effect of the personality disposition of unmitigated communion on functional disability (Danoff-Burg, Revenson, Trudeau, & Paget, 2004). Rather than focusing solely on coping processes as contributors to adjustment, researchers testing more complex models (i.e., examining mediation and moderation) in longitudinal designs are producing stronger and more ecologically relevant findings (e.g., Schiaffino & Revenson, 1992).

Social Resources and Interpersonal Support

A wealth of research over the past two decades has demonstrated that the quality of interpersonal relationships is a strong predictor of adjustment to chronic disease (Cohen, Underwood, & Gottlieb, 2000; Sarason, Sarason, & Gurung, 2001; Schmaling & Sher, 2000; Wills & Fegan, 2001). Most of the adaptive tasks of chronic disease require help from others. Thus, patients need an available and satisfying network of interpersonal relations on which they can count for both emotional sustenance and more practical help during periods of pain, disability, and uncertainty. Broadly defined, *social support* refers to the processes by which interpersonal relationships promote psychological well-being and protect people from health declines, particularly when they are facing stressful life circumstances (Cohen, Gottlieb, & Underwood, 2000). Supportive behaviors involve demonstrations that one is loved, valued, and cared for, as well as the provision of helpful information or tangible assistance.

An important distinction has been made between structural aspects of social ties and the functional resources that flow through existing ties (e.g., Berkman & Glass, 1999). Examples of structural measures are marital status, frequency of social activities, size of the social network, and network density (i.e., how many network members know each other). In contrast, the functions of support include (1) expressing positive affect; (2) validating beliefs, emotions and actions; (3) encouraging communication of feelings; (4) providing information or advice; (5) providing material aid; and (6) reminding recipients that they are part of a meaningful social group. Although, in principle, functional measures of support should not be dependent on the size of the individual's social network, the networks and social activities of ill or disabled individuals often are restricted because of the disease. Yet social integration and satisfaction with one's social ties are related to disease adjustment in different ways. In a study of women with RA (Goodenow, Reisine, & Grady, 1990), perceptions that one received adequate emotional caring, task assistance, and ego support were related to home and family role functioning, whereas social integration was not. Similarly, in other studies of RA patients, Fitzpatrick and his colleagues (Fitzpatrick, Newman, Lamb, & Shipley, 1988; Fitzpatrick, Newman, Archer, & Shipley, 1991) found that satisfaction with one's social relationships was more strongly related to psychological well-being than measures of the availability of those relationships.

By and large, most of the work on the effects of social relationships on health has focused on its benefits. Yet, receiving, using, or requesting social support has its costs as well (Rook, 1998). In looking at the "negative" effects of social support, it is important to distinguish between negative social interactions and social support attempts that backfire. The former involves criticism ("You never handle your pain well") or angry outbursts ("*Your* pain is ruining *my* life!") that never were meant to be supportive or helpful. In contrast, many well-intended attempts at helping go awry, for example, giving advice or providing feedback that patients do not perceive as helpful. Support may be perceived as problematic when it is neither desired, needed, nor requested, or when the type of support offered does not match the recipient's needs (Revenson, 1993). It is also important to distinguish problematic support exchanges from the absence of support, where no offers of help or statements of concern are made.

The perception of network members as unreceptive to efforts to discuss stressful or traumatic events has been referred to as *social constraints*. According to Lepore's (2001) social-cognitive processing model, discussing stressful events in a supportive, uncritical social environment allows people to process their emotions, maintain or reestablish a positive self-concept, and find meaning. Disclosure of stressful experiences may regulate emotion by changing the focus of attention, increasing habituation to negative emotions, and facilitating positive cognitive reappraisals of threats (Stanton & Danoff-Burg, 2002). Persons with breast, colon, or prostate cancer who perceive that others are unreceptive to hearing about their experiences often have poorer psychological adjustment than those who view their social networks as more receptive (Lepore, 2001). Cordova and his colleagues (2001) found that social constraints were associated with lower well-being and greater depression among women with breast cancer (see also Stanton et al., 2000); similar findings among women with RA are reported by Danoff-Burg and her colleagues (2004).

The psychological benefits of supportive relationships have been examined in many studies of persons with chronic disease. Compared with those reporting less support, patients receiving more support from friends and family exhibit greater self-esteem and life satisfaction, cope more effectively, and exhibit fewer depressive symptoms. The relationship between social support and better psychosocial adjustment is robust across studies of populations with different disease durations, when extremely different measures of support are used, and in both cross-sectional and longitudinal analyses. Moreover, social support contributes to psychosocial adjustment after controlling for prior levels of adjustment (i.e., social support helps explain *changes* in psychosocial adjustment).

Two theoretical models have been used in the majority of studies to explain how social support affects psychological adjustment. The stress-buffering model holds that support acts as a protective factor at times of crisis, serving to cushion the individual against the deleterious effects of stress. In contrast, the direct effects model proposes that support is beneficial regardless of the degree of stress experienced (i.e., more support is correlated with a better outcome across the board). Overall, empirical evidence for the direct effects model is found when support is conceptualized in terms of social integration (structural measures), whereas the stress-buffering model seems to describe the data when the functions of support are measured (Cohen & Wills, 1985).

However, more recent conceptualizations and empirical tests reach the conclusion that social support affects adjustment outcomes through a number of physiological, emotional, and cognitive pathways (see Wills & Fegan, 2001, Figure 12.3, for an array of mediational models). Social support enables recipients to use effective coping strategies by helping them come to a better understanding of the problem faced, increasing motivation to take instrumental action, and reducing emotional stress, which may impede other coping efforts (see also Taylor, this volume; Thoits, 1986). Support may encourage the performance of positive health behaviors, thus preventing or minimizing disease and symptom reporting. Or it may minimize physiological reactivity to stress or boost immune function.

Support from family members also may serve to enhance lay or professional treatment interventions. An elegantly designed study of patients with RA by Radojevic, Nicassio, and Weissman (1992) examined social support as an adjuvant to other intervention techniques. Patients were randomly assigned to one of three conditions (cognitive behavioral therapy with family support, cognitive behavioral therapy without family support, education with family support) or a no-treatment control group. In the behavior therapy conditions, patients were taught cognitive coping techniques (e.g., visual imagery), relaxation, and deep breathing. The behavior therapy with family support condition taught family members how to reinforce behavioral techniques and coping. In the education with family support condition, videotaped information was presented to patients and their family members, and group leaders facilitated discussions but did not provide behavioral training. Although there was general improvement across the study period, patients assigned to the two behavior therapy conditions had decreased severity and number of swollen joints (postintervention and 2 months later) compared with participants assigned to the education with family support or control conditions. More important, immediately after treatment, the behavior therapy with family support condition showed greater improvement than all other groups on disease status and maintained its initial treatment gains.

Another theoretical perspective suggests that social support is most beneficial when it matches the characteristics of the stressor faced. The matching hypothesis (Cutrona & Russell, 1990) maintains that certain types of social support are beneficial when they fit the contextual features of the stressor, including desirability, controllability, duration, timing, and social roles. The matching hypothesis also suggests that the effectiveness of support may hinge on a fit between the recipient's support needs and the amount or type of support received. For example, a recently diagnosed patient may desire concrete information to make a medical decision; a more disabled patient may prefer help with activities in daily living combined with companionship (Lanza, Cameron, & Revenson, 1995). Alternately, misfit may involve discrepancies between amount and quality of support desired and received; if the support provided exceeds the support required, feelings of infantilization or dependency may ensue

(Revenson, 1993). Who is providing support may be another critical aspect of the matching hypothesis. Different people serve different supportive functions within the network, so that it is the support network *as a whole* that fulfills the individual's needs (Dakof & Taylor, 1990, Lanza et al., 1995).

Most studies of the effects of support on adjustment to disease have been cross-sectional; thus, whether support benefits can be maintained over the lifetime course of a chronic disease is at question. Social support is often conceptualized and measured as fairly stable, whereas stressors, coping efforts, and patterns of psychological adjustment are assumed to fluctuate as disease status changes. Yet the composition of patients' social networks— even the closest family ties—may change over time in quantity or quality. For example, in a longitudinal study of breast cancer survivors, women who were treated with breast-conserving surgery reported less social support 3 months after surgery than women who were treated with mastectomy, although there had been no differences in perceived support immediately after surgery (Levy et al., 1992). Whether this is a result of the fact that women who had breast-conserving surgery were younger or that others saw them as healthier and as needing less support could not be discerned. Understanding how social supports, social constraints, and negative interpersonal interactions operate to influence adjustment and health end points over the course of chronic disease is a rich area for study.

Macro-Level Contextual Factors

Previously, we suggested that adaptational processes could be understood only in conjunction with the life context in which disease occurs. Although myriad contextual factors might shape adjustment to chronic disease, we focus on several macro-level factors that have been shown to affect health-behavior processes: socioeconomic status (SES), culture, ethnicity, and gender roles (see also Whitfield, Weidner, Clark, & Anderson, 2002; Yali & Revenson, 2004). These contextual influences cannot be neatly separated from each other and most likely affect health outcomes through more proximal mechanisms. Culture influences health, for example, by shaping health beliefs and cognitions (Landrine & Klonoff, 1992), which are strengthened by feedback from social ties and socialization practices (Berkman & Glass, 1999).

Berkman and Glass (1999) distinguish between upstream and downstream contextual factors that affect health (see also Link & Phelan, 1995). In their conceptual model, culture, SES, politics, and social change (e.g., urbanization) affect social network structure; these are the upstream or more distal contextual factors. Social networks, in turn, provide opportunities for psychosocial mechanisms (e.g., social support, access to resources) to influence health through behavioral and physiological pathways; these are the downstream or more proximal factors. Taylor, Repetti, and Seeman (1997) propose a similar conceptualization. In their model, SES and race most likely affect health indirectly through their influence on key environments, including the physical environment in which one lives and works and the social environment of interpersonal relationships. A contextual approach (Anderson & McNeilly, 1991; Ickovics, Thayaparan, & Ethier, 2001; Revenson, 1990, 2003) recognizes the interdependence of individuals' behavior and their life situations, as well as the complex associations *among* contexts. At the same time as they are independent determinants of adjustment, contextual variables are seen as setting the stage on which personality, appraisal, and coping processes operate.

Socioeconomic Status

Although the United States has prided itself on being a classless society in which anyone can better her or his life circumstances, disparities between the "haves" and "have-nots" are marked and growing. According to data from the Congressional Budget Office, income disparities grew more sharply between 1995 and 1997 than in any other 2-year period since 1979 (Shapiro & Greenstein, 2001). In social science research, socioeconomic status has been conceptualized alternately as financial status (income), occupational status, or educational status (or some combination of these), or the position in society into which one is born (which creates hierarchies of majority and minority statuses). In the past, ethnic minority group status was used as an indicator of SES, but more recent research has attempted to untangle the unique influences of ethnicity and social class.

Adler and her colleagues (1994) provided compelling data to show that socioeconomic status is an important correlate—if not determinant—of health status, morbidity, and mortality. Reviewing a number of large-scale studies in the United States and Western Europe, they documented an inverse graded association between SES and morbidity, mortality, and prevalence and course of disease at all levels of SES; that is, morbidity and mortality do not increase only at the lowest levels of SES, but rather a graded relationship occurs at all levels of SES. However, it still holds that rates of chronic disease are higher among less prosperous groups, as are rates of activity restrictions and the extent of impairment and decrement in functional abilities that stem from chronic disease.

Socioeconomic status affects health outcomes both independently and through its linkages with psychosocial factors, such as attitudes and behaviors, and access to and quality of medical care, particularly preventive care. That is, persons of lower SES may not only experience more psychosocial risks and deficits in the care they receive, but also may be more vulnerable to them (Williams, 1990). Access to medical care, however, is not a sufficient explanatory variable for the SES-health gradient (Adler, Boyce, Chesney, Folkman, & Syme, 1993; Meyerowitz, Richardson, Hudson, & Leedham, 1998; Williams, 1990), and recent work has given greater attention to psychosocial and behavioral variables as mediating mechanisms. For example, SES has been linked both to risky health behaviors, such as stress, smoking, and alcohol use, and to more health-protective health behaviors, such as exercise, health attitudes, and social ties (Adler et al., 1994). Individuals of lower SES experience more stressful life events and events of greater magnitude and have fewer social and psychosocial resources to cope with them, which leads to poorer mental and physical health (Gallo & Matthews, 2003).

Living in poverty is often conceptualized as the low end of the socioeconomic scale, but poverty and its correlates (e.g., low education) may provide a qualitatively different context in which individuals cope with disease. In addition to signaling a lack of fundamental resources, poverty often creates a sense of helplessness and hopelessness. In a study of more than 1,400 individuals with RA followed over 5 years, Callahan, Cordray, Wells, and Pincus (1996) found that a higher sense of helplessness entirely mediated the relation between lower education and early mortality. The constant struggle for resources to meet basic human needs may severely constrain coping resources (e.g., Belle, 1982; Mullings & Wali, 2001) and obviate the "search for

meaning" in disease that is afforded more privileged groups. Clearly, more research needs to be conducted to understand the mechanisms behind the SES-health gradient.

Culture

A central component of context is culture: contexts, and the behaviors and interactions that take place within them, are infused with values, belief systems, and worldviews that emanate from cultural phenomena. The concept of culture is applicable across standard social categories, including race, gender, ethnicity, nationality, religious preference, sexual orientation, and disability status. Most conceptualizations of culture include external referents, such as customs, artifacts, and social institutions, and internal referents such as ideologies, belief systems, attitudes, expectations, and epistemologies.

Adaptation to disease occurs within one or more cultural contexts. Cultural contexts supply blueprints for adaptation to disease—how meaning is given to events, which behaviors are appropriate in which situations, and what competencies are valued by group members. These blueprints or cultural schemata provide the various cultural lenses that inform people's worldviews, for example, whether one should follow the advice of "traditional" medical providers or turn to culturally sanctioned healers (McClain, 1989). Cultural blueprints also shape cognitive appraisals of disease (Landrine & Klonoff, 1992), guide treatment decisions (Rubel & Garro, 1992), and determine how illness is defined and expressed. For example, in Latina cultures the condition of *nervios* blurs the distinction between physical and mental illness, and in some societies with high poverty rates or a totalitarian government the expression of illness is a behavioral manifestation of powerlessness, particularly among women (Low, 1985, 1995). Culture also may define the acceptability of particular coping responses, such as emotional expression or anger, and thus their value as adaptive mechanisms.

Ethnicity

Social science researchers typically use demographic markers or proxy variables (e.g., Hispanic, Black, nationality, immigrant status) to define ethnic minority groups or nonmainstream cultural groups and to denote health-promoting or health-damaging behaviors (Matthews, 1989). These demographic distinctions are then used in between-group studies to document group differences. Meyerowitz and her colleagues (1998) reviewed the literature on ethnic differences in cancer outcomes and predictors of those outcomes, and found differences in beliefs and attitudes, variables that are related to preventive behavior. They also found overall differences in screening behavior (clinical breast exams, Pap smears, mammography), delay in seeking treatment, and follow-up of abnormal findings, all of which can lead to being diagnosed at a later (and less treatable) stage of cancer, and subsequent lower survival rates and quality of life. Interactions with health care providers also differed among ethnic groups, which also are related to screening, follow-up, and treatment decisions.

It is to their credit that Meyerowitz and her coauthors do not stop at describing the ethnic group differences found—they critique their own review in terms of the studies used to make their conclusions (e.g., few studies and possibly biased samples). They examine macro-level contextual influences that might affect or be confounded with these findings, such as SES. Broad ethnic group markers are insufficient to define any cultural group (Marin & Marin, 1991; Vega, 1992), and between-group studies do little to illuminate adaptational processes. The norms, values, and experiences of different cultural subgroups, for example, Dominicans and Puerto Ricans, may be as large as those between racial or ethnic groups (Bernal & Enchautegui-de-Jesus, 1994). Moreover, individuals may be members of multiple cultural or social groups—that is, as defined by socioeconomic, regional, or other factors—that condition the meaning of cultural categories.

It is unlikely that simple proxy variables adequately capture the cultural blueprints for adaptation to disease inherent in an ethnic or cultural community. Data based on such nominal categories as ethnic group membership may not provide information about factors that may explain *why* group differences occur. For example, in a study of men who have sex with men (Valleroy et al., 2000), the HIV prevalence rate for Latinos was twice that of Whites and, for African Americans, prevalence was 6 times that of Whites. But these data do not inform us what it is *within* the groups that might account for the differences *between* the groups or why. As Meyerowitz and her colleagues (1998) have written, "The classification of people into racial or ethnic groups becomes meaningful only when the classification leads to a better understanding of the factors that have led to disparity in disease treatment and health outcome" (p. 49).

Moreover, ethnic categorization does not lead us to those answers when it is confounded with poverty or with SES. Poverty does not fully account for race differences in health; as explained earlier, these differences occur at every level of the SES gradient. Instead, our understanding of variation in health outcomes might increase if we consider the psychological manifestations of ethnicity, such as discrimination or racism, and the effects of these manifestations on health and adjustment to disease (Clark, Anderson, Clark, & Williams, 1999). For example, Guyll, Matthews, and Bromberger (2001) found that African American women who attributed interpersonal mistreatment to racial discrimination exhibited greater diastolic blood pressure reactivity to a laboratory stressor that bore similarities to an encounter with racial prejudice. Similarly, Lepore et al. (2006) found that relative to White American women, Black American women showed significantly greater diastolic blood pressure reactivity, slower systolic blood pressure recovery, and faster heart rate recovery in response to a racial stressor than to a nonracial stressor. These findings suggest that perceived racism may act as a stressor that adversely affects longer-term cardiovascular health outcomes, and that the effect may be mediated by pathogenic events associated with physiological reactivity.

Gender Roles

Many psychological theories of "healthy adjustment" are influenced by cultural beliefs about gender roles. For example, dominant assumptions of mental health are that one should fight an illness; use active, instrumental, problem-solving efforts; and be self-reliant, drawing on one's inner resources. These ways of coping not only are correlated with better adjustment in many studies but also constitute the definition of better adjustment. The finding that female chronic disease patients have lower psychological well-being than their male counterparts (e.g., DeVellis et al., 1997; Hagedoorn et al., 2000) mirrors the literature on gender differences in depression in the general population (Gore & Colten, 1991). Although depression is often related to pain, disability, and disease severity, these factors do not fully explain observed gender differences in adjustment to disease.

A few examples may help illustrate how gender socialization translates into differentially effective modes of coping with illness that ultimately affect adjustment. In the area of personality, the gender-linked personality orientations of *agency* and *communion* (and their extreme forms, *unmitigated agency* and *unmitigated communion*) have been explored with respect to adjustment to a number of chronic diseases (see Helgeson & Fritz, 1998; Helgeson, 1994, for reviews). Individuals with an agentic orientation focus more on themselves and use more instrumental, problem-solving strategies to cope with stress. Individuals with a more communal orientation focus on others' needs and interpersonal relationships, and are more emotionally expressive. Unmitigated agency involves an extreme orientation toward oneself without regard for others and difficulty expressing emotions; unmitigated communion refers to an extreme orientation toward others, in which individuals become overinvolved with others to the detriment of their own well-being. These personality orientations were conceptualized originally as gender-linked traits, such that agency (instrumentality) was seen as representing one aspect of masculinity and communion (expressiveness) as one aspect of femininity. Consistent with this conceptualization, men typically score higher than women on measures of agency, and women typically score higher than men on measures of communion.

Agency has been linked to better physical and mental health across a number of chronic diseases, including coronary heart disease (Helgeson, 1990, 1993), prostate cancer (Helgeson & Lepore, 1997), diabetes (Helgeson, 1994), and RA (Trudeau, Danoff-Burg, Revenson, & Paget, 2003). Unmitigated agency, however, has been related to greater difficulty in expressing emotions, which in turn was associated with negative general and cancer-related adjustment in a group of men with prostate cancer (Helgeson & Lepore, 1997). Unmitigated communion has been associated with delays in seeking early treatment for cardiac symptoms (Helgeson, 1990), failure to adhere to recommended lifestyle changes following hospital discharge for a first coronary event (Helgeson, 1993), poor health behavior, negative social interactions, and greater depression and cardiac symptoms following a first coronary event (Fritz, 2000), poorer metabolic control and greater psychological distress among female adolescents with diabetes (Helgeson & Fritz, 1996), and greater

functional disability and depressive symptoms among women and men with RA (Trudeau et al., 2003). Helgeson (1993, 1994) has suggested that an unbridled focus on others leads to self-neglect.

A number of researchers, coming from different theoretical perspectives, have concluded that interpersonal relationships are essential components of women's coping with major stressors such as disease (Revenson, 1994). Women draw on their support networks more often; these interpersonal contacts serve as a place to express emotions, acquire feedback on coping choices, and obtain assistance with life tasks, such as child care. Women are more likely to ask for support, use support, and not feel demeaned by it (Shumaker & Hill, 1991). Women's focus on interpersonal relationships may create both additional stresses (Wethington, McLeod, & Kessler, 1987) and benefits (Brown, Nesse, Vinokur, & Smith, 2003); women are often taking care of others while they, themselves, are coping with a chronic condition (Revenson, 2003; Revenson, Abraído-Lanza, Majerovitz, & Jordan, 2005). Studies of chronic diseases such as cancer, heart disease, and arthritis have found that women report more psychological distress than men whether they are the patient or the caregiver (Hagedoorn et al., 2000; Revenson, 2003; Rohrbaugh et al., 2002). A prominent explanation for this is that caring for others is a more central aspect of women's identity (Gilligan, 1982), and the loss of that role is too great a threat to self-esteem and well-being to abandon (Abraído-Lanza, 1997). Thus, whether they are the patient or the caregiving partner, women continue to focus on others and maintain their domestic roles, both of which can create added stress (Revenson, 2003).

It is difficult to isolate the effect of gender on adaptation to disease. Because many diseases vary in their prevalence among men and women, most studies of adaptation to disease include respondents of only one sex or couples in which either men or women have the chronic disease (e.g., men with prostate cancer and their wives). Thus, if we detect differences in adjustment to disease, we cannot disentangle the influences of the disease context and of gender, or conclude whether the experience of coping with the "same" disease differs for men and women. For example, the majority of studies of adaptation to myocardial infarction involve male patients and female spouses. After a heart attack, men tend to reduce their work activities and responsibilities and are nurtured by their wives. In contrast, after returning home from the hospital, women resume household responsibilities more quickly, including taking care of other family members, and report receiving a greater amount of help from adult daughters and neighbors than from their healthy husbands (Rose, Suls, Green, Lounsbury, & Gordon, 1996). Michela (1987) found such substantial differences in husbands' and wives' experience that he wrote, "*His* experience is filtered through concerns about surviving and recovering from the MI with a minimum of danger or discomfort, while *her* experience is filtered through the meaning of the marital relationship to her—what the marriage has provided and, hence, what is threatened by the husband's potential death or what is lost by his disability" (p. 272). Are these completely different *his* and *her* experiences, or are they experiences created by the role of patient versus partner/caregiver?

Gender seldom has been examined in conjunction with other contextual factors for their synergistic influences. For example, the literature on gender differences in mortality or morbidity rarely examines whether these gender differences are influenced by socioeconomic status. Yet the magnitude of socioeconomic gradients in health and mortality varies by gender; for example, cardiovascular mortality and morbidity exhibit a steeper gradient for women than for men (MacIntyre & Hunt, 1997). Moreover, gender often places constraints on financial, educational, and occupational aspirations (Coriell & Adler, 1996).

As is the case with ethnicity and other contextual factors, identifying contributors to and mechanisms for gender-related effects is essential. Taylor and her colleagues (2000) proposed a tend-and-befriend model to characterize stress responses that are more uniquely female. Drawing evidence from hundreds of studies of humans and other animals, they argued that adaptive responses to stress in females is likely to involve efforts to tend, that is, to nurture the self and others, and to befriend, that is, to create and maintain social networks in order to provide protection from external threats. The authors suggested that these behaviors are likely to be prompted by the biobehavioral attachment/caregiving system, which depends in part on hormonal mechanisms in interaction with social, cultural, and environmental input. The intersection of biological and environmental influences on gender

differences in adjustment to chronic disease is a promising area for study.

Interventions to Enhance Adjustment to Chronic Disease: Implications of the Person-Context Fit

The fact that adaptation is a function of both persons and their environments (French, Rodgers, & Cobb, 1974; Lewin, 1951/1997) suggests multiple points for intervention, some directed at changing persons, some aimed at changing environments, and others targeted toward improving person-environment fit. The macro-level contextual factors described earlier—SES, culture, ethnicity, and gender roles—cannot be changed (or changed easily) without social intervention. System-level interventions are necessary to decrease barriers to health care and socioeconomic disparities, for example. At the same time, practitioners can work toward improving the interpersonal context through teaching patients how to develop and maintain social ties, recognize and accept others' help and emotional encouragement, or change their appraisals of the support they are receiving. These goals are not mutually exclusive. For example, interventions that help patients positively evaluate the meaning of the disease in their lives often involve the goal of strengthening existing family ties.

Most psychosocial interventions are directed primarily toward individual-level change (although they often are conducted in a group format) and are multimodal, involving cognitive-behavioral, educational, and interpersonal support components. Reviews of such interventions demonstrate their success in enhancing adjustment, particularly in realms that are disease related. For example, a meta-analysis of 37 studies of psychoeducational (health education and stress management) interventions for coronary heart disease patients suggested that the programs yielded a 34% reduction in cardiac mortality; a 29% reduction in recurrence of myocardial infarction; and positive effects on depression, anxiety, and risk factors for heart disease, such as blood pressure, cholesterol, body weight, smoking, physical activity, and eating habits (Dusseldorp, van Elderen, Maes, Meulman, & Kraaij, 1999). Reviews provide examples of effective individual-level interventions for people with cancer (e.g., Andersen, 2002; Meyer & Mark, 1995), diabetes (Gonder-Frederick, Cox, & Ritterband, 2002), AIDS (Lutgendorf et al., 1995; Kelly & Kalichman, 2002), and arthritis (Keefe, Smith et al., 2002).

Many interventions for persons coping with chronic disease involve support groups—groups of patients, or patients and family members, that meet regularly to share feelings, teach coping skills, and provide information. Groups may be peer led or professionally led, and may be geared toward more emotional or more informational support provision. The provision of informational support is expected to strengthen one's sense of control over the disease, reduce feelings of confusion, and enhance decision making. Peer discussion is expected to provide emotional support and, as such, enhance self-esteem, minimize aloneness, and reinforce coping choices (Helgeson & Cohen, 1996). In reality, most groups provide both types of support, which is congruent with the needs expressed by many patients.

Upon the release of Spiegel and colleagues' (Spiegel, Bloom, Kraemer, & Gottheil, 1989) findings that a supportive-expressive group intervention for advanced breast cancer patients appeared to enhance survival as well as improving quality of life, a rush ensued to encourage breast cancer patients to join groups. As groups proliferated, however, it became clear that support groups were not good for everyone. Recent research has failed to replicate Spiegel's original effects on survival (e.g., Goodwin et al., 2001) and has shown that support groups may not be universally effective. For example, social comparisons with others who are better or worse off may impede adjustment. Although similar others who are coping well with their disease may serve as strong role models, others who are not coping well, particularly those at advanced stages of the disease, may prompt frightening fantasies of what lies ahead (e.g., Stanton, Danoff-Burg, Cameron, Snider, & Kirk, 1999). Thus, the effectiveness (and, on the flip side, unintended negative consequences) of support groups depends on both individual and disease-related contextual factors, including age, disease stage, and preexisting psychosocial and other resources (Helgeson, Cohen, Schulz, & Yasko, 1999, 2001; Hinrichsen, Revenson, & Shinn, 1985; Lanza & Revenson, 1986; Taylor et al., 2003).

Current theories of coping have not maximized their utility for the design of interventions (de Ridder & Schreurs, 2001), in part because we have tended to use a "one size fits all" mentality, ignoring contextual factors at all levels that shape adaptation. An exception is Folkman and colleagues' (1991) coping effectiveness training. Successful in improving such outcomes as perceived stress and burnout, effects mediated by an increase in coping self-efficacy (Chesney, Folkman, & Chambers, 1996; Chesney, Chambers, Taylor, Johnson, & Folkman, 2003) in HIV-positive men, this intervention included appraisal training to disaggregate global stressors into specific coping tasks and to distinguish between changeable and immutable aspects of stressors; coping training to tailor application of particular coping strategies to specific stressors; and social support training to increase effectiveness in choosing and maintaining support resources. Successful interventions often have been developed only after years of basic research on the nature of the disease juxtaposed with the nature of coping with disease-related stressors. For example, Keefe (Keefe, Smith, et al., 2002) developed a pain coping intervention for arthritis patients based on his research showing the adverse effects of catastrophizing on adjustment to disease.

In light of the evidence that most individuals who confront chronic disease adjust well, a fruitful intervention approach will involve targeting especially challenging points in the disease trajectory, specific islands of disruption, and individuals who are most at risk, for example, those with clinical levels of depression, low social support, or high social constraints. Identification of these targets for intervention can be informed by research on contributors to adjustment to chronic disease. Research on predictors of adjustment also can aid in understanding *how* interventions work (e.g., through altering coping strategies or illness-related cognitions), which will allow the design of more effective treatments. A 2002 special issue of the *Journal of Consulting and Clinical Psychology* on behavioral medicine/clinical health psychology calls for greater investigation of moderators of and mechanisms for intervention effects, greater attention in interventions to environmental influences on adjustment, and increased attention to both biological and specific psychosocial endpoints (Andersen, 2002; Christensen & Ehlers, 2002; Gonder-Frederick et al., 2002; Keefe,

Buffington, et al, 2002; Keefe, Smith, et al., 2002). Interventions that are responsive to the person-context fit hold promise for enhancing health and well-being in individuals and their loved ones contending with chronic disease.

Future Research in Adjustment to Chronic Disease: The Promise of Both Broad Integration and Fine-Grained Focus

If you are a student researcher reading this chapter, you might feel daunted by the multiplicity of intersecting factors that deserve consideration in research on adjustment to chronic disease. Actually, as researchers in the area for the past 20 years, *we* still feel daunted by this complexity. To the extent that a researcher attempts to examine both contextual and individual contributors to adjustment using methodologically sound research designs (i.e., longitudinal or experimental methods, clinical trials), she or he is likely to require large samples, relatively lengthy time frames, additional instrument development, and assurance that interventions are culturally anchored across diverse samples (Yali & Revenson, 2004). This is a tough enough challenge to send even the most seasoned researchers running in the opposite direction. However, progress in the social sciences can be gauged by "small wins" (Weick, 1984), which involve recasting large problems into smaller, less knotty problems that present controllable opportunities to produce visible results. We believe that we need both broad and narrowly focused research in this area, and we encourage the readers of this chapter to take the next steps.

We do not need another cross-sectional study of the relations of six coping strategies to distress in breast cancer patients, to take but one example of the type of research most commonly found in the field. Rather, theoretically guided and methodologically definitive research examining individual and contextual biopsychosocial predictors, moderators of, and mechanisms for adaptive and biologic outcomes in chronic disease are needed to advance the knowledge base. To realize this goal, multiple sources of expertise will need to be integrated in order to produce the best conceptual frameworks and research designs. This need is especially urgent with the advent of biobehavioral models of specific

diseases (e.g., Andersen, Kiecolt-Glaser, & Glaser, 1994) and increased interest in biobehavioral mediators and medical outcomes. Exemplars include understanding the biopsychosocial mechanisms underlying the effects of personality attributes (e.g., Gallo & Smith, 1999; Helgeson, 2003; Martin et al., 2002; Smith & Gallo, 2001) and interpersonal variables (e.g., Taylor, Dickerson, & Klein, 2002; Uchino, Cacioppo, & Kiecolt-Glaser, 1996) on outcomes of chronic disease; the link between spirituality and health (e.g., Seeman, Dubin, & Seeman, 2003); and the relation of depression to both chronic disease onset (e.g., Carney, Jones, Woolson, Noyes, & Doebbeling, 2003; Wulsin & Singal, 2003) and resulting morbidity and mortality (e.g., Brown, Levy, Rosberger, & Edgar, 2003; de Groot, Anderson, Freedland, Clouse, & Lustman, 2001; Kinder, Kamarck, Baum, & Orchard, 2002; Sullivan, LaCroix, Russo, & Walker, 2001; Van Tilberg et al., 2001). Studies such as these will require sophisticated research planning and implementation.

Interdisciplinary collaboration is a critical mechanism for pursuing research that is truly biopsychosocial (or biopsychosociocultural). A multidisciplinary team representing expertise in psychosocial and biological processes involved in specific diseases, relevant theoretical frameworks, and quantitative methods provides the basic vehicle for conducting such research. If we are to address the complex questions that we have posed in this chapter, then scholars from other social sciences (e.g., sociology, anthropology) and from public health, as well as patients and community gatekeepers, also will contribute to the team, offering knowledge of macro-level contextual factors and community-level interventions.

At the same time as integrative research is needed, investigations with a sharp, hypothesis-driven focus on unanswered questions in chronic disease (e.g., mechanisms for gender-related effects on adjustment to chronic disease; behavioral and biologic mechanisms for the relation between avoidant coping and disease outcomes) also can move the field forward. Such research may alternate between basic research with healthy samples responding to experimentally induced stressors, experimental and quasi-experimental investigations of populations experiencing chronic disease, and clinical intervention trials to document causal mechanisms more conclusively. Longitudinal studies focusing on in-depth analysis of single contributors to adjustment (e.g., upward and downward social comparison, benefit finding, emotional expression) can set the stage for research to understand how these processes work in context and with diverse populations. Particularly in new areas of inquiry, qualitative studies can frame research questions and provide a way to "get inside" patients' experiences of chronic disease. Qualitative methods also may provide feedback on our research directions, questions, and approaches, as in participatory action research, in which research participants also help design the research. Intensive, daily process methodologies also may illuminate interacting individual and contextual contributors to adjustment (e.g., Tennen, Affleck, Armeli, & Carney, 2000). These methodologies are particularly appropriate for diseases for which coping and self-management demands occur daily. Certainly, there is room for both large-scale research examining multiple and interacting determinants of adjustment to chronic disease, as well as sharply honed, microanalytic investigations of processes underlying both positive and negative adaptive outcomes.

Conclusion

How far has our knowledge of adjustment to chronic disease advanced over the past 40 years, since that seminal, observational study of adjustment to chronic disease appeared in the *Archives of General Psychiatry* (Visotsky et al., 1961)? We still study how it is possible to deal with such powerful, pervasive, and enduring stresses as are involved in chronic disease, though the focus now is not on polio but on life-threatening diseases such as cancer and AIDS, as well as on non-life-threatening but severely disabling conditions such as arthritis. Considerable progress is evident in the development of multifaceted conceptualizations and operationalizations of adjustment, theories to specify contributors to adaptation, and the knowledge base regarding specific factors that contribute to unfavorable outcomes (although we know less about determinants of favorable outcomes). We now know that understanding discrete coping behaviors is not enough; investigating the intersections of emotions, cognition, and culture with behavior in the context of interpersonal relationships and life roles may provide more adequate answers. We are just beginning to use this knowledge to guide clini-

cal interventions, though (in the spirit of twentieth-century American psychology) we still rely largely on individual treatment models. We have made small wins, and the biggest gains—adequately capturing the connections among biological, psychological, and sociocultural mechanisms—are still to come.

Acknowledgments. We thank Sharon Danoff-Burg, Steve Lepore, and Howard Friedman for their incisive comments on an earlier draft of this chapter.

References

Abraído-Lanza, A. F. (1997). Latinas with arthritis: Effects of illness, role identity, and competence on psychological well-being. *American Journal of Community Psychology, 25,* 601–627.

Abraído-Lanza, A. F., Guier, C., & Revenson, T. A. (1996). Coping and social support resources among Latinas with arthritis. *Arthritis Care and Research, 9,* 501–508.

Adler, N. E., Boyce, T., Chesney, M., Cohen, S., Folkman, S., Kahn, R. L., et al. (1994). Socioeconomic status and health: The challenge of the gradient. *American Psychologist, 49,* 15–24.

Adler, N. E., Boyce, T., Chesney, M., Folkman, S., & Syme, S. L. (1993). Socioeconomic inequalities in health: No easy solution. *Journal of the American Medical Association, 269,* 3140–3145.

Affleck, G., Tennen, H., Croog, S., & Levine, S. (1987). Causal attribution, perceived benefits, and morbidity after a heart attack: An 8-year study. *Journal of Consulting and Clinical Psychology, 55,* 29–35.

Affleck, G., Tennen, H., Pfeiffer, C., & Fifield, J. (1987). Appraisals of control and predictability in adapting to chronic disease. *Journal of Personality and Social Psychology, 53,* 273–279.

Affleck, G., Tennen, H., Zautra, A., Urrows, S., Abeles, M., & Karoly, P. (2001). Women's pursuit of personal goals in daily life with fibromyalgia: A value-expectancy analysis. *Journal of Consulting and Clinical Psychology, 69,* 587–596.

Andersen, B. L. (2002). Biobehavioral outcomes following psychological interventions for cancer patients. *Journal of Consulting and Clinical Psychology, 70,* 590–610.

Andersen, B. L., Anderson, B., & deProsse, C. (1989a). Controlled prospective longitudinal study of women with cancer: I. Sexual functioning outcomes. *Journal of Consulting and Clinical Psychology, 57,* 683–691.

Andersen, B. L., Anderson, B., & deProsse, C. (1989b). Controlled prospective longitudinal study of women with cancer: II. Psychological outcomes. *Journal of Consulting and Clinical Psychology, 57,* 692–697.

Andersen, B. L., Kiecolt-Glaser, J., & Glaser, R. (1994). A biobehavioral model of cancer stress and disease course. *American Psychologist, 49,* 389–404.

Andersen, B. L., Woods, X. A., & Copeland, L. J. (1997). Sexual self schema and sexual morbidity among gynecologic cancer survivors. *Journal of Consulting and Clinical Psychology, 65,* 221–229.

Anderson, N. B., & McNeilly, M. (1991). Age, gender, and ethnicity as variables in psychophysiological assessment: Sociodemographics in context. *Psychological Assessment, 3,* 376–384.

Anderson, R. J., Clouse, R. E., Freedland, K. E., & Lustman, P. J. (2001). The prevalence of comorbid depression in adults with diabetes: A meta-analysis. *Diabetes Care, 24,* 1069–1078.

Anderson, R. N., & Smith, B. L. (2003). Deaths: Leading causes for 2001. *National Vital Statistics Reports, 52(9),* Hyattsville, MD: National Center for Health Statistics.

Antoni, M. H., Cruess, D. G., Cruess, S., Lutgendorf, S., Kumar, M., Ironson, G., et al. (2000). Cognitive-behavioral stress management intervention effects on anxiety, 24-hr urinary norepinephrine, and T-cytotoxic/suppressor cells over time among symptomatic HIV-infected gay men. *Journal of Consulting and Clinical Psychology, 68,* 31–45.

Antoni, M. H., Lehman, J. M., Kilbourn, K. M., Boyers, A. E., Culver, J. L., Alferi, S. M., et al. (2001). Cognitive-behavioral stress management intervention decreases the prevalence of depression and enhances benefit finding among women under treatment for early-stage breast cancer. *Health Psychology, 20,* 20–32.

Belle, D. (1982). *Lives in stress: Women and depression.* Beverly Hills, CA: Sage.

Berkman, L. F., & Glass, T. (1999). Social integration, social networks, social support, and health. In L. F. Berkman & T. Glass (Eds.), *Social epidemiology* (pp. 137–173). New York: Oxford University Press.

Bernal, G., & Enchautegui-de-Jesus, N. (1994). Latinos and Latinas in community psychology: A review of the literature. *American Journal of Community Psychology, 22,* 531–557.

Blalock, S. J., DeVellis, B. M., & Giorgino, K. B. (1995). The relationship between coping and psychological well-being among people with osteoarthritis: A problem-specific approach. *Annals of Behavioral Medicine, 17,* 107–115.

Bonanno, G. A. (2004). Loss, trauma, and human resilience: Have we underestimated the human capacity to thrive after extremely aversive events? *American Psychologist, 59,* 20–28.

Bower, J. E., Kemeny, M. E., Taylor, S. E., & Fahey, J. L. (1998). Cognitive processing, discovery of meaning, CD4 decline, and AIDS-related mortality among bereaved HIV-seropositive men. *Journal of Consulting and Clinical Psychology, 66,* 979–986.

Brown, K. W., Levy, A. R., Rosberger, Z., & Edgar, L. (2003). Psychological distress and cancer survival: A follow-up 10 years after diagnosis. *Psychosomatic Medicine, 65,* 636–643.

Brown, S. L., Nesse, R. M., Vinokur, A. D., & Smith, D. M. (2003). Providing social support may be more beneficial than receiving it: Results from a prospective study of mortality. *Psychological Science, 14,* 320–327.

Callahan, L. F., Cordray, D. S., Wells, G., & Pincus, T. (1996). Formal education and five-year mortality in rheumatoid arthritis: Mediation by helplessness scale scores. *Arthritis Care and Research, 9,* 463–472.

Carney, C. P., Jones, L., Woolson, R. F., Noyes, R., & Doebbeling, B. N. (2003). Relationship between depression and pancreatic cancer in the general population. *Psychosomatic Medicine, 65,* 884–888.

Carver, C. S., Harris, S. D., Lehman, J. M., Durel, L. A., Antoni, M. H., Spencer, S. M., et al. (2000). How important is the perception of personal control? Studies of early stage breast cancer patients. *Personality and Social Psychology Bulletin, 26,* 139–149.

Carver, C. S., Pozo, C., Harris, S. D., Noriega, V., Scheier, M. F., Robinson, D. S., et al. (1993). How coping mediates the effect of optimism on distress: A study of women with early stage breast cancer. *Journal of Personality and Social Psychology, 65,* 375–390.

Carver, C. S., & Scheier, M. F. (1998). *On the self-regulation of behavior.* New York: Cambridge University Press.

Cassileth, B. R., Lusk, E. J., Strouse, T. B., Miller, D. S., Brown, L. L., Cross, P. A., et al. (1984). Psychosocial status in chronic illness: A comparative analysis of six diagnostic groups. *New England Journal of Medicine, 311,* 506–511.

Catz, S. L., & Kelly, J. A. (2001). Living with HIV disease. In A. Baum, T. A. Revenson, & J. E. Singer (Eds.), *Handbook of health psychology* (pp. 841–849). Mahwah, NJ: Erlbaum.

Cella, D. (2001). Quality-of-life measurement in oncology. In A. Baum & B. L. Andersen (Eds.), *Psychosocial interventions for cancer* (pp. 57–76). Washington, DC: American Psychological Association.

Centers for Disease Control and Prevention, U.S. Department of Health and Human Services. (2003). *About chronic disease.* Retrieved May 10, 2004, from http://www.cdc.gov/washington/overview/chrondis.htm

Centers for Disease Control and Prevention, U.S. Department of Health and Human Services. (February, 2004). *The burden of chronic diseases and their risk factors: National and state perspectives 2004.* Retrieved May 10, 2004, from http://www.cdc.gov/nccdphp/burdenbook2004

Chesney, M., Folkman, S., & Chambers, D. (1996). Coping effectiveness training for men living with HIV: Preliminary findings. *International Journal of STD and AIDS, 7*(Suppl 2), 75–82.

Chesney, M. A., Chambers, D. B., Taylor, J. M., Johnson, L. M., & Folkman, S. (2003). Coping effectiveness training for men living with HIV: Results from a randomized clinical trial testing a group-based intervention. *Psychosomatic Medicine, 65,* 1038–1046.

Christensen, A. J., & Ehlers, S. L. (2002). Psychological factors in end-stage renal disease: An emerging context for behavioral medicine research. *Journal of Consulting and Clinical Psychology, 70,* 712–724.

Clark, N. M., Becker, M. H., Janz, N. K., Lorig, K., Rakowski, W., & Anderson, L. (1991). Self-management of chronic disease by older adults. *Journal of Aging and Health, 3,* 3–27.

Clark, R., Anderson, N. B., Clark, V. R., & Williams, D. R. (1999). Racism as a stressor for African Americans: A biopsychosocial model. *American Psychologist, 54,* 805–816.

Cohen, S., Gottlieb, S. L., & Underwood, L. G. (2000). Social relationships and health. In S. Cohen, L. G. Underwood, & B. H. Gottlieb (Eds.), *Social support measurement and intervention* (pp. 3–25). New York: Oxford University Press.

Cohen, S., & Syme, S. L. (1986). *Social support and health.* New York: Academic Press.

Cohen, S., Underwood, L. G., & Gottlieb, B. H. (Eds.). (2000). *Social support measurement and intervention.* New York: Oxford University Press.

Cohen, S., & Wills, T. A. (1985). Stress, support and the buffering hypothesis. *Psychological Bulletin, 98,* 310–357.

Cordova, M. J., Andrykowski, M. A., Kenady, D. E., McGrath, P. C., Sloan, D. A., & Redd, W. H. (1995). Frequency and correlates of posttraumatic-stress-disorder-like symptoms after treatment for breast cancer. *Journal of Consulting and Clinical Psychology, 63,* 981–986.

Cordova, M. J., Cunningham, L. L., Carlson, C. R., & Andrykowski, M. A. (2001). Posttraumatic growth following breast cancer: A controlled comparison study. *Health Psychology, 20,* 176–185.

Coriell, M., & Adler, M. (1996). Socioeconomic status and women's health: How do we measure SES among women? *Women's Health: Research on Gender, Behavior, and Policy, 2,* 141–156.

Coyne, J. C., & Gottlieb, B. H. (1996). The mismeasure of coping by checklist. *Journal of Personality, 64,* 959–991.

Coyne, J. C., & Racioppo, M. W. (2000). Never the twain shall meet? Closing the gap between coping research and clinical intervention research. *American Psychologist, 55,* 655–664.

Coyne, J. C., Rohrbaugh, M. J., Shoham, V., Sonnega, J. S., Nicklas, J. M., & Cranford, J. A. (2001). Prognostic importance of marital quality for survival of congestive heart failure. *American Journal of Cardiology, 88,* 526–529.

Cutrona, C. E., & Russell, D. W. (1990). Type of social support and specific stress: Toward a theory of optimal matching. In B. R. Sarason, I. G. Sarason, & G. R. Pierce (Eds.), *Social support: An interactional view* (pp. 319–366). New York: Wiley.

Dakof, G., & Taylor, S. E. (1990). Victims' perceptions of social support: What is helpful from whom? *Journal of Personality and Social Psychology, 58,* 80–89.

Danoff-Burg, S., Ayala, J., & Revenson, T. A. (2000). Researcher knows best? Toward a closer match between the concept and measurement of coping. *Journal of Health Psychology, 5,* 183–194.

Danoff-Burg, S., & Revenson, T. A. (2005). Benefit-finding among patients with rheumatoid arthritis: Positive effects on interpersonal relationships. *Journal of Behavioral Medicine, 28,* 91–103.

Danoff-Burg, S., Revenson, T. A., Trudeau, K. J., & Paget, S. A. (2004). Unmitigated communion, social constraints, and psychological distress among women with rheumatoid arthritis. *Journal of Personality, 72,* 29–46.

Davidson, R. J., Jackson, D. C., & Kalin, N. H. (2000). Emotion, plasticity, context, and regulation: Perspectives from affective neuroscience. *Psychological Bulletin, 126,* 890–909.

de Groot, M., Anderson, R., Freedland, K. E., Clouse, R. E., & Lustman, P. J. (2001). Association of depression and diabetes complications: A meta-analysis. *Psychosomatic Medicine, 63,* 619–630.

de Ridder, D., & Schreurs, K. (2001). Developing interventions for chronically ill patients: Is coping a helpful concept? *Clinical Psychology Review, 21,* 205–240.

Derogatis, L. R., Morrow, G. R., Fetting, J., Penman, D., Piasetsky, S., Schmale, A. M., Henrichs, R., & Carnickle, C. L. M. (1983). The prevalence of psychiatric disorders among cancer patients. *Journal of the American Medical Association, 249,* 751–757.

DeVellis, B. M., & DeVellis, R. F. (2001). Self-efficacy and health. In A. Baum, T. A. Revenson, & J. E. Singer (Eds.), *Handbook of health psychology* (pp. 235–247). Mahwah, NJ: Erlbaum.

DeVellis, B. M., Revenson, T. A., & Blalock, S. (1997). Arthritis and autoimmune diseases. In S. Gallant, G. P. Keita, & R. Royak-Schaler (Eds.), *Health care for women: Psychological, social and behavioral issues* (pp. 333–347). Washington, DC: American Psychological Association.

Dickens, C., McGowan, L., Clark-Carter, D., & Creed, F. (2002). Depression in rheumatoid arthritis: A systematic review of the literature with meta-analysis. *Psychosomatic Medicine, 64,* 52–60.

Dorval, M., Maunsell, E., Deschenes, L., Brisson, J., & Masse, B. (1998). Long-term quality of life after breast cancer: Comparison of 8-year survivors with population controls. *Journal of Clinical Oncology, 16,* 487–494.

Dunkel-Schetter, C., Feinstein, L. G., Taylor, S. E., & Falke, R. L. (1992). Patterns of coping with cancer. *Health Psychology, 11,* 79–87.

Dusseldorp, E., van Elderen, T., Maes, S., Meulman, J., & Kraaij, V. (1999). A meta-analysis of psychoeducational programs for coronary heart disease patients. *Health Psychology, 18,* 506–519.

Eberhardt, M. S., Ingram, D. D., Makuc, D. M, Pamuk, E. R., Freid, V. M., Harper, S. B., et al. (2001). *Health, United States, 2001.* Hyattsville, MD: National Center for Health Statistics.

Echteld, M. A., van Elderen, T., & van der Kamp, L. J. T. (2003). Modeling predictors of quality of life after coronary angioplasty. *Annals of Behavioral Medicine, 26,* 49–60.

Epping-Jordan, J. E., Compas, B. E., & Howell, D. C. (1994). Predictors of cancer progression in young adult men and women: Avoidance, intrusive thoughts, and psychological symptoms. *Health Psychology, 13,* 539–547.

Eton, D. T., & Lepore, S. J. (2001). Prostate cancer and quality of life: A review of the literature. *Psycho-Oncology, 10,* 1–20.

Eton, D. T., Lepore, S. J., & Helgeson, V. (2001). Early quality of life in patients with localized prostate carcinoma: An examination of treatment-related, demographic and psychosocial factors. *Cancer, 92,*1451–1459.

Felton, B. J., & Revenson, T. A. (1984). Coping with chronic illness: A study of illness controllability and the influence of coping strategies on psychological adjustment. *Journal of Consulting and Clinical Psychology, 52,* 343–353.

Felton, B. J., Revenson, T. A., & Hinrichsen, G. A. (1984). Stress and coping in the explanation of psychological adjustment among chronically ill adults. *Social Science and Medicine, 18,* 889–898.

Fitzgerald, T. E., Tennen, H., Affleck, G., & Pransky, G. S. (1993). The relative importance of dispositional optimism and control appraisals in quality of life after coronary artery bypass surgery. *Journal of Behavioral Medicine, 16,* 25–43.

Fitzpatrick, R. (2004). Quality of life: Measurement. In N. B. Anderson (Ed.), *Encyclopedia of health and behavior* (pp. 685–690). Thousand Oaks, CA: Sage.

Fitzpatrick, R., Newman, S., Archer, R., & Shipley, M. (1991). Social support, disability, and depression: A longitudinal study of rheumatoid arthritis. *Social Science and Medicine, 33,* 605–611.

Fitzpatrick, R., Newman, S., Lamb, R., & Shipley, M. (1988). Social relationships and psychological well-being in rheumatoid arthritis. *Social Science and Medicine, 27,* 399–403.

Folkman, S., & Moskowitz, J. T. (2000). The context matters. *Personality and Social Psychology Bulletin, 26,* 150–151.

Folkman, S., Chesney, M., McKusick, L., Ironson, G., Johnson, D. S., & Coates, T. J. (1991). Translating coping theory into intervention. In J. Eckenrode (Ed.), *The social context of coping* (pp. 239–259). New York: Plenum.

Folkman, S., Chesney, M., Pollack, L., & Coates, T. (1993). Stress, control, coping, and depressive mood in human immunodeficiency virus-positive and -negative gay men in San Francisco. *Journal of Nervous and Mental Disease, 181,* 409–416.

Folkman, S., Moskowitz, J. T., Ozer, E. M., & Park, C. L. (1997). Positive meaningful events and coping in the context of HIV/AIDS. In B. H. Gottlieb (Ed.), *Coping with chronic stress* (pp. 293–314). New York: Plenum.

Fox, N. A. (1991). If it's not left, it's right: Electroencephalograph asymmetry and the development of emotion. *American Psychologist, 46,* 863–872.

French, J. R. P., Jr., Rodgers, W., & Cobb, S. (1974). Adjustment as person-environment fit. In G. V. Coelho, D. A. Hamburg, & J. E. Adams (Eds.), *Coping and adjustment* (pp. 316–333). New York: Basic Books.

Fritz, H. L. (2000). Gender-linked personality traits predict mental health and functional status following a first coronary event. *Health Psychology, 19,* 420–428.

Gallo, L. C., & Matthews, K. A. (2003). Understanding the association between socioeconomic status and physical health: Do negative emotions play a role? *Psychological Bulletin, 129,* 10–51.

Gallo, L. C., & Smith, T. W. (1999). Patterns of hostility and social support: Conceptualizing psychosocial risk factors as characteristics of the person and the environment. *Journal of Research in Personality, 33,* 281–230.

Ganz, P. A., Rowland, J. H., Desmond, K., Meyerowitz, B. E., & Wyatt, G. E. (1998). Life after breast cancer: Understanding women's health-related quality of life and sexual functioning. *Journal of Clinical Oncology, 16,* 501–514.

Gilligan, C. (1982). *In a different voice: Psychological theory and women's development.* Cambridge, MA: Harvard University Press.

Gonder-Frederick, L. A., Cox, D. J., & Ritterband, L. M. (2002). Diabetes and behavioral medicine: The second decade. *Journal of Consulting and Clinical Psychology, 70,* 611–625.

Goodenow, C., Reisine, S. T., & Grady, K. E. (1990). Quality of social support and associated social and psychological functioning in women with rheumatoid arthritis. *Health Psychology, 9,* 266–284.

Goodwin, P. J., Leszcz, M., Ennis, M., Koopmans, J., Vincent, L., Guther, H., et al. (2001). The effect of group psychosocial support on survival in metastatic breast cancer. *New England Journal of Medicine, 345,* 1719–1726.

Gore, S., & Colten, M. E. (1991). Gender, stress, and distress. In J. Eckenrode (Ed.), *The social context of coping* (pp. 139–163). New York: Plenum.

Guyll, M., Matthews, K. A., & Bromberger, J. T. (2001). Discrimination and unfair treatment: Relationship to cardiovascular reactivity among African American and European American women. *Health Psychology, 20,* 315–325.

Hagedoorn, M., Kuijer, R. G., Buunk, B. P., DeJong, G. M., Wobbes, T., & Sanderman, R. (2000). Marital satisfaction in patients with cancer: Does support from intimate partners benefit those who need it most? *Health Psychology, 19,* 274–282.

Hamburg, D. A., & Adams, J. E. (1967). A perspective on coping behavior: Seeking and utilizing information in major transitions. *Archives of General Psychiatry, 17,* 277–284.

Helgeson V. S. (1990). The role of masculinity in a prognostic predictor of heart attack severity. *Sex Roles, 22,* 755–774.

Helgeson V. S. (1992). Moderators of the relation between perceived control and adjustment to chronic illness. *Journal of Personality and Social Psychology, 63,* 656–666.

Helgeson V. S. (1993). Implications of agency and communion for patient and spouse adjustment to a first coronary event. *Journal of Personality and Social Psychology, 64,* 807–816.

Helgeson V. S. (1994). Relation of agency and communion to well-being: Evidence and potential explanations. *Psychological Bulletin, 116,* 412–428.

Helgeson, V. S. (2003). Cognitive adaptation, psychological adjustment, and disease progression among angioplasty patients: 4 years later. *Health Psychology, 22,* 30–38.

Helgeson, V. S., & Cohen, S. (1996). Social support and adjustment to cancer: Reconciling descriptive, correlational, and intervention research. *Health Psychology, 15,* 135–148.

Helgeson, V. S., Cohen, S., Schulz, R., & Yasko, J. (1999). Education and peer discussion group interventions and adjustment to breast cancer. *Archives of General Psychiatry, 56,* 340–347.

Helgeson, V. S., Cohen, S., Schulz, R., & Yasko, J. (2000). Group support interventions for women with breast cancer: Who benefits from what?. *Health Psychology, 19,* 107–114.

Helgeson, V. S., Cohen, S., Schulz, R., & Yasko, J. (2001). Long-term effects of educational and peer discussion group interventions on adjustment to breast cancer. *Health Psychology, 20,* 387–392.

Helgeson, V. S., & Fritz, H. L. (1996). Implications of communion and unmitigated communion for adolescent adjustment to Type I diabetes. *Women's Health: Research on Gender, Behavior, and Policy, 2,* 169–194.

Helgeson, V. S., & Fritz, H. L. (1998). A theory of unmitigated communion. *Personality and Social Psychology Review, 2,* 173–183.

Helgeson, V. S., & Lepore, S. L. (1997). Men's adjustment to prostate cancer: The role of agency and unmitigated agency. *Sex Roles, 37,* 251–267.

Hinrichsen, G. A., Revenson, T. A., & Shinn, M. (1985). Does self-help help? An empirical investigation of scoliosis peer support groups. *Journal of Social Issues, 41,* 65–87.

Holland, J. C., & Lewis, S. (2000). *The human side of cancer: Living with hope, coping with uncertainty.* New York: HarperCollins.

Ickovics, J. R., & Park, C. (1998). Paradigm shift: Why a focus on health is important. *Journal of Social Issues, 54,* 237–244.

Ickovics, J. R., Thayaparan, B., & Ethier, K. A. (2001). Women and AIDS: A contextual analysis. In A. Baum, T. A. Revenson, & J. E. Singer (Eds.), *Handbook of health psychology* (pp. 817–839). Mahwah, NJ: Erlbaum.

Institute for the Future. (2000). *Health and health care 2010: The forecast, the challenge.* San Francisco: Jossey-Bass.

Jacobsen, P. B., Sadler, I. J., Booth-Jones, M., Soety, E., Weitzner, M. A., & Fields, K. K. (2002). Predictors of posttraumatic stress disorder symptomatology following bone marrow transplantation for cancer. *Journal of Consulting and Clinical Psychology, 70,* 235–240.

Janoff-Bulman, R., & Berger, A. R. (2000). The other side of trauma: Towards a psychology of appreciation. In J. H. Harvey & E. D. Miller (Eds.), *Loss and trauma: General and close relationship perspectives* (pp. 29–44). Philadelphia: Taylor and Francis.

Janoff-Bulman, R., & Frantz, C. M. (1997). The impact of trauma on meaning: From meaningless world to meaningful life. In M. Power & C. R. Brewin (Eds.), *The transformation of meaning in psychological therapies* (pp. 91–106). New York: Wiley.

Katz, R. C., Flasher, L., Cacciapaglia, H., & Nelson, S. (2001). The psychosocial impact of cancer and lupus: A cross-validation study that extends the generality of "benefit-finding" in patients with chronic disease. *Journal of Behavioral Medicine, 24,* 561–571.

Keefe, F. J., Buffington, A. L. H., Studts, J. L., & Rumble, M. E. (2002). Behavioral medicine: 2002 and beyond. *Journal of Consulting and Clinical Psychology, 70,* 852–856.

Keefe, F. J., Smith, S. J., Buffington, A. L. H., Gibson, J., Studts, J. L., & Caldwell, D. S. (2002). Recent advances and future directions in the biopsychosocial assessment and treatment of arthritis. *Journal of Consulting and Clinical Psychology, 70,* 640–655.

Kelly, J. A., & Kalichman, S. C. (2002). Behavioral research in HIV/AIDS primary and secondary prevention: Recent advances and future directions. *Journal of Consulting and Clinical Psychology, 70,* 626–639.

Kiecolt-Glaser, J. K., McGuire, L., Robles, T. F., & Glaser, R. (2002). Emotions, morbidity, and mortality: New perspectives from psychoneuroimmunology. *Annual Review of Psychology, 53,* 83–107.

Kinder, L. S., Kamarck, T. W., Baum, A., & Orchard, T. J. (2002). Depressive symptomatology and coronary heart disease in Type I diabetes mellitus: A study of possible mechanisms. *Health Psychology, 21,* 542–552.

Landrine, H., & Klonoff, E. (1992). Culture and health-related schemas: A review and proposal for interdisciplinary integration. *Health Psychology, 11,* 267–276.

Lanza, A. F., Cameron, A. E., & Revenson, T. A. (1995). Helpful and unhelpful support among individuals with rheumatic diseases. *Psychology and Health, 10,* 449–462.

Lanza, A. F., & Revenson, T. A. (1993). Social support interventions for rheumatoid arthritis patients: The cart before the horse? *Health Education Quarterly, 20,* 97–117.

Lazarus, R. S. (1991). *Emotion and adaptation.* New York: Oxford University Press.

Lazarus, R. S., & Folkman, S. (1984). *Stress, appraisal, and coping.* New York: Springer.

Lazarus, R. S., & Launier, R. (1978). Stress-related transactions between person and environment. In L. A. Pervin & M. Lewis (Eds.), *Perspectives in interactional psychology* (pp. 287–327). New York: Plenum.

Lazarus, R. S. (1981). The stress and coping paradigm. In C. Edisdorfer, D. Cohen, A. Kleinman, & P. Maxim (Eds.), *Models for clinical psychopathology* (pp. 177–214). New York: Spectrum Medical and Scientific Books.

Lepore, S. J. (2001). A social-cognitive processing model of emotional adjustment to cancer. In A. Baum & B. L. Andersen (Eds.), *Psychosocial interventions for cancer* (pp. 99–116). Washington, DC: American Psychological Association.

Lepore, S. J., & Eton, D. T. (2000). Response shifts in prostate cancer patients: An evaluation of suppressor and buffer models. In C. Schwartz & M. Sprangers (Eds.), *Adaptations to changing health: Response shift in quality-of-life research* (pp. 37–51). Washington, DC: American Psychological Association.

Lepore, S. J., & Helgeson, V. S. (1998). Social constraints, intrusive thoughts, and mental health after prostate cancer. *Journal of Behavioral Medicine, 17,* 89–106.

Lepore, S. J., Revenson, T. A., Weinberger, S., Weston, P., Frisina, P. Robertson, R., et al. (2006). Effects of social stressors on cardiovascular reactivity in Black and White women. *Annals of Behavioral Medicine, 31,* 120–127.

Leventhal, H., Leventhal, E. A., & Cameron, L. (2001). Representations, procedures, and affect in illness self-regulation: A perceptual-cognitive model. In A. Baum, T. A. Revenson, & J. E. Singer (Eds.), *Handbook of health psychology* (pp. 19–47). Mahwah, NJ: Erlbaum.

Levine, J., Warrenburg, S., Kerns, R., Schwartz, G., Delaney, R., Fontana, A., et al. (1987). The role of denial in recovery from coronary heart disease. *Psychosomatic Medicine, 49,* 109–117.

Levy, S. M., Haynes, L. T., Herberman, R. B., Lee, J., McFeeley, S., & Kirkwood, J. (1992). Mastectomy versus breast conservation surgery: Mental health effects at long-term follow-up. *Health Psychology, 11,* 349–354.

Lewin, K. (1951/1997). *Resolving social conflicts and field theory in social science.* Washington, DC: American Psychological Association.

Link, B. G., & Phelan, J. (1995). Social conditions as fundamental causes of disease. *Journal of Health and Social Behavior, 36* (extra issue), 80–94.

Low, S. (1985). Culturally interpreted symptoms or culture-bound syndromes: A cross-cultural review of nerves. *Social Science and Medicine, 21,* 187–196.

Low, S. (1995). Embodied metaphors: Nerves as lived experience. In T. Csordas (Ed.), *Embodiment and experience: The existential ground of culture and self* (pp. 139–162). Cambridge, England: Cambridge University Press.

Lustman, P. J. (1988). Anxiety disorders in adults with diabetes mellitus. *Psychiatric Clinics of North America, 11,* 419–432.

Lustman, P. J., Anderson, R. J., Freedland, K. E., de Groot, M., Carney, R. M., & Clouse, R. E. (2000). Depression and poor glycemic control: A meta-analytic review of the literature. *Diabetes Care, 23,* 934–942.

Lutgendorf, S. K., Antoni, M. H., Schneiderman, N., Ironson, G., & Fletcher, M. A. (1995). Psychosocial interventions and quality of life changes across the HIV spectrum. In J. E. Dimsdale & A. Baum (Eds.), *Quality of life in behavioral medicine research* (pp. 205–239). Hillsdale, NJ: Erlbaum.

MacIntyre, S., & Hunt, K. (1997). Socio-economic position, gender and health: How do they interact? *Journal of Health Psychology, 2,* 315–334.

Maes, S., Leventhal, H., & De Ridder, D. T. D. (1996). Coping with chronic diseases. In M. Zeidner & N. Endler (Eds.), *Handbook of coping: Theory, research, applications* (pp. 221–251). New York: Wiley.

Majerovitz, S. D., & Revenson, T. A. (1994). Sexuality and rheumatic disease: The significance of gender. *Arthritis Care and Research, 7,* 29–34.

Manne, S. L., & Zautra, A. J. (1989). Spouse criticism and support: Their association with coping and psychological adjustment among women with rheumatoid arthritis. *Journal of Personality and Social Psychology, 56,* 608–617.

Marin, G., & Marin, B.V. (1991). *Research with Hispanic populations.* Thousand Oaks, CA: Sage.

Martin, L. R., Friedman, H. S., Tucker, J. S., Tomlinson-Keasey, C., Criqui, M. H., & Schwartz, J. E. (2002). A life course perspective on childhood cheerfulness and its relation to mortality risk. *Personality and Social Psychology Bulletin, 28,* 1155–1165.

Matthews, K. A. (1989). Are sociodemographic variables markers for psychological determinants of health? *Health Psychology, 8,* 641–648.

McClain, C. S. (Ed.). (1989). *Women as healers: Cross-cultural perspectives.* New Brunswick, NJ: Rutgers University Press.

Meyer, T. J., & Mark, M. M. (1995). Effects of psychosocial interventions with adult cancer patients: A meta-analysis of randomized experiments. *Health Psychology, 14,* 101–108.

Meyerowitz, B. E., Richardson, J., Hudson, S., & Leedham, B. (1998). Ethnicity and cancer outcomes: Behavioral and psychosocial considerations. *Psychological Bulletin, 123,* 47–70.

Michela, J. L. (1987). Interpersonal and individual impacts of a husband's heart attack. In A. Baum &

J. E. Singer (Eds.), *Handbook of psychology and health* (Vol. 5, pp. 255–301). Hillsdale, NJ: Erlbaum.

Montgomery, G. H., & Bovbjerg, D. H. (2001). Specific response expectancies predict anticipatory nausea during chemotherapy for breast cancer. *Journal of Consulting and Clinical Psychology, 69,* 831–835.

Moos, R. H., & Schaefer, J. A. (1984). The crisis of physical illness. In R. Moos (Ed.), *Coping with physical illness* (pp. 3–26). New York: Plenum.

Moskowitz, J. T. (2003). Positive affect predicts lower risk of AIDS mortality. *Psychosomatic Medicine, 65,* 620–626.

Mullings, L., & Wali, A. (2001). *Stress and resilience: The social context of reproduction in central Harlem.* New York: Kluwer Academic Publishers.

Nayfield, S. G., Ganz, P. A., Moinpour, C. M., Cella, D. F., & Hailey, B. J. (1992). Report from a National Cancer Institute (USA) workshop on quality of life assessment in cancer clinical trials. *Quality of Life Research, 1,* 203–210.

Nerenz, D. R., & Leventhal, H. (1983). Self-regulation theory in chronic illness. In T. G. Burish & L. A. Bradley (Eds.), *Coping with chronic disease: Research and applications* (pp. 13–37). New York: Academic Press.

Neugarten, B. (1979). Time, age and the life cycle. *American Journal of Psychiatry, 136,* 887–894.

Newman, S., Fitzpatrick, R., Revenson, T. A., Skevington, S., & Williams, G. (1996). *Understanding rheumatoid arthritis.* London: Routledge and Kegan Paul.

O'Leary, V., & Ickovics, J. (1995). Resilience and thriving in response to challenge: An opportunity for a paradigm shift in women's health. *Women's Health: Research on Gender, Behavior, and Policy, 1,* 121–142.

Orbell, S., Jonston, M., Rowley, D., Espley, A., & Davey, P. (1998). Cognitive representations of illness and functional and affective adjustment following surgery for osteoarthritis. *Social Science and Medicine, 47,* 93–102.

Osowiecki, D. M., & Compas, B. E. (1999). A prospective study of coping, perceived control and psychological adjustment to breast cancer. *Cognitive Therapy and Research, 23,* 169–180.

Park, C. L., & Folkman, S. (1997). Meaning in the context of stress and coping. *Review of General Psychology, 1,* 115–144.

Polonsky, W. H., Anderson, B. J., Lohrer, P. A., Welch, G., Jacobson, A. M., Aponte, J. E., et al. (1995). Assessment of diabetes-related distress. *Diabetes Care, 18,* 754–760.

Radojevic, V., Nicassio, P. M., & Weisman, M. H. (1992). Behavioral intervention with and without family support for rheumatoid arthritis. *Behavior Therapy, 23*, 13–30.

Ramsey, S. D., Andersen, M. R., Etzioni, R., Moinpour, C., Peacock, S., Potosky, A., et al. (2000). Quality of life in survivors of colorectal carcinoma. *Cancer, 88*, 1294–1303.

Revenson, T. A. (1990). All other things are *not* equal: An ecological perspective on the relation between personality and disease. In H. S. Friedman (Ed.), *Personality and disease* (pp. 65–94). New York: Wiley.

Revenson, T. A. (1993). The role of social support with rheumatic disease. In S. Newman & M. Shipley (Eds.), Psychological aspects of rheumatic disease. *Balliere's Clinical Rheumatology, 7*(2), 377–396. London: Bailliere Tindal.

Revenson, T. A. (1994). Social support and marital coping with chronic illness. *Annals of Behavioral Medicine, 16*, 122–130.

Revenson, T. A. (2001). Chronic illness adjustment. In J. Worrell (Ed.), *Encyclopedia of women and gender* (Vol. 1, pp. 245–256). San Diego, CA: Academic Press.

Revenson, T. A. (2003). Scenes from a marriage: Examining support, coping, and gender within the context of chronic illness. In J. Suls & K. Wallston (Eds.), *Social psychological foundations of health and illness* (pp. 530–559). Oxford, England: Blackwell.

Revenson, T. A., Abraído-Lanza, A. F., Majerovitz, S. D., & Jordan, C. (2005). Couples' coping with chronic illness: What's gender got to do with it? In T. A. Revenson, K. Kayser, & G. Bodenmann (Eds.), *Emerging perspectives on couples' coping with stress* (pp. 137–156). Washington, DC: American Psychological Association.

Revenson, T. A., Schiaffino, K. M., Majerovitz, S. D., & Gibofsky, A. (1991). Social support as a double-edged sword: The relation of positive and problematic support to depression among rheumatoid arthritis patients. *Social Science and Medicine, 33*, 807–813.

Roberts, M. A. (Ed.). (1995). *Handbook of pediatric psychology*. New York: Guilford.

Rohrbaugh, M. J., Cranford, J. A., Shoham, V., Nicklas, J. M., Sonnega, J., & Coyne, J. C., (2002). Couples coping with congestive heart failure: Role and gender differences in psychological distress. *Journal of Family Psychology, 16*, 3–13.

Rook, K. S. (1998). Investigating the positive and negative sides of personal relationships: Through a lens darkly? In B. H. Spitzberg & W. R. Cupach (Eds.), *The dark side of close relationships* (pp. 369–393). Mahwah, NJ: Erlbaum.

Rose, G., Suls, J., Green, P. J, Lounsbury, P., & Gordon, E. (1996). Comparison of adjustment, activity, and tangible social support in men and women patients and their spouses during the six months post-myocardial infarction. *Annals of Behavioral Medicine, 18*, 264–272.

Roth, S., & Cohen, L. J. (1986). Approach, avoidance, and coping with stress. *American Psychologist, 41*, 813–819.

Rubel, A. J., & Garro, L. C. (1992). Social and cultural factors in the successful control of tuberculosis. *Public Health Reports, 107*, 626–636.

Sarason, B. R., Sarason, I. G., & Gurung, R. A. R. (2001). Close personal relationships and health outcomes: A key to the role of social support. In B. R. Sarason & S. Duck (Eds.), *Personal relationships: Implications for clinical and community psychology* (pp. 15–41). Chichester, England: Wiley.

Sarason, S. B. (1989). *The making of an American psychologist*. San Francisco: Jossey-Bass.

Scheier, M. F., & Bridges, M. W. (1995). Person variables and health: Personality predispositions and acute psychological states as shared determinants for disease. *Psychosomatic Medicine, 57*, 255–268.

Scheier, M. F., & Carver, C. S. (1985). Optimism, coping and health: Assessment and implications of generalized outcome expectancies. *Health Psychology, 4*, 219–247.

Scheier, M. F., Matthews, K. A., Owens, J. F., Magovern, G. J., Lefebvre, R. C., Abbott, R. A., et al. (1989). Dispositional optimism and recovery from coronary artery bypass surgery: The beneficial effects on physical and psychological well-being. *Journal of Personality and Social Psychology, 57*, 1024–1040.

Schiaffino, K. M., & Revenson, T. A. (1992). The role of perceived self-efficacy, perceived control, and causal attributions in adaptation to rheumatoid arthritis: Distinguishing mediator vs. moderator effects. *Personality and Social Psychology Bulletin, 18*, 709–718.

Schiaffino, K. M., Revenson, T. A., & Gibofsky, A. (1991). Assessing the role of self-efficacy beliefs in adaptation to rheumatoid arthritis. *Arthritis Care and Research, 4*, 150–157.

Schmaling, K. B. & Sher, T. G. (Eds.) (2000). *The psychology of couples and illness*. Washington, DC: American Psychological Association.

Schulz, R., O'Brien, A. T., Bookwala, J., & Fleissner, I. C. (1995). Psychiatric and physical morbidity effects of dementia caregiving: Prevalence, correlates and causes. *Gerontologist, 35*, 771–791.

Seeman, T. E., Dubin, L. F., & Seeman, M. (2003). Religiosity/spirituality and health: A critical review of the evidence for biological pathways. *American Psychologist, 58*, 53–63.

Shapiro, I., & Greenstein, R. (2001). The widening income gulf. Center on Budget and Policy Priorities. Retrieved May 10, 2004, from http://www.cbpp.org/9-4-99tax-rep.htm

Shnek, Z. M., Irvine, J., Stewart, D., & Abbey, S. (2001). Psychological factors and depressive symptoms in ischemic heart disease. *Health Psychology, 20,* 141–145.

Shumaker, S., & Hill, D. R. (1991). Gender differences in social support and physical health. *Health Psychology, 10,* 102–111.

Siegel, K., & Schrimshaw, E. W. (2000). Perceiving benefits in adversity: Stress-related growth in women living with HIV/AIDS. *Social Science and Medicine, 51,* 1543–1554.

Smith, B. W., & Zautra, A. J. (2002). The role of personality in exposure and reactivity to interpersonal stress in relation to arthritis disease activity and negative affect in women. *Health Psychology, 21,* 81–88.

Smith, T. W., & Gallo. L. C. (2001). Personality traits as risk factors for physical illness. In A. Baum, T. A. Revenson, & J. E. Singer (Eds.), *Handbook of health psychology* (pp. 139–173). Mahwah, NJ: Erlbaum.

Smyth, J., Stone, A., Hurewitz, A., & Kaell, A. (1999). Effects of writing about stressful experiences on symptom reduction in patients with asthma or rheumatoid arthritis: A randomized trial. *Journal of the American Medical Association, 281,* 1304–1309.

Snyder, C. R., Harris, C., Anderson, J. R., Holleran, S. A., Irving, L. M., Sigmon, S. T., et al. (1991). The will and the ways: Development and validation of an individual-differences measure of hope. *Journal of Personality and Social Psychology, 60,* 570–585.

Somerfield, M. R., & McCrae, R. (2000). Stress and coping research: Methodological challenges, theoretical advances, and clinical applications. *American Psychologist, 55,* 620–625.

Specter, M. (2002, July 15). The long ride. *New Yorker,* 48–58.

Spelten, E. R., Sprangers, M. A. G., & Verbeek, J. H. A. M. (2002). Factors reported to influence the return to work of cancer survivors: A literature review. *Psycho-Oncology, 11,* 124–131.

Spencer, S. M., Lehman, J. M., Wynings, C., Arena, P., Carver, C. S., Antoni, M. H., et al. (1999). Concerns about breast cancer and relations to psychosocial well-being in a multiethnic sample of early-stage patients. *Health Psychology, 18,* 159–168.

Spiegel, D., Bloom, J. R., Kraemer, H. C., & Gottheil, E. (1989). Effect of psychosocial treatment on survival of patients with metastatic breast cancer. *Lancet, 2,* 888–890.

Stanton, A. L., & Danoff-Burg, S. (2002). Emotional expression, expressive writing, and cancer. In S. Lepore & J. Smyth (Eds.). *The writing cure: Theory and research on the expressive writing paradigm* (pp. 31–51). Washington, DC: American Psychological Association.

Stanton, A. L., Collins, C. A., & Sworowski, L. A. (2001). Adjustment to chronic illness: Theory and research. In A. Baum, T. A. Revenson, & J. E. Singer (Eds.), *Handbook of health psychology* (pp. 387–403). Mahwah, NJ: Erlbaum.

Stanton, A. L., Danoff-Burg, S., Cameron, C. L., & Ellis, A. P. (1994). Coping through emotional approach: Problems of conceptualization and confounding. *Journal of Personality and Social Psychology, 66,* 350–362.

Stanton, A. L., Danoff-Burg, S., Cameron, C. L., Bishop, M. M., Collins, C. A., Kirk, S. B., et al. (2000). Emotionally expressive coping predicts psychological and physical adjustment to breast cancer. *Journal of Consulting and Clinical Psychology, 68,* 875–882.

Stanton, A. L., Danoff-Burg, S., Cameron, C. L., Snider, P., & Kirk, S. B. (1999). Social comparison and adjustment to cancer: An experimental examination of upward affiliation and downward evaluation. *Health Psychology, 18,* 151–158.

Stanton, A. L., & Snider, P. R. (1993). Coping with a breast cancer diagnosis: A prospective study. *Health Psychology, 12,* 16–23.

Stanton, A. L., Tennen, H., Affleck, G., & Mendola, R. (1992). Coping and adjustment to infertility. *Journal of Social and Clinical Psychology, 11,* 1–13.

Stewart, A. L., Greenfield, S., Hays, R. D., Wells, K., Rogers, W. H., Berry, S. D., et al. (1989). Functional status and well-being of patients with chronic conditions: Results from the Medical Outcomes Study. *Journal of the American Medical Association, 262,* 907–913.

Sullivan, M. D., LaCroix, A. Z., Russo, J. E., & Walker, E. A. (2001). Depression and self-reported physical health in patients with coronary disease: Mediating and moderating factors. *Psychosomatic Medicine, 63,* 248–256.

Suls, J., & Fletcher, B. (1985). The relative efficacy of avoidant and nonavoidant coping strategies: A meta-analysis. *Health Psychology, 4,* 249–288.

Taylor, K. L., Lamdan, R. M., Siegel, J. E., Shelby, R., Moran-Klimi, K., & Hrywna, M. (2003). Psychological adjustment among African American breast cancer patients: One-year follow-up results of a randomized psychoeducational group intervention. *Health Psychology, 22,* 316–323.

Taylor, S. E., Dickerson, S. S., & Klein, L. C. (2002). Toward a biology of social support. In C. R.

Snyder & S. J. Lopez (Eds.), *Handbook of positive psychology* (pp. 556–569). New York: Oxford University Press.

Taylor, S. E., Klein, L. C., Lewis, B. P., Gruenewald, T. L., Gurung, R. A. R., & Updegraff, J. A. (2000). Biobehavioral responses to stress in females: Tend-and-befriend, not fight-or-flight. *Psychological Review, 107,* 411–429.

Taylor, S. E. (1983). Adjustment to threatening events: A theory of cognitive adaptation. *American Psychologist, 38,* 1161–1173.

Taylor, S. E., Repetti, R., & Seeman, T. E. (1997). Health psychology: What is an unhealthy environment and how does it get under the skin? *Annual Review of Psychology, 48,* 411–447.

Tedeschi, R. G., & Calhoun, L. G. (1995). *Trauma and transformation: Growing in the aftermath of suffering.* Thousand Oaks, CA: Sage.

Tedeschi, R. G., & Calhoun, L. G. (2004). Posttraumatic growth: Conceptual foundations and empirical evidence. *Psychological Inquiry, 15,* 1–18.

Tennen, H., & Affleck, G. (1990). Blaming others for threatening events. *Psychological Bulletin, 108,* 209–232.

Tennen, H., & Affleck, G. (2000). The perception of personal control: Sufficiently important to warrant careful scrutiny. *Personality and Social Psychology Bulletin, 26,* 152–156.

Tennen, H., & Affleck, G. (2002). Benefit-finding and benefit-reminding. In C. R. Snyder & S. J. Lopez (Eds.), *Handbook of positive psychology* (pp. 584–597). New York: Oxford University Press.

Tennen, H., Affleck, G., Armeli, S., & Carney, M. A. (2000). A daily process approach to coping: Linking theory, research, and practice. *American Psychologist, 55,* 626–636.

Thoits, P. A. (1986). Social support as coping assistance. *Journal of Consulting and Clinical Psychology, 54,* 416–423.

Thompson, S. C., & Janigian, A. S. (1988). Life schemes: A framework for understanding the search for meaning. *Journal of Social and Clinical Psychology, 7,* 260–280.

Thompson, S. C., & Kyle, D. J. (2000). The role of perceived control in coping with the losses associated with chronic illness. In J. H. Harvey & E. D. Miller (Eds.), *Loss and trauma: General and close relationship perspectives* (pp. 131–145). Philadelphia: Brunner-Routledge.

Thompson, S. C., Nanni, C., & Levine, A. (1994). Primary versus secondary and central versus consequence-related control in HIV-positive men. *Journal of Personality and Social Psychology, 67,* 540–547.

Thompson, S. C., Sobolew-Shubin, A., Galbraith, M. E., Schwankovsky, L., & Cruzen, D. (1993). Maintaining perceptions of control: Finding perceived control in low-control circumstances. *Journal of Personality and Social Psychology, 64,* 293–304.

Tobin, D. L., Holroyd, K. A., Reynolds, R. V., & Wigal, J. K. (1989). The hierarchical factor structure of the Coping Strategies Inventory. *Cognitive Therapy and Research, 13,* 343–361.

Tomich, P. L., & Helgeson, V. S. (2002). Five years later: A cross-sectional comparison of breast cancer survivors with healthy women. *Psycho-Oncology, 11,* 154–169.

Tomich, P. L., & Helgeson, V. S. (2004). Is finding something good in the bad always good? Benefit finding among women with breast cancer. *Health Psychology, 23,* 16–23.

Trudeau, K. J., Danoff-Burg, S., Revenson, T. A., & Paget, S. (2003). Gender differences in agency and communion among patients with rheumatoid arthritis. *Sex Roles, 49,* 303–311.

Uchino, B. N., Cacioppo, J. T., & Kiecolt-Glaser, J. K. (1996). The relationship between social support and physiological processes: A review with emphasis on underlying mechanisms and implications for health. *Psychological Bulletin, 119,* 488–531.

Valleroy, L. A., MacKellar, D. A., Karon, J. M., Rosen, D. H., McFarland, W., Shehan, D. A., et al. (2000). HIV prevalence and associated risks in young men who have sex with men. *Journal of the American Medical Association, 284,* 198–204.

Van Tilberg, M. A. L., McCaskill, C. C., Lane, J. D., Edwards, C. L., Bethel, A., Feinglos, M. N., et al. (2001). Depressed mood is a factor in glycemic control in type I diabetes. *Psychosomatic Medicine, 63,* 551–555.

van't Spijker, A., Trijsburg, R. W., & Duivenvoorden, H. J. (1997). Psychological sequelae of cancer diagnosis: A meta-analytical review of 58 studies after 1980. *Psychosomatic Medicine, 59,* 280–293.

Vega, W. A. (1992). Theoretical and pragmatic implications of cultural diversity for community research. *American Journal of Community Psychology, 20,* 375–391.

Visotsky, H. M., Hamburg, D. A., Goss, M. E., & Lebovits, B. Z. (1961). Coping behavior under extreme stress: Observations of patients with severe poliomyelitis. *Archives of General Psychiatry, 5,* 27–52.

Vitaliano, P. P., Zhang, J., & Scanlan, J. M. (2003). Is caregiving hazardous to one's physical health? A meta-analysis. *Psychological Bulletin, 129,* 946–972.

Waltz, M., Badura, B., Pfaff, H., & Schott, T. (1988). Marriage and the psychological consequences of a heart attack: A longitudinal study of adaptation to chronic illness after 3 years. *Social Science and Medicine, 27,* 149–158.

Wegner, D., & Pennebaker, J. (Eds.). (1992). *Handbook of mental control.* New York: Prentice-Hall.

Weick, K. (1984). Small wins: Redefining the scale of social problems. *American Psychologist, 39,* 40–49.

Wethington, E., McLeod, J. D., & Kessler, R. (1987). The importance of life events for explaining sex differences in mental health. In R. C. Barnett, L. Biener, & G. K. Baruch (Eds.), *Gender and stress* (pp. 144–155). New York: Free Press.

Whitfield, K. E., Weidner, G., Clark, R., & Anderson, N. B. (2002). Sociodemographic diversity and behavioral medicine. *Journal of Consulting and Clinical Psychology, 70,* 463–481.

Williams, D. R. (1990). Socioeconomic differentials in health: A review and redirection. *Social Psychology Quarterly, 53,* 81–99.

Williamson, G. M. (2000). Extending the activity restriction model of depressed affect: Evidence from a sample of breast cancer patients. *Health Psychology, 19,* 339–347.

Wills, T. A., & Fegan, M. F. (2001). Social networks and social support. In A. Baum, T. A. Revenson, & J. E. Singer (Eds.), *Handbook of health psychology* (pp. 139–173). Mahwah, NJ: Erlbaum.

Wortman, C. B., & Silver, R. C. (1989). The myths of coping with loss. *Journal of Clinical and Consulting Psychology, 57,* 349–357.

Wortman, C. B., & Silver, R. C. (2001). The myths of coping with loss revisited. In M. S. Stroebe, R. O. Hansson, W. Stroebe, & H. Schut (Eds.), *Handbook of bereavement research: Consequences, coping, and care* (pp. 405–429). Washington, DC: American Psychological Association.

Wulsin, L. R., & Singal, B. M. (2003). Do depressive symptoms increase the risk for the onset of coronary disease? A systematic quantitative review. *Psychosomatic Medicine, 65,* 201–210.

Yali, A. M., & Revenson, T. A. (2004). How changes in population demographics will impact health psychology: Incorporating a broader notion of cultural competence into the field. *Health Psychology, 23,* 147–155.

Young, L. D. (1992). Psychological factors in rheumatoid arthritis. *Journal of Consulting and Clinical Psychology, 60,* 619–627.

Zautra, A. J., Burleson, M. H., Matt, K. S., Roth, S., & Burrows, L. (1994). Interpersonal stress, depression, and disease activity in rheumatoid arthritis and osteoarthritis patients. *Health Psychology, 13,* 139–148.

Zautra, A. J., & Manne, S. L. (1992). Coping with rheumatoid arthritis: A review of a decade of research. *Annals of Behavioral Medicine, 14,* 31–39.

Zautra, A. J., Smith, B., Affleck, G., & Tennen, H. (2001). Examinations of chronic pain and affect relationships: Applications of a dynamic model of affect. *Journal of Consulting and Clinical Psychology, 69,* 785–796.

10

Karen S. Rook, Susan T. Charles,
and Jutta Heckhausen

Aging and Health

In the past century, economically developed nations experienced unprecedented changes in the age structure of their populations, as a result of improved public health measures and medical advances that extended life expectancy. Throughout human history there have always been individuals who lived to an advanced age, but such survival was unusual before the twentieth century. During the twentieth century, life expectancy increased markedly and birth rates declined, ushering in an era of dramatic societal aging among developed nations. Since 1900, for example, the total population of the United States tripled in size, but the population of people over age 65 grew 11-fold (National Center for Health Statistics [NCHS], 1999a, 1999b). Average life expectancy at birth in the United States was 49.24 years in 1900, whereas it is now 74.8 years for men and 80.1 years for women (Hoyert, Kung, & Smith, 2005). Similarly, in 1900 only 4% of the population in the United States was greater than 65 years of age, but that figure has risen to 12.4% and is expected to climb to 20% by the year 2030 (American Administration on Aging [AAA], 2001). With the overall growth of the population, these percentage increases represent a very substantial, and still expanding, increase in the absolute numbers of people living to age 65 and beyond.

Accompanying this demographic shift has been a change in the major threats to health, and corresponding changes in medical research and treatment. Infectious and parasitic acute illnesses have been replaced by chronic, degenerative illnesses as the dominant health concerns in modern societies, and it is older adults who are most likely to experience chronic conditions (Merck Institute of Aging & Centers for Disease Control and Prevention [MIAH/CDD], 2004). Many of these chronic conditions, moreover, have roots in long-standing behaviors or lifestyles that compromise health over time. The traditional medical model, in which disease is conceptualized as the result of specific pathogens or physical changes that can be treated by medical technology, is not well suited to address the chronic conditions that contribute to morbidity and mortality in later adulthood. Instead, health researchers have turned to the biopsychosocial model of health, in which health and illness in old age are viewed as resulting not only from biological and physical factors but also from the cumulative effects of a lifetime of psychological, social, and behavioral processes (Engel, 1977; Suls & Rothman, 2004). This model recognizes the biological trajectory of decline throughout the adult life span and the fact that physical changes increase older adults' susceptibility to acute and chronic conditions. In addition, this model acknowledges that psychological and social processes interact over time with biological changes to influence physical functioning, onset and progression of disease, and adaptation to illness (Engel, 1977).

The biopsychosocial model can be applied to people of all ages, but this chapter focuses on older adults. The chapter is organized in three main sections. In the first section, we emphasize the biological component of the model, discussing trajectories of physical functioning and health in old age, including physical decline, morbidity, and mortality. We provide illustrations of normative changes that occur with age in the functioning of organ and sensory systems, noting the considerable variability in aging processes that exists within and across people. We then consider how these primary aging processes affect older adults' vulnerability to chronic illnesses and mortality. This leads to a discussion of how aging processes affect older adults' experiences of illness and medical intervention, as well as their perceptions of their physical health and their ability to carry out daily activities.

The second section of the chapter focuses on the psychosocial component of the biopsychosocial model, emphasizing psychosocial factors that influence physical health and functioning in old age. We approach this complex topic by illustrating several classes of psychosocial factors that influence health in later life, including ones that (1) operate very early in life to increase the risk of illness and disability in later adulthood, (2) emerge in later adulthood to influence concurrent health status, (3) influence adaptation to illness and disease in later adulthood, and (4) influence the optimal strategies for and benefits derived from health promotion and rehabilitation in late adulthood. A review of research that bears on these different classes of psychosocial factors is beyond the scope of the chapter, but we illustrate each one with a relevant research example.

Finally, in the third section of the chapter, we discuss two scenarios that researchers have projected for the health and well-being of future cohorts of older adults. One scenario forecasts that any future increases in life expectancy will be accompanied by corresponding gains in health and declines in disability. Another scenario projects that potential increases in life expectancy are unlikely to be unaccompanied by such health gains and,

instead, will yield only added years of illness and disability and a correspondingly greater societal burden of health care. These starkly different scenarios should serve as a call to arms, in a sense, for researchers who wish to contribute to efforts to forestall the darker forecast. We link our discussion of these different scenarios to alternative conceptions of what constitutes successful aging, and we conclude by highlighting the important role that health psychologists have to play in identifying the conditions and processes that prevent premature death, decrease the duration and severity of disability, and help to preserve well-being when functional limitations develop in later life.

Given the breadth and complexity of the topic of health and aging, this chapter necessarily considers some issues at the expense of others. We emphasize findings and conclusions derived from research conducted primarily in modern, economically developed nations, and these findings may not generalize to less developed nations. Similarly, we provide only a limited treatment of the substantial heterogeneity that exists in the elderly population, although we highlight well-documented sociodemographic variations in health and illness in later life. Cognitive functioning and mental health in later adulthood are integrally linked to physical health, but these topics, too, are beyond the scope of the chapter (see Craik & Salthouse, 2000, and Gatz, Kasl-Godley, & Karel, 1996, for comprehensive reviews). Finally, we emphasize the individual level of analysis, given our background as psychologists and the focus of this volume on health psychology. A more complete treatment of the topic of aging and health ultimately will require integration of research on individual and social structural factors that interact to influence health and functioning over the life span (Riley, 1998).

Physical Functioning and Health in Old Age

It is an unavoidable fact that biological and physiological functioning decline throughout the adult life span. Considerable intra- and interindividual variability exists in the rate and extent of change, however, making these declines difficult to characterize. Organ systems and functional abilities decline at different rates, and people also vary in the rate and extent of physical changes they experience over time (Rowe & Kahn, 1987; Shock et al., 1984). Complicating matters further, the implications of such declines for susceptibility to illness and for daily activities also vary. Some declines are unalterable, whereas others are potentially reversible. In addition, some declines can be mitigated by compensatory gains in other areas of physiological functioning. The changes that accompany normal aging, referred to as *primary aging,* generally can be characterized as relatively benign (M. E. Williams, 1994); these changes should be distinguished from pathological processes that accompany disease, or changes referred to as *secondary aging* (Birren & Cunningham, 1985; see Blumenthal, 2003, for a more complete discussion of the aging-disease distinction).

Primary Aging

Age-related declines in the functioning of sensory and organ systems have been documented extensively, with many declines beginning as early as the middle to late 20s (see review by Whitbourne, 1996). For example, hearing undergoes changes with age, making it more difficult to understand sounds at higher frequencies, and vision also changes, resulting in greater difficulty focusing on close objects and seeing under conditions of glare or low illumination (National Institute on Aging [NIA], 1996). The size and efficiency of many organs decrease, and the percentage of fat within organs increases. Lung capacity, for example, diminishes by about 40% from age 20 to 70 (NIA, 1996). Such decreases in organ size or capacity can signal changes in biological functioning. For example, the thymus gland shrinks considerably with age, resulting in fewer or less efficient T cells in the bloodstream. This decrease in a gland important to the immune system may contribute to increased susceptibility to, and prolonged recovery from, infections in later life (Terpenning & Bradley, 1991).

Primary aging also includes declines in higher-order regulatory processes, which may influence older adults' susceptibility to environmental challenges and other stressors. *Homeostasis* refers to the automatic and constantly occurring adjustments that the human body makes to maintain equilibrium, such as adjusting body temperature to changes in room temperature. With advancing age, maintaining homeostasis becomes more difficult,

and this may increase older adults' vulnerability to morbidity and mortality. Greater difficulty regulating body temperatures with age, for example, may lead to conditions that partly account for the elevated death rates among older adults during significant heat waves (Semenza et al., 1996).

Variability and Malleability of Physical Decline

Declines in organ functioning and homeostatic processes tend to be gradual, however, and they also vary considerably within and across individuals (see review by Rowe & Kahn, 1998). For example, an older person may exhibit marked decline in one area, such as pulmonary functioning, but little decline in other areas. Chronological age per se is an imperfect predictor of the nature or extent of decline in physiological functioning, as some older individuals exhibit few of the typical changes associated with aging, whereas others exhibit many changes.

In addition, declines in functioning in some areas may be offset by gains in other areas. For example, among adults who are free of heart disease, the ability of the heart to pump blood rapidly during periods of cardiovascular demand (such as exercise) declines with age, but overall blood flow declines relatively little because the volume of blood pumped with each stroke increase with age (NIA, 1993). Similarly, although neuronal loss or damage occurs with age, the brain appears to adapt by increasing the number or density of synapses between brain cells (Scheibel, 1996). Moreover, with the proper interventions, some declines are preventable and reversible. For example, in the absence of exercise, muscle mass declines by more than 20% for both men and women from age 30 to age 70, but regular exercise has been found to be effective in preventing such losses (NIA, 1996).

Reserve Capacity and Everyday Functioning

The existence of a reserve capacity in most organ systems minimizes the impact of common age-related declines on everyday activities. This extra capacity allows organ systems to function at 4 to 10 times their normal capacity, if needed, under stressful conditions (Fries & Crapo, 1981). Kidney functioning declines by 30% after age 30, for example, but the remaining capacity is more than adequate to allow wastes to be extracted from the bloodstream under ordinary circumstances (NIA, 1996). In the context of very stressful life circumstances or extreme environmental conditions, however, the demands on an organ system may overwhelm even this reserve capacity, leading to organ failure. Cardiovascular functioning that is sufficient to support an older person's daily walks, for example, may be insufficient to support his or her efforts to shovel snow or lift heavy boxes, increasing the risk of a heart attack. Thus, despite common declines in physical functioning, older adults often do not experience substantial adverse effects on their ability to carry out daily activities. Such adverse effects become evident most often when older adults exert themselves beyond their customary levels of activity, such as walking up a steep flight of stairs or fighting an illness.

Reserve capacity is not a static resource, however, but tends to decline with age (Fries, 1980; Rowe & Kahn, 1998). This decline may be partly responsible for the fact that older adults are more adversely affected by, and even more likely to die from, conditions that tend not to be lethal at younger ages, such as influenza or pneumonia (Koivula, Sten, & Makela, 1999).

Primary Aging and Acute Illness

Primary aging refers to age-related declines in physical functioning, not disease processes. Declines in reserve capacity and homeostasis make older adults more vulnerable, however, to the effects of acute disease processes (Sahyoun, Lentzner, Hoyert, & Robinson, 2001). Acute illnesses tend to be more common in young adulthood, but they often affect older adults more severely. More than 5% of deaths among older adults are attributable to conditions such as pneumonia, influenza, and septicemia, and researchers believe that the death rate from these conditions has increased in recent years (Sahyoun et al., 2001). Some epidemiologists have cautioned, moreover, that infectious diseases may be reemerging as significant causes of morbidity and mortality in economically developed nations due to increased international trade and migration, ecological disruption, and the spread of antibiotic-resistant pathogens (Barrett, Kuzawa, McDade, & Armelagos, 1998). If this should prove to be the case, existing views of the dominant threats to health in later life might require revision.

Secondary Aging

The fact that progressive declines in physiological functioning are common in later adulthood makes it challenging to distinguish changes that reflect intrinsic processes of aging (primary aging) from those that reflect the accumulated effects of disease, disuse, or exposure to environmental hazards (secondary aging). For example, osteoarthritis was once considered a normative age change, or the result of primary aging (Bennett, Waine, & Bauer, 1942). Only in the past 20 years did researchers determine that this condition represents a disease process that is associated with but not caused by age (e.g., Dequeker, 1989; Oddis, 1996). Atherosclerosis, in contrast, is now regarded as an essentially universal change that occurs with advancing age, or an outcome of primary aging (NIA, 1996). Distinguishing between changes that result from primary aging and those that result from secondary aging requires longitudinal studies that span decades (T. F. Williams, 1992).

Early and influential examples of longitudinal studies undertaken for this purpose include the Duke Longitudinal Study of Aging (Busse et al., 1985) and the Baltimore Longitudinal Study of Aging (NIA, 1993, 1996; Shock et al., 1984). Both studies were initiated in the 1950s, and both administered extensive batteries of physiological and psychological tests to participants on a regular basis over a period of decades. The Baltimore Longitudinal Study, for example, which began in 1958 and is still ongoing, brings participants ranging in age from their 20s to their 90s to Baltimore every 2 years to undergo as many as 100 different assessments of physiological, psychological, and social functioning; the study has yielded more than 800 scientific papers to date (NIA, 1996). Longitudinal studies have proved to be crucial to efforts to identify the timing and predictors of significant health-related changes in later life, such as the transitions between physical decline, functional impairment, and disability, as well as possible transitions between disease and recovery (Verbrugge, Reoma, & Gruber-Baldini, 1994). For example, Fozard, Metter, and Brant (1990) observed that major transitions in the rate of decline in strength occur in young and middle adulthood, rather than in old age.

Allostatic Load

The cumulative effects of stressors experienced over the course of a lifetime may contribute to secondary aging by causing permanent shifts in the organism's ability to regulate its physiological parameters (such as blood pressure or immune functioning) in response to external demands (Robinson-Whelen, Kiecolt-Glaser, & Glaser, 2000). Allostatic load is defined as the accumulated wear and tear on the body that results from having to adapt repeatedly to physical and psychological stressors (McEwen & Stellar, 1993). It is commonly measured by relatively stable indicators of physiological reactivity to physiological dysregulation, such as cholesterol levels, body mass index, glucose levels, or blood-clotting ability (McEwen & Stellar, 1993): The greater the number of these risk factors at elevated levels, the greater the allostatic load. The precursors of high allostatic load may begin with conditions that develop relatively early in life, such as childhood obesity or hypertension. Stressful life events experienced throughout the life span can lead to gradual alterations in the various components of allostatic load.

The physiological toll of severe or persistent stressors affects all age groups, but allostatic load generally increases with age, with significant implications for the health of older adults. Allostatic load predicts cognitive decline and increased functional impairment among older adults (Seeman, Singer, Rowe, Horwitz, & McEwen, 1997). The generally higher allostatic load among older adults, coupled with age-related declines in reserve capacity and in the ability to maintain homeostasis, can contribute to higher morbidity and mortality among older adults even when their stress levels resemble those of younger age groups.

Secondary Aging and Chronic Illness

Secondary aging is generally attributed to the cumulative effects of disease, disuse, or exposure to hazards; as such, it is closely linked to chronic illness in later life. Chronic illnesses last for long periods of time, cannot be cured, and have the potential to interfere with daily functioning and to detract from the quality of life. Unlike acute illnesses, chronic illnesses are more common in later adulthood, and approximately 80% of adults older than 65 have at least one chronic condition (Centers for Disease Control and Prevention [CDC]; 2003). Like acute conditions, chronic conditions tend to be associated with greater medical complications and greater restrictions of activity among older adults (AARP, 2001; MIAH/CDC, 2004). For

example, having one or more chronic conditions is associated with restrictions of daily activities among fewer than 10% of people under the age of 45 as compared with 25% of those aged 65 to 74 and 45% of those aged 75 and older (Schiller & Bernadel, 2004). The greater prevalence of chronic health problems in later life is partly attributable to the aging of young and middle-aged adults with disabilities, but it primarily reflects the increased incidence of chronic illness in later adulthood (Lollar & Crews, 2003).

The most common chronic conditions in the United States for both older men and women include arthritis, hypertension, heart disease, cataracts, diabetes, and sensory impairments (vision or hearing loss; AARP, 2001; MIAH/CDC, 2004). Some chronic conditions are age related, such as heart disease; others are not, such as paraplegia resulting from a spinal cord injury, but they may have significantly greater physical complications at advanced ages (e.g., Gerhard, Bergstrom, Charlifue, Menter, & Whiteneck, 1993). Chronic conditions experienced in old age tend to be more disabling, to require more care, and to be more difficult and costlier to treat than the conditions that affect younger age groups (NAAS, 1999a). In fact, chronic conditions account for about half of all disability among older adults in the United States (Merck Institute of Aging/Gerontological Society of America [MIAH/GSA], 2002) and contribute to older adults' greater health care utilization (including hospitalization) and expenditures (AARP, 2001). Although some chronic illnesses may not impact daily life significantly (e.g., successfully controlled hypertension), others can be debilitating and affect daily functioning (e.g., chronic obstructive pulmonary disease).

The chronic illnesses from which older adults suffer tend to be degenerative and to develop relatively slowly over many years or decades (Kaplan, Haan, & Wallace, 1999). Chronic illness may exist at a subclinical level for many years in middle adulthood and old age, before symptoms become evident or severe in late life (Fries & Crapo, 1981). For example, the onset of coronary heart disease may begin in young adulthood, with the advent of elevated cholesterol and small arterial plaques. The underlying coronary disease processes may progress with the development of larger arterial plaques in middle age before symptoms appear or adversely affect functioning. Although the progression from symptom onset to disability may unfold relatively slowly over time, this transition can be hastened by risk factors that are relatively acute, such as sudden stress or vasospasm in the case of cardiovascular disease (Kaplan et al., 1999). Whether age at the time of onset influences the severity and subsequent course of a disease (e.g., development of prostate cancer at age 75 versus age 60) is an issue that has just begun to receive attention (Siegler, Bastian, & Bosworth, 2001).

Comorbidity

Many older adults must deal with multiple chronic conditions simultaneously (Jaur & Stoddard, 1999; Kaplan et al., 1999), and these conditions may affect each other. For example, diabetes increases the risk of heart disease and also reduces the likelihood of survival after a heart attack or stroke (Wallace & Lemke, 1991). Similarly, arthritis may discourage physical exercise, and the lack of physical exercise may aggravate a coexisting condition, such as diabetes. Syndrome X is a cluster of coexisting disorders that generally includes glucose intolerance/non-insulin-dependent diabetes mellitus, hypertriglyceridemia, and hypertension. This syndrome is not uncommon among older adults, unfortunately, and is related to an increased risk of coronary artery disease and subsequent mortality (Kaplan, 1992). Comorbidity with mental health problems, particularly depression, is common, as well, potentially accelerating the rate of decline and complicating treatment plans (Bruce, Seeman, Merrill, & Blazer, 1994). More generally, comorbidity may affect the manifestation, detection, and outcomes of various conditions (Kaplan et al., 1999).

Frailty

Advancing age, coupled with declining reserves in multiple organ systems, increases the likelihood that an older adult will be regarded as frail. *Frailty* does not yet have a strict definition, but physicians use the term to refer to older adults "who have become fragile without a dominant chronic illness" (Fries, 2004, p. M604). Frailty is often characterized by wasting of the body (unintentional weight loss of 10 or more pounds), general muscular weakness (reduced grip strength, for example), slow walking speed, and low physical activity (Fried et al. 2001). Older adults regarded as frail tend to be older than 85 and to have an increased risk of falls, injuries, hospitalization, institutionalization, and

mortality. Gillick (2001) described a "cycle of frailty" characterized by a pattern of declining physiological reserves that decrease an older person's ability to "withstand acute illness or emotional upheaval or physical dislocation" (p. M135). Frailty is associated, therefore, with an increased risk of falls, hospitalization, disability, and mortality.

Mortality

In the United States, the leading causes of death among adults aged 65 and older are heart disease, cancer, stroke, chronic obstructive pulmonary disease, pneumonia and influenza, and diabetes (Himes, 2001). Together, these conditions account for 75% of the deaths among older adults, with just two conditions—heart disease and cancer—accounting for more than half of the deaths among older adults. Additionally, the progressive declines in organ reserves that cause frailty make frail older adults increasingly vulnerable to small perturbations that may cause death (Fries, 2004). Fries (2004, p. 604) has referred to frailty as "the ultimate competing risk for mortality, that of 'old age.'" It is not surprising, given the association between advanced age and both chronic illness and frailty, that death has come to be a phenomenon that is concentrated in later life in most developed nations. In the United States, for example, approximately three-quarters of all deaths occur among people aged 65 and older (Sahyoun et al., 2001).

It is important to bear in mind, of course, that death is not concentrated in later adulthood in all regions of the world. Extreme poverty and high rates of disease in many areas of the developing world have contributed to a problem of "shortevity" rather than "longevity" (Butler, 2002). In less economically developed nations, infectious diseases still figure prominently as causes of mortality, and life expectancies are correspondingly short (Butler, 2002). In Sierra Leone, for example, the average life expectancy is only 40 years (Butler, 2002), and the disability-adjusted life expectancy (the number of years of life expected to be lived in full health) is only 25 years (Mathers, Sadana, Salomon, Murray, & Lopez, 2001).

Moreover, even in economically developed societies, researchers worry about the extent to which gains in life expectancy can be sustained. On the one hand, reductions in such behavioral risk factors as cigarette smoking contributed to significant decreases in death rates due to heart disease and stroke over the past two decades in the United States (Himes, 2001). Mortality rates for cancer also declined in recent decades for men, due largely to decreases in lung cancer attributed to reduced rates of smoking. Yet during this same time period, rates of smoking among women increased, causing lung cancer to replace breast cancer as the dominant cause of cancer deaths among women (Himes, 2001). Burgeoning rates of obesity in the population also cast a troubling shadow over the longevity gains observed until now in the United States, as obesity elevates the risk for a number of serious chronic conditions (Wadden, Brownell, & Foster, 2002). In fact, an analysis of the implications of high rates of childhood obesity for life expectancy offered the chilling forecast that the current generation of children may be the first in modern history to lead sicker and shorter lives than those of their parents (Olshansky et al., 2005).

Disease Manifestation and Perceptions

The manifestations and perceptions of symptoms of disease may differ for younger and older people. Myocardial infarctions, for example, are more often "clinically silent" in older adults, relative to younger adults, but are no less serious (Kaplan et al., 1999). Other chronic diseases or disease events may go undetected for longer periods in later life because their symptom manifestations are more subtle or vague (Kaplan et al., 1999). Perceptions and reports of pain appear to change with age, with older adults exhibiting greater reticence to report pain (although not under conditions of strong pain stimulation; Yong, Gibson, Horne, & Helme, 2001), less confidence in their judgments of pain sensations, and greater reluctance to label sensations as painful (Yong et al., 2001). Evidence suggests that older adults tend to "normalize" at least some of the physical symptoms they experience, attributing them to aging rather than to illness (George, 2001; Stoller, 1993). Older people also sometimes misconstrue symptoms of disease or acute disease events (such as a heart attack or ulcer) as normal aspects of aging (Leventhal & Prohaska, 1986; Stoller, 1993), thus delaying diagnosis and treatment. Some researchers have expressed concern that an ethic of "stoicism" could lead older adults to minimize the significance of symptoms of potentially serious health problems, deferring or failing to seek appropriate medical care as a result. Distress about physical symptoms may be a necessary precondition to motivate older adults to seek care (Cameron, Leventhal, & Leventhal, 1983).

Medical Intervention

The primary focus of medical intervention traditionally has been on curing illness rather than providing palliative care or assisting with the management of a chronic, degenerative disease process. Yet the epidemiological and demographic revolutions that have occurred in developed nations, and that are under way in many developing nations (Murray & Lopez, 1996), are prompting a shift in public health priorities, from the prevention and treatment of communicable diseases to the prevention and management of chronic conditions, pain, and disability.

Efforts to treat chronic illnesses often frustrate both the physician and the patient. Besides being frustrating, treating older adults is often more challenging than treating younger adults. Understanding age-related changes in biological and physiological processes is vital for successful medical treatment, yet such information has been scarce until relatively recently. Norms, diagnostic criteria, and treatment plans for a variety of conditions have been based on predominantly middle-aged men (Meyerowitz & Hart, 1995). Determining appropriate medication dosages for older adults is often difficult, for example, because older adults generally have a greater percentage of fatty tissue and a slower metabolism than do middle-aged adults, and both of these factors magnify drug effects. Metabolism in the liver declines, as does kidney blood flow and functioning, resulting in reduced renal clearance and a potential increase in the accumulation of drugs in the bloodstream (Kaplan et al., 1999). Thus, medication may have longer-lasting effects in older adults as compared with younger age groups, and smaller doses may achieve the desired therapeutic effects (Steiner, 1996). Comorbidity often increases the complexity of medication regimens, with a corresponding increase in the number of medications taken and the risk of drug interactions and compliance problems (Roberts & Snyder, 2001).

Achieving adherence to medical regimens also presents unique challenges in later life. Older adults often need to recall and synchronize multiple medication schedules, and they may experience added difficulties reading medication labels or instructions, opening medication packaging (e.g., child-proof bottles), and swallowing large medication capsules (Miller, 2003). Some older adults also attempt to self-regulate drug dosages based on their perceptions of their health status, believing, for example, that they can forgo blood pressure medication for hypertensive illness on days when they do not feel stressed. Such mistaken beliefs can have grave health consequences.

Medical researchers and practitioners have called for fundamental changes in prevailing approaches to the management of chronic disease. Some have urged consideration of models in which patients function less as passive recipients of health care than as active partners who collaborate with health care providers in the complex and continuous processes of managing chronic disease over time (Holman, 2002). Arguments for such a partnership model grow out of recognition that the course of chronic disease in individual patients is characterized by considerable uncertainty and that patients often have greater awareness than do physicians of potentially important trends and transitions in their disease progression. This greater awareness of internal states can be joined with the physicians' knowledge base to make more effective joint decisions about care and to allow for interventions at an early stage when the patient's illness course begins to departs from an expected trajectory (Kane, 2001). In addition, the long-term management of chronic illnesses requires patients to understand and accept more responsibility and a wider range of practices than is typically the case with acute illness, and this, too, is likely to require an effective partnership between patients and physicians (Holman, 2002; Kane, 2001).

Advances in medical technology also have begun to allow forms of medical care to be administered at home that were once the province of hospitals and nursing homes, such as inhalation therapies and intravenous medication regimens (Kane, 1995). Such home-based "high-tech" health care has the potential to contain treatment costs, but it creates new challenges for individual patients and their family caregivers, including the need to understand and properly administer technologically complex care and the need to adapt to a medicalized home environment (Kane, 1995). Technologies have begun to emerge that allow for the remote monitoring of patients' health status; they have the potential to improve patient care by increasing the

ease and efficiency of ongoing health-status monitoring and the regularity of patient-physician exchanges (Wasson et al., 1992). Such technologies have the potential to be particularly useful for elderly patients whose chronic conditions restrict mobility and make visits to physicians' offices arduous ordeals. Yet here, too, a great deal remains to be learned about patients' understanding and acceptance of remote-monitoring technologies and the psychological impacts of such regular health-status monitoring and feedback. This discussion illustrates that medical care practices are beginning to undergo transformations in response to population aging and the ascendance of chronic disease as the dominant threat to health in developed countries (Kane, 1995).

Implications of Age-Related Declines for Functional Health and Self-Rated Health

As noted earlier, the declines in physiological functioning and health status that often occur with advancing age do not inevitably impair older adults' day-to-day functioning and qualify of life. The impact of such changes is typically gauged by examining how they affect older adults' ability to carry out their daily activities (functional health) and how they influence older adults' evaluations of their health (self-rated health). Moreover, as indicated earlier, the heterogeneity that exists within the elderly population makes broad generalizations difficult. Bearing this caveat in mind, we will describe some of the common patterns that have been documented in the literature and will highlight departures from these patterns that have been associated with sociodemographic variations.

We also wish to note that the patterns we discuss, such as statistics regarding the percentage of older adults who exhibit some degree of functional impairment, are often interpreted in two different ways. For example, a statistic indicating that 21% of older adults experience difficulty performing at least some tasks that are essential to maintaining independence (AARP, 2001) is applauded by some as evidence that 79% of older adults experience no such difficulties. For others, the 21% figure commands attention and is regarded as a cause for concern because it translates into huge numbers of people, in an absolute sense, who may be on a health trajectory that culminates in the loss of independence. This basic tension between emphasizing the "good" or "bad" news about aging recurs throughout the literature on aging and health and, indeed, throughout much of the history of gerontology (Carstensen & Charles, 2003). This is a theme to which we will turn in the concluding section of the chapter because it is tied centrally to differing conceptions of what constitutes optimal aging.

Functional Health

Chronic conditions generally do not take a substantial toll on older adults' daily functioning until relatively advanced old age. Among persons aged 65 to 74, only 29% report limiting their daily activities because of a chronic condition, but this figure rises to 51% among those aged 75 and older (AARP, 2001). A more complete view of the impact of chronic illness and declines in physiological function emerges when researchers examine older adults' ability to carry out everyday tasks of living. The terms *activities of daily living* (ADLs) and *instrumental activities of daily living* (IADLs) have come to refer to two classes of everyday activities that reflect the ability to carry out self-care tasks. ADLs refer to self-care activities that are necessary to live alone (e.g., bathing, dressing, feeding) but not necessarily to live independently. IADLs refer to more demanding activities that allow people to function independently in the community, such as shopping, preparing meals, and managing personal finances (Nagi, 1965; Katz, 1983). A person who is able to complete ADLs but not IADLs, for example, may live alone but would need someone to help them with IADLs. ADL impairment, in contrast, is most strongly linked to the need for long-term care. About 14% of adults aged 65 and older have difficulty carrying out at least some activities of daily living, and 21% have difficulty carrying out instrumental activities of living (AARP, 2001). In the population aged 25 to 64, the corresponding figures are much lower—roughly 3% and 4%, respectively (AARP, 2001).

More recently, researchers have moved beyond simply attempting to document the percentage of older adults with particular kinds of functional limitations to investigate the stages in the transition from minor to major impairment, and factors that hasten or slow these transitions (Femia, Zarit, & Johansson, 2001). Theoretical models have been developed to guide such investigations. A prominent model developed by Verbrugge and Jette (1994) describes the disablement process as involving a progression from a pathological condition (disease onset or injury) to impairment (dysfunction in specific bodily systems) to functional limitations (difficulties performing basic activities of daily living, such as handling objects or ambulating) to disability (difficulties performing instrumental activities of daily life, such as personal care or meal preparation). Empirical evidence has confirmed some of the core assumptions of this model, such as the assumption that functional limitations represent a major cause of subsequent disability, and that some limitations (such as lower body limitations) are more consequential than other (such as upper body limitations; Lawrence & Jette, 1996; Penninx et al., 2000). Interestingly, however, additional evidence suggests that some older adults experience disability even in the absence of identifiable functional limitations (Fried, Ettinger, Lind, Newman, & Gardin, 1994). For these individuals, factors other than physical impairment appear to contribute to the development of disability. Potential candidates include social isolation, depression, and poor self-rated health (Femia et al., 2001).

Self-Rated Health

Interest in self-rated health in later life has grown in recent years both because it is a legitimate dimension of health in its own right and because it has been found to predict important health outcomes. For example, self-rated health has been found to predict the severity of disability in later life, after controlling for functional limitations (Femia et al., 2001) and, further, has been found to predict mortality, after controlling for physical health, chronic illnesses, and functional limitations (Deeg & Bath, 2003; Strawbridge & Wallhagen, 1999). Significant associations have been found between older adults' ratings of their health and objective assessments of their health (e.g., Fillenbaum, 1979), although self-reported health often predicts mortality better than these measures or even physician ratings (e.g., Benyamini & Idler, 1999; Borawski, Kinney, & Kahana, 1996).

Despite the age-related declines in physiological functioning and increases in chronic illness that we have discussed, older adults' perceptions of their health tend, on average, to be positive (although sociodemographic variations, discussed later, qualify this conclusion). In 2001, 42% of adults aged 65 to 74 described their health as "excellent" or "very good"; this represents an increase from 35% in 1982 (MIAH/GSA, 2002). Chronic illness does detract from self-rated health, particularly among women (NAAS, 1999a), but even older adults with chronic conditions often rate their health more favorably than might be expected given their physical impairments.

The positive nature of older adults' appraisals of their health may partly reflect their tendency to evaluate their health with reference to age peers rather than with reference to their own health at a younger age (Robinson-Whelen & Kiecolt-Glaster, 1997). When asked to compare themselves with others their own age, older adults' ratings are decidedly more favorable (Roberts, 1999). In addition, most older adults do not identify themselves as "old," and they tend to regard their life circumstances, including their own health, as better than those of age peers (National Council on Aging, 2002; Smith, Shelley, & Dennerstein, 1994). Research also suggests that self-rated health is based on more than functional health and, rather, reflects positive mood and engagement in social activities, suggesting that the full "illness-wellness continuum" is important in understanding how older adults appraise their health status (Benyamini, Idler, Leventhal, & Leventhal, 2000). Older adults' evaluations of their health are not always so positive, however, and they vary across sociodemographic groups, as discussed in the next section.

Sociodemographic Variations in Health, Illness, and Mortality

Later life represents an expansive time frame, including people from age 65 to those older than 100, and it includes a heterogeneous group of people who have accumulated diverse life experiences. Age itself is an important source of variation within the elderly population, and gerontological researchers often have found it useful to distinguish between the "young-old" (often defined as those aged 65 to 80) and the "old-old" (defined as those older than 80 or 85). Compared with the young-old, the old-old tend to have more chronic conditions and to experience more adverse effects of both acute and chronic illnesses. The higher rates of chronic illness and disability among the oldest members of the

elderly population, coupled with the fact that more people are surviving to very advanced old age with conditions that formerly would have resulted in an earlier death (MIAH/GSA, 2002), may account for their somewhat less positive health assessments. The percentage of people describing their health as "excellent" or "very good" drops to 34% among those aged 75 to 84 and to 28% among those aged 85 and older, as compared with 43% of those aged 65 to 74 (MIAH/CDC, 2004). Additionally, the proportion of the old-old who describe their health as "excellent" or "very good" has declined slightly over time, in contrast to the gains seen for the young-old (AARP, 2001). The health status of the very old is of special interest to gerontological researchers because individuals aged 85 and older constitute the fastest-growing segment of the elderly population.

The great heterogeneity among older adults in terms of other sociodemographic characteristics results in different trajectories of health, which often underscore how differences throughout the life span affect the health experience. Unfortunately, groups that historically have faced discrimination also commonly experience poorer health outcomes in old age. These differences become apparent when people report on their health. Older African Americans less often describe their health as "excellent" or "very good" than do their European American counterparts, and few of the gains in self-reported health noted earlier in this discussion for European Americans generalize to African Americans. For example, only 26% of African Americans aged 65 to 74 endorsed these positive health descriptions in 1992, a figure that had increased by only 2% from 1982 (AARP, 2001).

Women live longer than men, but they experience more, if less lethal, chronic conditions (Verbrugge, 2001). Consistent with this, women generally rate their health less favorably and report more restrictions of activity and more days of bed rest when they feel ill (Verbrugge, 1989, 2001). This gender difference in self-rated health is evident across the life span, leading Verbrugge (1989) to conclude that women feel sicker for more of their lives than do men of the same age; women survive to live longer, but one price for this greater longevity is a higher prevalence and duration of disability (Stuck et al., 1999). Across a number of studies, older women have been found to exhibit more activity limitations because of underlying health conditions than have men (Verbrugge, 2001). From this perspective, the everyday burden of chronic illness in later life seems to be greater for women than for men (Verbrugge, 1985). Older men are more likely than older women to suffer from heart disease, in contrast, which poses a greater risk of death and partly accounts for the greater longevity of women (Gold, Malmberg, McClearn, Pedersen, & Berg, 2002).

Analyses of racial and ethnic differences in health and illness in later adulthood often are limited to comparisons between European Americans and African Americans, although Hispanic Americans are sometimes included, as well. In these studies, members of ethnic minority groups generally have high rates of chronic illness. African American men are at higher risk for hypertension and experience more rapid progression of end-organ damage from hypertension than do European American men (see review by Wagner, 1998). They also exhibit greater cardiovascular reactivity to stressors (Guyll, Matthews, & Bromberger, 2001), another possible precursor to heart disease. Similarly, elderly Hispanic Americans and African Americans have higher rates of diabetes than do elderly European Americans (MIAH/CDC, 2004), as well as higher rates of strokes and heart attacks (Cooper et al., 2000).

The major causes of death among older adults exhibit relatively little variability across sociodemographic groups, but the rank ordering of specific causes varies. Diabetes emerges as a more prominent cause of death among older African Americans and American Indians, for example, than among other groups of older adults (Sahyoun et al., 2001). More important, members of ethnic minority groups generally exhibit higher rates of mortality than do European Americans for almost every condition, as a result of lifelong experiences of economic hardship and discrimination that limit access to adequate health care and increase exposure to stress and environmental hazards (Williams & Collins, 1995). Consistent with this, life expectancies are shorter for members of ethnic minority groups. For example, life expectancies calculated at birth for African American men and women are roughly 7 and 5 years shorter, respectively, than for their European American counterparts (Himes, 2001). Life expectancies calculated at age 65 or beyond, among those who have survived to old age, often narrow or reveal a reverse pattern, with African Americans of advanced age living longer than age-matched European Americans (e.g., Corti et al., 1999). This reversal, which has come to be known

as the *racial crossover* in mortality, may reflect robustness in the population of African Americans of advanced old age, although data-quality issues need to be ruled out (Lynch, Brown, & Harmsen, 2003). The possibility of a mortality crossover does not, in any event, belie the significant disadvantages in health status and overall life expectancy experienced by members of many ethnic minority groups.

Such findings have led some researchers to conclude that real gains in the overall health of the elderly population will not be achieved until these disparities in health and longevity are addressed (Sahyoun et al., 2001). This will require research directed toward identifying modifiable behavioral risk factors and developing intervention strategies that take into account ethnic and cultural diversity, as well as life stage. Such work is needed not only to address current health disparities but also to anticipate and plan for the changing makeup of future elderly cohorts, which will be characterized by considerably greater racial, ethnic, and socioeconomic diversity than is the case now (NAAS, 1999b).

Psychosocial Factors and Physical Health

Psychosocial factors are intimately linked to physical functioning, as reviewed extensively in this volume. In this section, we illustrate some of the many ways that psychosocial factors affect health in later life. Our discussion emphasizes four pathways through which psychosocial factors influence physical health in old age, including (1) psychosocial factors that operate early in life to influence health status in later adulthood, (2) psychosocial factors in later adulthood that influence concurrent health status, (3) psychosocial factors that influence adaptation to illness and disease in later adulthood, and (4) psychosocial factors that influence health promotion and rehabilitation in late adulthood. For each of these four pathways, we provide an example to illustrate the kinds of interrelationships that have been reported in the literature.

Psychosocial Factors Early in Life That Influence Health Status in Later Adulthood

The importance of psychosocial factors for health in old age begins early in life. For example, it is now widely accepted that unhealthy behaviors and life-styles account for a substantial proportion of deaths in the United States, with estimates often converging on a figure of 50% (McGinnis & Foege, 1993; U.S. Department of Health and Human Services [USDHHS], 1979). Many important health behaviors that have consequences for health and illness in later adulthood represent established patterns that emerge in childhood and young adulthood, with adverse health effects often becoming evident by middle adulthood (Gatz, Harris, & Turk-Charles, 1995). Other psychosocial factors that predict morbidity may begin even earlier in the life course, with some researchers arguing that the precursors of risk factors for cardiovascular disease and other chronic illnesses common to old age are present at birth (e.g., Sandman, Wadhwa, Chicz-DeMet, Porto, & Garite, 1999).

The Example of Personality

Stable tendencies to respond to environmental stimuli in characteristic ways emerge early in life, and some of these characteristic ways of responding contribute to pathological processes that elevate the risk for future chronic disease. Some personality theorists, accordingly, argue that the foundation for links between personality, or temperament, and illness emerges early in life, arguably being pre-programmed at birth (McCrae et al., 2000). The predisposition to react strongly to events causes heightened physiological arousal, which may increase susceptibility to disease. People who are high on the dimension of trait hostility, for example, exhibit greater physiological reactivity to negative events than do people who are low on this dimension (Suarez, Kuhn, Schanberg, Williams, & Zimmermann, 1998). Over time, this wear and tear on organ systems associated with greater physiological reactivity can jeopardize physical health, with the cumulative effects being revealed in old age (Wilson, Mendes de Leon, Bienias, Evans, & Bennett, 2004).

Researchers argue that personality is strongly related to multiple dimensions of health (see review by Friedman, this volume; Friedman & Booth-Kewley, 1987; but see Cassileth 1985, 1990). In longitudinal studies that cover most of the adult life span, for example, pessimism and optimism expressed by men in their 20s have been found to predict their health in middle and old age (Peterson, Seligman, & Valliant, 1988). Men who were more pessimistic and less optimistic had worse health

beginning in middle age. Similarly, childhood personality variables have been found to predict all-cause mortality after age 50 (Friedman, this volume; Friedman, Tomlinson-Keasey, & Schwartz, 1993; Friedman et al., 1995). People who were lower in conscientiousness were more likely to die, as were those who were higher on the personality dimension of agreeableness. Wilson and his colleagues (Wilson et al., 2004) found conscientiousness and neuroticism to be related to the risk of mortality even in a relatively homogeneous elderly sample (elderly Catholic clergy members), in which the distribution of personality scores might be expected to be somewhat truncated. Although personality factors have not proved to be the sole causes of mortality in such research, their predictive power appears to be equivalent to that of biological factors such as obesity, hypertension, and tobacco use (Friedman et al., 1993; Friedman et al., 1995).

Personality also may influence vulnerability to health problems across the life span through it connections with health behavior. For example, conscientiousness may predispose people to avoid dangerous, impulsive behaviors, and agreeableness may lead people to engage in unhealthy but social behaviors, such as drinking alcohol, smoking, and eating to excess (Booth-Kewley & Vickers, 1994). Although people who score high on agreeableness are more likely to smoke and drink than are people who score low on this measure, these health behaviors do not completely explain the relationship between agreeableness and longevity (Martin et al., 2002). In addition, the likelihood of fatal accidents based on impulsive behavior appears to be lower among those high in conscientiousness, but again this explanation does not explain the relationship between conscientiousness and mortality (Friedman et al., 1995). Of course, poor health behaviors can lead to poor health at all ages, but the effects become stronger as time passes and when people are most physically vulnerable, which is usually at the end of the life span.

Psychosocial Factors in Later Adulthood That Influence Concurrent Health Status

Psychosocial factors also may operate to influence concurrent health status in later life. Some factors, such as the nature of day-to-day affective experience or the quality of one's interactions with social network members, influence health and well-being in other life stages and, therefore, do not necessarily have unique effects in old age. For example, affective experience has been found to be associated with sympathetic nervous system activation (e.g., Levenson, 1992) and changes in immune functioning in both older and younger adults (e.g., Futterman, Kemeny, Shapiro, Polonsky, & Fahey, 1992; see review by Herbert & Cohen, 1993). Similarly, the quality of one's interactions with social network members has been demonstrated to have important implications for health and well-being across the life span (see reviews by Berkman, Glass, Brissette, & Seeman, 2000; House, Landis, & Umberson, 1988; Seeman, 1996, Uchino, Cacioppo, & Kiecolt-Glaser, 1996), including old age (e.g., Antonucci, 2001; Seeman, 2000).

Yet the changing circumstances of later adulthood can create challenges that are relatively unique to this life stage or that alter previously stable psychosocial processes. For example, the loss or disruption of close relationships is a common experience in later life, with nearly 60% of women and 22% of men likely to be widowed by their mid-70s (U.S. Bureau of the Census, 2004). The loss of friends is common, as well. In one longitudinal study, 59% of men and 42% of women older than 85 reported that a close friend had died in the preceding year (Johnson & Troll, 1994). Such losses disrupt existing support networks and have the potential to detract from health and well-being (Goldman, Koreman, & Weinstein, 1995), creating adaptational demands in their own right (Rook, 2000; Zettel & Rook, 2004).

Similarly, although affective experiences influence health across the life course, the nature of affective experiences and the processes of emotion regulation exhibit developmental shifts. In the following section, we examine some of the commonalities and differences across age groups in the interplay between emotion and health.

The Example of Emotion

The association between physical health and emotion is often similar among age groups, and studies have found evidence for bidirectional causation, where both health and emotion influence each other (Diefenbach, Leventhal, Leventhal, & Patrick-Miller, 1996). For example, negative mood states have been found to predict physical health symptoms 6 months later (Leventhal, Hansell, Diefenbach, Leventhal, &

Glass, 1996). Conversely, self-rated physical health has been found to predict subsequent depressive symptoms (Aneshensel, Frerichs, & Huba, 1984). Additionally, as functional status and physical conditions improve for older adults, so does their affective well-being (Lieberman et al., 1999).

Given these associations between affect and health, perhaps one of the more counterintuitive findings in gerontology is what is *not* happening in the interplay of age-related losses, health status, and emotion. Older adults experience more losses than do younger adults in multiple areas of their lives, including social, economic, and health domains. Friends and family members die, retirement is often accompanied by reductions in social prestige and income, and chronic conditions increase. In addition, older adults experience reductions in physical reserve capacity, loss of homeostasis, and greater allostatic load, all risk factors that lead to greater physical vulnerability. In view of these changes, older adults might be expected to report reduced life satisfaction and lower affective well-being compared with younger adults. Surprisingly, this is not the case. Older adults do not differ from younger adults in life satisfaction or affective well-being, and they report less negative affect and relatively stable (and sometimes higher) levels of positive affect (Charles, Reynolds, & Gatz, 2001; Mroczek & Kolarz, 1998). In fact, older adults with chronic illnesses arguably fare better than do younger adults on measures of affective well-being. In a study comparing middle-aged and older adults with chronic illnesses, older adults engaged in less emotional expression and hostility and were more likely to focus on adaptive processes such as minimizing the threat of the disease (Folkman, Lazarus, Pimley, & Novacek, 1987).

To understand this paradox of old age, researchers have examined how emotional processes change throughout the life span. Socioemotional selectivity theory explains these findings and predicts enhanced emotion regulation in old age. According to this theory, all people have a conscious or unconscious awareness of how much time they have left to live, and chronological age is associated with this recognition of limited time. When time is limited, as in advanced old age, people focus on emotional goals, seeking to minimize involvement in emotionally unrewarding activities and focusing, instead, on emotionally meaningful experiences (Carstensen &

Charles, 1998). Research supporting socioemotional selectivity theory has documented a developmental shift that occurs starting in young adulthood, where emotional goals gradually increase in importance throughout the adult life span (e.g., Carstensen, 1992). Threats to health and longevity shift one's focus to emotionally meaningful events (Carstensen & Fredrickson, 1998) and may lead to increased efforts to attain emotional goals.

In a related vein, Leventhal and his colleagues (Leventhal, Rabin, Leventhal, & Burns, 2001) argue that emotional reactions to potential health threats influence ensuing plans for dealing with the threats and may become action goals themselves. Older adults have been found to be more risk averse in this regard, as reflected in a shorter latency from the onset of physical symptoms to the seeking of medical care (Leventhal, Leventhal, Schaefer, & Easterling, 1993). Less tolerance for the emotional distress and uncertainty associated with an unknown risk appears to underlie older adults' vigilant, risk-averse approach to potential health threats and may partly explain, as well, older adults' greater adherence to treatment regimens and generally lower rates of health-compromising behavior (Leventhal et al., 2001).

Thus, emotional experiences and the processes of emotion regulation are related to health status and the management of potential health threats in later life. We have emphasized affective processes that exhibit distinct developmental trends over the life span, but it is also important to recognize that genes and temperament contribute a degree of stability to affective processes. Emotions are physiological phenomena that can be influenced by the same factors that determine physical health and reserve capacity (Leventhal, Leventhal, Contrada, 1998). This genetic influence persists into old age, suggesting that genes continue to play an important role in the associations between psychosocial factors and both objective and subjective dimensions of health, despite older adults' greater lifetime exposure to environmental influences (Lichtenstein & Pedersen, 1995; Lichtenstein, Pedersen, Plomin, de Faire, & McClearn, 1989). The recognition that biologically based tendencies and psychosocial factors interact to influence the health-emotion relationship in old age underscores, yet again, the complexities of studying health in old age and the usefulness of the biopsychosocial approach in understanding these interrelationships.

Psychosocial Factors That Influence Adaptation to Illness and Disease in Later Adulthood

A key challenge in later life, and an important area of inquiry for health psychologists, is the process of adapting to declining health. How older people seek to adapt to such declines has significant implications for their quality of life and sense of self-worth, as well as for subsequent health and functioning. Adaptation to chronic illness is a broad topic with many facets, and it is reviewed extensively elsewhere (see Stanton & Revenson, this volume). We accordingly limit our attention to psychosocial factors, and specifically processes of primary and secondary control, that hold promise for understanding how older adults seek to preserve their psychological well-being in the face of declining health.

The Example of Control Strivings and Processes

Theoretical models of developmental regulation provide a useful framework for thinking about how people respond to losses of health and functional capabilities with advancing age. The life-span theory of control (Heckhausen & Schulz, 1995; Schulz & Heckhausen, 1996) differentiates between primary control strategies directed toward maintaining and expanding control of tangible outcomes in the environment and in one's own physical state, and secondary control strategies directed toward influencing one's internal psychological resources, such as one's motivation, emotional balance, or hopefulness. When outcomes are controllable, adaptive behavior is aimed at achieving primary control through a variety of goal-engagement strategies (Heckhausen, 1999; Heckhausen & Schulz, 1995). In contrast, when outcomes are uncontrollable, the adaptive form of control striving is to disengage from the futile goal and to focus instead on ameliorating the adverse effects of the loss of control on one's internal resources. Such goal disengagement protects resources from being expended on unattainable goals and allows them to be directed toward other goals.

The control model of developmental regulation has been applied to study responses to disease and disability in adulthood and old age (Chipperfield, Perry, & Menec, 1999; Wrosch, Heckhausen, & Lachman, 2000; Wrosch, Schulz, & Heckhausen,

2002). In a large study of different age groups, older and middle-aged adults reported both greater persistence (primary control strivings) and more positive reappraisal (self-protective disengagement from primary control strivings) than did young adults (Wrosch et al., 2000). The finding of continued primary control striving regarding health problems among older and middle-aged adults is noteworthy because it suggests that, even though primary control potential regarding health outcomes may decline with age, these individuals continue to engage in health maintenance behavior. At the same time, however, primary control strivings contributed less to the psychological well-being of middle-aged and older adults than did strategies of positive reappraisal. Thus, health-related primary control strivings were still used by aging individuals, albeit with less effectiveness.

This conclusion was reinforced and extended in a study of older adults by Chipperfield and her colleagues (1999), which found that primary control strategies had positive health consequences for the young-old but more negative consequence for the old-old. The oldest participants are likely to have suffered more chronic conditions, and such uncontrollable health problems would have rendered primary control attempts futile and wasteful of psychological resources. Primary control behavior has been associated with beneficial psychological outcomes in a study in which older adults were experiencing acute, controllable illnesses (Wrosch et al., 2002). Specifically, health-promoting behavior was associated with less depressive symptomatology in this group, both at baseline and at a 14-month follow-up assessment. Thus, primary control striving appears to be adaptive for controllable physical illnesses.

Conclusive evidence is not yet available regarding the effects of control strategies when individuals face uncontrollable health declines and increasing functional limitations. In such conditions, disengagement from primary control strategies and greater reliance on secondary control strategies may be crucial to maintain emotional well-being and to protect motivational resources for primary control striving directed toward other outcomes (see also the model in Schulz, Heckhausen, & O'Brien, 2000). Disengagement from primary control has its limits, however, and at more severe levels of disability, the control system may fail to compensate for the losses, thus increasing the individual's vulnerability to

anxiety, despair, and eventually clinical depression. Research on the use and consequences of different control strategies in diverse populations of individuals with chronic and/or life-threatening conditions may allow us to identify the major steps and shifts in individuals' control strategies when facing chronic, progressive disease. Several lines of defense may exist, each with its own cycle of initial primary control striving, superseded by compensatory secondary control strategies when primary control potential is compromised (Heckhausen, 2002).

Psychosocial Factors That Affect Health Promotion and Rehabilitation in Later Adulthood

Psychosocial factors influence health in later adulthood not only by influencing psychological adaptation to declining health, as discussed earlier, but also by the influencing the degree of success that is experienced in efforts to initiate and sustain health-enhancing behavior, whether in the context of prevention or treatment and rehabilitation. In this section, we consider whether modifiable risk factors for disease onset or progression known to be important in earlier life stages retain their importance in later life, and whether efforts to modify them have comparable benefits in later life. We also consider unique issues that arise in considering health promotion with older adults, and we illustrate how psychosocial factors may affect health behavior change efforts in later life by considering the role of social network influences.

It is often assumed that potentially modifiable risk factors that predict disease onset or progression in young adulthood and middle age have less relevance in later life. A review by Kaplan et al. (1999) suggests that this belief is not substantiated by available evidence. The association between some risk factors and disease does decline with age (e.g., smoking and ischemic stroke), but the association between other risk factors and disease persists or even increases with age (e.g., elevated systolic blood pressure and coronary heart disease); other risk factors exhibit no consistent age-related associations with disease outcomes (Kaplan et al., 1999). Even in advanced old age, some known risk factors continue to predict an increased risk of morbidity and mortality. For example, elevated cholesterol has been found to be a risk factor for mortality even among even among men aged 75 to

97 (Sorkin, Andres, Muller, Baldwin, & Fleg, 1992), and pharmacological interventions to lower lipid levels have been found to reduce the probability of coronary events among high-risk individuals aged 65 and older (Dombrook-Lavender, Pieper, & Roth, 2004; though see Muldoon, Kaplan, & Manuck, 2000). Risk-factor modification in middle and later adulthood does appear to yield significant health benefits (Rowe & Kahn, 1998) in cases where the modifiable factor plays a concurrent role in the disease process.

In a related vein, some researchers question whether preventive health behaviors in old age are as effective in younger ages or whether they constitute an example of too little, too late (e.g., Keysor & Jette, 2001). Health promotion and disease prevention tend to be targeted toward younger age groups, reflecting the belief that health-promoting behavior yields few discernible benefits for older adults. The title of an editorial in the *Journal of Gerontology: Medical Sciences* suggests an alternative view: "It's Never Too Late: Health Promotion and Illness Prevention in Older Persons" (Morley & Flaherty, 2002). Health behavior change and risk factor modification have been shown to have benefits even in old age, contributing to improved health and slowing the progression of disease (Fries, 2003; Kaplan et al., 1999; Leventhal et al., 2001; Rakowski, 1992, 1997; Smith, Orleans, & Jenkins, 2004). Improvements in aerobic fitness and in arterial stiffness have been obtained in later life with vigorous physical exercise (Vaitkevicius et al., 1993; see review by Singh, 2002). Similarly, moderate to intense resistance training, even among relatively frail or disabled older adults, has been shown to reduce disability and arthritis pain, increase gait stability, and reduce rates of injurious falls (Singh, 2002). Olshansky, Hayflick, and Carnes (2002) concluded in this regard that health and fitness can be enhanced in later life, as in other life stages, "primarily through the avoidance of behaviors . . . that accelerate the expression of age-related diseases, and by the adoption of lifestyles . . . that take advantage of a physiology that is inherently modifiable" (B295).

The effectiveness of specific strategies to promote health is likely to vary across age groups, however, and the identification and evaluation of age-appropriate strategies represent important priorities for future research (Smith et al., 2004). As noted earlier, comorbidity is common in later life, and a preexisting condition may limit the effectiveness of a behavioral intervention intended to address a different condition (Rakowski, 1992). For example, engaging in daily walks or other physical exercise in the context of a cardiac rehabilitation program may be discomforting or hazardous for an older person with impaired vision. Shortness of breath associated with chronic obstructive pulmonary disease can cause anxiety and a reluctance to engage in physical activity that might trigger episodes of breathlessness, leading to further cardiopulmonary deconditioning. To increase physical activity, it may be necessary for health care providers to anticipate and address older patients' concerns about breathing-related symptoms (Cousins, 2000; Leventhal et al., 2001). Moreover, health is itself a resource for initiating and maintaining lifestyle modifications, and even highly motivated older adults may lack the energy and physical reserves to engage in preventive behaviors (Rakowski, 1992). Low rates of physical exercise among older adults, relative to the other age groups, represent an exception to the general tendency for older adults to engage in fewer health-risk behaviors; possible explanations may be found in older adults' subjective experience of exercise programs as draining rather than augmenting energy reserves (Brownlee, Leventhal, & Leventhal, 1996), their potential misinterpretation of some of the physical effects of exercise as cardiac symptoms (Leventhal et al., 2001), and perceived or real environmental barriers to exercise (Leventhal et al., 2001; Rakowski, 1992). Rakowski (1992) also has cautioned against assuming that the formats for physical exercise favored by many young and middle-aged adults, such as sports club facilities or other group settings that afford little privacy, will necessarily be preferred by older adults.

More generally, the design and evaluation of strategies for promoting health in later life must take into account older adults' representations of and experiences with health threats and options for managing health risks, as well as the physical and social environments in which health promotion efforts occur. We explore the role of the social environment later, in a brief discussion of the role of social network members in health promotion and rehabilitation in later life (see Siegler, Bastian, Steffens, Bosworth, & Costa, 2002, for a discussion of the patient-physician relationship as another important element of the social environment for health promotion in later life).

The Example of Social Network Influences

People's efforts to manage a health threat by making changes in their health behavior probably rarely occur in a vacuum; rather, their efforts are likely to be observed and, often, shaped by members of the social environment, such as family members and friends. Moreover, efforts to modify health behaviors and adhere to a treatment regimen in the context of a chronic disease, such as diabetes, often must be sustained over a period of many years and, to be effective, must be capable of being renewed in the wake of setbacks. Social network members have the potential to facilitate or interfere with lifestyle modification and treatment adherence over time.

Most discussions of the role of social networks in health promotion and rehabilitation have emphasized the emotional and instrumental support provided by close relationships. A substantial literature has documented the health benefits of social support among various patient groups, including individuals diagnosed with cardiovascular disease (e.g., Coyne et al., 2001; Kulik & Mahler, 1993), cancer (e.g., Helgeson & Cohen, 1996), diabetes (e.g., Williams & Bond, 2002), and arthritis (e.g., Druley & Townsend, 1998). A meta-analysis that focused specifically on the implications of social support for adherence to physician-prescribed treatment regimens revealed that social support, particularly practical support, was significantly related to greater adherence (DiMatteo, 2004). A similar benefit was observed in studies that assessed the participants' family environments, with greater family cohesiveness associated with greater adherence.

This meta-analysis also revealed that family conflict was associated with less adherence, serving as a reminder that social networks can be a source of stress and demands, as well as support (cf. Rook, 1994). Ironically, distressing interactions that occur with social network members in the context of efforts to make and sustain health behavior changes sometimes result from support attempts that go awry over time (Coyne, Wortman, & Lehman, 1988; Lewis & Rook, 1999). Research on the effects of health-related social control, or social regulation, in close relationships has recently gained momentum and offers a way to conceptualize some of the well-intentioned efforts of social network members that have the effect of inadvertently undermining rather than enhancing health behavior change and treatment adherence.

Social control involves efforts by social network members to regulate the health behaviors of a focal person, either by discouraging an established health-compromising behavior or by encouraging the development of a health-enhancing behavior (Rook, 1990; Umberson, 1987). Early work on health-related social control was guided by the view that social control should contribute to physical health by fostering better health behaviors yet, at the same time, might detract from psychological health by constraining target individuals' autonomy. Hughes and Gove (1981) stated this "dual-effects hypothesis" succinctly: "Constraint may be the source of considerable frustration; at the same time it tends to reduce the probability of problematic or maladaptive behaviors" (p. 71). Subsequent formulations of the dual-effects hypothesis have elaborated on the expectation of adverse psychological effects by noting that social network members' efforts to regulate a target person's health behavior convey, even if implicitly, a message that the target person's capacity for self-regulation is deficient (Franks et al., in press; Rook, 1990, 1995).

Empirical research testing the effects of health-related social control in older adults (Rook, Thuras, & Lewis, 1990; Tucker, 2002) and other age groups (e.g., Lewis & Rook, 1999; Tucker & Anders, 2001; Westmaas, Wild, & Ferrence, 2002) has yielded mixed evidence for the dual-effects hypothesis. Of the few studies that have examined social control specifically in the context of chronic illness management, evidence generally suggests that social control is associated with worse (rather than better) health behavior, with greater psychological distress, and with less health-related self-efficacy (Franks et al., in press; Helgeson, Novak, Lepore, & Eton, 2004). It seems plausible that social network members' attempts to be supportive of a patient's efforts to adhere to a prescribed medical regimen give way over time to more controlling, and even coercive, strategies to induce behavior change if the patient's own efforts have little success (Franks et al., in press; Rook, 1990, 1995).

This discussion has focused on the potential roles of social network members, particularly those involving close relationships, in older adults' efforts to initiate and sustain changes in important health behaviors. Enduring behavior change is often difficult to achieve, and it is not surprising that frustrations develop, not only among those attempting to effect their own behavior change but also among the people who are close to them. The fact that social network interactions at such times have the potential to be problematic does not mean that they cannot be powerfully supportive and health enhancing at other times. Nonetheless, understanding how an important aspect of older adults' social environment—their close social relationships—may affect health promotion is likely to benefit from considering potential negative, as well positive, influences (Seeman, 2000).

Projections for the Health Status of Future Older Adults

A key question that surfaces in many discussions of the health of the elderly population is what the future holds. Will the future bring continued increases in life expectancy, and if so, will the added years of life represent a time of good health or only a time of extended disability? The answers to these questions have important implications for public health planning and priorities, as well as for the lives of older individuals, potentially affecting their personal longevity expectations, health behavior and health care utilization, financial and retirement decisions, residential changes, and planning and decision making in other important areas of their lives. Developing scientific models that allow such forecasts for the future to be offered with any degree of certainty is a difficult undertaking; it is not surprising that scientific opinion is mixed regarding the most probable future scenarios (e.g., see review by Robine & Michel, 2004, and commentaries published in the same issue).

Life Expectancy of Future Elderly Cohorts

Scientists disagree regarding the prospects for further increases in human life expectancy. Some argue that further increases are unlikely, at least on a scale that resembles the dramatic increases that occurred in the twentieth century (e.g., Fries, 1980; Olshansky et al., 2002). Arguments mustered in support of this position (see Fries & Crapo, 1981) have included evidence of apparently finite life spans in many species, an apparent limit in the number times that human cells can divide and replicate (the Hayflick limit), and the failure to find scientific validation for the claims of extraordinary old age among pre-

sumably long-lived peoples in various regions of the world. Other scientists challenge some of these data and argue, in contrast, that the preponderance of available evidence supports the conclusion that human life expectancy will continue to increase (Vaupel et al., 1998). The Hayflick limit already has been overturned in laboratory experiments in recent years through genetic engineering. Caloric restriction has been found to increase the life span of rodents and nonhuman primates, although extrapolation to humans is not yet warranted (Olshansky et al., 2002). The substantial growth in the number of centenarians now alive challenges the notion that further increases in average life expectancy cannot be achieved (Oeppen & Vaupel, 2002). Moreover, some scientists note that the actual empirical record of mortality improvements points to gains in life expectancy of approximately 2.5 years per decade for more than a century, and it is reasonable to expect continued gains in the future (Oeppen & Vaupel, 2002; but see Fries, 2003). Oeppen and Vaupel (2002) concluded that "modest annual increments in life expectancy will never lead to immortality, . . . but centenarians may become commonplace within the lifetimes of people alive today" (p. 1031). They caution, as well, that underestimating possible increases in life expectancy is risky from a public policy standpoint because even modest increases can translate into large numbers of very old individuals, contributing to a burgeoning demand for health care services.

Extending the human life span will have limited value, of course, unless this is accompanied by corresponding improvements in the health status of older adults. Closely tied to questions about the life expectancy of future elderly cohorts, therefore, are questions about the probable health status of such future cohorts.

Health Status of Future Elderly Cohorts

Many medical researchers and epidemiologists predict, with some caveats, that the health of future cohorts of older adults in developed nations such as the United States will be better than that of current and past cohorts. This optimistic projection is based on declines in recent decades in the rates of some chronic diseases and disability in the older population (AARP, 2001). As noted earlier, mortality due to heart disease declined in the United States in the 1980s and 1990s, reflecting a reduction in rates of smoking and improved control of hypertension. Lung cancer mortality has declined among older men as a result of declining rates of smoking (NAAS, 1999b), and the prevalence of some other chronic conditions is declining (Rowe, 1997). Levels of education have increased among older adults (U.S. Department of Health and Human Services [USDHHS], 2001). All these factors, coupled with improvements in medical care and technology, may have contributed to a decline in the prevalence of disability in the elderly population in recent years (NAAS, 1999a; Waidmann & Liu, 2000), although they may not fully account for it (Fries, 2002a).

Such patterns are consistent with the "compression of morbidity" hypothesis first proposed in the early 1980s (Fries, 1980; Fries & Crapo, 1981). This hypothesis posited that the burden of illness in an aging society can be reduced most effectively not through efforts to find cures for the leading causes of disability and mortality but, instead, through efforts to postpone the onset of chronic illness to a time in life that approaches the average age of death. The duration of time spent living with chronic illness, accordingly, would be compressed into fewer years, with correspondingly less pain and disability. Notably, the total number of years lived does not increase in this scenario; rather, by delaying functional decline, the period of life that is relatively free of disability (i.e., active life expectancy) is extended. Postponing the onset of chronic illness would require an emphasis on the prevention or modification of well-established behavioral risk factors for disease. Fries (2002b, 2003) took stock of evidence bearing on the compression of morbidity hypothesis and concluded that little evidence of such compression was apparent in the 1980s, but more promising evidence began to emerge by the 1990s, including declining rates of some chronic illness and disability in older adults. More compelling evidence for the compression of morbidity hypothesis has emerged from studies indicating that the age of disability onset began to shift in the 1990s to later ages among individuals with fewer behavioral risk factors, such as smoking, lack of exercise, and obesity. This postponement was found to correspond to 7 to 8 years in several studies and was related not only to substantially reduced disability but also to reduced medical care costs among individuals exhibiting fewer behavioral risk factors (Fries, 2002b). Additional, and also compelling, support for the compression of morbidity perspec-

tive has emerged from analyses indicating that disability rates declined more sharply during this period than did mortality rates (Fries, 2003, 2004).

The optimism engendered by these signs of a compression of morbidity in later adulthood (Fries, 1980; Rowe, 1997) is tempered, however, by other developments that threaten to undo these trends toward improved health. Increased rates of smoking among women, for example, suggest that future cohorts of elderly women may experience higher rates of lung cancer mortality (NAAS, 1999b). Similarly, soaring rates of childhood and adult obesity have the potential to contribute to a significant increase in the prevalence of chronic illness and disability among future cohorts of older adults. In addition, the old-old constitute the fastest-growing segment of the elderly population (Kinsella & Velkoff, 2001), and this traditionally has been the age group in which rates of functional impairment and disability are highest (MIAH/GSA, 2002; USDHHS, 2001). Thus, even though rates of disability have declined among older adults overall, the growing size of the 85 and older subgroup is anticipated to lead to an increase in the sheer number of people with disability and an increase in the burden of care for families and society (NAAS, 1999b; Waidmann & Liu, 2000). The number of disabled older adults living in and out of institutions, for example, is estimated to increase by 300% from 1985 to 2050 (Manton, Corder, & Stallard, 1997).

Even the widely cited declines in rates of disability among older adults appear, on closer scrutiny, to provide a basis for more guarded optimism. These declines in disability do not appear to have followed a linear or accelerating trajectory; additionally, they apply only to routine care disability and not to severe personal care disability (Freedman, Martin, & Schoeni, 2002; Schoeni, Freedman, & Wallace, 2001). Equally important, the gains in health that have been observed in later life in recent decades have not been evenly distributed across the elderly population. Fewer gains have been observed among older adults with less education and lower socioeconomic status and among older members of ethnic minority groups (AARP, 2001; Schoeni et al., 2001).

Prospects for an Antiaging Medicine

The declining physical vigor and increasing risk of disability that accompany old age, despite the gains in selected areas that some groups have begun to enjoy, lead many people to invest hope in the prospect that a viable antiaging medicine will emerge someday. This hope can be traced, in various permutations, through centuries of human history (Binstock, 2004; Haber, 2004). However, several groups of biogerontologists have joined forces to condemn an antiaging industry that exploits fears of aging by marketing an astonishing variety of products and therapies purported to extend longevity and to prevent or reverse the physical signs of aging. (e.g., Butler et al., 2002; Binstock, 2004; Hayflick, 2004; Olshansky et al., 2002). These scientists soundly reject claims of the validity of any existing antiaging remedies, and most express strong doubts that effective interventions for halting or reversing fundamental aging processes will emerge in the foreseeable future. Still others suggest that public debate and discussion should begin now to consider the social and ethical implications of possible antiaging remedies that could be discovered to be effective at some point in the future (Binstock, 2004).

Conclusion: Resilient Aging in the Absence of a Fountain of Youth

Hopes for the discovery of a fountain of youth that could undo the effects of aging and guarantee a disease-free old age have long fueled human imagination, but such hopes lack a foundation in modern biomedical science and, thus, remain elusive. In the absence of a fountain of youth, more realistic prospects and goals for successful, or resilient, aging should command our attention. These include the prevention of premature deaths associated with modifiable risk factors, the postponement of functional impairment and disability to later ages, and the preservation of independence and psychological well-being to the fullest extent possible even after the onset of functional limitations.

Successful aging, therefore, is unlikely to involve a process of growing old with minimal illness or impairment, and conceptions of successful aging have been evolving to reject both overly pessimistic and overly optimistic views. The concept of successful aging was propelled to a place of prominence in the gerontological literature by Rowe and Kahn (1987) in the late 1980s. They argued that many of the decrements often attributed to aging

were, in fact, the result of disease. They juxtaposed this concept of "usual aging" with the concept of "successful aging," or growing old without disease-related decrements. This formulation of successful aging, and its explicit contrast with usual aging, excited many researchers and practitioners, who were pleased by the challenge it presented to prevailing notions of what is possible in later life. It also stimulated a considerable amount of empirical work directed toward identifying the biopsychosocial determinants of successful aging. Critics of the concept of successful aging, however, felt that it inadvertently championed an elite few whose genetic or socioeconomic advantages made healthy aging possible (Masoro, 2001). Other critics objected that the concept of successful aging, as originally defined by Rowe and Kahn (1987), precluded the possibility that individuals with disabilities acquired early in life could age successfully (Strawbridge, Wallhagen, & Cohen, 2002).

Rowe and Kahn (1998) subsequently expanded their definition of successful aging to include three main components: a low probability of suffering from disease or a disease-related disability, a high level of cognitive and physical functioning, and active engagement with life. This expanded definition has blunted much of the criticism and has broadened the appeal of the construct, although some gerontologists favor models of successful aging that emphasize the processes by which well-being is preserved in the face of age-related declines in health and functioning (Baltes, 1997; Baltes & Baltes, 1990; Baltes & Carstensen, 1996; Heckhausen & Schulz, 1995). These models of successful aging, thus, are compatible rather than contradictory, with complementary emphases on adaptive outcomes and processes, and Kahn (2002) has urged the theoretical integration of these different models.

A common element of many current perspectives on what it means to age well is an emphasis, explicit or implicit, on resilience. Resilience is defined as succeeding in the face of adversity (Ryff, Singer, Love, & Essex, 1998). Being resilient in later adulthood is contingent not on health status per se but, rather, on how people manage health-related challenges. Given the virtual inevitability of physical decline with advancing age, an individual's capacity to deal with its consequences for everyday activities and psychological health is a key determinant of successful, or resilient, aging. In this sense, successful aging is not merely a state but a process over time (Menec, 2003; von Farber et al., 2001). Successful aging may be evaluated, moreover, with reference to subjective and objective criteria, and these sets of criteria may differ and may follow distinctive trajectories over time (Baltes & Baltes, 1990; von Farber et al., 2001).

Health psychologists have a great deal to contribute to the understanding and promotion of processes and conditions that are important in efforts to prevent premature death, postpone disability, and encourage resilience in the face of physical declines and functional limitations. Such work has both tremendous importance and considerable urgency in view of the burgeoning of the elderly population that lies ahead. Underscoring this urgency, Fries (2003) observed that "our greatest national health problem is the health of the elderly" (p. 458), and Kane (2004) warned, "Whatever the final shape of the morbidity and disability projections, they will be dwarfed in the United States by the demographic shifts of an aging baby boomer population" (p. 608). Given the centrality of behavioral and psychosocial factors to health and adaptation in later adulthood, and given their expertise in these areas, health psychologists can make significant contributions to efforts to meet the challenges of population aging. At the same time, health psychology as a discipline is likely to be enriched by adopting a life-span perspective on health and by integrating concepts and methods from research on aging and adult development (Siegler et al., 2002; Smith, Kendall, & Keefe, 2002).

References

American Administration on Aging. (2001). *A profile of older Americans: 2001.* U.S. Department of Health and Human Services. Washington, DC: U.S. Government Printing Office.

American Association of Retired Persons (AARP). (2001). *The health of people age 50 and older.* Washington, DC: American Association of Retired Persons.

Aneshensel, C. S., Frerichs, R. R., & Huba, G. J. (1984). Depression and physical illness: A multiwave, nonrecursive causal model. *Journal of Health and Social Behavior, 25,* 350–371.

Antonucci, T. C. (2001). Social relations: An examination of social networks, social support, and sense of control. In J. E. Birren & K. Warner Schaie (Eds.), *Handbook of the psychology of aging* (5th ed., pp. 427–453). San Diego, CA: Academic Press.

Baltes, P. B. (1997). On the incomplete architecture of human ontogeny: Selection, optimization, and compensation as a foundation of developmental theory. *American Psychologist, 52,* 366–380.

Baltes, P. B., & Baltes, M. (1990). Psychological perspectives on successful aging: The model of selective optimization with compensation. In P. B. Baltes & M. Baltes (Eds.), *Successful aging: Perspectives from the behavioral sciences* (pp. 1–34). New York: Cambridge University Press.

Baltes, M. M., & Carstensen, L. L. (1996). The process of successful aging. *Ageing and Society, 16,* 397–422.

Barrett, R., Kuzawa, C. W., McDade, T., & Armelagos, G. J. (1998). Emerging and re-emerging infectious diseases: The third epidemiologic transition. *Annual Review of Anthropology, 27,* 247–271.

Bennett, G. A., Waine, H., & Bauer, W. (1942). *Changes in the knee joint at various ages.* New York: Commonwealth Fund.

Benyamini, Y., & Idler, E. L. (1999). Community studies reporting association between self-rated health and mortality. *Research on Aging, 21,* 392–401.

Benyamini, Y., Idler, E. L., Leventhal, H., & Leventhal, E. A. (2000). Positive affect and function as influences on self-assessments of health: Expanding our view beyond illness and disability. *Journal of Gerontology: Psychological Sciences, 55,* P107–P116.

Berkman, L. F., Glass, T., Brissette, I., & Seeman, T. E. (2000). From social integration to health: Durkheim in the new millennium. *Social Science and Medicine, 51,* 843–857.

Binstock, R. H. (2004). Anti-aging medicine and research: A realm of conflict and profound societal implications. *Journal of Gerontology: Biological Sciences, 59,* B523–B533.

Birren, J. E., & Cunningham, W. (1985). Research on the psychology of aging: Principles, concepts, and theory. In J. E. Birren & K. W. Schaie (Eds.), *Handbook of the psychology of aging* (2nd ed., pp. 3–34). New York: Van Nostrand Reinhold.

Blumenthal, H. T. (2003). The aging-disease dichotomy: True or false? *Journal of Gerontology: Medical Sciences, 58,* 138–145.

Booth-Kewley, S., & Vickers, R. R. (1994). Associations between major domains of personality and health behavior. *Journal of Personality, 62,* 281–298.

Borawski, E. A., Kinney, J. M., & Kahana, E. M. (1996). The meaning of older adults' health appraisals. *Journal of Gerontology: Social Sciences, 51,* S157–S170.

Brownlee, S., Leventhal, E. A., & Leventhal, H. (1996). Self-regulation, health, and behavior. In J. E. Birren (Ed.), *Encyclopedia of gerontology*

(Vol. 2, pp. 467–477). San Diego, CA: Academic Press.

Bruce, M. L., Seeman, T. E., Merrill, S. S., & Blazer, D. G. (1994). The impact of depressive symptomatology on physical disability: MacArthur Studies of Successful Aging. *American Journal of Public Health, 84,* 1796–1799.

Busse, E. W., Maddox, G. L., Buckley, C. E., Burger, P. C., George, L. K., Marsh, G. R. L., et al. (1985). *The Duke longitudinal studies of normal aging: 1955–1980.* New York: Springer.

Butler, R. N. (2002). Report and commentary from Madrid: The United Nations World Assembly on Ageing. *Journal of Gerontology: Medical Sciences, 57,* M770–M771.

Butler, R. N., Fossel, M., Harman, S. M., Heward, C. B., Olshansky, S. J., Perls, T. T., et al. (2002). Is there an antiaging medicine? *Journal of Gerontology: Biological Sciences, 57,* B333–B338.

Cameron, L., Leventhal, E. A., Leventhal, H. (1993). Symptom representations and affect as determinants of care seeking in a community-dwelling, adult sample population. *Health Psychology, 12,* 171–179.

Carstensen, L. L. (1992). Social and emotional patterns in adulthood: Support for socioemotional selectivity theory. *Psychology and Aging, 7,* 331–338.

Carstensen, L. L., & Charles, S. T. (1998). Emotion in the second half of life. *Current Directions in Psychological Science, 7,* 144–149.

Carstensen, L. L., & Charles, S. T. (2003). Human aging: Why is even good news taken as bad? In L. Aspinwall & U. Staudinger (Eds.), *A psychology of human strengths: Perspectives on an emerging field* (pp. 75–86). Washington, DC: American Psychological Association.

Carstensen, L. L., & Fredrickson, B. F. (1998). Influence of HIV status and age on cognitive representations of others. *Health Psychology, 17,* 494–503.

Cassileth, B. R. (1985). Psychosocial correlates of survival in advanced malignant disease? *New England Journal of Medicine, 312,* 1551–1555.

Cassileth, B. R., (1990). Mental health quackery in cancer treatment. Special Issue: Unvalidated, fringe, and fraudulent treatment of mental disorders. *International Journal of Mental Health, 19,* 81–84.

Centers for Disease Control and Prevention. (2003). Public health and aging: Trends in aging—United States and worldwide. *Morbidity and Mortality Weekly Report, 52,* 101–106.

Charles, S. T., Reynolds, C., & Gatz, M. (2001). Age-related differences and change in positive and negative affect over twenty-three years.

Journal of Personality and Social Psychology, 80, 136–151.

Chipperfield, J. G., Perry, R., & Menec, V. H. (1999). Primary and secondary control enhancing strategies: Implications for health in later life. *Journal of Aging and Health, 11,* 517–539.

Cooper, R., Cutler, J., Desvigne-Nickens, P., Fortmann, S. P., Friedman, L., Havlik, R., et al. (2000). Trends and disparities in coronary heart disease, stroke, and other cardiovascular diseases in the United States: Findings of the National Conference on Cardiovascular Disease Prevention. *Circulation, 102,* 3137–3147.

Corti, M. C., Guralnik, J. M., Ferrucci, L., Izmirlian, G., Leville, S. G., Pahor, M., et al. (1999). Evidence for a black-white crossover in all-cause and coronary heart disease mortality in an older population: The North Carolina EPESE. *American Journal of Public Health, 89,* 308–314.

Cousins, S. O. (2000). My heart couldn't take it: Older women's beliefs about exercise benefits and risks. *Journal of Gerontology: Psychological Sciences, 55,* P283–P294.

Coyne, J. C., Rohrbaugh, M. J., Shoham, V., Sonnega, J. S., Nicklas, J. M., & Cranford, J. A. (2001). Prognostic importance of marital quality for survival of congestive heart failure. *American Journal of Cardiology, 88,* 526–529.

Coyne, J. C., Wortman, C. B., & Lehman, D. R. (1988). The other side of support: Emotional overinvolvement and miscarried helping. In B. H. Gottlieb (Ed.), *Marshalling social support: Formats, processes, and effects* (pp. 305–330). Newbury Park, CA: Sage.

Craik, F. I. M., & Salthouse, T. A. (Eds). (2000). *The handbook of aging and cognition* (2nd ed.). Mahwah, NJ: Erlbaum.

Deeg, D. J. H., & Bath, P. A. (2003). Self-rated health, gender, and mortality in older persons: Introduction to a special issue. *Gerontologist, 43,* 369–371.

Dequeker, J. (1989). Triggering factors for pathological joint changes. In G. Ehrlich & G. Gallacchi (Eds.), *The elderly rheumatic patient: Diagnostic, prognostic and therapeutic aspects. Report of a symposium held during the XIth European Congress of Rheumatology, Athens, 1987* (pp. 18–28). Lewiston, NY: Huber.

Diefenbach, M. A., Leventhal, E. A., Leventhal, H., & Patrick-Miller, L. (1996). Negative affect relates to cross-sectional but not longitudinal symptom reporting: Data from elderly adults. *Health Psychology, 15,* 282–288.

DiMatteo, R. M. (2004). Social support and patient adherence to medical treatment. *Health Psychology, 23,* 207–218.

Dombrook-Lavender, K. A., Pieper, J. A., & Roth,

M. T. (2004). Primary prevention of coronary heart disease in the elderly. *Annals of Pharmacotherapy, 37,* 1653–1663.

Druley, J. A., & Townsend, A. L. (1998). Self-esteem as a mediator between spousal support and depressive symptoms: A comparison of healthy individuals and individuals coping with arthritis. *Health Psychology, 17,* 255–261.

Engel, G. L. (1977). The need for a new medical model: A challenge for biomedicine. *Science, 196,* 129–136.

Femia, E. E., Zarit, S. H., & Johansson, B. (2001). The disablement process in very late life: A study of the oldest-old in Sweden. *Journal of Gerontology: Psychological Sciences, 56,* P12–P23.

Fillenbaum, G. G. (1979). Social context and self-assessments of health among the elderly. *Journal of Health and Social Behavior, 20,* 45–51.

Folkman, S., Lazarus, R. S., Pimley, S., & Novacek, J. (1987). Age differences in stress and coping processes. *Psychology and Aging, 2,* 171–184.

Fozard, J. L., Metter, E. J., & Brant, L. J. (1990). Next steps in describing aging and disease in longitudinal studies. *Journal of Gerontology, 45,* P116–P127.

Franks, M. M., Stephens, M. A. P., Rook, K. S., Franklin, B. A., Keteyian, S. J., & Artinian, N. T. (in press). Spouses' provision of health-related support and control to patients participating in cardiac rehabilitation. *Journal of Family Psychology.*

Freedman, V. A., Martin, L. G., & Schoeni, R. F. (2002). Recent trends in disability and functioning among older adults in the United States: A systematic review. *Journal of the American Medical Association, 288,* 3137–3146.

Fried, L. P., Ettinger, W. H., Lind, B., Newman, A. B., & Gardin, J. (1994). Physical disability in older adults: A physiological approach. *Journal of Clinical Epidemiology, 47,* 747–760.

Fried, L. P., Tangen, C. M., Walston, J., Newman, A. B., Hirsch, C., Gottdiener, J., et al. (2001). Frailty in older adults: Evidence for a phenotype. *Journal of Gerontology: Medical Sciences, 56,* M146–M156.

Friedman, H. S., & Booth-Kewley, S. (1987). The "disease-prone personality": A meta-analytic view of the construct. *American Psychologist, 42,* 539–555.

Friedman, H. S., Tomlinson-Keasey, C., & Schwartz, J. E. (1993). Does childhood personality predict longevity? *Journal of Personality and Social Psychology, 65,* 176–185.

Friedman, H. S., Tucker, J. S., Schwartz, J. E., Martin, L. R., Tomlinson-Keasey, C., Wingard, D.L., et al. (1995). Childhood conscientiousness and longevity: Health behaviors and cause of death.

Journal of Personality and Social Psychology, 68, 696–703.

Fries, J. F. (1980). Aging, natural death, and the compression of morbidity. *New England Journal of Medicine, 303,* 130–135.

Fries, J. F. (2002a). Editorial: Reducing disability in old age. *Journal of the American Medical Association, 288,* 3164–3165.

Fries, J. F. (2002b). Successful aging: An emerging paradigm of gerontology. *Clinics in Geriatric Medicine, 18,* 371–382.

Fries, J. F. (2003). Measuring and monitoring success in compressing morbidity. *Archives of Internal Medicine, 139,* 455–459.

Fries, J. F. (2004). Robine and Michel's "Looking forward to a general theory on population aging": Commentary. *Journal of Gerontology: Medical Sciences, 59,* M603–M605.

Fries, J. F., & Crapo, L. M. (1981). *Vitality and aging.* San Francisco: Freeman.

Futterman, A. D., Kemeny, M. E., Shapiro, D. P., Polonsky, W., & Fahey, J. L. (1992). Immunological variability associated with experimentally-induced positive and negative affective states. *Psychological Medicine, 22,* 231–238.

Gatz, M., Harris, J. R., & Turk-Charles, S. (1995). The meaning of health for older women. In A. L. Stanton & S. J. Gallant (Eds.), *The psychology of women's health: Progress and challenges in research and application* (pp. 491–529). Washington, DC: American Psychological Association.

Gatz, M., Kasl-Godley, J. E., & Karel, M. J. (1996). Aging and mental disorders. In J. E. Birren & K. W. Schaie (Eds.), *Handbook of the psychology of aging* (4th ed., pp. 365–382). San Diego, CA: Academic Press.

Gerhard, K. A., Bergstrom, E., Charlifue, S. W., Menter, R. R., & Whiteneck, G. G. (1993). Long-term spinal cord injury: Functional changes over time. *Archives of Physical Medicine and Rehabilitation, 74,* 1030–1034.

George, L. K. (2001). The social psychology of health. In R. H. Binstock & L. K. George (Eds.), *Handbook of aging and the social sciences* (pp. 217–237). San Diego, CA: Academic Press.

Gillick, M. (2001). Pinning down frailty. *Journal of Gerontology: Medical Science, 56,* M134–M135.

Ginzberg, E. (1999). U.S. health care: A look ahead to 2025. *Annual Review of Public Health, 20,* 55–66.

Gold, C. H., Malmberg, B., McClearn, G. E., Pedersen, N. L., & Berg, S. (2002). Gender and health: A study of older unlike-sex twins. *Journal of Gerontology: Social Sciences, 57,* S168–S176.

Goldman, N., Koreman, S., & Weinstein, R. (1995). Marital status and health among the elderly. *Social Science and Medicine, 40,* 1717–1730.

Guyll, M., Matthews, K .A., & Bromberger, J. T. (2001). Discrimination and unfair treatment: Relationship to cardiovascular reactivity among African American and European American women. *Health Psychology, 20,* 315–325.

Haber, C. (2004). Life extension and history: The continual search for the fountain of youth. *Journal of Gerontology: Biological Sciences, 59,* 512–522.

Hayflick, L. (2000). The illusion of cell immortality. *British Journal of Cancer, 83,* 841–846.

Hayflick, L. (2004). "Anti-aging" is an oxymoron. *Journal of Gerontology: Biological Sciences, 59,* 573–578.

Heckhausen, J. (1999). *Developmental regulation in adulthood: Age-normative and sociostructural constraints as adaptive challenges.* New York: Cambridge University Press.

Heckhausen, J. (2002). Developmental regulation of life-course transitions: A control theory approach. In L. Pulkkinen & A. Caspi (Eds.), *Paths to successful development: Personality in the life course* (pp. 257–280). Cambridge, England: Cambridge University Press.

Heckhausen, J., & Schulz, R. (1995). A life-span theory of control. *Psychological Review, 102,* 284–304.

Helgeson, V. S., & Cohen, S. (1996). Social support and adjustment to cancer: Reconciling descriptive, correlational, and intervention research. *Health Psychology, 15,* 135–148.

Helgeson, V. S., Novak, S. A., Lepore, S. J., & Eton, D. T. (2004). Spouse social control efforts: Relations to health behavior and well-being among men with prostate cancer. *Journal of Social and Personal Relationships, 21,* 53–68.

Herbert, T. B., & Cohen, S. (1993). Stress and immunity in humans: A meta-analytic review. *Psychosomatic Medicine, 55,* 364–379.

Himes, C. L. (2001). Elderly Americans. *Population Bulletin, 56,* 3–42.

Holman, H. (2002). Patients as partners in managing chronic disease. *British Medical Journal, 320,* 526–527.

House, J. S., Landis, K. R., & Umberson, D. (1988). Social relationships and health. *Science, 241,* 540–545.

Hoyert, D. L., Kung, H. C., & Smith, B. L. (2005). *Deaths: Preliminary data for 2003.* National Vital Statistics Reports, 53 (15). Hyattsville, MD: National Center for Health Statistics.

Hughes, M., & Gove, W. R. (1981). Living alone, social integration, and mental health. *American Journal of Sociology, 87,* 48–74.

Jaur, L., & Stoddard, S. (1999). *Chartbook on women and disability in the U.S.* Washington, DC: National Institute on Disability and Rehabilitation Research.

Johnson, C. L., & Troll, L. (1994). Constraints and facilitators to friendships in late late life. *Gerontologist, 34,* 79–87.

Kahn, R. L. (2002). On "Successful aging and well-being: Self-rated compared with Rowe and Kahn." *The Gerontologist, 42,* 725–726.

Kane, R. L. (1995). Comment: Health care reform and the care of older adults. *Journal of the American Geriatrics Society, 43,* 718–719.

Kane, R. L. (2001). Meeting the challenge of chronic care. *Drugs Today, 37,* 581–585.

Kane, R. L. (2004). Robine and Michel's "Looking forward to a general theory on population aging": Commentary. *Journal of Gerontology: Medical Sciences, 59,* M608.

Kaplan, G. A., Haan, M. N., & Wallace, B. R. (1999). Understanding changing risk factor associations with increasing age in adults. *Annual Review of Public Health, 20,* 89–108.

Kaplan, N. M. (1992). Syndromes X: Two too many. *American Journal of Cardiology, 69,* 1643–1644.

Katz, S. (1983). Assessing self-maintenance: Activities of daily living, mobility and instrumental activities of daily living. *Journal of the American Geriatrics Society, 31,* 721–727.

Keysor, J. J., & Jette, A. M. (2001). Have we oversold the benefit of late-life exercise? *Journal of Gerontology: Medical Sciences, 56,* M412–M423.

Kinsella, K., & Velkoff, V. A. (2001). *An aging world.* U.S. Census Bureau, Series P95/01–1. Washington, DC: U.S. Government Printing Office.

Koivula, I., Sten, M., & Makela, P. H. (1999). Prognosis after community-acquired pneumonia in the elderly. *Archives of Internal Medicine, 159,* 1550–1555.

Kulik, J. A., & Mahler, H. I. M. (1993). Emotional support as a moderator of adjustment and compliance after coronary artery bypass surgery: A longitudinal study. *Journal of Behavioral Medicine, 16,* 45–63.

Lawrence, R. H., & Jette, A. M. (1996). Disentangling the disablement process. *Journal of Gerontology: Social Sciences, 51,* S173–S182.

Levenson, R. W. (1992). Autonomic nervous system differences among emotions. *Psychological Science, 3,* 23–27.

Leventhal, E. A., Hansell, S., Diefenbach, M., Leventhal, H., & Glass, D. C. (1996). Negative affect and self-reports of physical symptoms: Two longitudinal studies of older adults. *Health Psychology, 15,* 282–288.

Leventhal, E. A., Leventhal, H., Schaefer, P., & Easterling, D. (1993). Conservation of energy, uncertainty reduction, and swift utilization of medical care among the elderly. *Journal of Gerontology: Psychological Sciences, 48,* P78–P86.

Leventhal, E. A., & Prohaska, T. R. (1986). Age, symptom interpretation, and health behavior. *Journal of the American Geriatrics Society, 34,* 185–191.

Leventhal, H., Leventhal, E. A., & Contrada, R. J. (1998). Self-regulation, health, and behavior: A perceptual-cognitive approach. *Psychology and Health, 13,* 717–733.

Leventhal, H., Rabin, C., Leventhal, E. A., & Burns, E. (2001). Health risk behaviors and aging. In J. E. Birren & K. Warner Schaie (Eds.), *Handbook of the psychology of aging* (5th ed., pp. 186–214). San Diego, CA: Academic Press.

Lewis, M. A., & Rook, K. S. (1999). Social control in personal relationships: Impact on health behaviors and psychological distress. *Health Psychology, 18,* 63–71.

Lichtenstein, P., & Pedersen, N. P. (1995). Social relationship, stressful life events, and self-reported physical health: Genetic and environmental influences. *Psychology and Health, 10,* 295–319.

Lichtenstein, P., Pedersen, N. P., Plomin, R., de Faire, U., & McClearn, G. E. (1989). Type A behavior pattern, related personality traits and self-reported coronary heart disease. *Personality and Individual Differences, 10,* 419–426.

Lieberman, D., Galinsky, D., Fried, V., Grinshpun, Y., Mytlis, N., Tylis, R., et al. (1999). Geriatric Depression Screening Scale (GDS) in patients hospitalized for physical rehabilitation. *International Journal of Geriatric Psychiatry, 14,* 549–555.

Lollar, D. J., & Crews, J. E. (2003). Redefining the role of public health in disability. *Annual Review of Public Health, 24,* 195–208.

Lynch, S. M., Brown, J. S., & Harmsen, K. G. (2003). Black-white differences in mortality compression and deceleration and the mortality crossover reconsidered. *Research on Aging, 25,* 456–483.

Manton, K. G., Corder, L., & Stallard, E. (1997). Chronic disability trends in the elderly United States populations: 1982–1994. *Proceedings of the National Academy of Sciences, Medical Sciences, 94,* 2593–2598.

Martin, L., Friedman, H. S., Tucker, J. S., Tomlinson-Keasey, C., Criqui, M. H., & Schwartz, J. E. (2002). A life course perspective on childhood cheerfulness and its relation to mortality risk. *Personality and Social Psychology Bulletin, 28,* 1155–1165.

Masoro, E. J. (2001). "Successful aging": Useful or misleading concept? *Gerontologist, 41,* 415–418.

Mathers, C. D., Sadana, R., Salomon, J. A., Murray, C. J. L., & Lopez, A. D. (2001). Healthy life expectancy in 191 countries, 1999. *Lancet, 357,* 1685–1690.

McCrae, R. R., Costa, P. T., Ostendorf, F., Angleitner, A., Hrebickova, M., Avia, M. D., et al. (2000). Nature over nurture: Temperament, personality, and life span development. *Journal of Personality and Social Psychology, 78,* 173–186.

McEwen, B. S., & Stellar, E. (1993). Stress and the individual: Mechanisms leading to disease. *Archives of Internal Medicine, 153,* 2093–2101.

McGinnis, J. M., & Foege, W. H. (1993). Actual causes of death in the United States. *Journal of the American Medical Association, 270,* 2207–2212.

Menec, V. H. (2003). The relation between everyday activities and successful aging: A 6-year longitudinal study. *Journal of Gerontology: Social Sciences, 58,* S74–S82

Merck Institute of Aging and Health, & Centers for Disease Control and Prevention. (2004). *The state of aging and health in America.* Washington, DC: Merck Institute of Aging and Health.

Merck Institute of Aging and Health, & Gerontological Society of America. (2002). *The state of aging and health in America.* Washington, DC: Gerontological Society of America.

Meyerowitz, B. E., & Hart, S. L. (1995). Women and cancer: Have assumptions about women limited our research agenda? In A. L. Stanton & S. J. Gallant (Eds.), *The psychology of women's health: Progress and challenges in research and application* (pp. 51–84). Washington, DC: American Psychological Association.

Miller, C. A. (2003). Safe medication practices: Administering medications to elders who have difficulty swallowing. *Geriatric Nursing, 24,* 378–379.

Morley, J. E., & Flaherty, J. H. (2002). It's never too late: Health promotion and illness prevention in older persons. *Journal of Gerontology: Medical Sciences, 57,* M338–M342.

Mroczek, D. K., & Kolarz, C. M. (1998). The effect of age on positive and negative affect: A developmental perspective on happiness. *Journal of Personality and Social Psychology, 75,* 1333–1349.

Muldoon, M. F., Kaplan, J. R., & Manuck, S. B. (2000). Uncertain health effects of cholesterol reduction in the elderly. In S. B. Manuck, R. J. Jennings, B. S. Rabin, & A. Baum (Eds.), *Behavior, health and aging* (pp. 225–244). Mahwah, NJ: Erlbaum.

Murray, C. J. L., & Lopez, A. D. (1996). Evidence-based health policy: Lessons from the Global Burden of Disease Study. *Science, 274,* 740–743.

Nagi, S. (1965). Some conceptual issues in disability and rehabilitation. In M. Sussman (Ed.), *Sociology and rehabilitation* (pp. 100–113). Washington, DC: American Sociological Association.

National Academy on an Aging Society. (1999a). Chronic and disabling conditions. *Challenges for the 21st Century, 1,* 1–6. Washington, DC: National Academy on an Aging Society.

National Academy on an Aging Society.(1999b). *Demography is not destiny.* Washington, DC: National Academy on an Aging Society.

National Academy on an Aging Society. (2000). At risk: Developing chronic conditions in later life. *Challenges for the 21st Century, 4,* 1–6. Washington, DC: National Academy on an Aging Society.

National Center for Health Statistics. (1999a). *Health, United States, 1999, with health and aging chartbook.* Hyattsville, MD: National Center for Health Statistics.

National Center for Health Statistics. (1999b). *U.S. decennial life tables for 1989–1991: Vol. 1, No. 3. Some trends and comparisons of United States life table data; 1900–1991.* Hyattsville, MD: National Center for Health Statistics.

National Council on the Aging. (2002). *American perceptions of aging in the 21st century: The NCOA's continuing study of the myths and realities of aging.* Washington, DC: The National Council on the Aging, Inc.

National Institute on Aging. (1993). *In search of the secrets of aging.* Bethesda, MD: U.S. Government Printing Office.

National Institute on Aging. (1996). *In search of the secrets of aging* (2nd ed.). Bethesda, MD: U.S. Government Printing Office.

Oddis, C. V. (1996). New perspectives on osteoarthritis. *American Journal of Medicine, 100,* 10S–15S.

Oeppen, J., & Vaupel, J. W. (2002). Broken limits to life expectancy. *Science, 296,* 1029–1031.

Olshanksy, S. J., Hayflick, L., & Carnes, B. A. (2002). Position statement on human aging. *Journal of Gerontology: Biological Sciences, 57,* B292–B297.

Olshansky, S. J., Passaro, D. J., Hershow, R. C., Layden, J., Carnes, B. A., Brody, J., et al. (2005). A potential decline in life expectancy in the United States in the 21st century. *New England Journal of Medicine, 352,* 1138–1145.

Penninx, B. W. J. H., Ferrucci, L., Leveille, S. G., Rantanen, T., Pahor, M., & Guralnik, J. M. (2000). Lower extremity performance in nondisabled older persons as a predictor of subsequent hospitalization. *Journal of Gerontology: Medical Sciences, 55,* M691–M697.

Petersen, C., Seligman, M. E., & Valliant, G. (1988). Pessimistic explanatory style is a risk factor for physical illness: A thirty-five-year longitudinal study. *Journal of Personality and Social Psychology, 55,* 23–27.

Rakowski, W. (1992). Disease prevention and health promotion with older adults. In M. Ory, R. Abeles, & P. Lipman (Eds.), *Aging, health, and behavior* (pp. 239–275). Newbury Park, CA: Sage.

Rakowski, W. (1997). Health behavior in the elderly. In D. S. Gochman (Ed.), *Handbook of health behavior research III: Demography, development, and diversity* (pp. 97–117). New York: Plenum.

Riley, M. W. (1998). Letter to the editor. *Gerontologist, 38,* 151.

Roberts, G. (1999). Age effects and health appraisal: A meta-analysis. *Journal of Gerontology: Social Sciences, 54,* S24–S30.

Roberts, J., & Snyder, D. L. (2001). Drug interactions. In G. L. Maddox, R. C. Atchley, J. G. Evans, C. E. Finch, R. A. Kane, M. D. Mezey, et al. (Eds.), *Encyclopedia of aging: A comprehensive multidisciplinary resource in gerontology and geriatrics* (3rd ed., pp. 310–313). New York: Springer.

Robine, J. M., & Michel, J. P. (2004). Looking forward to a general theory on population aging. *Journal of Gerontology: Medical Sciences, 59,* M590–M597.

Robinson-Whelen, S., & Kiecolt-Glaser, J. (1997). The importance of social versus temporal comparison appraisals among older adults. *Journal of Applied Social Psychology, 27,* 959–966.

Robinson-Whelen, S., Kiecolt-Glaser, J. K., & Glaser, R. (2000). Effects of chronic stress on immune function and health in the elderly. In S. B. Manuck & R. Jennings (Eds.), *Behavior, health, and aging* (pp. 69–82). Mahwah, NJ: Erlbaum.

Rook, K. S. (1990). Social networks as a source of social control in older adults' lives. In H. Giles, N. Coupland, & J. Wiemann (Eds.), *Communication, health, and the elderly* (pp. 45–63). Manchester, England: University of Manchester Press.

Rook, K. S. (1994). Assessing the health-related dimensions of older adults' social relationships. In M. P. Lawton & J. Teresi (Eds.), *Annual review of gerontology and geriatrics* (Vol. 14, pp. 142–181). New York: Springer.

Rook, K. S. (1995). Social support, companionship, and social control in older adults' social networks: Implications for well-being. In J. Nussbaum & J. Coupland (Eds.), *Handbook of communication and aging research* (pp. 437–463). Mahwah, NJ: Erlbaum.

Rook, K. S. (2000). The evolution of social relationships in later adulthood. In S. Qualls & N. Abeles (Eds.), *Psychology and the aging revolution* (pp. 173–191). Washington, DC: American Psychological Association.

Rook, K. S., Thuras, P., & Lewis, M. (1990). Social control, health risk taking, and psychological distress among the elderly. *Psychology and Aging, 5,* 327–334.

Rose, M. R. (1999). Can human aging be postponed? *Scientific American, 281,* 106–111.

Rowe, J. W. (1997). The new gerontology. *Science, 278,* 367.

Rowe, J. W. (2002). On "Successful aging and well-being: Self-rated compared with Rowe and Kahn." *Gerontologist, 42,* 725–726.

Rowe, J. W., & Kahn, R. L. (1987). Human aging: Usual and successful. *Science, 237,* 143–149.

Rowe, J. W., & Kahn, R. L. (1998). *Successful aging.* New York: Pantheon.

Ryff, C., Singer, B., Love, G. D., & Essex, M. J. (1998) Resilience in adulthood and later life: Defining features and dynamic processes. In J. Lomranz (Ed.), *Handbook of aging and mental health: An integrative approach* (pp. 6996). New York: Plenum.

Sahyoun, N. R., Lentzner, H., Hoyert, D., & Robinson, K. N. (2001). Trends in causes of death among the elderly. *Aging Trends, 1,* 1–9. Hyattsville, MD: National Center for Health Statistics.

Sandman, C., Wadhwa, P. D., Chicz-DeMet, A., Porto, M., & Garite, T. J. (1999). Maternal corticotropin-releasing hormone and habituation in the human fetus. *Developmental Psychobiology, 34,* 163–173.

Scheibel, A. B. (1996). Structural and functional changes in the aging brain. In J. E. Birren & K. W. Schaie (Eds.), *Handbook of the psychology of aging* (4th ed., pp. 105–128). San Diego, CA: Academic Press.

Schiller J. S., & Bernadel, L. (2004). *Summary health statistics for the U.S. population: National Health Interview Survey, 2002.* National Center for Health Statistics. Vital Health Statistics 10(220). Washington, DC: U.S. Government Printing Office.

Schoeni, R. F., Freedman, V. A., & Wallace, R. B. (2001). Persistent, consistent, widespread, and robust? Another look at recent trends in old-age disability. *Journal of Gerontology: Social Sciences, 55,* S206–S218.

Schulz, R., & Heckhausen, J. (1996). A life-span model of successful aging. *American Psychologist, 51,* 702–714.

Schulz, R., Heckhausen, J., & O'Brien, A. (2000). Negative affect and the disablement process in late life: A life-span control theory approach. In S. B. Manuck, R. Jennings, B. S. Rabin, & A. Baum (Eds.), *Behavior, health, and aging* (pp. 119–133). Mahwah, NJ: Erlbaum.

Seeman, T. E. (1996). Social ties and health. *Annals of Epidemiology, 6,* 442–451.

Seeman, T. E. (2000). Health promoting effects of friends and family: The impact of the social environment on health outcomes in older adults. *American Journal of Health Promotion, 14,* 362–370.

Seeman, T. E., Singer, B. H., Rowe, J. H., Horwitz, R. I., & McEwen, B. S. (1997). Price of adaptation-Allostatic load and its health consequences: MacArthur studies of successful aging. *Archives of Internal Medicine, 157,* 2259–2268.

Seeman, T. E., Singer, B. H., Ryff, C. D., Diengerg-Love, G., & Levy-Storms, L. (2002). Social relationships, gender, and allostatic load across two age cohorts. *Psychosomatic Medicine, 64,* 395–406.

Semenza, J. C., Rubin, C. H., Falter, K. H., Selanikio, J. D., Flanders, D. W., Howe, H. L., et al. (1996). Heat-related deaths during the July 1995 heat wave in Chicago. *New England Journal of Medicine, 335,* 84–90.

Shock, N. W., Greulich, R. C., Andres, R. A., Arenberg, D., Costa, P. T., Jr., Lakatta, E. W., et al. (1984). *Normal human aging: The Baltimore Longitudinal Study of Aging.* Washington, DC: U.S. Department of Health and Human Services.

Siegler, I. C., Bastian, L. A., & Bosworth, H. B. (2001). Health, behavior, and aging. In A. Baum, T. A. Revenson, & J. E. Singer (Eds.), *Handbook of health psychology* (pp. 469–476). Mahwah, NJ: Erlbaum.

Siegler, I. C., Bastian, L. A., Steffens, D. C., Bosworth, H. B., & Costa, P. T. (2002). Behavioral medicine and aging. *Journal of Consulting and Clinical Psychology, 70,* 843–851.

Singh, M. A. F. (2002). Exercise comes of age: Rationale and recommendations for a geriatric exercise prescription. *Journal of Gerontology: Medical Sciences, 57,* M262–M282.

Smith, A. M. A., Shelley, J. M., & Dennerstein, L. (1994). Self-rated health: Biological continuum or social discontinuity? *Social Science and Medicine, 39,* 77–83.

Smith, T. W., Kendall, P. C., & Keefe, F. J. (2002). Behavioral medicine and clinical health psychology: Introduction to the special issue, A view from the decade of behavior. *Journal of Consulting and Clinical Psychology, 70,* 459–462.

Smith, T. W., Orleans, C. T., & Jenkins, C. D. (2004). Prevention and health promotion: Decades of progress, new challenges, and emerging agenda. *Health Psychology, 23,* 126–133.

Sorkin, J. D., Andres, R., Muller, D. C., Baldwin, H. L., & Fleg, J. L. (1992). Cholesterol as a risk factor for coronary heart in disease in elderly men: The BLSA. *Annals of Epidemiology, 2,* 59–67.

Steiner, J. F. (1996). Pharmacotherapy problems in the elderly. *Journal of the American Pharmaceutical Association, 36,* 431–437.

Stoller, E. P. (1993). Interpretations of symptoms by older people: A health diary study of illness behavior. *Journal of Aging and Health, 5,* 58–81.

Strawbridge, W. J., & Wallhagen, M. I. (1999). Self-rated health and mortality over three decades: Results from a time-dependent covariate analysis. *Research on Aging, 21,* 402–416.

Strawbridge, W. J., Wallhagen, M. I., & Cohen, R. D. (2002). Successful aging and well-being: Self-rated compared with Rowe and Kahn. *Gerontologist, 42,* 727–733

Stuck, A. E., Walthert, J. M., Nikolaus, T., Buela, C. J., Hohmann, C., & Beck, J. C. (1999). Risk factors for functional status decline in community-living elderly people: A systematic literature review. *Social Science and Medicine, 48,* 445–469.

Suarez, E. C., Kuhn, C. M., Schanberg, S. M., Williams, R. B., & Zimmermann, E. A. (1998). Neuroendocrine, cardiovascular, and emotional responses of hostile men: The role of interpersonal challenge. *Psychosomatic Medicine, 60,* 78–88.

Suls, J., & Rothman, A. (2004). Evolution of the biopsychosocial model: Prospects and challenges for health psychology. *Health Psychology, 23,* 119–125.

Terpenning, M. S., & Bradley, S. F. (1991). Why aging leads to increased susceptibility to infection. *Geriatrics, 46,* 77–80.

Tucker, J. S. (2002). Health-related social control within older adults' relationships. *Journal of Gerontology: Psychological Sciences, 57,* P387–P395.

Tucker, J. S., & Anders, S. L. (2001). Social control of health behaviors in marriage. *Journal of Applied Social Psychology, 31,* 467–485.

Uchino, B. N., Cacioppo, J. T., & Kiecolt-Glaser, J. K. (1996). The relationship between social support and physiological processes: A review with emphasis on underlying mechanisms and implications for health. *Psychological Bulletin, 119,* 488–531.

Umberson, D. (1987). Family status and health behaviors: Social control as a dimension of social integration. *Journal of Health and Social Behavior, 28,* 306–319.

U.S. Bureau of the Census. (2004). *Statistical Abstract of the U.S. Section 1: Population* Washington, DC: U.S. Government Printing Office.

U.S. Department of Health and Human Services. (1979). *Healthy people: The surgeon general's report on health promotion and disease prevention.* Washington, DC: U.S. Government Printing Office.

U.S. Department of Health and Human Services. (2001). *A profile of older Americans: 2001.* Washington, DC: U.S. Government Printing Office.

Vaitkevicius, P. V., Fleg, J. L., Engel, J. H., O'Connor, F. C., Wright, J. G., Lakatta, L. E., et al. (1993). Effects of age and aerobic capacity on arterial stiffness in healthy adults. *Circulation, 88,* 1456–1462.

Vaupel, J. W., Carey, J. R., Christensen, K., Johnson, T. E., Yashin, A. I., Holm, N. V., et al. (1998). Biodemographic trajectories of longevity. *Science, 280,* 855–860.

Verbrugge, L. M. (1989). The twain meet: Empirical explanations of sex differences in health and mortality. *Journal of Health and Social Behavior, 30,* 282–304.

Verbrugge, L. M. (2001). Sex differences in health. In G. L. Maddox, R. C. Atchley, J. G. Evans, C. E. Finch, R. A. Kane, M. D. Mezey, et al. (Eds.), *Encyclopedia of aging: A comprehensive multidisciplinary resource in gerontology and geriatrics* (3rd ed., pp. 850–854). New York: Springer.

Verbrugge, L. M., & Jette, A. M. (1994). The disablement process. *Social Science and Medicine, 38,* 1–14.

Verbrugge, L. M., Reoma, J. M., & Gruber-Baldini, A. L. (1994). Short-term dynamics of disability and well-being. *Journal of Health and Social Behavior, 35,* 97–117.

von Farber, M., Bootsma-van der Wiel, A., van Exel, E., Gussekloo, J., Lagaay, A. M., van Dongen, E., et al. (2001). Successful aging in the oldest old: Who can be characterized as successfully aged? *Archives of Internal Medicine, 161,* 2694–2700.

Wadden, T. A., Brownell, K. D., & Foster, G. D. (2002). Obesity: Responding to the global epidemic. *Journal of Consulting and Clinical Psychology, 70,* 510–525.

Wagner, L. (1998). Hypertension in African-Americans. *Clinical Excellence for Nurse Practitioners: The International Journal of NPACE, 2*(4):225–231.

Waidmann, T. A., & Liu, K. (2000). Disability trends among elderly persons and implications for the future. *Journal of Gerontology: Social Sciences, 55,* S298–S307.

Wallace, R. B., & Lemke, J. H. (1991). The compression of comorbidity. *Journal of Aging and Health, 3,* 237–246.

Wasson, J., Gaudette, C., Whaley, F., Sauvigne, A., Baribeau, P., & Welch, H. G. (1992). Telephone care as a substitute for routine clinic follow-up. *Journal of the American Medical Association, 267,* 1788–1829.

Westmaas, J. L., Wild, T. C., & Ferrence, R. (2002). Effects of gender in social control of smoking cessation. *Health Psychology, 21,* 368–376.

Whitbourne, S. K. (1996). Psychological perspectives on the normal aging process. In L. L. Carstensen, B. A. Edelstein, & L. Dornbrand (Eds.), *The practical handbook of clinical gerontology* (pp. 3–25). Thousand Oaks, CA: Sage.

Williams, D. R., & Collins, C. (1995). U.S. socioeconomic and racial differences in health: Patterns and explanations. *Annual Review of Sociology, 21,* 349–386.

Williams, K. E., & Bond, M. J. (2002). The roles of self-efficacy, outcome expectancies and social support in the self-care behaviors of diabetics. *Psychology, Health, and Medicine, 7,* 127–141.

Williams, M. E. (1994). Clinical management of the elderly patient. In W. R. Hazzard, E. L. Bierman, J. P. Blass, W. H. Ettinger Jr., & J. B. Halter (Eds.), *Principles of geriatric medicine and gerontology* (3rd ed., pp. 195–201). New York: McGraw-Hill.

Williams, T. F. (1992). Aging versus disease: Which changes seen with age are the result of "biological aging"? *Generations, 16,* 21–25.

Wilson, R. S., Mendes de Leon, C. F., Bienias, J. L., Evans, D. A., & Bennett, D. A. (2004). Personality and mortality in old age. *Journal of Gerontology: Psychological Sciences, 59,* P110–P116.

Wrosch, C., Heckhausen, J., & Lachman, M. E. (2000). Primary and secondary control strategies for managing health and financial stress across adulthood. *Psychology and Aging, 15,* 387–399.

Wrosch, C., Schulz, R., & Heckhausen, J. (2002). Health stresses and depressive symptomatology in the elderly: The importance of health engagement control strategies. *Health Psychology, 21,* 340–348.

Yong, H. H., Gibson, S. J., de L. Horne, D. J., & Helme, R. D. (2001). Development of a Pain Attitudes Questionnaire to assess stoicism and cautiousness for possible age differences. *Journal of Gerontology: Psychological Sciences, 56,* P279–P284.

Zettel, L. A., & Rook, K. S. (2004). Substitution and compensation in the social networks of older women. *Psychology and Aging, 19,* 433–443.

James W. Pennebaker

and Cindy K. Chung

Expressive Writing, Emotional Upheavals, and Health

There is a long history in psychology and medicine linking the occurrence of traumatic experiences with subsequent physical and mental health problems. What is it about a trauma that influences health? Several candidates immediately come to mind. Psychologically, personal upheavals provoke intense and long-lasting emotional changes. The unexpected events are generally associated with cognitive disruption, including rumination and attempts to understand what happened and why. Socially, traumas are known to cause wholesale disruptions in people's social networks. Behaviorally, and perhaps because of the social and psychological changes, traumas are often associated with lifestyle changes such as unhealthy smoking, drinking, exercise, sleeping, and eating patterns. Each of these psychological, social, and behavioral effects is associated with a host of biological changes, including elevations in cortisol, immune disruption, cardiovascular changes, and a cascade of neuro-transmitter changes.

Individuals who are highly reactive to novel stimuli (Vaidya & Garfield, 2003), are highly anxious (Miller, 2003), avoidant, and self-blaming (Sutker, Davis, Uddo, & Ditta, 1995), and high in hypnotic ability (Bower & Sivers, 1998) may be particularly susceptible to traumatic experiences.

Similarly, the more extreme the trauma and the longer time over which it lasts are predictors of post-traumatic stress disorder (PTSD) incidence (e.g., Breslau, Chilcoat, Kessler, & Davis, 1999). It is also generally agreed that people most prone to PTSD have had a history of depression, trauma, and other PTSD episodes in the past even prior to their most recent traumatic experience (cf. Miller, 2003).

Perhaps more surprising than the discovery of the trauma-illness link is the realization that most people do not become sick after a trauma. In a classic article, Wortman and Silver (1989) summarized several studies showing that at least half of people who have faced the death of a spouse or child did not experience intense anxiety, depression, or grief. Numerous studies report that at least 65% of male and female soldiers who have lived through horrific battles or war-zone stress never show any evidence of PTSD (Keane, 1998; Murray, 1992). Multiple studies with individuals who have survived major motor vehicle accidents (Brom, Kleber, & Hofman, 1993) or witnessed tragic airplane accidents (Carlier & Gersons, 1997) find that the majority of research participants did not experience depression or PTSD in the weeks or months after their experiences. Across studies, 40% to 80% of rape survivors did not evidence symptoms of PTSD

(Kilpatrick, Resnick, Saunders, & Best, 1998; Resnick, Kilpatrick, & Lipovsky, 1991).

Why is it that some people seem to deal with major upheavals better than others? What is the profile of healthy coping? This, of course, is a central question among trauma researchers. We know, for example, that people with an intact social support group weather upheavals better than others (e.g., Murray, 1992). Beyond basic genetic predispositions, do some people adopt certain coping strategies that allow them to move past an upheaval more efficiently? If such coping strategies exist, can they be trained? If such techniques are available, how do they work?

Given that as many as 30% of people who face massive traumatic experiences will experience PTSD, what can we, as researchers and clinicians, do to reduce this rate? It is likely that many (perhaps most) PTSD-prone individuals will not benefit from any simple interventions. The nature of their trauma, their genetic, biological, and/or personality predispositions, or pretrauma life experiences will override social or psychological therapies. Nevertheless, some PTSD-prone individuals as well as the majority of distressed but subclinical cases may benefit by focusing on their psychological and social worlds in the wake of their traumatic experiences.

As we lay out in this chapter, there is reason to believe that when people transform their feelings and thoughts about personally upsetting experiences into language, their physical and mental health often improves. The links to PTSD are still tenuous. However, an increasing number of studies indicate that having people write about traumas can result in healthy improvements in social, psychological, behavioral, and biological measures. As with the trauma-illness link, however, there is probably not a single mediator that can explain the power of writing. One promising candidate that is proposed concerns the effects of translating emotions into language format, or, as we suggest, a metaphoric translation of an analog experience into a digital one.

Emotional Upheavals, Disclosure, and Health

Not all traumatic events are equally toxic. By the 1960s, Holmes and Rahe (1967) suggested that the health impact of a trauma varied with the degree to which the trauma disrupted a person's life. Interestingly, the original scales tapping the health risks of traumas generally measured socially acceptable traumas—death of spouse, loss of job. No items asked if the participant had been raped, had had a sexual affair, or had caused the death of another. By the mid-1980s, investigators started to notice that upheavals that were kept secret were more likely to result in health problems than those that could be spoken about more openly. For example, individuals who were victims of violence and who had kept silent about this experience were significantly more likely to have adverse health effects than those who openly talked with others (Pennebaker & Susman, 1988). In short, having any type of traumatic experience is associated with elevated illness rates; having any trauma and not talking about it further elevates the risk. These effects actually are stronger when controlling for age, sex, and social support. Apparently, keeping a trauma secret from an intact social network is more unhealthy than not having a social network to begin with (cf. Cole, Kemeny, Taylor, & Visscher, 1996).

If keeping a powerful secret about an upsetting experience is unhealthy, can talking about it—or in some way putting it into words—be beneficial? This is a question we asked two decades ago. Going on the untested assumption that most people would have had at least one emotional upheaval that they had not disclosed in great detail, we began a series of studies that involved people writing and, in some cases, talking about these events.

In the first study, people were asked to write about a trauma or about superficial topics for 4 days, 15 minutes per day. We found that confronting the emotions and thoughts surrounding deeply personal issues promoted physical health, as measured by reductions in physician visits in the months following the study, fewer reports of aspirin usage, and overall more positive long-term evaluations of the effect of the experiment (Pennebaker & Beall, 1986). The results of that initial study have led to a number of similar disclosure studies, in our laboratory and by others, with a wide array of intriguing results. Next we briefly review the paradigm and basic findings.

The Basic Writing Paradigm

The standard laboratory writing technique has involved randomly assigning participants to one of two or more groups. All writing groups are asked to write about assigned topics for 1 to 5 consecutive days, for 15 to 30 minutes each day. Writing is generally done in the laboratory, with no feedback given. Those assigned to the control conditions are typically asked to write about superficial topics, such as how they use their time. The standard instructions for those assigned to the experimental group are a variation on the following:

> For the next three days, I would like for you to write about your very deepest thoughts and feelings about the most traumatic experience of your entire life. In your writing, I'd like you to really let go and explore your very deepest emotions and thoughts. You might tie this trauma to your childhood, your relationships with others, including parents, lovers, friends, or relatives. You may also link this event to your past, your present, or your future, or to who you have been, who you would like to be, or who you are now. You may write about the same general issues or experiences on all days of writing or on different topics each day. Not everyone has had a single trauma but all of us have had major conflicts or stressors—and you can write about these as well. All of your writing will be completely confidential. Don't worry about spelling, sentence structure, or grammar. The only rule is that once you begin writing, continue to do so until your time is up.

Whereas the original writing studies asked people to write about traumatic experiences, later studies expanded the scope of writing topics to general emotional events or to specific experiences shared by other participants (e.g., diagnosis of cancer, losing a job, coming to college). The amount of time people have been asked to write has also varied tremendously, from 10 minutes to 30 minutes for 3, 4, or 5 days—sometimes within the same day to once per week for up to 4 weeks.

The writing paradigm is exceptionally powerful. Participants—from children to the elderly, from honor students to maximum-security prisoners—disclose a remarkable range and depth of human experiences. Lost loves, deaths, sexual and physical abuse incidents, and tragic failures are common themes in all our studies. If nothing else, the paradigm demonstrates that when individuals are given the opportunity to disclose deeply personal aspects of their lives, they readily do so. Even though a large number of participants report crying or being deeply upset by the experience, the overwhelming majority report that the writing experience was valuable and meaningful in their lives.

Interest in the expressive writing method has grown over the years. The first study was published in 1986. By 1996, approximately 20 studies had been published. By 2006, well over 150 have been published in English-language journals. Although many studies have examined physical health and biological outcomes, an increasing number have explored writing's effects on attitude change, stereotyping, creativity, working memory, motivation, life satisfaction, school performance, and a variety of health-related behaviors. It is beyond the scope of this chapter to provide a detailed review of the findings of the writing paradigm. Rather, we briefly summarize some of the more promising findings before focusing on the underlying mechanisms that may be at work.

Effects of Disclosure on Health-Related Outcomes

Researchers have relied on a variety of physical and mental health measures to evaluate the effect of writing. Writing or talking about emotional experiences relative to writing about superficial control topics has been found to be associated with significant drops in physician visits from before to after writing among relatively healthy samples. Over the last decade, as the number of expressive writing studies has increased, several meta-analyses either have been conducted or are being conducted as of this writing.

The original expressive writing meta-analysis, based on 14 studies using healthy participants, was published by Joshua Smyth (1998). Smyth's primary conclusions were that the writing paradigm is associated with positive outcomes with a weighted mean effect size of $d = .47$ ($r = .23, p < .0001$), noting that this effect size is similar to or larger than those produced by other psychological interventions. The highest significant effect sizes ($p < .0001$) were for psychological ($d = .66$) and physiological ($d = .68$) outcomes, which were greater than those for health ($d = .42$) and general functioning ($d = .33$) outcomes. A nonsignificant effect size was found for health behaviors. Smyth also found that longer intervals between writing sessions produced larger overall effect sizes, and that males benefited more from writing than did females.

Almost 7 years after Smyth's article was published, another meta-analysis by Meads (2003) was released by the Cochran Commission. In an analysis of dozens of studies, the author concluded that there was not sufficient evidence to warrant adopting the writing method as part of clinical practice. One problem that the report underscored was the lack of any large randomized clinical trials (RCTs) that were based on large, clearly identified samples. Coming from a medical background, the Meads article was befuddled by the fact that most of the experimental studies of expressive writing were more theory oriented and not aimed at clinical application. Since the release of the Meads paper, new waves of RCTs are now being conducted with a diverse group of patient populations.

Most recently, Frisina, Borod, and Lepore (2004) performed a similar meta-analysis on nine writing studies using clinical populations. They found that expressive writing significantly improved health outcomes ($d = .19$, $p < .05$). However, the effect was stronger for physical ($d = .21$, $p = .01$) than for psychological ($d = .07$, $p = .17$) health outcomes. The authors suggested that a possible reason for these small effect sizes was the heterogeneity of the samples. Writing was less effective for psychiatric than for physical illness populations.

Researchers have relied on a variety of physical and mental health measures to evaluate the effect of writing. Across multiple studies in laboratories around the world, writing or talking about emotional experiences relative to writing about superficial control topics has been found to be associated with significant drops in physician visits from before to after writing among relatively healthy samples. Writing and/or talking about emotional topics has also been found to influence immune function in beneficial ways, including T-helper cell growth (using a blastogenesis procedure with the mitogen PHA), antibody response to Epstein-Barr virus, and antibody response to hepatitis B vaccinations (for reviews, see Lepore & Smyth, 2002; Pennebaker & Graybeal, 2001; Sloan & Marx, 2004b).

Activity of the autonomic nervous system is also influenced by the disclosure paradigm. Among those participants who disclose their thoughts and emotions to a particularly high degree, skin conductance levels are significantly lower during the trauma disclosures than when participants are describing superficial topics. Systolic blood pressure and heart

rate drop to levels below baseline following the disclosure of traumatic topics but not superficial ones (Pennebaker, Hughes, & O'Heeron, 1987). In short, when individuals talk or write about deeply personal topics, their immediate biological responses are congruent with those seen among people attempting to relax. McGuire, Greenberg, and Gevirtz (2005) have shown that these effects can carry over to the long term in participants with elevated blood pressure. One month after writing, those who participated in the emotional disclosure condition exhibited lower systolic and diastolic blood pressure (DBP) than before writing. Four months after writing, DBP remained lower than baseline levels.

Similarly, Sloan and Marx (2004a) found that participants in a disclosure condition exhibited greater physiological activation, as indexed by elevated cortisol levels, during their first writing session, relative to controls. Physiological activation then decreased and was similar to that of controls in subsequent writing sessions. The initial elevation in cortisol from the first writing session predicted improved psychological but not physical health at 1 month follow-up. It is possible that confronting a traumatic or distressing experience led to reactions aimed for in exposure-based treatments (e.g., Foa, Rothbaum, & Furr, 2003).

Behavioral changes have also been found. Students who write about emotional topics evidence improvements in grades in the months following the study (e.g., Lumley & Provenzano, 2003). Senior professionals who have been laid off from their jobs get new jobs more quickly after writing (Spera, Buhrfeind, & Pennebaker, 1994). Consistent with the direct health measures, university staff members who write about emotional topics are subsequently absent from their work at lower rates than controls. Interestingly, relatively few reliable changes emerge using self-reports of health-related behaviors. That is, in the weeks after writing, experimental participants do not exercise more or smoke less. The one exception is that the study with laid off professionals found that writing reduced self-reported alcohol intake.

Self-reports also suggest that writing about upsetting experiences, although painful in the days of writing, produces long-term improvements in mood and indicators of well-being compared with controls. Although some studies have failed to find clear mood or self-reported distress effects, Smyth's

(1998) meta-analysis on written disclosure studies indicates that, in general, writing about emotional topics is associated with significant reductions in distress.

Procedural Differences That Affect Expressive Writing

Writing about emotional experiences clearly influences measures of physical and mental health. In recent years, several investigators have attempted to define the boundary conditions of the disclosure effect. Some of the most important findings are as follows.

Topic of Disclosure

Although two studies have found that health effects only occur among individuals who write about particularly traumatic experiences (Greenberg & Stone, 1992; Lutgendorf, Antoni, Kumar, & Schneiderman, 1994), most studies have found that disclosure is more broadly beneficial. Choice of topic, however, may selectively influence outcomes. Although virtually all studies find that writing about emotional topics has positive effects on physical health, only certain assigned topics appear to be related to changes in grades. For beginning college students, for example, when they are asked to write specifically about emotional issues related to coming to college, both health and college grades improve. However, when other students are asked to write about emotional issues related to traumatic experiences in general, only health—and not academic performance—improves (see Pennebaker, 1995; Pennebaker & Keough, 1999).

Over the last decade, an increasing number of studies have experimented with more focused writing topics. Individuals diagnosed with breast cancer, lung cancer, or HIV have been asked to write specifically about their living with the particular disease (e.g., de Moor et al., 2002; Mann, 2001; Petrie et al., 2004; Stanton & Danoff-Burg, 2002). Similarly, people who have lost their job have been asked to write about that experience (Spera et al., 1994). In each case, however, participants are asked to write about this topic in a very broad way and are encouraged to write about other topics that may be only remotely related. For example, in the job layoff project, participants in the experimental conditions were asked to explore their thoughts and feelings about losing their jobs. Fewer than half of the essays dealt directly with the layoff. Others dealt with marital problems and issues with children, money, and health.

It has been our experience that traumatic experiences often bring to the fore other important issues in people's lives. As researchers, we assume that, say, the diagnosis of a life-threatening disease is the most important issue for a person to write about in a cancer-related study. However, for many, this can be secondary to a cheating husband, an abusive parent, or some other trauma that may have occurred years earlier. We recommend that writing researchers and practitioners provide sufficiently open instructions to allow people to deal with whatever important topics they want to write about. As described in greater detail later, the more that the topic or writing assignment is constrained, the less successful it usually is.

Topic Orientation: Focusing on the Good, the Bad, or the Benefits

There are a number of theoretical and practical reasons to assume that some strategies for approaching emotional upheavals might be better than others. With the growth of the field of positive psychology, several researchers have reported on the benefits of having a positive or optimistic approach to life (Carver & Scheier, 2002; Diener, Lucas, & Oishi, 2002; Seligman, 2000). Particularly persuasive have been a series of correlational studies on benefit finding—that is, people who are able to find benefits to negative experiences generally report less negative affect, milder distress, fewer disruptive thoughts, and greater meaningfulness in life. People who engage in benefit finding fare better on objective physical and mental health outcomes (e.g., children's developmental test scores, recurrence of heart attacks) even after controlling for a host of possible confounding factors (for a review, see Affleck & Tennen, 1996). Being able to see things in a positive light, then, might be a critical component to successful adjustment.

In one study examining adjustment to college, Cameron and Nicholls (1998) had participants previously classified as dispositional optimists or pessimists write in one of three conditions: a self-regulation condition (writing about thoughts and feelings toward coming to college and then formulating coping strategies), a disclosure condition (writing about thoughts and feelings only), or a control task (writing about trivial topics). Overall, participants in the disclosure task had higher GPA scores at follow-up, but only those in the self-regulation task experienced less negative affect and better adjustment to college over the control participants. Optimists visited their doctors less in the following month if they had participated in either of the experimental writing conditions. On the other hand, only pessimists in the self-regulation condition had significantly fewer visits to the doctor after the study. With the added encouragement of formulating coping strategies, pessimists may be able to reap the same health benefits from writing about their thoughts and feelings as optimists naturally might do.

When confronting traumatic experiences, is it best to ask people to simply write about them or to write about the positive sides of the experiences? Several studies have addressed this question. Particularly interesting has been a series of studies by Laura King and her colleagues in which participants were asked to write about intensely positive experiences (IPEs) or control topics. Those who wrote about IPEs reported significantly better mood and fewer illness-related health center visits than did those who wrote about trivial topics (Burton & King, 2004). In another study, students were asked to write about traumas in the standard way (King & Miner, 2000). In the benefit-finding condition, participants were encouraged to focus on the benefits that have come from the trauma. Finally, in the mixed condition, participants were asked to first write about the trauma, and then to switch to the perceived benefits arising from the trauma experience. Counter to predictions, the trauma-only and benefits-only participants evidenced health improvements, whereas the mixed group did not. It could be that writing about the perceived benefits is enough to organize thoughts and feelings about a trauma, and to cope effectively. However, as evidenced from the mixed condition, if people are not able to integrate their perceived benefits into their trauma story in their own way, writing may be ineffective.

Several unpublished studies from our own lab paint a similar picture about the problems of constraining participants' orientations. For her dissertation, Cheryl Hughes (1994) asked students to write about either the positive or the negative aspects of their coming to college for 3 days. Neither group evidenced any benefits of writing compared with a nonemotional control condition. Indeed, both groups complained that there were some real negative (in the positive condition) and positive (in the negative condition) aspects of coming to college that they also wanted to write about. Similarly, in an unpublished project by Lori Stone (2002), students were asked to write about their thoughts and feelings about the September 11 attacks. In one condition, they received the standard unconstrained instructions. In a second condition, participants were asked to focus on their own feelings on one day and on other perspectives on alternating days. The perspective-switching instructions proved to be less beneficial than the unconstrained methods.

Although several variations on the expressive writing method have been tested, none have been found to be consistently superior to the original trauma writing or other methods that encourage participants to freely choose their writing topic. Forcing individuals to write about a particular topic or in a particular way may cause them to focus on the writing itself rather than on the topic and the role of their emotions in the overall story.

Writing Versus Talking Alone Versus Talking to Others

Most studies comparing writing alone to talking either into a tape recorder (Esterling, Antoni, Fletcher, Marguiles, & Schneiderman, 1994) or to a therapist in a one-way interaction (Murray, Lamnin, & Carver, 1989; Donnelly & Murray, 1991) find comparable biological, mood, and cognitive effects. Talking and writing about emotional experiences are both superior to writing about superficial topics.

A striking exception to this was a study by Gidron, Peri, Connolly, and Shalev (1996) in which a group of 14 Israeli PTSD patients were randomly assigned to write about either traumas ($N = 8$) or superficial topics ($N = 6$) on three occasions. After writing, experimental participants were asked to discuss their most traumatic events to a group, whereas controls were asked to describe a daily routine. Unlike all other published writing studies, this one found that experimental participants were significantly more distressed, with poorer health, at the 5-week follow-up. Because other studies have been conducted with participants coping with PTSD, the findings are not due solely to the nature of the participants or the disorder. Rather, reading or discussing one's traumas in a group format after writing may pose unexpected problems. Clearly, additional research is needed to help understand this process.

Actual or Implied Social Factors

Unlike psychotherapy and everyday discussions about traumas, the writing paradigm does not employ feedback to the participant. Rather, after individuals write about their own experiences, they are asked to place their essays into an anonymous-looking box with the promise that their writing will not be linked to their name. In one study comparing the effects of having students write either on paper that would be handed in to the experimenter or on a magic pad (wherein the writing disappears when the person lifts the plastic writing cover), no autonomic or self-report differences were found (Czajka, 1987). The benefits of writing, then, occur without explicit social feedback. Nevertheless, the degree to which people write holding the belief that some symbolic other person may "magically" read their essays can never be easily determined.

Typing, Handwriting, and Finger Writing

Although no studies have compared ways of writing on health outcomes, a few have explored whether mode of writing can influence people's ratings of the expressive writing procedure itself. Brewin and Lennard (1999), for example, reported that writing by hand produced more negative affect and led to more self-rated disclosure than did typing. One possibility is that writing by hand is slower and encourages individuals to process their thoughts and feelings more deeply. Recently, the first author has tested the idea of finger writing. In finger writing exercises, people are asked to use their finger and to "write" about a trauma as if they were holding a pen. Over the last 2 years, six expressive writing workshops have been given in Wisconsin, Sweden, Australia, England, the Netherlands, and England that involved a total of 227 participants (mean age = 44.5, SD = 12.3; 73% female) in groups ranging from 28 to 71 people.

In each workshop, participants have been asked to write for 5 to 10 minutes about an emotional topic on three occasions. For two of the three times, people are asked to write using a pen and one time with their finger. At the conclusion of the 4- to 6-hour workshop, individuals are asked to rate "how valuable and meaningful" each of the writing exercises had been. Along a 7-point unipolar scale, where 7 equals a great deal, the mean rating for the finger writing has been 5.81 (SD = 2.30) and the mean for the two pen-writing occasions has been 5.84. Interestingly, women significantly prefer the finger writing to a greater degree than do men. When queried about their preference for finger writing, many women reported that it allowed them to freely express some of their most secret thoughts. Indeed, in every workshop, several people reported that they used more swear words when finger writing than when writing with a pen.

Timing: How Long After a Trauma

In the last 30 years, advances in emergency medicine have been astounding. Although we know how to treat people medically in the first hours and days after a trauma, our knowledge about psychological interventions during the same period has grown very little. Without the guidance of any research, several groups have created immediate crisis intervention businesses. Perhaps the most successful, known as critical incident stress management (CISM; e.g., Mitchell & Everly, 1996), argues that people victimized by trauma should be attended to within the first 72 hours after the event has occurred. Although the CISM system has many components, the most interesting and controversial encourages individuals to openly acknowledge their emotions and thoughts concerning the trauma within a group. The CISM system has now been adopted by thousands of businesses, governmental organizations, and other groups around the world. Despite the intuitive appeal of CISM, there is very little evidence that it works. Indeed, most studies suggest that it is more likely to cause harm than benefits (e.g. McNally, Bryant, & Ehlers, 2003).

The CISM findings as well as other projects interested in self-disclosure immediately following an upheaval have relevance for the timing for an expressive writing intervention. For example, one study asked women who had recently given birth to talk about their deepest thoughts, feelings, and fears to their midwives. These women were actually more likely to subsequently experience depression than women not asked to talk about these topics (Small, Lumley, Donohue, Potter, & Waldenström, 2000). Women who were asked to write about the treatment they were undergoing for breast cancer during the last week of radiation treatment evidenced no benefits for any measures compared with controls (Walker, Nail, & Croyle, 1999).

Is there an optimal time after a trauma that expressive writing would most likely work? Unfortunately, no parametric studies have been conducted on this question. Over the years, we have been involved in several projects that have attempted to tap people's natural disclosure patterns in the days and weeks after upheavals. For example, using a random-digit dialing in the weeks and months after the 1989 Loma Prieta earthquake in the San Francisco Bay area, we asked different groups of people the number of times that they had thought about and talked about the earthquake in the previous 24 hours. We used a similar method a year later to tap people's responses to the declaration of war with Iraq during the first Persian Gulf War. In both cases, we found that people talked with one another at very high rates in the first 2 to 3 weeks. By the 4th week, however, talking rates were extremely low. Rates of thinking about the earthquake and war showed a different pattern: It took considerably longer (about 8 weeks) before people reported thinking about them at low rates (from Pennebaker & Harber, 1993).

More recently, we have analyzed the blogs of almost 1,100 frequent users of an Internet site in the 2 months before and 2 months after the September 11 terrorist attacks. Rates of writing increased dramatically for about 2 weeks after the attacks. More striking was the analysis of word usage. Use of first-person singular (*I, me,* and *my*) dropped almost 15% within 24 hours of the attacks and remained low for about a week. However, over the next 2 months, *I*-word usage remained below baseline (Cohn, Mehl, & Pennebaker, 2004). Use of first-person singular is significant because it correlates with depression (Rude, Gortner, & Pennebaker, 2004). What was striking was that these bloggers—who expressed an elevated rate of negative moods in the days after 9/11—were generally quite healthy. They were psychologically distancing themselves from the emotional turmoil of the event.

Considering the current evidence, it is likely that defenses such as denial, detachment, distraction, and distancing may, in fact, be quite healthy in the hours and days after an upheaval. A technique such as expressive writing may be inappropriate until several weeks or months later. Indeed, we now encourage clinicians to delay their use of expressive writing until at least 1 to 2 months after an upheaval or until they think their patient is thinking "too much" about the event. Obsessing and ruminating about a trauma a few weeks after it has occurred is probably not too much. Thinking about it at the same high rate 6 months later might in fact signal that expressive writing might be beneficial.

Timing Between Writing Sessions

Different experiments have variously asked participants to write for 1 to 5 days, ranging from consecutive days to sessions separated by a week, ranging from 10 to 45 minutes for each writing session, for anywhere from 1 to 7 sessions. In Smyth's (1998) meta-analysis, he found a trend suggesting that the more days over which the experiment takes place, the stronger the impact on outcomes. Two subsequent studies that actually manipulated the times between writing failed to support Smyth's findings.

The first, by Sheese, Brown, and Graziano (2004), asked students to write either once per week for 3 weeks or for 3 continuous days about traumatic experiences or superficial topics. Although the experimental-control difference was significant for health center differences, no trend emerged concerning the relative benefits of once a week versus daily writing. More recently, the authors randomly assigned 100 students to write either about major life transitions or about superficial topics. Participants wrote three times, for 15 minutes each time, either once a day for 3 days, once an hour for 3 hours, or three times in a little more than an hour (Pennebaker & Chung, 2005). Immediately after the last writing session and again at 1 month follow-up, no differences were found between the daily versus three-times-in-1-hour condition. Indeed, at follow-up, the three experimental groups evidenced lower symptom reports ($p = .05$, one-tailed test) than the controls after controlling for the prewriting symptom levels.

Time Until Follow-Up

Another suspect for inconsistent or null results across writing studies is the varied duration between the final writing session and the follow-up assessment. Expressive writing outcomes have been measured up to about 6 months after the writing sessions are completed. While some psychological and physical health changes may be immediately apparent, they may be fleeting. On the other hand, some effects may take days, weeks, months, or even years to emerge as significant changes on various health measures, if at all. The timing of improvements may also vary as a function of sampling characteristics. In an expressive writing study examining those suffering from asthma or rheumatoid arthritis (RA), health benefits were seen in asthmatics in the experimental writing condition as early as 2 weeks after writing. However, the health profile of individuals with RA in the experimental writing condition did not differ from those in the control condition until the 4-month assessment period (Smyth, Stone, Hurewitz, & Kaell, 1999).

Considering all the other variants on the writing method already mentioned, it would be difficult to come up with a standard time for follow-up. Instead, knowing the general time course of proposed underlying mechanisms and providing multiple convergent measures to validate specific outcomes may be a more practical approach in thinking about follow-up assessments.

Individual Differences

No consistent personality measures have distinguished who does versus who does not benefit from writing. A number of variables have been unrelated to outcomes, including age, anxiety (or negative affectivity), and inhibition or constraint. A small number of studies that have either preselected participants or performed a median split on a particular variable have reported some effects. However, given the large number of studies, these effects should probably be viewed as promising rather than definitive.

Christensen et al. (1996) preselected students on hostility and found that those high in hostility benefited more from writing than those low in hostility. Some studies have found that individuals high on alexithymia (a trait that taps the inability of people to label or feel particular negative emotions) tended to benefit from writing more than those low on alexithymia (Paez, Velasco, & Gonzalez, 1999; Solano, Donati, Pecci, Persicheeti, & Colaci, 2003). However, later research by Lumley (2004) suggests that unlike the participants in the aforementioned studies, alexithymics suffering from chronic illnesses or elevated stress may not reap the same benefits after writing.

Finally, there has been a great deal of interest in knowing if sex differences exist in the potential benefits of expressive writing. Smyth's (1998) meta-analysis revealed that males tend to benefit more from the writing paradigm than do females. Several

studies have explored this with reasonably large samples—usually with college students—and have not replicated the meta-analytic results. Clearly, more studies are needed, using more diverse samples.

Educational, Linguistic, or Cultural Effects

Within the United States, the disclosure paradigm has benefited senior professionals with advanced degrees at rates comparable to rates of benefit in maximum-security prisoners with 6th-grade educations (Spera et al., 1994; Richards, Beal, Seagal, & Pennebaker, 2000). Among college students, we have not found differences as a function of the student's ethnicity or native language. The disclosure paradigm has produced positive results among French-speaking Belgians (Rimé, 1995), Spanish-speaking residents of Mexico City (Domínguez, Valderrama, & Pennebaker, 1995), multiple samples of adults and students in the Netherlands (Schoutrop, Lange, Brosschot, & Everaerd, 1997), and English-speaking New Zealand medical students (Petrie, Booth, Pennebaker, Davison, & Thomas, 1995).

Summary

When individuals write or talk about personally upsetting experiences in the laboratory, consistent and significant health improvements are found. The effects include both subjective and objective markers of health and well-being. The disclosure phenomenon appears to generalize across settings, many individual difference factors, and several Western cultures and is independent of social feedback.

Why Does Expressive Writing Work?

Psychology, like most sciences, is dedicated to understanding how things work. We are also driven by the law of parsimony and assume that, ideally, a single explanatory mechanism for a phenomenon should exist. If you are expecting a clean and simple explanatory world, we have some very bad news: There is no single reason that explains the effectiveness of writing. Over the last two decades, a daunting number of explanations have been put forward, and many have been found to be partially correct.

Ultimately, there is no such thing as a single cause for a complex phenomenon. The reason is twofold. First, any causal explanation can be dissected at multiple levels of analysis, ranging from social explanations to changes in neurotransmitter levels. Second, an event that takes weeks or even months to unfold will necessarily have multiple determinants that can inhibit or facilitate the process over time.

In this section, we briefly summarize some of the more compelling explanations for the expressive writing–health relationship. Many of these processes occur simultaneously or may influence one another.

Individual and Social Inhibition

The first expressive writing projects were guided by a general theory of inhibition (cf. Pennebaker & Beall, 1986). Earlier studies had discovered that people who had experienced one or more traumas in their lives were more likely to report health problems if they did not confide in others about their traumas than if they had done so (e.g., Pennebaker & Susman, 1988). The inhibition idea was that the act of inhibiting or in some way holding back thoughts, emotions, or behaviors is associated with low-level physiological work—much the way that Sapolsky (2004) or Selye (1978) thought about stress. Further, people were especially likely to inhibit their thoughts and feelings about traumatic experiences that were socially threatening. Hence, individuals who had experienced a sexual trauma would be far less likely to talk about it with others than if they had experienced the death of a grandparent.

Following the logic of inhibition, it was assumed that if people were encouraged to talk or write about a previously inhibited event, health improvements would be seen. Perhaps, we reasoned, once people put the experience into words, they would no longer have the need to inhibit. Despite the helpfulness of the theory in generating interesting and testable hypotheses, the supporting evidence has been decidedly mixed. Several studies attempted to evaluate the degree to which people wrote about secret versus more public traumas and previously disclosed versus not previously disclosed events. In no case did these factors differentially predict improvements in health (e.g., Greenberg & Stone, 1992; Pennebaker, Kiecolt-Glaser, & Glaser, 1988).

Promising research in this vein has been conducted by Steve Lepore and his colleagues (e.g., Lepore, Fernandez-Berrocal, Ragan, & Ramos, 2004; Lepore, Ragan, & Jones, 2000). Across several studies, they find that people who are encouraged to talk about an emotional experience—such as a movie—are less reactive to the movie if what they say is validated. That is, if their comments about seeing the movie on the first occasion are supported by another person, they find the movie less aversive on a second screening on another day. However, if another person disagrees with their thoughts and feelings about the movie, the participants are more biologically aroused on a second screening—even though they are watching the movie alone.

Ultimately, real-world inhibitory processes are almost impossible to measure. For example, people have great difficulty in evaluating the degree to which they have been actively holding back in telling others about an emotional experience. Some people who do not tell others about an upsetting experience may never think about the event, and others do. Of those who think about it, some may want to tell others; others may not. Of these various cases, it is not clear which people are inhibiting or even who might benefit most from writing. Although experimental studies may be effective in demonstrating the potential dangers of inhibition, the task of isolating these psychological processes in the real world will be a far more difficult enterprise. As described in a later section on the social dynamics of expressive writing, one potential strategy is to simply track changes in people's social behaviors after expressive writing in order to infer the possibility of inhibition.

Emotions and Emotional Expression

Emotional reactions are part of all important psychological experiences. From the time of Breuer and Freud (1957/1895), most therapists have explicitly or tacitly believed that the activation of emotion is necessary for therapeutic change. The very first expressive writing study found that if people just wrote about the facts of a trauma, they did not evidence any improvement (Pennebaker & Beall, 1986). Consistent with an experiential approach to psychotherapeutic change, emotional acknowledgment ultimately fosters important cognitive changes (Ullrich & Lutgendorf, 2002).

Although experiencing emotions while writing is clearly a necessary component of the expressive writing effects, cognitive work is required as well.

As an example, students were randomly assigned either to express a traumatic experience using bodily movement, or to express an experience using movement and then write about it, or to exercise in a prescribed manner for 3 days, 10 minutes per day (Krantz & Pennebaker, 1995). Whereas the two movement expression groups reported that they felt happier and mentally healthier in the months after the study, only the movement-plus-writing group evidenced significant improvements in physical health and grade point average. The mere emotional expression of a trauma is not sufficient. Health gains appear to require translating experiences into language.

Habituation to Emotional Stimuli

A variation on the emotional expression idea is that the benefits of writing accrue because individuals habituate to the aversive emotions associated with the trauma they are confronting. The role of habituation to emotional stimuli has a long and rich history in classical conditioning and a variety of behavioral therapies (e.g., Wolpe, 1968). More nuanced approaches have been proposed by Edna Foa and her colleagues (e.g., Foa & Kozak, 1986; Meadows & Foa, 1999). Repeated exposure to emotional stimuli can help to extinguish the classically conditioned link between an event and people's reactions to it. At the same time, these authors note, people change in their understanding and/or representation of it.

Another test of a habituation model would be to see if people who wrote about the same topic in the same general way from essay to essay would benefit more than people who changed topics. In earlier studies (e.g., Pennebaker & Francis, 1996), judges evaluated the number of different topics people wrote about across a 3-day writing study. Number of topics was unrelated to health improvements. A more elegant strategy involved the use of latent semantic analysis (LSA; Landauer, Foltz, & Laham, 1998). LSA, a technique developed by experts in artificial intelligence, is able to mathematically evaluate the similarity of content of any sets of text, such as essays. Using LSA, we attempted to learn if the content similarity of essays written by people in the experimental conditions in three previous writing studies was related to health improvements. The answer is no. If anything, the more similar the writing content was from day to

day, the less likely people's health was to improve (Campbell & Pennebaker, 2003).

A pure habituation argument is probably insufficient in explaining the expressive writing effects. The findings from the emotion-only condition in the Pennebaker and Beall (1986) study together with the expressive movement-only condition in the Krantz and Pennebaker (1995) experiment suggest that the mere activation of emotions associated with a trauma can provide only limited benefits. Beyond any habituation processes, some form of cognitive change is also important.

Language and Emotions: Toward an A-to-D Theory of Emotional Processing

What happens when emotions or emotional experiences are put into words? Research has shown that verbally labeling an emotion may itself influence the emotional experience. Keltner, Locke, and Audrain (1993) found that after reading a depressing story, participants who were given the opportunity to label their emotions subsequently reported higher life satisfaction than those who did not label them. Berkowitz and Troccoli (1990) found that after labeling their own emotions, participants were more magnanimous in evaluating others than if they were not given the emotion-labeling opportunity. These approaches are consistent with findings by Schwarz (1990), who has demonstrated that defining and making attributions for internal feelings can affect the feelings themselves. Similarly, Wilson (2002) summarized several studies indicating that when individuals focus on their feelings, the correspondence between attitudes and behaviors increases, whereas attending to the reasons for one's attitudes reduces attitude-behavior consistency.

Indeed, changing any sensory experience into language affects the experience. In an important study on language's effects on sensory experience, Schooler and Engstler-Schooler (1990) suggested that once an individual attempts to translate a picture into words, it changes the memory of the picture. Most experiences are like pictures. Sights, sounds, smells, and feelings are often vague, complicated, and dynamic. To provide a detailed image of any experience would require more than the presumed 1,000-word limit. However, because language is flexible, relatively few words or even several thousand words can be used to describe a single experience.

The problem of capturing an experience with language is comparable to the engineering difficulty of defining an analog signal using digital technology. In the world of measuring skin conductance, for example, a person's fingers will change in their sweatiness almost continuously. As can be seen in Figure 11.1a, skin conductance level (SCL), as measured by an old-fashioned polygraph, initially increases after the person hears a loud tone and then gradually returns to normal. For this signal to be computer analyzed, the analog line must be converted into numbers using an analog-to-digital (A-to-D) converter. To convert the line to numbers, however, one needs to decide how frequently the numbers should be sampled.

Assume the tick marks on the x-axis refer to seconds, meaning that the entire graph encompasses 15 seconds. Should one sample SCL 200 times per second, once per second, once every 5 seconds? Obviously, the more times one samples, the truer the representation of the line will be (see Figure 11.1b). However, sampling at such a high frequency can be a tremendous waste of time and computer space, since most of the adjacent read-

Figure 11.1. Skin conductance level in response to a loud tone (a) measured with a polygraph, and digitally sampled (b) at a high frequency and (c) at a low frequency.

(a)

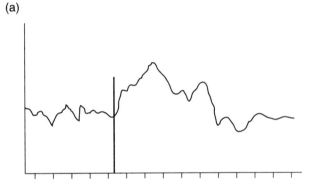

(b)

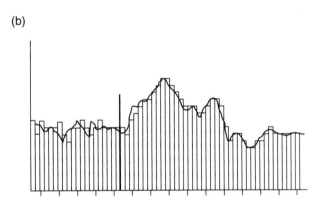

(c)

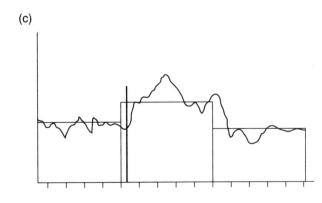

ings will be redundant. Similarly, if the sampling rate is once every 5 seconds, most of the information regarding the change in SCL will be lost (see Figure 11.1c).

Verbally labeling an emotion is much like applying a digital technology (language) to an analog signal (emotion and the emotional experience). Assume that novel or emotion-provoking experiences tend to remain in awareness either until they are cognitively understood or until they extinguish with time. It is hypothesized that if an emotion or experience remains in analog form, it cannot be understood or conceptually tied to the meaning of an event. The only way by which an emotion or experience in non-linguistic form can leave awareness is through habituation, extinction, or the introduction of a new or competing emotion. Once an experience is translated into language, however, it can be processed in a conceptual manner. In language format, the individual can assign meaning, coherence, and structure. This would allow for the event to be assimilated and, ultimately, resolved and/or forgotten, thereby alleviating the maladaptive effects of incomplete emotional processing on health.

Following from the foregoing reasoning, if an experience and its emotions are described too briefly, the experience will not adequately capture or represent the event (hereafter referred to as *verbal underrepresentation*). In this case, it would be predicted that the many parts of the experience that were not represented in the brief linguistic description would continue to be processed until they gradually extinguished over time. If a moderate number of words are used to describe the experience (*moderate representation*), its representation should adequately mirror the event. This should reduce the degree to which the event takes up cognitive capacity and, at the same time, enhance self-regulation, coping, and health. On the other hand, if the emotional event is described in exhaustive detail (*overrepresentation*), the experience is essentially reconfigured in its entirety, but in a new format.

The argument, based on the A-to-D emotion theory, is that once an event is adequately represented in language format, the verbal/conceptual processing takes over. In theory, one could argue that the ideal way to talk about an emotional event is to employ language in the form of moderate representation. The moderate representation view is that the most efficient way to process an event is to use as few words as possible that adequately cap-

ture the entire emotional experience. The event, then, would be summarized in a relatively tight way that would allow for later leveling and sharpening. Alternatively, the overrepresentation view would argue that representing the event in detailed linguistic form would lessen the possibility for reappraisal or assimilation into broader knowledge structures and identity.

In recent years, Lisa Feldman Barrett has distinguished between individuals who describe their emotion experience using highly differentiated emotion terms and those who more or less categorize their emotion experience using like-valenced terms interchangeably (Barrett, 1995; Barrett, 1998). In her studies, participants are asked to keep a daily diary for 2 weeks to rate their most intense emotional experience each day on several affect terms using a Likert scale. Emotional differentiation is reflected by a small correlation between positive-emotions words (e.g., *happiness, joy, enthusiasm, amusement*) and a small correlation between negative-emotions words (e.g., *nervous, angry, sad, ashamed, guilty*). Barrett, Gross, Christensen, and Benvenuto (2001) showed that the more individuals differentiated their negative emotions, the more they endorsed engaging in various emotion regulation strategies (situation selection, situation modification, attentional deployment, cognitive change, and response modulation) over the course of the study, especially for more intense negative emotion experiences. These findings provide support for the A-to-D theory. That is, individuals who more precisely identify a verbal label representing their actual emotion experience are more likely to make attributions and effectively plan for future actions.

Use of Emotion Words in Writing

The A-to-D approach is a valuable working model by which to understand the connection between emotional experience and its translation into words. A complementary approach to the understanding of emotional processes in the expressive writing paradigm is to look at the words people use while describing traumatic experiences. If we merely counted the ways people use emotion words in natural text, could we begin to capture the underlying emotional processes that occur during writing?

Although a number of computerized text analysis programs have been developed (for a review, see Pennebaker, Mehl, & Niederhoffer, 2003), we are most familiar with Linguistic Inquiry and Word Count (LIWC), which was initially created to analyze essays from emotional writing studies. LIWC was developed by having groups of judges evaluate the degree to which about 2,000 words or word stems were related to each of several dozen categories (for a full description, see Pennebaker, Francis, & Booth, 2001). The categories include negative-emotion words (*sad, angry*), positive-emotion words (*happy, laugh*), causal words (*because, reason*), and insight words (*understand, realize*). For each essay, LIWC computes the percentage of total words that these and other linguistic categories represent.

The LIWC program enabled language explorations into previous writing studies, linking word usage among individuals in the experimental conditions with various health and behavioral outcomes (Pennebaker, Mayne, & Francis, 1997). One re-analysis of data was based on six writing studies: two studies involving college students writing about traumas where blood immune measures were collected (Pennebaker et al., 1988; Petrie et al., 1995); two studies of first-year college students who wrote about their deepest thoughts and feelings about coming to college (Pennebaker, Colder, & Sharp, 1990; Pennebaker & Francis, 1996); one study of maximum-security prisoners in a state penitentiary (Richards et al., 2000); and one study using professional men who had unexpectedly been laid off from their jobs after more than 20 years of employment (Spera et al., 1994).

Analyzing the use of negative- and positive-emotion word use yielded two important findings. First, the more that people used positive-emotion words, the more their health improved. Negative-emotion word use, however, was curvilinearly and not linearly related to health change after writing. Individuals who used a moderate number of negative emotions in their writing about upsetting topics evidenced the greatest drops in physician visits in the months after writing. The curvilinear emotion indices were computed using the absolute value of the difference between each person's emotion word use and the means of the sample. The simple correlations between change in physician visits with the curvilinear negative emotion index was $r(152) = .27$, $p < .05$, whereas the positive words were unrelated, $r = -.14$, *ns*.

Individuals who use very few negative emotion words or who use a very high rate of them are the ones most likely to remain sick after writing, com-

pared with those who use a moderate number of negative emotion words. The findings support the A-to-D theory and, in many ways, also square with other literatures. Individuals who maintain verbal underrepresentation and tend to use very few negative emotion words are most likely to be characterized as repressive copers (cf. Schwartz & Kline, 1995) or alexithymics (Lumley, Tojek, & Macklem, 2002). Those who overuse negative emotion words may well be the classic high negative affect individuals described by Watson and Clark (1984). That is, those individuals who describe their negative conditions in such detail may simply be in a recursive loop of complaining without attaining closure (overrepresentation). Indeed, as discussed later, this may be exacerbated by the inability of these individuals to develop a story or narrative (Nolen-Hoeksema, 2000).

Beyond Emotions: The Construction of a Story

One of the basic functions of language and conversation is to communicate coherently and understandably. By extension, writing about an emotional experience in an organized way is healthier than doing so in a chaotic way. Indeed, growing evidence from several labs suggest that people are most likely to benefit if they can write a coherent story (e.g., Smyth, True, & Souto, 2001). Any technique that disrupts the telling of the story or the organization of the story is undoubtedly detrimental.

Unfortunately, we are not yet at the point of being able to precisely define what is meant by coherent, understandable, or meaningful when it comes to writing about emotional upheavals (cf. Graybeal, Seagal, & Pennebaker, 2002). One person's meaning may be another's rumination. Many times in our own research we have been struck by how a person appears to be writing in a way that avoids dealing with what we see as a central issue. Nevertheless, the person's health improves, and he or she exclaims how beneficial the study was. Meaning, then, may ultimately be in the eye of the writer.

Although talking about the upsetting experience will help to organize and give it structure, talking about such a monumental experience may not always be possible. Others may not want to or even be able to hear about it. Within the discourse literature, particular attention has been paid to the role of written language in demanding more integration and structure than spoken language (Redeker, 1984; see also Brewin & Lennard, 1999). It would follow that writing—and to a lesser degree talking—about traumatic experiences would require a structure that would become apparent in the ways people wrote or talked about the events.

The Components of a Story: The Analysis of Cognitive Words

It is beyond the bounds of this chapter to explore the philosophical definitions of knowledge, narrative, or meaning. For current purposes, knowledge of an event can encompass a causal explanation of it or the ability to understand the event within a broader context. The degree to which individuals are able to cognitively organize the event into a coherent narrative is a marker that the event has achieved knowledge status. In many ways, it is possible to determine the degree to which people have come to know their emotions and experiences by the language they use. Words or phrases such as "I now realize that . . ." or "I understand why . . ." suggest that people are able to identify when they have achieved a knowing state about an event.

The LIWC analyses find promising effects for changes in insight and causal words over the course of emotional writing (see also Klein & Boals, 2001; Petrie, Booth, & Pennebaker, 1998). Specifically, people whose health improves, who get higher grades, and who find jobs after writing go from using relatively few causal and insight words to using a high rate of them by the last day of writing. In reading the essays of people who show this pattern of language use, judges often perceive the construction of a story over time (Graybeal et al., 2002). Building a narrative, then, may be critical in reaching understanding or knowledge. Interestingly, those people who start the study with a coherent story that explained some past experience generally do not benefit from writing.

Those who use more insight and causal words in their emotional writing tend to gain the most improvements in working memory and, at the same time, report drops in intrusive thinking about negative events (Klein & Boals, 2001). Consistent with the A-to-D emotion theory, for those in the experimental condition, the writing experience packages the event in a way that frees their minds for other cognitive tasks. Another way to interpret the salutary effects of using insight and causal words is that,

together with the use of positive-emotion words, this type of language reflects a positive reappraisal of events, which fuels cognitive broadening (Fredrickson, 1998, 2001). Narrating an emotional event into the bigger picture might help to integrate the experience into one's greater knowledge structures and personal identity.

Either way, the findings are consistent with current views on narrative and psychotherapy (e.g., Mahoney, 1995) in suggesting that it is critical for the client to create and come to terms with a story to explain and understand behavioral or mental problems and their history. Merely having a story may not be sufficient, since the quality of stories and the people themselves change over time. A story, then, is a type of knowledge. Further, a narrative that provides knowledge must label and organize the emotional effects of an experience as well as the experience itself.

Writing as a Way to Change Perspective

A central tenet of all insight-oriented therapies is that through psychotherapy people are able to develop a better understanding of their problems and reactions to them (e.g., Rogers, 1940). Inherent in this understanding is the ability to stand back and look at oneself from different perspectives. Although most therapists would agree with the importance of shifting perspectives, the difficulty for a researcher is in devising a way to track this shift. Some recent linguistic analyses offer some promising new strategies.

As described earlier, latent semantic analysis, or LSA, is a powerful mathematical tool that allows investigators to determine the similarity of any sets of essays. LSA was originally designed to look at the linguistic content of text samples. Consequently, most LSA applications routinely delete all noncontent words. These noncontent or "junk" words include pronouns, prepositions, conjunctions, articles, and auxiliary verbs. A more formal designation of junk words would be function words or particles. Function words can be thought of as the glue that holds content words together. Rather than reflecting what people are saying, these function words connote how they are speaking. In short, function words reflect linguistic style (cf. Pennebaker & King, 1999; Pennebaker et al., 2003).

Is it possible that people's linguistic styles can predict who benefits from writing? Using LSA, we discovered that the answer is yes. Analyzing three previous expressive writing studies, we discovered that the more that people change in their use of function words from day to day in their writing, the more their health improved (Campbell & Pennebaker, 2003). Closer analyses revealed that these effects were entirely due to changes in pronoun use. Specifically, the more that people oscillated in their use of first-person singular pronouns (*I, me, my*) and all other personal pronouns (e.g., *we, you, she, they*), the more their health improved. If individuals wrote about emotional upheavals across the 3 to 4 days of writing but approached the topic in a consistent way—as measured by pronoun use—they were least likely to show health improvements. The findings suggest that the switching of pronouns reflects a change in perspective from one writing day to the next. Interestingly, it does not matter if people oscillate between an I-focus to a we- or them-focus or vice versa. Rather, health improvements merely reflect a change in the orientation and personal attention of the writer.

A note on causality is in order. The various studies that have examined the relationship between word use and health outcomes in the emotional writing conditions imply a causal arrow: People who change perspectives, use positive emotion words, and construct a story ultimately evidence better health. Caution is necessary, however, in interpreting these findings. The use of these word patterns may simply reflect some underlying cognitive and emotional changes occurring in the person. As noted earlier, some studies have attempted to get people to write with more positive emotion words, changing perspectives, and even constructing a story. These manipulations have not been particularly successful. The issues of mediation, moderation, and emergent properties of word use, cognitive and emotional activity, and long-term health will provide fertile grounds for research in the years to come.

Expressive Writing and Social Dynamics

One of the popular appeals of the expressive writing paradigm is that it sounds almost magical. Write for 15 minutes a day for 3 days (a total of 45 minutes), and your health will improve for months. You may also get a job, fall in love, and make better grades. This is a bit of an overstatement. When people write about emotional upheavals for 3 or 4 days, they report thinking about the topics quite frequently. Many spontaneously tell us that they have been dreaming about the topics. Expressive writing's effects exist beyond the walls of the experiment.

Even more striking have been some of the social changes that occur as a result of expressive writing. Across multiple studies, individuals report that they talk to others about their writing topics. Many years ago, we conducted a study with Holocaust survivors and asked them to tell their stories orally. Prior to the study, approximately 70% reported that they had not talked about their experiences during World War II in any detail to anyone. After the interview, all participants were given a copy of their videotaped testimony. A month later, the average person reported watching the videotape 2.3 times and showing it to 2.5 other people (Pennebaker, Barger, & Tiebout, 1989). Disclosure begets disclosure.

Recently, we have developed a digital recording device called the Electronically Activated Recorder (EAR; Mehl, Pennebaker, Crow, Dabbs, & Price, 2003), which has been engineered to record for 30 seconds every 12 to 13 minutes. The recordings are then transcribed and rated by judges concerning where the participant is and what he or she is doing. Recently, Youngsuk Kim (2005) had 95 bilingual students either write about traumatic experiences or participate in control tasks for 4 days, 15 minutes each day. Prior to writing and assignment to condition, individuals wore the EAR for 2 days. Approximately 1 month after writing, they wore the EAR again for 2 days. Overall, those who wrote about emotional upheavals talked more with others after writing than before writing. An earlier pilot study of approximately 50 students had found a similar effect (Pennebaker & Graybeal, 2001).

Across the various studies, we are now becoming convinced that one of the powers of expressive writing is that it brings about changes in people's social lives. Consider that writing has been shown to increase working memory and that these effects apparently last several weeks (Klein & Boals, 2001). After people write about troubling events, they devote less cognitive effort to them. This allows them to be better listeners, better friends. Their writing may also encourage people to talk more openly with others about the secrets that they have been keeping.

The Big Picture: Life Course Correction

Part of the human experience is that we all deal with a variety of major and minor life issues. Often we are caught off guard by an upheaval and do not have sufficient time to think about it or to explore the broader implications the event might have on us and those around us. One reason we believe that expressive writing has been effective is that it serves as a life course correction. Occasionally, most of us benefit from standing back and examining our lives. This requires a perspective shift and the ability to detach ourselves from our surroundings. If we are still in the midst of a massive upheaval, it is virtually impossible to make these corrections.

The idea of expressive writing as a life course correction has not been tested empirically. The idea is certainly consistent with McAdam's (2001) life story approach. It is also relevant to work in autobiographical memory (e.g., Neisser & Fivush, 1994; Conway, 1990). There are times when we are forced to stop and look back at our lives and evaluate what issues and events have shaped who we are, what we are doing, and why.

Summary and Conclusions

The purpose of this chapter has been to provide a broad overview of the expressive writing paradigm. Since its first use in the 1980s, dozens of studies have been exploring the parameters and boundary conditions of its effectiveness. Perhaps most interesting has been the growing awareness that its value cannot be explained by a single cause or theory. Expressive writing ultimately sets off a cascade of effects. For this chapter and certainly for this book, one of the more important effects is an improvement in physical health.

There is a certain irony that the original explanation for the writing phenomenon was inhibition. In the 1980s, we believed that when people did not talk about emotional upheavals, the work of inhibition ultimately led to stress and illness. The explanation was partially correct. Now, however, we are all beginning to appreciate the nuances of the problem. Not talking about a traumatic experience is also associated with a breakdown of one's social network, a decrease in working memory, sleep disruptions, alcohol and drug abuse, and an increased risk for additional traumatic experiences. Expressive writing or the unfettered talking about a trauma can often short-circuit this process.

Writing forces people to stop and reevaluate their life circumstances. The mere act of writing also demands a certain degree of structure, as well as the basic labeling or acknowledging of their emotions. A particularly rich feature of the process is that these inchoate emotions and emotional experiences are translated into words. This analog-to-digital process demands a different representation of the events in the brain, in memory, and in the ways people think on a daily basis.

All these cognitive changes provide the potential for people to come to a different understanding of their circumstances. The cognitive changes themselves now allow individuals to begin to think about and use their social worlds differently. They talk more; they connect with others differently. They are now better able to take advantage of social support. And with these cognitive and social changes, many of their unhealthy behaviors abate. As recent data suggest, expressive writing promotes sleep, enhanced immune function, reduced alcohol consumption, and so on.

Despite the large number of promising studies, expressive writing is not a panacea. The overall effect size of writing is modest at best. We still do not know for whom it works best, when it should be used, or when other techniques should be used in its place. One of the difficulties of studying expressive writing is that the best studies have found that writing influences slow-moving but important outcome measures such as physician visits, illness episodes, and other real-world behaviors that may take months to see. Self-report outcomes, although common and easy to use, generally do not bring about extremely strong findings. Future researchers would be wise to try to agree on one or more outcome measures that are sufficiently robust and also easy to measure.

After two decades of research on expressive writing, two strategies must continue to grow. The first is applying the method to large samples of people with differing diagnoses using rigorous RCT designs. This "big science, big medicine" approach is essential. At the same time, we should continue to nurture innovative smaller science. It will be the individual labs around the world that will ultimately identify the boundary conditions of the phenomenon and the underlying mechanisms that explain its effectiveness.

Acknowledgments.   Preparation of this chapter was aided by a grant from the National Institutes of Health (MH52391).

References

Affleck, G., & Tennen, H. (1996). Construing benefits from adversity: Adaptational significance and dispositional underpinnings. *Journal of Personality, 64,* 899–922.

Barrett, L. F. (1998). Discrete emotions or dimensions? The role of valence focus and arousal focus. *Cognition and Emotion, 12,* 579–599.

Barrett, L. F. (1995). Valence focus and arousal focus: Individual differences in the structure of affective experience. *Journal of Personality and Social Psychology, 69,* 153–166.

Barrett, L. F., Gross, J., Christensen, T. C., & Benvenuto, M. (2001). Knowing what you're feeling and knowing what to do about it: Mapping the relation between emotion differentiation and emotion regulation. *Cognition and Emotion, 15,* 713–724.

Barrett, L. F., & Salovey, P. (2002). *The wisdom in feeling: Psychological processes in emotional intelligence.* New York: Guilford.

Berkowitz, L., & Troccoli, B. T. (1990). Feelings, direction of attention, and expressed evaluations of others. *Cognition and Emotion, 4,* 305–325.

Bower, G. H., & Sivers, H. (1998). Cognitive impact of traumatic events. *Developmental and Psychopathology, 10,* 625–653.

Breslau, N., Chilcoat, H. D., Kessler, R. C., & Davis, G. C. (1999). Previous exposure to trauma and PTSD effects of subsequent trauma: Results from the Detroit Area Survey of Trauma. *American Journal of Psychiatry, 156,* 902–907.

Breuer, J., & Freud, S. (1957). *Studies on hysteria* (J. Strachey, Trans.). New York: Basic Books. (Original work published 1895)

Brewin, C. R., & Lennard, H. (1999). Effects of mode of writing on emotional narratives. *Journal of Traumatic Stress, 12,* 355–361.

Brom, D., Kleber, R. J., & Hofman, M. C. (1993). Victims of traffic accidents: Incidence and prevention of post-traumatic stress disorder. *Journal of Clinical Psychology, 49,* 131–140.

Burton, C. M., & King, L. A. (2004). The health benefits of writing about intensely positive experiences. *Journal of Research in Personality, 38,* 150–163.

Cameron, L. D., & Nicholls, G. (1998). Expression of stressful experiences through writing: Effects of a self-regulation manipulation for pessimists and optimists. *Health Psychology, 17,* 84–92.

Campbell, R. S., & Pennebaker, J. W. (2003). The secret life of pronouns: Flexibility in writing style and physical health. *Psychological Science, 14,* 60–65.

Carlier, I. V. E., & Gersons, B. P. R. (1997). Stress reactions in disaster victims following the Bijlmermeer plane crash. *Journal of Traumatic Stress, 10,* 329–335.

Carver, C. S., & Scheier, M. F. (2000). Optimism. In C. R. Snyder & S. J. Lopez (Eds.), *Handbook of positive psychology* (pp. 231–243). London: Oxford University Press.

Christensen, A. J., Edwards, D. L., Wiebe, J. S., Benotsch, E. G., McKelvey, L., Andrews, M., et al. (1996). Effect of verbal self-disclosure on natural killer cell activity: Moderating influence of cynical hostility. *Psychosomatic Medicine, 58,* 150–155.

Clark, L. F. (1993). Stress and the cognitive-conversational benefits of social interaction. *Journal of Social and Clinical Psychology, 12,* 25–55.

Cohn, M. A., Mehl, M. R., & Pennebaker, J. W. (2004). Linguistic markers of psychological change surrounding September 11, 2001. *Psychological Science, 15,* 687–693.

Cole, S. W., Kemeny, M. E., Taylor, S . E., & Visscher, B. R. (1996). Elevated physical health risk among gay men who conceal their homosexual identity. *Health Psychology, 15,* 243–251.

Conners, C. K. (1985). The Conners Rating Scales: Instruments for the assessment of childhood psychopathology. In J. Sattler (Ed.), *Assessment of academic achievement and special abilities* (pp. 328–399). San Diego, CA: Jerome Sattler.

Conway, M. A. (1990). *Autobiographical memory: An introduction.* Buckingham, England: Open University Press.

Czajka, J. A. (1987). *Behavioral inhibition and short term physiological responses.* Unpublished masters thesis. Southern Methodist University.

Damasio, A. R. (1998). Emotion in the perspective of an integrated nervous system. *Brain Research Reviews, 26,* 83–86.

De Moor, C., Sterner, J., Hall, M., Warneke, C., Gilani, Z., Amato, R., et al. (2002). A pilot study of the effects of expressive writing on psychological and behavioral adjustment in patients enrolled in a phase II trial of vaccine therapy for metastatic renal cell carcinoma. *Health Psychology, 21,* 615–619.

Diener, E., Lucas, R., & Oishi, S. E. (2002). Subjective well-being: The science of happiness and well-being. In C. R. Snyder & S. J. Lopez (Eds.), *Handbook of positive psychology* (pp. 463–473). London: Oxford University Press.

Domínguez, R. B., Valderrama, I. P., & Pennebaker, J. W. (1995). Escribiendo sus secretos, promoción de la salud mental empleando técnicas no invasivas antiguas con enfoques contemporáneos. In E. Mendez (Ed.), *Compartiendo experiencias de terapia con hipnosis,* pp. 49–66. Mexico City, Mexico: Instituto Milton H. Erickson.

Donnelly, D. A., & Murray, E. J. (1991). Cognitive and emotional changes in written essays and therapy interviews. *Journal of Social and Clinical Psychology, 10,* 334–350.

Esterling, B. A., Antoni, M. H., Fletcher, M. A., Margulies, S., & Schneiderman, N. (1994). Emotional disclosure through writing or speaking modulates latent Epstein-Barr virus antibody titers. *Journal of Consulting and Clinical Psychology, 62,* 130–140.

Foa, E. B., & Kozak, M. J. (1986). Emotional processing of fear: Exposure to corrective information. *Psychological Bulletin, 99,* 20–35.

Foa, E. B., Rothbaum, B. O., & Furr, J. M. (2003). Augmenting exposure therapy with other CBT procedures. *Psychiatric Annals, 33,* 47–53.

Francis, M. E., & Pennebaker, J. W. (1992). Putting stress into words: Writing about personal upheavals and health. *American Journal of Health Promotion, 6,* 280–287.

Fredrickson, B. L. (1998). What good are positive emotions? *Review of General Psychology: Special Issue: New Directions in Research on Emotion, 2,* 300–319.

Fredrickson, B. L. (2001). The role of positive emotions in positive psychology: The broaden-and-build theory of positive emotions. *American Psychologist, 56,* 218–226.

Frisina, P. G., Borod, J. C., & Lepore, S. J. (2004). A meta-analysis of the effects of written emotional disclosure on the health outcomes of clinical populations. *Journal of Nervous and Mental Disease, 192,* 629–634.

Gidron, Y., Peri, T., Connolly, J. F., & Shalev, A. Y. (1996). Written disclosure in posttraumatic stress disorder: Is it beneficial for the patient? *Journal of Nervous and Mental Disease, 184,* 505–507.

Graybeal, A., Seagal, J. D., & Pennebaker, J. W. (2002). The role of story-making in disclosure writing: The psychometrics of narrative. *Psychology and Health, 17,* 571–581.

Greenberg, M. A., & Stone, A. A. (1992). Emotional disclosure about traumas and its relation to health: Effects of previous disclosure and trauma severity. *Journal of Personality and Social Psychology, 63,* 75–84.

Greenberg, M. A., Wortman, C. B., & Stone, A. A. (1996). Emotional expression and physical health: Revising traumatic memories fostering self-regulation? *Journal of Personality and Social Psychology, 71,* 588–602.

Heberlein, A. S., Adolphs, R., Pennebaker, J. W., & Tranel, D. (2003). Effects of damage to right-hemisphere brain structures on spontaneous emotional and social judgments. *Political Psychology, 24,* 705–726.

Holmes, T. H., & Rahe, R. H. (1967). The Social Readjustment Rating Scale. *Journal of Psychosomatic Research, 11,* 213–218.

Hughes, C. F. (1994). Effects of expressing negative and positive emotions and insight on health and adjustment to college (Doctoral dissertation, Southern Methodist University). *Dissertation Abstracts International: Section B: The Sciences and Engineering, 54,* 3899.

Keane, T. M. (1998). Psychological effects of military combat. In B. P. Dohrenwend (Ed.), *Adversity, stress, and psychopathology* (pp. 52–65). London: Oxford University Press.

Keltner, D., Locke, K. D., & Audrain, P. C. (1993). The influence of attributions on the relevance of negative feelings to personal satisfaction. *Personality and Social Psychology Bulletin, 19,* 21–29.

Kilpatrick, D. G., Resnick, H. S., Saunders, B. E., & Best, C. L. (1998). Rape, other violence against women, and posttraumatic stress disorder. In B. P. Dohrenwend (Ed.), *Adversity, stress, and psychopathology* (pp. 161–176). London: Oxford University Press.

Kim, Y. (2005). Effects of expressive writing among Mexican and Korean bilinguals on social, physical, and mental well-being. (Doctoral dissertation, The University of Texas at Austin).

King, L. A., & Miner, K. N. (2000). Writing about the perceived benefits of traumatic events: Implications for physical health. *Personality and Social Psychology Bulletin, 26,* 220–230.

Klein, K., & Boals, A. (2001). Expressive writing can increase working memory capacity. *Journal of Experimental Psychology: General, 130,* 520–533.

Krantz, A., & Pennebaker, J. W. (1995). Bodily versus written expression of traumatic experience. Unpublished manuscript.

Labov, W., & Fanshel, D. (1977). *Therapeutic discourse.* New York: Academic Press.

Landauer, T. K., Foltz, P. W., & Laham, D. (1998). An introduction to Latent Semantic Analysis. *Discourse Processes, 25,* 259–284.

Ledoux, J. (1999). Can neurobiology tell us anything about human feelings? In D. Kahneman & E. Diener (Eds.), *The foundations of hedonic psychology* (pp. 489–499). New York: Russell Sage Foundation.

Lepore, S. J., Fernandez-Berrocal, P., Ragan, J., & Ramos, N. (2004). It's not that bad: Social challenges to emotional disclosure enhance adjustment to stress. *Anxiety, Stress and Coping: An International Journal, 17,* 341–361.

Lepore, S. J., Ragan, J., & Jones, S. (2000). Talking facilitates cognitive-emotional processes of adaptation to an acute stressor. *Journal of Personality and Social Psychology, 78,* 499–508.

Lepore, S. J., & Smyth, J. M. (2002). *Writing cure: How expressive writing promotes health and emotional well-being.* Washington, DC,: American Psychological Association.

Lumley, M. A. (2004). Alexithymia, emotional disclosure, and health: A program of research. *Journal of Personality, 72,* 1271–1300.

Lumley, M. A., & Provenzano, K. M. (2003). Stress management through written emotional disclosure improves academic performance among college students with physical symptoms. *Journal of Educational Psychology, 95,* 641–649.

Lumley, A., Tojek, T. M., & Macklem, D. J. (2002). Effects of written emotional disclosure among repressive and alexithymic people. In S. J. Lepore, & J. M. Smyth (Eds.), *The writing cure: How expressive writing promotes health and emotional well-being* (pp. 75–95). Washington, DC: American Psychological Association.

Lutgendorf, S. K., Antoni, M. H., Kumar, M., & Schneiderman, N. (1994). Changes in cognitive coping strategies predict EBV-antibody titre change following a stressor disclosure induction. *Journal of Psychosomatic Research, 38,* 63–78.

Mahoney, M. J. (1995). *Cognitive and constructive psychotherapies: Theory, research, and practice.* New York: Springer.

Mann, T. (2001). Effects of future writing and optimism on health behaviors in HIV-infected women. *Annals of Behavioral Medicine, 23,* 26–33.

McAdams, D. P. (2001). The psychology of life stories. *Review of General Psychology, 5,* 100–122.

McGuire, K. M. B., Greenberg, M. A., & Gevirtz, R. (2005). Autonomic effects of expressive writing in individuals with elevated blood pressure. *Journal of Health Psychology, 10,* 197–207.

McNally, R. J., Bryant, R. A., & Ehlers, A. (2003). Does early psychological intervention promote recovery from posttraumatic stress? *Psychological Science in the Public Interest, 4,* 45–79.

Meadows, E. A., & Foa, E. B. (1999). Cognitive-behavioral treatment of traumatized adults. In P. A. Saigh & J. D. Bremner (Eds.), *Posttraumatic stress disorder: A comprehensive text* (pp. 376–390). Needham Heights, MA: Allyn and Bacon.

Meads, C. (2003, October). *How effective are emotional disclosure interventions? A systematic review with meta-analyses.* Paper presented at the 3rd International Conference on The (Non)Expression of Emotions in Health and Disease. Tilburg, Netherlands.

Mehl, M., Pennebaker, J. W., Crow, D. M., Dabbs, J., & Price, J. (2001). The Electronically Activated Recorder (EAR): A device for sampling naturalistic daily activities and conversations. *Behavior Research Methods, Instruments, and Computers, 33,* 517–523.

Miller, M. W. (2003). Personality and the etiology and expression of PTSD: A three-factor model perspective. *Clinical Psychology: Science and Practice, 10,* 373–393.

Mitchell, J. T., & Everly, G. S. *Critical Incident Stress Debriefing (CISD): An operations manual.* Ellicott City, MD: Chevron, 1996.

Mumford, E., Schlesinger, H. J., & Glass, G. V. (1983). Reducing medical costs through mental health treatment: Research problems and recommendations. In A. Broskowski, E. Marks, & S. H. Budman (Eds.), *Linking health and mental health* (pp. 257–273). Beverly Hills, CA: Sage.

Murphy, F. C., Nimmo-Smith, I., & Lawrence, A. D. (2003). Functional neuroanatomy of emotions: A meta-analysis. *Cognitive, Affective, and Behavioral Neuroscience, 3,* 207–233.

Murray, E. J., Lamnin, A. D., & Carver, C. S. (1989). Emotional expression in written essays and psychotherapy. *Journal of Social and Clinical Psychology, 8,* 414–429.

Murray, J. B. (1992). Posttraumatic stress disorder: A review. *Genetic, Social, and General Psychology Monographs, 118,* 313–338.

Neisser, U., & Fivush, R. (1994). *The remembering self: Construction and accuracy in the self-narrative.* New York: Cambridge University Press.

Nolen-Hoeksema, S. (2000). The role of rumination in depressive disorders and mixed anxiety/depressive symptoms. *Journal of Abnormal Psychology, 109,* 504–511.

Paez, D., Velasco, C., & Gonzalez, J. L. (1999). Expressive writing and the role of alexithymia as a dispositional deficit in self-disclosure and psychological health. *Journal of Personality and Social Psychology, 77,* 630–641.

Pennebaker, J. W. (1993). Putting stress into words: Health, linguistic, and therapeutic implications. *Behaviour Research and Therapy, 31,* 539–548.

Pennebaker, J. W. (1995). *Emotion, disclosure, and health.* Washington, DC: American Psychological Association.

Pennebaker, J. W. (1997). Writing about emotional experiences as a therapeutic process. *Psychological Science, 8,* 162–166.

Pennebaker, J. W., Barger, S. D., & Tiebout, J. (1989). Disclosure of traumas and health among Holocaust survivors. *Psychosomatic Medicine, 51,* 577–589.

Pennebaker, J. W., & Beall, S. (1986). Confronting a traumatic event: Toward an understanding of inhibition and disease. *Journal of Abnormal Psychology, 95,* 274–281.

Pennebaker, J. W., & Chung, C. K. (2005). *Variations in expressive writing formats.* Unpublished technical report. Austin: University of Texas at Austin.

Pennebaker, J. W., Colder, M., & Sharp, L. K. (1990). Accelerating the coping process. *Journal of Personality and Social Psychology, 58,* 528–537.

Pennebaker, J. W., & Francis, M. E. (1996). Cognitive, emotional, and language processes in disclosure. *Cognition and Emotion, 10,* 601–626.

Pennebaker, J. W., Francis, M. E., & Booth, R. J. (2001). *Linguistic Inquiry and Word Count (LIWC): LIWC2001.* Mahwah, NJ: Erlbaum.

Pennebaker, J. W., & Graybeal, A. (2001). Patterns of natural language use: Disclosure, personality, and social integration. *Current Directions, 10,* 90–93.

Pennebaker, J. W., & Harber, K. D. (1993). A social stage model of collective coping: The Persian Gulf War and other natural disasters. *Journal of Social Issues, 49,* 125–145.

Pennebaker, J. W., Hughes, C. F., & O'Heeron, R. C. (1987). The psychophysiology of confession: Linking inhibitory and psychosomatic processes. *Journal of Personality and Social Psychology, 52,* 781–793.

Pennebaker, J. W., & Keough, K. A. (1999). Revealing, organizing, and reorganizing the self in response to stress and emotion. In R. Ashmore & L. Jussim (Eds.), *Self and social identity* (Vol. 2, pp. 101–121). New York: Oxford University Press.

Pennebaker, J. W., Kiecolt-Glaser, J., & Glaser, R. (1988). Disclosure of traumas and immune function: Health implications for psychotherapy. *Journal of Consulting and Clinical Psychology, 56,* 239–245.

Pennebaker, J. W., & King, L. A. (1999). Linguistic styles: Language use as an individual difference. *Journal of Personality and Social Psychology, 77,* 1296–1312.

Pennebaker, J. W., Mayne, T. J., & Francis, M. E. (1997). Linguistic predictors of adaptive bereavement. *Journal of Personality and Social Psychology, 72,* 166–183.

Pennebaker, J. W., Mehl, M. R., & Niederhoffer, K. G. (2003). Psychological aspects of natural language use: Our words, our selves. *Annual Review of Psychology, 54,* 547–577.

Pennebaker, J. W., & Susman, J. R. (1988). Disclosure of traumas and psychosomatic processes. *Social Science and Medicine, 26,* 327–332.

Petrie, K. P., Booth, R. J., & Pennebaker, J. W. (1998). The immunological effects of thought suppression. *Journal of Personality and Social Psychology, 75,* 1264–1272.

Petrie, K. J., Booth, R., Pennebaker, J. W., Davison, K. P., & Thomas, M. (1995). Disclosure of trauma and immune response to hepatitis B vaccination program. *Journal of Consulting and Clinical Psychology, 63,* 787–792.

Petrie, K. J., Fontanilla, I., Thomas, M. G., Booth, R. J., & Pennebaker, J. W. (2004). Effect of written emotional expression on immune function in patients with human immunodeficiency virus infection: A randomized trial. *Psychosomatic Medicine, 66,* 272–275.

Redeker, G. (1984). On differences between spoken and written language. *Discourse Processes, 7,* 43–55.

Resnick, H. S., Kilpatrick, D. G., & Lipovsky, J. A. (1991). Assessment of rape-related posttraumatic stress disorder: Stressor and symptom dimensions. *Psychological Assessment, 3,* 561–572.

Richards, J. M., Beal, W. E., Segal, J. D., & Pennebaker, J. W. (2000). Effects of disclosure of traumatic events on illness behavior among psychiatric prison inmates. *Journal of Abnormal Psychology, 109,* 156–160.

Rimé, B. (1995). Mental rumination, social sharing, and the recovery from emotional experience. In J. W. Pennebaker (Ed.), *Emotion, disclosure, and health* (pp. 271–291). Washington, DC: American Psychological Association.

Rogers, C. R. (1940). The processes of therapy. *Journal of Consulting Psychology, 4,* 161–164.

Rude, S. S., Gortner, E. M., & Pennebaker, J. W. (2004). Language use of depressed and depression-vulnerable college students. *Cognition and Emotion, 18,* 1121–1133.

Salovey, P., & Mayer, J. D. (1989–90). Emotional Intelligence. *Imagination, Cognition and Personality, 9,* 185–211.

Sapolsky, R. M. (2004). *Why zebras don't get ulcers.* New York: Holt.

Schooler, J. W., & Engstler-Schooler, T. Y. (1990). Verbal overshadowing of visual memories: Some things are better left unsaid. *Cognitive Psychology, 22,* 36–71.

Schoutrop, M. J. A., Lange, A., Brosschot, J., & Everaerd, W. (1997). Overcoming traumatic events by means of writing assignments. In A. Vingerhoets, F. van Bussel, & J. Boelhouwer (Eds.), *The (non)expression of emotions in health and disease* (pp. 279–289). Tilburg, Netherlands: Tilburg University Press.

Schwartz, G. E., & Kline, J. P. (1995). Repression, emotional disclosure, and health: Theoretical, empirical, and clinical considerations. In J. W. Pennebaker (Ed.), *Emotion, disclosure, and health* (pp. 177–194). Washington, DC: American Psychological Association.

Schwarz, N. (1990). Feelings as information: Informational and motivational functions of affective states. In E. T. Higgins & R. M. Sorrentino (Eds.), *Handbook of motivation and cognition: Foundations of social behavior* (Vol. 2, pp. 527–561). New York: Guilford.

Seligman, M. E. P. (2000). Positive psychology. In J. E. Gillman (Ed.), *Science of optimism and hope: Research essays in honor of Martin E. P. Seligman* (pp. 415–429). Philadelphia: Templeton Foundation Press.

Seyle, H. (1978). *The stress of life.* Oxford, England: McGraw Hill.

Sheese, B. E., Brown, E. L., & Graziano, W. G. (2004). Emotional expression in cyberspace: Searching for moderators of the Pennebaker disclosure effect via email. *Health Psychology, 23,* 457–464.

Singer, J. A., & Salovey, P. (1993). *The remembered self: Emotion and memory in personality.* New York: Free Press.

Sloan, D. M., & Marx, B. P. (2004a). A closer examination of the structured written disclosure procedure. *Journal of Consulting and Clinical Psychology, 72,* 165–175.

Sloan, D. M., & Marx, B. P. (2004b). Taking pen to hand: Evaluating theories underlying the written disclosure paradigm. *Clinical Psychology: Science and Practice, 11,* 121–137.

Small, R., Lumley, J., Donohue, L., Potter, A., & Waldenström, U. (2000). Randomised controlled trial of midwife led debriefing to reduce maternal depression after operative childbirth. *British Medical Journal, 321,* 1043–1047.

Smith, M. L., Glass, G. V., & Miller, R. L. (1980). *The benefits of psychotherapy.* Baltimore: Johns Hopkins University Press.

Smyth, J. M. (1998). Written emotional expression: Effect sizes, outcome types, and moderating variables. *Journal of Consulting and Clinical Psychology, 66,* 174–184.

Smyth, J. M., Stone, A. A., Hurewitz, A., & Kaell, A. (1999). Effects of writing about stressful experiences on symptom reduction in patients with asthma or rheumatoid arthritis: A randomized trial. *Journal of the American Medical Association, 281,* 1304–1309.

Smyth, J. M., True, N., & Souto, J. (2001). Effects of writing about traumatic experiences: The necessity for narrative structuring. *Journal of Social and Clinical Psychology, 20,* 161–172.

Solano, L., Donati, V., Pecci, F., Persicheeti, S., & Colaci, A. (2003). Post-operative course after papilloma resection: Effects of written disclosure of the experience in subjects with different alexithymia levels. *Psychosomatic Medicine, 65,* 477–484.

Spera, S. P., Buhrfeind, E. D., & Pennebaker, J. W. (1994). Expressive writing and coping with job loss. *Academy of Management Journal, 37,* 722–733.

Springer, S. P., & Deutsch, G. (1998). *Left brain, right brain: Perspectives from cognitive neuroscience (5th ed.).* New York: Freeman/Times Books/Henry Holt.

Stanton, A. L., & Danoff-Burg, S. (2002). Emotional expression, expressive writing, and cancer. In S. J. Lepore & J. M. Smyth (Eds.), *Writing cure: How expressive writing promotes health and emotional well-being* (pp. 31–51). Washington, DC: American Psychological Association.

Stone, L. (2002, January). *Expressive writing and perspective change: Applications to September 11.* Poster presented at the 2003 conference for the Society for Personality and Social Psychology, Savannah, GA.

Sutker, P. B., Davis, J. M., Uddo, M., & Ditta, S. R. (1995). War zone stress, personal resources, and PTSD in Persian Gulf War returnees. *Journal of Abnormal Psychology, 104,* 444–452.

Taylor, L., Wallander, J., Anderson, D., Beasley, P., & Brown, R. (2003). Improving chronic disease utilization, health status, and adjustment in adolescents and young adults with cystic fibrosis. *Journal of Clinical Psychology in Medical Settings, 10,* 9–16.

Ullrich, P. A., & Lutgendorf, S. L. (2002). Journaling about stressful events: Effects of cognitive processing and emotional expression. *Annals of Behavioral Medicine, 24,* 244–250.

Vaidya, N. A., & Garfield, D. A. S. (2003). A comparison of personality characteristics of patients with posttraumatic stress disorder and substance dependence: Preliminary findings. *Journal of Nervous and Mental Disease, 191,* 616–618.

Vano, A. M., & Pennebaker, J. W. (1997). Emotion vocabulary in bilingual Hispanic children: Adjustment and behavioral effects. *Journal of Language and Social Psychology, 16,* 191–200.

Walker, B. L., Nail, L. M., & Croyle, R. T. (1999). Does emotional expression make a difference in reactions to breast cancer? *Oncology Nursing Forum, 26,* 1025–1032.

Watson, D., & Clark, L. A. (1984). Negative affectivity: The disposition to experience aversive emotional states. *Psychological Bulletin, 96,* 465–490.

Wilson, T. D. (2002). *Strangers to ourselves: Discovering the adaptive unconscious.* Cambridge, MA: Belknap Press at Harvard University Press.

Wolpe, J. (1968). Psychotherapy by reciprocal inhibition. *Conditional Reflex, 3,* 234–240.

Wortman, C. B., & Silver, R. C. (1989). The myths of coping with loss. *Journal of Consulting and Clinical Psychology, 57,* 349–357.

Camille B. Wortman

and Kathrin Boerner

Beyond the Myths of Coping with Loss:
Prevailing Assumptions Versus Scientific Evidence

The death of a loved one is a ubiquitous human experience and is often regarded as a serious threat to health and well-being. Coming to terms with personal loss is considered to be an important part of successful adult development (Baltes & Skrotzki, 1995). In this chapter, we draw from our own research and that of others to explore how people are affected by the death of a loved one. In our judgment, such losses provide an excellent arena in which to study basic processes of stress and adaptation to change. Unlike many stressful life experiences, bereavement cannot be altered by the coping efforts of survivors. Indeed, the major coping task faced by the bereaved is to reconcile themselves to a situation that cannot be changed and find a way to carry on with their own lives. By learning more about how people react to a loved one's death, and how they come to terms with what has happened, we can begin to clarify the theoretical mechanisms through which major losses can have deleterious effects on subsequent mental and physical health.

In our judgment, one of the most fascinating things about studying bereavement is the extraordinary variability that has been found regarding how people react to the death of a loved one. Some people are devastated and never again regain their psychological equilibrium; others emerge from the loss relatively unscathed and perhaps even strengthened (Elison & McGonigle, 2003; Parkes & Weiss, 1983). Yet at this point, we know relatively little about the diverse ways that people respond to the loss of a loved one, and why some people react with intense and prolonged distress while others do not. Do people who have the most rewarding and satisfying relationships with their loved one suffer the most following the loved one's death? Or is it those with conflictual or ambivalent relationships who experience the most distress following the loss of a loved one, as clinicians have frequently argued (see, e.g., Freud, 1917/1957; Parkes & Weiss, 1983; Rando, 1993). Among those who fail to show distress following the loss, is this best understood as denial, lack of attachment, or resilience in the face of loss?

Over the years, we carried out several systematic evaluations of common assumptions about coping with loss that appear to be held by professionals in the field as well as laypersons (Bonanno & Kaltman, 2001; Wortman & Silver, 1987, 1989, 2001). We identified these assumptions by reviewing some of the most important theoretical models of the grieving process, such as Freud's (1917/1957) grief work perspective and Bowlby's (1980) early attachment model (see Bonanno & Kaltman, 1999;

Wortman & Silver, 2001). In addition, we examined books and articles written by and for clinicians and other health care providers that describe the grieving process (see, e.g., Jacobs, 1993; Malkinson, Rubin, & Witztum, 2000; Rando, 1993). Finally, we reviewed books and articles written by and for bereaved individuals themselves (e.g., Gowell, 1992; Sanders, 1999). The following assumptions were identified:

1. Bereaved persons are expected to exhibit significant distress following a major loss, and the failure to experience such distress tends to be seen as indicative of a problem (e.g., that the bereaved person will experience a delayed grief reaction).
2. Positive emotions are implicitly assumed to be absent during this period. If they are expressed, they tend to be viewed as an indication that people are denying or covering up their distress.
3. Following the loss of a loved one, the bereaved must confront and "work through" their feelings about the loss. Efforts to avoid or deny feelings are maladaptive in the long run.
4. It is important for the bereaved to break down their attachment to the deceased loved one.
5. Within a year or two, the bereaved will be able to come to terms with what has happened, recover from the loss, and resume their earlier level of functioning.

Because these assumptions about the grieving process seemed to be firmly entrenched in Western culture, we anticipated that they would be supported by the available data. However, our reviews provided little support for any of these assumptions. For this reason, we labeled them "myths of coping with loss."

Initially, studies in the field of grief and loss were plagued by major methodological shortcomings, including the use of convenience samples, low response rates, attrition, and the failure to include control respondents. There was a dearth of scientific evidence on important concepts like "working through" and recovery from loss. Hence, in our earliest papers discussing these assumptions (Wortman & Silver, 1987, 1989), it was difficult to evaluate the validity of some of them. Over the past few decades, however, research on bereavement has

burgeoned. In fact, just in the last 10 years, approximately 5,000 articles have appeared on grief and/or bereavement. In addition to a large number of sound empirical studies, two editions of an influential handbook of bereavement have appeared in the literature (Stroebe, Hansson, Stroebe, & Schut, 2001; Stroebe, Stroebe, & Hansson, 1993). As a result of the accumulation of research evidence, as well as related theoretical developments in the field of bereavement, some shifts have occurred in prevailing views about how people cope with the loss of a loved one. In this chapter, we review these developments.

In the first section of the chapter, we provide a brief review of the most influential theories of grief and loss, some of which have contributed to the myths of coping, while others have helped generate new questions about the grieving process. In the second section, we discuss each myth of coping, summarizing available evidence and highlighting ways the myths have changed over time as research evidence has accumulated. In these sections, we also identify what we believe to be the most important new areas of research. In the final section, we discuss the implications of this work for researchers, clinicians, and the bereaved themselves. In so doing, we consider the efficacy of grief counseling or therapy. We also address the question of what physicians, funeral directors, employers, and friends can do to support the bereaved in their efforts to deal with the loss.

Theories of Grief and Loss

Many different theoretical formulations have influenced the current understanding of the grief process (for a more detailed review, see Archer, 1999; Bonanno & Kaltman, 1999; Rando, 1993; Stroebe & Schut, 2001).

Classic Psychoanalytic View

One of the most influential approaches to loss has been the classic psychoanalytic model of bereavement, which is based on Freud's (1917/1957) seminal paper, "Mourning and Melancholia." According to Freud, the primary task of mourning is the gradual surrender of psychological attachment to the deceased. Freud believed that relinquishment of the love object involves a painful internal struggle. The individual experiences intense yearning for the lost loved one yet is faced with the reality of that person's absence. As thoughts and memories are reviewed, ties to the loved one are gradually withdrawn. This process, which requires considerable time and energy, was referred to by Freud as "the work of mourning." At the conclusion of the mourning period, the bereaved individual is said to have "worked through" the loss and to have freed himself or herself from an intense attachment to an unavailable person. Freud maintained that when the process has been completed, the bereaved person regains sufficient emotional energy to invest in new relationships and pursuits. This view of the grieving process has dominated the bereavement literature over much of the past century and only more recently has been called into question (Bonanno & Kaltman, 1999; Stroebe, 1992–1993; Wortman & Silver, 1989). For example, it has been noted that the concept of grief work is overly broad and lacks clarity because it fails to differentiate between such processes as rumination, confrontative coping, and expression of emotion (Stroebe & Schut, 2001).

Attachment Theory

Another theoretical framework that has been extremely influential is Bowlby's attachment theory (Bowlby, 1969, 1973, 1980; see also Fraley & Shaver, 1999; Shaver & Tancredy, 2001). In this work, Bowlby integrated ideas from psychodynamic thought, from the developmental literature on young children's reactions to separation, and from work on the mourning behavior of primates. Bowlby maintained that during the course of normal development, individuals form instinctive affectional bonds or attachments, initially between child and parent and later between adults. He believed that the nature of the relationship between a child and his or her mother or caregiver has a major impact on subsequent relationships. He suggested that when affectional bonds are threatened, powerful attachment behaviors are activated, such as crying and angry protest. Unlike Freud, Bowlby believed that the biological function of these behaviors is not withdrawal from the loved one but rather reunion. However, in the case of a permanent loss, the biological function of assuring proximity with attachment figures becomes dysfunctional. Consequently, the bereaved person struggles between the opposing forces of activated attachment behavior and the reality of the loved one's absence.

Bowlby maintained that in order to deal with these opposing forces, the mourner goes through four stages of grieving: initial numbness, disbelief, or shock; yearning or searching for the deceased, accompanied by anger and protest; despair and disorganization as the bereaved gives up the search, accompanied by feelings of depression and hopelessness; and reorganization or recovery as the loss is accepted, and there is a gradual return to former interests. By emphasizing the survival value of attachment behavior, Bowlby was the first to give a plausible explanation for responses such as searching or anger in grief. Bowlby was also the first to maintain that there is a relationship between a person's attachment history and how he or she will react to the loss of a loved one. For example, children who endured frequent separations from their parents may form anxious and highly dependent attachments as adults, and may react with intense, and prolonged grief when a spouse or partner dies (see Shaver & Tancredy, 2001, or Stroebe, Schut, & Stroebe, 2005a, for a more detailed discussion). Because it provides a framework for understanding individual differences in response to loss, Bowlby's attachment model has continued to be influential in the study of grief and loss.

Stages of Grief

Another aspect of Bowlby's work that has been influential in determining how we think about grief is his idea that grieving involves stages of reaction to loss. Drawing from this work, several theorists have proposed that people go through stages or phases in coming to terms with loss (see, e.g., Horowitz, 1976, 1985; Ramsay & Happee, 1977; Sanders, 1989). Perhaps the most well known of these models is the one proposed by Kübler-Ross (1969) in her highly influential book *On Death and Dying*. This model, which was developed to explain how dying persons react to their own impending death, posits that people go through denial, anger, bargaining, depression, and ultimately acceptance. It is Kübler-Ross's model that popularized stage theories of bereavement. For many years, stage models have been taught in medical, nursing, and social work schools, and in many cases, these models are firmly entrenched among health care professionals. Kübler-Ross's model has also appeared in articles in newspapers and magazines written for bereaved persons and their family members. As a result, stage models have strongly influenced the common understanding of grief in our society.

Beyond Stage Models

As research has begun to accumulate, it has become clear that there is little support for the view that there are systematic stages. In contrast, the evidence shows that the reaction to loss varies considerably from person to person, and that few people pass through the stages in the expected fashion (see Archer, 1999, or Attig, 1996, for a review). Several major weaknesses of stage models have been identified (Neimeyer, 1998). First, they cannot account for the variability in response that follows a major loss. Second, they place grievers in a passive role. Third, such models fail to consider the social or cultural factors that influence the process. Fourth, stage models focus too much attention on emotional responses to the loss and not enough on cognitions and behaviors. Finally, stage models tend to pathologize people who do not pass through the stages. If people do not reach a state of acceptance, for example, they may be led to believe that they are not coping appropriately with the loss. As a result of these and other critiques and an absence of empirical support, most researchers have come to believe that the idea of a fixed sequence of stages is not particularly useful (Stroebe, Hansson, et al., 2001).

More recent theoretical models, such as Neimeyer's model of meaning reconstruction (Neimeyer, 1997, 1999), have attempted to address these shortcomings by portraying grief as a more idiosyncratic process in which people strive to make sense of what has happened. For example, Neimeyer (2000, 2006) has maintained that major losses challenge a person's sense of identity and narrative coherence. Narrative disorganization can range from relatively limited and transient to more sweeping and chronic, depending on the nature of the relationship and the circumstances surrounding the death. According to Neimeyer, a major task of grief involves reorganizing one's life story to restore coherence and maintain continuity between the past and the future.

Stress and Coping Approach

Over the past two decades, a theoretical orientation referred to as the stress and coping approach, or the cognitive coping approach (Lazarus & Folkman, 1984; see also Carver, this volume), has become highly influential in the field of bereavement. Stress and coping theorists maintain that life changes like the death of a loved one become distressing if a person appraises the situation as taxing or exceeding his or her resources. An important feature of this model is that it highlights the role of cognitive appraisal in understanding how people react to loss. A person's appraisal, or subjective assessment of what has been lost, is hypothesized to influence his or her emotional reaction to the stressor and the coping strategies that are employed. As Folkman (2001) has indicated, however, there is surprisingly little research on specific coping strategies that people use to deal with loss and the impact of these various strategies.

To explain why a given loss has more impact on one person than another, stress and coping researchers have focused on the identification of potential risk or protective factors, such as a history of mental health problems, optimism, social support, or financial assets (see Stroebe & Schut, 2001, for a review). The appraisal of the loss, as well as the magnitude of physical and mental health consequences that result from the loss, are thought to depend on these factors. Those with fewer risk factors, and more coping resources, are expected to recover more quickly and completely. Originally, the model focused primarily on negative emotions that were generated as a result of experiencing a stressful life event. In an important revision of the model, Folkman (2001) has incorporated positive emotions, which are believed to sustain coping efforts over time.

Toward More Comprehensive Models of Bereavement

Stage models and the stress and coping model can be applied to bereavement, but they were not developed specifically to account for people's reactions to the loss of a loved one. Within the past few years, two new theoretical models have been developed: Bonanno's four-component model (Bonanno & Kaltman, 1999), and Stroebe and Schut's (1999, 2001) dual-process model. Not only do these models focus specifically on bereavement, but each attempts to integrate elements from diverse theoretical approaches into a comprehensive model. Bonanno's goal was to develop a conceptually sound and empirically testable framework for understanding individual differences in grieving. He identified four primary components of the grieving process—the context in which the loss occurs (e.g., was it sudden or expected, timely or untimely); the subjective meanings associated with the loss (e.g., was the bereaved person resentful that he or she had to care for the loved one prior to the death?); changes in the representation of the lost loved one over time (e.g., does the bereaved person maintain a continuing connection with the deceased?); and the role of coping and emotion regulation processes that can mitigate or exacerbate the stress of loss. Bonanno's model makes the prediction that recovery is most likely when negative grief-related emotions are regulated or minimized and when positive emotions are instigated or enhanced (Bonanno, 2001). This hypothesis, which is diametrically opposed to what would be derived from the psychodynamic approach, has generated considerable interest and support in recent years.

The dual-process model of coping with bereavement (Stroebe & Schut, 1999, 2001) indicates that following a loved one's death, bereaved people alternate between two different kinds of coping: loss-oriented coping and restoration-oriented coping. While engaged in loss-oriented coping, the bereaved person focuses on and attempts to process or resolve some aspect of the loss itself. Restoration-oriented coping involves attempting to adapt to or master the challenges inherent in daily life, including life circumstances that may have changed as a result of the loss. Stroebe and Schut (1999, 2001) have proposed that each of these coping orientations is associated with certain advantages and disadvantages, and that by alternating between them, the disadvantages of employing one strategy too long can be minimized. They have suggested that early in the process, most people focus primarily on loss-oriented coping but that over time, there is a shift to more restoration-oriented coping. They have also maintained that the model provides a way to understand individual differences in coping. For example, they pointed out that there is considerable evidence to indicate that women tend to be more loss-oriented than men (Stroebe & Schut, 2001), thus suggesting a possible explanation for gender differences in response to loss. As Archer (1999) has noted, one of the most important features of this model is that it provides an alternative to the view that grief is resolved solely through confrontation with the loss.

Throughout the years, the theoretical models discussed here have influenced and, at the same time, have been influenced by the empirical work on coping with loss. For example, accumulating evidence regarding variability in response to loss led researchers to move away from traditional grief

models and instead employ a stress and coping framework that can account for divergent responses to loss. In return, the empirical evidence that has come out of this effort to account for variability in response to loss has led to further theoretical development. For example, the most recent bereavement models have incorporated new insights about what questions are important to study and allow specific predictions as to how to address these questions. The following sections provide a review of the empirical work that in some ways has been the "engine" behind recent changes in our thinking about bereavement.

Revisiting the "Myths of Coping"

Over the past decade, bereavement research has continued to become more methodologically sophisticated, with many researchers employing powerful longitudinal designs to study the impact of loss. Some longitudinal studies have examined the reactions of the bereaved from a few months after the loss through the first 5 years (e.g., Bonanno, Keltner, Holen, & Horowitz, 1995; Murphy, Johnson, Chung, & Beaton, 2003; Murphy, Johnson, & Lohan, 2002). Others have focused on people whose loved one is ill, and have assessed relevant variables before and at various intervals after the death (e.g., Folkman, Chesney, Collette, Boccellari, & Cooke, 1996; Nolen-Hoeksema & Larson, 1999; Nolen-Hoeksema, McBride, & Larson, 1997; Schulz, Mendelson, & Haley, 2003). Still others have followed large community samples across time and studied those who became bereaved during the course of the study (e.g., Bonanno et al., 2002; Carnelley, Wortman & Kessler, 1999; Lichtenstein, Gatz, Pederson, Berg, & McClearn, 1996; Mendes de Leon, Kasl, & Jacobs, 1994). Most studies have relied solely on respondents' assessments of key variables such as depression. However, some have used clinical assessments, and a few have included nonverbal data (e.g., Bonanno & Keltner, 1997) or assessments from others (e.g., Bonanno, Moskowitz, Papa, & Folkman, 2005).

The vast majority of bereavement studies have focused on the loss of a spouse. In the past decade, however, important new studies have appeared on reactions to the loss of a child (e.g., Dyregrov, Nordanger, & Dyregrov, 2003; Murphy, 1996; Murphy et al., 1999; Murphy, Johnson, & Lohan,

2003); parent (e.g., Silverman, Nickman, & Worden, 1992); and sibling (e.g., Balk, 1983; Batten & Oltjenbruns, 1999; Cleiren, 1993; Hogan & DeSantis, 1994). In one study, reactions to various kinds of familial loss were compared (Cleiren, 1993; Cleiren, Diekstra, Kerkhof, & van der Wal, 1994). Most studies have focused on respondents who are heterogeneous with respect to cause of death. However, some have examined reactions to specific losses, such as parents whose children experienced a sudden, traumatic death (e.g., Dyregrov et al., 2003; Murphy, Johnson, & Lohan, 2003), or gay male caregivers whose partners died of AIDS (e.g., Folkman, 1997a; Folkman et al., 1996; Moskowitz, Folkman, & Acree, 2003; Moskowitz, Folkman, Collette, & Vittinghoff, 1996). A few studies have compared two or more groups of respondents who lost loved ones under different circumstances (e.g., natural causes, accident, or suicide; e.g., Cleiren, 1993; Dyregrov et al., 2003; Middleton, Raphael, Burnett, & Martinek, 1998; Murphy, Johnson, Wu, Fan, & Lohan, 2003). Consequently, it is now possible to determine whether the "myths of coping" hold true across different kinds of deaths that occur under varying conditions.

Of course, there are still some areas where relatively little is known. For example, the vast majority of studies on the loss of a spouse focus on middle-aged or elderly white women. This is ironic, since the available evidence (see, e.g., Miller & Wortman, 2002; Stroebe, Stroebe, & Schut, 2001) suggests that men are more vulnerable to the effects of conjugal loss than are women. In recent years, there has been increasing interest in how men grieve (see, e.g., Martin & Doka, 2000), and in gender differences in grieving (see, e.g., Wolff & Wortman, 2006; Wortman, Wolff, & Bonanno, 2004). There are very few studies on reactions to the death of a sibling, despite evidence that this is a profound loss, particularly for adult women (Cleiren, 1993). With few exceptions (e.g., Carr, 2004), there is also a paucity of studies that include Blacks or Hispanics. Hence, it is difficult to determine whether the findings reported in the literature will generalize to these or other culturally diverse groups.

In the material to follow, each assumption about coping with loss is discussed in some detail. As we will show, beliefs about some of these assumptions have shifted over time as the evidence has continued to accumulate. For example, because several studies have identified a variety of common grief

patterns among the bereaved, researchers have become more skeptical about the assumption that most people go through a period of intense distress following a loss. In the discussion to follow, each myth is updated, the available evidence is presented, and gaps in our knowledge base are identified.

The Expectation of Intense Distress

Description

The most prevalent theories in the area, such as classic psychoanalytic models (e.g., Freud, 1917/1957) and Bowlby's (1980) attachment model, are based on the assumption that at some point, people will confront the reality of their loss and go through a period of depression. Many books written by grief researchers, as well as those written by and for the bereaved, also convey the view that following the death of a loved one, most people react with intense distress or depression. For example, Sanders (1999) has maintained that once the bereaved person has accepted the reality of the loss, he or she will go through a phase of grief that can seem frightening "because it seems so like clinical depression" (p. 78). Similarly, Shuchter (1986) has indicated that "virtually everyone whose spouse dies exhibits some signs and symptoms of depression" (p. 170). It is anticipated that depression or distress will decrease over time as the bereaved comes to terms with the loss.

Historically, the failure to exhibit grief or distress following the loss of a spouse has been viewed as an indication that the grieving process has gone awry (e.g., Deutsch, 1937; Marris, 1958). Bowlby (1980) identified "prolonged absence of conscious grieving" (p. 138) as one of two possible types of disordered mourning, along with chronic mourning. Marris (1958) has indicated that "grieving is a process which 'must work itself out' . . . if the process is aborted from too hasty a readjustment . . . the bereaved may never recover" (p. 33). In recent years, some investigators have challenged the assumption that the failure to experience distress is indicative of pathology. For example, M. Stroebe, Hansson, and Stroebe (1993) have argued that there are many possible reasons why a bereaved person may fail to exhibit intense distress that would not be considered pathological (e.g., early adjustment following an expected loss; relief that the loved one is no longer suffering).

However, available evidence suggests that most practicing clinicians continue to maintain, either explicitly or implicitly, that there is something wrong with individuals who do not exhibit grief or depression following the loss of a loved one. In a survey of expert clinicians and researchers in the field of loss (Middleton, Moylan, Raphael, Burnett, & Martinek, 1993), a majority (65%) endorsed the belief that "absent" grief exists, that it typically stems from denial or inhibition, and that it is generally maladaptive in the long run. An important component of this view is that it assumes that if people fail to experience distress shortly after a loss, problems or symptoms of distress will erupt at a later point. For example, Bowlby (1980) has argued that individuals who have failed to mourn may suddenly, inexplicably become acutely depressed at a later time (see also Rando, 1984; Worden, 2002). These authors have also maintained that the failure to grieve will result in subsequent health problems (Bowlby, 1980; Worden, 2002).

Consistent with the notion that "absent" grief signals unhealthy denial and repression of feelings, there is a great deal of clinical literature to suggest that people who have lost a loved one, but who have not begun grieving, will benefit from clinical intervention designed to help them work through their unresolved feelings (see, e.g., Bowlby, 1980; Deutsch, 1937; Jacobs, 1993; Lazare, 1989; Rando, 1993; Worden, 2002). In a report published by the Institute of Medicine, for example, Osterweis, Solomon, and Green (1984) concluded that "professional help may be warranted for persons who show no evidence of having begun grieving."(p. 136). Similarly, Jacobs (1993) has suggested that the bereaved individuals who experience "inhibited grief . . . ought to be offered brief psychotherapy by a skilled therapist" (p. 246).

The failure to exhibit distress following the loss of a loved one has also been viewed as evidence for character weakness in the survivor. In a classic paper, Deutsch (1937) maintained that grief-related affect was sometimes absent among individuals who were not emotionally strong enough to begin grieving. Osterweis et al. (1984) emphasized that clinicians typically assume "that the absence of grieving phenomena following bereavement represents some form of personality pathology" (p. 18). Similarly, Horowitz (1990) has stated that those who show little overt grief or distress following a loss are "narcissistic personalities" who "may be too developmentally immature to have an adult type of relationship and so cannot exhibit an adult type of

mourning at its loss" (p. 301; see also Raphael, 1983). It has also been suggested that some people fail to exhibit distress because they were only superficially attached to their spouses (Fraley & Shaver, 1999; Rando, 1993).

Evidence for Intense Distress

Among people who have faced the loss of a loved one, is it true that distress is commonly experienced? Will distress or depression emerge at a later date among those who fail to exhibit distress in the first several weeks or months following the loss? We identified several studies that provide information bearing on these questions. Most of these studies focused on the loss of a spouse (Boerner, Wortman, & Bonanno, 2005; Bonanno, Moskowitz, et al., 2005; Bonanno et al., 2002; Bonanno & Field, 2001; Bonanno et al., 1995; Bournstein, Clayton, Halikas, Maurice & Robins, 1973; Lund et al., 1985–1986; Vachon, Rogers, et al., 1982; Vachon, Sheldon, et al., 1982; Zisook & Shuchter, 1986); two examined reactions to the loss of a child (Bonanno, Moskowitz, et al., 2005; Wortman & Silver, 1993); and another two focused on response to loss following a time of caregiving for a chronically ill loved one (Bonanno, Moscowitz, et al., 2005; Schulz et al., 2003). These studies assessed depression or other forms of distress in the early months following the death, and then again anywhere from 13 to 60 months after the loss. The construct of depression/distress was operationalized differently in the different studies. For example, some studies utilized the SCL-90 depression subscale and/or *DSM*-based SCID (e.g., Bonanno, Moscowitz, et al., 2005); other studies used the CESD depression scale (e.g., Bonanno et al., 2002). For each study, the investigators determined a cutoff score to classify respondents as high or low in distress or depression.

The longitudinal studies identified here provide evidence regarding the prevalence of different patterns of grief. "Normal" or "common" grief, which involves moving from high distress to low distress over time, was found among 41% of participants in a study on loss of a child from SIDS (Wortman & Silver, 1987), and anywhere between 9% and 41% in studies on conjugal loss (35% in Bonanno et al., 1995; 29% in Bournstein et al., 1973; 9% in Lund, Caserta, & Dimond, 1986; 41% in Vachon, Rogers, et al., 1982; and 20% in Zisook & Shuchter, 1986). Furthermore, in these studies, evidence for "minimal" or "absent" grief, which involves scoring low in distress consistently over time, was found for 26% (Wortman & Silver, 1987), 41% (Bonanno et al., 1995), 57% (Bournstein et al., 1973), 30% (Vachon, Rogers, et al., 1982), 78% (Lund et al., 1986), and 65% of respondents (Zisook & Shuchter, 1986).

In a recent prospective study on conjugal loss among older adults that included data from 3 years pre-loss to 18 months postloss (Bonanno et al., 2002; Bonanno, Wortman, & Nesse, 2004), nearly half of the participants (46%) experienced low levels of distress consistently over time and were labelled "resilient." Only 11% showed "normal" or "common" grief. Another trajectory in this study referred to as "depressed-improved" reflected elevated distress before the loss and improvement after the loss (10%). A similar pattern of reduced distress levels following the loss was detected in a prospective study on care-givers of dementia patients that included both pre- and postloss data (Schulz et al., 2003).

Taken together, in all studies, less than half of the sample showed "normal" grief, and in many, such a reaction was shown by only a small minority of respondents. In fact, in the prospective study on conjugal loss by Bonanno et al. (2002), the relatively small proportion of those who showed "normal" grief (11%) was almost equal to those who showed a depressed-improved pattern of being more distressed before the loss, followed by improvement after the loss (10%). Most important, however, the available evidence shows that "minimal" or "absent" grief is very common. The number of respondents failing to show elevated distress or depression at the initial or final time point was sizable, ranging from one quarter of the sample to more than three quarters of the sample. In fact, a recent comparison of nonbereaved and bereaved individuals (who lost either a child or a spouse; Bonanno, Moskowitz, et al., 2005) showed that, in terms of distress levels, slightly more than half of the bereaved did not significantly differ from the matched sample of married individuals when assessed at 4 and 18 months postloss.

It should be noted that category labels such "minimal" or "absent" grief do not mean that there was absolutely no distress at any moment after the loss, but rather that despite brief spikes in distress around the time of the death (Bonanno, Moskowitz et al., 2005) or a short period of daily variability in levels of well-being (Bisconti, Bergeman, & Boker,

2004), people who showed these patterns had generally low distress levels and managed to function at or near their normal levels (Bonanno, 2005). The prevalence of the "minimal" or "absent" grief reaction alone calls into question the assumption that failure to show distress following a loss is pathological. In fact, it suggests that learning more about why many people do not exhibit significant distress following a loss should become an important research priority.

Studies with Assessment of Mild Depression

When we have described these findings in the past (e.g., Bonanno et al., 2002; Wortman & Silver, 1989, 2001), it was sometimes suggested that the data may underestimate those who show significant distress following a loss. This is because the studies we reviewed classify respondents as depressed only if their score exceeds a cutoff believed to reflect clinically significant levels of depression. Respondents who do not exhibit major depression may still be evidencing considerable distress or depression. The previous studies do not speak to this issue, since they do not include measures of mild depression.

Fortunately, such measures have been included in a number of studies. For example, Bruce, Kim, Leaf, and Jacobs (1990) assessed dysphoria as well as depression in a study of conjugally bereaved individuals (aged 45 and older). Dysphoria was defined as feeling "sad, blue, depressed or when you lost all interest and pleasure in things you usually cared about or enjoyed" for 2 weeks or more. About 60% of the respondents had experienced dysphoria. However, a significant minority (almost 40%) did not go through even a 2-week period of sadness following their loss. Similarly, Zisook, Paulus, Shuchter, and Judd (1997) conducted a study of elderly widowers and widows in which their ratings on symptom inventories were used to classify them into *DSM-IV* categories of major depression, minor depression, subsyndromal depression (endorsing any two symptoms from the symptom list), and no depression (endorsing one or no items reflecting depression). Two months after the partner's death, 20% were classified as showing major depression, 20% were classified as exhibiting minor depression, and 11% were classified as evidencing subsyndromal depression. Forty-nine percent of the respondents were classified as evidencing no depression (for similar results, see Cleiren, 1993). These studies provide compelling evidence that following the death of a spouse, a substantial percentage of people do not show significant distress.

Delayed Grief

Is it true that if the bereaved do not become depressed following a major loss, a "delayed grief reaction," or physical health problems, will emerge at some point in the future? The data from the longitudinal studies we identified fail to support this view. In two studies, there were no respondents showing a delayed grief reaction (Zisook & Shuchter, 1986; Bonanno et al., 1995; Bonanno & Field, 2001). In the remaining studies, the percentage of respondents showing delayed grief was .02%, 1%, 2%, 2.5%, and 5.1%, respectively (Boerner et al., 2005; Bournstein et al., 1973; Lund et al., 1986; Wortman & Silver, 1987; Vachon, Rogers, et al., 1982). It should be noted that in two of these studies (Lund et al., 1986; Zisook & Shuchter, 1986), bereaved respondents were interviewed at frequent intervals during the course of the study. There were very few respondents who moved from low distress to high distress on any subsequent interview. These studies indicate that "delayed grief" does not occur in more than a small percentage of cases. Nor do physical symptoms appear to emerge among those who fail to experience distress soon after the loss. Both the Boerner et al. (2005) and Bonanno and Field (2001) studies are convincing on this point, because conjugally bereaved individuals were assessed over a 4- and 5-year period, respectively, using multiple outcome measures. Data failing to support the "delayed grief" hypothesis were also obtained by Middleton et al. (1996). Based on cluster analyses of several bereaved samples, she concluded that "no evidence was found for . . . delayed grief." Nonetheless, in the previously described survey conducted by Middleton et al. (1993), a substantial majority of researchers and clinicians (76.6%) indicated that delayed grief does occur.

Predictors of "Minimal" Distress

The hypothesis that some people fail to become distressed following a loss because they were not attached to the loved one, or because they were cold and unfeeling, has only recently been subject to empirical research. Bonanno et al. (2002) tested the prediction that those who reported low levels of depression from pre-loss through 18 months of bereavement (resilient group) would score higher on

pre-loss measures of avoidant/dismissive attachment than those in other groups (depressed-improved, common grief, chronic grief, and chronic depression). They also examined whether those in the resilient group would evaluate their marriage less positively and more negatively, and whether they would be rated by interviewers as less comfortable and skillful socially, and as exhibiting less warmth compared with the other groups at the pre-loss time point. The resilient group did not appear to differ from the other groups on any of these variables. A follow-up study yielded similar results with respect to variables on processing the loss (Bonanno et al., 2004). For example, the resilient group scored relatively high on comfort from positive memories of the deceased, a finding that also argues against the view that they were not strongly attached to the deceased. Furthermore, in their recent study on the loss of spouse or child, Bonanno, Moskowitz, et al. (2005) found that the friends of bereaved participants who showed resilience following the death rated them more positively, and reported having more contact and closer relations with them. Taken together, these findings do not support and even contradict the hypothesis that the absence of intense distress following loss is a sign of lack of attachment to the deceased or the inability to maintain close relationships.

Thus, available evidence clearly indicates that the so-called normal grief pattern is not as common as was assumed in the past, and that a significant proportion of bereaved individuals experience relatively little distress following a loss, without showing delayed grief or other signs of maladjustment. It should be noted, however, that such a reaction is far more prevalent following some kinds of losses than others. For example, elderly people who lose a spouse are more likely to show consistently low distress than younger individuals who lose a spouse or parents who lose a child. In fact, research on the loss of a child under sudden or violent circumstances suggests that it is normative to experience intense distress following such a loss. In her study on the violent death of a child, for example, Murphy (1996) found that 4 months after the loss, more than 80% of the mothers and 60% of the fathers rated themselves as highly distressed. Thus, there is clear evidence that both the nature of the death and the circumstances surrounding the loss play a critical role in people's response to loss. These and other factors associated with long-term difficulties in adaptation to loss will be discussed in the section on recovery.

Future Directions

Given the prevalence of resilience or low distress following a loss, we need to learn more about the potential costs and benefits of this response. As described previously, there is evidence that for the bereaved person, resilience, or showing consistently low distress following the loss, appears to be an adaptive response. However, it would be interesting to address whether there are any disadvantages associated with resilience. For example, participants who showed the resilient pattern may have had a way of approaching life that made them less vulnerable to life stressors but also less attentive to others' concerns. If so, this could result in lower pre-loss marital satisfaction among their spouses. The best way to test these ideas would be to draw on prospective data of couples or multiple family members, in which each person's perspective on the relationship is assessed prior to the loss and at various points thereafter. Such data would provide the opportunity to learn what the deceased person thought about his or her relationship with the "resilient person."

It would also be worthwhile to consider the social implications of a resilient pattern in response to loss. In some cases, the resilient person may elicit negative reactions from others because others expect the bereaved to show more distress. Others may interpret low levels of distress as an indication of aloofness or indifference. In other cases, showing resilience may reflect positively on the bereaved because it is easier for others to be with a less distressed person. Another intriguing question is what happens in families or other social groups when one person shows a low distress pattern after a loss, whereas the other members in this social system experience intense distress. In such a case, would those who are more distressed be likely to benefit from the presence or availability of a resilient person? Or would the lack of congruence in the experience of individual members be more likely to lead to misunderstandings and individual coping efforts that interfere with one another? These questions are likely to assume considerable importance in couples following the death of a child. For example, one spouse may feel uncomfortable expressing feelings of distress about the loss if it appears that the partner is not as distressed (e.g., Wortman, Battle, & Lemkau, 1997). Future work addressing these questions would make an important contribution because people rarely face a loss in a social vacuum.

Positive Emotions Are Typically Absent

Description

The most important theories of grief and loss, such as Freud's (1917/1957) psychoanalytic model and Bowlby's (1980) attachment model, emphasize the importance of working through the emotional pain associated with the loss. Amid the despair and anguish that often accompany grief, positive emotions may seem unwarranted, even inappropriate (Fredrickson, Tugade, Waugh, & Larkin, 2003). When they are mentioned at all, positive emotions are typically viewed as indicative of denial and as an impediment to the grieving process (Deutsch, 1937; Sanders, 1993; see Keltner & Bonanno, 1997, for a review). With notable exceptions (e.g., Folkman, 1997b; Folkman & Moskowitz, 2000; Fredrickson, 2001; Lazarus, Kanner, & Folkman, 1980), theories focusing specifically on the grieving process, or more generally on coping with adversity, have failed to consider the role that may be played by positive emotions.

In the 1980s, Wortman and her associates became interested in whether positive emotions were experienced by people who had encountered major losses, and if so, whether they could perhaps sustain hope and facilitate adjustment. Therefore, they decided to measure positive as well as negative emotions in two studies, one focusing on permanent paralysis following a spinal cord injury, and one focusing on loss of a child as a result of sudden infant death syndrome (SIDS); see Wortman & Silver, 1987, for a more detailed discussion). In conducting the first study, they encountered extreme resistance from the hospital staff, who felt it was "ridiculous" to ask people who were permanently disabled about their positive emotions. In the second study, they experienced similar problems from their interviewers, who did not want to ask people who had lost a child how many times they had felt happy in the past week. Only through careful pilot work and much persuading were they able to convince the staff, and the interviewers, that the project was indeed feasible and worthwhile.

Evidence for Positive Emotions Following Loss

Both of these studies provided evidence that positive emotions are quite prevalent following major loss. At 3 weeks following the death of their infant to SIDS, parents reported experiencing positive emotions such as happiness as frequently as they experienced negative feelings. By the second interview, conducted 3 months after the infant's death, positive affect was more prevalent than negative affect, and this continued to be the case at the third interview, conducted at 18 months after the loss. Respondents were asked to describe the intensity as well as the frequency of their feelings. These measures were included so that the investigators could determine whether negative feelings, while no more prevalent than positive ones, were more intense. However, this did not turn out to be the case. At all three interviews, feelings of happiness were found to be just as intense as feelings of sadness. In fact, at the second and third interviews, respondents reported that their feelings of happiness were significantly more intense than their feelings of sadness.

Subsequent studies have corroborated that positive emotions are surprisingly prevalent during bereavement. For example, when caregivers of men who died of AIDS were asked to talk about their experiences, about 80% evidenced positive emotions during the conversation, whereas only 61% conveyed negative emotions (Folkman, 1997a, 2001; Folkman & Moskowitz, 2000; Stein, Folkman, Trabasso, & Christopher-Richards, 1997). Except for just before and just after the death, caregivers' reports regarding positive states of mind were as high as community samples (Folkman, 1997a). A recent study examining positive affect scores of caregivers from 8 months pre-loss to 8 months post-loss demonstrated the presence of positive emotions even within a few weeks before and after the death (Bonanno, Moskowitz, et al., 2005). Comparable findings have been obtained from a study that went beyond self-report data. At 6 months post-loss, Bonanno and Keltner (1997) coded facial expressions of conjugally bereaved respondents while they were talking about their relationship with the deceased. Videotapes of the interviews were then coded for the presence of genuine or "Duchenne" laughs or smiles, which involve movements in the muscles around the eyes. Positive emotion was exhibited by the majority of participants. Moreover, the presence of positive affect was associated with reduced grief at 14 and 25 months post-loss. Those who exhibited Duchenne laughs or smiles also evoked more favorable responses in observers (Keltner & Bonanno, 1997). In addition to rating them more positively overall, observers rated those who engaged in laughs and smiles as healthier, better adjusted, less frustrating, and more amusing. These findings suggest that one way positive emotions may facilitate coping with loss is by eliciting positive responses from those in the social environment.

Revised Stress and Coping Model

Drawing on her research on caregivers of men who died of AIDS, Folkman (1997b) concluded that it is important to learn more about how positive psychological states are generated and maintained during a major loss, as well as how they help to sustain coping efforts. In her revision of Lazarus and Folkman's (1984) model of the coping process, Folkman (1997b, 2001) has proposed that when people are distressed as a result of a loss event, they can generate positive emotions by infusing ordinary events with positive meaning. This observation came about in an interesting way. In her study of caregiving partners of men with AIDS, Folkman (1997a) had initially focused exclusively on stressful aspects of the caregiving situation. Respondents were questioned about these every 2 months. Shortly after the study began, several participants "reported that we were missing an important part of their experience by asking only about stressful events; they said we needed to ask about positive events as well if we were to understand how they coped with the stress of caregiving" (p. 1215). Consequently, Folkman added a question in which respondents were asked to describe "something you did, or something that happened to you, that made you feel good and that was meaningful to you and helped you get through the day" (p. 1215). Such events were reported by 99.5% of the respondents. Events focused on many different aspects of daily life, such as enjoying a good meal, receiving appreciation for something done for one's partner, or going to the movies with friends. Folkman has hypothesized that events of this sort generate positive emotion by helping people feel connected and cared about, by providing a sense of achievement and self-esteem, and by providing a respite or distraction from the stress of caregiving. She has suggested that the coping processes that generate positive emotions, and the positive emotions themselves, are likely to help sustain coping efforts in dealing with a stressful situation. Recent empirical evidence is consistent with this prediction. Positive affect not only is quite prevalent at times of adversity but also appears to ameliorate bereavement-related distress (Bonanno, Moskowitz, et al., 2005; Moskowitz et al., 2003). For example, in a recent study on the role of daily positive emotions during bereavement, Ong, Bergeman, and Bisconti (2004) found that the stress-depression correlation was significantly reduced on days in which more positive emotion was experienced.

Broaden-and-Build Theory of Positive Emotions

Another theory that has important implications for understanding the role that positive emotions may play in coping with loss is Fredrickson's broaden-and-build theory of positive emotions (Fredrickson, 1998, 2001; Fredrickson et al., 2003). Fredrickson has maintained that positive emotions can broaden people's attention, thinking, and behavioral repertoire, bringing about an increase in flexibility, creativity, and efficiency and thereby improving their ways of coping with stress. She suggests that over time, this helps people to accumulate important resources, including physical resources (e.g., health), social resources (e.g., friendships), intellectual resources (e.g., expert knowledge), and psychological resources (e.g., optimism). In brief, her work suggests that efforts to cultivate positive emotions in the aftermath of a stressful life experience will pay off in the short run, by improving the person's subjective experience, undoing physiological arousal, and enhancing coping, and in the long term by building enduring resources.

Future Directions

In subsequent work, it will be important to learn more about how people cultivate and maintain positive emotions in the midst of coping with a major loss. Are there particular strategies that people use to generate and maintain such emotions during a crisis? Are those with certain personality characteristics or belief systems (e.g., those with particular spiritual beliefs) more likely than others to experience positive emotions in the context of adversity? We also need to know more about the impact of positive emotions on adaptation to a

major life event such as bereavement. Specific hypotheses could be derived from the Frederickson model, addressing the mechanisms through which positive emotions are thought to improve coping with stress. For example, one could assess whether those who experience positive emotions following a loss indeed show higher flexibility, creativity, and efficiency in terms of their thinking and coping behavior, and determine whether this buffers the negative impact of the loss on people's adjustment. As Folkman (1997b) has pointed out, it may be the case that positive psychological states must reach a certain level of intensity or duration in order to sustain or facilitate coping with loss. Future work in this area is particularly important because strategies that help generate positive emotions in the face of loss are a concrete tool that can be taught as part of an intervention (cf. Fredrickson, 2001). It will also be important to learn more about difficulties the bereaved may encounter in experiencing or expressing positive emotions following a loss. For example, some people may feel guilty if they enjoy something because their loved one is "missing out" on enjoyable experiences. Experiencing or expressing positive emotions may also make people feel that they are being disloyal toward their loved one.

The Importance of Working Through the Loss

Description

Among researchers as well as practitioners in the field of grief and loss, it has been commonly assumed that to adjust successfully to the death of a loved one, a person must "work through" the thoughts, memories, and emotions associated with the loss. The term *grief work* was originally coined by Freud (1917/1957), who maintained that "working through" our grief is critically important—a process we neglect at our peril. Although there is some debate about what it means to "work through" a loss, most grief theorists assert that it involves an active, ongoing effort to come to terms with the death. Implicit in our understanding of grief work is that it is not possible to resolve a loss without it. As Rando (1984) has stated, "For the griever who has not attended to his grief, the pain is as acute and fresh ten years later as it was the day after" (p. 114). Attempts to deny the implications of the loss, or block feelings or thoughts about it, are generally regarded as unproductive. As noted earlier, this view of the grieving process has constituted the dominant perspective on bereavement for the past half century (Bonanno, 2001). It is only within the past several years that investigators have begun to question these ideas (see, e.g., Bonanno & Kaltman, 1999; Stroebe, 1992–1993; Wortman & Silver, 1989, 2001).

However, an examination of the most influential books on grief therapy suggests that clinicians still regard "working through" as a cornerstone of good treatment (see, e.g., Rando, 1993; Worden, 2002). Consequently, a major treatment goal for clinicians typically involves facilitating the expression of feelings and thoughts surrounding the loss (see Bonanno, 2001, for a more detailed discussion). Clinicians have also emphasized the importance of expressing negative feelings that are directed toward the deceased, such as anger or hostility (see, e.g., Lazare, 1989; Raphael, 1983). In fact, practitioners have frequently argued against the use of sedative drugs in the early phases of mourning because they may interfere with the process of "working through" the loss (see Jacobs, 1993, for a more detailed discussion). As Jacobs (1993) has indicated, such attitudes are prevalent among practicing clinicians despite the fact that there is "little or no evidence for the idea" (p. 254).

Evidence on "Working Through"

Over the past decade, several studies relevant to the construct of "working through" have appeared in the literature. These studies have assessed such constructs as confronting thoughts and reminders of the loss versus avoiding reminders and using distraction (e.g., Bonanno et al., 1995; Bonanno & Field, 2001; M. Stroebe & Stroebe, 1991); thinking about one's relationship with the loved one (e.g., Nolen-Hoeksema et al., 1997); verbally expressing or disclosing feelings of grief or distress (e.g., Lepore, Silver, Wortman, & Wayment, 1996); exhibiting negative facial expressions (e.g., Bonanno & Keltner, 1997; Keltner & Bonanno, 1997); or expressing one's feelings through writing about the loss (Lepore & Smyth, 2002; Pennebaker, Zech, & Rime, 2001; Smyth & Greenberg, 2000). These studies have provided limited support for the notion that "working through" is important for adjustment to the death of a loved one. Some have found support for the grief work hypothesis on only a few dependent measures, some have not found any support for this hypothesis, and some have reported findings that directly contradict this hypothesis.

Confronting Versus Avoiding Loss

In one of the earliest studies on grief work, M. Stroebe and Stroebe (1991) assessed five kinds of behaviors associated with confronting the loss of one's spouse or with avoidance (e.g., disclosed one's feelings to others; avoided reminders), at 4 to 7 months, 14 months, and 2 years post-loss. At the final time point, there were no differences between widows who had showed evidence for confronting their loss at either of the first two time points and those who did not. However, for two of the five measures (those assessing distraction and suppression), widowers who confronted their grief showed lower subsequent depression. Overall, these results provide limited support for the grief work hypothesis, leading M. Stroebe and Stroebe (1991) to conclude that the statement "'Everyone needs to do grief work' is an oversimplification" (p. 481).

In another study comparing those who used avoidant versus more confrontative coping styles (Bonanno et al., 1995; Bonanno & Field, 2001), respondents who had lost a spouse were asked to talk about their relationship to the deceased, and their feelings about the loss, at the 6–month point following their loss. Physiological data assessing cardiovascular reactivity were also collected. Respondents who evidenced emotional avoidance (i.e., little emotion relative to their physiological reactivity) showed low levels of interviewer-rated grief throughout the 2-year study. Among respondents who initially showed emotional avoidance, there was no evidence of delayed grief. Although respondents with an avoidant style did show higher levels of somatic complaints at 6 months post-loss, these symptoms did not persist beyond the 6-month assessment and were not related to medical visits.

In a study of gay men who lost a partner to AIDS, Nolen-Hoeksema and colleagues (1997) examined the impact of thinking about one's relationship with the partner versus avoiding such thoughts. Those who had thought about their life without their partner, and how they had changed as a result of the loss, showed more positive morale shortly after the death than those who did not, but showed more depression over the 12 months following the loss.

Taken together, the results of these studies suggest that many respondents did not make an active, ongoing effort to confront the loss but nonetheless evidenced good adjustment following bereavement. Apparently, focusing attention away from one's emotional distress can be an effective means of coping with the loss of a loved one.

Talking About Negative Feelings

A study by Bonanno and Keltner (1997) casts doubt on the value of expressing negative feelings. These investigators assessed the expression of negative emotion in two ways: through self-report and through facial expressions. An advantage of studying facial expressions is that they can be assessed independently of self-report and even without participant awareness. Those who expressed negative feelings or manifested negative facial expressions while talking about the decreased 6 months post-loss showed higher interviewer-rated grief 14 months post-loss. This was particularly the case for facial expressions of anger, the emotion most consistently believed by grief work theorists to require expression (Belitsky & Jacobs, 1986).

As Bonanno (2001) has indicated, it was not clear from this study whether the expression of negative emotions actually influenced subsequent grief, or whether individuals in a more acute state of grief merely tended to express more negative emotions—in other words, the expression of negative affect may have simply been a by-product of grief. To address this concern, Bonanno (2001) reanalyzed the facial data controlling for the initial level of grief and distress, which enabled him to isolate the extent to which expressing negative emotion was related to subsequent grief. Even under these stringent conditions, facial expressions of negative emotion were still related to increased grief at 14 months post-loss. These studies by Bonanno and his associates suggest that minimizing the expression of negative emotion results in reduced grief over time, which is just the opposite of what the grief work hypothesis would predict.

Writing About Negative Feelings

One problem in interpreting the previously described findings by Bonanno has been identified by Pennebaker et al. (2001). These investigators have pointed out that the best predictor of future distress is current distress, and that it is important to differentiate among those studies where distress is a reflection of grief from those studies where respondents participate in an intervention that allows them to work through their grief.

To provide a more convincing test of the value of expression, Pennebaker and his associates developed a writing intervention that provides the opportunity for people to engage in emotional expression following trauma or loss. Participants are asked to write essays expressing their deepest thoughts and feelings about the most traumatic event they can remember. Control participants are asked to write about innocuous topics, such as their plans for the day. Typically, participants write for 20 to 30 minutes on several consecutive days (see, e.g., Pennebaker & Beall, 1986). When given these instructions, people are indeed willing to write about experiences that are very traumatic and upsetting. According to Pennebaker et al. (2001), "Deaths, abuse incidents, and tragic failures are common themes" (p. 530).

It has been shown that writing has a positive impact on such health outcomes such as health center visits and immunologic status. Although the literature on the impact of writing on mood and psychological well-being is somewhat mixed (see Pennebaker et al., 2001, for a review), a meta-analysis suggested that overall, mood and psychological well-being being improve following writing. The results also suggested that writing can affect health outcomes as well as behavioral changes, such as an improvement in grades, or the ability to get a new job after being laid off. Hence, the results illustrate that the impact of writing is not restricted to any one outcome. Smyth's (1998) study suggested that the effects produced by the writing task are substantial, and are similar in magnitude to other psychological interventions.

Do these writing effects apply to individuals who have lost a loved one? Pennebaker et al. (2001) have estimated that across the studies conducted in his lab, approximately 20% of participants write about the death of a close friend or family member. According to these investigators, people who write about death benefit as much as people who write about other topics. However, studies focusing on the value of emotional expression among the bereaved have produced inconclusive findings (see M. Stroebe, Stroebe, Schut, Zech, & van den Bout, 2002, for a review). For example, Segal, Bogaards, Becker, and Chatman (1999) conducted a study with elderly people who had lost a spouse an average of 16 months previously. Respondents were instructed to talk into a tape recorder about the loss and to express their deepest feelings. When compared with a delayed treatment control condition, those who expressed their feelings showed a slight but nonsignificant improvement in hopelessness. No significant effects emerged on other measures of distress such as depression and intrusion/avoidance.

Two studies by Range and her associates (Kovac & Range, 2000; Range, Kovac, & Marion, 2000) also fail to support the value of written emotional expression among the bereaved. In the first study (Range et al., 2000), undergraduates who had experienced the loss of a friend or family member as a result of an accident or a homicide were asked to write about their deepest thoughts and feelings surrounding the death. A control group was asked to write about a trivial issue. The results revealed that both groups showed improvements in symptoms of depression, anxiety, and grief during the course of the study. There was no indication of greater improvement among respondents who were assigned to express their feelings. There were also no differences among the two groups in doctor visits. In the second study, people who had lost a loved one to suicide were invited to express their deepest feelings or to write about a trivial issue. The study included many dependent measures such as intrusion/avoidance, doctors' visits, and grief. On the majority of measures, there were no differences between the groups. Similar results were also obtained in an intervention study by Bower, Kemeny, Taylor, and Fahey (2003). Women who had lost a close relative to breast cancer were assigned to write about the death or about neutral topics. Writing did not appear to facilitate adaptation to the loss.

Stroebe et al. (2002) conducted two exceptionally well-designed studies to determine whether expression of emotions facilitates recovery among the bereaved. In the first study, the authors focused on disclosures of emotion made by the bereaved in everyday life. A large sample of people who had lost a spouse were asked to complete a questionnaire designed to assess disclosure of emotion to others at four points over a 2-year period. The results provided no evidence that disclosure facilitated adjustment to loss. In the second study, people who lost a spouse from 4 to 8 months previously were randomly assigned to one of three writing conditions or to a control no-writing condition. Participants in the first writing condition were instructed to focus on their emotions. Those in the second condition were told to focus on problems and difficulties they have to deal with as a result of the death. The final group was asked to focus on both their feelings and problems. The results of this study

provided no evidence whatsoever for a general beneficial effect of emotional expression. None of the experimental groups was better off than control respondents on any measures.

To determine whether the emotional expression of grief may be beneficial under specific conditions, M. Stroebe et al. (2002) further examined whether writing effects were a function of the type of loss. When they compared bereaved participants who expected the loss with those who had encountered a sudden, unexpected loss, there was no indication that emotional expression through writing was more beneficial for the latter group. They also investigated whether the expression of emotions may work only among people who have not yet had much opportunity to disclose their feelings. However, they found no evidence to suggest that those who had rarely disclosed their feelings in the past benefited more from the writing intervention than those who had disclosed their feelings more frequently. In fact, these investigators found that it was low disclosers who were less likely to suffer from intrusive thoughts, and who had fewer doctor visits, than high disclosures.

Traditional, Conditional, or Modified Grief Work Hypothesis

In a study on grief processing and deliberate grief avoidance among bereaved spouses and parents in the United States and the People's Republic of China, Bonanno, Papa, Lalande, Zhang, and Noll (2005) tested different versions of the grief work hypothesis, using a comprehensive measure of grief processing that included thinking and talking about the deceased, having positive memories, expressing feelings, and searching for meaning. These authors also used a measure of grief avoidance that included avoidance of thinking, talking, and expressing feelings about the deceased. This study addressed (a) the traditional hypothesis that grief processing was a necessary step toward positive adjustment, and that the absence of grief processing reflects avoidance or denial; (b) the conditional hypothesis that grief work may be beneficial for those with severe grief; and (c) another modified hypothesis that grief work was more akin to rumination, with the prediction that those who scored high on grief processing initially would continue to score high on this measure and show poorer adjustment at the 18-month follow-up than those who did not score high on initial grief processing.

Support was found for the third but not for the first two hypotheses. Moreover, grief processing and grief avoidance were independent predictors of outcome in both cultures, which indicates that they can coexist rather than represent opposite ends of one dimension. Grief processing and avoidance each predicted poorer adjustment for U.S. participants, even for those who had shown more severe grief initially The authors interpreted this as contradictory to both the traditional and the conditional grief work hypothesis but as consistent with the grief work as rumination hypothesis. Grief processing and avoidance did not emerge as significant predictors of outcome among the Chinese participants, which may have reflected cultural differences in terms of mourning rituals and practices. Overall, the authors concluded that these findings cast doubt on the usefulness of grief processing and argued that it may be inadvisable to encourage the bereaved to focus on processing the loss.

When reviewing the different studies that have tested the grief work hypothesis, it is important to keep in mind how grief work was conceptualized in each study, and how this may have affected the findings. For example, it is possible that Bonanno, Papa, et al. (2005) failed to find positive effects of grief processing because their grief processing measure included the expression of feelings, which, as discussed previously, has been found to predict worse outcome in some studies, and searching for meaning, which may be regarded as reflective of ruminative thinking. There is evidence that rumination, if defined as engaging in thoughts and behaviors that maintain one's focus on negative emotions (Nolen-Hoeksema, 1991), heightens distress, interferes with problem solving, and may drive away potential supporters.

Future Directions

In future work, it will be important to include separate assessments of constructs pertaining to working through, such as thinking about the loss, talking about what has happened, crying, or searching for meaning. This would help to clarify how these constructs are related to one another and to identify the role played by each in the process of recovery. When comparing findings from different studies on this issue, and in particular when drawing conclusions about adaptiveness, it is extremely important to be clear about what kind of grief processing is talked about in each specific case. This also leads to the more general question regarding what kind of grief processing may be beneficial for whom, and under which circumstances. For example, one reason the literature on "working through" may be so inconsistent is because some studies may have included people who did not need to "work through" what happened, some who may have been reluctant to engage fully in the process, and some who were made worse by being required to confront the trauma. Those who may have difficulty expressing their emotions seem to benefit the most from interventions such as writing about their experience (Lumley, Tojeck, & Macklem, 2002; Norman, Lumley, Dooley, & Diamond, in press). Furthermore, it is possible that "working through" may be more beneficial for certain kinds of events, such as those that are particularly traumatic and/or likely to shatter the survivors' views of the world. We also need to know more about the conditions under which emotional expression reduces the bereaved person's distress, helps him or her to gain insight or cognitively structure what has happened, and helps to elicit support and encouragement from others. Hopefully, subsequent research will assist us in specifying the conditions under which "working through" one's loss is more or less likely to be beneficial, and if it is indicated, how this grief processing needs to be done in order to truly facilitate recovery and adjustment.

Breaking Down Attachments

Description

According to the traditional view on grief, espoused by Freud (1917/1957) and other psychoanalytic writers (e.g., Volkan, 1971), it is necessary to disengage from the deceased in order to get on with life. These writers believed that for grief work to be completed, the bereaved person must withdraw energy from the deceased and thus free him- or herself from attachment to an unavailable person. This view remained influential for many years, with its advocates maintaining that if attachments are not broken down, the bereaved will be unable to invest their energy in new relationships or activities. It is generally believed that bereaved people accomplish this task by carefully reviewing thoughts and memories of the deceased, as well as both positive and negative aspects of the relationship (see, e.g., Rando, 1993; Raphael, 1983). Clinicians have traditionally maintained that the failure to break down bonds with the deceased is indicative of a need for treatment. In fact, relinquishing the tie to the deceased has been a major goal of grief therapy (see, e.g., Raphael & Nunn, 1988; Sanders, 1989).

During the past decade, this view has been called into question (see Stroebe & Schut, 2005, for a review). Indeed, an increasing number of researchers now believe that it is normal to maintain a continuing connection to the deceased, and that such a connection may actually promote good adjustment to the loss (Attig, 1996; Klass, Silverman, & Nickman, 1996; Neimeyer, 1998; Shmotkin, 1999). Others have maintained that it is time to move beyond the dichotomy of disengagement versus continuing connection (Boerner & Heckhausen; 2003; Russac, Steighner, & Canto, 2002). For example, Boerner and Heckhausen (2003) conceptualized adaptive bereavement as a process of transforming mental ties to the deceased that involves features of both disengagement and continuing connection. They further proposed that this process of transforming the relationship occurs by substituting mental representations of the deceased for the lost relationship. Such mental representations may simply reflect experiences that are retrieved from memory (e.g., remembering what the deceased said in a particular situation). Others may be newly constructed by adding new aspects to one's preexisting image (e.g., imagining what the deceased would say). Boerner and Heckhausen (2003) also noted that different ways of transforming the relationship may be more or less adaptive for a particular person. Stroebe and Schut (2005) extended this view by arguing that certain types of continuing bonds, as well as certain types of relinquishing bonds, can be helpful or harmful. Their notion of relinquishing ties, however, is one of "relocating" rather than "forgetting" the deceased, reflecting the idea of transforming the nature of the relationship to symbolic, internalized, imagined levels of relatedness (Boerner & Heckhausen, 2003; Shuchter & Zisook, 1993; Stroebe & Schut, 2005).

Historically, one of the first theorists to question the importance of breaking down attachments was Bowlby (1980). In his later writings, Bowlby maintained that continuing attachments to the deceased, such as sensing his or her presence or talking with him or her, can provide an important sense of continuity and facilitate adjustment to the loss. A similar view has been expressed by Hagman (1995, 2001), who argued that there had been too

much emphasis on relinquishment of the bond with the deceased. In fact, Hagman indicated that in some cases, it is more adaptive to restructure one's memories of the deceased so as to allow a continuing connection. In their influential book, *Continuing Bonds,* Klass et al.(1996) also emphasized the potential value of maintaining a connection with the deceased. These investigators noted that their training led them to expect grief resolution to be accompanied by breaking down attachments to the deceased. However, this is not what they found in their research or in their clinical work. Instead, their work indicated that most people experienced a continuing connection with the deceased and that these connections "provided solace, comfort, and support, and eased the transition from the past to the future" (p. xvii).

Just as it was previously maintained that breaking the bond between the bereaved and deceased should be an important goal of therapy, many clinicians now argue that such bonds should be facilitated as part of bereavement counseling. Silverman and Nickman (1996) concluded that the tie between the bereaved and the deceased loved one should be viewed as a strengthening resource, and that it should be explicitly encouraged in bereavement interventions. Along similar lines, Fleming and Robinson (1991) have argued that it is important for the bereaved to confront such questions as what he or she has learned from the deceased, and how he or she has changed as a result of the relationship with the deceased. Neimeyer (2000, 2001) has proposed a number of innovative methods for developing an ongoing connection with the deceased, such as writing a biographical sketch of the deceased or writing letters to the deceased along with imaginary answers, which are to be written by the bereaved from the deceased person's perspective. Other investigators have provided specific suggestions about how to learn more about the deceased and his or her possible influence on one's life. For example, Attig (2000) has indicated that it can be helpful to explore records such as letters or diaries, as well as sharing memories with others who knew the deceased. He has suggested that the bereaved can benefit considerably by talking with people who may have a different perspective on the deceased. For example, a wife might seek out opportunities to talk with her deceased husband's coworkers, or parents may make an effort to talk with the friends of their deceased adolescent son.

Evidence for Prevalence and Types of Continuing Connections

Does empirical evidence support the view that continuing attachments to the deceased are common, and that they facilitate good adjustment? Since the 1970s, studies have appeared in the literature suggesting that many forms of attachment to the deceased are common (see, e.g., Glick, Weiss, & Parkes, 1974; Parkes & Weiss, 1983; Rees, 1971). The most frequently studied forms of attachment include sensing the presence of the deceased, seeing the deceased as protecting or watching over oneself, and talking to the deceased (see Klass & Walter, 2001, for a review). For example, Zisook and Shuchter (1993) found that 13 months after their spouse's death, 63% of the respondents indicated that they feel their spouse is with them at times, 47% indicated that he or she is watching out for them, and 34% reported that they talk with their spouse regularly. Similar results have been reported by Stroebe and Stroebe (1991), who found that 2 years following the death of a spouse, a third of the bereaved still sensed the presence of the deceased. Results suggesting a continuing connection between the deceased and the bereaved have also been reported by Bonanno, Mihalecz, and LeJeune (1999) in a study of the emotional themes that emerge during bereavement. These investigators have reported that 6 months after the loss, more than 80% of the bereaved described emotional themes indicative of an enduring positive bond. Similar findings were obtained by Richards, Acree, and Folkman (1999) in their study of bereavement among caregivers of men who died of AIDS. These investigators reported that 3 to 4 years post-loss, 70% of the bereaved caregivers reported an ongoing inner relationship with their deceased partner. Continuing ties with the deceased took many forms: some deceased partners were thought to serve as guides, some were believed to be present at times, and some "talked with" the bereaved partner. A sense of closeness with the deceased persisted even though most of the men had made life changes (e.g., changing jobs or living situations). As Richards et al. (1999) have indicated, "The continued relationship to the deceased did not appear to be an aspect of clinging to the past but, rather, a part of a reorganized present where the deceased assumed a new position in the living partner's world scheme" (pp. 122–123).

Data from the Harvard Child Bereavement Study (Silverman & Worden, 1992) indicate that it is common for children to maintain a connection with deceased parents. Silverman and Nickman (1996) reported that 4 months after losing a parent, 74% of the children had located their parent in heaven, and most viewed the parent as watching out for them. Moreover, nearly 60% of the children reported that they talked with the deceased parent, and 43% indicated that they received an answer. A year following the loss, these attachment behaviors were still very prevalent, with nearly 40% of the children indicating that they talked with their deceased parent.

There has also been interest in connections in which the deceased loved one serves as a moral compass or guide (see, e.g., Klass & Walter, 2001; Marwit & Klass, 1996). Although this form of continuing bond has received less study than those mentioned earlier, Glick, Weiss, and Parkes (1974) found that at 1 year following the loss, 69% of those who lost a spouse expressed agreement with the statement that they try to behave as the deceased would want them to. Similarly, Stroebe and Stroebe (1991) found that at 2 years following the death of their spouse, half of the respondents indicated that they consulted the bereaved when they had to make a decision. Several similar kinds of attachment behavior have been described in the literature, including relying on the deceased as a role model, incorporating virtues of the deceased into one's character, working to further the deceased's interests or values, and reflecting on the deceased person's life and/or death to clarify current values or value conflicts (Marwit & Klass, 1996; Normand, Silverman, & Nickman, 1996).

In a related study, Field, Gal-Oz, and Bonanno (2003) assessed a wide variety of attachment behaviors. They included such items as attempting to carry out the deceased's wishes, having inner conversations with the deceased, taking on the spouse's values or interests, using the spouse as a guide in making decisions, reminiscing with others about the spouse, experiencing the spouse as continuing to live through oneself, having fond memories of the spouse, and seeing the spouse as a loving presence in one's life. The results indicated that most of these types of connection were quite prevalent even at 5 years after the loss. On average, participants endorsed these items in the range of "moderately true." Items that received the highest scores included keeping things that belonged to one's spouse, enjoying reminiscing with others about one's spouse, seeing the spouse as a loving presence in one's life, expressing awareness of the positive influence of one's spouse on who one is today, and having fond memories of one's spouse. Items endorsed less frequently at 5 years post-loss included seeking out things that remind one of his or her spouse, awareness of taking on one's spouse's values or interests, and having conversations with one's spouse.

Continuing Connections and Adaptation

Although many studies have examined the prevalence of continuing connections to the deceased among the bereaved, only a few have examined the relationship between such connections and adaptation to the loss. These studies have yielded inconclusive evidence. In studies assessing the frequency of sensing the presence of the deceased or talking with him or her, the majority of respondents experience these encounters as comforting (Klass & Walter, 2001). Silverman and Nickman (1996) have also noted that the ties that children developed with their deceased parents were apparently beneficial. Many children made spontaneous comments such as "It feels good to think about him." In fact, when the children were asked what they would advise another bereaved child to do, they gave answers such as "Just think of them as often as you can." However, as other investigators have noted (cf. Fraley & Shaver, 1999), a significant number of survivors report that ongoing connections are not always comforting. For example, nearly 60% of the children in the study by Silverman and Nickman (1996) indicated that they were "scared" by the idea that their parents could watch them from heaven. In fact, some children regarded their deceased parent as a ghost whose presence was frightening and unpredictable (Normand, Silverman, & Nickman, 1996). In a follow-up analysis of these data, Silverman, Baker, Cait, and Boerner (2003) found that many of the children who showed emotional and behavioral problems after the loss had a continuing bond with the deceased that was primarily negative. These "high-risk" children carried troubling legacies related to their deceased parent's health, personality, or role in the family. Health-related legacies, for example, reflected children's fear that they will die from the same condition or disease that killed their parent. Role-related legacies reflected children's sense that they needed to assume the role

in the family that was once filled by the parent, creating a burden that was clearly too heavy for these children.

Datson and Marwit (1997) found that 60% of those who had lost a loved one within the previous 4 years reported sensing the presence of their deceased loved one at some point, and the vast majority (86%) regarded the experience as comforting. However, those who reported that they had sensed the presence of their loved one scored higher in neuroticism than those who did not. These findings suggest that, in some cases, sensing the presence of the deceased loved one may be more an indication of greater distress than a sign of good adjustment.

In a study by Field, Nichols, Holen, and Horowitz (1999), interviewers rated the extent to which bereaved individuals manifested four different kinds of attachment behaviors 6 months after the loss. Those who tended to maintain the deceased person's possessions as they were when he or she was alive, or who tended to make excessive use of the deceased's possessions for comfort, exhibited more severe grief symptoms over the course of the 25-month study. These respondents also showed less of a decrease in grief symptoms over time. Attachment strategies that involved sensing the deceased spouse's presence, or seeking comfort through memories of their loved one, were not related to the intensity of grief. These findings suggest that whether continuing bonds are adaptive or maladaptive may depend on the form that the connection takes.

To address this question, Field et al. (2003) conducted a follow-up study on this same sample, in which they assessed a wide variety of attachment behaviors at 5 years post-loss (see earlier discussion). Results showed that each of the continuing bond items, as well as a composite score based on all of the items that were assessed, was associated with more severe grief. There was a strong positive correlation between continuing bonds assessed 5 years after the death and grief assessed at the same time point. The relationship between continuing bonds and other forms of well-being was much weaker, suggesting that the relationship between continuing bonds and adjustment is largely restricted to grief-restricted measures.

In another study, Field and Friedrichs (2004) examined the use of attachment behaviors as a way of coping with the death of a husband. Fifteen early-bereaved widows (4 months post-loss) and

15 later-bereaved widows (more than 2 years) completed continuing bond and mood measures four times each day for 14 consecutive days. Greater use of continuing bond coping was related to more positive mood among the later- but not the early-bereaved, and more negative mood in both groups. Furthermore, in time-lagged analyses, greater use of continuing bond coping was predictive of a shift toward more negative mood among early-bereaved but not among later-bereaved widows. These findings suggest that continuing bond coping may be less effective in mood regulation earlier than later on after the death. As the authors noted, however, neither this nor the prior two studies allowed for a investigation of the direction of causality between continuing bonds and grief symptoms. Hence, it is not clear whether continuing bonds are simply correlates of bereavement-related distress or whether the formation of such bonds in fact plays a causal role in impending adjustment to bereavement. Nonetheless, when considered together, these studies raise questions about whether continuing bonds should be regarded as exclusively adaptive.

In summary, our belief in the value of continuing attachments between the bereaved and the deceased has shifted markedly over the past few decades. Initially, it was believed that it was essential to break down ties to the deceased. At present, such ties are widely regarded as normal and generally beneficial. Because so few studies have examined the role such ties may play in adjustment to loss, there is virtually no evidence to support this current view. In fact, the few studies that have explored the matter suggest that it would be a mistake to regard continuing bonds as uniformly adaptive.

Future Directions

In future work, it will be important to learn more about whether certain kinds of continuing bonds may facilitate good adjustment while others do not. Some types of behaviors may in fact reflect the presence of continuing bonds, whereas others may signal the presence of other psychological processes. Maintaining the deceased person's possessions as they were, for example, may reflect failure to accept the loss rather than a continuing attachment to the deceased. Results of the studies by Field et al. (1999, 2003) also suggest that whether continuing bonds are adaptive may depend on how much time has elapsed since the death. At this point, we do not know whether those who make the best adjust-

ments to a loss experience continuing bonds for several years into the future, or whether these bonds gradually fade over time as the bereaved become involved in other relationships and activities. By examining a large and representative class of continuing bonds from shortly after the loss through the next several years, it should be possible to address critical questions about the possible causal role continuing bonds may play in facilitating adjustment. Such questions could also be addressed through experimental studies in which respondents are randomly assigned to participate in exercises believed to promote continuing bonds, such as discussions about what the deceased loved one has meant to them.

Even if continuing bonds are generally found to facilitate adjustment, there may be conditions under which this is not the case. Negative legacies from past relationships can be related to aspects of the deceased's life (e.g., health aspects, or burdensome roles that were once filled by the deceased), or to aspects of the relationship with the deceased (e.g., if the relationship was abusive or destructive in other ways). If the bereaved is left with such a negative legacy, what kind of a connection to the deceased, if any, should the bereaved attempt to develop? In some cases, perhaps reviewing the relationship, and the negative legacy that is attached to this relationship, can help the bereaved to attain important self-knowledge. However, it may be this self-knowledge (e.g., I deserved to be with someone who treated me better) rather than a positive tie with the deceased that is helpful to the person under such conditions.

In the process of clarifying the relationship between various continuing bonds and adjustment, it would be valuable to have a greater understanding about how particular sorts of connections are experienced and perceived by the bereaved. For example, although it is common for the bereaved to talk with the deceased and to report that this is comforting, little is known about what transpires in such conversations or what psychological needs they may fulfill. It will also be important to determine whether there are circumstances that might impede or facilitate the development of continuing bonds that facilitate adjustment. For example, the opportunity to talk with others who knew and valued the deceased may help to facilitate the development of such bonds. However, it may be more difficult for the bereaved to develop such bonds following a loss that cannot be acknowledged or shared (Boerner & Heckhausen, 2003).

Expectations About Recovery

Description

Traditionally, it has been believed that once people have completed the process of "working through" the loss and "relinquishing their ties to the deceased," they will reach a state of recovery. Most prior work has conceptualized recovery in terms of a return to prebereavement or baseline levels of psychological distress. As Weiss (1993) has emphasized, however, it is important to examine a broader set of indicators when trying to determine whether a person has recovered from a loss. These include freedom from intrusive or disturbing thoughts and the ability to encounter reminders without intense pain; the ability to give energy to everyday life; the ability to experience pleasure when desirable, hoped-for or enriching events occur; hopefulness about the future and being able to make and carry out future plans; and the ability to function well in social roles such as spouse, parent, and member of the community.

In the past, bereavement has been viewed as a time-limited process, with people resuming "normal life" once they reach the end point (Malkinson, 2001). It was assumed that in most cases, grief work would be completed in approximately 12 months (Malkinson, 2001; Wortman & Silver, 2001). Those who failed to recover after an "appropriate" amount of time were often viewed as displaying "chronic" grief (see, e.g., Jacobs, 1993), a pattern of grieving that has been regarded as an indication of "pathological mourning" (Middleton et al., 1993). Over the past decade, however, this view of the recovery process has begun to change. Malkinson (2001) has noted that at this point, the 12-month time period is viewed as "mythological" and that there is wide recognition that the process can take far longer.

Moreover, recovery is no longer viewed as a process with a discrete end point. As widows and widowers sometimes express it, "You don't get over it, you get used to it" (Weiss, 1993, p. 277). Several investigators have pointed out that terms like *resolution* and *recovery* are becoming unpopular, and that they are not applicable to most losses because they imply a once-and-for-all closure that does not occur (see, e.g., Rando, 1993; Klass, Silverman, & Nickman, 1996; Stroebe, Hansson, et al.,

2001; Weiss, 1993). Similarly, there is a growing consensus that bereaved individuals may never return to their pre-loss state. Weiss (1993) has argued that a major loss will almost invariably produce changes in a person's character. Miller and Omarzu (1998) have suggested that returning to one's pre-loss state may not be an optimal goal. As Malkinson (2001) has expressed it, recovery can be "a lifelong process of struggling to find the balance between what was and what is" (p. 675).

Evidence for Chronicity

Empirical evidence suggests that while most bereaved individuals do not seem to experience intense distress for extended periods of time (see the earlier section on the expectation of intense distress), a significant minority of people develop long-term difficulties. This was found in the six longitudinal studies mentioned previously that included two postloss time points and provided evidence for different patterns of grief. "Chronic" grief, which involved scoring high in distress at both time points, was found among 30% of participants in the study on the loss of a child from SIDS (Wortman & Silver, 1987), and anywhere between 8% and 26% in studies on conjugal loss (24% in Bonanno et al., 1995; 13% in Bournstein et al., 1973; 8% in Lund et al., 1986; 26% in Vachon, Rogers, et al., 1982; and 20% in Zisook & Shuchter, 1986). It should be noted that the highest percentage of respondents showing a pattern of consistently high levels of distress following the loss came from the study on death of a child to SIDS (Wortman & Silver, 1987). Another important consideration is the striking difference among the studies on conjugal loss in the percentage of respondents evidencing chronic grief. This may be related to differences in the age of the respondents, and hence the timeliness of the loss. For example, the study by Lund et al. (1986) focused on elderly bereaved, whereas the study by Vachon, Rogers, et al. (1982) focused on loss of a spouse at midlife.

In our prospective work on conjugal loss (Bonanno et al., 2002), the availability of pre-loss data made it possible to further distinguish a chronic grief pattern, scoring low before the loss and consistently high afterward (16%), from chronic depression (8%), which involved scoring high at all pre- and postloss time points. To further characterize the nature of these patterns, Bonanno et al. (2002) identified their pre-loss predictors. Chronic grievers were likely to have had healthy spouses, to rate their marriage positively, and to show high levels of pre-loss dependency (e.g., agreeing that no one could take the spouse's place). The chronically depressed group was less positive about their marriage than chronic grievers, but as dependent on their spouse. Further analyses examined the context and processing of the loss at 6 and 18 months post-loss (Bonanno et al., 2004). Results suggest that chronic grief stems from an enduring struggle with cognitive and emotional distress related to the loss, whereas chronic depression results more from enduring emotional difficulties that are exacerbated by the loss. For example, at 6 months postloss, chronic grievers were more likely to report current yearning and emotional pangs, and they reported thinking and talking about the deceased more often than did chronically depressed individuals.

Most classic grief theorists (e.g., Jacobs, 1993) discuss the notion of chronic grief but fail to indicate how long it typically takes and whether it abates. To address this issue, we conducted a follow-up analysis investigating whether the chronic grievers and the chronically depressed would remain distressed up to 48 months post-loss (Boerner et al., 2005). Overall, the chronic grief group experienced a more intense and prolonged period of distress than, for example, did the common grief group. Measures of outcome and processing the loss measures, however, indicated a turn toward better adjustment by the 48–month time point, which suggests that this group does not remain chronically distressed as a result of the loss. In contrast, the chronically depressed group clearly demonstrated long-term problems, with little indication of improvement between 18 and 48 months. This group not only showed the poorest adjustment 4 years after the loss but also struggled the most with questions about meaning. These differential findings for the chronic grief and chronic depression group underscore the need to further refine the criteria that are used to identify those who are at risk for long-term problems.

Risk Factors

Over the past decade, it has become increasingly clear that reactions to loss are highly variable, but that a significant minority shows enduring effects. Consequently, researchers have become interested in identifying factors that may promote or impede successful adjustment to the loss of a loved one.

Studying risk factors has the potential to advance bereavement theory by helping to clarify the mechanisms through which loss influences subsequent mental and physical health. Perhaps even more important, knowledge about risk factors can aid in the identification of people who may benefit from bereavement interventions.

Several broad classes of risk factors have been studied in the literature (see Archer, 1999; Jordan & Neimeyer, 2003; and Stroebe & Schut, 2001, for reviews). These include *demographic factors,* such as age, gender, and socioeconomic status; *background factors,* including whether the respondent has a history of mental health problems or substance abuse, or has experienced prior losses or traumas; *factors describing the type and nature of the relationship,* such as whether it was a child, spouse, or sibling who was lost and whether the relationship was emotionally close or conflictual; *personal and social resources,* including personality traits, attachment history, religiosity, and social support; and *the context in which the loss occurs,* which refers to the circumstances surrounding the death, whether the surviving loved one was involved in caregiving, the type and quality of the death, and the presence of concomitant stressors such as ill health of the surviving loved one. A comprehensive review of these risk factors is beyond the scope of this chapter. However, in this section, we wish to highlight selected areas of research on risk factors that we believe are of emerging interest and importance.

Most of the research on *gender differences* following the loss of a loved one has focused on the loss of a spouse. There is clear evidence that in comparison to married controls, widowed men are more likely to become depressed and to experience greater mortality than are widowed women (see Stroebe, Stroebe, et al., 2001, and Miller & Wortman, 2002, for reviews). Interestingly, such deaths are especially likely among younger bereaved men. Major causes of death among bereaved men include alcohol-related illness, accidents and violence, suicide, and chronic ischemic heart disease.

One possible explanation for these gender differences is that men may benefit more from marriage than do women, and may therefore be more adversely affected when the marriage ends. Consistent with this view, several studies have shown that women typically have many more close social relationships than men, who rely primarily on their wives for support. In addition, women usually perform more housework and child care than do men. Because men often rely on their wives in these domains, they may find it difficult to handle these matters on their own. Research suggests that while social ties and household responsibilities are related to gender differences following conjugal loss, they account for relatively little variance in the relationship between widowhood and mortality or depression (Miller & Wortman, 2002).

A second mechanism has been suggested by Umberson (1987, 1992), who has demonstrated that women typically take greater responsibility for their partner's health care, diet, nutrition, and exercise than do men. For example, married women are typically the ones who schedule doctor appointments and regular checkups for themselves and their spouses. They are also more likely to monitor whether their husbands are taking prescribed medications, and to offer reminders if necessary. Married women are also more likely to place constraints on negative health behavior, such as drinking and driving. Umberson concludes that the poor health of men following the death of their spouse is caused in part by the loss of this positive influence on their health behavior.

Several comparative studies of different *kinship relationships* have shown that the loss of a child results in more intense and prolonged grief and depression than the loss of a spouse, parent, or sibling (see Stroebe & Schut, 2001, for a review). Available research suggests that mothers are more adversely affected than fathers by the loss of a child (see Archer, 1999, for a more detailed discussion). In most studies focusing on the death of a child, mothers typically report higher levels of grief, psychological distress, preoccupation with the loss, intrusive thoughts, and feelings of guilt than do fathers (see, e.g., Dyregrov et al., 2003).

Virtually all of the studies that have examined how bereavement is affected by the *nature of the relationship* have focused on the loss of a spouse. Historically, clinical writings on loss have maintained that chronic grief results from conflict in the marital relationship or feelings of ambivalence toward the spouse (see, e.g., Bowlby, 1980; Freud, 1917/1957; Parkes & Weiss, 1983). However, well-controlled studies fail to provide support for this view (Bonanno et al., 2002; Carr et al., 2000). Clinicians have also maintained that excessive dependency on one's spouse is a risk factor for chronic grief (see, e.g., Lopata, 1979; Parkes & Weiss, 1983).

Available evidence suggests that this is indeed the case. In the Bonanno et al. (2002) study described earlier, chronic grievers showed significantly higher levels of dependency on their spouse as well as general interpersonal dependency than did respondents in some of the other trajectory groups. It would be interesting to determine whether the nature of the relationship is an important risk factor in other kinds of relationships. For example, do parents have more difficulty resolving their grief following the death of an adolescent child if the relationship was conflictual?

Regarding personal and social resources, some of the most important work linking personality with bereavement outcome has been conducted by Nolen-Hoeksema and her colleagues (see, e.g., Nolen-Hoeksema & Larson, 1999; Nolen-Hoeksema, 2001). In a study on coping with conjugal loss, she identified two personality variables that played an important role: dispositional optimism and a ruminative coping style. Those who scored high on dispositional optimism (i.e., the tendency to be optimistic in most circumstances) showed a greater decline in symptoms of depression following the loss, and were also more likely to find meaning or benefit in the loss than were pessimists. As mentioned earlier, a ruminative coping style involves a tendency to "engage in thoughts and behaviors that maintain one's focus on one's negative emotions and the possible causes and consequences of those emotions" (Nolen-Hoeksema, 2001, p. 546). Nolen-Hoeksema's findings indicate that those who engage in rumination following loss show little decrease in distress over time. Although bereaved ruminators believed that focusing on the loss would solve their problems, this was not the case: They were significantly less likely to become actively engaged in effective problem solving than were nonruminators.

In recent years, there has been increasing interest in the role that religious or spiritual beliefs may play in dealing with a loved one's death (see Stroebe & Schut, 2001, for a more detailed discussion). Many investigators have suggested that religious beliefs may ease the sting of death, and facilitate finding meaning in the loss, by providing a ready framework of beliefs for incorporating negative events (Pargament & Park, 1995). It has also been argued that specific tenets of one's faith, such as the belief that the deceased is in a better place, or that the survivor and deceased will be reunited in the afterlife, may mitigate the distress associated with the death of a loved one. Unfortunately, most of the studies that have examined variables of this sort are methodologically weak, and the results are conflictual. However, there are indications in the literature that religious beliefs facilitate finding meaning in the death of a child (McIntosh, Silver, & Wortman, 1993; Murphy, Johnson, & Lohan, 2003). Moreover, available evidence suggests that those with spiritual beliefs are more likely to use positive reappraisal and effective problem solving than those who do not hold such beliefs (Richards et al., 1999; Richards & Folkman, 1997).

As noted earlier, there is also a great deal of interest in the relationship between a person's attachment style and his or her reaction to the loss of a loved one (see Shaver & Tancredy, 2001, and Stroebe, Schut, & Stroebe, 2005a, for a more detailed discussion). For example, Shaver and Tancredy (2001) have maintained that individuals with a secure attachment style find it easy to be close to others, and typically react to loss with normal but not overwhelming grief. Those with an insecure-dismissing orientation to relationships have difficulty trusting others or allowing themselves to depend on others, and are "compulsively independent" (Stroebe, Stroebe, & Schut, in press, p. 21). These individuals would be expended to suppress and avoid attachment-related emotions, and to show relatively little distress following a major loss. Those with an anxious or preoccupied orientation to relationships have a strong desire to be close to others but are often preoccupied or worried that their partner will abandon them. Such individuals would be expected to react to the loss with intense distress and to remain upset and preoccupied with the loss. Although few studies have tested these hypotheses, some limited evidence suggests that attachment style may be important. For example, Wayment and Vierthaler (2002) found that persons with a secure attachment style showed lower levels of depressive symptoms following the loss of a loved one than those with a preoccupied style, who expressed more distress and were more likely to engage in rumination.

At present, some of the most exciting work on risk factors has focused on various factors associated with *the context in which the death occurs.* One contextual factor that is generating increasing research interest concerns the *circumstances under which the death occurs.* Accumulating evidence clearly

suggests that grief is more likely to be intense and prolonged following the sudden, traumatic loss of a spouse or child.

In an early study examining the effects of losing a spouse or child in a motor vehicle accident 4 to 7 years previously (Lehman, Wortman, & Williams, 1987), comparisons between the bereaved and control respondents, matched on a case-by-case basis, revealed significant differences on depression and other psychiatric symptoms, role functioning, and quality of life. The bereaved experienced more strain in dealing with surviving children and family members, and felt more vulnerable to future negative events. Bereavement was associated with an increased mortality rate, a decline in financial status, and, in the case of bereaved parents, a higher divorce rate. A majority of respondents indicated that they were still experiencing painful thoughts and memories about their loved one.

Another study focusing on how parents are affected by the sudden, traumatic loss of a child (Murphy et al., 2002) found that 5 years postloss, a majority of mothers and fathers met diagnostic criteria for mental distress. Compared with normative samples, about three times as many mothers (28%) and twice as many fathers (13%) met diagnostic criteria for post-traumatic stress disorder (PTSD). In a follow-up study, Murphy, Johnson, Wu, et al. (2003) examined the influence of type of death (accident, suicide, homicide) and time since death on parent outcome. Those who lost a child through homicide were more likely to manifest symptoms of PTSD. However, a majority of parents reported that it took them 3 or 4 years to put the loss into perspective and continue with their lives, and this assessment was not affected by the child's cause of death.

Similar results were obtained in a study by Dyregrov et al. (2003), who focused on parents who lost a child as a result of suicide, sudden infant death syndrome (SIDS), or an accident. The results showed that one and a half years after the death of their child, a considerable proportion of parents showed symptoms of PTSD and complicated grief reactions. Rates of problems were highest for those who lost loved ones through accidents or suicide. As many as 78% of these parents were "above the risk zone of maladaptive symptoms of loss and long-term dysfunction" (p. 155). On the basis of these findings, the authors concluded that "to lose a child suddenly and in traumatic circumstances is a devastating experience for the survivors, most often resulting in a tremendous and long-lasting impact" (p. 156).

Available evidence also suggests that the sudden, traumatic death of a spouse is associated with intense and prolonged distress. In addition to the aforementioned study by Lehman et al., two more recent studies help to clarify the impact of such losses. Zisook, Chentsova-Dutton, and Shuchter (1998) followed a large number of respondents longitudinally for the first 2 years after losing a spouse. Those whose spouse died as a result of an accident, homicide, or suicide were more likely to develop PTSD symptoms than those who experienced a sudden, unexpected death due to natural causes (e.g., heart attack). Those who scored high on PTSD symptomology also scored high on depression. Similarly, Kaltman and Bonanno (2003) compared respondents whose spouses died of natural causes with those who experienced the death of a spouse as a result of an accident, homicide, or suicide. The latter group manifested a significantly higher number of PTSD symptoms as long as 25 months after the loss. Moreover, those who lost a loved one through natural causes showed a decline in depressive symptoms, whereas those who lost a loved one as a result of an accident or suicide showed no drop in depressive symptoms over the 2-year course of the study. Among the natural death cohort, there were no significant differences in PTSD symptoms or the persistence of depression between bereaved individuals who had sudden, unexpected losses and those who had expected losses.

Taken together, these studies provide compelling evidence that the death of a spouse or child under traumatic or violent circumstances is linked to more intense and prolonged grief. It is important to note that such deaths are associated with PTSD symptoms as well as symptoms of depression. This means that in addition to dealing with such symptoms as yearning for the deceased and profound sadness, survivors of sudden, traumatic losses must contend with such symptoms as intrusive thoughts and flashbacks, feelings of detachment or estrangement, irritability, and problems in concentration.

The studies reviewed here have focused primarily on the untimely death of a spouse or child. Do the circumstances under which the death occurs have an impact on survivors when a loved one dies following a life-threatening illness or when an elderly person dies? For people aged 65 and older, chronic illnesses such as cancer, heart disease, and diabetes account for more than 60% of all deaths. Over the past decade, a great deal of research has focused on the impact of caregiving (see Carr, Wortman, & Wolff, 2006, for a review). Studies have shown that caregivers are more stressed and depressed and have lower levels of well-being than noncaregivers (Pinquart & Sorensen, 2003a, 2003b). Depressive symptoms increase as the number of hours one engages in caregiving increases (Schulz et al., 2001). In recent years, investigators have begun to examine the impact of caregiving on adjustment to the loss following the loved one's death. This research demonstrates that the relationship between caregiving and adjustment to bereavement is complex. Although stressful caregiving is associated with poor psychological adjustment when the spouse is alive, overly taxed caregivers tend to rebound to relatively high levels of functioning after the loss (Schulz et al., 2003). A minority of strained caregivers demonstrated intense and prolonged grief, and investigators are attempting to uncover the determinants of this reaction. Caregivers who are most energized by their caregiving role, and who find meaning in what they are doing, often have a difficult time adjusting to the loss (Boerner, Schulz, & Horowitz, 2004). These studies suggest that those who are at the greatest risk of distress during the dying process may fare relatively well in the post-loss period.

In an important paper, Carr (2003) has pointed out that policymakers and care providers are becoming increasingly concerned with helping dying people to experience a "good death." According to Carr (2003), a "good death" is characterized by physical comfort, support from one's loved ones, acceptance, and appropriate medical care. Carr is one of the first bereavement researchers to suggest that whether a loved one dies a "good death" may have implications for the grief experienced by surviving family members. In analyses based on the Changing Lives of Older Couples (CLOC) data, she found that those who reported that their spouses were in severe pain showed elevated levels of yearning, anxiety, and intrusive thoughts following the loss. Those who believed that their spouse's medical care was negligent reported elevated anger symptoms.

Several studies have shown that there are unique stresses associated with caring for a loved one who is dying (see Carr et al., 2006, for a more detailed discussion). For example, Prigerson and her associates (2003) examined quality of life among hospice-based dying patients and their caregivers, who included spouses and children. The caregivers had cared for their relatives for 2 years, on average, prior to the hospice admission. More than three quarters of the caregivers reported that they had witnessed the patient in severe pain or discomfort, and 62% said they had witnessed this daily. Nearly half reported that their loved one was unable to sleep or unable to eat or swallow on a daily basis. These findings are particularly striking when one considers that one of the core goals of hospice care is pain management. Several studies have shown that family members report more positive evaluations of their spouse's quality of care at the end of life and better psychological adjustment following the death when their loved one spent his or her final weeks using in-home hospice services rather than receiving care in nursing homes, hospitals, or at home with home health nursing services (see, e.g., Teno, Clarridge, & Casey, 2004). In fact, a study by Christakis and Iwashyna (2003) indicates that hospice use can reduce the increased mortality of risk associated with bereavement. These investigators conducted a matched cohort study with a sample of nearly 200,000 respondents in the United States. At 18 months after the loss, there were significantly fewer deaths among wives whose husbands had received hospice care than among those whose husbands received other types of care (typically a combination of home care with occasional hospital stays). Mortality was also lower for husbands whose wives received hospice care, but the effect fell short of statistical significance. These studies suggest that sites of care that provide hospice care may be more conducive to a "good death" for the patient and, consequently, his or her surviving loved ones.

Complicated Grief As a Distinct Psychiatric Disorder

Despite the progress that has been made in identifying risk factors for chronic grief, there are no standard guidelines to determine how complications following bereavement should be diagnosed and when they should be treated. Among theorists as well as clinicians, there has been a long-standing awareness that bereavement can result in psychiatric problems. As Jacobs (1993) has indicated, most

research has focused on the prevalence of clinically significant depression and anxiety disorders among the bereaved. More recently, as was described earlier, researchers have become interested in the prevalence of PTSD following the loss of a loved one, particularly among survivors of sudden, traumatic losses.

In an important new line of research, Prigerson and her associates (e.g., Prigerson, 2004; Jacobs, Mazure, & Prigerson, 2000; see Lichtenthal, Cruess, & Prigerson, 2004, for a review) have focused on the empirical development of diagnostic criteria to identify those individuals who exhibit chronic grief, and who would benefit from clinical intervention. Drawing from epidemiological, pharmacological, and clinical case studies, these investigators have identified a unique pattern of symptoms called *complicated grief* (CG). They have maintained that these symptoms are associated with enduring mental and physical health problems that are typically slow to resolve, and that can persist for years if left untreated. To obtain a diagnosis of CG, individuals must experience intense yearning for the deceased daily over the past month. They must also experience 4 of 8 additional symptoms during the past month: trouble accepting the death, difficulty trusting others, excessive bitterness, feeling uneasy about moving forward, feeling detached from others, viewing life as empty, feeling that the future holds no meaning without the deceased, and feeling on edge since the death. These symptoms must cause marked and persistent dysfunction in social, occupational, or other important roles, and the symptom disturbance must last at least 6 months. Research has shown that these symptoms form a unified cluster and that they are distinct from depression, anxiety, or PTSD. For example, feeling sad and blue is characteristic of depression but not of CG, and avoidance and hyperarousal are characteristic of PTSD but not of CG. Unlike these other disorders, vulnerability to CG is believed to be rooted in insecure attachment styles that are developed in childhood. Consistent with this notion, evidence has shown that childhood abuse and serious neglect are significantly associated with CG during widowhood (Silverman, Johnson, & Prigerson, 2001).

Evidence has shown that the prevalence of CG among individuals who have lost a loved one is between 10% and 20%. The symptoms of CG typically last for several years. They are predictive of morbidity (e.g., suicidal thoughts and behaviors, incidence of cardiac events, high blood pressure), adverse health behaviors (e.g., increased alcohol consumption and use of tobacco), and impairments in the quality of life (e.g., loss of energy). Interestingly, bereaved people with CG are significantly less likely to visit a mental health or physical health care professional than those without grief complications; perhaps people with severe mental anguish have difficulty mobilizing themselves to go into treatment.

Future Directions

We now know that a significant minority of individuals experience enduring difficulties following the loss of a loved one, and we have a reasonably good understanding of the risk factors for grief complications. However, important questions remain unanswered about exactly how people do recover from a loss. As Archer (1999) has observed, "It is commonly believed that it is not time itself that is the healer but some process which occurs during this time" (p. 108). At this point, however, there is considerable confusion about what this process involves. It is now clear that some people recover from a loss without "working through" the implications of what has happened. What other processes play an important role in facilitating acceptance of what has happened, the ability to encounter reminders without distress, and the ability to become engaged in new interests and pursuits?

In evaluating the impact of a major loss, it is important to recognize that the survivor may also be coping with additional losses. The death of child, for example, may require surviving parents to face the loss of their hopes and dreams for the future, the loss of their belief in God as a benevolent protector, and the loss of their beliefs in their ability to control outcomes that are important. The death of a spouse is often accompanied by concurrent stressors, including loss of income or struggling with tasks formerly performed by the deceased.

Although most research on the enduring effects of loss has focused on mental and physical health problems, there is increasing recognition that losses can bring about positive psychological changes (Tedeschi & Calhoun, 1996, 2004). Several researchers have documented, for example, that following the loss of a spouse, the surviving spouse reports greater feelings of self-confidence, a greater awareness of one's strengths, and a greater inclination to try new experiences (see Wortman, 2004, for a review). It less clear whether sudden, traumatic losses

of a spouse or child are accompanied by personal growth. There are some indications that survivors of trauma resent the implication that they should be able to find something good in what has happened, and that others' exhortations to this effect often heighten survivors' feelings of inadequacy and shame (see Wortman, 2004, for a more detailed discussion).

Conclusions and Implications

In previous papers, we have described several common assumptions about coping with loss that appear to be held by professionals in the field as well as by laypersons. We conducted a careful evaluation of each assumption and concluded that most were not supported, and were often contradicted, by the available data. Indeed, this is why these assumptions were originally referred to as "myths of coping with loss."

It has been almost 20 years since the first articles on the myths of coping appeared in the literature (Wortman & Silver, 1987, 1989). As the scientific evidence pertaining to these myths has continued to accumulate, there have been some shifts in the prevailing views about how people cope with loss. The main purpose of this chapter has been to summarize the most important research bearing on the validity of each "myth of coping," and also to highlight how the myths themselves have changed over time.

In the material to follow, we first summarize how, in our judgment, these assumptions are currently viewed by researchers. We then examine the extent to which the myths of coping are still influential among practicing clinicians. We discuss the relationship between belief in these myths and grief counseling and therapy as it is currently practiced in the United States today. In particular, we highlight extensive research evidence suggesting that treatment for grief is in most cases ineffective, and in some cases harmful. We then consider the extent to which the myths of coping are continuing to influence other health care providers who come into contact with the bereaved, such as clergy and general practitioners. Next, we consider the extent to which these myths of coping are maintained by the bereaved themselves and their potential support providers. Finally, we explore whether these beliefs impact the amount and quality of support the bereaved are likely to receive.

Implications for Research

Over time, it appears that researchers' assumptions about the process of coping with loss have changed in important ways. For example, most researchers would probably agree that a large minority of respondents fail to experience even mild depression following an important loss, that delayed grief is rare, that positive emotions are common following a loss and are associated with a good recovery, that not everyone may need to actively confront their thoughts and feelings about the loss, that continuing attachment to the loved one is normal, and that recovery from a loss is highly variable and depends on many factors, including the nature of the relationship and the circumstances surrounding the death.

Awareness of this body of work is leading researchers to ask new and important questions about the process of coping with loss. As was noted earlier, for example, many of the early studies on grief focused solely on depression and other negative emotions and symptoms; questions about positive emotions experienced during grieving were typically not included. At this point, however, researchers not only are including measures of positive emotions but also are attempting to identify the role that such emotions may play in facilitating adjustment to a loss. In terms of outcome measures, it has become clear that we must examine the possibility that losses can bring about enduring positive changes, such as increased self-confidence and independence, altered life priorities, and enhanced compassion for others suffering similar losses (for a more detailed discussion of growth following loss, see Wortman, 2004).

Despite these advances, it is important for researchers to ask themselves whether they may hold assumptions or beliefs about the coping process that are limiting the scope of their scientific inquiry into loss. In a collaborative study called the Americans' Changing Lives, for example (see Nesse, Wortman, & House, 2006), personal interviews were conducted with a national sample of people who had lost a spouse anywhere from 3 months to 60 years previously. Several of the investigators wanted to eliminate questions about widowhood for all respondents whose loss occurred longer than 10 years ago, assuming that there would be no effects after that point. Ultimately, the decision was made to ask these questions of all respondents. This was fortu-

nate because the results enhanced our knowledge about the ways such losses continue to influence the surviving spouse. For example, several decades after the loss, it was common for people to have thoughts and conversations about their spouse that made them feel sad or upset (see Carnelley, Wortman, Bolger, & Burke, in press).

Implications for Treatment

Earlier, we have attempted to argue that in most cases, researchers no longer take the prevailing cultural assumptions about coping with loss at face value and instead appear to recognize the extraordinary variability in response to loss. It is less clear, however, whether the accumulation of research findings has filtered down to clinicians or other health care providers working with the bereaved, to potential support providers of the bereaved, or to the bereaved themselves.

Clinicians

A review of books and articles written for and by clinicians indicates that assumptions about the importance of going through a period of distress, and of working through the loss, are still widely held. For example, in what is perhaps the most widely used book on grief counseling written for clinicians and other mental health professionals, Worden (2002) indicates that not allowing negative feelings to be experienced frequently leads to complicated bereavement. As he expressed it, "It is necessary to acknowledge and work through this pain or it can manifest itself through physical symptoms or some form of aberrant behavior" (p. 30).

There has been a proliferation of grief counseling and therapy, which is reflected in wide offerings of workshops, professional conferences, and publications, as well as in countless individual and group-based treatments offered in virtually all communities (Neimeyer, 2000). As Neimeyer (2000) has indicated, most people assume that grief counseling is "a firmly established, demonstrably effective service, which, like psychotherapy in general, seems to have found a secure niche in the health care field" (p. 542). And indeed, most clinicians who treat the bereaved believe that what they do is helpful and necessary (Jordan & Neimeyer, 2003). In a ground-breaking paper, Jordan and Neimeyer (2003) have examined the empirical evidence bearing on these claims. They carefully examine the results of one narrative review and three meta-analytic reviews focusing on the impact of bereavement interventions. Although these reviews have focused on somewhat different sets of studies and have employed a variety of analytic approaches, all have come to basically the same conclusion: that the scientific basis for the efficacy of grief counseling is quite weak (for a more detailed discussion of these reviews and their implications, see Jordan & Neimeyer, 2003, and Stroebe, Schut, & Stroebe, 2005b).

All three of the studies using meta-analytic techniques found small effect sizes for bereavement interventions. For example, Neimeyer (2000) found an overall effect size of .13 across the 23 studies they included. This means that the average participant in grief therapy was better off than only 55% of bereaved people who received no treatment. This effect size is far smaller than the effect size for other types of therapeutic evaluations that have been studied. Moreover, they found clear evidence that such interventions can have a negative impact: They found that 38% of participants showed apparent deterioration as a result of the treatment and would have had a better outcome if they had been assigned to the control, rather than the treatment, condition. As Jordan and Neimeyer (2003) have noted, this rate is far higher than that obtained in most psychotherapy outcome studies, where there is an average rate of deterioration of about 5%. Treatment outcome was not related to such variables as the length of treatment, the level of training of the therapist (professional vs. nonprofessional), or the type of treatment approach (individual, family, or group).

Fortner and Neimeyer (as reported in Neimeyer, 2000) did find a more substantial, but still modest, positive effect size (.38) among studies dealing with grief following a sudden, traumatic death or chronic grief, and the potential for deterioration was substantially lower for these groups (.17%). Similar findings emerged from Schut et al.'s (2001) narrative review. Among those who were defined as being at high risk for developing bereavement-related problems (e.g., those who had experienced the sudden, traumatic death of a loved one, those who lost a child, or those who evidenced high levels of symptoms prior to the intervention), a modest positive effect was found. Schut et al. (2001) found the most positive effects for those intervention studies that focused on bereaved individuals who had already developed a complicated grief reaction.

Jordan and Neimeyer (2003) have pointed out that there are many possible ways of understanding this pattern of findings. Some studies may have failed to find a robust positive effect for grief counseling because the studies were small, and there may not have been enough statistical power to detect differences between groups. In other studies, findings may not have emerged because the treatment offered did not include enough sessions (most included 8–12 sessions). Alternatively, the intervention may not have been offered at the most appropriate time. Neimeyer (2000) found that interventions that were delivered shortly after the death had significantly smaller effect sizes than those delivered at a later time. Jordan and Neimeyer (2003) have suggested that there may be a "critical window of time" (p. 774) when it is best to offer interventions, perhaps 6 to 18 months after the loss, "before problematic patterns of adjustment have become entrenched" (p. 774). These investigators also emphasized that the types of counseling needed shortly after the loss may differ from what is needed a year or more after the loss, noting that investigators should try to customize the type of intervention to particular points in the bereavement trajectory.

Taken together, these findings suggest that in many cases, people may not need therapy following a loved one's death, but that some subgroups are likely to benefit substantially from treatment. It would be useful to develop interventions that are designed specifically to address the problems of mourners in high-risk categories, such as those who have experienced the sudden, traumatic loss of a spouse or child, or those who have already developed complicated grief. Shear and her associates (2005) have recently completed a randomized, clinical trial comparing an intervention designed for people with complicated grief to a more standard treatment for depression (interpersonal therapy). The multifaceted complicated grief intervention draws from research on the treatment of PTSD. For example, clients are given exercises to help them confront avoided situations. In addition, they are asked to tell their story into a tape recorder and to play it back during the week. The average length of treatment was 19 weeks. Although both treatments produced improvement in complicated grief symptoms, there was a higher response rate and a faster time to response in the complicated grief treatment. This treatment would appear to hold considerable promise for people who are struggling with complicated grief.

Perhaps the main implication of this work for practicing clinicians is that they should not assume that one type of intervention will work best for everyone. As Jordan and Neimeyer (2003) have emphasized, "It is a truism that grief is unique to each individual, yet this wisdom is rarely reflected in the design and delivery of services to the bereaved" (p. 782). They suggest that treating clinicians focus more attention on such issues as whether the client has experienced previous traumas or losses, as well as the client's personality structure, coping style, and available support resources.

This work suggests that it is essential for program administrators to focus their efforts on identifying high-risk mourners. This task could be facilitated by the development of screening tools that make it possible to identify people at risk for subsequent problems. As was described earlier, Prigerson and her associates (1995) have developed an Inventory of Complicated Mourning that has predictive validity regarding those who are likely to develop complicated grief. It would be useful to have screening tools that could quickly and reliably assess other risk factors and resources, such as trauma history and available social support.

One consistent finding that has emerged from the intervention studies reviewed here is that those who seek treatment are likely to show better results from grief therapy than those who are recruited into a treatment (see Stroebe, Schut, & Stroebe ., 2005b, for a more detailed discussion). It is not clear whether this occurs because those who seek treatment are more likely to have serious problems and hence benefit more from the treatment, or whether other important factors underlie this effect. However, as was noted earlier, there is evidence to indicate that individuals with complicated grief are less likely to seek treatment than those whose grief is not associated with complications. This suggests that those most in need of help may be least likely to seek and obtain it. At this point, little is known about what percentage of high-risk mourners seek help. It would also be highly useful to understand the reasons that high-risk mourners often do not seek help. Clearly, it is important for administrators and policymakers to find ways of reaching out to high-risk mourners who do not avail themselves of treatment.

Other Care Providers

Studies on help seeking among the bereaved have shown that only a small percentage of those who experience major mental health problems following bereavement seek professional help (see Jacobs, 1993, for a more detailed discussion). To the extent that they seek assistance at all, bereaved individuals are far more likely to approach physicians, nurses, or clergymen than they are to seek formal grief counseling or therapy. Hence, it is important to ask whether these care providers may hold assumptions about the grieving process that interfere with their ability to provide effective help and support to the bereaved.

There is evidence to suggest that physicians and nurses do not receive much training about grief, and an examination of commonly used textbooks suggests that such books often perpetuate the myths of coping. For example, books written for nurses and physicians frequently maintain that people go through stages of emotional response as they come to terms with the loss, and that failure to exhibit distress is indicative of a problem (see, e.g., Potter & Perry, 1997). Clearly, it is important for care providers to recognize that particularly with certain kinds of loss, it is normative to exhibit little distress, and that this may be indicative of resilience.

How much do physicians and clergy know about the risk factors associated with complications of bereavement? Do they know, for example, that a large percentage of parents who experience the sudden, traumatic loss of a child experience high levels of symptoms for years after the loss? If they are not aware of these findings, they may convey to bereaved parents that they should be over the loss, thus contributing to the burden such parents are already shouldering. In our experience, it is common for physicians and those in the clergy to assume that prolonged grief is indicative of a weakness or coping failure on the part of the bereaved. It is also important for physicians and clergymen to have a good understanding of the symptomology that accompanies particular types of loss. For example, they could be far more helpful to those who encounter sudden, traumatic losses if they understand that such losses are often accompanied by post-traumatic stress symptoms. Many studies have suggested that following the traumatic death of a loved one, survivors are frightened by such symptoms as loss of memory, concentration problems, and intrusive thoughts or images of the deceased (Dyregrov et al., 2003), Physicians and clergymen are in a unique position to normalize disturbing symptoms among bereaved who are not receiving grief therapy or treatment. Bereaved individuals are likely to benefit from learning that their symptoms are understandable, given what they have been through, and do not convey mental illness or coping failure.

Knowledge of risk factors not only would help to ensure that bereaved people are treated more compassionately by their physicians and clergymen but also would increase the likelihood that those who would benefit from counseling are encouraged to seek help. At present, little is known about how common it is for these care providers to make referrals, or whether they are knowledgeable about how or where to refer bereaved people for grief counseling.

Considering the impact of bereavement on mortality, particularly among men who lose their spouses, it would also be prudent for clergy to encourage these men to see their physicians. These men would benefit from encouragement, from physicians as well as clergymen, to take other positive steps to maintain their health. Clergymen may also be in a good position to mobilize support for the bereaved, particularly for widowed men who may have relied primarily on their wives for support and companionship.

The Bereaved and Their Support Providers

At the present time, what expectations or assumptions about the grieving process are prevalent among laypersons? When a person experiences a loss, does he or she expect to go through stages of grief, beginning with intense distress? If intense distress is not experienced, is this a source of concern? How knowledgeable are laypersons about the symptoms of grief, and how do they judge and evaluate their own reactions? Do they believe that it is necessary to "work through" the loss, and if so, what kinds of behaviors do they engage in to facilitate this? Do they assess their progress according to a timetable concerning when they think they should be recovered? Are laypersons aware that symptoms are more intense and prolonged following certain kinds of losses, or do they hold themselves up to unrealistically high standards and judge themselves harshly if they are not able to move on within a year or so? Given that most bereaved do not seek grief counseling or therapy, where do they turn for assistance, and to what extent are they able

to obtain information and/or support that is beneficial? It is also important to ascertain whether certain assumptions or beliefs about coping with loss are held by members of the bereaved person's support network and, if so, whether these facilitate or impede the receipt of effective support.

Unfortunately, few studies have focused on these questions, and at present little is known about how the grief process is viewed by the bereaved, or by those in their support network. However, there are some indications in the literature that many laypersons still believe in stages of emotional response. Elison and McGonigle (2003) describe a case in which one woman asked her therapist to do something to make her angry. When the therapist asked why she should do so, the client replied, "My neighbor told me that at this stage, I should be angry, and I'm not. "I'm afraid I'm not doing this right" (p. xxiii).

It also appears that laypersons have strong expectations that the bereaved will go through a period of intense distress. Those who do not appear to be showing enough distress may elicit judgmental reactions from others. A person who fails to react with sufficient distress may also be thought to be "in denial," with friends conveying the sentiment that "it hasn't hit her yet." Elison and McGonigle (2003) have pointed out that in cases of deaths that occur under suspicious circumstances, failure to show distress may be shown as evidence as guilt. They maintained that the failure of John and Patty Ramsey to show distress following the murder of their daughter, JonBenet, "convicted them in the court of public opinion."

In their insightful book *Liberating Losses,* Elison and McGonigle (2003) describe several situations in which people feel relieved or liberated following the loss of a loved one. For example, they note that it is common to experience feelings of relief after a long period of caregiving. Such feelings are also prevalent when a person has been involved in a relationship with someone who has been a constant source of criticism, abuse, or oppression. In these cases, the death may be viewed as a "God given divorce" (see also Sanders, 1999). Elison and McGonigle (2003) note how outsiders' comments are often unhelpful. For example, a friend may say "it's okay to cry," or "You must miss him terribly," thus making the survivor feel even more guilty and conspicuous. Or they may make comments like, "I can't believe you're getting rid of his things already," implying that the survivor's reactions are inappropriate.

Regarding expectations about recovery, some studies suggest that the bereaved judge themselves harshly if they continue to show intense distress beyond the first few months. A frequent complaint of the bereaved is that others expect them to be recovered from the loss after the first few months or so. There is also evidence that others attempt to encourage a prompt recovery following the loss, and that the bereaved do not find this helpful (Ingram et al., 2001; Lehman, Ellard, & Wortman, 1986). For example, following the death of a spouse, friends might try to arouse the surviving spouse's interest in new activities or in the resumption of old hobbies or interests. It is also common for others to bring up the topic of remarriage. Discussions of this topic are often initiated within a few days or weeks of the spouse's death.

Other kinds of responses that are frequently made by potential support providers but that are not regarded as helpful by the bereaved include attempts to block discussions about the loss or displays of feelings (e.g., "Crying won't bring him back"); minimization of the problem (e.g., "You had so many good years together"); invoking a religious or philosophical perspective (e.g., "God needed him more than you did"); giving advice (e.g., "You should consider getting a dog; they're wonderful companions"); and identification with feelings (e.g., "I know how you feel—I lost my second cousin"). It is also common for those in the support network to ask inappropriate questions. They may ask about such matters as how the death occurred (e.g., "Was he wearing a seat belt?"); about financial matters (e.g., "How are you going to spend all of that insurance money?"); or about the loved one's possessions (e.g., "What are you going to do with his tools?"). Studies have shown that unsupportive social interactions account for a significant amount of the variance in depression among the bereaved, beyond the variance explained by the level of present grief (Ingram et al., 2001). Such comments are more likely to be made by relatives or close friends than they are among casual acquaintances of the survivor (see Wortman, Wolff, & Bonanno, 2004, for a more detailed discussion).

What types of responses from support providers do the bereaved regard as beneficial? Research indicates that they value the opportunity to talk with others about their feelings when they elect to do so (Lehman et al., 1986; Marwit & Carusa, 1998). In fact, there is evidence that if people want to talk about the loss and are blocked from doing so, they become more depressed over time (Lepore et al., 1996). The bereaved also find it helpful when others convey a supportive presence (e.g., "I am here for you") or express concern (e.g., "I care what happens to you"). Tangible assistance, such as help with errands or meals, is typically regarded as helpful. Finally, contact with a similar other is judged to be very helpful. Unlike those who have not experienced such a loss, they may have a more accurate understanding of what the bereaved has been through. Contact with similar others can also reassure the bereaved that their own feelings and behaviors are normal.

In our judgment, it would be beneficial for the bereaved themselves, and their potential support providers, to have greater awareness of the extraordinary variability in responses to loss. We believe that awareness of the conditions under which the bereaved may fail to experience or exhibit distress, or may experience grief that is more intense and prolonged than the norm, would also have a positive impact. Hopefully, greater understanding of the available research will result in treatment of the bereaved that is less judgmental and more compassionate.

References

Archer, J. (1999). *The nature of grief: The evolution and psychology of reactions to loss.* New York: Routledge.

Attig, T. (1996). *How we grieve: Relearning the world.* New York: Oxford University Press.

Attig, T. (2000). Anticipatory mourning and the transition to loving in absence. In T. A. Rando (Ed.), *Clinical dimensions of anticipatory mourning: Theory and practice in working with dying, their loved ones, and their caregivers* (pp. 115–133). Champaign, IL: Research Press.

Balk, D. (1983). Adolescents' grief reactions and self-concept perceptions following sibling death: A study of 33 teenagers. *Journal of Youth and Adolescence, 12,* 137–161.

Baltes, M. M., & Skrotzki, E. (1995). Tod im Alter: Eigene Endlichkeit und Partnerverlust [Death in old age: Finality and loss of spouse]. In R. Oerter & L. Montada (Eds.), *Entwicklungspsychologie* (3rd ed., pp. 1137–1146). Munich, Germany: PVU.

Batten, M., & Oltjenbruns, K. A. (1999). Adolescent sibling bereavement as a catalyst for spiritual bereavement as a catalyst for spiritual development: A model for understanding. *Death Studies, 23,* 529–546.

Belitsky, R., & Jacobs, S. (1986). Bereavement, attachment theory, and mental disorders. *Psychiatric Annals, 16,* 276–280.

Bisconti, T. L., Bergeman, C. S., & Boker, S. M. (2004). *Social support as a predictor of variability: An examination of recent widows' adjustment trajectories.* Manuscript submitted for publication.

Boerner, K., & Heckhausen, J. (2003). To have and have not: Adaptive bereavement by transforming mental ties to the deceased. *Death Studies, 27,* 199–226.

Boerner, K., Schulz, R., & Horowitz, A. (2004). Positive aspects of caregiving and adaptation to bereavement. *Psychology and Aging, 19,* 668–675.

Boerner, K., & Wortman, C. B., & Bonanno, G. (2005). Resilient or at risk? A four-year study of older adults who initially showed high or low distress following conjugal loss. *Journal of Gerontology: Series B: Psychological Sciences and Social Sciences, 60B,* P67–P73.

Bonanno, G. A. (2001). Grief and emotion: A social-functional perspective. In M. S. Stroebe & R. O. Hansson (Eds.), *Handbook of bereavement research: Consequences, coping, and care* (pp. 493–515). Washington, DC: American Psychological Association.

Bonanno, G. A. (2005). Resilience in the face of potential trauma. *Current Directions in Psychological Science, 14,* 135–138.

Bonanno, G. A., & Field, N. P. (2001). Evaluating the delayed grief hypothesis across 5 years of bereavement. *American Behavioral Scientist, 44,* 798–816.

Bonanno, G. A., & Kaltman, S. (1999). Toward an integrative perspective on bereavement. *Psychological Bulletin, 125,* 760–786.

Bonanno, G. A., & Kaltman, S. (2001). The varieties of grief experience. *Clinical Psychology Review, 21,* 705–734.

Bonanno, G. A., & Keltner, D. (1997). Facial expressions of emotion and the course of conjugal bereavement. *Journal of Abnormal Psychology, 106,* 126–137.

Bonanno, G. A., Keltner, D., Holen, A., & Horowitz, M. J. (1995). When avoiding unpleasant emotion might not be such a bad thing: Verbal-autonomic response dissociation and midlife conjugal bereavement. *Journal of Personality and Social Psychology, 46,* 975–985.

Bonanno, G. A., Mihalecz, M. C., & LeJeune, J. T.

(1999). The core emotion themes of conjugal loss. *Motivation and Emotion, 23,* 175–201.

Bonanno, G. A., Moskowitz, J. T., Papa, A., & Folkman, S. (2005). Resilience to loss in bereaved spouses, bereaved parents, and bereaved gay men. *Journal of Personality and Social Psychology, 88,* 827–843.

Bonanno, G. A., Papa, A., Lalande, K., Zhang, N., & Noll, J. G. (2005). Grief processing and deliberate grief avoidance: A prospective comparison of bereaved spouses and parents in the United States and the People's Republic of China. *Journal of Consulting and Clinical Psychology, 73,* 86–98.

Bonanno, G. A., Rennicke, C., & Dekel, S. (in press). Self-enhancement among high-exposure survivors of the September 11th terrorist attack: Resilience or social maladjustment? *Journal of Personality and Social Psychology.*

Bonanno, G. A., Wortman, C. B., Lehman, D., Tweed, R., Sonnega, J., Carr, D., et al. (2002). Resilience to loss, chronic grief, and their pre-bereavement predictors. *Journal of Personality and Social Psychology, 83,* 1150–1164.

Bonanno, G. A., Wortman, C. B., & Nesse, R. M. (2004). Prospective patterns of resilience and maladjustment during widowhood. *Psychology and Aging, 19,* 260–271.

Bournstein, P. E., Clayton, P. J., Halikas, J. A., Maurice, W. L., & Robins, E. (1973). The depression of widowhood after thirteen months. *British Journal of Psychiatry, 122,* 561–566.

Bower, J. E., Kemeny, M. E., Taylor, S. E., & Fahey, J. L. (2003). Finding positive meaning and its association with natural killer cell cytotoxicity among participants in a bereavement-related disclosure intervention. *Annals of Behavioral Medicine, 25,* 146–155.

Bowlby, J. (1969). *Attachment.* (*Attachment and loss, Vol. 1*). New York: Basic Books.

Bowlby, J. (1973). *Separation: Anxiety and anger.* (*Attachment and loss, Vol. 2*). New York: Basic Books.

Bowlby, J. (1980). *Loss: Sadness and depression.* (*Attachment and loss, Vol. 3*). New York: Basic Books.

Bruce, M. L., Kim, K, Leaf, P. J., & Jacobs, S. (1990). Depressive episodes and dysphoria resulting from conjugal bereavement in a prospective community sample. *American Journal of Psychiatry, 147,* 608–611.

Carnelley, K. B., Wortman, C. B., Bolger, N., & Burke, C. T. (in press). The time course of adjustment to widowhood: Evidence from a national probability sample. *Journal of Personality and Social Psychology.*

Carnelley, K. B., Wortman, C. B., & Kessler, R. C.

(1999). The impact of widowhood on depression: Findings from a prospective survey. *Psychological Medicine, 29,* 1111–1123.

Carr, D. (2003). A "good death" for whom? Quality of spouse's death and psychological distress among older widowed persons. *Journal of Health and Social Behavior, 44,* 215–232.

Carr, D. (2004). Black/white differences in psychological adjustment to spousal loss among older adults. *Research on Aging, 26,* 591–622.

Carr, D., House, J. S., Kessler, R. C., Nesse, R. M., Sonnega, J., & Wortman, C. (2000). Marital quality and psychological adjustment to widowhood among older adults: A longitudinal analysis. *Journal of Gerontology: Series B: Psychological Sciences and Social Sciences, 55B,*S197–S207.

Carr, D., Wortman, C. B., & Wolff, K. (2006). How Americans die. In D. Carr, R. Nesse, & C. B. Wortman (Eds.), *Spousal bereavement in late life* (pp. 49–78). New York: Springer.

Christakis, N., & Iwashyna, T. (2003). The health impact on health care on families: A matched cohort study of hospice use by decedents and mortality outcomes in surviving, widowed spouses. *Social Science and Medicine, 57,* 465–574.

Cleiren, M. P. H. D. (1993). *Bereavement and adaptation: A comparative study of the aftermath of death.* Philadelphia: Hemisphere.

Cleiren, M., Diekstra, R., Kerkhof, A., & van der Wal, J. (1994). Mode of death and kinship in bereavement: Focusing on "who" rather than "how." *Crisis, 15*(1), 22–36.

Datson, S. L., & Marwit, S. J. (1997). Personality constructs and perceived presence of deceased loved ones. *Death Studies, 21,* 131–146.

Deutsch, H. (1937). Absence of grief. *Psychoanalytic Quarterly, 6,* 12–22.

Dyregrov, K., Nordanger, D., & Dyregrov, A. (2003). Predictors of psychosocial distress after suicide, SIDS and accidents. *Death Studies, 27,* 143–165.

Elison, J., & McGonigle, C. (2003). *Liberating losses: When death brings relief.* Cambridge, MA: Perseus.

Field, N. P., & Friedrichs, M. (2004). Continuing bonds in coping with the death of a husband. *Death Studies, 28,* 597–620.

Field, N. P., Gal-Oz, E., & Bonanno, G. A. (2003). Continuing bonds and adjustment at 5 years after the death of a spouse. *Journal of Consulting and Clinical Psychology, 71,* 110–117.

Field, N. P., Nichols, C., Holen, A., & Horowitz, M. J. (1999). The relation of continuing attachment to adjustment in conjugal bereavement. *Journal of Consulting and Clinical Psychology, 67,* 212–218.

Fleming, S., & Robinson, P. J. (1991). The application of cognitive therapy to the bereaved. In T. M. Vallis & J. L. Howes (Eds.), *The challenge of cognitive therapy: Applications to nontraditional populations* (pp. 135–158). New York: Plenum.

Folkman, S. (1997a). Introduction to the special section: Use of bereavement narratives to predict well-being in gay men whose partner died of AIDS—Four theoretical perspectives. *Journal of Personality and Social Psychology, 72,* 851–854.

Folkman, S. (1997b). Positive psychological states and coping with severe stress. *Social Science and Medicine, 45,* 1207–1221.

Folkman, S. (2001). Revised coping theory and the process of bereavement. In M. S. Stroebe & R. O. Hansson (Eds.), *Handbook of bereavement research: Consequences, coping, and care* (pp. 563–584). Washington, DC: American Psychological Association.

Folkman, S., Chesney, M., Collette, L., Boccellari, A., & Cooke, M. (1996). Postbereavement depressive mood and its prebereavement predictors in HIV+ and HIV–gay men. *Journal of Personality and Social Psychology, 70,* 336–348.

Folkman, S., & Moskowitz, J. T. (2000). Stress, positive emotion, and coping. *Current Directions in Psychological Science, 9,* 115–118.

Fraley, R. C., & Shaver, P. R. (1999). Loss and bereavement: Bowlby's theory and recent controversies concerning "grief work" and the nature of detachment. In J. Cassidy & P. R. Shaver (Eds.), *Handbook of attachment theory and research: Theory, research, and clinical applications* (pp. 735–759). New York: Guilford.

Fredrickson, B. L. (1998). What good are positive emotions? *Review of General Psychology, 2,* 300–319.

Fredrickson, B. L. (2001). The role of positive emotions in positive psychology: The broaden-and-build theory of positive emotions. *American Psychologist, 56,* 218–226.

Fredrickson, B. L., Tugade, M. M., Waugh, C. E., & Larkin, G. R. (2003). What good are positive emotions? A prospective study of resilience and emotions following the terrorist attacks on the United States on September 11, 2001. *Journal of Personality and Social Psychology, 84,* 365–376.

Freud, S. (1917/1957). Mourning and melancholia. In J. Strachey (Ed.), *The standard edition of the complete works of Sigmund Freud* (Vol. 14, pp. 152–170). London: Hogarth Press.

Glick, I. O., Weiss, R. S., & Parkes, C. M. (1974). *The first year of bereavement.* New York: Wiley.

Gowell, E. C. (1992). *Good grief rituals: Tools for healing.* New York: Station Hill Press.

Hagman, G. (1995). Mourning: A review and reconsideration. *International Journal of Psycho-Analysis, 76,* 909–925.

Hagman, G. (2001). Beyond decathexis: Toward a new psychoanalytic understanding and treatment of mourning. In R. A. Neimeyer (Ed.), *Meaning, reconstruction and the experience of loss* (pp. 13–31). Washington, DC: American Psychological Association.

Hogan, N. S., & DeSantis, L. (1994). Things that help and hinder adolescent sibling bereavement. *Western Journal of Nursing Research, 16,* 132–153.

Horowitz, M. J. (1976). *Stress response syndromes.* Oxford, England: Jason Aronson.

Horowitz, M. J. (1985). Anxious states of mind induced by stress. In A. H. Tuma & J. D. Maser (Eds.), *Anxiety and the anxiety disorders* (pp. 619–631). Hillsdale, NJ: Erlbaum.

Horowitz, M. J. (1990). A model of mourning: Change in schemas of self and other. *Journal of American Psychoanalytic Association, 38,* 297–324.

Ingram, K. M., Jones, D. A., & Smith, N. G. (2001). Adjustment among people who have experienced AIDS-related multiple loss: The role of unsupportive social interactions, social support, and coping. *Omega: Journal of Death and Dying, 43,* 287–309.

Jacobs, S. (1993). *Pathological grief: Maladaptation to loss.* Washington, DC: American Psychiatric Press.

Jacobs, S., Mazure, C., & Prigerson, H. (2000). Diagnostic criteria for traumatic grief. *Death Studies, 24,* 185–199.

Jordan, J. R., & Neimeyer, R. A. (2003). Does grief counseling work? *Death Studies, 27,* 765–786.

Kaltman, S., & Bonanno, G. A. (2003). Trauma and bereavement: Examining the impact of sudden and violent death. *Journal of Anxiety Disorders, 17,* 131–147.

Keltner, D., & Bonanno, G. A. (1997). A study of laughter and dissociation: Distinct correlates of laughter and smiling during bereavement. *Journal of Personality and Social Psychology, 73,* 687–702.

Klass, D., Silverman, P. R., & Nickman, S. L. (1996). *Continuing bonds: New understandings of grief.* Philadelphia: Taylor and Francis.

Klass, D., & Walter, J. (2001). Processes of grieving: How bonds are continued. In M. S. Stroebe & R. O. Hansson (Eds.), *Handbook of bereavement research: Consequences, coping, and care* (pp. 431–448). Washington, DC: American Psychological Association.

Kovac, S. H., & Range, L. M. (2000). Writing projects: Lessening undergraduates' unique suicidal bereavement. *Suicide and Life-Threatening Behavior, 30,* 50–60.

Kübler-Ross, E. (1969). *On death and dying.* New York: Springer.

Lazare, A. (1989). Bereavement and unresolved grief. In A. Lazare (Ed.), *Outpatient psychiatry: Diagnosis and treatment* (2nd ed., pp. 381–397). Baltimore: Williams and Wilkins.

Lazarus, R., & Folkman, S. (1984). *Stress, appraisal, and coping.* New York: Springer.

Lazarus, R. S., Kanner, A. D., & Folkman, S. (1980). Emotions: A cognitive-phenomenological analysis. In R. Plutchik & H. Kellerman (Eds.), *Emotions: Theory, research, and experience* (Vol. 1, pp. 189–217). New York: Academic Press.

Lehman, D. R., Ellard, J. H., & Wortman, C. B. (1986). Social support for the bereaved: Recipients' and providers' perspectives on what is helpful. *Journal of Consulting and Clinical Psychology, 54,* 438–446.

Lehman, D. R., Wortman, C. B., & Williams, A. F. (1987). Long-term effects of losing a spouse or child in a motor vehicle crash. *Journal of Personality and Social Psychology, 52,* 218–231.

Lepore, S. J., Silver, R. C., Wortman, C. B., & Wayment, H. A. (1996). Social constraints, intrusive thoughts, and depressive symptoms among bereaved mothers. *Journal of Personality and Social Psychology, 70,* 271–282.

Lepore, S. J., & Smyth, J. M. (2002). *The writing cure: How expressive writing promotes health and emotional well-being.* Washington: American Psychological Association.

Lichtenstein, P., Gatz, M., Pedersen, N. L., Berg, S., & McClearn, G. E. (1996). A co-twin control study of response to widowhood. *Journal of Gerontology. Series B, Psychological Sciences and Social Sciences, 51,* 279–289.

Lichtenthal, W. G., Cruess, D. G., & Prigerson, H. G. (2004). A case for establishing complicated grief as a distinct mental disorder in *DSM-V. Clinical Psychology Review, 24,* 637–662.

Lopata, H. Z. (1979). *Women as widows: Support systems.* New York: Elsevier.

Lumley, M. A., Tojeck, T. M., & Macklem, D. J. (2002). The effects of written and verbal disclosure among repressive and alexithymic people. In S. J. Lepore & J. M. Smyth (Eds.), *The writing cure: How expressive writing promotes health and emotional well-being* (pp. 75–95). Washington, DC: American Psychological Association.

Lund, D. A., Dimond, M. F., Caserta, M. S., Johnson, R. J., Poulton, J. L., & Connelly, J. R. (1985–1986). Identifying elderly with coping difficulties after two years of bereavement. *Omega, 16,* 213–224.

Lund, D. A., Caserta, M. S., & Dimond, M. F. (1986). Impact of bereavement on the self-conceptions of older surviving spouses. *Symbolic Interaction, 9,* 235–244.

Malkinson, R. (2001). Cognitive-behavioral therapy of grief: A review and application. *Research on Social Work Practice, 11,* 671–698.

Malkinson, R., Rubin, S. S., & Witztum, E. (2000). *Traumatic and nontraumatic loss and bereavement:*

Clinical theory and practice. Madison, CT: Psychosocial Press.

Marris, P. (1958). *Widows and their families.* London: Routledge and Kegan Paul.

Martin, J. L, & Doka, K. (2000). *Men don't cry . . . women do: Transcending gender stereotypes of grief.* Philadelphia: Brunner/Mazel.

Marwit, S. J., & Carusa, S. S. (1998). Communicated support following loss: Examining the experiences of parental death and parental divorce in adolescence. *Death Studies, 22,* 237–255.

Marwit, S. J., & Klass, D. (1996). Grief and the role of the inner representation of the deceased. In D. Klass & P. R. Silverman (Eds.), *Continuing bonds: New understandings of grief* (pp. 297–309). Philadelphia: Taylor and Francis.

McIntosh, D., Silver, R., & Wortman, C. B. (1993). Religion's role in adjustment to a negative life event: Coping with the loss of a child. *Journal of Personality and Social Psychology, 65,* 812–821.

Mendes de Leon, C. F., Kasl, S. V., & Jacobs, S. (1994). A prospective study of widowhood and changes in symptoms of depression in a community sample of the elderly. *Psychological Medicine, 24,* 613–624.

Middleton, W., Burnett, P., Raphael, B., & Martinek, N. (1996). The bereavement response: A cluster analysis. *British Journal of Psychiatry, 169,* 167–171.

Middleton, W., Moylan, A., Raphael, B., Burnett, P., & Martinek, N. (1993). An international perspective on bereavement related concepts. *Australian and New Zealand Journal of Psychiatry, 27,* 457–463.

Middleton, W., Raphael, B., Burnett, P., & Martinek, N. (1998). A longitudinal study comparing bereavement phenomena in recently bereaved spouses, adult children and parents. *Australian and New Zealand Journal of Psychiatry, 32,* 235–241.

Miller, E. D., & Omarzu, J. (1998). New directions in loss research. In J. Harvey (Ed.), *Perspectives on loss: A sourcebook* (pp. 3–20). Washington, DC: Taylor & Francis.

Miller, E., & Wortman, C. B. (2002). Gender differences in mortality and morbidity following a major stressor: The case of conjugal bereavement. In G. Weidner, S. M. Kopp, & M. Kristenson (Eds.), *Heart disease: Environment, stress and gender.* NATO Science Series, Series I: Life and Behavioural Sciences. Volume 327. Amsterdam: IOS Press.

Moskowitz, J. T., Folkman, S., & Acree, M. (2003). Do positive psychological states shed light on recovery from bereavement? Findings from a 3-year longitudinal study. *Death Studies, 27,* 471–500.

Moskowitz, J. T., Folkman, S., Collette, L., & Vittinghoff, E. (1996). Coping and mood during AIDS-related caregiving and bereavement. *Annals of Behavioral Medicine, 18,* 49–57.

Murphy, S. A. (1996). Parent bereavement stress and preventive intervention following the violent deaths of adolescent or young adult children. *Death Studies, 20,* 441–452.

Murphy, S. A., Das Gupta, A., Cain, K. C., Johnson, L. C., Lohan, J., Wu, L., et al. (1999). Changes in parents' mental distress after the violent death of an adolescent or young adult child: A longitudinal prospective analysis. *Death Studies, 23,* 129–159.

Murphy, S. A., Johnson, L. C., Chung, I., & Beaton, R. D. (2003). The prevalence of PTSD following the violent death of a child and predictors of change 5 years later. *Journal of Traumatic Stress, 16,* 17–25.

Murphy, S. A., Johnson, L. C., & Lohan, J. (2002). The aftermath of the violent death of a child: An integration of the assessment of parents' mental distress and PTSD during the first 5 years of bereavement. *Journal of Loss and Trauma, 7,* 203–222.

Murphy, S. A., Johnson, L. C., & Lohan, J. (2003). Finding meaning in a child's violent death: A five-year prospective analysis of parents' personal narratives and empirical data. *Death Studies, 27,* 381–404.

Murphy, S. A., Johnson, L. C., Wu, L., Fan, J. J., & Lohan, J. (2003). Bereaved parents' outcomes 4 to 60 months after their children's death by accident, suicide, or homicide: A comparative study demonstrating differences. *Death Studies, 27,* 39–61.

Neimeyer, R. A. (1997). Problems and prospects in constructivist psychotherapy. *Journal of Constructivist Psychology, 10,* 51–74.

Neimeyer, R. A. (1998). *Lessons of loss: A guide to coping.* Boston: McGraw-Hill.

Neimeyer, R. A. (1999). Narrative strategies in grief therapy. *Journal of Constructivist Psychology, 12,* 65–85.

Neimeyer, R. A. (2000). Searching for the meaning of meaning: Grief therapy and the process of reconstruction. *Death Studies, 24,* 541–558.

Neimeyer, R. A. (2001). *Meaning, reconstruction and the experience of loss.* Washington, DC: American Psychological Association.

Neimeyer, R. A. (2006). Widowhood, grief and the quest for meaning: A narrative perspective on resilience. In D. Carr, R. M. Nesse, & C. B. Wortman (Eds.), *Spousal bereavement in late life* (pp. 227–252). New York: Springer.

Nesse, R. M., Wortman, C. B., & House, J. S. (2006). Introduction: A history of the Changing Lives of

Older Couples Study. In D. Carr, R. Nesse, & C. B. Wortman (Eds.), *Spousal Bereavement in Late Life* (pp. xxi–xxxi). New York: Springer.

Nolen-Hoeksema, S. (1991). Responses to depression and their effects on the duration of depressive episodes. *Journal of Abnormal Psychology, 100,* 569–582.

Nolen-Hoeksema, S. (2001). Ruminative coping and adjustment to bereavement. In M. S. Stroebe & R. O. Hansson (Eds.), *Handbook of bereavement research: Consequences, coping, and care* (pp. 545–562). Washington, DC: American Psychological Association.

Nolen-Hoeksema, S., & Larson, J. (1999). *Coping with loss.* Mahwah, NJ: Erlbaum.

Nolen-Hoeksema, S., McBride, A., & Larson, J. (1997). Rumination and psychological distress among bereaved partners. *Journal of Personality and Social Psychology, 72,* 855–862.

Norman, S. A., Lumley, M. A., Dooley, J. A., & Diamond, M. P. (in press). For whom does it work? Moderators of the effects of written emotional disclosure in women with chronic pelvic pain. *Psychosomatic Medicine.*

Normand, C. L., Silverman, P. R., & Nickman, S. L. (1996). Bereaved children's changing relationships with the deceased. In D. Klass & P. R. Silverman (Eds.), *Continuing bonds: New understandings of grief* (pp. 87–111). Philadelphia: Taylor and Francis.

Ong, A. D., Bergeman, C. S., & Bisconit, T. L. (2004). The role of daily positive emotions during conjugal bereavement. *Journals of Gerontology: Series B: Psychological Sciences and Social Psychology, 59B,* 168–176.

Osterweis, M., Solomon, F., & Green, F. (1984). *Bereavement: Reactions, consequences, and care.* Washington, DC: National Academy Press.

Pargament, K. I., & Park, C. L. (1995). Merely a defense? The variety of religious means and ends. *Journal of Social Issues, 51,* 13–32.

Parkes, C. M., & Weiss, R. S. (1983). *Recovery from bereavement.* New York: Basic Books.

Pennebaker, J. W., & Beall, S. K. (1986). Confronting a traumatic event: Toward an understanding of inhibition and disease. *Journal of Abnormal Psychology, 95,* 274–281.

Pennebaker, J. W., Zech, E., & Rime, B. (2001). Disclosing and sharing emotion: Psychological, social, and health consequences. In M. S. Stroebe & R. O. Hansson (Eds.), *Handbook of bereavement research: Consequences, coping, and care* (pp. 517–543). Washington, DC: American Psychological Association.

Pinquart, M., & Sorenson, S. (2003a). Differences between caregivers and noncaregivers in psychological health and physical health: A meta-analysis. *Psychology and Aging, 18,* 250–267.

Pinquart, M., & Sorenson, S. (2003b). Associations of stressors and uplifts of caregiving with caregiver burden and depressive mood: A meta-analysis. *Journals of Gerentology: Series B: Psychological Sciences and Social Sciences, 58B,* P112–P128.

Potter, P. A., & Perry, A. G. (1997). *Fundamentals of nursing: Concepts, process, and practice* (4th ed.). St. Louis, MO: Mosby.

Prigerson, H. (2004). Complicated grief: When the path of adjustment leads to a dead-end. *Bereavement Care, 23,* 38–40.

Prigerson, H. G., Cherlin, E., Chen, J. H., Kasl, S. V., Hurzeler, R., & Bradley, E. H. (2003). The stressful caregiving adult reactions to experiences of dying (SCARED) scale: A measure for assessing caregiver exposure to distress in terminal care. *American Journal of Geriatric Psychiatry, 11,* 309–319.

Prigerson, H. G., Maciejewski, P. K., Reynolds, C. F., III, Bierhals, A. J., Newsom, J. T., Fasiczka, A., et al. (1995). Inventory of Complicated Grief: A scale to measure maladaptive symptoms of loss. *Psychiatry Research, 59*(1–2), 65–79.

Ramsay, R. W., & Happee, J. A. (1977). The stress of bereavement: Components and treatment. In C. D. Spielberger, & I. G. Sarason (Eds.), *Stress and anxiety: IV* (pp. 53–64). Oxford, UK: Hemisphere.

Rando, T. A. (1984). *Grief, dying, and death.* Champaign, IL: Research Press.

Rando, T. A. (1993). *Treatment of complicated mourning.* Champaign, IL: Research Press.

Range, L. M., Kovac, S. H., & Marion, M. S. (2000). Does writing about the bereavement lessen grief following sudden, unintentional death? *Death Studies, 24,* 115–134.

Raphael, B. (1983). *The anatomy of bereavement.* New York: Basic Books.

Raphael, B., & Nunn, K. (1988). Counseling the bereaved. *Journal of Social Issues, 44,* 191–206.

Rees, W. D. (1971). The hallucinations of widowhood. *British Medical Journal, 4,* 37–41.

Richards, T., Acree, M., & Folkman, S. (1999). Spiritual aspects of loss among partners of men with AIDS: Postbereavement follow-up. *Death Studies, 23,* 105–127.

Richards, T. A., & Folkman, S. (1997). Spiritual aspects of loss at the time of a partner's death from AIDS. *Death Studies, 21,* 527–552.

Russac, R. J., Steighner, N. S., & Canto, A. (2002). Grief work versus continuing bonds: A call for paradigm integration or replacement? *Death Studies, 26,* 463–478.

Sanders, C. M. (1989). *Grief: The mourning after.* New York: Wiley.

Sanders, C. M. (1993). Risk factors in bereavement outcome. In M. Stroebe, W. Stroebe, & R. O. Hansson (Eds.), *Handbook of bereavement: Theory, research and intervention* (pp. 255–267). New York: Cambridge University Press.

Sanders, C. M. (1999). *Grief: The mourning after* (2nd ed.). New York: Wiley.

Schulz, R., Beach, S. R., Lind, B., Martire, L. M., Zdaniuk, B., Hirsch, C., et al. (2001). Involvement in caregiving and adjustment to death of a spouse: Findings from the caregiver health effects study. *Journal of the American Medical Association, 285,* 3123–3129.

Schulz, R., Mendelson, A. B., & Haley, W. E. (2003). End-of-life care and the effects of bereavement on family caregivers of persons with dementia. *New England Journal of Medicine, 349,* 1936–1942.

Schut, H., Stroebe, M. S., van den Bout, J., & Terheggen, M. (2001). The efficacy of bereavement interventions: Determining who benefits. In M. S. Stroebe, R. O. Hansson, W. Stroebe, & H. Schut (Eds.), *Handbook of bereavement research: Consequences, coping, and care* (pp. 705–737). Washington, DC: American Psychological Association.

Segal, D. L., Bogaards, J. A., Becker, L. A., & Chatman, C. (1999). Effects of emotional expression on adjustment to spousal loss among older adults. *Journal of Mental Health and Aging, 5,* 297–310.

Shaver, P. R., & Tancredy, C. M. (2001). Emotion, attachment, and bereavement: A conceptual commentary. In M. S. Stroebe, R. O. Hansson, W. Stroebe, & H. Schut (Eds.), *Handbook of bereavement research: Consequences, coping, and care* (pp. 63–88). Washington, DC: American Psychological Association.

Shear, K., Frank, E., Houck, P. R., & Reynolds, C. F., III. (2005). Treatment of complicated grief: A randomized controlled trial. *Journal of the American Medical Association, 293,* 2601–2608.

Shmotkin, D. (1999). Affective bonds of adult children with living versus deceased parents. *Psychology and Aging, 14,* 473–482.

Shuchter, S. R. (1986). *Dimensions of grief: Adjusting to the death of a spouse.* San Francisco, CA: Jossey-Bass.

Shuchter, S. R., & Zisook, S. (1993). The course of normal grief. In M. S. Stroebe & W. Stroebe (Eds.), *Handbook of bereavement: Theory, research, and intervention* (pp. 23–43). New York: Cambridge University Press.

Silverman, P. R., Baker, J., Cait, C., & Boerner, K. (2003). The effects of negative legacies on the adjustment of parentally bereaved children and adolescents. *Omega: Journal of Death and Dying, 46,* 335–352.

Silverman, P. R., Johnson, J., & Prigerson, H. G. (2001). Preliminary explorations of the effects of prior trauma and loss on risk for psychiatric disorders in recently widowed people. *Israel Journal of Psychiatry and Related Sciences, 38,* 202–215.

Silverman, P. R., & Nickman, S. L. (1996). Children's construction of their dead parents. In D. Klass, P. R. Silverman, & S. L. Nickman (Eds.), *Continuing bonds: New understandings of grief* (pp. 73–86). Philadelphia: Taylor and Francis.

Silverman, P. R., Nickman, S., & Worden, J. W. (1992). Detachment revisited: The child's reconstruction of a dead parent. *American Journal of Orthopsychiatry, 62,* 494–503.

Silverman, P. R., & Worden, J. W. (1992). Children's reactions in the early months after the death of a parent. *American Journal of Orthopsychiatry, 62,* 93–104.

Smyth, J. M. (1998). Written emotional expression: Effect sizes, outcome types, and moderating variables. *Journal of Consulting and Clinical Psychology, 66,* 174–184.

Smyth, J. M., & Greenberg, M. A. (2000). Scriptotherapy: The effects of writing about traumatic events. In P. R. Duberstein & J. M. Masling (Eds.), *Psychodynamic perspectives on sickness and health* (pp. 121–160). Washington, DC: American Psychological Association.

Stein, N. L., Folkman, S., Trabasso, T., & Christopher-Richards, A. (1997). Appraisal and goal processes as predictors of well-being in bereaved care-givers. *Journal of Personality and Social Psychology, 72,* 863–871.

Stroebe, M. S. (1992–1993). Coping with bereavement: A review of the grief work hypothesis. *Omega: Journal of Death and Dying, 26,* 19–42.

Stroebe, M. S., Hansson, R. O., & Stroebe, W. (1993). Contemporary themes and controversies in bereavement research. In M. S. Stroebe, W. Stroebe, & R. O. Hansson (Eds.), *Handbook of bereavement: Theory, research, and intervention* (pp. 457–476). Cambridge, England: Cambridge University Press.

Stroebe, M. S., Hansson, R. O., Stroebe, W., & Schut, H. (Eds.). (2001). *Handbook of bereavement research: Consequences, coping, and care.* Washington, DC: American Psychological Association.

Stroebe, M., & Schut, H. (1999). The dual process model of coping with bereavement: Rationale and description. *Death Studies, 23,* 197–224.

Stroebe, M. S., & Schut, H. (2001). Meaning making in the dual process model of coping with bereavement. In R. A. Neimeyer (Ed.), *Meaning reconstruction and the experience of loss* (pp. 55–

73). Washington, DC: American Psychological Association.

Stroebe, M., & Schut, H. (2005). To continue or relinquish bonds: A review of consequences for the bereaved. *Death Studies, 29,* 477–494.

Stroebe, M., Schut, H., & Stroebe, W. (2005a). Attachment in coping with bereavement: A theoretical integration. *Review of General Psychology, 9,* 48–66.

Stroebe, W., Schut, H., & Stroebe, M. S. (2005b). Grief work, disclosure, and counseling: Do they help the bereaved? *Clinical Psychology Review, 25,* 395–414.

Stroebe, M., & Stroebe, W. (1991). Does "grief work" work? *Journal of Consulting and Clinical Psychology, 59,* 479–482.

Stroebe, M. S., Stroebe, W., & Hansson, R. O. (Eds.). (1993). *Handbook of bereavement: Theory, research, and intervention.* New York: Cambridge University Press.

Stroebe, M., Stroebe, W., & Schut, H. (2001). Gender differences in adjustment to bereavement: An empirical and theoretical review. *Review of General Psychology, 5,* 62–83.

Stroebe, M., Stroebe, W., & Schut, H. (in press). Reactions to loss: New directions. *Psychological Inquiry.*

Stroebe, M., Stroebe, W., Schut, H., Zech, E., & van den Bout, J. (2002). Does disclosure of emotion facilitate recovery from bereavement? Evidence from two prospective studies. *Journal of Consulting and Clinical Psychology, 70,* 169–178.

Tedeschi, R. G., & Calhoun, L. G. (1996). The Posttraumatic Growth Inventory: Measuring the positive legacy of trauma. *Journal of Traumatic Stress, 9,* 455–472.

Tedeschi, R. G., & Calhoun, L. G. (2004). Target article: "Posttraumatic growth: Conceptual foundations and empirical evidence." *Psychological Inquiry, 15,* 1–18.

Teno, J. M., Clarridge, B. R., & Casey, V. (2004). Family perspectives on end-of-life care at the last place of care. *Journal of the American Medical Association, 29,* 88–93.

Umberson, D. (1987). Family status and health behaviors: Social control as a dimension of social integration. *Journal of Health and Social Behavior, 28,* 306–319.

Umberson, D. (1992). Gender, marital status and the social control of health behavior. *Social Science and Medicine, 34,* 907–917.

Vachon, M. L. S., Rogers, J., Lyall, W. A., Lancee, W. J., Sheldon, A. R., & Freeman, S. J. J. (1982). Predictors and correlates of adaptation to conjugal bereavement. *American Journal of Psychiatry, 139,* 998–1002.

Vachon, M. L. S., Sheldon, A. R., Lancee, W. J., Lyall, W. A. L., Rogers, J., & Freeman, S. J. J. (1982). Correlates of enduring distress patterns following bereavement: Social network, life situation and personality. *Psychological Medicine, 12,* 783–788.

Volkan, V. (1971). A study of a patient's "re-grief work" through dreams, psychological tests and psychoanalysis. *Psychiatric Quarterly, 45,* 244–273.

Wayment, H. A., & Vierthaler, J. (2002). Attachment style and bereavement reactions. *Journal of Loss and Trauma, 7,* 129–149.

Weiss, R. S. (1993). Loss and recovery. In M. S. Stroebe, W. Stroebe, & R. O. Hansson (Eds.), *Handbook of bereavement: Theory, research, and intervention* (pp. 271–284). New York: Cambridge University Press.

Wolff, K., & Wortman, C. B. (2006). Psychological consequences of spousal loss among the elderly. In D. Carr, R. Nesse, & C. B. Wortman (Eds.). *Spousal bereavement in late life* (pp. 81–115). New York: Springer.

Worden, J. W. (2002). *Grief counseling and grief therapy: A handbook for the mental health practitioner* (3rd ed.). New York: Springer.

Wortman, C. B. (2004). Post-traumatic growth: Progress and problems. *Psychological Inquiry, 15,* 81–90.

Wortman, C. B., Battle, E. S., & Lemkau, J. P. (1997). Coming to terms with sudden, traumatic death of a spouse or child. In R. C. Davis & A. J. Lurigio (Eds.), *Victims of crime* (pp. 108–133). Thousand Oaks, CA: Sage.

Wortman, C. B., & Silver, R. C. (1987). Coping with irrevocable loss. In G. R. VandenBos & B. K. Bryant (Eds.), *Cataclysms, crises, and catastrophes: Psychology in action (Master Lecture Series), 6,* 189–235. Washington, DC: American Psychological Association.

Wortman, C. B., & Silver, R. C. (1989). The myths of coping with loss. *Journal of Consulting and Clinical Psychology, 57,* 349–357.

Wortman, C. B., & Silver, R. C. (1993). Reconsidering assumptions about coping with loss: An overview of current research. In S. H. Filipp, L. Montada, & M. Lerner (Eds.), *Life crises and experiences of loss in adulthood.* Hillsdale, NJ: Erlbaum.

Wortman, C. B., & Silver, R. C. (2001). The myths of coping with loss revisited. In M. S. Stroebe, R. O. Hansson, W. Stroebe, & H. Schut (Eds.), *Handbook of bereavement research: Consequences, coping, and care* (pp. 405–430). Washington, DC: American Psychological Association.

Wortman, C. B., Wolff, K., & Bonanno, G. (2004). Loss of an intimate partner through death. In D.

Mashek & A. Aron (Eds.) *The handbook of closeness and intimacy*. Mahwah, NJ: Erlbaum.

Zisook, S., Chentsova-Dutton, Y., & Shuchter, S. R. (1998). PTSD following bereavement. *Annals of Clinical Psychiatry, 10,* 157–163.

Zisook, S., Paulus, M., Shuchter, S. R., & Judd, L. L. (1997). The many faces of depression following spousal bereavement. *Journal of Affective Disorders, 45,* 85–94.

Zisook, S., & Shuchter, S. R. (1986). The first four years of widowhood. *Psychiatric Annals, 16,* 288–294.

Zisook, S., & Shuchter, S. R. (1993). Major depression associated with widowhood. *American Journal of Geriatric Psychiatry, 1,* 316–326.

13

Judith A. Hall and Debra L. Roter

Physician-Patient Communication

The Physician-Patient Relationship and the Biopsychosocial Model of Health

Everyone who has been a medical patient—and of course this is everyone—knows that interactions with physicians can be rewarding and productive, but often such interactions are upsetting and frustrating. Patients who are sick are worried or uncomfortable, and even if they are not sick (as at a checkup visit) they are often aggravated by the inconvenience of going, waiting, and talking to the doctor. Encounters with doctors are highly charged, and patients often remember—and recount for family and friends—every word exchanged at important moments in the medical visit. Patients also remember, usually too late, things they wished they or the doctor had talked about. Patients' focus on how they communicate with their doctor should not, of course, be a surprise considering that most of what doctors and patients do is talk. However, the medical profession has come rather slowly to a full awareness of the centrality of talk, and of communication more broadly, to the practice of medicine.

Research on the communication process in medical interactions still lacks status in medical curricula on a par with other, more traditional areas of research and knowledge. Communication in medical visits, unlike communication in clinical and counseling psychology, has never held center stage. Whereas in mental health visits it is understood that, much of the time, the talk is inseparable from the therapy, in the field of medicine it is more likely to be assumed that good medicine rests on the cognitive skills of the clinician (e.g., diagnostic ability and knowledge base), in combination with technology and physiologically based treatments. Of course these are extremely important. But without understanding the role of communication, one cannot progress toward improving a host of widely acknowledged problems, including dissatisfaction, doctor shopping, litigation, poor adherence to medical regimens, skipping appointments, poor understanding and recall of information, and ultimately less than optimal resolution of health problems. The present chapter offers a summary of the burgeoning behavioral science literature on communication in physician–patient relationships, including its description, antecedents, and consequences. This literature makes clear the wide range of psychological and sociodemographic factors pertinent to this communication and the important health-related outcomes that are to some extent dependent on its quality. A more thorough treatment of this research literature is available in Roter and Hall (in press).

The physician-patient relationship and its expression through the medical dialogue have been described or alluded to in the history of medicine since the time of the Greeks (Emanuel, 1961) and in the modern medical and social sciences literature for the past 50 years (Engel, 1977; Freidson, 1970; Parsons, 1951; Szasz & Hollender, 1956). Nevertheless, historians of modern medicine have tracked an undeniable decline in the centrality of communication to the care process. In his study of the history of doctors and patients, Shorter (1985) attributes the denigration of communication to the ascendancy of the molecular and chemistry-oriented sciences as the predominant twentieth-century medical paradigm. This change was fundamental in directing medical inquiry away from the person of the patient to the biochemical makeup and pathophysiology of the patient. It was not coincidental that the practice of interviewing patients from a written outline designed around a series of yes-no hypothesis-testing questions replaced unstructured medical histories at this point in the history of medicine.[1]

The resulting loss of focus on the patient as person was well captured in Kerr White's (1988) lament that physicians failed to recognize that "apples are red and sweet as well as being composed of cells and molecules" (White, 1988, p. 6). Lacking a pathway to collaboration and partnership, many see the need for fundamental reform in medicine's vision. Just as the molecular and chemistry-oriented sciences were adopted as the twentieth-century medical paradigm, incorporation of the patient's perspective into medicine's definition of patient need has been suggested as the medical paradigm of the twenty-first century (White, 1988). George Engel's articulation of the biopsychosocial model of medical interviewing in the 1970s (Engel, 1977, 1988), later translated into a patient-centered clinical method by McWhinney (1988, 1989), has given substance to "patient-centeredness" as a key philosophy underlying medical communication curricula and research (Lipkin, Putnam, & Lazare, 1995; Mead & Bower, 2000).

Patient-centeredness has been defined both loosely and also somewhat inconsistently by different authors. At the heart of all conceptions are two key notions. The first is that the patient is a whole person, not just a set of symptoms or an organ system. Emotional and psychosocial issues are there-

fore to be accorded the attention they deserve as causes, exacerbators, and consequences of the state of a person's health. It follows from such a perspective that the patient's expectancies, beliefs, attitudes, values, experiences, and cultural background (as well as other sociodemographic characteristics, such as gender) move to the forefront as influences on the process of care and as matters on which the patient is a crucial source of information and decision-making authority. The patient is thus a player in a much more active way than an earlier "doctor-centric" paradigm, in which the physician assesses the facts of a situation and decides what is to be done, would allow. The acknowledgment that patients are experts on their own experience, values, and history is reflected in the title of Tuckett, Boulton, Olson, and Williams's (1985) book on physician-patient communication: *Meetings Between Experts.*

The second key aspect of the patient-centered approach is that communication is the vehicle by which medical care takes place, and it is therefore a subject deserving of intense scrutiny by researchers, medical educators, and clinicians in practice and their patients. Indeed, the two key elements we have identified can be joined in a parsimonious definition of medical care as the combination of mutual expertise and interpersonal communication in the service of solving health issues.

Although widely used, the term *patient-centered medicine* has been criticized as representing a semantic disregard for the powerful nature of the patient-provider relationship. The Pew-Fetzer Task Force on Advancing Psychosocial Health Education (Tresolini, 1994) suggests the more encompassing term *relationship-centered medicine* as recognizing the role of relationships in the optimal integration and synthesis of both the biomedical and lifeworld perspectives. According to this perspective, the relationship itself is part of the therapeutic picture, and this in turn depends not just on the patient's attributes (values, background, etc.) but also on those of the physician, in a dynamic relation with the patient. Thus, just as the patient-centered perspective puts a face on the patient, so the relationship-centered perspective puts a face on the physician as well. Medical care is seen as a dynamic process between individuals, not just a formulaic or role-based interchange.

A further expansion of the concept of relationship-centered care can be characterized as medically functional, facilitative, responsive, informative, and participatory (Cohen-Cole, 1991; Kurz, Silverman, & Draper, 1998; Lipkin et al., 1995; M. Stewart et al., 1995; Stone, 1979). The relative importance of each of these characteristics may vary depending on the care setting, the health status of the patient, and the nature and extent of prior relationship, as well as other exigencies.

First, the *medically functional* aspect of relationship-centered care is the extent to which the relationship fulfills the medical management functions of the visit within the constraints of a given health delivery system. Provision of quality care demands accomplishment of basic medical tasks. If the relationship inhibits performance of these tasks, it fails both patients and physicians in a primary way. Included among these tasks are structuring the visit, efficient use of time and resources, smooth organization and sequencing of the visit, and team building among health professionals (Kurz et al., 1998; M. Stewart et al., 1995), as well as technical tasks related to physical exam, diagnosis, and treatment.

Second, the relationship must be *facilitative* in eliciting the patient's full spectrum of concerns and visit agenda. Within this context the patient's ability to tell the story of his or her illness holds the key to the establishment and integration of the patient's perspective in all subsequent care. Telling the story is the method by which the meaning of the illness and the patient's response to it are integrated and interpreted by both doctor and patient. Particularly critical is elicitation in the psychosocial realm of experience. A patient's experience of illness is often reflected in how illness affects quality of life and daily function, family, social and professional functioning and relations, and feelings and emotions. Awareness of how these coping challenges are faced is critical to the finding of common ground and establishment of authentic dialogue (Cohen-Cole, 1991; Kurz et al., 1998; Lazare, Putnam, & Lipkin, 1995; M. Stewart et al., 1995).

Third, the visit must be *responsive* to the patient's emotional state and concerns. Physicians are not simply expert consultants; they are also individuals to whom people go when they are particularly vulnerable. Support, empathy, concern, and legitimation, as well as explicit probes regarding feelings and emotions, are important elements of rapport building and are key to a patient feeling known and understood (Cohen-Cole, 1991; Kurz et al., 1998; Lazare et al., 1995; Roter et al., 1995; M. Stewart et al., 1995).

Fourth, the relationship must be *informative,* providing both technical information and expertise and behavioral recommendations in a manner that is understandable, useful, and motivating. A singularly consistent finding in studies of doctors and patients conducted over the past 25 years has been that patients want as much information as possible from their physicians. Receiving information appears to be as important in contributing to the patient's capacity to cope with the overwhelming uncertainty and anxieties of illness as it is in making a substantive contribution to directing patient actions (Roter & Hall, 1992).

Finally, the fifth element of the relationship is that it must be *participatory*. Physicians have a responsibility and obligation to help patients assume an authentic and responsible role in the medical dialogue and in decision making. The first definition of *doctor* in *Webster's* is "teacher." The word *teacher* implies helping, but this help is not limited to the usual clinical sense of providing correct diagnosis and treatment, or empathy and reassurance. A teacher helps by equipping learners (patients) with what they need to help themselves; this includes not just information but also confidence in the value of their own contributions. The educator model is more egalitarian and collaborative than the traditional doctor-patient model, and as such is core to the building of a mutual partnership (Freire, 1970). Moreover, patient participation and autonomy can be traced back even farther to how physicians were educated in medical school—whether on an autonomy-promotive or controlling (authoritarian) model (G. C. Williams & Deci, 1998).

The Theoretical and Philosophical Basis of the Therapeutic Relationship

The relationship center of care can be viewed from another perspective. Bioethicists Emanuel and Emanuel (1992) suggest that power relations in medical visits are expressed through several key elements, including (1) who sets the agenda and goals of the visit (the physician, the physician and patient in negotiation, or the patient); (2) the role of patients' values (assumed by the physician to be consistent with their own, jointly explored by the patient and physician, or unexamined); and (3) the functional role assumed by the physician (guardian, adviser, or consultant). Application of these core elements can be useful in recognizing the variety of power relations expressed in models of the doctor-patient relationship.

The upper left quadrant of Table 13.1, demonstrating mutuality, reflects the strengths and resources of each participant on a relatively even footing. Inasmuch as power in the relationship is balanced, the goals, agenda, and decisions related to the visit are the result of negotiation between partners; both the patient and the physician become part of a joint venture. The medical dialogue is the vehicle through which patient values are explicitly articulated and explored. Throughout this process the physician acts as a counselor or adviser.

Most prevalent, but not necessarily most efficient or desirable, the prototype of paternalism is shown in the lower left quadrant. In this model of relations, physicians dominate agenda setting, goals, and decision making in regard to both information and services; the medical condition is defined in biomedical terms, and the patient's voice is largely absent. The physician's obligation is to act in the patient's "best interest." The determination of best interest, however, is largely based on the assumption that patient values and preferences are the same as those of the physician. The guiding model is that of physician as guardian, acting in the patient's best interest regardless of patient preferences.

The top right quadrant of the table represents consumerism. Here the more typical power relationship between doctors and patients may be reversed. Patients set the goal and agenda of the visit and take sole responsibility for decision making. Patient demands for information and technical services are accommodated by a cooperating physician. Patient values are defined and fixed by the

patient and unexamined by the physician. This type of relationship redefines the medical encounter as a marketplace transaction. *Caveat emptor,* "let the buyer beware," rules the transaction, with power resting in the buyer (patient) who can make the decision to buy (seek care) or not, as seen fit (Haug & Lavin, 1983). The physician role is limited to technical consultant with the obligation to provide information and services contingent on patient preferences (and within professional norms).

When patient and physician expectations are at odds or when the need for change in the relationship cannot be negotiated, the relationship may come to a dysfunctional standstill, a kind of relationship default, as represented in the lower right quadrant of the table. Default can be seen as characterized by unclear or contested common goals, obscured or unclear examination of patient values, and an uncertain physician role. It is here that medical management may be least effective, with neither the patient nor the physician sensing progress or direction. A frustrated and angry patient may make inappropriate time and service demands and ultimately drop out of care because of failed expectations. For physicians, these visits represent the most frustrating aspects of medicine, reflecting "the difficult and hateful patient." Unless recalibration of the relationship is undertaken with direct intervention, the relationship is likely to continue to unravel and ultimately fail.

It can be argued that, because different forms of relationship can bring some benefit, it should be left to patients to decide which form they prefer (Haug & Lavin, 1983; Quill, 1983). A different perspective, however, can be taken. Even when patients and physicians have mutually agreed upon a paternalistic relationship, questions regarding the appropriate-

Table 13.1. Prototypes of the Physician-Patient Relationship

	Physician power	
Patient power	*High physician power*	*Low physician power*
High patient power	MUTUALITY	CONSUMERISM
Goals and agenda	Negotiated	Patient set
Patient values	Jointly examined	Unexamined
Physician's role	Adviser	Technical consultant
Low patient power	PATERNALISM	DEFAULT
Goals and agenda	Physician set	Unclear
Patient values	Assumed	Unclear
Physician's role	Guardian	Unclear

ness of the relationship may still be raised. Patients and doctors are often on so unequal a footing that few patients can really play an equal role with physicians in shaping the relationship. The possibility exists, then, that patients may adopt a passive patient role without being fully aware of alternatives or able to negotiate a more active stance (President's Commission, 1982). Certainly they lack role modeling by their physicians much of the time. According to a study of community practicing physicians, a full three quarters of physicians did not promote a participatory style of interaction with their patients (Gotler et al., 2000).

Just as the paternalistic model can be criticized for its narrow exclusion of the patient's perspective, fault can also be found with the consumerist model as too narrowly limiting the physician's role. Patients may limit physician participation in decision making without appreciating the full benefit in terms of both decision making and coping that could be added by the inclusion of the physician's perspective (Roter & Hall, 1992; Schneider, 1998).

Relatively little is known about what kinds of patients are likely to prefer more or less passive and dependent relationships with their physicians. Several patient sociodemographic variables do appear to be associated with a more dependent relationship preference; the strongest of these is older age (alternatively, earlier age-cohort). Male gender, lower income, and lower level of occupation are also associated with this preference (Arora & McHorney, 2000; Ende, Kazis, Ash, & Moskowitz, 1989; Haug & Lavin, 1983). Other investigators have suggested that the wide gap in educational background and socioeconomic status between most patients and physicians contributes to the deference of lower social class patients and their adoption of a passive and dependent role in the doctor-patient relationship (Waitzkin, 1985). Ende and colleagues (Ende et al., 1989; Ende, Kazis, & Moskowitz, 1990) also suggest that illness severity plays a crucial role in patient deference to physicians in medical decision making, even for physicians when they are patients themselves.

There are significant nurturing and supportive aspects to a dependent or paternalistic doctor-patient relationship. Patients may draw comfort and support from a doctor-"father" figure. Indeed, the supportive nature of paternalism appears to be all the more important when patients are very sick and at their most vulnerable (Ende et al., 1989; Ende

et al., 1990). Relief of the burden of worry is curative in itself, some argue, and the trust and confidence implied by this model allow the doctor to do "medical magic." There is also evidence that idealization of the physician can have an important therapeutic effect, as placebo studies have demonstrated. Respondents who reported having greater faith in doctors, and being more dependent on them, were much less likely than others to adopt a consumerist orientation (Hibbard & Weeks, 1985, 1987).

In many regards, the primary methodological challenge to the field is the transition from the conceptual underpinnings of relationship-centered care to operational indicators that are observable and measurable elements of communication. Indeed, a number of measurement systems address at least some component of relationship-centered care consistent with the characteristics listed earlier (Roter, 2000a). Although none of the systems is explicitly contradictory with other systems or suggests exclusivity in its measurement, there has been little attempt to find common measurement ground. This is problematic; no single magic measurement bullet is evident or likely to emerge soon.

How Physician-Patient Communication Is Studied

A debate of long-standing intensity concerning the assessment of medical dialogue centers on the distinctions between qualitative and quantitative evaluative approaches (Roter & Frankel, 1992). In a qualitative approach, a narrative account of medical interaction or a verbatim transcript of a medical exchange is studied in terms of the substantive themes that emerge, with reliance on interpretation of the underlying meaning embodied in the discourse. In contrast, in a quantitative approach one gives numerical values to events, behaviors, verbal statements, and personal/situational characteristics using instruments and methods that aim for objectivity and reliability, and that allow for statistical analysis. The heat of the debate is derived not merely from a disagreement over the relative advantages and disadvantages of qualitative and quantitative methods but from the broader perception that these approaches reflect incompatible paradigms. Advocates of each of these methods not only have argued their own relative merits but also have maintained unusually critical and intellectually isolated positions.

A well-recognized list of attributes distinguishes the quantitative and qualitative paradigms and their adherents. The quantitative worldview is characterized as hypothetico-deductive, particularistic, atomistic, objective, and outcome oriented; its researchers are logical positivists. In contrast, the qualitative worldview is characterized as social anthropological, inductive, holistic, subjective, and process oriented; its researchers are phenomenologists (Reichardt & Cook, 1969). An allegiance to a particular paradigm implies not only a worldview but also a paradigm-specific method of inquiry and even styles of presentation.

The extension of the qualitative and quantitative paradigm controversy to evaluation of medical dialogue has been made by several authors. Quantitative approaches have been characterized as reflective and consistent with the biomedical model's emphasis on scientific method, and a tendency to translate observations into numbers. For instance, quantitative researchers typically present statistical summaries and correlates of objectively measured patient and provider behaviors. Qualitatively inclined researchers, on the other hand, rarely assign numerical values to their observations but prefer instead to record data in the language of their subjects, almost always presenting actual speech through verbatim transcripts of audio and video recordings.

There is a certain parallelism between the systems of open-sea navigation described by the cultural anthropologist Thomas Gladwin (1964) and the debate among researchers of the medical encounter over qualitative and quantitative methods. The system of navigation represented by the European tradition is distinguished by the plotting of a course prior to a journey's beginning that subsequently guides all decisions regarding location. The extent to which the journey "stays the course" is a testament to the navigator's skill. The islanders of Truk face the problem of managing long distances over uncertain conditions in a very different manner than the Europeans. The Trukese navigator has no preestablished plan of any kind; rather, experience from previous voyages and information at hand during the current sailing trip account completely for Trukese navigational expertise.

As argued elsewhere (Roter & Frankel, 1992), it is our view that the paradigmatic perspective that promotes mutual exclusivity is in error; we see no inherent logic to the limitations established by tra-

dition, other than tradition itself. Much of the debate in medical interaction research has focused on comparing methods independent of particular contexts, questions, or outcomes. Although it is quite clear that the methods used by Gladwin's navigators differ in both kind and degree, it is also the case that they both solve the same practical problem successfully. The value of Gladwin's analysis is that it includes both context and outcome as determinants of methodological utility. It also raises a caution about attempts to understand one set of methodological practices in the terms used to describe another. The presence or absence of mapmaking skills is essentially irrelevant to the Trukese navigator, as is the ability or inability of European navigators to read local wave patterns. Methods of research, like those of navigation, are open to description in their own terms and should be judged on the extent to which they succeed in answering the questions they raise in the context in which they were raised. Thus, the qualitative and quantitative methods may each be best suited to answer certain kinds of questions. Moreover, respect for alternative methods does not preclude combining methods to maximize discovery and insight. The question for researchers should be one of practical utility and theoretical relevance: Under what conditions does each method, or a combination of methods, make sense and advance the theory and practice of medical care?

Qualitative Approaches

A wide variety of approaches to qualitative assessment of patient-physician interaction is evident in the literature, with several of these reflecting particular theoretical and methodological roots and the use of formalized transcription and analytic guidelines (Mishler, 1984; Sacks, Schegloff, & Jefferson, 1974). The three primary formalized approaches are discourse analysis, conversational analysis, and narrative analysis. Although there is a good deal of overlap, discourse analysis approaches tend to focus on how talk within medical interactions changes, establishes, or maintains social/power relationships, while conversational analysis addresses structural features of talk that obligate participants to certain courses of action, for instance, turn-taking rules and question-and-answer sequences. Narrative analysis focuses on the stories of participants' experiences (Roter & McNeilis, 2003). Other approaches are more ad hoc in nature and idiosyncratic in their methods (Roter & Frankel, 1992). Nevertheless, the common ground shared across all qualitative approaches is the preservation of the verbatim record of spoken dialogue in the participants' own words.

Beckman and Frankel's (1984) study of the opening segments of medical visits is perhaps the most frequently cited qualitative study in medical communication and represents an integrated qualitative-quantitative assessment of patient-physician interaction. These segments were evaluated for total number of patient concerns expressed, number of concerns expressed before physician interruption, time from onset of the study segment to the point of interruption if present, and the total time for the study segment. The studied segment usually began with the physician's solicitation of the chief complaint and ended with the physician's recount of the history of the present illness, or a patient statement indicating completion of concerns.

Overall, patients completed their statements in only 23% of the visits analyzed. Only one of the interrupted patients completed his or her statement. For the other 69% of patients, the interruption appeared to halt the spontaneous flow of information from the patient and marked a transition to a series of closed-ended, physician-initiated questions, although there was no evidence that the patients had finished answering the opening question, "What problems are you having?" On average, patients were interrupted 18 seconds after they began to speak, most often after the expression of a single stated concern.

The following two transcript excerpts from the Beckman and Frankel study provide good examples of completed and interrupted statements:

D: How you been doing?
P: Oh, well, I been doing okay, except for Saturday, well Sunday night. You know I been kinda nervous off and on but I had a little incident at my house Saturday and it kinda shook me up a little bit.
D: Okay.
P: And, my ulcer, it's been burning me off and on like when I eat something if it don't agree, then I'll find out about it.
D: Right, okay.
P: But lately I've been getting this funny, like I'll lay down on my back, and my heart'll go "brr" you know like that. Like it's skipping a beat or something, and then it'll just start on back off

beating like when I get upset it'll just start beating boom-bom-bom and it'll just go back to its normal beat.
D: Okay.
P: Is that normal?
D: That's, that's a lot of things. Anything else that's bothering you?
P: No.

In contrast to this segment, the following exchange was interrupted by the physician after the first stated problem:

D: What brings you here today?
P: My head is killing me.
D: Have you had headaches before?

The first exchange took less than 60 seconds; it required three acknowledgment statements and a question by the physician to confirm that the patient was finished. In that short period of time the patient provided an uninterrupted statement of concerns and stated her agenda for the visit. The authors argue that premature interruption, as in the second example, could give the physician an incomplete picture of the patient's needs, resulting in an inappropriate treatment plan and use of time. For instance, in a similar study (Marvel, Epstein, Flowers, & Beckman, 1999), investigators found that patients who completed their statement of concern in the opening moments of the encounter were significantly less likely to raise concerns toward the end of the visit. It is interesting to note that while most interruptions occurred within 5 to 50 seconds of the physician's initial question, most completed statements took less than 1 minute, and no patients took more than 3 minutes to complete their statement.

The Beckman and Frankel and Marvel et al. studies highlight not only insightful use of qualitative analysis but also a hybrid methodology that allowed them to quantify key aspects of the communication process for purposes of description as well as prediction. These studies can thus be seen as a prototype of a combined qualitative-quantitative approach.

Quantitative Approaches to Interaction Analysis

It is only since the mid-1960s that the actual dynamics of the therapeutic dialogue have been observed in any systematic manner and an attempt to recast this aspect of medicine as science has been made. The evolution of methodological and technological sophistication has made observation and analysis of the medical visit easier over the years; indeed, the number of empirical studies of doctor-patient communication doubled from 1982 to 1987 (Roter, Hall, & Katz, 1988). A review of studies directly assessing provider-patient communication and its correlates found 28 different analysis systems used in 61 studies (Roter et al., 1988). Half the studies used audiotape as their primary method of observation; the remaining studies were equally likely to use videotape or impartial observers. There was a great deal of diversity in the content and process analysis approaches applied to the medical interactions. More than half the investigators employed an analysis system uniquely designed for their current study; the other investigators used a coding approach, usually with some minor modifications, employed in a prior study by the same or other investigators. The most commonly used process analysis systems were those of Bales, Roter, and Stiles, respectively (see later in section), but even these were used in only 5 to 7 studies each.

A more recent review of communication assessment instruments, covering the period 1986 to 1996, identified a total of 44 instruments (Boon & Stewart, 1998). Approximately one third of these were designed to evaluate medical student performance in communication skills training programs; of these, only 3 were used by an investigator other than the system's author, although not within the past 15 years. Also identified in the review were 28 systems used primarily for assessment of communication in research studies. In this category, 4 systems based on an analysis of an empirical record were used by multiple investigators. As was true in the earlier review, the most commonly used systems were those of Bales, Stiles, and Roter. In addition, Stewart's patient-centered method was found to be used by multiple investigators.

A brief overview of each of these four systems is provided here.

Bales's Process Analysis System

Concerned with group dynamics, Bales (1950) developed an analysis scheme for assessing patterns of interaction, communication, and the decision-making processes of small groups. Since its original conceptualization, Bales's scheme has been more widely modified than any other single approach to

increase understanding of the dynamics of the medical encounter. Bales's approach focuses on ways in which the process and structure of communication among persons in a group reflect how they differentially participate in problem solving. The theoretical rationale of this method conceives of problem solving in two domains, the task area and the socioemotional area. Interaction is described in terms of 12 mutually exclusive categories; 6 are conceived as affectively neutral and ascribed to the task dimension (e.g., gives suggestion or asks for orientation), and 6 are viewed as representing the socioemotional dimension of communication, divided into positive and negative affective categories (e.g., agrees or disagrees; shows tension release or shows tension).

Analysis using Bales's method is based on literal transcripts of the verbal events of the encounter that are operationally defined as the smallest discriminable speech segment to which the rater can assign classification. A unit may be as short as a single word or as long as a lengthy sentence; compound sentences are usually divided at the conjunction, and sentence clauses are scored as separate units when they convey a single item of thought or behavior, such as an acknowledgment, evaluation, or greeting. Inasmuch as Bales's system was originally devised as a method for studying group interaction, many researchers who derived theoretical direction from the system substantially changed the substantive categories to more directly reflect dyadic medical interaction. Nevertheless, the first studies of medical dialogue in which Bales's Process Analysis System was applied in the late 1960s and 1970s are still cited as the seminal studies in doctor-patient communication (Davis, 1969, 1971; Freemon, Negrete, Davis, & Korsch, 1971; Korsch, Gozzi, & Francis, 1968). Additional work in the 1980s with adults (M. Stewart, 1984) was also closely modeled on Bales's system.

Stiles's Verbal Response Mode (VRM)

An alternative theoretical approach to Bales's Process Analysis, based on linguistic theory, was introduced by William Stiles as the Verbal Response Mode (Stiles, 1992). Like Bales's system, the VRM taxonomy is a general-purpose system for coding speech acts and consequently is not specific to medical encounters. The unit of analysis is a speech segment (similar to Bales's system), defined grammatically to be equivalent to one psychological unit of experience, or a single utterance.

The system forms a taxonomy that implies a particular interpersonal intent or micro-relationship between communicator and recipient. There are three principles of classification: the source of experience, operationalized as attentiveness (to the other speaker) or informativeness (speaker's own experience); presumption about experience, operationalized as directive (controlling dialogue) or acquiescent (deferring to the other's viewpoint); and, finally, the frame of reference, defined as presumptuous (presuming knowledge about the other person) or unassuming (not presuming particular knowledge). Each of these classification principles is dichotomous, taking the value of either "the speaker" or "the other." The taxonomy assigns language segments to the following categories: disclosure, edification, advisement, confirmation, question, acknowledgment, interpretation, and reflection. Using this taxonomy, each speech segment is coded twice, once with respect to its grammatical form, or literal meaning, and once with respect to its communicative intent, or pragmatic meaning. Thus, there are 64 possible form-intent combinations—8 pure modes in which form and intent coincide, and 56 mixed modes in which they differ.

Reliability of VRM coding appears to be good, with reports of 81% agreement for form and 66% for intent (based on Cohen's kappa) in a study of parent-child interaction (Stiles & White, 1981), and an average of 78% agreement over categories was reported in a Dutch study of primary care visits (Meeuwesen, Schaap, & van der Staak, 1991).

The VRM has been used by its author and others in studies in the United States, the United Kingdom, and the Netherlands. As noted by Stiles in his review, these studies included patients in primary care, patients with particular types of problems, including hypertension, expectant mothers, breast cancer patients, those with a psychological component to their physical complaint, and the institutionalized aged (Stiles, 1992). (See Stiles, 1992, for a more exhaustive review of VRM studies.)

Roter Interaction Analysis System (RIAS)

The RIAS is derived loosely from social exchange theories related to interpersonal influence, problem solving (Bales, 1950; Emerson, 1976), and reciprocity (Ben-Sira, 1980; Davis, 1969; Gouldner, 1960; Roter & Hall, 1989). It provides a tool for viewing the dynamics and consequences of patients' and providers' exchange of resources through their medical dialogue. The social exchange orientation is consistent with health education and empowerment perspectives that view the medical encounter as a "meeting between experts" grounded in an egalitarian model of patient-provider partnership that rejects expert-domination and passive patient roles (Freire, 1983; Roter, 1987; Roter & Hall, 1991; Roter, 2000a, 2000b; Tuckett et al., 1985; Wallerstein & Bernstein, 1988).

A useful framework for organizing and grounding RIAS-coded communication in the clinical encounter is the functional model of medical interviewing (Cohen-Cole, 1991). Task behaviors fall within two of the medical interview functions: "Gathering Data" to understand the patient's problems and "Educating and Counseling" patients about their illness and motivating patients to adhere to treatment. Affective behaviors generally reflect the third medical interview function of "Building a Relationship" through the development of rapport and responsiveness to the patient's emotions. A fourth function of the visit can be added, "Activating and Partnership Building," to enhance patients' capacity to engage in an effective partnership with their physician. Although not explicitly defined by the authors of the functional model, the use of verbal strategies to help patients integrate, synthesize, and translate between the biomedical and psychosocial paradigms of the therapeutic dialogue deserves special note. The "activating" function facilitates the expression of patients' expectations, preferences, and perspectives so that they may more meaningfully participate in treatment and management decision making (Roter, 2000a).

The RIAS is applied to the smallest unit of expression or statement to which a meaningful code can be assigned, generally a complete thought, expressed by each speaker throughout the medical dialogue. These units are assigned to mutually exclusive and exhaustive categories that reflect the content and form of the medical dialogue. Form distinguishes statements that are primarily informative (information giving), persuasive (counseling), interrogative (closed and open-ended questions), affective (social, positive, negative, and emotional), and process-oriented (partnership building, orientations, and transitions). In addition to form, content areas are specified for exchanges about medical condition and history, therapeutic regimen, lifestyle behaviors, and psychosocial topics relating to social relations and feelings and emotions.

In addition to the verbal categories of exchange, coders rate each speaker on a 6–point scale reflecting a range of affective dimensions, including anger, anxiety, dominance, interest, and friendliness. These ratings have been found to reflect voice tone channels that are largely independent of literal verbal content (Hall, Roter, & Rand, 1981).

The system is flexible and responsive to study context by allowing for the addition of tailored categories. Coders may also mark the phases of the visit so that the opening, history segment, physical exam, counseling and discussion segment, and closing are specified and communication falling within these parts of the visit can be analyzed and summarized separately (e.g., Roter, Lipkin, & Korsgaard, 1991).

Since the unit of analysis is the smallest unit of expression or statement to which a meaningful code can be assigned, and these are mutually exclusive and exhaustive, the RIAS categories can be used individually or combined to summarize the dialogue in a variety of ways. For instance, medical questions and psychosocial questions can be separately tallied, subclassified as open or closed, combined to form superordinate categories, or made into ratios (e.g., open to closed questions, biomedical to psychosocial questions). Similar groupings can be derived from information-giving and counseling categories. Other variable combinations represent composites of partnership building, emotional talk, and positive talk. Patient-centeredness scores can be computed by calculating a ratio of patient versus physician communication control: the sum of physician information giving (including both biomedical and psychosocial) and patient psychosocial information giving and question asking divided by the sum of physician question asking and patient biomedical information giving. This is similar to the approach taken in several of our own studies (Roter et al., 1997; Wissow et al., 1998) and by other investigators (Greenfield, Kaplan, & Ware, 1985).

The RIAS code definitions are straightforward and intuitive. Very basic training is accomplished over a 3-day period, with acceptable levels of reliability and speed generally achieved with 60 to 80 hours of practice. Experienced RIAS coders average 3 times real time for an uncomplicated coding task; a 20-minute visit can be expected to be coded in about an hour. Coders apply the RIAS directly to audio or video tape, without transcription, using direct entry software that can be applied to digitized audio or video files or used with analog audio or videotape recordings.

The RIAS has demonstrated substantial reliability and predictive validity with respect to a variety of patient outcomes. In the author's own studies, the reliability has ranged across categories from roughly .70 to .90 based on Pearson correlation coefficients, with lower reliabilities reflecting infrequent categories (Levinson, Roter, Mullooly, Dull, & Frankel, 1997; Roter, Hall, & Katz, 1987; Roter et al., 1997; Wissow et al., 1998). Other researchers have reported similar reliabilities (Bensing & Dronkers, 1992; Inui, Carter, Kukull, & Haigh, 1982; Mead & Bower, 2000; Van Dulmen, Verhaak, & Bilo, 1997).

The RIAS system has been used widely in the United States and Europe, as well as in Asia, Africa, and Latin America, in primary care and in specialty practice, and in relation to many correlates; examples are physicians' malpractice experience (Levinson et al., 1997), physicians' satisfaction (Roter et al., 1997; Suchman, Roter, Green, & Lipkin, 1993), and patients' satisfaction (Bertakis, Roter, & Putnam, 1991; Hall, Irish, Roter, Ehrlich, & Miller, 1994b; Roter et al., 1987; Roter, 1991; Roter et al., 1997). It has also been used to evaluate several types of communication training programs, including residency and medical student training (Kalet, Earp, & Kowlowitz, 1992; Roter, Cole, Kern, Barker, & Grayson, 1990) and continuing medical education (Roter et al., 1995). (An annotated list of more than 100 RIAS-related studies is available on the RIAS Web site: https://rias.org.)

Stewart's Patient-Centered Measure

Developed specifically to assess the behaviors of patients and doctors according to the patient-centered clinical method (McWhinney, 1989; M. Stewart et al., 1995), a method of scoring the "patient-centeredness" of audiotaped or videotaped medical encounters was developed (Brown, Weston, & Stewart, 1989; Levenstein, McCracken, McWhinney, Stewart, & Brown, 1986; M. Stewart et al., 1995). The scoring procedure is described in detail elsewhere (Brown, Stewart, & Tessier, 1995; Henbest & Stewart, 1989; M. Stewart et al., 1995); briefly, scores range from 0 (not at all patient-centered) to 100 (very patient-centered) based on assessment of three main components. The first component is "understanding of the patient's disease and experience" (statements related to symptoms, prompts, ideas, expectations, feelings, and impact on function). Every pertinent statement (as many as are applicable), for each of the six elements, made by the patient is recorded verbatim on the coding sheet. The coder assigns a score to the statement as to whether the physician provided preliminary exploration (yes or no) or further exploration (yes or no), or cut off discussion (yes or no). The second component, "understanding the whole person," explores the context of a patient's life setting (e.g., family, work, social supports) and stage of personal development (e.g., life cycle). The third component is "finding common ground" (mutual understanding and agreement on the nature of the problems and priorities, the goals of treatment and management, and the roles of the doctor and patient).

Interrater reliability, reported by the system's authors, ranges between .69 and .83 (Brown, Stewart, McCracken, McWhinney, & Levenstein, 1986; M. Stewart et al., 1996). Mead and Bower (2000) report an intraclass correlation coefficient of .58 for the system in their study.

Comparison Studies

Two studies have contrasted multiple coding systems in an attempt to compare these approaches and draw some conclusions regarding their relative practical and predictive value, or to validate one approach through its comparison with another. In the first of these studies, Bales's original Process Analysis System, the RIAS, and the VRM were compared by Inui et al. (1982). The three interaction analysis systems were applied to 101 new-patient visits to a general medical clinic for which patient knowledge, satisfaction, recall of prescribed medications, and compliance had been determined. The investigators found that the explanatory power of the three systems differed. For instance, Bales's system explained 19% of the variation between patients who took prescribed drugs correctly, compared with 28% for the RIAS and none for the VRM. Explanation of variation in knowledge was somewhat better for the RIAS than for Bales's system and the VRM, and satisfaction also favored the RIAS and Bales's system.

In the second study, three measures of patient-centeredness were applied to the same sample of 55 videotaped general practitioner consultations (Mead & Bower, 2000). The RIAS was used to construct a single summary measure of patient-centeredness as a ratio of patient-centered categories of talk (all physician and patient questions and information giving about psychosocial or lifestyle-related issues, physician information about biomedical topics, all patient biomedical questions, all physician emotionally focused talk, and physician partnership talk) divided by physician-centered categories of talk (summation of all physician question asking, physician directive statements, and patient biomedical information giving). The second measure of patient-centeredness was devised using the Henbest and Stewart coding approach (1989), and the third measure was a global rating scale designed by the authors for use in the Euro-Communication Study, a six-nation comparative study of physician-patient communication (Mead & Bower, 2000). Correlations were of similar magnitude between the Euro-Communication rating scale and the RIAS (Pearson correlation = .37; $p < .01$) and between the Euro-Communication rating scale and the Henbest and Stewart measure (Pearson correlation = .37; $p < .01$), and somewhat lower between the RIAS and Henbest and Stewart measure (Pearson correlation = .21; $p < .12$).

The Euro-Communication rating scale was significantly correlated with five variables: physician age, perceived acquaintance with the patient, consultation length, proportion of patient-directed eye gaze in the consultation, and physician ratings of the importance of psychological factors. The RIAS was also significantly correlated with all these variables, with the exception of general practitioner age. In addition, the RIAS was correlated with the patient's score on the General Health Questionnaire, a validated measure of emotional distress (Goldberg & Williams, 1988), patient age, and patient health status. The Henbest and Stewart measure was significantly associated with only one of the measures—patient-directed eye gaze.

Profile of the Medical Visit

Despite the differences in approaches to assessment of the medical dialogue just described, there is a large degree of overlap in the variables that are extracted from these studies. In our review of 61 published studies in the field prior to 1987 (Hall, Roter, & Katz, 1988; Roter et al., 1988), we found 247 unique communication variables abstracted from observations of patient and physician interaction.

Few of the variables, at least in the form in which they were reported, were common to more than 1 or 2 studies. However, virtually all the variables fit within five mutually exclusive categories: information giving, question asking, social conversation, positive talk, and negative talk. An additional category, partnership building, was necessary for physician interaction only. A more recent review of communication studies addressing physician gender differences produced a very similar array of variables and subsuming categories (Roter, Hall, & Aoki, 2001).

How do these categories translate into a portrait of the medical encounter? We addressed this question in an earlier summary across a variety of studies (Roter & Hall, 1992). First, reviewing physician talk, we found that what physicians do most is give information (38% of all utterances on average). This includes all forms of information giving, including the mere reciting of facts ("Your blood pressure is high today, 180/95"); counseling ("It is very important that you take all the medication I am prescribing. You have to get your blood pressure under control, and this medication will do it, but only if you take it as you are supposed to"); and directions and instructions ("Put your clothes back on and sit down. Now, take these pills twice a day for a week and drink plenty of water"). Each of these has a different intent—to inform, to persuade, or to control (respectively). From our own work it appears that the giving of facts constitutes about half of this category, and both counseling and directing patient behavior contribute in equal parts to the remainder.

Question asking by physicians also accounts for a good proportion of the visit (23% of the physician's utterances); this is usually done during history taking and mostly consists of closed-ended questions. Closed-ended questions are those questions for which a one-word answer, usually yes or no, is expected (e.g., "Are your leg symptoms worse after standing for several minutes?"). In contrast, open-ended questions are those that allow patients some discretion in the direction they may take in answering (e.g., "Tell me about your leg pain. What seems to be the problem?").

Closed questions limit responses to a narrow field set by the physician; the patient knows that an appropriate response is one or two words and does not normally elaborate any further. In contrast, open questions suggest to the patient that elaboration is appropriate and that the field of inquiry is wide enough to include the patient's thoughts about what might be relevant. These two types of questions have very different implications for control of the medical visit; closed questions imply high physician control of the interaction, whereas open questions are much less controlling. In routine practice, closed questions outnumber open questions by a factor of two or three, perhaps because they are thought to be less time-consuming and more efficient at providing the information needed to make a diagnosis.

Positive talk constitutes a smaller share of physician talk (15% of the utterances) and serves two functions. One is obvious. Approval (e.g., "Your blood pressure is great! You've been doing a good job on your diet and taking your pills"), shared laughter, encouragement, and empathy all increase a positive bond between speakers. The second purpose of statements in this category is to signal that the listener is attentive and eager for the speaker to continue. Often included are communications more aptly described as noises than words; hm, huh, aha, and ahh serve this purpose. The Beckman and Frankel study described earlier found that the more a physician used these noises in the first 90 seconds of the visit, the more likely the physician was to uncover fully the patient's major concerns and reason for the visit (Beckman & Frankel, 1984). Patients readily defer to the physician and are easily diverted from giving their thoughts. Attentive noises, however, encourage elaboration so that a patient's full agenda for the visit can be revealed.

Partnership building (about 11% of utterances) represents the physician's attempts to engage the patient more fully in the medical dialogue. These may be considered, in some respect, as attempts to activate the patient, perhaps directed at particularly passive or noncommunicative patients.

Social, nonmedical conversation constitutes some 6% of interaction. It includes greetings, casual remarks, and niceties ("Hello Mr. Waller, nice to see you. That was some baseball game last night"). This talk is important as a social amenity—it is usually positive, and we are accustomed to greetings and a certain amount of chitchat in most encounters, at least initially, to put people at ease.

Finally, negative talk is quite rare from physicians (less than 2% of utterances). This includes disagreements, confrontations, and antagonistic remarks ("You've gained weight since your last visit and I am disappointed in you. You're not really trying at all"). However, although negative talk is not often made explicit by physicians, a negative message can be expressed in other ways. Professional etiquette and training discourage unpleasantness and the high emotions that may arise from direct criticisms and contradictions. Reprimands may be expressed as forceful counseling or imperatives on the need to follow recommendations better. For the unsuccessful dieter, for instance, this could mean exhortation for the patient to do better on his or her diet and to follow a prescribed regimen. The physician may also express displeasure in an angry, anxious, or dominant tone of voice or may cut patients off in various verbal and nonverbal ways.

It should not be surprising to find that about half of patient talk is information giving, much of it in response to the physician's questions. What is surprising, however, is how little interaction, only some 7%, is devoted to the patient's questions. This is particularly troubling because many studies have demonstrated that patients often have questions they would like to ask but simply do not. It has been suggested that this reticence may reflect a reluctance to appear foolish or inappropriate, or it may be that physicians, in myriad ways, signal that the time is not right to ask questions. The right time, however, is never quite there. Whatever the reason, patients ask questions relatively rarely.

Though the proportion of positive talk was roughly equivalent for physicians and patients, negative talk reported in the studies we reviewed was seven times greater for patients than for physicians. It is notable how much more frequent direct contradiction or criticism of the physician is by the patient than vice versa. Patients may be more direct in this regard than their physicians because they have fewer communication options; they cannot easily express their disagreements through lecture, counseling, or imperatives. However, patients engage in more positive as well as negative talk. The expression of these emotionally laden statements generally marks greater interpersonal engagement. The patient is likely to have a far greater emotional investment in the proceedings than the physician, and this is expressed in both positive and negative terms.

Correlates of Physician-Patient Communication

Individuals coming together in medical dialogue bring with them all their personal characteristics —their personalities, social attitudes and values, personal histories, gender, sexual orientation, age, education, ethnicity, and physical and mental health, to name a few. This applies to the physician as well as to the patient, though research on physician characteristics is less common owing to typically small physician samples in communication studies. Furthermore, the end points we might wish to measure, such as satisfaction or clinical outcomes, have many determinants. Always, when interpreting nonexperimental comparisons such as constitute most of the literature on physician-patient communication, it is important not to make assumptions about the causal relations among variables. Even when potentially confounding variables (such as sociodemographic variables or health status) are controlled for statistically, strong inferences of causality are often not justified. Causation may lie in unmeasured variables, and even when one has measured the right variables, complex paths of causation can exist. A given behavior could have many different origins— it may be caused by a stable or transient characteristic of the person engaging in it, by how that person responds to the other person's characteristics, or by how that person is treated by the other person, to name a few possibilities. To illustrate those just named, a patient may act negative because he feels sick, because he does not like his physician's ethnicity, or because the physician is inconsiderate and he is responding in kind. The physician-patient interaction is a prime setting for the operation of interpersonal self-fulfilling prophecies (Rosenthal & Rubin, 1978). Such processes not only are illustrative of complex reciprocal causation but also are generally out of awareness, producing possible errors of attribution. Another example of likely reciprocal causation is the physician's liking for the patient; physicians like some of their patients more than others, and this seems to be related to patient characteristics (e.g., gender and health status) and to the patient's satisfaction with the physician (Hall, Epstein, DeCiantis, & McNeil, 1993; Hall, Horgan, Stein, & Roter, 2002).

In the sections that follow, we present research relating physician-patient communication to some of the antecedent and outcome variables that have been frequently studied.

Predictors of Communication

Patient Health

The state of a patient's physical and mental health is related to both patient and physician communication (Bertakis, Callahan, Helms, Rahman, & Robbins, 1993; Hall, Roter, Milburn, & Daltroy, 1996). When the patient is more distressed, either physically or mentally, both the patient and the physician engage in less social conversation and make more emotionally concerned statements, engage in more psychosocial discussion, and ask more biomedical questions. Sicker patients also provide more biomedical information. The research also suggests that physicians may respond ambivalently to sicker patients; physicians report less satisfaction after visits with sicker patients, and they report liking sicker patients less than they do healthier patients (Hall 2006). This apparent ambivalence, in conjunction with numerous findings showing that people with worse health status are less satisfied with their care (as reviewed by Hall, Feldstein, Fretwell, Rowe, & Epstein, 1990), raises the question of whether physicians produce dissatisfaction in their sicker patients by displaying negative behaviors toward them. Hall et al. (1998) used structural equation modeling to test this hypothesis and an alternative hypothesis that the dissatisfaction stems directly from the sicker patient's negative outlook. In general, the direct path was supported over the physician-mediated path, with one exception: Physicians' curtailing of social conversation with sicker patients accounted for some of these patients' dissatisfaction. This is unfortunate, for in curtailing this "expendable" category of interaction in the service of devoting time to more pressing medical issues, physicians may unknowingly undermine their relationships with the very patients for whom the quality of the relationship may matter most.

Physician Gender

A large amount of research conducted in nonclinical settings has found gender differences in communication style (e.g., Brody & Hall, 2000; Dindia & Allen, 1992; Eagly & Johnson, 1990; Hall, 1984). Indeed, the magnitude of gender differences in non-verbal expression rivals or exceeds the gender dif-

ferences found for a wide range of other psychological traits and behaviors. Men have been shown to engage in less smiling and laughing, less interpersonal gazing, greater interpersonal distances and less direct body orientation, less nodding, less hand gesturing, and fewer back-channel responses (interjections such as "mm-hmm," which serve to facilitate a partner's speech); they also have more restless lower bodies, more expansive arm movements, and weaker nonverbal communication skills (in terms of accuracy in judging the meanings of cues and expressing emotions accurately through nonverbal cues) than do women. Men have also been found to use less verbal empathy, to be less democratic as leaders, and to engage in less personal self-disclosure than do women. Also relevant is research suggesting that women report experiencing many emotions both more frequently and more intensely than do men, and refer more to emotions in their language.

There are several reasons to investigate the communication behavior of male and female physicians. Of most practical significance is the relevance of the "female" behavioral repertoire to the goals of medical education in the era of the biopsychosocial model. The concept of relationship-centered medicine, with its emphasis on viewing the patient as a whole person, is reminiscent of "female" interaction goals such as minimizing status differentials, sharing personal information, relating effectively to emotional concerns, and showing sensitivity to others' needs and states. Furthermore, it appears that patients experience better clinical outcomes when their physicians have a more patient-centered approach (M. Stewart, 1996).

In undertaking a review of communication differences between male and female physicians, we entertained two contrasting hypotheses (Roter, Hall, & Aoki, 2002). The first was that the gender differences commonly seen in nonclinical settings would not be present in physicians. Considering that medical school is still widely regarded as a highly "masculine" institution, we considered it possible that selection bias (resulting from either self-selection or school admissions policies) would produce female physicians whose behavioral style is similar to that of male physicians. Furthermore, even without this bias the process of medical education (learning to suppress one's feelings, exert authority, and generally model oneself on the "male" physician prototype) might level out initial differences. The second hypothesis was that male and female physicians would behave much like men and women in other walks of life. Finding such differences among physicians would attest to the strength of gender-role socialization across the life span.

Observational studies of physician-patient communication typically have many fewer physicians than patients, with a ratio of two to one in favor of male over female physicians. This, plus the relative recency of interest in the role of gender in the process of care, means that only two dozen or so studies have systematically compared the communication styles of male versus female physicians using objective methods based on audio/video recordings or neutral third-party observers.

Our review of this literature generally supported the second hypothesis. Male and female physicians did not differ in how much biomedical information they conveyed, but male physicians' talk included less psychosocial discussion. Male physicians also asked fewer questions of all sorts, engaged in fewer partnership-building behaviors (enlisting the patient's active participation and reducing physician dominance), produced less positively toned talk and less talk with emotional content, used less positive nonverbal behavior (e.g., smiling and nodding), and had overall shorter visits than did female physicians. Consistent with these direct observational effects, male physicians report liking their patients less than female physicians report (Hall et al., 1993; Hall et al., 2002) and hold less patient-centered values than female physicians (where a patient-centered response would be to believe that the patient's expectations, feelings, and life circumstances are critical elements in the treatment process; Krupat et al., 2000).

Although the effect sizes for these gender differences are often small, nevertheless they could have an important impact when generalized over many medical visits and many patients. To the extent that male physicians' behavior and attitudes are less patient-centered than those of female physicians, there may be implications for overall quality of care and health outcomes. And, considering that the gender differences among physicians closely mirror those found in the general population, it should come as no surprise that female physicians seem to have fewer barriers to overcome when learning to apply the biopsychosocial model in medical practice (Roter & Hall, 2004).

Meta-analytic review has also shown that in primary care practice, patients communicate differently toward male versus female physicians as well, in a pattern that either matches or complements the effects just described (Hall & Roter, 2002). Patients talk more to female than male physicians, disclose more biomedical and psychosocial information, and make more positive statements. Patients also behave more assertively toward female physicians, perhaps as a response to female physicians' more participatory and status-leveling style (Roter et al., 2002).

In spite of the communication style differences suggesting that female physicians are more patient centered, patients are not consistently more satisfied with female physicians; in fact, the literature is very inconsistent with findings favoring both men and women physicians. We are not yet in a position to explain this variation. Possibly, the fact that female physicians engage in higher levels of desirable, patient-centered behaviors is offset by masculine-biased values and expectations that put female physicians at a disadvantage in patients' eyes; alternatively, even though female physicians are more patient centered than male physicians, they still may violate the female stereotype in not being as "soft" and approachable as patients expect women to be (Hall et al., 1994b). Thus, female physicians may experience something of a double bind. However, we believe social attitudes are changing rapidly as more women enter medicine and as patients develop less paternalistic expectations regarding their medical care.

Patient Gender

Among patients with chronic disease, females are more likely than males to prefer an active role in medical decision making (Arora & McHorney, 2000). Indeed, this preference appears to be borne out in practice, as female patients report that they experience more opportunity for decision making in their relations with their physicians than male patients report (Kaplan, Gandek, Greenfield, Rogers, & Ware, 1995). In that study, patient participation in decision making was particularly low when male patients interacted with male physicians, a finding consistent with the finding that in male patient–male physician interactions the contribution of the patient relative to the physician is the least of all gender combinations (Hall, Irish, Roter, Ehrlich, & Miller, 1994a).

Waitzkin (1985) found that female patients were given more information than male patients, and that the information was given in a more comprehensible manner. The same data set also revealed that the greater amount of information directed toward women was largely in response to women's tendency to ask more questions in general and to ask more questions following the doctor's explanation (Wallen, Waitzkin, & Stoeckle, 1979). Similar conclusions were reached by Pendleton and Bochner (1980), who found in an English study that female patients were given more information than males and that this information was in answer to their more frequent questions. These findings are consistent with those relating to patient activation described earlier.

Investigators have also found that female patients receive more positive talk and more attempts to include them in discussion than males. In one study, physicians were more likely to express "tension release" (mainly laughter) with female patients and to ask them about their feelings more (M. Stewart, 1983).

Although stereotypes about females' agreeableness and politeness might lead to the expectation that they would be more satisfied with care than men, the literature does not support this expectation (Hall & Dornan, 1990). Indeed, the trend suggests, if anything, less satisfaction among women than among men (Hall & Dornan, 1990; Hargraves et al., 2001; Thi, Briançon, Empereur, & Guillemin, 2002).

Patient Age

Visits with elderly patients are complex. Older patients are plagued by multiple and complicated medical problems, as well as hearing impairment and sometimes dementia. Stressful life events of old age often occur simultaneously in the elderly, resulting in depression, fear of losing independence and control, and threats to self-esteem and identity (Greene & Adelman, 1996). As their health declines, the elderly are confronted with the treatment and management of debilitating or life-threatening conditions and are asked to make difficult decisions regarding end-of-life planning. While faced with these challenges, the elderly may be at a special disadvantage in fully understanding the complex choices they are asked to make. The elderly typically demonstrate lower levels of literacy and have had less exposure to formal education than younger birth cohorts (Gazmararian et al., 1999).

Particularly relevant to these decision-making demands, older patients appear to experience medi-

cal visits in which they are more passive and less actively engaged in the treatment decision-making process. The Medical Outcomes Study (MOS; Kaplan et al., 1995), based on surveys of more than 8,000 patients sampled from the practices of 344 physicians, found that patients aged 75 and over reported significantly less participatory visits with their doctors than all but the youngest age cohorts of patients (those younger than 30 years). Interestingly, the most participatory visits were evident among only slightly younger patient groups, including those aged 65 to 74, and the middle-aged group ranging from 45 to 64 years. In addition to age, both poor health status and lower educational achievement were associated with lower reports of participation. Thus, the oldest patients may be at triple risk for low levels of participatory engagement with their doctors; each of these factors—cohort expectations, health status, and educational attainment—may act alone and in concert to diminish the likelihood that full patient-physician partnerships will develop.

As measured by physician time during interviews, elderly patients do not receive greater physician attention (Keeler, Solomon, Beck, Mendenhall, & Kane, 1982; Mann et al., 2001; Radecki, Kane, Solomon, Mendenhall, & Beck, 1988). However, older patients visit physicians three times more often than their younger counterparts, so cumulatively they may accrue more physician contact. There is some indication, however, that how the time is spent may differ. Several investigators have concluded that older patients appear to have an advantage over younger patients in communication with physicians. A meta-analysis of more than 40 studies published between 1965 and 1985 in which videotapes or audiotapes of medical visits were analyzed found consistent relationships between patient age and physicians' interviewing skills (Roter et al., 1988; Hall et al., 1988). The review found that older patients received more information, more total communication, and more questions concerning drugs than did younger patients.

Studies comparing communication directed toward older and younger patients found differences in what topics were addressed and the emotional tone of the visit. Greene and colleagues found physicians were less responsive to the psychosocial issues the elderly raised during visits than to similar concerns of younger patients (Greene, Hoffman, Charon, & Adelman, 1987). Inadequate response in this domain may be associated with patient or physician reticence to introduce psychosocial problems into an already complicated biomedical visit, and a tendency to attribute sensory failings to the aging process. Other studies, however, have not reported similar results. Mann et al. (2001) found no decrease in counseling on medical or psychosocial topics, or physician satisfaction with patient visits, with increasing age of patients. However, many studies have found that increasing age is associated with higher levels of patient satisfaction (see meta-analysis of Hall & Dornan, 1990).

Older patient visits are distinguished from those of younger adults by the frequent presence of a visit companion; estimates of the percentages of all visits that include a companion range between 20% and 57% (Prohaska & Glasser, 1996). There are only a few empirical studies of the effect of companions on the dynamics of exchanges in discussions, but their presence appears to change communication patterns (Roter, 2003; Tates & Meeuwesen, 2001). Greene et al. (1987) found that when a companion was present, older patients raised fewer topics, were less responsive to topics they did raise, and were less assertive and expressive. Moreover, patients were sometimes excluded completely from the conversation when a companion was present. Additional communication difficulties have been identified, including a tendency for a family member to take on the information-giving role in the visit, sometimes contradicting the patient or disclosing information the patient had not wanted revealed (Hasselkus, 1994). It appears that the content, tone, and nature of the medical discussion may be shaped by the roles adopted by the patient companion; these may range from advocate and supporter to antagonist (Adelman, Greene, & Charon, 1987; Greene, Adelman, Friedmann, & Charon, 1994).

We know little about moderating effects of the visit companion's age, gender, or relationship to the patient on communication dynamics in the medical encounter. An intriguing question is what is the effect on communication of having "baby boomers" as companions in the medical visits of their aging parents, compared with spouses or contemporaries acting as visit companions. We might speculate that these adult children bring a higher level of consumerism to their encounters that can dominate the visit and perhaps contribute to a verbal withdrawal by the patient from the medical dialogue (as described by Greene et al., 1987); alternatively, the presence of a consumerist companion may spur assertive behavior on the part of some patients.

Patient Ethnicity and Social Class

Physicians deliver less information, less supportive talk, and less proficient clinical performance to Black and Hispanic patients and patients of lower economic class than they do to more advantaged patients, even in the same care settings (Bartlett et al., 1984; A. Epstein, Taylor, & Seage, 1985; Hooper, Comstock, Goodwin, & Goodwin, 1982; Ross, Mirowsky, & Duff, 1982; Waitzkin, 1985; Wasserman, Inui, Barriatua, Carter, & Lippincott, 1984). Race discordance between physicians and patients (e.g., an African American patient seen by a White physician) is associated with patient reports of lowered involvement, less partnership, lower levels of trust, and lower levels of satisfaction, as well as with shorter length and more negative affect (e.g., Cooper-Patrick et al., 1999; Cooper et al., 2003; Young & Klingle, 1996).

Interpreting sociodemographic effects is complex. Inadequacies of communication in visits involving minority or low-income patients may result because physicians devalue them and their needs; poor performance may also stem from erroneous beliefs about the expectations, capacities, and desires of such patients. Also, as a result of cultural norms or lack of confidence, such patients may not request or demand a high level of performance from their physicians (which could, of course, confirm whatever stereotypes the physicians may already have; van Ryn, 2002).

Physician and Patient Training

Educators and researchers have often commented on the ironic fact that physicians perform thousands of medical interviews during their career with virtually no formal training in communication skills (R. Epstein, Campbell, Cohen-Cole, McWhinney, & Smilkstein, 1993). The assumption was, for a long time, that physicians naturally have adequate skill or that skill inevitably develops through frequent experience. Now medical educators agree that training is necessary, that a solid foundation of behavioral science research exists to support training programs, and that training improves the communication of physicians. Communication skills training during medical school has been shown to have effects lasting as long as 5 years (Maguire, Fairburn, & Fletcher, 1986).

Despite variations in the length and format of physician training programs, all or most of these programs focus on the principles of relationship-centered medicine as defined in this chapter (e.g., Bensing & Sluijs, 1985; Cohen-Cole, 1991; Novack, Dube, & Goldstein, 1992; Putnam, Stiles, Jacob, & James, 1988; Roter et al., 1995). For example, the study of Novack et al. (1992) found improvements in sensitivity to psychosocial aspects of the patient's illness, ability to relate to patients, ability to elicit information from patients, and ability to communicate empathy. Roter et al.'s (1995) training program emphasized physicians' ability to recognize and handle psychosocial problems; after only 8 hours of training, physicians did better with their actual patients (who were audiotaped several weeks after training) in terms of emotion handling, recognizing psychological problems, and taking a problem-solving approach, with no increase in the overall length of the medical visit.

Smith et al. (2000) have developed a standardized training program for primary care residents that has produced very encouraging results in terms of residents' knowledge, attitudes, self-confidence, skills in interviewing patients and dealing with relationships, skills in managing and communicating with somatizing patients, and skills in educating patients. Elements in Smith's training program include setting the stage (e.g., welcoming the patient, using the patient's name, introducing self, removing barriers to communication, putting the patient at ease); agenda setting (e.g., indicating time available, indicating own needs, obtaining list of all issues the patient wants to discuss, summarizing and finalizing the agenda); nonfocused interviewing (e.g., appropriate use of open- and closed-ended questions, observing the patient's cues); and focused interviewing (e.g., symptom discovery, learning personal context of symptoms, addressing emotions).

In contrast to the many programs aimed at physicians and many published evaluations of such programs, relatively little research has tried to intervene with patients to improve the communication process. Classic is Roter's (1977) waiting-room intervention to increase patients' question asking. As described later, the waiting-room interventions by Greenfield and colleagues also influenced patients' behaviors during the medical visit. Recently, an even simpler intervention, consisting of a mailed booklet designed to heighten patients' awareness and skills in communicating with their physicians,

had significant effects on patients' information seeking and success in obtaining information, and on how much information they gave to their physicians (Cegala, McClure, Marinelli, & Post, 2000). In a systematic review of intervention studies, Harrington, Noble, and Newman (2004) concluded that patients' rate of participation is often increased by interventions, more so for face-to-face than written interventions (such as a booklet or workbook).

Outcomes of Communication

From a functional perspective, the assessment of physician-patient communication serves the purpose of predicting important outcomes for patients. In the following sections, we describe three categories of outcomes—satisfaction, adherence, and health status/quality of life. These categories do not, of course, exhaust all the desirable short-term and long-term effects of communication processes within medical care. Others include recall of medical advice, physician-patient concordance (e.g., about the purpose of the visit), relief of worry, physician satisfaction, self-confidence, and sense of control (Beckman, Kaplan, & Frankel, 1989).

It is important to be reminded again of the causal uncertainties intrinsic to correlational data. As indicated earlier, experimentally controlled studies are rare in this literature. Even quite strong and consistent predictive relations do not necessarily mean direct causal paths.

Satisfaction

Satisfaction with medical care is mostly measured with reference to a medical visit that has just occurred. However, the referent can also be a less recent visit, a particular physician, one's care in general, or doctors in general. The latter approach, because it does not emphasize the patient's own experience, is sometimes favored because it produces average levels of satisfaction that are not as extremely high as typically found with physician-specific or visit-specific measures (Hall & Dornan, 1988). This ceiling effect has often been noted as a problem for two reasons. The first is psychometric, in that a restriction of range may attenuate correlations with other variables of interest. The second relates to validity: The extremely high level of satisfaction found in many studies seems to contradict the everyday impression that many patients are disappointed and frustrated with their interactions with physicians. Despite the ceiling effect, which can be extreme, the validity of patient satisfaction measurement is supported by many correlations with antecedent, process, and outcome variables, as we shall see.

Though much satisfaction research has proceeded without a strong theoretical basis (Cleary & McNeil, 1988), it is reasonable to think of satisfaction as the end result of the patient's comparing ideal hopes, realistic expectations, and actual care. Satisfaction has been operationally defined with many instruments that tap a dozen or so aspects of care in addition to overall satisfaction. Some aspects are asked about frequently (e.g., physician's humaneness and physician's informativeness) and some very infrequently (e.g., outcome of care and physician's attention to psychosocial problems; Hall & Dornan, 1988). Though instruments often cover noninterpersonal aspects of care such as access, availability, facilities, and bureaucracy (Hall & Dornan, 1988), satisfaction with physician behavior during the medical visit is most relevant to the present chapter.

Physicians' behaviors are typically classified as task related/cognitive versus socioemotional/affective. For example, not answering all the patient's questions or using too much jargon would be considered task-related failings, whereas treating the patient disrespectfully or acting in a hurry would be considered socioemotional failings. This distinction can be difficult to draw, however, when one considers, first, that task-related behaviors have affective significance (the patient attributes a respectful or caring attitude to the physician who answers all questions) and, second, that the biopsychosocial model specifically places attention to the patient's psychosocial concerns within the scope of physicians' task obligations (Roter & Hall, 1992; Roter et al., 1987).

Satisfaction instruments are typically designed with psychometric standards in mind (e.g., reliability) and typically consist of Likert-scaled items (agree-disagree) or direct evaluative scales (not satisfied to very satisfied). Though investigators often conceptualize satisfaction as multifactorial, nevertheless different aspects of satisfaction tend to be highly related, and often a one-dimensional structure emerges, though sometimes the distinction between technical and interpersonal aspects is revealed (Hagedoorn et al., 2003; Marshall, Hays, Sherbourne, & Wells, 1993; Roter et al., 1987).

The term *satisfaction* suggests a response that is both affective (how did this experience make me feel?) and evaluative (did this experience meet my standards of quality?), and indeed instruments often capture these elements. However, about half of all satisfaction studies operationally define "satisfaction" in terms of factual descriptions (e.g., my physician seemed to be in a hurry; my physician answered all of my questions) that embody "satisfaction" only to the extent that the investigator makes assumptions about what values and expectations are held by the patient (Hall & Dornan, 1988). Thus, the patient whose physician does not seem to be in a hurry is assumed to be the more satisfied. This could be a wrong assumption if the patient was not particularly troubled by that aspect of the physician's behavior. Measures designed on this format are positively related to those that ask the patient to evaluate their care or indicate satisfaction directly, supporting their use as satisfaction measures. Nevertheless, it is interesting to point out the conceptual ambiguity of items that in one context would be taken as description of the physician's behavior and in another context as an affective response to the physician's behavior (Hall & Dornan, 1988). Obviously, to treat descriptions of physician behavior as "satisfaction" poses difficulties when one seeks to identify which physician behaviors lead to satisfaction.

Satisfaction has been examined in many studies of physician-patient communication, and many relations have been uncovered. The studies of DiMatteo and colleagues stand out as strongly suggesting a role for physicians' nonverbal expression and judgment abilities in determining patients' satisfaction. These studies are especially interesting because they are the only ones that have measured physicians' communication skills as general traits, that is, in terms of scores on tests of nonverbal communication skill. Physicians' ability to express emotions through nonverbal cues (e.g., facial expressions and tones of voice) and their ability to judge the meanings of such nonverbal expressions predicted their patients' satisfaction (DiMatteo, Taranta, Friedman, & Prince, 1980). Though research has not directly observed how these more nonverbally skilled physicians interacted with their patients, one can speculate that they listened well; picked up on cues of anxiety, pain, and unspoken concerns; and were able to show the emotions they wish to show, as well as suppress outward displays of undesired emotions. Though we cannot yet trace which physician behaviors account for the correlations between tested skills and patient satisfaction, many studies have found significant relations between physician behaviors measured during the medical visit and patient satisfaction measured after the visit. Speaking broadly, many findings can be subsumed under several main categories of physician behavior (see reviews by Hall et al., 1988; Ong, de Haes, Hoos, & Lammes, 1995; Thompson, 1994; S. Williams, Weinman, & Dale, 1998). Greater satisfaction is associated with a physician style that includes more information giving, more supportive behavior (partnership building, positive talk, psychosocial and emotional talk, and more nonverbal immediacy—e.g., gaze, forward lean, and closer distance), and more social (nonmedical) talk. Greater physician competence in both task and socioemotional domains predicts satisfaction, suggesting that patients are able to discriminate on objective quality dimensions. Longer visits predict satisfaction, which may be no surprise considering that the previously named categories together account for most physician-patient conversation. On the patient's side, higher levels of activation also contribute to improvements in satisfaction (Bertakis et al., 1998).

Consistent with these behavioral predictors, physician attitudes also predict satisfaction. Krupat et al. (2000) found that patients were more satisfied when their physicians responded favorably to items such as "Patients should be treated as if they were partners with the doctor, equal in power and status." Krupat et al. (2000) also tested the important hypothesis that optimal outcomes occur when the physician and patient share congruent values about the balance of power. Satisfaction was particularly low when the patient placed higher value on shared power than the physician did.

Several physician behaviors have emerged as negative predictors of satisfaction. Whereas psychosocial questioning is very well received by patients, there is evidence that more questioning on biomedical topics is associated with lower satisfaction (Roter et al., 1987; Bertakis et al., 1991). At least two interpretations of this finding are possible. One is that more biomedical questioning by the physician occurs when the patient's health is worse, and as discussed earlier, poor health is associated with lower satisfaction. Thus, the relation may be spurious. Another interpretation is that more biomedical questioning by the physician is indicative of greater physician dominance, with the questions (which are most often the closed, yes-no type) reflecting physician control over the substance of the dialogue. Indeed, a number of studies find that greater physician dominance predicts lower satisfaction, whether measured objectively (as in a higher ratio of physician-to-patient talk; Bertakis et al., 1991) or in patients' ratings of physician dominance (Buller & Buller, 1987; Burgoon et al., 1987).

There are few intervention studies in the satisfaction literature; Hall and Dornan (1988) found that only 14% of the 221 satisfaction studies in their meta-analysis had experimental designs. Many studies report simple correlations that do not attempt to control statistically for potentially confounding variables. One needs to be cautious, therefore, in assuming that causality goes from communication behavior to patients' subsequent satisfaction. When controlled studies are done, they do support a causal interpretation; for example, interventions aimed at improving physicians' communication skills have been shown to produce not only changes in physician behavior but also improvements in patient satisfaction (Evans, Kiellerup, Stanley, Burrows, & Sweet, 1987). But even so, there can be other causal paths, such as when low patient satisfaction is expressed in negative behaviors, which are then reciprocated by the physician.

At its extreme, low satisfaction can culminate in a malpractice suit. Research finds that disappointment in one's relationship with a physician often overshadows the objective severity of the physician's errors of medical judgment. Objectively measured quality of care does not appear to be the primary determinant in a patient's decision to initiate a malpractice claim. It is estimated that fewer than 2% of patients who have suffered a significant injury due to negligence initiate a malpractice claim (Localio, Lawthers, & Brennan, 1991). There is evidence that patients and families are more likely to sue a physician when faced with a bad outcome if they felt that the physician failed to communicate in a timely and open manner or perceived the physician as being uncaring or indifferent (Beckman, Markakis, Suchman, & Frankel, 1994). How communication may actually differ between physicians who were never sued and those who were was addressed in a study by Levinson et al. (1997). The routine medical visits of primary care physicians who had never been sued were compared with those with a lifetime malpractice experience of at least two suits. Interaction analysis of the physician visits (using the RIAS) found that never-sued doctors had longer visits, engaged in more laughter, were more likely to orient the patient to what to expect in regard to the flow of the visit, and used more partnership-type exchanges (asking for the patient's opinion, understanding of what was said and expectations for the visit; showing interest in patient disclosures; and paraphrasing and interpreting what the patient said) than physicians who had been sued.

As mentioned, most research on patient satisfaction has been conducted in primary care, outpatient settings. But a growing body of research in oncology seems to indicate findings similar to those found in primary care. For example, Ong, Visser, Lammes, and de Haes (2000) found that cancer patients' satisfaction was related to the affective quality of the consultation. Like most patients, those with cancer typically want more information than they get, are unsure of their diagnosis and prognosis, and are unsure of what diagnostic tests are needed and what they mean; indeed, oncologists themselves report being stressed by their poor training in communication (Fallowfield & Jenkins, 1999). A smaller amount of attention has been paid to studying communication issues for hospitalized patients, some of whom of course also have cancer; again, the preference for receiving information is high and predictive of satisfaction (Krupat, Fancey, & Cleary, 2000), and patients complain of inadequate time talking with nurses and doctors, not being told about hospital routine, not being told whom to ask for help, and not getting enough information about post-discharge care (Delbanco et al., 1995).

Adherence

The extent to which patients follow their treatment or lifestyle recommendations and show up for scheduled visits has long been a subject of concern for health services researchers because failure in either of these areas is likely to jeopardize health and waste health resources (Becker, 1985). For many years, the term *compliance* was used by investigators, but more recently, in keeping with changes in how the field conceptualizes the physician-patient relationship, *adherence* has become the preferred term. As long as the implicit model of the relationship was a paternalistic one in which influence was assumed to flow one way, it followed that the patient's job was to do what the doctor said to

do (i.e., comply). With the advent of other models of patienthood, a wider range of goals and commitments is now considered relevant to health outcomes. Accordingly, the term *adherence* suggests that the patient may engage in behaviors relevant to self-set and mutually negotiated goals, as well as physician-set goals.

Research finds that adherence is shockingly low, as reviewed by Haynes, Taylor, and Sackett (1979) and subsequently corroborated by many other reviewers. Estimates of nonadherence rates with prescribed therapeutic regimens typically range from 30% to 60%, with most researchers agreeing that at least 50% of patients for whom drugs are prescribed fail to receive full benefit through inadequate adherence (Rogers & Bullman, 1995). Adherence rates may be improving, however. In the largest quantitative synthesis of this literature done to date, DiMatteo (2004) reported that the rate of patient adherence is generally increasing. Studies conducted after 1980 yielded an average adherence rate of 75%, representing an improvement of 13 percentage points over the rates found for studies published before that period. This is a clinically relevant change reflecting an increasing awareness of the role of adherence in influencing medical outcomes.

In addition to adherence problems, it has been estimated that almost one third of patients who received prescriptions were using them in a manner that posed a serious threat to their health (Boyd, Covington, Stanaszek, & Coussons, 1974). Nevertheless, doctors infrequently suspect that their patients are not taking their drugs exactly as prescribed, and are poor at estimating their patients' rate of adherence; patients rarely volunteer adherence information to their doctor; doctors do not often explicitly ask, and instead are likely to blame nonadherence on the patient's personality (Becker, 1985; Steele, Jackson, & Gutmann, 1990).

Measures of adherence are varied and include self-reports of medication adherence, diet, exercise, and prevention; physiological outcomes (such as blood pressure and blood glucose) that are deemed to be sensitive to medication and/or lifestyle adherence; indirect measures such as refill records and pill counts; and utilization measures, which include appointment making, appointment keeping, and use of preventive services such as mammography (Roter et al., 1998). These measures have variable validity; self-reports of adherence, for example, may be exaggerated (though research suggests they are positively related to other methods of assessment; Becker, 1985), and physiological indicators are subject to influences other than adherence to regimen.

Not surprisingly, research has found correlations between physician-patient communication and adherence. DiMatteo, Hays, and Prince (1986) found that the patients of physicians who were more sensitive to nonverbal cues (as measured with a standardized test) were more adherent to their scheduled appointments than patients of less sensitive physicians. We do not yet know how it is that such physicians induce better adherence, but it is known that patients are more adherent when their physicians deliver more information, ask more questions about adherence (but fewer questions overall), and engage in more positive talk (Hall et al., 1988). In this context, the patient intervention study of Roter (1977), mentioned earlier, is relevant: Patients who were encouraged by the investigator to ask more questions during their medical visit were subsequently more likely to keep their scheduled appointments than were untrained patients. Although it is possible that improvements in appointment keeping was a benefit of the added information patients received from their physicians, other findings of the study suggest that the higher rates of appointment keeping were related to an enhanced internal sense of control in health-related matters. The patients who participated in the activation intervention scored significantly higher than other patients on a measure of health locus of control.

The sources of patients' nonadherence are many, with some related to deficiencies in the physician-patient relationship. Patients need to understand the treatment recommendations, believe in them, and have the ability to follow them. When they do not understand what they are to do or doubt a recommendation's usefulness, they ignore it; and when they lack appropriate circumstances or supports, they are less likely to follow through as recommended (DiMatteo, 1994; DiMatteo & DiNicola, 1982; DiMatteo, Reiter, & Gambone, 1994).

Poor adherence can also be the end result of reciprocity processes between patient and physician. Roter and Hall (1992) suggested that resentment toward a disappointing or aggravating physician can lead patients to reciprocate the negativity by not doing what the physician wants. Unfortunately, in deciding how to behave, a patient may be more influenced by the anticipated satisfaction of

"getting even" with the doctor than by the likely damage to his or her own health resulting from nonadherence. Though our emphasis has been on communication skill as a physician trait, it is possible of course that situational stresses and other contextual variables impair physician performance as well. Consistent with such an interpretation, when physicians were less satisfied with their jobs, their patients reported poorer treatment adherence as much as 2 years later (DiMatteo et al., 1993).

Many intervention studies have been designed to improve adherence. A meta-analysis of 153 studies classified the intervention strategies broadly as educational, behavioral, and affective (Roter et al., 1998). Educational interventions could emphasize pedagogical methods intended to increase patients' knowledge through one-to-one and group teaching, as well as the use of written and audiovisual materials. Behaviorally focused interventions were designed to change adherence by targeting, shaping, or reinforcing specific behavioral patterns and included skill-building and practice activities, behavioral modeling and contracting, packaging and dosage modifications, and mail and telephone reminders. Affectively focused strategies attempted to influence adherence through appeals to feelings and emotions or social relationships and social supports, including family support, counseling, and supportive home visits. Interventions were further subclassified according to how many distinct components and strategies were represented.

The meta-analysis found that interventions had positive effects that ranged from small to large in magnitude. Overall effects were almost always significant regardless of whether the outcome measures were physiological indicators such as disease severity, direct indicators such as blood or urine tests, indirect indicators such as refill records, subjective measures such as self-reports, or utilization measures such as appointment keeping. Larger studies produced smaller effects, possibly because they used less tailored or less intensive interventions. Interventions profited from combining more than one kind of strategy, for example, educational plus behavioral. Finally, interventions appeared to be effective across a variety of diagnostic categories (cancer, hypertension, diabetes, and mental health problems), though some kinds of interventions worked better than others for different diagnoses.

All in all, it is encouraging that interventions can do some good considering that adherence is also influenced by many extraneous factors, including personality, health beliefs, and sociodemographic factors. The question that is most germane to the present chapter is whether it is possible and practical for physicians to incorporate adherence-improving activities in routine practice. We strongly believe that it is, and that a large part of the battle consists in simply persuading physicians to increase their currently low level of discussing the topic with their patients. Once that barrier is overcome, it should be relatively easy to teach physicians to engage in a few targeted behaviors. Furthermore, studies showing that satisfaction and adherence are positively related and our earlier discussion of reciprocity suggest that the quality of the physician-patient relationship itself can motivate adherence, above and beyond any particular adherence-inducing behaviors enacted by the physician.

An example of the potential for incorporating simple interventions into routine practice is the study of Cegala, Marinelli, and Post (2000), in which a workbook was mailed to patients before their scheduled visit that was designed to instruct them in seeking, verifying, and providing information during the medical visit and to give patients the opportunity to write down their concerns and questions. Adherence, as determined in a telephone survey 2 weeks later, was significantly greater than in two control groups.

Health and Quality of Life

Some of the same measures that are used as indicators of adherence are also used as health status end points, for example, glucose, blood pressure, and cholesterol control. A number of self- or physician-reported measuring instruments exist, typically checklists of health conditions. Other measures of health status are more global, reflecting a patient's or an observer's (typically a physician's) assessment of health on various dimensions, including physiological, emotional, cognitive, and social (Hall et al., 1996; Jenkinson, 1994; A. Stewart & Ware, 1992). Measures of health status serve also as predictor measures and covariates in many studies.

Research finds that behaviors that can collectively be considered relationship centered, including physician informativeness, partnership building, and emotional rapport and support, are related to a range of health outcomes such as improvements in emotional health, symptom resolution, physical functioning and quality-of-life assessments, physi-

ological indicators of disease management (blood pressure, blood sugar), and pain control (Arora, 2003; M. Stewart, 1996). For example, blood pressure control improved more if patients were allowed to tell their whole story to their doctor and the doctor provided more information to the patient (Orth, Stiles, Scherwitz, Hennrikus, & Vallbona, 1987); health status improved more over time when the physician's communication style included more psychosocial counseling (Bertakis et al., 1998).

Consistent with these results, a meta-analysis of randomized studies of the effects of psychosocial interventions on health and quality of life in cancer patients found positive and significant effects for a range of outcomes, including emotional adjustment, functional adjustment, and reduction in disease- and treatment-related symptoms (Meyer & Mark, 1995). These positive effects were evident across a range of psychosocial interventions, including cognitive-behavioral methods, informational-educational methods, and various kinds of counseling and verbal psychotherapy. The impact on disease outcomes was also positive but not significant (there were few studies in this category).

More striking still are experimental studies showing that communication interventions can have significant effects on health outcomes. In one study, a research assistant reviewed the medical record with the patient, helped the patient identify decisions to be made, rehearsed negotiation skills, encouraged the patient to ask questions, reviewed obstacles such as embarrassment and intimidation, and after the visit gave the patient a copy of the medical record for that visit. In a sample of diabetic patients, such an intervention reduced blood sugar, reduced patients' reports of functional limitations (mobility, role functions, physical activities), and improved patients' perceptions of their overall health (Greenfield, Kaplan, Ware, Yano, & Frank, 1988). Mechanisms accounting for these effects are not entirely understood because the intervention contained a number of elements but are likely related both to information exchange and to feelings of empowerment; in that study, experimental patients elicited more information from physicians, talked more, and were more assertive. Encouraging results have occurred in similarly designed studies using different patient populations, for example, patients with ulcer disease (Kaplan, Greenfield, & Ware, 1989). C. G. Williams and Deci (2001) intervened experimentally with physicians' manner of communicating about smoking cessation and found that an autonomy-supportive style increased patient participation, which then reduced smoking rates for as long as 30 months after the visit.

A review of studies on the relation between physician behavior style and patients' health outcomes in chronic disease made a distinction between studies that measured how much the physician elicited and discussed patients' beliefs versus how much the physician tried to activate the patient to take control in the consultation and the management of the illness (Michie, Miles, & Weinman, 2003). Studies involving patient activation showed more consistent effects.

Interventions to improve physicians' communication skills also hold promise to improve health status. As mentioned earlier, Roter et al. (1995) randomly assigned community-based physicians either to an 8–hour course on improving their recognition and management of psychosocial distress in primary care or to a control group. Patients of trained physicians showed improvements in their emotional distress for as long as 6 months after the intervention.

Although only a relatively small number of studies relate communication process to health outcomes, some studies allow an inference about ultimate health effects by showing that communication is related to important proximal variables or that patient reports of physician behavior predict health outcomes. A good example regarding a proximal variable is the pediatric study of Wissow, Roter, and Wilson (1994) in which parents were more likely to disclose information about their child's mental health when the pediatricians asked more questions about psychosocial issues, expressed support, and displayed interest and attention while listening. If we assume that disclosure of a psychosocial problem is the first step toward treating and relieving it, then such a study again points to physician communication as a potent influence in this process. An example based on patient reports of physician behavior is G. C. Williams, Freedman, and Deci's (1998) study in which diabetic patients' reports of autonomy-supportive behaviors by their physicians predicted improvements in their glucose levels.

Yet another pathway to improved health outcomes is through adherence to medical regimens; though one would like to assume that adherence promotes health, this should not be a foregone conclusion, because many factors contribute to

health outcomes. Fortunately, the meta-analysis of DiMatteo, Giordani, Lepper, and Croghan (2002) demonstrated that better adherence is associated with better health outcomes, especially when adherence is to a nonmedication regimen. Tracing the path backward from adherence to communication, these results further support the idea that communication has an important impact on health status.

Limitations in Research to Date

There are a number of fundamental issues with which the field must contend for progress to continue. Among these important considerations are the need for guiding theoretical models, current methodological limitations, and the application of research methods and results to physician training and assessment.

First and primary among these issues is the lack of theoretical models to guide investigators (see Hall et al., 1988; Roter & Hall, 1992; Roter, 2000a). This deficit has contributed to the largely exploratory nature of this work, with little conceptual framing of the studies' meaning. In this regard the application of meta-analytic methods can be helpful in uncovering common underlying dimensions in this body of research. Many of the coding systems are complementary and could potentially be combined in creative and powerful ways. Furthermore, measurement approaches must be subject to both construct and predictive validity. In particular, they must be designed to capture the theoretical constructs that guide a study's hypotheses. A recent review concluded, for example, that even though investigators are eager to study patient involvement in decision making, few instruments exist that are specifically designed to measure this process in medical visits (Elwyn et al., 2001).

Second, methodological limitations are evident in all individual systems of interaction analysis. There has yet to be developed a practical approach that can account for interaction *sequence* in our analysis. A basic assumption has been that summary profiles based on frequencies of verbal behaviors engaged in during the encounter adequately reflect the communication process. However, as pointed out by Inui and Carter (1985), this is analogous to describing *Hamlet* as a play in which the principal characters include ghosts, witches, lords, ladies, officers, soldiers, sailors, messengers, and attendants—one of whom is already dead, one of whom dies by drowning, one by poisoned drink, two by poisoned sword, and one by sword and by drink! The schism between qualitative and quantitative methods continues to stymie progress in both these areas. We need to develop new models of analysis that are integrative rather than parallel or competing. New computer technologies, but even more so nontraditional thinking, may be the key to this needed breakthrough.

Along these same lines, the design of research in the field has been quite narrow and almost entirely cross-sectional, with little attention to longitudinality or continuity of care; two exceptions are studies by M. Stewart (1995) and van Dulmen et al. (1997). In a meta-analysis reported earlier, only 40% of the studies even specified whether the patient and physician were previously acquainted (Roter et al., 1988). Our current work is moving in this direction; we have analyzed the health maintenance visits of 192 new babies over a 1-year period (for a total of 700 visits) to 30 pediatricians. Surprisingly, we found that a longitudinal relationship was not associated with more frequent discussion of psychosocial topics or with improved physician awareness of maternal distress (Wissow et al., 2000). Although there is reason to believe that continuity of care provides great advantages to the therapeutic relationship (it is related to patient satisfaction, for example), we really know very little about continuity's black box. In fact, it may be that there are some negative aspects of continuity, such as the presumptuousness of familiarity, labeling, and simply the need for a fresh perspective. Better specification of the ongoing relationship can be accomplished through more conscientious reporting by investigators and through more creative research designs.

Third, investigators have some responsibility to make their research methods and findings accessible to the clinical audience. More intervention studies are needed in which teaching methods are evaluated in light of actual changes in physicians' communication style and, further, validated against changes in patient outcomes. Those physicians responsible for training in clinical interviewing courses could particularly benefit from this area of work by collaborating with researchers to develop analysis schemes pertinent to quality-of-care assessment. Application of research to patient interventions is also an important and relatively underdeveloped focus. Many studies that addressed patient interven-

tions found favorable effects. This is clearly an area that needs further elaboration and has tremendous potential for health education trials.

Future Directions

The field needs more experience in analyzing relationships under stress, for example, under circumstances of trauma or terminal illness. Most of what we know about patient-physician communication has been described within the context of routine primary care. As mentioned earlier, a growing and important body of studies with cancer patients will help us better understand nonroutine care and the management of life-threatening illness episodes. Insight into these areas is important because it could improve the care of large numbers of patients who will remain outside of the primary care system, as well as improve coordination and integrate care for the majority of patients straddling primary and specialty care.

Integration of psychotherapeutic techniques and theories into communication assessment and primary care training will help push forward the field in meeting the challenges of psychosomatic and psychosocial distress among so many primary care patients. Communication researchers must also confront emerging ethical and philosophical issues. These include decision-making processes related to conditions of uncertainty such as end-of-life planning, enrollment in clinical trials, treatment of the cognitively impaired, and decisions regarding genetic testing and its consequences.

Insight is needed into the social context of the therapeutic relationship, with attention to issues of gender, social class, and ethnicity. Of these social context variables, gender has received the most attention within communication studies, although as noted earlier the number of studies is still small. Virtually unknown are the effects of physicians' social class, ethnicity, and culture on patients of the same or different backgrounds.

Knowledge of the basic social psychology of the therapeutic relationship continues to mature but still shows vulnerable gaps. We cannot yet consistently increase patient understanding and recall, improve participatory decision making, or optimize adherence and commitment to therapeutic regimens. These are continuing and critical challenges for communication researchers.

We must embrace the challenge of new interactive computer technologies into all levels of our work. Use of interactive CD-ROMs, Web-based programming, and interactive videos foreshadows this tremendously exciting new frontier.

Finally, one further issue is worthy of consideration: The basic characteristics of the provider-patient relationship may be undergoing substantial evolutionary change (Inui & Carter, 1985). There is considerable evidence that patients are becoming more consumerist in orientation, and particularly the new generation of patients is likely to directly challenge physician authority within the medical encounter (Haug & Lavin, 1983). There is, likewise, evidence that physicians may be accommodating their patients with a more egalitarian relationship and tolerance for patient participation in decision making. The implications of these changes are tremendous, and they must be given full and serious consideration in conceptualizing how the patient-physician relationship may be articulated in the medical encounter. Important strides have been made in the understanding of doctor-patient relations, but challenges remain. The most significant of these challenges is to push forward our conceptual and methodological imagination to approach the field in new and meaningful ways.

Note

1. We refer throughout this chapter to *physicians* and *doctors* (terms we use interchangeably), but a great deal of what we report is relevant to a wide range of health professionals, including nurses, dentists, physical and occupational therapists, and pharmacists. Furthermore, each of these professions has been the focus of its own communication research.

References

Adelman, R. D., Greene, M. G., & Charon, R. (1987). The physician elderly patient companion triad in the medical encounter. *Gerontologist, 27,* 729–734.

Arora, N. K. (2003). Interacting with cancer patients: The significance of physicians' communication behavior. *Social Science & Medicine, 57,* 791–806.

Arora, N. K., & McHorney, C. A. (2000). Patient preferences for medical decision-making: Who really wants to participate? *Medical Care, 38,* 335–341.

Bales, R. F. (1950). *Interaction process analysis.* Cambridge, MA: Addison-Wesley.

Balint, M. (1964). *The doctor, his patient, and the illness* (2nd ed.). New York: International Universities Press.

Bartlett, E. E., Grayson, M., Barker, R., Levine, D. M., Golden, A., & Libber, S. (1984). The effects of physician communication skills on patient satisfaction, recall, and adherence. *Journal of Chronic Diseases, 37,* 755–764.

Becker, M. H. (1985). Patient adherence to prescribed therapies. *Medical Care, 23,* 539–555.

Beckman, H., Kaplan, S. H., & Frankel, R. (1989). Outcome based research on doctor-patient communication: A review. In M. Stewart & D. Roter (Eds.), *Communicating with medical patients* (pp. 223–227). Newbury Park, CA: Sage.

Beckman, H. B., & Frankel, R. M. (1984). The effect of physician behavior on the collection of data. *Annals of Internal Medicine, 101,* 692–696.

Beckman, H. B., Markakis, K. M., Suchman, A. L., & Frankel, R. M. (1994). The doctor-plaintiff relationship: Lessons from plaintiff depositions. *Archives of Internal Medicine, 154,* 1365–1370.

Bensing, J. M., & Dronkers, J. (1992). Instrumental and affective aspects of physician behavior. *Medical Care, 30,* 283–298.

Bensing, J. M., & Sluijs, E. M. (1985). Evaluation of an interview training course for general practitioners. *Social Science & Medicine, 20,* 737–744.

Ben-Sira, Z. (1980). Affective and instrumental components in the physician-patient relationship: An additional dimension of interaction theory. *Journal of Health and Social Behavior, 21,* 170–181.

Bertakis, K. D., Callahan, E. J., Helms, L. J., Azari, R., & Robbins, J. A., & Miller, J. (1998). Physician practice styles and patient outcomes: Differences between family practice and general internal medicine. *Medical Care, 36,* 879–891.

Bertakis, K. D., Callahan, E. J., Helms, L. J., Azari, R., & Robbins, J. A. (1993). The effect of patient health on physician practice style. *Family Medicine, 25,* 530–535.

Bertakis, K. D., Roter, D. L., & Putnam, S. M. (1991). The relationship of physician medical interview style to patient satisfaction. *Journal of Family Practice, 32,* 175–181.

Boon, H., & Stewart, M. (1998). Patient-physician communication assessment instruments: 1986 to 1996 in review. *Patient Education and Counseling, 35,* 161–176.

Boyd, J. R., Covington, T. R., Stanaszek, W. F., & Coussons, R. T. (1974). Drug defaulting: Part I. Determinants of compliance. *American Journal of Hospital Pharmacy, 31,* 485–491.

Brody, L. R., & Hall, J. A. (2000). Gender, emotion, and expression. In M. Lewis & J. Haviland-Jones (Eds.), *Handbook of emotions* (2nd ed., pp. 338–349). New York: Guilford.

Brown, J. B., Stewart, M. A., McCracken, E. C., McWhinney, I. R., & Levenstein, J. H. (1986). The patient-centered clinical method: 2. Definition and application. *Family Practice: An International Journal, 3,* 75–79.

Brown, J. B., Stewart, M., & Tessier, S. (1995). *Assessing communication between patients and doctors: A manual for scoring patient-centered communication.* Working paper series (Paper No. 95). University of Western Ontario, Centre for Studies in Family Medicine, London, Ontario, Canada.

Brown, J. B., Weston, W. W., & Stewart, M. A. (1989). Patient-centered interviewing. Part II: Finding common ground. *Canadian Family Physician, 35,* 153–157.

Buller, M. K., & Buller, D. B. (1987). Physicians' communication style and patient satisfaction. *Journal of Health and Social Behavior, 28,* 375–388.

Burgoon, J. K., Pfau, M., Parrott, R., Birk, T., Coker, R., & Burgoon, M. (1987). Relational communication, satisfaction, compliance-gaining strategies, and compliance in communication between physicians and patients. *Communication Monographs, 54,* 307–324.

Cegala, D. J., Marinelli, T., & Post, D. (2000). The effects of patient communication skills training on compliance. *Archives of Family Medicine, 9,* 57–64.

Cegala, D. J., McClure, L., Marinelli, T. M., & Post, D. M. (2000). The effects of communication skills training on patients' participation during medical interviews. *Patient Education and Counseling, 41,* 209–222.

Cleary, P. D., & McNeil, B. J. (1988). Patient satisfaction as an indicator of quality care. *Inquiry, 25*(Spring), 25–36.

Cohen-Cole, S. (1991). *The medical interview: The three function approach.* St. Louis, MO: Mosby.

Cooper, L. A., Roter, D. L., Johnson, R. L., Ford, D. E., Steinwachs, D. M., & Powe, N. R. (2003). Patient-centered communication, ratings of care, and concordance of patient and physician race. *Annals of Internal Medicine, 139,* 907–915.

Cooper-Patrick, L., Gallo, J. J., Gonzales, J. J., Vu, H. T., Powe, N. R., Nelson, C., et al. (1999). Race, gender, and partnership in the patient-physician relationship. *Journal of the American Medical Association, 282,* 583–589.

Davis, M. (1969). Variations in patients' compliance with doctors' advice: An empirical analysis of patterns of communication. *American Journal of Public Health, 58,* 274–288.

Davis, M. (1971). Variation in patients' compliance with doctors' orders: Medical practice and doctor-patient interaction. *Psychiatry in Medicine, 2,* 31–54.

Delbanco, T. L., Stokes, D. M., Cleary, P. D., Edgman-Levitan, S., Walker, J. D., Gerteis, M., et al. (1995). Medical patients' assessments of their care during hospitalization: Insights for internists. *Journal of General Internal Medicine, 10,* 679–685.

DiMatteo, M. R. (1994). Enhancing patient adherence to medical recommendations. *Journal of the American Medical Association, 271,* 79–83.

DiMatteo, M. R. (2004). Variations in patients' adherence to medical recommendations: A quantitative review of 50 years of research. *Medical Care, 42,* 200–209.

DiMatteo, M. R., Giordani, P. J., Lepper, H. S., & Croghan, T. W. (2002). Patient adherence and medical treatment outcomes: A meta-analysis. *Medical Care, 40,* 794–811.

DiMatteo, M. R., Hays, R. D., & Prince, L. M. (1986). Relationship of physicians' nonverbal communication skills to patient satisfaction, appointment noncompliance, and physician workload. *Health Psychology, 5,* 581–594.

DiMatteo, M. R., & DiNicola, D. D. (1982). *Achieving patient compliance.* New York: Pergamon Press.

DiMatteo, M. R., Reiter, R. C., & Gambone, J. C. (1994). Enhancing medication adherence through communication and informed collaborative choice. *Health Communication, 6,* 253–265.

DiMatteo, M. R., Sherbourne, C. D., Hays, R. D., Ordway, L., Kravitz, R. L., McGlynn, E. A., et al. (1993). Physicians' characteristics influence patients' adherence to medical treatment: Results from the Medical Outcomes Study. *Health Psychology, 12,* 93–102.

DiMatteo, M. R., Taranta, A., Friedman, H. S., & Prince, L. M. (1980). Predicting patient satisfaction from physicians' nonverbal communication skills. *Medical Care, 18,* 376–387.

Dindia, K., & Allen, M. (1992). Sex differences in self-disclosure: A meta-analysis. *Psychological Bulletin, 112,* 106–124.

Eagly, A. H., & Johnson, B. T. (1990). Gender and leadership style: A meta-analysis. *Psychological Bulletin, 108,* 233–256.

Elwyn, G., Edwards, A., Mowle, S., Wensing, M., Wilkinson, C., Kinnersley, P., et al. (2001). Measuring the involvement of patients in shared decision-making: A systematic review of instruments. *Patient Education and Counseling, 43,* 5–22.

Emanuel, E. J., & Emanuel, L. L. (1992). Four models of the physician-patient relationship. *Journal of the American Medical Association, 267*, 2221–2226.

Emanuel, E. J., trans. Plato (1961). In E. Hamilton & H. Cairns (Eds.), *The collected dialogues.* Princeton, NJ: Princeton University Press.

Emerson, R. M. (1976). Social exchange theory. *Annual Review of Public Health, 2*, 335–362.

Ende, J., Kazis, L., Ash, A., & Moskowitz, M. A. (1989). Measuring patients' desire for autonomy: Decision making and information-seeking preferences among medical patients. *Journal of General Internal Medicine, 4*, 23–30.

Ende, J., Kazis, L., & Moskowitz, M. A. (1990). Preferences for autonomy when patients are physicians. *Journal of General Internal Medicine, 5*, 506–509.

Engel, G. L. (1977). The need for a new medical model: A challenge for biomedicine. *Science, 196*, 129–136.

Engel, G. L. (1988). How much longer must medicine's science be bound by a seventeenth century world view? In K. White (Ed.), *The task of medicine: Dialogue at Wickenburg* (pp. 113–136). Menlo Park, CA: Henry J. Kaiser Family Foundation.

Epstein, A. M., Taylor, W. C., & Seage, G. R. (1985). Effects of patients' socioeconomic status and physicians' training and practice on patient-doctor communication. *American Journal of Medicine, 78*, 101–106.

Epstein, R. M., Campbell, T. L., Cohen-Cole, S. A., McWhinney, I. R., & Smilkstein, G. (1993). Perspectives on patient-doctor communication. *Journal of Family Practice, 37*, 377–388.

Evans, B. J., Kiellerup, F. D., Stanley, R. O., Burrows, G. D., & Sweet, B. (1987). A communication skills programme for increasing patients' satisfaction with general practice consultations. *British Journal of Medical Psychology, 60*, 373–378.

Fallowfield, L., & Jenkins, V. (1999). Effective communication skills are the key to good cancer care. *European Journal of Cancer, 35*, 1592–1597.

Freemon, B., Negrete, V., Davis, M., & Korsch, B. (1971). Gaps in doctor patient communication. *Pediatric Research, 5*, 298–311.

Freidson, E. (1970). *Professional dominance.* Chicago: Aldine.

Freire, P. (1970). *Pedagogy of the oppressed.* New York: Seabury

Freire, P. (1983). *Education for critical consciousness.* New York: Continuum.

Gazmararian, J .A., Baker, D .W., Williams, M. V., Parker, R. M., Scott, T. L., Green, D. C., et al. (1999). Health literacy among Medicare enrollees in a managed care organization. *Journal of the American Medical Association, 281*, 545–551.

Gladwin, T. (1964). Culture and logical process. In W. H. Goodenough (Ed.), *Explorations in cultural anthropology: Essays in honor of George Peter Murdock* (pp. 167–177). New York: McGraw-Hill.

Goldberg, D., & Williams, P. (1988). *A user's guide to the General Health Questionnaire.* Windsor, Berkshire, UK: NFER-Nelson.

Gotler, R. S., Flocke, S. A., Goodwin, M. A., Zyzanski, S. J., Murray, T. H., & Stange, K. C. (2000). Facilitating participatory decision-making: What happens in real-word community practice? *Medical Care, 38*, 1200–1209.

Gouldner, A .W. (1960). The norm of reciprocity: A preliminary statement. *American Sociological Review, 26*, 161–179.

Greene, M. G., & Adelman, R. D. (1996). Psychosocial factors in older patients' medical encounters. *Research on Aging, 18*, 84–102.

Greene, M. G., Adelman, R. D., Friedmann, E., & Charon, R. (1994). Older patient satisfaction with communication during an initial medical encounter. *Social Science & Medicine, 38* , 1279–1283.

Greene, M. G., Hoffman, S., Charon, R., & Adelman, R. D. (1987). Psychosocial concerns in the medical encounter: A comparison of the interactions of doctors with their old and young patients. *Gerontologist, 27*, 164–168.

Greenfield, S., Kaplan, S., & Ware, J. E. Jr. (1985). Expanding patient involvement in care: Effects on patient outcomes. *Annals of Internal Medicine, 102*, 520–528.

Greenfield, S., Kaplan, S. H., Ware, J. E., Jr., Yano, E. M., & Frank, H. J. L. (1988). Patients' participation in medical care: Effects on blood sugar control and quality of life in diabetes. *Journal of General Internal Medicine, 3*, 448–457.

Hagedoorn, M., Uijl, S. G., Van Sonderen, E., Ranchor, A. V., Grol, B. M. F., Otter, R., et al. (2003). Structure and reliability of Ware's Patient Satisfaction Questionnaire. III: Patients' satisfaction with oncological care in the Netherlands. *Medical Care, 41*, 254–263.

Hall, J. A. (1984). *Nonverbal sex differences: Communication accuracy and expressive style.* Baltimore: Johns Hopkins University Press.

Hall, J. A. (2006). How big are nonverbal gender differences? The case of smiling and sensitivity to nonverbal cues. In K. Dindia & D. J. Canary (Eds.), *Sex differences and similarities in communication* (2nd ed., pp. 59–81). Mahwah, NJ: Erlbaum.

Hall, J. A., & Dornan, M. C. (1988). Meta-analysis of satisfaction with medical care: Description of research domain and analysis of overall satisfaction levels. *Social Science & Medicine, 27*, 637–644.

Hall, J. A., & Dornan, M. C. (1990). Patient socio-demographic characteristics as predictors of satisfaction with medical care: A meta-analysis. *Social Science & Medicine, 30,* 811–818.

Hall, J. A., Epstein, A. M., DeCiantis, M. L., & McNeil, B. J. (1993). Physicians' liking for their patients: More evidence for the role of affect in medical care. *Health Psychology, 12,* 140–146.

Hall, J. A., Feldstein, M., Fretwell, M. D., Rowe, J. W., & Epstein, A. M. (1990). Older patients' health status and satisfaction with medical care in an HMO population. *Medical Care, 28,* 261–270.

Hall, J. A., Horgan, T. G., Stein, T. S., & Roter, D. L. (2002). Liking in the physician-patient relationship. *Patient Education and Counseling, 48,* 69–77.

Hall, J. A., Irish, J. T., Roter, D. L., Ehrlich, C. M., & Miller, L. H. (1994a). Gender in medical encounters: An analysis of physician and patient communication in a primary care setting. *Health Psychology, 13,* 384–392.

Hall, J. A., Irish, J. T., Roter, D. L., Ehrlich, C. M., & Miller, L. H. (1994b). Satisfaction, gender, and communication in medical visits. *Medical Care, 32,* 1216–1231.

Hall, J. A., Milburn, M. A., Roter, D. L., & Daltroy, L. H. (1998). Why are sicker patients less satisfied with their medical care? Tests of two explanatory models. *Health Psychology, 17,* 70–75.

Hall, J. A., & Roter, D. L. (2002). Do patients talk differently to male and female physicians? A meta-analytic review. *Patient Education and Counseling, 48,* 217–224.

Hall, J. A., Roter, D. L., & Katz, N. R. (1988). Meta-analysis of correlates of provider behavior in medical encounters. *Medical Care, 26,* 657–675.

Hall, J. A., Roter, D. L., Milburn, M. A., & Daltroy, L. H. (1996). Patients' health as a predictor of physician and patient behavior in medical visits: A synthesis of four studies. *Medical Care, 34,* 1205–1218.

Hall, J. A., Roter, D. L., & Rand, C. S. (1981). Communication of affect between patient and physician. *Journal Health and Social Behavior, 11,* 18–30.

Hargraves, J. L., Wilson, I. B., Zaslavsky, A., James, C., Walker, J. D., Rogers, G., et al. (2001). Adjusting for patient characteristics when analyzing reports from patients about hospital care. *Medical Care, 39,* 635–641.

Harrington, J., Noble, L. M., & Newman, S. P. (2004). Improving patients' communication with doctors: A systematic review of intervention studies. *Patient Education and Counseling, 52,* 7–16.

Hasselkus, B. R. (1994). Three-track care: Older patients, family member, and physician in the medical visit. *Journal of Aging Studies, 8,* 291–307.

Haug, M., & Lavin, B. (1983). *Consumerism in medicine: Challenging physician authority.* Beverly Hills, CA: Sage.

Haynes, R. B., Taylor, D. W., & Sackett, D. L. (1979). *Compliance in health care.* Baltimore: Johns Hopkins University Press.

Henbest, R. J., & Stewart, M. A. (1989). Patient-centeredness in the consultation I: A method for measurement. *Family Practice: An International Journal, 6,* 249–253.

Hibbard, J. H., & Weeks, E. C. (1985). Consumer use of physician fee information. *Journal of Health and Human Resources Administration, 7,* 321–335.

Hibbard, J. H., & Weeks, E. C. (1987). Consumerism in health care: Prevalence and predictors. *Medical Care, 25,* 1019–1032.

Hooper, E. M., Comstock, L. M., Goodwin, J. M., & Goodwin, J. S. (1982). Patient characteristics that influence physician behavior. *Medical Care, 20,* 630–638.

Inui, T. S., & Carter, W. B. (1985). Problems and prospects for health services research on provider patient communication. *Medical Care, 23,* 521–538.

Inui, T. S., Carter, W. B., Kukull, W. A., & Haigh, V. H. (1982). Outcome-based doctor-patient interaction analysis: I. Comparison of techniques. *Medical Care, 10,* 535–549.

Jenkinson, C. (Ed.). (1994). *Measuring health and medical outcomes.* London: UCL Press.

Kalet, A., Earp, J., & Kowlowitz, V. (1992). How well do faculty evaluate the interviewing skills of medical students? *Journal of General Internal Medicine, 7,* 499–505.

Kaplan, S. H., Gandek, B., Greenfield, S., Rogers, W., & Ware, J. E. (1995). Patient and visit characteristics related to physicians' participatory decision-making style: Results from the Medical Outcomes Study. *Medical Care, 33,* 1176–1183.

Kaplan, S. H., Greenfield, S., & Ware J. E., Jr. (1989). Assessing the effects of physician-patient interactions on the outcomes of chronic disease. *Medical Care, 27,* S110–S127.

Keeler, E. B., Solomon, D. H., Beck, J. C., Mendenhall, R. C., & Kane, R. L. (1982). Effect of patient age on duration of medical encounter with physicians. *Medical Care, 20,* 1101–1108.

Korsch, B. M., Gozzi, E. K., & Francis, V. (1968). Gaps in doctor-patient communication: I. Doctor-patient interaction and patient satisfaction. *Pediatrics, 42,* 855–871.

Krupat, E., Fancey, M., & Cleary, P. D. (2000). Information and its impact on satisfaction among surgical patients. *Social Science & Medicine, 51,* 1817–1825.

Krupat, E., Rosenkranz, S. L., Yeager, C. M., Barnard,

K., Putnam, S. M., & Inui, T. S. (2000). The practice orientations of physicians and patients: The effect of doctor-patient congruence on satisfaction. *Patient Education and Counseling, 39,* 49–59.

Kurz, S. M., Silverman, J. D., & Draper, J. D. (1998). *Teaching and learning communication skills in medicine.* Oxford, England: Radcliffe Medical Press.

Lazare, A , Putnam, S. M., & Lipkin, M. (1995). Three functions of the medical interview. In M. Lipkin, S. Putnam, & A. Lazare (Eds.), *The medical interview: Clinical care, education, and research* (pp. 3–19). New York: Springer-Verlag.

Levenstein, J. H., McCracken, E. C., McWhinney, I. R., Stewart, M. A., & Brown, J. B. (1986). The patient-centered clinical method. I. A model for the doctor-patient interaction in family medicine. *Family Practice, 3,* 24–30.

Levinson, W., Roter, D. L., Mullooly, J., Dull, V., & Frankel, R. (1997). Doctor-patient communication: A critical link to malpractice in surgeons and primary care physicians. *Journal of the American Medical Association, 277,* 553–559.

Lipkin, M., Putnam, S., & Lazare, A. (Eds.). (1995). *The medical interview: Clinical care, education, and research.* New York: Springer-Verlag.

Localio, A. R., Lawthers, A. G., & Brennan, T .A. (1991). Relation between malpractice claims and adverse events due to negligence: Results of the Harvard Medical Practice Study III. *New England Journal of Medicine, 325,* 245–251.

Maguire, P., Fairburn, S., & Fletcher, C. (1986). Consultation skills of young doctors: Benefits of feedback training in interviewing as students persist. *British Medical Journal, 292,* 1573–1576.

Mann, S., Sripathy, K., Siegler, E., Davidow, A., Lipkin, M., & Roter, D. L. (2001). The medical interview: Differences between adult and geriatric outpatients. *Journal of the American Geriatric Society, 49,* 65–71.

Marshall, G. N., Hays, R. D., Sherbourne, C. D., & Wells, K. B. (1993). The structure of patient satisfaction with outpatient medical care. *Psychological Assessment, 5,* 477–483.

Marvel, M. K., Epstein, R. M., Flowers, K., & Beckman, H. B. (1999). Soliciting the patient's agenda: Have we improved? *Journal of the American Medical Association, 281,* 283–287.

McWhinney, I. (1988). Through clinic method to a more humanistic medicine. In K. White (Ed.), *The task of medicine: Dialogue at Wickenburg* (pp. 218–231). Menlo Park, CA: Henry J. Kaiser Family Foundation.

McWhinney, I. (1989). The need for a transformed clinical method. In M. Stewart & D. Roter (Eds.), *Communicating with medical patients* (pp. 25–40). Newbury Park, CA: Sage.

Mead, N., & Bower, P. (2000). Measuring patient-centeredness: A comparison of three observation-based instruments. *Patient Education and Counseling, 39,* 71–80.

Meeuwesen, L., Schaap, C., & van der Staak, C. (1991). Verbal analysis of doctor-patient communication. *Social Science & Medicine, 10,* 1143–1150.

Meyer, T. J., & Mark, M. M. (1995). Effects of psychosocial interventions with adult cancer patients: A meta-analysis of randomized experiments. *Health Psychology, 14,* 101–108.

Michie, S., Miles, J., & Weinman, J. (2003). Patient-centredness in chronic illness: What is it and does it matter? *Patient Education and Counseling, 51,* 197–206.

Mishler, E. G. (1984). *The discourse of medicine: Dialectics of medical interviews.* Norwood, NJ: Ablex.

Novack, D. H., Dube, C., & Goldstein, M. G. (1992). Teaching medical interviewing: A basic course on interviewing and the physician-patient relationship. *Archives of Internal Medicine, 152,* 1814–1820.

Ong, L. M. L., de Haes, J. C. J. M., Hoos, A. M., & Lammes, F. B. (1995). Doctor-patient communication: A review of the literature. *Social Science & Medicine, 40,* 903–918.

Ong, L. M. L., Visser, M. R. M., Lammes, F. B., & de Haes, J. C. J. M. (2000). Doctor-patient communication and cancer patients' quality of life and satisfaction. *Patient Education and Counseling, 41,* 145–156.

Orth, J. E., Stiles, W. B., Scherwitz, L., Hennrikus, D., & Vallbona, C. (1987). Patient exposition and provider explanation in routine interviews and hypertensive patients' blood pressure control. *Health Psychology, 6,* 29–42.

Parsons, T. (1951). *The social system.* Glencoe, IL: Free Press.

Pendleton, D. A., & Bochner, S. (1980). The communication of medical information in general practice consultations as a function of patients' social class. *Social Science & Medicine, 14A,* 669–673.

President's Commission for the Study of Ethical Problems in Medicine and Biomedical and Behavioral Research. (1982). *Making health care decisions and ethical and legal implications of informed consent in the patient-practitioner relationship* (Vol. 1). Washington, DC: U.S. Government Printing Office.

Prohaska, T. R., & Glasser, M. (1996). Patients' views of family involvement in medical care decisions and encounters. *Research on Aging, 18,* 52–69.

Putnam, S. M., Stiles, W. B., Jacob, M. C., & James, S. A. (1988). Teaching the medical interview: An intervention study. *Journal of General Internal Medicine, 3,* 38–47.

Quill, T. E. (1983). Partnerships in patient care: A contractual approach. *Annals of Internal Medicine, 98,* 228–234.

Radecki, S. E., Kane, R. L., Solomon, D. H., Mendenhall, R. C., & Beck, J. C. (1988). Do physicians spend less time with older patients? *Journal of the American Geriatrics Society, 36,* 713–718.

Reichardt, C. S., & Cook, T. D. (1969). *Qualitative and quantitative methods in evaluation research.* Beverly Hills, CA: Sage.

Rogers, P. G., & Bullman, W. R. (1995). Prescription medicine compliance: A review of the baseline of knowledge. A report of the National Council on Patient Information and Education. *Journal of Pharmacoepidemiology, 2,* 3–36.

Rosenthal, R., & Rubin, D. B. (1978). Interpersonal expectancy effects: The first 345 studies. *Behavioral and Brain Sciences, 3,* 377–386.

Ross, C. E., Mirowsky, J., & Duff, R. S. (1982). Physician status characteristics and client satisfaction in two types of medical practice. *Journal of Health and Social Behavior, 23,* 317–329.

Roter, D. (1977). Patient participation in the patient-provider interaction: The effects of patient question asking on the quality of interaction, satisfaction, and compliance. *Health Education Monographs, 5,* 281–315.

Roter, D. (1987). An exploration of health education's responsibility for a partnership model of client-provider relations. *Patient Education and Counseling, 9,* 25–31.

Roter, D. L. (1991). Elderly patient–physician communication: A descriptive study of content and affect during the medical encounter. *Advances in Health Education, 3,* 179–190.

Roter, D. L. (2000a). The enduring and evolving nature of the patient-physician relationship. *Patient Education and Counseling, 39,* 5–15.

Roter, D. L. (2000b). The medical visit context of treatment decision-making and the therapeutic relationship. *Health Expectations, 3,* 17–25.

Roter, D. L. (2003). Observations on methodological and measurement challenges in the assessment of communication during medical exchanges. *Patient Education and Counseling, 50,* 17–21.

Roter, D. L., Cole, K. A., Kern, D. E., Barker, L. R., & Grayson, M. (1990). An evaluation of residency training in interviewing skills and the psychosocial domain of medical practice. *Journal of General Internal Medicine, 5,* 347–354.

Roter, D., & Frankel, R. (1992). Quantitative and qualitative approaches to the evaluation of the medical dialogue. *Social Science & Medicine, 34,* 1097–1103.

Roter, D. L., & Hall, J. A. (1989). Studies of doctor-patient interaction. *Annual Review of Public Health, 10,* 163–180.

Roter, D. L., & Hall, J. A. (1991). Health education theory: An application to the process of patient-provider communication. *Health Education Research Theory and Practice, 6,* 185–193.

Roter, D. L., & Hall, J. A. (1992). *Doctors talking with patients/patients talking with doctors: Improving communication in medical visits.* Westport, CT: Auburn House.

Roter, D. L., & Hall, J. A. (2004). Physician gender and patient-centered communication: A critical review of empirical research. *Annual Review of Public Health, 25,* 497–519.

Roter, D. L., & Hall, J. A. (in press). *Doctors talking with patients/patients talking with doctors: Improving communication in medical visits* (2nd ed.). Westport, CT: Pergamon.

Roter, D. L., Hall, J. A., & Aoki, Y. (2002). Physician gender effects in medical communication: A meta-analytic review. *Journal of the American Medical Association, 288,* 756–764.

Roter, D. L., Hall, J. A., & Katz, N. R. (1987). Relations between physicians' behaviors and analogue patients' satisfaction, recall, and impressions. *Medical Care, 25,* 437–451.

Roter, D. L., Hall, J. A., & Katz, N. R. (1988). Patient-physician communication: A descriptive summary of the literature. *Patient Education and Counseling, 12,* 99–119.

Roter, D. L., Hall, J. A., Kern, D. E., Barker, L. R., Cole, K. A., & Roca, R. P. (1995). Improving physicians' interviewing skills and reducing patients' emotional distress. *Archives of Internal Medicine, 155,* 1877–1884.

Roter, D. L., Hall, J. A., Merisca, R., Nordstrom, B., Cretin, D., & Svarstad, B. (1998). Effectiveness of interventions to improve patient compliance: A meta-analysis. *Medical Care, 36,* 1138–1161.

Roter, D., Lipkin, M., Jr., & Korsgaard, A. (1991). Gender differences in patients' and physicians' communication during primary care medical visits. *Medical Care, 29,* 1083–1093.

Roter, D. L., & McNeilis, K. S. (2003). The nature of the therapeutic relationship and the assessment and consequences of its discourse in routine medical visits. In T. Thompson, A. Dorsey, K. Miller, & R. Parrott (Eds.), *Handbook of health communication.* Mahwah, NJ: Erlbaum.

Roter, D. L., Stewart, M., Putnam, S., Lipkin, M., Stiles W., & Inui, T. (1997). Communication patterns of primary care physicians. *Journal of the American Medical Association, 270,* 350–355.

Sacks, H., Schegloff, E. A., & Jefferson, G. (1974). A simplest systematic for the organization of turn-taking in conversation. *Language, 50,* 696–735.

Schneider, C. E. (1998). *The practice of autonomy: Patients, doctors, and medical decisions.* New York: Oxford University Press.

Shorter, E. (1985). *Bedside manners.* New York: Simon and Schuster.

Smith, R. C., Marshall-Dorsey, A. A., Osborn, G. G., Shebroe, V , Lyles, J. S., Stoffelmayr, B. E., et al. (2000). Evidence-based guidelines for teaching patient-centered interviewing. *Patient Education and Counseling, 39,* 27–36.

Steele, D. J., Jackson, T. C., & Gutmann, M. C. (1990). Have you been taking your pills? The adherence monitoring sequence in the medical interview. *Journal of Family Practice, 30,* 294–299.

Stewart, A. L., & Ware, J. E., Jr. (Eds.). (1992). *Measuring functioning and well-being: The Medical Outcomes Study approach.* Durham, NC: Duke University Press.

Stewart, M. (1983). Patient characteristics which are related to the doctor-patient interaction. *Family Practice, 1,* 30–35.

Stewart, M. (1995). Patient-doctor relationships over time. In M. Stewart, J. B. Brown, W. W. Weston, I. McWhinney, C. L. McWilliam, & T. R. Freeman (Eds.), *Patient-centered medicine: Transforming the clinical method* (p. 216–228). Thousand Oaks, CA: Sage.

Stewart, M., Brown, J. B., Donner, A., McWhinney, I. R., Oates, J., & Weston, W. (1996). *The impact of patient-centered care on patient outcomes in family practice: Final report.* Ontario, Canada: Health Services Research, Ministry of Health.

Stewart, M., Brown, J. B., Weston, W. W., McWhinney, I., McWilliam, C. L., & Freeman, T. R. (Eds.). (1995). *Patient-centered medicine: Transforming the clinical method.* Thousand Oaks, CA: Sage.

Stewart, M A. (1984). What is a successful doctor-patient interview? A study of interactions and outcomes. *Social Science & Medicine, 19,* 167–175.

Stewart, M. A. (1996). Effective physician-patient communication and health outcomes: A review. *Canadian Medical Association Journal, 152,* 1423–1433.

Stiles, W. B. (1992). *Describing talk: A taxonomy of verbal response modes.* Newbury Park, CA: Sage.

Stiles, W. B., & White, M. L. (1981). Parent-child interaction in the laboratory: Effects of role, task, and child behavior pathology on verbal response mode use. *Journal of Abnormal Child Psychology, 9,* 229–241.

Stone, G. C. (1979). Patient compliance and the role of the expert. *Journal of Social Issues, 35*(1), 34–59.

Suchman, A. L, Roter, D. L., Green, M., & Lipkin, M.,

Jr. (1993). Physician satisfaction with primary care office visits. *Medical Care, 31,* 1083–1092.

Szasz, P. S., & Hollender, M. H. (1956). A contribution to the philosophy of medicine: The basic model of the doctor-patient relationship. *Archives of Internal Medicine, 97,* 585–592.

Tates, K., & Meeuwesen, L. (2001). Doctor-parent-child communication: A (re)view of the literature. *Social Science & Medicine, 52,* 839–851.

Thi, P. L. N., Briançon, S., Empereur, F., & Guillemin, F. (2002). Factors determining inpatient satisfaction with care. *Social Science & Medicine, 54,* 493–504.

Thompson, T. L. (1994). Interpersonal communication and health care. In M. L. Knapp & G. R. Miller (Eds.), *Handbook of interpersonal communication* (2nd ed., pp. 696–725). Thousand Oaks, CA: Sage.

Tresolini, C. P., and the Pew-Fetzer Task Force on Advancing Psychosocial Health Education. (1994). *Health professions education and relationship-centered care.* San Francisco: Pew Health Professions Commission.

Tuckett, D., Boulton, M., Olson, C., & Williams, A. (1985). *Meetings between experts.* New York: Tavistock.

Van Dulmen, A. M., Verhaak, P. F. M., & Bilo, H. J. G. (1997). Shifts in doctor-patient communication during a series of outpatient consultations in non-insulin-dependent diabetes mellitus. *Patient Education and Counseling, 30,* 227–237.

van Ryn, M. (2002). Research on the provider contribution to race/ethnicity disparities in medical care. *Medical Care, 40,* I140–I151.

Waitzkin, H. (1985). Information giving in medical care. *Journal of Health and Social Behavior, 26,* 81–101.

Wallen, J., Waitzkin, H., & Stoeckle, J. D. (1979). Physician stereotypes about female health and illness: A study of patient's sex and the informative process during medical interviews. *Women & Health, 4,* 135–146.

Wallerstein, N., & Bernstein, E. (1988). Empowerment education: Freire's ideas adapted to health education. *Health Education Quarterly, 15,* 379–394.

Wasserman, R. C., Inui, T. S., Barriatua, R. D., Carter, W. B., & Lippincott, P. (1984). Pediatric clinicians' support for parents makes a difference: An outcome-based analysis of clinician-parent interaction. *Pediatrics, 74,* 1047–1053.

White, K. (1988). Physician and professional perspectives. In K. White (Ed.), *The task of medicine: Dialogue at Wickenburg* (pp. 30–46). Menlo Park, CA: Henry J. Kaiser Family Foundation.

Williams, G. C., Freedman, Z. R., & Deci, E. L.

(1998). Supporting autonomy to motivate patients with diabetes for glucose control. *Diabetes Care, 21,* 1644–1651.

Williams, G. C., & Deci, E. L. (1998). The importance of supporting autonomy in medical education. *Annals of Internal Medicine, 129,* 303–308.

Williams, G. C., & Deci, E. L. (2001). Activating patients for smoking cessation through physician autonomy support. *Medical Care, 39,* 813–823.

Williams, S., Weinman, J., & Dale, J. (1998). Doctor-patient communication and patient satisfaction: A review. *Family Practice, 15,* 480–492.

Wissow, L. S., Roter, D., Bauman, L. J., Crain, E., Kercsmar, C., Weiss, K., et al. (1998). Patient–provider communication during the emergency department care of children with asthma. *Medical Care, 36,* 1439–1450.

Wissow, L. S., Roter, D., Larson, S., Wang, M-C, Hwang, W. T., & Johnson, R. (2000, July). *Longitudinal pediatric care and discussion of maternal psychosocial issues.* Paper presented at the Mental Health Services Research Meetings, Washington, DC. (Abstract pages 52–53).

Wissow, L. S., Roter, D. L., & Wilson, M. E. H. (1994). Pediatrician interview style and mothers' disclosure of psychosocial issues. *Pediatrics, 93,* 289–295.

Young, M., & Klingle, R. S. (1996). Silent partners in medical care: A cross-cultural study of patient participation. *Health Communication, 8,* 29–53.

Robert M. Kaplan

Uncertainty, Variability, and Resource Allocation in the Health Care Decision Process

Health psychology has played a tentative role in the enterprise of health care. Health psychologists have concerned themselves with how patients adapt to illness or how psychological factors might contribute to a medical diagnosis (Friedman, 2002; Sarafino, 2002; Taylor, 1999). They have also studied how diagnosis affects mood, cognitive functioning, and other psychological variables. It is typically assumed that diagnoses are correct and that all patients placed in diagnostic categories should receive treatment. Considerable effort has been devoted to training patients to adhere to physician orders or instructions. It is assumed that physician orders describe the most likely path to positive patient outcomes. Rarely has the patient's perspective been given equal consideration. For example, health psychology devotes insufficient attention to whether treatment results in improved health, damaged health through side effects, or reduced financial resources, or to how patients can gain equal partnership in decisions concerning their medical care.

One common assumption is that medical diagnoses are "correct." By correct, we assume that a diagnosis identifies true pathology and that identification of this problem initiates a course of action that will result in patient improvement. The physician plays a mechanical role. He or she finds the problem and then proceeds to fix it. This chapter argues that medicine is not a mechanical science. Instead, it is a social science that requires complex decisions based on ambiguous evidence. There is often uncertainty about the correctness of the diagnosis, uncertainty regarding whether treatments will make patients better, and variability in beliefs that treatments are safe. This chapter focuses on uncertainty, variability, and resource allocation. First, evidence will be presented to show that there is substantial variability in physician decisions. Several lines of research will be reviewed to demonstrate remarkable variation in the decisions to use diagnostic tests and therapeutic interventions. Second, it will be argued that physician decisions are influenced by incentives to increase the number of patients receiving a chronic disease diagnoses through aggressive testing and through changes in the definition of what we label as "disease." These incentives can have substantial impacts on health care costs, patient anxiety, and the organization and delivery of health care. Third, because of these problems, patients need to be much more active in sharing decisions about their own care. The final section of the chapter will review the emerging literature on shared medical decision making.

Expenditures and Outcomes

Good health is, perhaps, the most valued state of being. In many ways we orient our lives in order to achieve wellness for ourselves and for our families and friends. Health services are used to achieve better health, to maintain good health, or to prevent health-damaging conditions. Because these services come at a cost, we are willing to use financial resources to purchase health. But are we using our resources wisely in the pursuit of better population health? To address this question, we must consider the financial implications of purchasing health care. A good starting point is the comparison of medical decisions and health care expenditures in the United States in relation to other countries.

Health care costs in the United States have grown exponentially since 1940. Although there was a temporary slowdown in the early 1990s, the rate of increase began to accelerate again by the turn of the century. Health care in the United States now consumes about 14.5% of the gross domestic product (GDP), whereas no other country in the world spends more than 10%. Although the rate of growth has slowed, the Institute for the Future estimates that health care expenditures will increase at a rate of 6.4% annually and will account for 15.6% of the GDP by 2010 (Future, 2000). Figure 14.1, based

on data reported to the Organization for Economic Development and Cooperation (OEDC), shows that the expense of health care in the United States exceeds that in virtually all developed countries.

One of the most unexplored assumptions is that greater expenditure will result in greater health benefit. We know from international studies that developed countries that spend considerably less than the United States on health care have about equal health outcomes. The United Kingdom, for example, spends about half as much per capita on health care as the United States. However, life expectancy in the United Kingdom (80.4 years for women, 74.4 years for men) is slightly longer than it is in the United States (79.5 years for women, 73.9 years for men), and infant mortality is slightly lower (5.6/1,000 vs. 6.9/1,000; 2003 OECD data www .OECD.org). Among 13 countries in one comparison, the United States ranked 12th when compared on 16 health indicators (Starfield, 2000).

Within the United States, there is considerable variability in spending. For example, using data from the Medicare program, per capita spending ranges from a low of $2,736 in Oregon to a high of $6,307 in Alaska. State-level data are also available on the average quality of health care. Quality is typically defined as adherence to defined standards of patient care. For example, it is possible to estimate the extent to which physicians adhere to defined

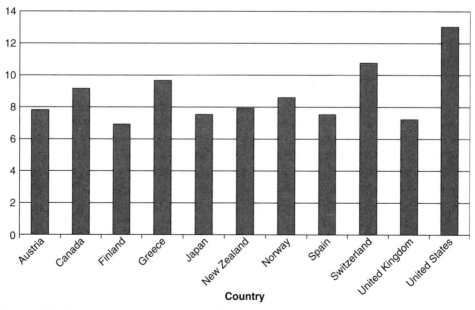

Figure 14.1. Percentage of GDP devoted to health (OECD data, 2003).

practice guidelines. The association between per capita spending and quality across the United States is shown in Figure 14.2. As the figure demonstrates, the relationship goes in the wrong direction. Spending more does not buy better quality of care. Adjusting for socioeconomic status does not alter this finding.

Another, related assumption is that patients will be better off if they have access to high-technology centers. For example, neonatal intensive care units (NICUs) offer dramatic benefits to premature and low birth rate infants. It is assumed that there will be more NICUs in areas where there are concentrations of low birth weight infants. However, systematic evaluation of this issue suggests that the concentration of neonatologists and specialized units is unrelated to the areas where there is a need for these services (Goodman et al., 2002).

We would assume that babies born in areas of plentiful care have a higher chance of survival. However, evidence suggests that this is not the case. It does appear that survival is poor for low birth rate infants born in areas in the bottom 20% of NICU availability. Beyond this lower quintile, however, being born in a area with a high density of NICUs makes very little difference (Goodman et al., 2002). The reason for this finding may be that we may have more neonatologists and NICUs than necessary. For example, the number of births per neonatologist ranges from 390 to 8,197. In many areas of the country, there are simply too many neonatologists and not enough work for them to do. In other words, we may have significantly overtrained and overinvested in neonatal intensive care. With an overabundance of providers, some unnecessary procedures may be done. Further, building an overabundance of NICUs might use resources that could have been applied for other purposes. For example, many communities that have an oversupply of NICUs do not support appropriate prenatal care due to lack of resources. Spain has many fewer NICUs than the United States, but it devotes more resources to supportive care. Spain's infant mortality rate is lower than the rate of the United States (3.9 vs. 6.9/1,000; OECD 2003 data).

Opportunity Cost Problem

Managed care and other pressures have forced new competition among health care providers. Health care resources are limited, and there is constant pressure to spend more on attractive new treatments or diagnostic procedures. Without containment, health care could grow to the point where it

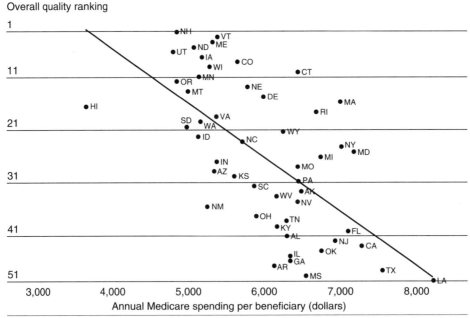

Figure 14.2. Per capita spending by states and estimates of quality of care (from Baicker, Chandra, Skinner, & Wennberg, 2004).

would use such a large portion of the GDP that there would not be enough money left for high-quality public services in other sectors, such as education, energy, or national defense (Blumenthal, 2001). Although most provider groups understand that health care costs must be contained, few acknowledge that their own expenditures should be subject to evaluation. Successful lobbying to obtain reimbursement for a specific service may necessarily mean that another service is excluded.

Suppose, for example, that the amount that can be spent on health care is fixed, and $3 of each $100 (3%) is devoted to behavioral services. If psychologists are able to get $10 of each $100 spent on their services, there will be less to spend on other non-behavioral health services. This is called the *opportunity cost problem*. Opportunity costs are the forgone opportunities that are surrendered when resources are used to support a particular decision. If we spend a lot of money in one sector of health care, we necessarily spend less money elsewhere. How do we decide which services should get more and which should get fewer resources?

When confronted with the choice between two good programs, it is always tempting to support both. The difficulty is that it costs more to offer multiple programs. No public policy has ever been shown to effectively control costs in the American health care system (Blumenthal, 2001). The cost of programs is represented in the fees for health insurance or the cost of health care to taxpayers. A society can choose to offer as many health programs as it wants. However, more programs require more funding. Employees do not want the fees for their health insurance to rise, and taxpayers do not want tax increases. The goal of formal decision models is to get higher-quality health care without increasing costs.

Uncontrollable Demand for Heath Care

There are many explanations for why it is difficult to control health care costs (Kronick & California Program on Access to Care, 1999). Providing an exhaustive list of these explanations is beyond the scope of this chapter. However, two important issues will be probed. First, the demand for health care is elastic, expandable, and perhaps infinite. It might be argued that health concerns should receive

first priority in the allocation of public resources. Once population health is achieved, policymakers can move on to other priorities, such as education, national defense, or homeland security. However, if all desired health services were provided, resources would be exhausted quickly, and there may be insufficient resources to address other societal concerns. The problem is compounded by a continual supply of new expensive services and products. Further, we have no assurance that investments in health care will improve population health because many services produce limited benefits.

Many have argued that society has a moral obligation to provide all necessary services for those who are sick and in need of help. The challenge is in determining how many people are in need of help and whether services will really help them. The medical care system has been motivated to expand the number of people who are "sick" and, therefore, in need of medical service. This has been accomplished through screening programs that identify disease at very early phases. Once an individual is identified as "sick," it is incumbent upon the system to treat the problem. In many cases, however, attention to early stages of disease may offer little or no benefit. Mass screening programs may produce harm, but not for the obvious reasons. There is little evidence that they harm people physiologically. The concern is connected to opportunity costs. Some expensive programs may divert significant resources away from public health and behavioral programs that might offer greater potential to improve population health.

How Much Health Care Do We Need? The Geographic Distribution of Health Services

The difference in disease rates in various communities is complicated by another variable. Society has often assumed that if a doctor diagnoses an illness, the illness exists. Further, we assume that any qualified doctor, presented with the same problem, will come to the same diagnosis. However, there is substantial evidence that there is variability in diagnosis. Professionals make errors in diagnosis, but we assume that these errors are random. Thus, if the distribution of disease is the same in different communities, we would expect the rates of reporting to be roughly equivalent. However, physicians vary markedly in the rates of illness they detect and the rates of service they recommend. Wennberg and his colleagues have devoted the past quarter century to the description of this problem (Wennberg, 1996; Wennberg & Gittelsohn, 1982). They report that a major factor in the use of medical services is supplier-induced demand; providers create demand for their services by diagnosing illnesses. When new diagnostic technologies gain acceptance from physician groups, new epidemics of "disease" appear. One of the earliest documented cases on supplier-induced demand was described by Glover in the United Kingdom. Glover recorded the rates of tonsillectomy in the Hornse Burrough school district. In 1928, 186 children in the district had their tonsils surgically removed. The next year, the doctor who enthusiastically supported tonsillectomy was replaced by another physician who was less attracted to the procedure. In 1929 the number of tonsillectomies was reduced to only 12 (Wennberg, 1990).

Often, surgeons agree on the need to perform surgery. For example there are high-consensus diagnoses, such as resection of the colon for colon cancer and surgery for appendicitis. Other areas of high agreement might include amputation of a toe with gangrene, removal of well-defined tumors, or intervention to repair a compound fracture. For most surgical procedures, however, there is substantial discretion, and rates for surgery vary (Birkmeyer et al., 2003; Finlayson, Laycock, & Birkmeyer, 2003; Pope, Birkmeyer, & Finlayson, 2002).

Boston Versus New Haven: A Case Example

Boston, Massachusetts, and New Haven, Connecticut, are similar in numerous ways. Both are traditional New England cities that have multiethnic populations. The two cities have approximately the same climate, and each is home to a prestigious Ivy League university. Because the cities are near one another, we would expect that the costs of medical care would be approximately the same. Using data from the mid-1970s, Wennberg and colleagues (Wennberg, Freeman, & Culp, 1987) demonstrated that, in fact, medical care costs in Boston were nearly twice as high as those in New Haven.

Figure 14.3 shows the distribution of hospital expenditures in Connecticut cities and in Massachusetts cities in the 1970s. In 1975, Medicare was

paying $324 per recipient per month for people in Boston and only $155 per month for residents of New Haven. The situation has not changed much. In 1989, per capita hospital expenditures for acute care were $1,524 for residents of Boston and $777 for those living in New Haven. By 2000, medical care in the United States had changed, but most differences between practice in Boston and New Haven remained.

Further study by Wennberg and his colleagues showed that Boston has more hospital capacity than does New Haven. In Boston there are 4.3 hospital beds for every 1,000 residents, whereas in New Haven there are fewer than 2.3 beds per 1,000 residents. Residents of Boston are more likely to be hospitalized for a wide variety of acute medical conditions than are residents of New Haven. For medical conditions such as pneumonia or congestive heart failure, Bostonians are more likely to be cared for as hospital inpatients, but residents of New Haven were treated outside the hospital.

Boston is rich with medical institutions. New Haven has only one major medical school (Yale), whereas Boston has three (Harvard, Tufts, and Boston University). Further, the Harvard Medical School is associated with a variety of teaching hospitals. Boston has four hospitals associated with different religious establishments; there is only one religious-affiliated hospital in New Haven.

The Boston–New Haven comparison is particularly interesting from a public policy perspective. U.S. Medicare is a federal program that aims to provide equal benefit to all its recipients. Yet, on average, Medicare spends twice as much in Boston as it does in New Haven (Wennberg et al., 1987). Are New Haven residents getting a bad deal? Because the government spends less on New Haven residents, it might be argued that the health of New Haven residents will suffer because they receive insufficient medical attention. However, evidence does not show that residents of Boston are any healthier than residents of New Haven. In fact, some evidence implies that Boston residents may be worse off. For example, people in Boston are more likely to be rehospitalized for the same condition than are people in New Haven (Fisher, Wennberg, Stukel, & Sharp, 1994). Residents of Boston appear to have more complications from medical treatment. In this case, more may not necessarily be better; indeed, there is some evidence that more may be worse (Fisher & Welch, 1999).

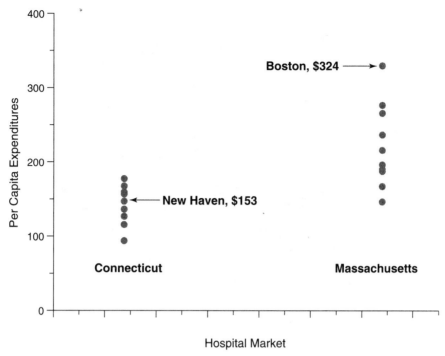

Figure 14.3. Hospital expenditures in Connecticut and Massachusetts (from Wennberg, 1990).

A group of investigators at the Dartmouth Medical School created an atlas of maps that show health care utilization broken down by geographic region. The atlas attempts to link the substantial variation in service to a variety of other factors. Figure 14.4 for example, shows Medicare spending mapped by hospital service area. It shows that Medicare spends about twice as much per recipient in southern Texas as it does in New Mexico. Yet we have no evidence that people in southern Texas get better health care or have better health outcomes than people in Albuquerque. One factor that does not explain the variation is the prevalence of disease in the different communities. On the other hand, some evidence suggests that the availability of doctors and hospitals informs how much medical service a community will receive. *The Dartmouth Atlas of Health Care* also shows remarkable variability in the distribution of physicians and physician specialists. For example, there are 43.9 psychiatrists per 1,000 persons in White Plains, New York, and there are 38.4 in San Francisco. Manhattan is not far behind (35.5). On the other hand, there are only 2.8 psychiatrists per 1,000 persons in Oxford, Mississippi, and 3.0 per 1,000 in Fort Smith, Arkansas. The map shows that psychiatrists tend to

live in major metropolitan areas and to be focused on the West or East Coast. They have a strong concentration in New England. There is also a substantial concentration near the ski areas of Colorado and in southeast Arizona (Wennberg, 1998).

Some medical conditions are associated with higher variation and use than are others. For example, variation for problems such as fracture of the hip is not large. Patients who fracture their hip are likely to be admitted to the hospital wherever they live. However, as the maps show, most problems are associated with high variation. The Dartmouth group estimates that 80% of patients who are admitted to hospitals have been diagnosed with high-variation medical conditions such as pneumonia, chronic obstructive pulmonary disease, gastroenteritis, and congestive heart failure. They argue that hospital capacity has a major influence on the likelihood that a patient will be hospitalized. This relationship is illustrated in Figure 14.5, which shows the relationship between hospital beds per 1,000 residents and hospital discharges for ambulatory care–sensitive conditions. The figure suggests that the bed supply explains more that half of the variance in discharges for conditions such as pneumonia, heart failure, and

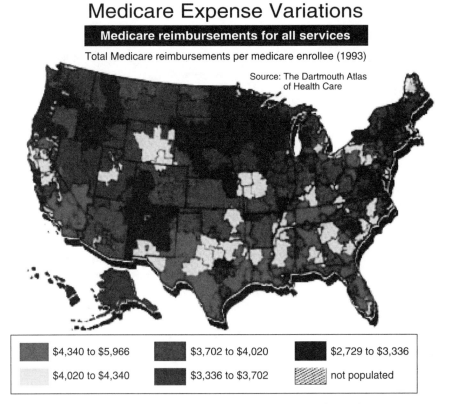

Medicare Expense Variations

Medicare reimbursements for all services

Total Medicare reimbursements per medicare enrollee (1993)

Source: The Dartmouth Atlas
of Health Care

■ $4,340 to $5,966	■ $3,702 to $4,020	■ $2,729 to $3,336
▫ $4,020 to $4,340	■ $3,336 to $3,702	▨ not populated

Figure 14.4. *Dartmouth Atlas of Health Care* map of hospital costs by hospital service area (1993).

chronic obstructive pulmonary disease. The correlation between hospital beds and admissions is a remarkable .75. In hospital referral regions where there are fewer than 2.5 beds per 1,000 residents, the hospital discharge rate for high-variation conditions was 145 per 1,000. Among regions that had more 4.5 beds per 1,000 residents, the rate was 219.8. More beds mean more hospital discharges. These data indicate that the decision to admit individuals to the hospital is influenced by factors other than their medical condition. When beds are available, they are more likely to be used. When more hospital beds are used, health care costs go up.

It seems plausible that communities with greater hospital resources are better able to care for their populations. More health care should lead to more health. However, several analyses have shown that people are slightly more likely to die in communities where more acute hospital care is used. An obvious explanation is that these communities have people who are older, sicker, or poorer. However, careful analyses controlled for age, sex, race, in-

come, and a variety of variables related to illness and the need for care. None of these variables was able to explain the relationship (Fisher et al., 2003). In other words, the analysis suggests that more is not better. In fact, it implies that more may be worse.

Is Preventive Medicine Using the Wrong Model?

How could there be so much variation in the use of medical care services? Are some doctors missing important diagnoses and others diagnosing diseases that do not exist? Following the dictum that all who are sick must receive treatment, it might be argued that everyone with a medical diagnosis must be given the very best treatment. Nowhere is this more apparent than in the field of clinical preventive medicine, which is moving toward more aggressive screening and treatment of mild-spectrum disease. We define mild-spectrum as values close to the population norm. One thrust of preventive medicine has been

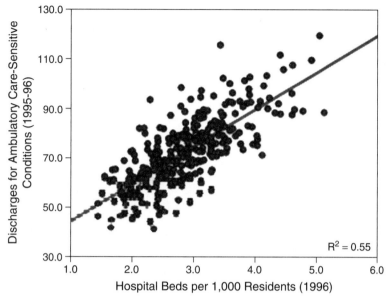

Figure 14.5. Hospital beds and discharges for ambulatory care–sensitive conditions (from *The Dartmouth Atlas of Health Care*, p. 129).

directed toward the use of high-cost pharmaceutical products for the management of large numbers of patients. There are many alternative uses of the same resources, including public health approaches that might prevent risk factors from developing in the first place. These approaches may not be part of the medical care system but might produce substantial health benefit. For example, programs to prevent youths from using cigarettes may produce substantial public health benefit even though they do not require medical diagnosis or the use of medical or surgical treatments (R. M. Kaplan, 2000).

Disease is often characterized as a binary variable. A "diagnosis" is either present or absent. However, many biological variables are normally distributed in the population. Clinical judgment and evidence-based reviews have been used to set cut points that divide these continuous distributions into disease-nondisease dichotomies. Little is known about the effect of setting different disease cut points upon costs and health outcomes.

Finding Better Ways to Make Health Care Decisions

If the decisions made in heath care are not optimal in terms of resource use and patient outcomes, how

might a better system be designed? The remainder of this chapter introduces decision models that might contribute to this problem. Before reviewing applications of the models, two conceptual issues will be introduced. The first is a conceptualization of health outcomes, and the second is "disease reservoir model" that probes our understanding of the need for health services.

Defining Health Outcomes

The traditional biomedical model of health and the outcomes model focus on different measures for the evaluation of health care. The traditional biomedical model is regarded as successful if disease is found and fixed. The Outcomes Model of health care suggests that resources should be used to make people live longer and feel better (R. M. Kaplan, 2000). Finding and fixing disease may or may not contribute to this objective.

In order to quantify the benefits of health care, it is necessary to build a comprehensive model of health benefit. Traditional measures of health outcome were very general. They included life expectancy, infant mortality, and disability days. The difficulty with these indicators is that they did not reflect most of the benefits of health care. For example, life expectancy and infant mortality are good measures because they allow for comparisons between programs with different specific objectives. The difficulty is that neither is sensitive to minor variations in health status. Treatment of most common illnesses may have relatively little effect on life expectancy. Infant mortality, although sensitive to socioeconomic variations, does not register the effect of health services delivered to people who are older than 1 year.

Survival analysis, which gives a unit of credit for each year of survival, is an attractive generic measure of health status. Suppose, for example, that a person has a life expectancy of 80 years and dies prematurely at age 50. In survival analysis, the person is scored as 1.0 for each of the first 50 years and 0 for each year thereafter. The problem is that years with disability are scored the same as those years in perfect health. For example, a person with severe arthritis who is alive is scored exactly the same as someone in perfect health. To address this problem, we have proposed using adjusted survival analysis, a method that allows us to summarize outcomes in terms of quality-adjusted life years (QALYs). In quality-adjusted survival analysis, years of wellness are scored on a continuum ranging from 0 for death to 1.0 for optimum function (R. M. Kaplan, 1994).

QALYs are measures of life expectancy with adjustments for quality of life (Gold, 1996; R. M. Kaplan, 1990, 1994; Weinstein, Siegel, Gold, Kamlet, & Russell, 1996). QALYs integrate mortality and morbidity to express health status in terms of equivalents of well years of life. If a woman dies of breast cancer at age 50 and one would have expected her to live to age 75, the disease was associated with 25 lost life years. If 100 women died at age 50 (and also had a life expectancies of 75 years), 2,500 (100 times 25 years) life years would be lost.

Death is not the only outcome of concern in cancer. Many adults suffer from the disease, leaving them somewhat disabled over long periods of time. Although they are still alive, the quality of their lives has diminished. QALYs take into consideration the quality-of-life consequences of these illnesses. For example, a disease that reduces quality of life by one half will take away 0.5 QALYs over the course of one year. If it affects two people, it will take away 1 year (or 2 times 0.5) over a 1-year period. A pharmaceutical treatment that improves quality of life by 0.2 for each of five individuals will result in the equivalent of one QALY if the benefit is maintained over a 1-year period. The basic assumption is that 2 years scored as 0.5 add up to the equivalent of 1 year of complete wellness. Similarly, 4 years scored as 0.25 are equivalent to 1 completely well year of life. A treatment that boosts a patient's health from 0.5 to 0.75 produces the equivalent of 0.25 QALYs. If applied to four individuals, and the duration of the treatment effect is 1 year, the effect of the treatment would be equivalent to 1 completely well year of life. This system has the advantage of considering both benefits and side effects of programs in terms of the common QALY units. Although QALYs are typically assessed for patients, they can also be measured for others, including caregivers who are placed at risk because they experience stressful life events. The Institute of Medicine recommended that population health metrics be used to evaluate public programs and to assist the decision-making process (Field & Gold, 1998).

In addition to health benefits, programs also have costs. Resources are limited, and good policy requires allocation to maximize life expectancy and health-related quality of life. Thus, in addition to measuring health outcomes, costs must also be considered. Methodologies for estimating costs have now become standardized (Gold, 1996; R. M. Kaplan, 1990, 1994; Weinstein et al., 1996). From an administrative perspective, cost estimates include all costs of treatment and costs associated with caring for any side effects of treatment. Typically economic discounting is applied to adjust for using current assets to achieve a future benefit. From a social perspective, costs are broader and may include costs of family members staying home from work to provide care. Comparing programs for a given population with a given medical condition, cost-effectiveness is measured as the change in costs of care for the program compared with the existing therapy or program, relative to the change in health measured in a standardized unit such as the QALY. The difference in costs over the difference in effectiveness is the *incremental cost-effectiveness* and is usually expressed as the cost/QALY. Since the objective of all programs is to produce QALYs, the cost/QALY ratio can be used to show the relative efficiency of different programs (R. Kaplan & Anderson, 1996).

When Finding and Fixing Disease Does Not Matter: The Disease Reservoir Hypothesis

Using a traditional biomedical approach, much of contemporary preventive medicine is oriented toward finding disease early and applying aggressive treatments. However, there may be circumstances in which early detection of disease does not lead to improvement in patient outcomes. To understand this, it may be valuable to introduce an idea known as the *disease reservoir hypothesis.*

Undiagnosed disease is probably quite common, particularly among older people. Cancers of the breast and prostate have been identified in as many as 30% (breast) and 40% (prostate) of older adults who die from other causes (Black & Welch, 1997). Only about 3% of elderly men will die of prostate cancer, and only about 3% of elderly women will die of breast cancer. Autopsy studies consistently show that more than 90% of young adults who died early in life from noncardiovascular causes have fatty streaks in their coronary arteries indicating the initiation of coronary disease (Strong et al., 1999). The harder we look, the more likely it is that cases will be found. A very sensitive test for prostate cancer may detect disease in 10 men for each man who will eventually die of this condition. Advanced magnetic resonance imaging (MRI) technology has revealed surprisingly high rates of undiagnosed stroke. One cross-sectional study of 3,502 men and women over age 65 found that 29% had evidence of mild stokes and that 75% had plaque in their carotid arteries (Manolio et al., 1999).

As diagnostic technology improves, the health care system will be challenged because these common problems will be identified in many individuals who may not benefit from treatment. The problem has been fiercely debated in relation to cancer screening tests such as mammography and prostate-specific antigen (PSA; Welch & Black, 1997; Welch, Schwartz, & Woloshin, 2000).

According to the American Cancer Society, screening and early detection of cancers save lives (*Cancer Facts and Figures—2002,* 2002). It is believed that there is a reservoir of undetected disease that might be eliminated through more aggressive intervention. Screening guidelines have been proposed, and those who fail to adhere to these guidelines are regarded as irresponsible. One recent national survey found that 87% of adults think that cancer screening is almost always a good idea, and 74% believe that early detection saves lives. Nearly 70% of the respondents considered a 55-year-old woman who did not get a mammogram to be irresponsible (Schwartz, Woloshin, Fowler, & Welch, 2004). Although early detection messages have been pushed for more than a century (Aronowitz, 2001), evidence that early detection results in better outcomes is very limited (Welch, 2001).

To better understand the problem, it is necessary to understand the natural history of disease. Public health campaigns assume that disease is binary; either a person has the "diagnosis," or they do not. However, most diseases are processes. It is likely that chronic disease begins long before it is diagnosed. For example, if smokers are screened for lung cancer, many cases can be identified. However, clinical trials have shown that the course of the disease is likely to be the same for those who are screened and those not subjected to screening, even though screening leads to more diagnosis and treatment (Marcus et al., 2000).

Black and Welch make the distinction between disease and pseudodisease (Black & Welch, 1997). Pseudodisease is disease that will not affect life duration or quality of life at any point in a patient's lifetime. When the disease is found, it is often "fixed" with surgical treatment. However, the fix may have consequences, often leaving the patient with new symptoms or problems. The outcomes model considers the benefits of screening and treatment from the patient's perspective (R. M. Kaplan, 2000). Often, using information provided by patients, we can estimate the quality-adjusted life expectancy for a population and determine if they are better off with or without screening and treatment (R. M. Kaplan, 1997).

The Value of Screening

Screening tests are often used to detect disease early. Although screening is clearly worthwhile for detecting cases of disease, some of these cases will actually be pseudodisease. Cases of pseudodisease are unlikely to benefit from clinical intervention, raising questions about whether resources commonly devoted to early disease detection might be better used for other purposes. To illustrate the complexity of these decisions, three case examples will be offered: prostate cancer, breast cancer, and heart disease.

Prostate Cancer Screening

The disease reservoir hypothesis helps explain controversies surrounding several cancer screening tests. One example of the differences between the traditional biomedical model and the outcomes models concerns screening and treatment for prostate cancer. Most cancer prevention efforts follow a traditional "find it–fix it" secondary prevention model. The identification of cancer dictates treatment, which in turn is evaluated by changes in biological process or disease activity. In the case of prostate cancer, a digital rectal exam may identify an asymmetric prostate, leading to a biopsy and the identification of prostate cancer. Diagnosis of cancer often leads to a radical prostectomy (surgical removal of the prostate gland). The success of the surgery would be confirmed by eradication of the tumor, reduced PSA, and patient survival.

Studies have demonstrated that serum PSA is elevated in men with clinically diagnosed prostate cancer (J. E. Fowler Jr., Bigler, & Farabaugh, 2002; Schroder & Wildhagen, 2002; Vis, 2002) and that high PSA levels have positive predictive value for prostate cancer. Despite the promise of PSA screening, there are also significant controversies. Prostate cancer is common for men aged 70 and older (Lu-Yao, Friedman, & Yao, 1997; Lu-Yao & Greenberg, 1994). Averaging data across eight autopsy studies, it has been estimated that the prevalence of prostate cancer is as high as 39% in 70- to 79-year-old men (Lu-Yao et al., 1997; Lu-Yao & Greenberg, 1994). The treatment of this disease varies dramatically from country to country and within regions of the United States. For example, radical prostatectomy was done nearly twice as often in the Pacific Northwest as it was in New England a few years ago (Lu-Yao et al., 1997), although the disparities have declined slightly in recent years (Bubolz, Wasson, Lu-Yao, & Barry, 2001). Yet survival rates and deaths from prostate cancer are no different in the two regions. PSA screening finds many cases. In the great majority of cases, however, the men would have died of another cause long before developing their first symptom of prostate cancer. In other words, much of the prostate cancer that is detected is probably pseudodisease.

Several decision models have been developed to assess the value of screening and treatment of prostate cancer. One model considered three options for the treatment of prostate cancer: radical prostatectomy (surgical removal of the prostate gland), external beam radiation therapy, and "watchful waiting." Both radical prostatectomy and radiation therapy carry high risks of complications that may reduce life satisfaction. For example, there are significant increases in the chances of becoming impotent and/or incontinent (F. J. Fowler Jr., Barry, Lu-Yao, Wasson, & Bin, 1996; F. J. Fowler Jr. et al., 1998). Watchful waiting, on the other hand, does not require therapy, but only evaluation and supervision by a physician. The watchful waiting option has been used least often because it does not treat the cancer (F. J. Fowler et al., 1998).

Decision models have been used to estimate QALYs under these three treatment options. For example, one decision model was used to estimate whether prostatectomy results in longer quality-adjusted survival in men with clinically localized prostate cancer. The analysis considered the QALYs with conservative treatment and prostatectomy for men aged 55, 60, and 65 with clinically localized well, moderately, and poorly differentiated prostate cancer. Well-differentiated cancer cells have a regular cell structure and are associated with a good prognosis. Poorly differentiated cancers have an irregular cell structure and are associated with a high chance of spread.

Figure 14.6 summarizes the results of the analysis. For men with well-differentiated tumors, conservative treatment (waiting) was about equivalent to prostatectomy. For men with moderately differentiated tumors, prostatectomy was preferred to conservative treatment. This was also so for men with poorly differentiated tumors. In terms of QALYs, conservative therapy may be the most appropriate approach for well-differentiated cancer. Men with moderately differentiated cancer had a marginal benefit from prostatectomy at age 55 and 60, but the benefit did not extend to men beyond the age of 65.

With poorly differentiated cancer, all men appeared to benefit from surgery. However, the model also showed that in many cases the results are altered when different values are used to weight the quality-of-life outcomes. For example, if men have moderately differentiated cancer but assign a low quality-of-life value to impotence, the model is more likely to recommend conservative treatment. For men less concerned about the quality-of-life effects of impotence, the model suggests that surgery may

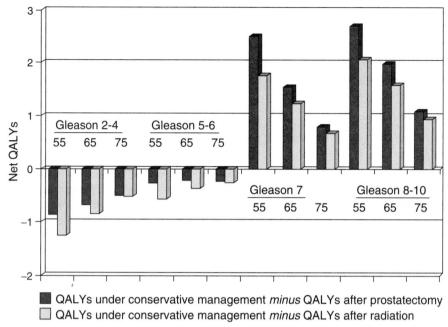

☐ QALYs under conservative management *minus* QALYs after prostatectomy
☐ QALYs under conservative management *minus* QALYs after radiation

Figure 14.6. Net quality-adjusted life years at ages 55, 65, and 75. QALYs after prostatectomy or RT (radiation therapy) minus QALYs under conservative management for patients diagnosed at 55, 65, or 75 years old. Conservative management was preferred for well differentiated cancers (Gleason scores 2–4 and 5–6) (negative net QALYs). Prostatectomy or RT was preferred over conservative management for moderately differentiated and poorly differentiated cancers (Gleason score 7 and 8–10). Treatment benefit decreased with increasing age (from Bhatnagar et al., 2004).

be the best option (Bhatnagar, Kaplan, Stewart, & Bonney, 2001).

Similar decision models have been used to evaluate screening for prostate cancer. Using QALYs as an outcome measure, simulations suggest there are few benefits of screening. For example, Krahn and colleagues (1994) estimated the population benefit of programs to screen 70-year-old men for prostate cancer. They found that the benefits, on average, were improvements in the life expectancy from a few hours to 2 days. However, when they adjusted the life expectancy for quality of life, they discovered that screening programs actually reduced quality-adjusted life days. The reason for this negative impact is that screening identifies many men who would have died of other causes. These men, once identified with prostate cancer, are then likely to engage in a series of treatments that would significantly reduce their quality of life. For these men, the treatment causes harm without producing substantial benefits. Because the traditional model and the outcomes model focus on different

outcome measures, they come to different conclusions about the value of screening.

Screening for Breast Cancer

Controversy surrounding the use of screening mammography for women 40 to 50 years of age is another example. *The Dartmouth Atlas of Health Care* systematically reviews variation in the use of a wide variety of medical services. One example is the use of techniques for the diagnosis and treatment of breast cancer. There is controversy about the age for initiating screening for breast cancer using mammography (Gelmon & Olivotto, 2002; McLellan, 2002; Miettinen et al., 2002; Nystrom et al., 2002). However, the analyses consistently show that screening women older than 50 produces health benefit. Among women between the ages of 50 and 74, periodic screening results in significantly lower rates of death from breast cancer (Navarro & Kaplan, 1996). Thus, screening of women of Medicare age is commonly advocated. Nevertheless, there is substantial variation in the percentage of female Medicare recipients who had had one or more mammograms. For example, in Michigan and Florida, mammograms are done routinely. In Lansing, Michigan, nearly 35% of all women had received mammograms, and similarly high rates were observed in Fort Lauderdale and Sarasota, Florida. On the other hand, only 13% of the women in Oklahoma City had obtained mammograms, and a variety of cities had similar rates. Salt Lake, for example, had a rate of 13.4% (Wennberg, 1998).

For women diagnosed with breast cancer, there is substantial variation in the treatments delivered. In 1992–1993 more than 100,000 women in the Medicare program had surgery for breast cancer. For women who have breast cancer, the surgeon has at least two major options: lumpectomy, which involves removal of the tumor, or mastectomy, which requires either the removal of a larger portion of tissue (partial mastectomy) or complete removal of the breast (total mastectomy). Clinical trials have shown little or no difference in survival rates between women who receive lumpectomy followed by radiation or chemotherapy and women who receive total mastectomy. Because the outcomes are likely to be similar, the woman's own preference should play an important role in the decision process. However, *The Dartmouth Atlas of Health Care* shows that there are some regions in the country where mastectomy is typically done and other regions where lumpectomy is typically done. For example, considering the proportion of women who had breast sparing surgery (lumpectomy), women were 33 times more likely to have lumpectomy if they lived in Toledo, Ohio, than if they lived in Rapid City, South Dakota (48% vs. 1.4%). Figure 14.7 shows the variation map for breast-sparing surgery. The proportion of women having breast-sparing surgery in Patterson, New Jersey, and Ridgewood, New Jersey, was 37.8% and 34.8%, respectively. At the other extreme, only 1.9% had breast-sparing surgery in Ogden, Utah, as did 3.8% in Yakima, Washington. In general, breast-sparing surgery is more widely used in the Northeast than anywhere else in the United States, and the rates tend to be low in the South, Midwest, and Northwest.

Surgery rates are affected by the number of new cases detected. Evidence also suggests that cancer screening rates vary from community to community. Mammography offers an excellent example. In February 2002, Health and Human Services secretary Tommy Thompson used endorsement of mammography for women 40 years of age and older as

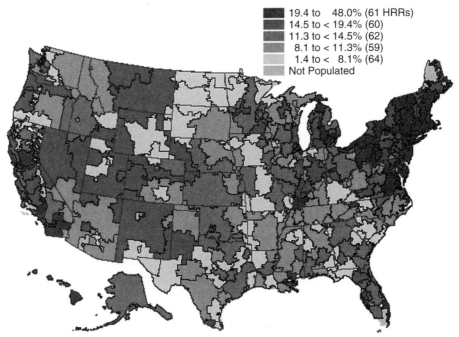

Figure 14.7. Percentage of inpatient breast cancer surgery in Medicare women that was breast sparing by hospital referral region (HRR), 1992–1993; *Dartmouth Atlas of Health Care*).

evidence supporting the Bush administration's commitment to preventive medicine. Thompson held a press conference to advise women, "If you are 40 or older, get screened for breast cancer with mammography every one to two years." However, the public health benefit of promoting screening mammography for 40- to 50-year-old women may be somewhat limited. Clinical trials and meta-analyses have failed to show a population benefit of screening women in this age-group (Barton et al., 2001; Fletcher, 1997; Gelmon & Olivotto, 2002; McLellan, 2002; Miettinen et al., 2002; Nystrom et al., 2002).

In January 1997, the National Institutes of Health (NIH) convened a panel to make recommendations about the use of screening mammography for women 40 to 50 years of age. In contrast to diagnostic testing used when a woman is in a high-risk group or has felt a lump, screening mammography is used to evaluate asymptomatic women. The panel suggested that evidence did not support screening mammography for 40–50 year old women. The conclusion of the panel review shocked the American Cancer Society. The headline of *USA Today* (January 24, 1997) read, "Mammogram Panel Only Adds to Furor." Commentators on morning talk shows were outraged by the committee's decision. Richard Klausner, the director of the National Cancer Institute, decided to disregard the report of his own expert panel. Shortly thereafter, the American Cancer Society appointed a panel of experts chosen because each already believed that screening was valuable for 40- to 50-year-old women. To no one's surprise, this ACS panel recommended that 40- to 50-year-old women should be screened (Fletcher, 1997).

The controversy died down for a brief time but reemerged in 2002. Two Norwegian epidemiologists reanalyzed earlier trials and classified studies by methodological quality. In their analysis they noted that the only studies supporting screening mammography for women of any age were of low quality, and that those studies not supporting screening mammography tended to have greater methodological rigor (Olsen & Gotzsche, 2001). The findings are summarized in Figure 14.8. Remarkably, there appeared to be no benefit at all for screening—the relative risk ratio was nearly 1.0. Although the analysis was conducted as part of the highly respected Cochrane collaboration, the Cochrane group disowned the analysis in the wake of a public controversy, although the protocol for

the study had been approved by the group before the results were known (Horton, 2001). Even though many scholars agree with the Norwegian investigators, the controversy continues. For example, data from a key Swedish study have been reanalyzed and shown to support screening mammography (Nystrom et al., 2002). However, all reviews of the data indicate that any benefit of screening mammography are very small and that screening offers little or no benefit in terms of increasing life expectancy when all causes of mortality are considered (Black, Haggstrom, & Welch, 2002). Decisions are very difficult to evaluate in individual cases. For example, many women get screened, have surgical treatment, and go on to live long and healthy lives. In many cases these women attribute their survival to early detection and treatment. However, it is difficult to determine whether the screening saved their lives, or if the outcomes would have been the same without screening. The clinical trials indicate that the contribution of screening is very small.

Since many experts believe the benefit of screening is very small, we must call on decision analysis to evaluate whether the policies promoted by the American Cancer Society and by Secretary Thompson are a good use of public resources. The cost-effectiveness of mammography has been estimated in several analyses. These analyses are difficult because most meta-analyses fail to show that screening mammography has any benefit for 40- to 49-year-old women (there is less debate about the value of screening for women 50 to 69 years of age). Under the assumption of no benefit, the cost/QALY goes toward infinity because the model would require division by zero. Using studies suggesting some benefit of mammography for women 40 to 49 years of age, Eddy (1989, 1997) estimated the cost to produce a quality-adjusted year of life as $240,000. One analysis used newer data to evaluate the cost-effectiveness of guidelines requiring screening for women aged 40 to 49 (Salzmann, Kerlikowske, & Phillips, 1997). They noted that screening women 50 to 64 years of age produces a QALY at about $21,400. By contrast, the expected benefit of screening women 40 to 49 years of age increases life expectancy by only 2.5 days at a cost of $676 per woman, resulting in an incremental cost utility of $105,000/QALY.

Analyses in all aspects of health care suggest that there is plenty of disease to be discovered and that newer technology will find even more cases.

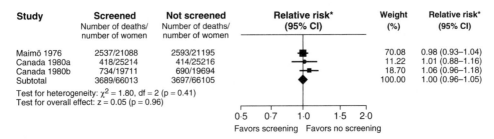

Study	Screened Number of deaths/ number of women	Not screened Number of deaths/ number of women	Relative risk* (95% CI)	Weight (%)	Relative risk* (95% CI)
Maimö 1976	2537/21088	2593/21195		70.08	0.98 (0.93–1.04)
Canada 1980a	418/25214	414/25216		11.22	1.01 (0.88–1.16)
Canada 1980b	734/19711	690/19694		18.70	1.06 (0.96–1.18)
Subtotal	3689/66013	3697/66105		100.00	1.00 (0.96–1.05)

Test for heterogeneity: $\chi^2 = 1.80$, df = 2 (p = 0.41)
Test for overall effect: z = 0.05 (p = 0.96)

0·5 0·7 1·0 1·5 2·0
Favors screening   Favors no screening

Figure 14.8. Relative risk and confidence intervals for mammography randomized controlled trials (from: Olsen & Gotzsche (2001). Cochrane review on screening for breast cancer with mammography. *Lancet* 358:1340–1342).

But are all these cases clinically important? The disease reservoir hypothesis leads to some controversial predictions concerning breast and prostate cancer screening. One hypothesis is that greater screening for disease will create the false appearance of epidemics. Figure 14.9a shows increases in breast cancer and Figure 14.9b increases in prostate cancer as a function of increased screening. With a reservoir of undetected disease, the more you look, the more you find. Figures 14.9a and 14.9b also show the mortality from breast cancer and prostate cancer. If these were true epidemics, we would expect increases in deaths from these serious diseases. However, in each case, mortality is relatively stable (R. M. Kaplan & Wingard, 2000).

Stable mortality rates appear to contradict the suggestion that survival from cancer is increasing and is attributable to better screening and treatment (*Cancer Facts and Figures—2002*, 2002). Although there appeared to be a small increase in prostate cancer deaths in the 1980s, it has since declined and may have been an artifact (J. E. Fowler et al., 2002). The disease reservoir hypothesis would argue that screening changes the point at which disease is detected (lead time) without necessarily changing the course of the illness. If the date of death is unchanged, earlier detection will make the interval between diagnosis and death appear longer even when screening has no effect on life expectancy. This is known as *lead-time bias*.

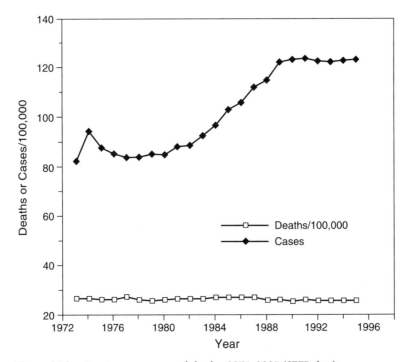

Figure 14.9a. Breast cancer cases and deaths: 1974–1995 (SEER data).

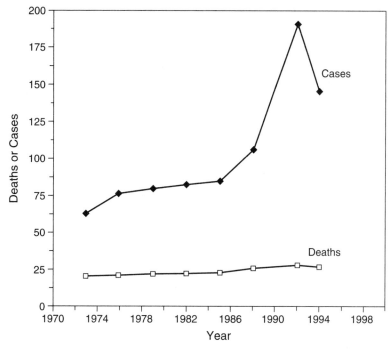

Figure 14.9b. Prostate cancer cases and deaths: 1972–1994 (SEER data).

Cholesterol Screening

The controversy over screening extends beyond cancer. In cancer screening, a judgment is made about whether or not a tumor is present. Clinicians sometimes challenge whether the tumor had meaningful clinical consequences. In many areas of medicine the definition of *disease* is somewhat arbitrary. Many biological processes are approximately normally distributed in the general population. Diagnostic thresholds are often set toward the tail of the distribution (see Figure 14.10). For example, total cholesterol values greater than 240 mg/dl were once used as the diagnostic threshold for hypercholesterolemia. Recently, diagnostic thresholds have been reduced, and some groups advocate treatment for individuals closer to the center of the distribution. In the total cholesterol example, the third National Health and Nutrition Examination Survey (NHANES III) showed that about 20% of the adult population have values above 240 mg/dl. However, more than half of the adult population has total cholesterol levels over 200 mg/dl. If some group advocated changing the diagnostic threshold from 240 to 200, the policy change would identify an additional 30% of the adult population as in need of treatment.

These are several other examples of the problem with changing disease definitions (R. M. Kaplan, Ganiats, & Frosch, 2004). The National Heart Lung and Blood Institute (NHLBI) has administered the National High Blood Pressure Education Program (NHBPEP) for more than three decades. In May 2003, the commission released its seventh national report, known as JNC-7 (Chobanian et al., 2003). Successive JNC reports have pushed for lower diagnostic thresholds for high blood pressure. JNC-6 defined high-normal blood pressure as systolic blood pressure of 130 to 139 mmHg and diastolic blood pressure 85 to 89 mmHg. JNC-7 goes a step further by defining a new condition known as *prehypertension*. Individuals in this category have a systolic blood pressure of 120 to 139 mmHg or a diastolic BP of 80 to 89 mmHg (Chobanian et al., 2003). Although many people will be labeled as prehypertensive, the report does not suggest the use of antihypertensive drugs in this category. Instead, behavioral intervention is indicated. On the surface, the rationale for creating the new category of prehypertension is compelling. Epidemiologic studies of adults between the ages of 40 and 70 years suggest that each increase in systolic BP of 20 mmHg

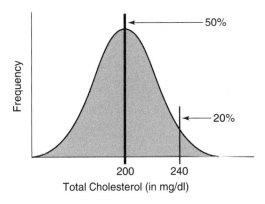

Figure 14.10. Percentage of U.S. population with total cholesterol over 240mg/dl and 200mg/dl (NHANES data).

and each increase in diastolic BP of 10 mmHg results in a doubling of risk for cardiovascular disease except for those with blood pressures lower than 115/75 mmHg (Lewington, Clarke, Qizilbash, Peto, & Collins, 2002). The report argued that management of blood pressure using medication results in a 40% reduction in the incidence of stroke, a 25% reduction in the incidence of myocardial infarction, and a 50% reduction in the incidence of heart failure (Neal, MacMahon, & Chapman, 2000). However, large clinical trials have not shown benefits for lowering high-normal to optimal blood pressure, and there are no outcome studies assessing the effects of behavioral interventions upon mortality. Further, it is unclear what benefit to expect from lifestyle intervention among those in the pre-hypertension range. Analysis of data from the National Health and Nutrition Examination Survey suggests that nearly 90% of older adults will qualify for a diagnosis of pre-hypertension or hypertension. Similar examples are available for type 2 diabetes (with a change in diagnostic threshold for fasting blood glucose from 140 mg/dl to 126 mg/dl), overweight (reduction of threshold to body mass index of 25), and several other health problems. Some common health problems, such as subsyndromal depression, could include as much as 50% of the adult population. This is important because those with the mildest disease (values closest to the mean) usually have the lowest risk of complications from their "disease," yet they often face the same risks of treatment side effects as those more clearly in need of therapy.

At the same time, pharmaceutical costs have become the strongest driver of increases in health care costs. The most recent evidence suggests that pharmaceutical costs rose twice as fast as other components of heath care expenditures during the 1990s (Liberman & Rubinstein, 2002). Currently, the costs of prescription medications for Medicare patients are rising about 20% each year. To address the policy issues, we need to understand the impact of lowering diagnostic thresholds upon population health status and health care costs. For most of these conditions, an expensive pharmaceutical product is available, with treatment costs approaching $3 per day. For older adults with a multiple diagnoses, the costs of medications may exceed the cost of food.

Given the lower potential benefit and the higher costs of treating the large number of patients with mild-spectrum conditions, the cost-effectiveness of treating mild-spectrum disease is less than for directing resources toward the severe-spectrum group. It is even less than treating the average group evaluated in clinical trials. For this reason, we must explore the incremental cost-effectiveness associated with changing diagnostic thresholds. Spending significant resources on mild-spectrum conditions may foreclose opportunities to invest in other aspects of health care. For example, the cost/QALY for treating some mild-spectrum condition might be $800,000/QALY. Using resources to screen and treat this hypothetical condition might reduce the opportunity to support a program that produces a QALY for $50,000. In other words, each QALY gained by pursuing mild-spectrum conditions might take resources away from a program that could produce 16 QALYs at the same cost.

Screening and treatment for high cholesterol offers an interesting case study. The National Cholesterol Education Program developed detailed guidelines on screening for high cholesterol ("Executive Summary of the Third Report of the National Cholesterol Education Program [NCEP] Expert Panel on Detection, Evaluation, and Treatment of High Blood Cholesterol in Adults [Adult Treatment Panel III]," 2001). A national campaign was developed with the emphasis on screening all Americans for high cholesterol. The evidence supporting this campaign came from two sources. First, epidemiologic investigations have shown significant correlations between elevated serum cholesterol and deaths from coronary heart disease (Grundy et al., 1997). Second, clinical trials have demonstrated that reductions in total cholesterol and in the low-density lipoprotein subfraction of cholesterol resulted in reductions in deaths from coronary heart disease (Van Horn & Ernst, 2001). The national policy was based on the mechanistic thinking that high cholesterol is bad and lower cholesterol improves health status. Consumers were led to believe that those with elevated cholesterol were likely to die of heart disease, whereas those with normal levels would survive.

Many difficulties in these analyses have now become apparent. First, the NCEP recommended cholesterol screening tests for all Americans independent of age, gender, or ethnicity. However, the clinical trials supporting the policies were based exclusively on middle-aged men, and there was no specific evidence for children or for older adults. A second concern was that systematic clinical trials consistently failed to demonstrate improvements in life expectancy resulting from cholesterol lowering (R. M. Kaplan, 1984). In all clinical trials, reductions in deaths from heart disease were offset by increases in deaths from other causes (Golomb, 1998; Golomb, Stattin, & Mednick, 2000; R. M. Kaplan & Golomb, 2001). For example, the Coronary Primary Prevention Trial (CPPT) showed that a drug effectively lowered cholesterol in comparison to placebo. Further, those taking the cholesterol-lowering medication were significantly less likely to die of heart disease than those taking the placebo. However, over the period these participants were followed, there were more deaths from other causes among those taking the drug, and the chances of being alive were comparable in the two groups ("The Lipid Research Clinics Coronary Primary Prevention Trial Results. I. Reduction in Incidence of Coronary Heart Disease," 1984). More recent evidence also demonstrates systematic increases in deaths from other causes for those taking cholesterol-lowering agents. Biological mechanisms for these increases have been proposed (Golomb, 1998).

In contemporary medicine, most patients with high cholesterol are treated with a class of expensive medications known as statins. Although the great majority of physicians encourage the use of statins, there is some controversy (R. M. Kaplan & Golomb, 2001). A meta-analysis based on studies published before the release of statins showed a mortality benefit with cholesterol-lowering treatment for high-risk populations; studies enrolling low-cardiac risk populations showed that cholesterol-lowering drugs may be associated with an increased risk of death (Smith, Song, & Sheldon, 1993). Although risk-benefit profiles may be more favorable for statins than for other cholesterol-lowering treatments, a truly low-risk primary prevention group has not been studied. Among statin trials, the study enrolling those at lowest risk for heart disease mortality showed no overall mortality benefit, but rather a nonsignificant trend toward harm (80 vs. 77 deaths; Downs et al., 1998).

The focus on overall mortality is important because reduced deaths from heart disease may be compensated for by increased risk of death from other causes (Annoura et al., 1999). Statins have been linked to modest but significant reductions in cognitive functioning (Muldoon et al., 2000), a finding of particular relevance to the older elderly—in whom cognitive function is potently related to survival (Frisoni, Fratiglioni, Fastbom, Viitanen, & Winblad, 1999). Other statin effects have been reported that may impact quality of life, including sleep disturbance, peripheral neuropathy, erectile dysfunction, pain (Bruckert, Giral, Heshmati, & Turpin, 1996), and depression (Davidson, Reddy, McGrath, Zitner, & MacKeen, 1996).

There have been several cost-utility analyses of cholesterol screening and treatment. Goldman and colleagues (Goldman, Weinstein, Goldman, & Williams, 1991) modeled the value of screening for high cholesterol and treatment with statin medications. Their model considered recurrent heart attack rates using data from the Framingham Heart Study. One simulation considered men with total cholesterol values in excess of 300 mg/dl but no other risk factors for heart disease. For these men the cost to produce a year of life was estimated to be between $71,000 and $135,000. For women, estimates ranged from $84,000 to $390,000 per life year. If the threshold for initiating treatment is lowered to 250 mg/dl, the cost to produce a year of life increases to between $105,000 and $270,000 for men. Campaigns have attempted to increase the number of adults undergoing medical treatment. Until recently, the threshold for a diagnosis of hypercholesterolemia was 240 mg/dl. Under that definition about one in five adults qualified. With the more recent push toward defining high cholesterol as greater that 200 mg/dl, about half of all adults will be deemed abnormal (Fisher & Welch, 1999). However, as shown by the simulations, the lower the diagnostic threshold, the less cost-effective screening and treatment will be.

What Opportunities Are Being Missed?

As noted previously, most resources in preventive medicine are devoted to screening programs. The public health benefits of many (but certainly not all) of these programs have been limited. The common feature of the screening programs is that they require a medical diagnosis. The intent is not to prevent disease but to diagnose established pathology at an early phase. Once diagnosed, the screened individual becomes a patient who requires significant medical attention. Changes in diagnostic thresholds assure that large proportions of the general population will become patients. Half of all adults qualify for a diagnosis of high serum cholesterol, and well over half qualify for a diagnosis of overweight or obesity. In many cases, changes in diagnostic thresholds allow large portions of the population the opportunity to enter a disease category from which they were previously excluded. Often the decision to lower diagnostic thresholds follows the availability of a high-cost pharmaceutical product to treat the condition. In many cases individuals with mild-spectrum conditions have very little potential to benefit from treatment.

While enormous resources are being devoted to screening approaches to preventive medicine, remarkably little effort has been devoted to true disease prevention. In primary prevention, diagnosis is irrelevant because there is no disease to diagnose. Intervention is typically behavioral and might include exercise, dietary change, or the avoidance or reduction of tobacco use. Interventions might also include public policy change such as water sanitation or highway improvements (G. A. Kaplan & Lynch, 1999). For example, there is mounting evidence that people are more physically active if they live in communities that are designed for walking and cycling (Saelens, Sallis, & Frank, 2003).

Shared Decision Making

This chapter argues that health care in the United States is too expensive and that resources are often used to treat pseudodiseases. A central component of the problem is that the role of uncertainty in medical decision making is underappreciated. Although patients accept treatment with high expectations of benefit, experienced health care providers may recognize that the potential benefit of many treatments is probabilistic. One approach to this problem is greater patient involvement in decisions about care. This section reviews the emerging study of shared medical decision making, in which choices of treatment pathways are a collaborative effort between provider and patient (Frosch & Kaplan, 1999).

In an ideal world, a patient could approach a physician with a list of symptoms and problems. The physician would identify the problem and administer a remedy. The service should be inexpensive and painless. However, this scenario is not common. For most medical decisions, judgments about disease are not perfectly reliable, and even when an early diagnosis is available, it is not always clear that treatment is the best option (Eddy, 1996). Choices about what treatments should be offered have typically been left to the physician. For a variety of reasons, however, patients are becoming activated in the decision process.

Shared decision making is the process by which the patients and physicians join in partnership to decide whether the patient should undergo diagnostic testing or receive therapy. Often, shared decision making involves formal decision aids that provide patients with detailed information about their options. The information is usually presented through interactive video disks, decision boards, descriptive consultations, or the Internet (O'Connor et al., 2003). Using these decision aids, patients complete exercises to inform them of the risks and benefits of treatment options. Sometimes they provide preferences for outcomes in the shared decision-making process (Frosch & Kaplan, 1999).

Decision aids are valuable for both patients and physicians. One of the challenges of contemporary primary care medicine is that patient visits are short. Typically, the entire visit is limited to 15 minutes. During this time, the physician must greet the patient, do routine evaluations such as taking blood pressure, review medical history, determine the presenting complaint, perform a physical examination, make a diagnosis, write a prescription, discuss treatment plans, write notes in the patient's chart, and move on to the next patient. If at the end of this interaction the patient asks the difficult questions such as, "Should I be on hormone replacement therapy?" or "Should I get a PSA test?" or "Do I need a mammogram?" the physician knows that there is not enough time to discuss the issue properly. For each of these issues, the literature is complex and conflicting. Instead of dealing with the complexity, it is much easier to simply say that the test or treatment is recommended. However, each of these decisions has important consequences for the patient.

Shared decision making is not patient decision making. In other words, there are technical aspects of medical decisions for which patients are not well equipped. For example, patients are not expected to know what approach to surgery is best or the advantages or disadvantages of particular medications. On the other hand, patients have a perspective that only they fully understand. For instance, surgical treatment of prostate cancer may make a man impotent. For some men, this is a major concern, even at older ages. Other men may not be sexually active, and for them impotence may not be a concern. The patient provides the perspective that is typically unknown to the physician. Use of decision aids allows these preferences to be expressed. The personal issues brought by the patient can be merged with the technical concerns of the physicians.

Because time in medical encounters is so limited, shared decision making often involves a referral to a decision laboratory. The doctor may advise the patient to use a decision aid, often under the supervision of another health care professional. Once the patient has interacted with the decision aid, he or she can return to the physician prepared to deal with the decision in a relatively short period of time.

Although shared decision making is a relatively new field, several decision aids have now been evaluated. In one example, Frosch, Kaplan, and Feletti (2001) considered a decision aid to help men decide whether they should be screened for prostate cancer using the PSA test. The men were all enrolled in a clinic that provides a wide variety of medical screening tests. In an experiment, the men were randomly assigned to one of four groups in a two-by-two factorial design. One factor was for use of a decision video. Men either watched or did not watch a video that systematically reviewed the risks and benefits of PSA screening. The video featured a debate between a urologist who favored PSA screening and an internist who opposed it. Further, the video systematically reviewed the probabilities of false positives, false negatives, and the risks of prostate cancer. It also systematically reviewed the evidence for the benefits of treatment for prostate cancer. The other factor in the experimental design was whether or not men had the opportunity to discuss the decision with others. The design re-

sulted in four groups: usual care, discussion alone, video alone, and video plus discussion. All men were asked if they wanted the PSA test, and medical records were obtained to determine whether the test was completed.

The study showed that there was a systematic effect of the video and discussion groups. In the usual care control group, virtually all men (97%) got the PSA test. In other words, with no new information, men will typically take the test. In the other groups, having more information lead to a conservative bias. In contrast to the usual care control, those in the other groups were more sensitive to the risks of the test in relation to its benefits. Among those participating in the discussion group, 82% got the PSA test. For those watching the video, 63% completed the test. Those watching the video and participating in those discussions had only a 50% PSA completion rate (see Figure 14.11). The study demonstrates that, as patients become better informed, they are less likely to take the PSA test. The study also obtained information on patient knowledge. As knowledge increased, the likelihood of getting the PSA test deceased, again stressing that better-informed patients make more conservative decisions.

There are a variety of other approaches to shared decision making. Sometimes, patient preferences for outcomes are measured directly. One example concerns treatment for prostate cancer. In this case, decision models can be used to simulate the likely benefit of a particular choice. These models often yield a decision map, which shows the best choice for a particular patient, given his or her medical history and individual values. Figure 14.12 is an example of one of these maps. This particular map considers patient preferences for becoming impotent. In this case, if the patient has a high disutility for impotence, with a utility value below .67, and the probability of impotence is greater than .8, watchful waiting is the appropriate choice. However, if the utility for impotence is higher (.85), probability of impotence being as high as .90 might be tolerated (Bhatnagar, Stewart, Bonney, & Kaplan, 2004).

The Internet offers significant advantages for shared decision making. Because medical knowledge changes so quickly, the Internet provides a great opportunity to continually update information. However, we do not know how effective the Internet is at delivering information. New evidence

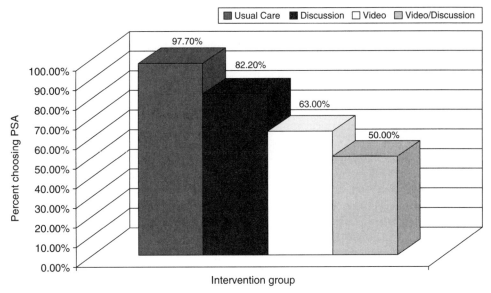

Figure 14.11. Men choosing PSA test by intervention group (from Frosch, Kaplan, & Felitti, 2001).

suggests that large proportions of the American population have Internet access. Yet how good a platform is the Internet for delivering shared decision making? In one study, 226 men, 50 years of age or older, who are scheduled for a complete physical exam, were randomly assigned to access a Web site or to view a 23-minute videotape about the risks and benefits of being screened for prostate cancer using the PSA test. Both methods of delivering the information were effective, but those watching the video were more likely to review the materials than those using the Internet. In addition, those watching the video were more likely to increase their knowledge about the PSA test and were more likely to decline the test than those assigned to the Internet group. Further, those who watched the video were more likely to express confidence that watchful waiting was the best treatment for prostate cancer. Thus, it appeared that the video may have been the best channel for delivering the information. However, using cookies from the Internet, it was possible to determine how much time each participant spent using the program. The analysis indicated that many of the men spent very little time with the Internet program. Among those men who participated in the entire Internet program, the results were identical to the results for those who watched the video. In other words, the Internet and the video worked about equally well if people exposed themselves to the entire program.

When motivated to use the Internet, patients can gain significant benefits (Frosch, Kaplan, & Felitti, 2003).

Conclusions

Contemporary health care is in crisis. Despite relentless increases in cost, there is little evidence that high expenditures are related to patient or population benefit. To address these problems, new methods must be applied to find the best use of limited resources. Preventive medicine is a medical specialty that should help address this problem by applying technologies that will prevent expensive episodes of illness. However, the primary focus of preventive medicine has been toward the identification of established disease at an early phase. The tools of preventive medicine emphasize medical diagnosis and pharmacological treatment. Analyses of many large-scale screening and treatment programs indicates that the benefits have been limited (R. M. Kaplan, 2000). Nevertheless, we are currently witnessing greater emphasis on population screening and lowering of diagnostic thresholds for many disease categories. This will result in significant increases in health care costs with unknown population health benefits.

A major contributor to the expense of contemporary heath care is that there is considerable uncertainty about the potential benefit of many preventive

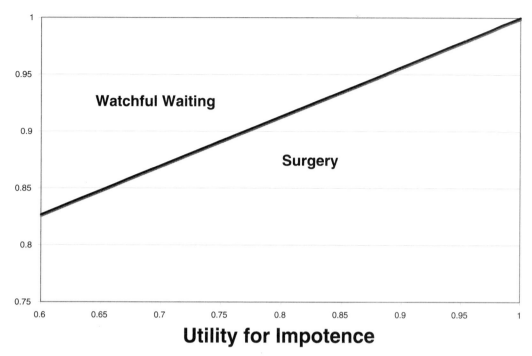

Figure 14.12. Decision map relating patient utility for impotence to treatment choice. Preferred alternatives for men age 55 with localized prostate cancer (original figure by R. M. Kaplan).

treatments. Typically, the safest option is to assume all minor health problems will grow into major health concerns. The favored option is to medically treat these conditions. However, the benefit of these treatments is typically uncertain, and the treatments usually carry some risks. Further, aggressive treatment of mild-spectrum conditions is costly, with little evidence of benefit at the population level.

Although the uncertain benefit of many programs for screening and treatment of mild-spectrum disease is well documented in the medical literature, most patients are unaware of the controversies. When there is uncertainty among providers, approaches to treatment are often highly variable. This is reflected in the medical care use maps. Typically the variation represents differences in physician preferences. Shared medical decision making is a new paradigm in health care that uses decision aids to help patients understand the risks and benefits of treatment. Early studies suggest that allowing patients a greater role in decision making usually results in more conservative decisions. The selection of less aggressive care results in reduced health care costs. Further, shared medical decision making typically results in greater patient satisfac-

tion. By offering a better basis for informed consent, shared medical decision making may also protect physicians from litigation.

Shared decision making is a new paradigm in medicine and health care. There will be ample opportunities to develop new methodologies and to evaluate the effect of these methods on patient outcomes, patient satisfaction, and medical care costs.

References

Annoura, M., Ogawa, M., Kumagai, K., Zhang, B., Saku, K., & Arakawa, K. (1999). Cholesterol paradox in patients with paroxysmal atrial fibrillation. *Cardiology, 92,* 21–27.

Aronowitz, R. A. (2001). Do not delay: Breast cancer and time, 1900–1970. *Milbank Quarterly 79,* 355–386.

Baicker, K., Chandra, A., Skinner, J. S., & Wennberg, J. E. (2004). Who you are and where you live: How race and geography affect the treatment of medicare beneficiaries. *Health Affairs (Millwood), Suppl Web Exclusive,* VAR33–44. Retrieved May 2, 2006, from http://content.healthaffairs.org/cgi/content/abstract/hlthaff.var.33.

Barton, M. B., Moore, S., Polk, S., Shtatland, E., Elmore, J. G., & Fletcher, S. W. (2001). Increased patient concern after false-positive mammograms: Clinician documentation and subsequent ambulatory visits. *Journal of General Internal Medicine, 16,* 150–156.

Bhatnagar, V., Kaplan, R., Stewart, S., & Bonney, W. (2001). Prostatectomy compared to conservative treatment for localized prostate cancer: A decision analysis. *Medical Decision Making, 21,* 548.

Bhatnagar, V., Stewart, S. T., Bonney, W. W., & Kaplan, R. M. (2004). Treatment options for localized prostate cancer: Quality adjusted life years and the effects of lead-time bias. *Urology, 63,* 103–109.

Birkmeyer, J. D., Stukel, T. A., Siewers, A. E., Goodney, P. P., Wennberg, D. E., & Lucas, F. L. (2003). Surgeon volume and operative mortality in the United States. *New England Journal of Medicine, 349,* 2117–2127.

Black, W. C., Haggstrom, D. A., & Welch, H. G. (2002). All-cause mortality in randomized trials of cancer screening. *Journal of the National Cancer Institute, 94,* 167–173.

Black, W. C., & Welch, H. G. (1997). Screening for disease. *American Journal of Roentgenology, 168,* 3–11.

Blumenthal, D. (2001). Controlling health care expenditures. *New England Journal of Medicine, 344,* 766–769.

Bruckert, E., Giral, P., Heshmati, H. M., & Turpin, G. (1996). Men treated with hypolipidaemic drugs complain more frequently of erectile dysfunction. *Journal of Clinical Pharmacy and Therapeutics, 21,* 89–94. ◦

Bubolz, T., Wasson, J. H., Lu-Yao, G., & Barry, M. J. (2001). Treatments for prostate cancer in older men: 1984–1997. *Urology, 58,* 977–982.

Cancer Facts and Figures—2002. (2002). Atlanta, GA: American Cancer Society.

Chobanian, A. V., Bakris, G. L., Black, H. R., Cushman, W. C., Green, L. A., Izzo, J. L., Jr., et al. (2003). The seventh report of the Joint National Committee on Prevention, Detection, Evaluation, and Treatment of High Blood Pressure: The JNC 7 report. *Journal of the American Medical Association, 289,* 2560–2572.

Davidson, K. W., Reddy, S., McGrath, P., Zitner, D., & MacKeen, W. (1996). Increases in depression after cholesterol-lowering drug treatment. *Behavioral Medicine, 22,* 82–84.

Downs, J. R., Clearfield, M., Weis, S., Whitney, E., Shapiro, D. R., Beere, P. A., et al. (1998). Primary prevention of acute coronary events with lovastatin in men and women with average cholesterol levels: Results of AFCAPS/TexCAPS.

Air Force/Texas Coronary Atherosclerosis Prevention Study. *Journal of the American Medical Association, 279,* 1615–1622.

Eddy, D. M. (1989). Screening for breast cancer. *Annals of Internal Medicine, 111,* 389–399.

Eddy, D. M. (1997). Breast cancer screening in women younger than 50 years of age: What's next? *Annals of Internal Medicine, 127,* 1035–1036.

Eddy, D. M. (2005). Evidence-based medicine: A unified approach. *Health Affairs (Millwood), 24*(1), 9–17.

Executive Summary of the Third Report of the National Cholesterol Education Program (NCEP) Expert Panel on Detection, Evaluation, and Treatment of High Blood Cholesterol in Adults (Adult Treatment Panel III). (2001). *Journal of the American Medical Association, 285,* 2486–2497.

Field, M. J., & Gold, M. R. (1998). *Summarizing population health.* Washington, DC: Institute of Medicine, National Academy Press.

Finlayson, S. R., Laycock, W. S., & Birkmeyer, J. D. (2003). National trends in utilization and outcomes of antireflux surgery. *Surgical Endoscopy, 17,* 864–867.

Fisher, E. S., & Welch, H. G. (1999). Avoiding the unintended consequences of growth in medical care: How might more be worse? *Journal of the American Medical Association, 281,* 446–453.

Fisher, E. S., Wennberg, D. E., Stukel, T. A., Gottlieb, D. J., Lucas, F. L., & Pinder, E. L. (2003). The implications of regional variations in Medicare spending. Part 2: Health outcomes and satisfaction with care. *Annals of Internal Medicine, 138,* 288–298.

Fisher, E. S., Wennberg, J. E., Stukel, T. A., & Sharp, S. (1994). Hospital readmissions rates for cohorts of Medicare beneficiaries in Boston and New Haven. *New England Journal of Medicine, 331,* 989–995.

Fletcher, S. W. (1997). Whither scientific deliberation in health policy recommendations? Alice in the Wonderland of breast-cancer screening. *New England Journal of Medicine, 336,* 1180–1183.

Fowler, F. J. Jr., Barry, M. J., Lu-Yao, G., Wasson, J. H., & Bin, L. (1996). Outcomes of external-beam radiation therapy for prostate cancer: A study of Medicare beneficiaries in three surveillance, epidemiology, and end results areas. *Journal of Clinical Oncology, 14,* 2258–2265.

Fowler, F. J. Jr., Bin, L., Collins, M. M., Roberts, R. G., Oesterling, J. E., Wasson, J. H., et al. (1998). Prostate cancer screening and beliefs about treatment efficacy: A national survey of primary care physicians and urologists. *American Journal of Medicine, 104,* 526–532.

Fowler, J. E. Jr., Bigler, S. A., & Farabaugh, P. B. (2002). Prospective study of cancer detection in Black and White men with normal digital rectal examination but prostate specific antigen equal or greater than 4.0 ng/mL. *Cancer, 94,* 1661–1667.

Friedman, H. S. (2002). *Health psychology* (2nd ed.). Upper Saddle River, NJ: Prentice Hall.

Frisoni, G. B., Fratiglioni, L., Fastbom, J., Viitanen, M., & Winblad, B. (1999). Mortality in non-demented subjects with cognitive impairment: The influence of health-related factors. *American Journal of Epidemiology, 150,* 1031–1044.

Frosch, D. L., & Kaplan, R. M. (1999). Shared decision making in clinical medicine: Past research and future directions. *American Journal of Preventive Medicine, 17*(4), 285–294.

Frosch, D. L., Kaplan, R. M., & Felitti, V. (2001). The evaluation of two methods to facilitate shared decision making for men considering the prostate-specific antigen test. *Journal of General Internal Medicine, 16*(6), 391–398.

Frosch, D. L., Kaplan, R. M., & Felitti, V. J. (2003). A randomized controlled trial comparing Internet and video to facilitate patient education for men considering the prostate specific antigen test. *Journal of General Internal Medicine, 18,* 781–787.

Future, I. F. T. (2000). *Health and health care 2010: The forecast, the challenge.* San Francisco: Jossey-Bass.

Gelmon, K. A., & Olivotto, I. (2002). The mammography screening debate: Time to move on. *Lancet, 359,* 904–905.

Gold, M. (1996). Panel on cost-effectiveness in health and medicine. *Medical Care, 34*(Suppl 12), DS197–DS199.

Goldman, L., Weinstein, M. C., Goldman, P. A., & Williams, L. W. (1991). Cost-effectiveness of HMG-CoA reductase inhibition for primary and secondary prevention of coronary heart disease. *Journal of the American Medical Association, 265,* 1145–1151.

Golomb, B. A. (1998). Cholesterol and violence: Is there a connection? *Annals of Internal Medicine, 128,* 478–487.

Golomb, B. A., Stattin, H., & Mednick, S. (2000). Low cholesterol and violent crime. *Journal of Psychiatric Research, 34,* 301–309.

Goodman, D. C., Fisher, E. S., Little, G. A., Stukel, T. A., Chang, C. H., & Schoendorf, K. S. (2002). The relation between the availability of neonatal intensive care and neonatal mortality. *New England Journal of Medicine, 346*(20), 1538–1544.

Grundy, S. M., Balady, G. J., Criqui, M. H., Fletcher, G., Greenland, P., Hiratzka, L. F., et al. (1997). Guide to primary prevention of cardiovascular diseases: A statement for healthcare professionals from the Task Force on Risk Reduction, American Heart Association Science Advisory and Coordinating Committee. *Circulation, 95,* 2329–2331.

Horton, R. (2001). Screening mammography: An overview revisited. *Lancet, 358,* 1284–1285.

Kaplan, G. A., & Lynch, J. W. (1999). Socioeconomic considerations in the primordial prevention of cardiovascular disease. *Preventive Medicine, 29*(6 Pt 2), S30–S35.

Kaplan, R. M. (1984). The connection between clinical health promotion and health status: A critical overview. *American Psychologist, 39,* 755–765.

Kaplan, R. M. (1990). Behavior as the central outcome in health care. *American Psychologist, 45,* 1211–1220.

Kaplan, R. M. (1994). The Ziggy theorem: Toward an outcomes-focused health psychology. *Health Psychology, 13,* 451–460.

Kaplan, R. M. (1997). Decisions about prostate cancer screening in managed care. *Current Opinion in Oncology, 9,* 480–486.

Kaplan, R. M. (2000). Two pathways to prevention. *American Psychologist, 55,* 382–396.

Kaplan, R. M., & Anderson, J. (1996). The general health policy model: An integrated approach. In B. Spilker (Ed.), *Quality of Life and Pharmacoeconomics in Clinical Trials* (pp. 309–322). New York: Raven.

Kaplan, R. M., Ganiats, T. G., & Frosch, D. L. (2004). Diagnostic and treatment decisions in US healthcare. *Journal of Health Psychology, 9,* 29–40.

Kaplan, R. M., & Golomb, B. A. (2001). Cost-effectiveness of statin medications. *American Psychologist, 56,* 366–367.

Kaplan, R. M., & Wingard, D. L. (2000). Trends in breast cancer incidence, survival, and mortality. *Lancet, 356,* 592–593.

Krahn, M. D., Mahoney, J. E., Eckman, M. H., Trachtenberg, J., Pauker, S. G., & Detsky, A. S. (1994). Screening for prostate cancer: A decision analytic view. *Journal of the American Medical Association, 272,* 773–780.

Kronick, R., & California Program on Access to Care. (1999). *Expansion of health care to the working poor.* Berkeley, CA: California Policy Research Center.

Lewington, S., Clarke, R., Qizilbash, N., Peto, R., & Collins, R. (2002). Age-specific relevance of usual blood pressure to vascular mortality: A meta-analysis of individual data for one million adults in 61 prospective studies. *Lancet, 360,* 1903–1913.

Liberman, A., & Rubinstein, J. (2002). Health care reform and the pharmaceutical industry: Crucial decisions are expected. *Health Care Management (Frederick), 20*(3), 22–32.

The Lipid Research Clinics Coronary Primary Prevention Trial results. I. Reduction in incidence of coronary heart disease. (1984). *Journal of the American Medical Association, 251,* 351–364.

Lu-Yao, G. L., Friedman, M., & Yao, S. L. (1997). Use of radical prostatectomy among Medicare beneficiaries before and after the introduction of prostate specific antigen testing. *Journal of Urology, 157,* 2219–2222.

Lu-Yao, G. L., & Greenberg, E. R. (1994). Changes in prostate cancer incidence and treatment in USA. *Lancet, 343,* 251–254.

Manolio, T. A., Burke, G. L., O'Leary, D. H., Evans, G., Beauchamp, N., Knepper, L., et al. (1999). Relationships of cerebral MRI findings to ultrasonographic carotid atherosclerosis in older adults: The Cardiovascular Health Study. CHS Collaborative Research Group. *Arteriosclerosis, Thrombosis, and Vascular Biology, 19,* 356–365.

Marcus, P. M., Bergstralh, E. J., Fagerstrom, R. M., Williams, D. E., Fontana, R., Taylor, W. F., et al. (2000). Lung cancer mortality in the Mayo Lung Project: Impact of extended follow-up. *Journal of the National Cancer Institute, 92,* 1308–1316.

McLellan, F. (2002). Independent US panel fans debate on mammography. *Lancet, 359,* 409.

Miettinen, O. S., Henschke, C. I., Pasmantier, M. W., Smith, J. P., Libby, D. M., & Yankelevitz, D. F. (2002). Mammographic screening: No reliable supporting evidence? *Lancet, 359,* 404–405.

Muldoon, M. F., Barger, S. D., Ryan, C. M., Flory, J. D., Lehoczky, J. P., Matthews, K. A., et al. (2000). Effects of lovastatin on cognitive function and psychological well-being. *American Journal of Medicine, 108,* 538–546.

Navarro, A. M., & Kaplan, R. M. (1996). Mammography screening: Prospects and opportunity costs. *Women's Health, 2,* 209–233.

Neal, B., MacMahon, S., & Chapman, N. (2000). Effects of ACE inhibitors, calcium antagonists, and other blood-pressure-lowering drugs: Results of prospectively designed overviews of randomised trials. Blood Pressure Lowering Treatment Trialists' Collaboration. *Lancet, 356,* 1955–1964.

Nystrom, L., Andersson, I., Bjurstam, N., Frisell, J., Nordenskjold, B., & Rutqvist, L. E. (2002). Long-term effects of mammography screening: Updated overview of the Swedish randomised trials. *Lancet, 359,* 909–919.

Olsen, O., & Gotzsche, P. C. (2001). Cochrane review on screening for breast cancer with mammography. *Lancet, 358*(9290), 1340–1342.

O'Connor, A. M., Drake, E. R., Wells, G. A., Tugwell, P., Laupacis, A., & Elmslie, T. (2003). A survey of the decision-making needs of Canadians faced with complex health decisions. *Health Expectancy, 6,* 97–109.

Pope, G. D., Birkmeyer, J. D., & Finlayson, S. R. (2002). National trends in utilization and in-hospital outcomes of bariatric surgery. *Journal of Gastrointestinal Surgery, 6,* 855–860; discussion 861.

Saelens, B. E., Sallis, J. F., & Frank, L. D. (2003). Environmental correlates of walking and cycling: Findings from the transportation, urban design, and planning literatures. *Annals of Behavioral Medicine, 25,* 80–91.

Salzmann, P., Kerlikowske, K., & Phillips, K. (1997). Cost-effectiveness of extending screening mammography guidelines to include women 40 to 49 years of age. *Annals of Internal Medicine, 127,* 955–965.

Sarafino, E. P. (2002). *Health psychology: Biopsychosocial interactions* (4th ed.). New York: Wiley.

Schroder, F. H., & Wildhagen, M. F. (2002). Low levels of PSA predict long-term risk of prostate cancer: Results from the Baltimore longitudinal study of aging. *Urology, 59,* 462.

Schwartz, L. M., Woloshin, S., Fowler, F. J., Jr., & Welch, H. G. (2004). Enthusiasm for cancer screening in the United States. *Journal of the American Medical Association, 291,* 71–78.

Smith, G. D., Song, F., & Sheldon, T. A. (1993). Cholesterol lowering and mortality: The importance of considering initial level of risk. *British Medical Journal, 306,* 1367–1373.

Starfield, B. (2000). Is US health really the best in the world? *Journal of the American Medical Association, 284,* 483–485.

Strong, J. P., Malcom, G. T., McMahan, C. A., Tracy, R. E., Newman, W. P., III, Herderick, E. E., et al. (1999). Prevalence and extent of atherosclerosis in adolescents and young adults: Implications for prevention from the Pathobiological Determinants of Atherosclerosis in Youth Study. *Journal of the American Medical Association, 281,* 727–735.

Taylor, S. E. (1999). *Health psychology* (4th ed.). Boston: McGraw-Hill.

Van Horn, L., & Ernst, N. (2001). A summary of the science supporting the new National Cholesterol Education Program dietary recommendations: What dietitians should know. *Journal of the American Dietetic Association, 101,* 1148–1154.

Vis, A. N. (2002). Does PSA screening reduce prostate cancer mortality? *Canadian Medical Association Journal, 166,* 600–601.

Weinstein, M. C., Siegel, J. E., Gold, M. R., Kamlet, M. S., & Russell, L. B. (1996). Recommendations of the Panel on Cost-Effectiveness in Health and Medicine. *Journal of the American Medical Association, 276,* 1253–1258.

Welch, H. G. (2001). Informed choice in cancer screening. *Journal of the American Medical Association, 285,* 2776–2778.

Welch, H. G., & Black, W. C. (1997). Using autopsy series to estimate the disease "reservoir" for ductal carcinoma in situ of the breast: How much more breast cancer can we find? *Annals of Internal Medicine, 127,* 1023–1028.

Welch, H. G., Schwartz, L. M., & Woloshin, S. (2000). Do increased 5-year survival rates in prostate cancer indicate better outcomes? *Journal of the American Medical Association, 284,* 2053–2055.

Wennberg, J. E. (1996). On the appropriateness of small-area analysis for cost containment: Researchers should abandon their microscopic inspection of medical practice and refocus their gaze on what patients want, what works, and how much is enough. *Health Affairs, 15,* 164–167.

Wennberg, J. E. ., & Gittelsohn, A. (1982). Variations in medical care among small areas. *Scientific American, 246,* 120–134.

Wennberg, J. E. (1990, May). *Small area analysis and the medical care outcome problem.* Paper presented at the Agency for Health Care Policy and Research conference, Research Methodology: Strengthening Causal Interpretations of Nonexperimental Data, Rockville, MD.

Wennberg, J. E. (1998). *The Dartmouth Atlas of Health Care in the United States.* Hanover, NH: Trustees of Dartmouth College.

Wennberg, J. E., Freeman, J. L., & Culp, W. J. (1987). Are hospital services rationed in New Haven or over-utilised in Boston? *Lancet, 1,* 1185–1189.

Index

Page numbers in bold indicate tables, those in italic indicate figures.

health. *See also* disease; social support
  and conscientiousness, 184
  cost of care and, 359
  defined, 127–128
  and delayed grief, 293
  demographic factors, 23–24
  doctor-patient communication, 325, 347
  and emotions, 246–247
  and expressive writing, 276
  expressive writing and grief, 298–299
  functional, 242
  genetic development and temperament, 177–178
  grief and, 291
  and health psychology, 16
  marriage benefits, 156–157
  patient-physician communication, 338–339
  personality and disease, 7, 16, 173–174
  positive affect and, 206
  psychosocial factors and old age, 244–249
  and racism, 218
  self-rated, 242–243
  and SES, 216–217
  and stress, 133, 137
  traumatic experiences and, 263–264
health belief model (HBM), 54–55
health care. *See also* disease; financial issues
  The Dartmouth Atlas of Health Care, 363
  in American history, 5–6
  decision making models, 365–366
  demand for care, 361
  demographic changes, 76
  and health psychology, 15, 358
  resources and pseudodisease, 376
  shared decision making, 378–379
  United States Agency for Health Care Policy and Research (AHCPR), 54
health costs. *See* financial issues
Health Insurance Plan, 10
health maintenance organizations (HMOs), 10
health psychology. *See also* measurement (health psychology)
  and aging, 235, 254
  Cannon and the wisdom of the body, 10
  definition, 15
  emergence of, 3, 5
  evolution and funding, 15–16
  and health care, 358
  historical development of, 12–14
  insurance reimbursements, 9
  perspectives on health, 16
  and public health, 10
Health Psychology (1979), handbook, 13
"Health Psychology: A New Journal for a New Field," 14
Health Psychology (journal), 14
Healthy for Life Project, 54

heart disease
  and aging, 238
  bereaved men, death of, 306–307
  decline of in U.S., 251
  and depression, 188
  and Down syndrome, 180
  Framingham Heart Study, 10, 375
  mortality rates, 76
  and optimism, 209
  post-traumatic growth, 206
  unmitigated communion, 219
  Western Collaborative Group study, 188
Helicobacter pylori, 7
Henbest and Stewart coding approach, 335
hepatitis B vaccine, 106
herpes simplex virus (HSV), 106–107, 147
heterogeneity, 22
hetero-method correlations, 35–37
high heart rate (HR) reactivity, 79–80
highly active antiretroviral therapy (HAART), 108–109
high-risk mourners, 313–314
hippocampus, 82, 84
Hippocrates, 4, 173–174
Hispanic Americans, 217–218, 244, 341
HIV infection
  benefit finding, 212
  coping effectiveness training, 221
  disease prediction, 107–110
  expressive writing, effects, 267
  and immune system cells, 96
  interventions, 56, 59
  mortality and ethnicity, 204
  and optimism, 209
  post-traumatic growth, 206
  self-representation and, 104–105, 110–111
  social support benefits, 146, 152
  support groups, 160
HMOs (health maintenance plan), 10
Hobfoll, Stevan, 120–121
Holocaust survivors, 278
homeostasis
  allostatic load, 238
  allostatic regulation, 80–81
  blood pressure, 78–80
  fight-or-flight response, 81, 174
  in older adults, 246
  and personality, 172
  primary aging, 236–237
  as process, 73
  self-healing personality, 175
  and Walter Cannon, 10–12, 78, 174
homicide, 76, 308
hopelessness, 217, 287, 299. *See also* emotions
hormones, 4
hospices, 4, 310